PEARSON   ALWAYS LEARNING

Writing for College and the Workplace

Custom Edition for Bryant & Stratton College

Taken from:

The Prentice Hall Guide for College Writers, Eleventh Edition
by Stephen P. Reid and Dominic DelliCarpini

*The Curious Researcher: A Guide to
Writing Research Papers*, Eighth Edition
by Bruce Ballenger

The Successful Writer's Handbook, Third Edition
by Kathleen T. McWhorter and Jane E. Aaron

The Little, Brown Compact Handbook, Ninth Edition
by Jane E. Aaron

Workplace Communications: The Basics, Sixth Edition
by George J. Searles

Cover Art: Courtesy of Pearson Education, Inc.

Taken from:

The Prentice Hall Guide for College Writers, Eleventh Edition
by Stephen P. Reid and Dominic DelliCarpini
Copyright © 2017, 2014, 2011 by Pearson Education, Inc.
New York, New York 10013

The Curious Researcher: A Guide to Writing Research Papers, Eighth Edition
by Bruce Ballenger
Copyright © 2015, 2012, 2009 by Pearson Education, Inc.
New York, New York 10013

The Successful Writer's Handbook, Third Edition
by Kathleen T. McWhorter and Jane E. Aaron
Copyright © 2015, 2012, 2009 by Pearson Education, Inc.
New York, New York 10013

The Little, Brown Compact Handbook, Ninth Edition
by Jane E. Aaron
Copyright © 2016, 2012, 2010 by Pearson Education, Inc.
New York, New York 10013

Workplace Communications: The Basics, Sixth Edition
by George J. Searles
Copyright © 2014, 2011, 2009 by Pearson Education, Inc.
New York, New York 10013

Pearson Learning Solutions, 330 Hudson Street, New York, New York 10013
A Pearson Education Company
www.pearsoned.com

Printed in the United States of America

3   17

000200010272039901

ISBN 10: 1-323-43547-6
ISBN 13: 978-1-323-43547-2

Contents

2   Clarity and Style   103

3 Punctuation 137

UNIT 2 The Writing Process 197

5 Writing in College 199

6 Prewriting 209

14   Summaries   371

15   Reflective Writing   385

UNIT 4   The Information Literacy Cycle   413

---

16   Information Literacy   415

UNIT 5   Writing Styles   513

UNIT 6   Writing for Your Career   621

Unit 1

Grammar & Mechanics

This image represents visually many key elements of the national debate about the cost of going to college—and how those costs affect perceptions of higher education's value. Think about the effect of each element in the image on the audience. What does the piggy bank represent? The glasses on the bank? The chalkboard and the graph that is drawn on it? Thinking about the effect of each element can not only put key parts of the debate on the table, but can also help you to better understand how a visual argument can be built upon the audience's disposition toward a particular image and its composition.

1

Sentences

Basic Grammar

Grammar describes how language works, and understanding it can help you create clear and accurate sentences. This section explains the kinds of words in sentences and how to build basic sentences, expand them, and classify them.

1.1 PARTS OF SPEECH

Successful writers . . .

- Recognize nouns and pronouns (pp. 4–5).
- Recognize verbs (p. 5).
- Recognize adjectives and adverbs (p. 6).
- Recognize prepositions, conjunctions, and interjections (pp. 7–10).

Taken from *The Successful Writer's Handbook,* Third Edition by Kathleen T. McWhorter and Jane E. Aaron.

All English words fall into eight groups, called **parts of speech:** nouns, pronouns, verbs, adjectives, adverbs, prepositions, conjunctions, and interjections. The following box summarizes the parts of speech.

The Parts of Speech		
Part of Speech	**What It Does**	**Examples**
Noun	Names persons, places, things, ideas, or qualities	Roosevelt, girl, Kip River, Koran, happiness, love
Pronoun	Substitutes for a noun	I, you, he, she, it, we, they, myself, who, which, everyone
Verb	Expresses actions, occurrences, or states of being	run, entertain, stop, become, be
Adjective	Describes or modifies nouns or pronouns	gentle, small, helpful
Adverb	Describes or modifies verbs, adjectives, other adverbs, or whole groups of words	daily, rather, helpfully, almost, really, someday
Preposition	Relates nouns or pronouns to other words in a sentence	about, at, down, for, of, with
Conjunction	Connects words, phrases, and clauses	and, or, but, for, although, because, if, whenever
Interjection	Expresses feelings or commands attention	hey, oh, well

In different sentences a word may serve as different parts of speech. For example:

The government sent <u>aid</u> to the city. [*Aid* is a noun.]

Governments <u>aid</u> citizens. [*Aid* is a verb.]

1.1a Recognizing Nouns

Nouns name. They may name a person (*Angelina Jolie, astronaut*), a thing (*chair, book, Mt. Rainier*), a quality (*pain, mystery, simplicity*), a place (*city, Washington, ocean, Red Sea*), or an idea (*reality, peace, success*).

Nouns can be sorted into two groups. The same noun may appear in more than one group.

- A *common noun* names a general class of things and does not begin with a capital letter: *earthquake, citizen, earth, fortitude, army.*
- A *proper noun* names a specific person, place, or thing and begins with a capital letter: *Oprah Winfrey, Washington Monument, El Paso, US Congress.*

1.1b Recognizing Pronouns

Most **pronouns** substitute for nouns and function in sentences as nouns do: *Susanne Ling enlisted in the Air Force when she graduated.*

Below are three types of pronouns:

- A *personal pronoun* **refers to one or more specific individuals or things:** *I, you, he, she, it, we,* and *they.*
- An *indefinite pronoun* **does not refer to a specific noun:** *anyone, everything, no one, somebody,* and so on. *No one came. Nothing moves. Everybody speaks.*
- A *relative pronoun* **relates a group of words to a noun or another pronoun:** *who, whoever, which, that. Everyone who attended received a prize. The book that won is a novel.*

The personal pronouns *I, he, she, we,* and *they* and the relative pronouns *who* and *whoever* change form depending on their function in the sentence. (See Pronoun Case, p. 54.)

1.1c Recognizing Verbs

Verbs express an action (*bring, change, grow*), an occurrence (*become, happen*), or a state of being (*be, seem*).

1 Forms of Verbs

Most verbs can be recognized by two changes in form:

- **Most verbs add** *-d* or *-ed* **to indicate a difference between present and past time:** *They play today. They played yesterday.* Some verbs indicate past time irregularly: *eat, ate; begin, began* (see pp. 26–28).
- **Most present-time verbs add** *-s* or *-es* **with subjects that are singular nouns or the pronouns he, she, it:** *The bear escapes. It runs. The woman begins. She sings. Be* and *have* change to *is* and *has.*

(See Verb Forms, pp. 24–39, for more on verb forms.)

2 Helping Verbs

Some verb forms combine with **helping verbs** to indicate time, possibility, obligation, necessity, and other kinds of meaning: *can run, was sleeping, had been working.* In these **verb phrases,** *run, sleeping,* and *working* are **main verbs**—they carry the principal meaning.

	Verb phrase	
	Helping	*Main*
Artists	can	train others to draw.
The techniques	have	changed little.

These are the most common helping verbs:

be able to	had better	must	used to
be supposed to	have to	ought to	will
can	may	shall	would
could	might	should	

Forms of *be*: be, am, is, are, was, were, been, being
Forms of *have*: have, has, had, having
Forms of *do*: do, does, did

See pp. 33–35 for more on helping verbs.

EXERCISE 1.1.1   Identifying Nouns, Pronouns, and Verbs

Identify the words that function as nouns (N), pronouns (P), and verbs (V) in the following sentences.

Example

```
P    V        N           N
We took the tour through the museum.
```

1. The film was a bore, and I slept through the last half.
2. Guests must register at the desk; otherwise, they cannot obtain a card.
3. The trees they planted are dying of disease.
4. The new speed limit has prevented many accidents.
5. Although I was absent for a month, I finished the semester with good grades.

1.1d Recognizing Adjectives and Adverbs

Adjectives describe or modify nouns and pronouns. They specify which one, what quality, or how many.

old city	generous one	two pears
adjective noun	adjective pronoun	adjective noun

Adverbs describe or modify verbs, adjectives, other adverbs, and whole groups of words. They specify when, where, how, and to what extent.

nearly   destroyed   too   quickly
adverb   verb   adverb   adverb

very   generous   Unfortunately, taxes will rise.
adverb   adjective   adverb   word group

An *-ly* ending often signals an adverb, but not always: *friendly* is an adjective; *never* and *not* are adverbs. The only way to tell whether a word is an adjective or an adverb is to determine what it modifies.

See pp. 68–79 for more on adjectives and adverbs.

| EXERCISE 1.1.2   Identifying Adjectives and Adverbs |

Circle the adjectives and underline the adverbs in the following sentences. Mark *a*, *an*, and *the* as adjectives.

Example

(Undue) stress can hit people when they least expect it.

1. The icy rain created glassy patches on the roads.
2. Happily, children played in the slippery streets.
3. Fortunately, no cars ventured out.
4. Wise parents stayed indoors where they could be warm and dry.
5. The dogs slept soundly near the warm radiators.

1.1e Recognizing Prepositions

Prepositions are connecting words that link a noun or pronoun to the rest of the sentence. Prepositions show relationships of place, direction, time, or manner: *in the room, down the stairs.*

A **prepositional phrase** begins with a preposition and includes its objects and modifiers. *The plants trailed down the stairs. The door to the room remained closed.* (See p. 16.)

Common Prepositions				
about	before	except for	of	throughout
above	behind	excepting	off	till
according to	below	for	on	to
across	beneath	from	onto	toward
after	beside	in	on top of	under
against	between	in addition to	out	underneath
along	beyond	inside	out of	unlike
along with	by	inside of	outside	until
among	concerning	in spite of	over	up
around	despite	instead of	past	upon
as	down	into	regarding	up to
aside from	due to	like	round	with
at	during	near	since	within
because of	except	next to	through	without

CULTURE LANGUAGE   The meanings and uses of English prepositions can be difficult to master. See pp. 127–28 for a discussion of prepositions in idioms, such as *proud of* and *angry with*. See pp. 38–39 for two-word verbs that include prepositions, such as *look after* or *look up*.

EXERCISE 1.1.3   Using Prepositions

Expand each of the following sentences by adding a prepositional phrase in the blank.

Example

A cat hid _____ when the garage door opened.

A cat hid <u>under the car</u> when the garage door opened.

1. The librarian explained that the books about Africa are located _____.
2. When the bullet hit the window, shards flew _____.
3. _____, there is a restaurant that serves green tea ice cream.
4. Heavy winds blowing _____ caused the waves to hit the house.
5. Stacks of books were piled _____.

1.1f Recognizing Conjunctions

Conjunctions are words that connect word groups or single words: *The audience grew quiet <u>when the actor appeared</u> <u>and</u> spoke.* The two types of conjunctions are subordinating and coordinating/correlative.

1 Subordinating Conjunctions

Subordinating conjunctions form sentences into word groups called **dependent clauses,** such as <u>*when the meeting ended*</u> or <u>*that she knew*</u>. These clauses serve as modifiers or nouns in sentences: *Everyone was relieved <u>when the meeting ended</u>. She said <u>that she knew the reason for the successful result</u>.* (See pp. 19–20.)

Common Subordinating Conjunctions			
after	even if	rather than	until
although	even though	since	when
as	if	so that	whenever
as if	if only	than	where
as long as	in order that	that	whereas
as though	now that	though	wherever
because	once	till	whether
before	provided	unless	while

CULTURE LANGUAGE   Learning the meanings of English subordinating conjunctions can help you to express your ideas clearly. Note that each one conveys its meaning on its own. It does not need help from another function word, such as the coordinating conjunction *and, but, for,* or *so.*

Faulty   <u>Even though</u> the parents are illiterate, <u>but</u> their children may read well. [*Even though* and *but* have the same meaning, so both are not needed.]

Revised   <u>Even though</u> the parents are illiterate, their children may read well.

2 Coordinating and Correlative Conjunctions

Coordinating and correlative conjunctions connect words or word groups of the same kind, such as nouns or whole sentences.

Coordinating conjunctions consist of a single word:

Coordinating Conjunctions			
and	nor	for	yet
but	or	so	

> Biofeedback <u>or</u> simple relaxation can relieve headaches.
>
> Relaxation works well, <u>and</u> it is inexpensive.

Correlative conjunctions are combinations of coordinating conjunctions and other words:

Common Correlative Conjunctions	
both . . . and	neither . . . nor
not only . . . but also	whether . . . or
not . . . but	as . . . as
either . . . or	

> <u>Both</u> biofeedback <u>and</u> relaxation can relieve headaches.
>
> The headache sufferer learns <u>not only</u> to recognize the causes of headaches <u>but also</u> to control those causes.

EXERCISE 1.1.4 Adding Connecting Words

Fill each blank in the following sentences with the appropriate connecting word: a preposition, a subordinating conjunction, or a coordinating conjunction. Consult the lists on p. 7 and opposite if you need help.

Example

A Trojan priest warned, "Beware _____ Greeks bearing gifts." (*preposition*)

A Trojan priest warned, "Beware <u>of</u> Greeks bearing gifts."

1. Just about everyone has heard the story _____ the Trojan Horse. (*preposition*)
2. This incident happened at the city of Troy _____ was planned by the Greeks. (*coordinating conjunction*)
3. The Greeks built a huge wooden horse _____ a hollow space big enough to hold many men. (*preposition*)
4. At night, they rolled the horse to the gate of Troy _____ left it there. (*coordinating conjunction*)
5. _____ the morning, the Trojans were surprised to see the enormous horse. (*preposition*)

6. They were amazed _____ they saw that the Greeks were gone. (*subordinating conjunction*)
7. _____ they were curious to examine this gift from the Greeks, they dragged the horse into the city and left it outside the temple. (*subordinating conjunction*)
8. In the middle of the night, the hidden Greeks emerged _____ the horse and began setting fires all over town. (*preposition*)
9. _____ the Trojan soldiers awoke and came out of their houses, the Greeks killed them one by one. (*subordinating conjunction*)
10. By the next morning, the Trojan men were dead _____ the women were slaves to the Greeks. (*coordinating conjunction*)

1.1g Recognizing Interjections

Interjections express feeling or command attention. They are rarely used in academic or business writing.

Oh, the meeting went fine.
They won seven thousand dollars! Wow!

1.2 THE SENTENCE

Successful writers . . .

- Recognize subjects and predicates (below).
- Recognize predicate patterns (p. 12).

The **sentence** is the basic unit of expression. It is a group of words that expresses a complete thought about something or someone. To be complete, a sentence must contain both a subject and a predicate.

1.2a Recognizing Subjects and Predicates

Most sentences make statements. First the **subject** names something. It identifies who or what the sentence is about. The subject is often a noun—a word that names a person, place, or thing. After the subject, the **predicate** indicates what the subject does or what happened to the subject. The predicate must include a verb (a word that expresses action or a state of being).

Subject	Predicate
Arethea	swam.

The **simple subject** consists of one or more nouns or pronouns; the **complete subject** also includes any modifiers. The **simple predicate** consists of one or more verbs; the **complete predicate** adds any words needed to complete the meaning of the verb plus any modifiers.

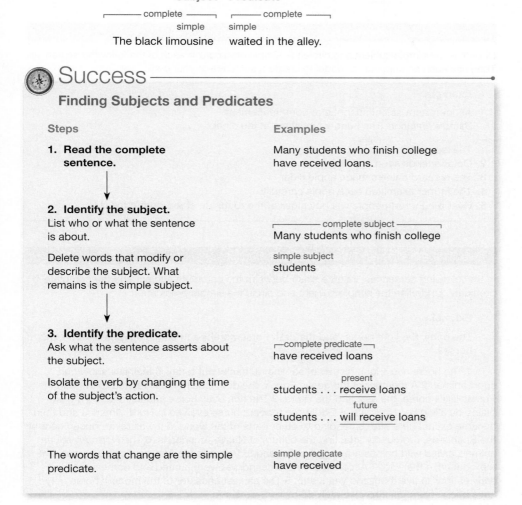

Subject   Predicate

┌——— complete ———┐ ┌——— complete ———┐
           simple simple
The black limousine   waited in the alley.

⊕ Success
Finding Subjects and Predicates

Steps	Examples
1. **Read the complete sentence.**	Many students who finish college have received loans.
2. **Identify the subject.** List who or what the sentence is about.	┌——— complete subject ———┐ Many students who finish college
Delete words that modify or describe the subject. What remains is the simple subject.	simple subject students
3. **Identify the predicate.** Ask what the sentence asserts about the subject.	┌—complete predicate—┐ have received loans
Isolate the verb by changing the time of the subject's action.	present students . . . <u>receive</u> loans
	future students . . . <u>will receive</u> loans
The words that change are the simple predicate.	simple predicate have received

A sentence may contain two or more simple subjects joined by a coordinating conjunction (*and, or, nor*). A sentence may also contain two or more verbs joined by a coordinating conjunction. These groupings are called a **compound subject** and a **compound predicate.**

compound
┌— subject —┐ ┌——— compound predicate ———┐
Joshua and Luis   unlocked their bikes and rode away.

The subject of a sentence in standard American English may be a noun (*music*) or a pronoun that refers to the noun (*it*), but not both. (See p. 100.)

Faulty   Some <u>music</u> it stirs emotions.

Revised   Some <u>music</u> stirs emotions.

EXERCISE 1.2.1   Identifying Subjects and Predicates

Underline the simple subject and circle the simple predicate in each of the following sentences. Then use each sentence as a model to create a sentence of your own.

Example

An important <u>scientist</u> (spoke) at commencement.
Sample imitation: The hungry family ate at the diner.

1. The leaves fell.
2. October ends soon.
3. The orchard owners made apple cider.
4. The farmer examined each apple carefully.
5. Over a hundred people will buy cider at the roadside stand during the fall.

EXERCISE 1.2.2   Identifying Subjects and Predicates

In the following sentences, insert a slash between the complete subject and the complete predicate. Underline the simple subject and circle the simple predicate.

Example

The <u>pony</u>, the light <u>horse</u>, and the draft <u>horse</u> /(are) the three main types of domestic horses.

1 The horse has a long history of serving humanity but today is mainly a show and sport animal. **2** A member of the genus *Equus*, the domestic horse is related to the wild Przewalski's horse, the ass, and the zebra. **3** The domestic horse and its relatives are all plains-dwelling herd animals. **4** Oddly, the modern horse evolved in North America and then became extinct here after spreading to other parts of the world. **5** It was reintroduced here by the Spaniards, profoundly affecting the culture of Native Americans. **6** The North American animals called wild horses are actually descended from escaped domesticated horses that reproduced in the wild. **7** According to records, horses were hunted and domesticated as early as four to five thousand years ago. **8** The earliest ancestor of the modern horse may have been eohippus, approximately 55 million years ago.

1.2b Recognizing Predicate Patterns

All English sentences are based on five patterns, each differing in the complete predicate (the verb and any words following it).

 The word order in English sentences may not correspond to the word order in the sentences of your native language. English, for instance, strongly prefers subject first, then verb, whereas some other languages prefer the verb first.

Pattern 1: The earth trembled.

In the simplest pattern the predicate consists only of an **intransitive verb,** a verb that does not require a following word to complete its meaning.

Subject	Predicate
	Intransitive verb
The earth	trembled.
The hospital	may close.

Pattern 2: The earthquake destroyed the city.

In pattern 2 the verb is followed by a **direct object**, a noun or pronoun that identifies who or what receives the action of the verb. A verb that requires a direct object to complete its meaning is called **transitive.**

Subject	Predicate	
	Transitive verb	*Direct object*
The earthquake	destroyed	the city.
Education	opens	doors.

CULTURE LANGUAGE   In standard American English, only transitive verbs may be used in the passive voice: *The city was destroyed by the earthquake.* (See pp. 45–46.) A dictionary says whether a verb is transitive or intransitive, often with an abbreviation such as *tr.* or *intr.* Some verbs (*begin, learn, read, write,* and others) can be both transitive and intransitive.

Pattern 3: The result was chaos.

In pattern 3 the verb is followed by a **subject complement**, a word that renames or describes the subject. A verb in this pattern is called a **linking verb** because it links its subject to the description following. The linking verbs include forms of *be,* the verbs of the senses (*feel, look, smell, sound, taste*), and a few others (*seem, appear, become, grow, remain, stay, prove*). Subject complements are usually nouns or adjectives.

Subject	Predicate	
	Linking verb	*Subject complement*
The result	was	chaos. [Noun.]
The man	became	an accountant. [Noun.]
The car	seems	expensive. [Adjective.]

Pattern 4: The government sent the city aid.

In pattern 4 the verb is followed by a direct object and an **indirect object,** a word identifying to or for whom the action of the verb is performed. The direct object and indirect object refer to different things, people, or places.

	Subject	Predicate		
		Transitive verb	*Indirect object*	*Direct object*
	The government	sent	the city	aid.
	One company	offered	its employees	bonuses.

A number of verbs can take indirect objects, including *send* and *offer* (preceding examples) and *allow, bring, buy, deny, find, get, give, leave, make, pay, read, sell, show, teach,* and *write.*

CULTURE LANGUAGE With some English verbs that express action done to or for someone, the indirect object must be turned into a phrase beginning with *to* or *for*. The phrase must come after the direct object. The verbs that require these changes include *admit, announce, demonstrate, explain, introduce, mention, prove, recommend, say,* and *suggest.*

Faulty
indirect object · direct object
The manual explains <u>workers</u> the new <u>procedure.</u>

Revised
direct object · *to* phrase
The manual explains the new <u>procedure</u> <u>to workers.</u>

Pattern 5: The citizens considered the earthquake a disaster.

In pattern 5 the verb is followed by a direct object and an **object complement,** a word that renames or describes the direct object. Object complements may be nouns or adjectives.

	Subject	Predicate		
		Transitive verb	*Direct object*	*Object complement*
	The citizens	considered	the earthquake	a disaster.
	Success	makes	some people	nervous.

EXERCISE 1.2.3   Identifying Sentence Parts

In the following sentences identify the subject (S) and verb (V) as well as any direct object (DO), indirect object (IO), subject complement (SC), or object complement (OC).

Example

S   ┌—V—┐   DO
Crime <u>statistics</u> <u>can cause</u> <u>surprise.</u>

1. The number of serious crimes in the United States decreased.
2. A decline in serious crimes occurred each year.
3. The Crime Index measures serious crime.
4. The FBI invented the index.
5. The four serious violent crimes are murder, robbery, rape, and aggravated assault.
6. Auto theft, burglary, arson, and larceny-theft are the four serious crimes against property.

7. The Crime Index gives the FBI a measure of crime.
8. The index shows trends in crimes and the people who commit them.
9. The nation's largest cities showed the largest decline in crime.
10. However, crime actually increased in smaller cities.

EXERCISE 1.2.4   Identifying Sentence Patterns

In the following sentences identify each verb as intransitive, transitive, or linking. Then identify each direct object (DO), indirect object (IO), subject complement (SC), and object complement (OC).

Example

```
         transitive
         verb        IO          DO              DO
Children give their parents both headaches and pleasures.
```

1. Many people find New York City exciting.
2. Tourists flock there each year.
3. Often they visit Times Square first.
4. The square's lights are astounding.
5. The flashing signs sell visitors everything from TVs to underwear.

1.3 PHRASES AND DEPENDENT CLAUSES

Successful writers . . .

- Recognize phrases: prepositional, verbal, appositive (p. 16).
- Recognize dependent clauses (p. 19).

Most sentences contain word groups that serve as adjectives, adverbs, or nouns and thus cannot stand alone as sentences.

- **A *phrase* lacks either a subject or a predicate or both.**

  in a panic

  wondering aloud

- **A *dependent clause* contains a subject and a predicate but begins with a subordinating word:**

```
subordinating
word          subject      predicate
when          prices       rise
```

1.3a Recognizing Phrases

1 Prepositional Phrases

A **prepositional phrase** consists of a preposition plus a noun, a pronoun, or a word group that functions as a noun, called the **object of the preposition.** A list of prepositions appears on p. 7.

prepo-
sition   object
Order a plate of spaghetti.

prepo-
sition   object
Juan ate with great enjoyment.

Prepositional phrases usually modify other words in the sentence.

In cooking class I prepared dishes from many countries.

EXERCISE 1.3.1   Identifying Prepositional Phrases

Underline each prepositional phrase in the following passage, and show or name the word that the phrase modifies.

Example

After an hour I finally arrived at the home of my professor.

The woman in blue socks ran from the police officer on horseback. She darted down Bates Street and then into the bus depot. At the depot the police officer dismounted from his horse and searched for the woman. The entrance to the depot and the interior were filled with travelers, however, and in the crowd she escaped. She boarded a bus on the other side of the depot and was soon riding across town.

EXERCISE 1.3.2   Sentence Combining: Prepositional Phrases

To practice writing sentences with prepositional phrases, combine each pair of sentences below into one sentence that includes one or two prepositional phrases. You will have to add, delete, and rearrange words. Each item has more than one possible answer.

Example

I will start working. The new job will pay the minimum wage.
I will start working at a new job for the minimum wage.

1. The prize money was hidden. It was concealed behind a painting.
2. The band members held a party. They invited one hundred people.
3. Alex received earrings. An unknown admirer gave them.
4. The wagging tail toppled the lamp. It was a dog's tail.
5. Everyone attended the lecture. Only Kayleah and Carlos did not go.

2 Verbal Phrases

Certain forms of verbs, called **verbals**, can serve as modifiers or nouns. Often these verbals appear with their own modifiers and objects in **verbal phrases**.

Note Verbals cannot serve as the only verbs in sentences. *The sun rises over the dump* is a sentence; *The sun rising over the dump* is a sentence fragment. (See pp. 86–89.)

Participial Phrases

Present participles end in *-ing*: *living, walking*. **Past participles** usually end in *-d* or *-ed*: *lived, walked*. **Participial phrases** are made from participles plus modifiers and objects. They usually serve as adjectives.

participle   noun
Strolling shoppers fill the malls.

noun   participial phrase
They make selections determined by personal taste.

Note With irregular verbs, the past participle may have a different ending—for instance, *hidden funds*. (See pp. 26–29.)

CULTURE LANGUAGE The present and past participles of English verbs that express feelings have different meanings. The present participle modifies the thing that causes the feeling: *It was a boring lecture*. The past participle modifies the thing that experiences the feeling: *The bored students slept*. See page 74.

Gerund Phrases

A **gerund** is the *-ing* form of a verb used as a noun. A **gerund phrase** is made up of a gerund and its modifiers and objects. Gerunds and gerund phrases can do anything that nouns can do, including serving as sentence subjects.

gerund
Shopping satisfies personal needs.

—gerund phrase —
Learning Arabic is challenging.

Infinitive Phrases

An **infinitive** is the plain form of a verb preceded by the word *to*: *to hide*. Infinitives and **infinitive phrases** serve as nouns or as modifiers (adjectives or adverbs).

infinitive phrase
—(sentence subject) —
To love one's enemies is admirable.

infinitive phrase
—(adjective) —
The season to sell bulbs is in the fall.

infinitive phrase
—(adverb) —
The swim team met to practice for the state championship.

In English sentences, infinitives and gerunds may follow some verbs and not others and may differ in meaning after a verb (see pp. 36–37).

The cowboy stopped to sing. [He stopped to do the activity.]

The cowboy stopped singing. [He finished the activity.]

EXERCISE 1.3.3   Identifying Verbals and Verbal Phrases

The following sentences contain participles, gerunds, and infinitives as well as participial, gerund, and infinitive phrases. Underline each verbal or verbal phrase.

Example

Laughing, the talk-show host prodded her guest to talk.

1. Encouraged by her teachers, Sophie applied to art school.
2. He is self-confident enough to laugh at his own faults.
3. Sliding and slipping, they moved across the ice to greet their friends.
4. Eating at a nice restaurant is a relaxing way to end a hectic week.
5. To fly was one of humankind's recurring dreams.
6. Because of the dwindling water supply, the remaining vacationers decided to leave for another campground.

EXERCISE 1.3.4   Sentence Combining: Verbals and Verbal Phrases

To practice writing sentences with verbals and verbal phrases, combine each of the following pairs of sentences into one sentence. You will have to add, delete, change, and rearrange words. Each item has more than one possible answer.

Example

My father took pleasure in mean pranks. For instance, he hid the neighbor's cat.

My father took pleasure in mean pranks such as hiding the neighbor's cat.

1. The highway leads into the town. It is lined with fast-food restaurants.
2. She worked hard at her job search. She called every lead she got.
3. The letter had been opened by mistake. It was lying on the table.
4. Children shop in supermarkets with their parents. This is an early experience that almost all children share.
5. I must get a job. I must support myself.

---

3 Appositive Phrases

An **appositive** is usually a noun that renames another noun. An **appositive phrase** includes modifiers as well. Both appositives and appositive phrases usually fall immediately after the nouns they rename.

appositive phrase
Bizen ware, a dark stoneware, is produced in Japan.

Appositives and appositive phrases sometimes begin with *that is, such as, for example,* or *in other words.*

appositive phrase

Bizen ware is used in the Japanese tea ceremony, that is, the Zen Buddhist observance that links meditation and art.

EXERCISE 1.3.5   Sentence Combining: Appositive Phrases

Combine each pair of sentences into one sentence that contains an appos-itive phrase. You will have to delete and rearrange words. Some items have more than one possible answer.

Example

The largest land animal is the elephant. The elephant is also one of the most intelligent animals.

The largest land animal, the elephant, is also one of the most intelligent animals.

1. Riley is a friendly guy. He is often invited to parties.
2. The part of Nathan Detroit is played by Frank Sinatra. Detroit is a gambler.
3. The story described a unicorn. That is the fabled horselike animal with one horn.
4. Cactus-growing attracts patient people. It is a hobby with no immediate rewards.
5. Edgar Allan Poe was a writer of fantastic, scary stories. He was also a poet and a journalist.

1.3b Recognizing Dependent Clauses

A **clause** is any group of words that contains both a subject and a predicate. There are two kinds of clauses, and the distinction between them is important.

- An *independent clause* (also called *main*) makes a complete statement and can stand alone as a sentence: *The sky darkened.*

- A *dependent clause* (also called *subordinate*) is just like a main clause *except* that it begins with a subordinating word: *when the sky darkened.* The subordinating word reduces the clause from a complete statement to a single part of speech: an adjective, adverb, or noun. Use dependent clauses to support the ideas in independent clauses, as described on p. 107.

Note A dependent clause punctuated as a sentence is a sentence fragment. (See pp. 86–89.)

Adjective Clauses

An **adjective clause** modifies a noun or pronoun. It usually begins with the relative pronoun *who, whom, whose, which,* or *that.* The relative pronoun is the subject or object of the clause it begins. The clause ordinarily comes immediately after the word it modifies.

adjective clause
Parents who cannot read may have bad memories of school.

adjective clause
One school, which is open year-round, helps parents learn to read.

Adverb Clauses

An **adverb clause** modifies a verb, an adjective, another adverb, or a whole word group. It always begins with a subordinating conjunction, such as *although, because, if,* or *when* (see p. 8 for a list).

adverb clause
The school began teaching parents when adult illiteracy gained national attention.

adverb clause   independent clause
Because it was directed at people who could not read, advertising had to be inventive.

Noun Clauses

A **noun clause** replaces a noun in a sentence and serves as a subject, object, or complement. It begins with *that, what, whatever, who, whom, whoever, whomever, when, where, whether, why,* or *how.*

sentence subject
Whether the program would succeed depended on door-to-door advertising.
noun clause

object of verb
Teachers explained in person how the program would work.
noun clause

EXERCISE 1.3.6 Identifying Clauses

Underline the dependent clauses in the following sentences and indicate whether each is used as an adjective, an adverb, or a noun.

Example

adjective clause   noun clause
The article that appeared online explained how one could build an underground house.

1. They were not interested in what the tour guide said.
2. The auctioneer opened the bidding once everyone was seated.
3. Whenever the economy is uncertain, people tend to become anxious.
4. Whoever wants to graduate must pass all the required courses.
5. I knew the ending would be unhappy when the main character started falling apart.

EXERCISE 1.3.7　Sentence Combining: Dependent Clauses

To practice writing sentences with dependent clauses, combine each of the following pairs of independent clauses into one sentence. Use either subordinating conjunctions or relative pronouns as appropriate, referring to the list of conjunctions on p. 8 if necessary. You will have to add, delete, and rearrange words. Each item has more than one possible answer.

Example

She did not have her tire irons with her. She could not change her bicycle tire.

<u>Because</u> she did not have her tire irons with her, she could not change her bicycle tire.

1. The critic reviewed the new spy movie. It was playing at the multiplex.
2. He is an accountant. He rarely makes mistakes.
3. We came to the gate. We had first seen the deer tracks there.
4. Someone is fickle. This person cannot be relied on.
5. James won the award. This still amazes us.
6. We can make no exceptions. You should know this.
7. The town government canceled the new playground. Then small children demonstrated in the streets.
8. Those dogs have a trainer. He gives them equal discipline and praise.
9. The basketball team has had a losing season. The team still shows promise.
10. He did not bother to undress for bed. He was too tired.

EXERCISE 1.3.8　Identifying Clauses

Underline the dependent clauses in the following paragraphs and identify each one as adjective (ADJ), adverb (ADV), or noun (N) by determining how it functions in its sentence.

Example

N (sentence subject)
<u>Whoever follows the Koran</u> refers to God as *Allah*, the Arabic word for God's name.

1 The Prophet Muhammad, who was the founder of Islam, was born about 570 CE in the city of Mecca. **2** He grew up in the care of his grandfather and an uncle because both of his parents had died when he was very young. **3** His extended family was part of a powerful Arab tribe that lived in western Arabia. **4** When Muhammad was about forty years old, he had a vision while he was in a cave outside Mecca. **5** He believed that God had selected him to be the prophet of a true religion for the Arab people. **6** Viewed as God's messenger, Muhammad attracted many followers before he lost the support of the clans of Mecca. **7** He and his followers moved to Medina, where they established an organized Muslim community that sometimes clashed with the Meccans and with Jewish clans. **8** Throughout his life Muhammad continued as the religious, political, and military leader of Islam as it spread in Asia and Africa. **9** He continued to have revelations, which are recorded in the sacred book of Muslims, the Koran.

1.4 SENTENCE TYPES

Successful writers . . .

- Recognize simple sentences (below).
- Recognize compound sentences (below).
- Recognize complex sentences (below).
- Recognize compound-complex sentences (facing page).

The four basic sentence structures vary in the number of independent clauses and dependent clauses. Each structure gives different emphasis to the main and supporting information in a sentence.

1.4a Recognizing Simple Sentences

A **simple sentence** consists of a single independent clause and no dependent clause.

Independent clause.

┌────────── independent clause ──────────┐
Last summer was unusually hot.

┌─────────────────────────── independent clause ───────────────────────────
The heat and lack of rain made many farmers leave the area for good or
────────────┐
forced them to work in town.

1.4b Recognizing Compound Sentences

A **compound sentence** consists of two or more independent clauses and no dependent clause.

Independent clause + **independent clause.**

independent clause   ┌────── independent clause ──────┐
Last July was hot, but August was even hotter.

┌────────── independent clause ──────────┐   ┌────────── independent clause ──────────┐
The hot sun scorched the earth, and the lack of rain killed many crops.

1.4c Recognizing Complex Sentences

A **complex sentence** consists of one independent clause and one or more dependent clauses.

Independent clause + **dependent clause.**

(Order varies)

independent clause ┌───────dependent clause──────────┐
Rain finally came, although many had left the area by then.

┌─── independent clause ──────────┐ ┌─── dependent clause ───┐
Those who remained were able to start anew because the government
────────────────┐
came to their aid.

1.4d Recognizing Compound-Complex Sentences

A **compound-complex sentence** has two or more independent clauses and at least one dependent clause.

Independent clause + **independent clause** + **dependent clause.**

(Order varies)

┌──── dependent clause ─────┐ ┌──── independent clause ────┐
When government aid finally came, many people had already been
────────────────┐ ┌────── independent clause ──────┐
reduced to poverty and others had been forced to move.

EXERCISE 1.4.1 Identifying Sentence Structures

Mark the independent clauses and dependent clauses in the following paragraphs. Then identify each sentence as simple, compound, complex, or compound-complex.

Example

┌──────── independent clause ─────────┐ ┌──── dependent clause ───┐
The human voice is produced in the larynx, which has two bands called
────────────┐
vocal cords. [Complex.]

1 Our world has many sounds, but they all have one thing in common. **2** They are all produced by vibrations. **3** Vibrations make the air move in waves, and these sound waves travel to the ear. **4** When the waves enter the ear, the auditory nerves convey them to the brain, and the brain interprets them. **5** Some sounds are pleasant, and others, which we call noise, are not. **6** Pleasant sounds, such as music, are produced by regular vibrations at regular intervals. **7** Most noises are produced by irregular vibrations at irregular intervals; an example is the barking of a dog.

8 Sounds, both pleasant and unpleasant, have frequency and pitch. **9** When an object vibrates rapidly, it produces high-frequency, high-pitched sounds. **10** People can hear sounds over a wide range of frequencies, but dogs, cats, and many other animals can hear high frequencies that humans cannot.

EXERCISE 1.4.2 Sentence Combining: Sentence Structures

Combine each of the following groups of simple sentences to produce the kind of sentence specified in parentheses. You will have to add, delete, change, and rearrange words.

Example

The traffic passed her house. It never stopped. (*Complex.*)
The traffic that passed her house never stopped.

1. Dinner was tasty. It did not fill us up. (*Compound.*)
2. The storm was predicted to be fierce. It passed by quickly. (*Complex.*)
3. The musical notes died away. Then a strange object filled the sky. (*Complex.*)
4. The wolves were afraid. They feared the fire. (*Simple.*)
5. We wanted the rumors to stop. We hoped for that. They did not. (*Compound-complex.*)

Verbs

Verbs express actions, conditions, and states of being. This section covers verbs' forms, tenses, mood, and voice and shows how to make verbs match their subjects.

1.5 VERB FORMS

Successful writers . . .

- Know the five basic verb forms (below and opposite).
- Use the correct forms of irregular verbs (p. 26).
- Distinguish between *sit* and *set, lie* and *lay*, and *rise* and *raise* (p. 30).
- Use the -*s* and -*ed* verbs forms when they are required (p. 31).
- Use helping verbs with main verbs appropriately (p. 33).
- Use a gerund or infinitive after a verb as appropriate (p. 36).
- Use the appropriate particles with two-word verbs (p. 38).

All verbs except *be* have five basic forms. The first three are the verb's principal parts:

- **The *plain form* is the dictionary form of the verb.** When the subject is a plural noun or the pronoun *I, we, you,* or *they,* the plain form indicates action that occurs in the present, occurs habitually, or is generally true.

  A few artists <u>live</u> in town today.

  They <u>hold</u> classes downtown.

Terms That Describe Verbs		
Term	Meaning	Examples
Tense	Shows time of the verb's action	*Present:* I kick. *Past:* He kicked. *Future:* I will kick.
Mood	Shows the attitude of the speaker or writer	I kick the ball. Kick the ball! I suggested that she kick the ball.
Voice	Makes the distinction between **active** (subject performs the action) and **passive** (subject is acted upon)	*Active:* I kick the ball. *Passive:* The ball is kicked.
Person	Shows whether the subject is speaking or being spoken to or about	*Subject speaking:* I/we kick the ball. *Subject spoken to:* You kick the ball. *Subject spoken about:* She kicks the ball.
Number	Indicates whether the subject is singular or plural	*Singular:* The girl kicks the ball. *Plural:* Girls kick the ball.

- **The *past-tense form* indicates that the action of the verb occurred before *now.*** It usually adds *-d* or *-ed* to the plain form, although some irregular verbs form it in other ways (see pp. 26–29).

  Many artists lived in town before this year.

  They held classes downtown. [Irregular verb.]

- **The *past participle* is the same as the past-tense form,** except in most irregular verbs. It combines with forms of *have* or *be* (*has tied, was tied*), or by itself it modifies nouns and pronouns (*the tied game*).

  Artists have lived in town for decades.

  They have held classes downtown. [Irregular verb.]

- **The *present participle* adds *-ing* to the verb's plain form.** It combines with forms of *be* (*is buying*), modifies nouns and pronouns (*the boiling water*), or functions as a noun (*Running exhausts me*).

  A few artists are living in town today.

  They are holding classes downtown.

- **The *-s form* ends in *-s* or *-es.*** When the subject is a singular noun, a pronoun such as *everyone,* or the personal pronoun *he, she,* or *it,* the *-s* form indicates action that occurs in the present, occurs habitually, or is generally true.

  The artist lives in town today.

  She holds classes downtown.

The verb *be* has eight forms rather than the five forms of most other verbs:

Plain form	be		
Present participle	being		
Past participle	been		
	I	*he, she, it*	*we, you, they*
Present tense	am	is	are
Past tense	was	was	were

CULTURE LANGUAGE   If standard American English is not your native language or dialect, you may have difficulty with verbs' *-s* forms (including those for *be*: *is, was*) or with the forms that indicate time (such as the past-tense form). See pages 31–32 and 39–42, respectively, for more on these forms.

Helping Verbs

Helping verbs, also called **auxiliary verbs,** combine with some verb forms to indicate time and other kinds of meaning, as in *can run*, *was sleeping*, *had been eaten*. These combinations are **verb phrases.** Since the plain form, present participle, or past participle in any verb phrase always carries the principal meaning, it is sometimes called the **main verb.**

Verb phrase

Helping   *Main*

Artists can   train others to draw.
The techniques have   changed little.

Following are the most common helping verbs:

be able to	have to	shall
be supposed to	may	should
can	might	used to
could	must	will
had better	ought to	would

Forms of *be*: be, am, is, are, was, were, been, being
Forms of *have*: have, has, had, having
Forms of *do*: do, does, did

CULTURE LANGUAGE   The helping verbs of standard American English may be problematic if you are accustomed to speaking another language or dialect. See pp. 33–35 for more on helping verbs.

1.5a Use the correct forms of *sing/sang/sung* and other irregular verbs.

Most verbs are **regular**: they form their past tense and past participle by adding *-d* or *-ed* to the plain form.

Plain form	Past tense	Past participle
live	lived	lived
act	acted	acted

About two hundred English verbs are **irregular**: they form their past tense and past participle in some irregular way. Check a dictionary under the verb's plain form if you have any doubt about its other forms. If the verb is irregular, the dictionary will list the plain form, the past tense, and the past participle in that order (*go, went, gone*). If the dictionary gives only two forms (as in *think, thought*), then the past tense and the past participle are the same.

Common Irregular Verbs		
Plain Form	**Past Tense**	**Past Participle**
arise	arose	arisen
be	was, were	been
become	became	become
begin	began	begun
bid	bid	bid
bite	bit	bitten, bit
blow	blew	blown
break	broke	broken
bring	brought	brought
burst	burst	burst
buy	bought	bought
catch	caught	caught
choose	chose	chosen
come	came	come
cut	cut	cut
dive	dived, dove	dived
do	did	done
dream	dreamed, dreamt	dreamed, dreamt
drink	drank	drunk
drive	drove	driven
eat	ate	eaten
fall	fell	fallen
find	found	found
flee	fled	fled
fly	flew	flown
forget	forgot	forgotten, forgot
freeze	froze	frozen
get	got	got, gotten
give	gave	given
go	went	gone
grow	grew	grown
hang (suspend)	hung	hung
have	had	had

(continued)

Common Irregular Verbs (continued)

Plain Form	Past Tense	Past Participle
hear	heard	heard
hide	hid	hidden
hold	held	held
keep	kept	kept
know	knew	known
lay	laid	laid
lead	led	led
leave	left	left
lend	lent	lent
let	let	let
lie	lay	lain
lose	lost	lost
pay	paid	paid
prove	proved	proved, proven
ride	rode	ridden
ring	rang	rung
rise	rose	risen
run	ran	run
say	said	said
see	saw	seen
set	set	set
shake	shook	shaken
shrink	shrank, shrunk	shrunk, shrunken
sing	sang, sung	sung
sink	sank, sunk	sunk
sit	sat	sat
sleep	slept	slept
slide	slid	slid
speak	spoke	spoken
spring	sprang, sprung	sprung
stand	stood	stood
steal	stole	stolen
swim	swam	swum
swing	swung	swung
take	took	taken
tear	tore	torn
throw	threw	thrown
wear	wore	worn
write	wrote	written

CULTURE LANGUAGE   Some English dialects use distinctive verb forms that differ from those of standard American English: for instance, *drug* for *dragged*, *growed* for *grew*, *come* for *came*, or *went* for *gone*. In situations requiring standard American English, use the forms in the list here or in a dictionary.

Faulty   They have <u>went</u> to the movies.

Revised   They have <u>gone</u> to the movies.

EXERCISE 1.5.1   Using Irregular Verbs

For each irregular verb in brackets, supply either the past tense or the past participle, as appropriate, and identify the form you used.

Example

Though we had [hide] the cash box, it was [steal].
Though we had <u>hidden</u> the cash box, it was <u>stolen</u>. [Two past participles.]

1. He [dream] that he [sing] the National Anthem at the opening game.
2. He [keep] bringing out more food until finally they had all [eat] too much.
3. Tyler [choose] a good spot and then Arun [hang] the picture.
4. After she had [speak] about interest rates, the economist [draw] some interesting conclusions.
5. Because the day was so dark, it seemed as though the sun had never [rise].
6. Before we could stop him, my cousin had [drink] all the chocolate milk and had [eat] all the cookies.
7. The fans were encouraged because their team had not [lose] a home game all season.
8. The wind [blow] and my hands almost [freeze].
9. If we had not [leave] the table, we would have [fall] asleep.
10. The dry spell was [break] when the rains [begin] again.

EXERCISE 1.5.2   Using Irregular Verbs

For each irregular verb in brackets, replace the plain form with the past tense or the past participle, as appropriate, and identify the form you used.

Example

Population has [be] a concern.
Population has <u>been</u> a concern. [Past participle.]

1 The world population had [grow] by two-thirds of a billion people in less than a decade. **2** Recently it [break] the 7 billion mark. **3** Population experts have [draw] pictures of a crowded future, predicting that the world population may have [slide] up to as many as 9.5 billion by the year 2050. **4** The supply of food, clean water, and land is of particular concern. **5** Even though the food supply [rise] in the last decade, the share to each person [fall]. **6** At the same time the water supply, which had actually [become] healthier in the twentieth century, [sink] in size and quality. **7** Changes in land use [run] nomads and subsistence farmers off their fields, while the overall number of species on earth [shrink] by 20%.

8 Yet not all the news is bad. **9** Recently some countries have [begin] to heed these and other problems and to explore how technology can be [drive] to help the earth and all its populations. **10** Population control has [find] adherents all over the world. **11** Crop management has [take] some pressure off lands with poor soil, allowing their owners to produce food, while genetic engineering promises to replenish food supplies that have [shrink]. **12** Some new techniques for waste processing have [prove] effective. **13** Land conservation programs have [give] endangered species room to reproduce and thrive.

1.5b Distinguish between *sit* and *set*, *lie* and *lay*, and *rise* and *raise*.

The forms of *sit* and *set*, *lie* and *lay*, and *rise* and *raise* are easy to confuse.

Plain form	Past tense	Past participle
sit	sat	sat
set	set	set
lie	lay	lain
lay	laid	laid
rise	rose	risen
raise	raised	raised

In each of these confusing pairs, one verb is intransitive (it does not take an object) and one is transitive (it does take an object). (See p. 13 for more on this distinction.)

Intransitive

The patients lie in their beds. [*Lie* means "recline" and takes no object.]

Visitors sit with the patients. [*Sit* means "be seated" or "be located" and takes no object.]

Patients' temperatures rise. [*Rise* means "increase" or "get up" and takes no object.]

Transitive

Nursing aides lay the dinner trays on tables. [*Lay* means "place" and takes an object, here *trays*.]

The aides set the trays down. [*Set* means "place" and takes an object, here *trays*.]

The aides raise the patients' beds. [*Raise* means "lift" or "bring up" and takes an object, here *beds*.]

Note The verb *lie* meaning "to tell an untruth" is a regular verb. Its past tense and past participle forms are *lied*: *Nikki lied to us. She has lied to us for many years.*

EXERCISE 1.5.3 Distinguishing between *sit/set, lie/lay, rise/raise*

Choose the correct verb from the pair given in brackets. Then supply the past tense or past participle, as appropriate.

Example

After I washed all the windows, I [lie, lay] down the squeegee and then I [sit, set] the table.

After I washed all the windows, I laid down the squeegee and then I set the table.

1. Yesterday afternoon the child [lie, lay] down for a nap.
2. The child has been [rise, raise] by her grandparents.
3. Most days her grandfather has [sit, set] with her, reading her stories.
4. She has [rise, raise] at dawn most mornings.
5. Her toys were [lie, lay] on the floor.

1.5c Use the *-s* and *-ed* forms of the verb when they are required.

Speakers of some English dialects and nonnative speakers of English sometimes omit the *-s* and *-ed* verb endings when they are required in standard American English. If you tend to omit these endings in writing, practice pronouncing them when speaking or when reading correct verbs aloud, such as those in the examples here. The spoken practice can help you remember the endings in writing.

1 Required *-s* Ending

Use the *-s* form of a verb when *both* of these situations apply:

- **The subject is a singular noun (*boy*), an indefinite pronoun (*everyone*), or *he, she*, or *it*.** These subjects are **third person,** used when someone or something is being spoken about.

    The letter asks [not ask] for a quick response.

    Everything costs [not cost] money.

- **The verb's action occurs in the present,** as in the preceding examples.

Be especially careful with the *-s* forms of *be* (*is*), *have* (*has*), and *do* (*does, doesn't*). These forms should always be used to indicate present time with third-person singular subjects.

The company is [not be] late in responding.

The proposal has [not have] problems.

The committee doesn't [not don't] have the needed data.

The contract does [not do] depend on the response.

In addition, *be* has an *-s* form in the past tense with *I* and third-person singular subjects:

> I was invited.
>
> The company was [not were] in trouble before.

Except for the past-tense *I was*, the pronouns *I and you* and all plural subjects do *not* take the *-s* form of present-tense verbs:

> I am [not is] a student.
>
> You are [not is] also a student.
>
> They are [not is] students, too.

2 Required *-ed* or *-d* Ending

The *-ed* or *-d* verb form is required in *any* of these situations:

- **The verb's action occurred in the past:**

  The company asked [not ask] for more time.

- **The verb form functions as a modifier:**

  The data concerned [not concern] should be retrievable.

- **The verb form combines with a form of the helping verb *be* or *have*:**

  The company is supposed [not suppose] to be the best.

  The law firm has developed [not develop] an excellent reputation.

Watch especially for a needed *-ed* or *-d* ending when it isn't pronounced clearly in speech, as in *asked, discussed, mixed, supposed, walked,* and *used.*

EXERCISE 1.5.4 Using *-s* and *-ed* Verb Endings

Supply the correct form of each verb in brackets. Be careful to include *-s* and *-ed* (or *-d*) endings where they are needed for standard English.

Example

Unfortunately, the roof on our new house already [leak].

Unfortunately, the roof on our new house already leaks.

1. A teacher sometimes [ask] too much of a student.
2. In high school I was once [punish] for being sick.
3. I had [miss] a week of school because of a serious case of the flu.
4. I [realize] that I would fail a test unless I had a chance to make up the class work.
5. I [discuss] the problem with the teacher.
6. He said I was [suppose] to make up the work while I was sick.
7. At that I [walk] out of the class.

8. I [receive] a falling grade then, but it did not change my attitude.

9. I [work] harder in the courses that have more understanding teachers.

10. Today I still balk when a teacher [make] unreasonable demands or [expect] miracles.

1.5d Use helping verbs with main verbs appropriately.

Helping verbs combine with main verbs in verb phrases: *The line should have been cut. Who was calling?*

1 Required Helping Verbs

Standard American English requires helping verbs in certain situations:

- **The main verb ends in *-ing*:**

  Faulty   Scientist conducting research.

  Revised   Scientists are conducting research.

- **The main verb is *been* or *be*:**

  Faulty   Researchers been fortunate in their discoveries.

  Revised   Researchers have been fortunate in their discoveries.

  Faulty   Some researchers be real-life Indiana Joneses.

  Revised   Some researchers could be real-life Indiana Joneses.

- **The main verb is a past participle such as *talked*, *begun*, or *thrown*:**

  Faulty   The medical errors reported in the news.

  Revised   The medical errors were reported in the news.

  Faulty   The dancers given interviews on TV.

  Revised   The dancers have given interviews on TV.

In these examples, omitting the helping verb creates an incomplete sentence, or sentence fragment (see pp. 86–89).

2 Combination of Helping Verb + Main Verb

Helping verbs and main verbs combine into verb phrases in specific ways.

Note The main verb in a verb phrase (the one carrying the main meaning) does not change to show a change in subject or time: *she has sung, you had sung*. Only the helping verb may change.

Form of *be* + Present Participle

Create the progressive tenses with *be, am, is, are, was, were, or been* followed by the main verb's present participle (ending in *-ing*).

Faulty	She is work on a new book.
Revised	She is working on a new book.

Faulty	She has been work on it for several months.
Revised	She has been working on it for several months.

Note Verbs that express mental states or activities rather than physical actions do not usually appear in the progressive tenses. These verbs include *adore, appear, believe, belong, have, hear, know, like, love, need, see, taste, think, understand,* and *want*.

Faulty	She is wanting to understand contemporary art.
Revised	She wants to understand contemporary art.

Form of *be* + Past Participle

Create the passive voice with *be, am, is, are, was, were, being, or been* followed by the main verb's past participle (usually ending in *-d* or *-ed* or, for irregular verbs, in *-t* or *-n*).

Faulty	Her last book was finish in four months.
Revised	Her last book was finished in four months.

Faulty	It was bring to the President's attention.
Revised	It was brought to the President's attention.

Note Only transitive verbs may form the passive voice.

Faulty	A philosophy conference was occurred that week. [*Occur* is not a transitive verb.]
Revised	A philosophy conference occurred that week.

Form of *have* + Past Participle

To create one of the perfect tenses, use the main verb's past participle preceded by a form of *have*, such as *has, had, have been,* or *will have had*.

Faulty	Some students have complain about the lab.
Revised	Some students have complained about the lab.

Faulty	Money has not been spend on the lab in years.
Revised	Money has not been spent on the lab in years.

Form of *do* + Plain Form

Always with the plain form of the main verb, three forms of *do* serve as helping verbs: *do, does, did*.

Faulty	Safety concerns <u>do exists</u>.
Revised	Safety concerns <u>do exist</u>.

Faulty	Didn't the lab <u>closed</u> briefly last year?
Revised	Didn't the lab <u>close</u> briefly last year?

Modal + Plain Form

The **modal** helping verbs convey ability, possibility, necessity, and other meanings. They include *be able to, be supposed to, can, could, had better, have to, may, might, must, ought to, shall, should, used to, will,* and *would.*

Use the plain form of the main verb with a modal unless the modal combines with another helping verb (usually *have*):

Faulty	The lab equipment <u>may causes</u> injury.
Revised	The lab equipment <u>may cause</u> injury.

Faulty	The equipment <u>could have fail</u>.
Revised	The equipment <u>could have failed</u>.

**EXERCISE 1.5.5   Using Helping Verbs   **

Add helping verbs in the following sentences where they are needed for standard American English.

Example

The school be opened to shelter storm victims.

The school <u>will</u> be opened to shelter storm victims.

1. For as long as I can remember, I been writing stories.
2. While I living with my grandparents one summer, I wrote mystery stories.
3. Nearly every afternoon I sat at the computer and wrote about two brothers who solved mysteries while their mother be working.
4. By the end of the summer, I written four stories.
5. I was very happy when one of my stories published in the school newspaper.

**EXERCISE 1.5.6   Using Helping Verbs   **

Add helping verbs to the following paragraph where they are needed for standard American English. If a sentence is correct as given, circle the number preceding it.

Example

Roberto training to work as a tutor.

Roberto <u>is</u> training to work as a tutor.

1 Each year thousands of new readers been discovering Agatha Christie's mysteries. **2** Christie, a well-loved writer who worked as a nurse during World War I, wrote more than sixty-five detective novels. **3** Christie never expected that her mysteries become as popular as they did. **4** Nor did she anticipate that her play, *The Mousetrap*, be performed for decades. **5** At her death in 1976, Christie been the best-selling English novelist for some time. **6** Her books still selling well to readers who like being baffled.

EXERCISE 1.5.7   Revising: Helping Verbs Plus Main Verbs   CULTURE LANGUAGE

Revise the following paragraph so that helping verbs and main verbs are used correctly for standard American English. If a sentence is correct as given, circle the number preceding it.

Example

The college testing service has test as many as five hundred students at one time.

The college testing service has <u>tested</u> as many as five hundred students at one time.

1 A report from the Bureau of the Census has confirm a widening gap between rich and poor. **2** As suspected, the percentage of people below the poverty level did increased over the last decade. **3** The richest 1% of the population is make 17% of all the income. **4** These households will keeping an average of $1.3 million each after taxes. **5** The average middle-income household will retain about $55,000.

1.5e Use a gerund or an infinitive after a verb as appropriate. CULTURE LANGUAGE

A **gerund** is the *-ing* form of a verb used as a noun: *Smoking is unhealthful.* An **infinitive** is the plain form of a verb preceded by *to*: *Try not to smoke.* Gerunds and infinitives may follow certain verbs but not others. Sometimes the use of a gerund or an infinitive with the same verb changes the meaning:

The woman stopped <u>eating</u>. [She no longer ate.]

The woman stopped <u>to eat</u>. [She paused in order to eat.]

1 Either Gerund or Infinitive

A gerund or an infinitive may follow these verbs with no significant difference in meaning: *begin, can't bear, can't stand, continue, hate, hesitate, like, love, prefer, start.*

The pump began <u>working</u>. The pump began <u>to work</u>.

2 Meaning Change with Gerund or Infinitive

With four verbs—*forget, remember, stop,* and *try*—a gerund has quite a different meaning from an infinitive.

The engineer stopped <u>watching</u> the pump. [She no longer watched.]

The engineer stopped <u>to watch</u> the pump. [She paused in order to watch.]

3 Gerund, Not Infinitive

Do not use an infinitive after these verbs: *admit, adore, appreciate, avoid, consider, deny, detest, discuss, dislike, enjoy, escape, finish, imagine, keep, mind, miss, practice, put off, quit, recall, resent, resist, risk, suggest, tolerate, understand.*

> **Faulty**   She suggested <u>to check</u> the pump.
>
> **Revised** She suggested <u>checking</u> the pump.

4 Infinitive, Not Gerund

Do not use a gerund after these verbs: *agree, ask, assent, beg, claim, decide, expect, have, hope, manage, mean, offer, plan, pretend, promise, refuse, say, wait, want, wish.*

> **Faulty**   She decided <u>checking</u> the pump.
>
> **Revised** She decided <u>to check</u> the pump.

5 Noun or Pronoun + Infinitive

Some verbs may be followed by an infinitive alone or by a noun or pronoun and an infinitive: *ask, beg, choose, dare, expect, help, need, promise, want, wish, would like.* A noun or pronoun changes the meaning.

> She expected <u>to watch</u>.
>
> She expected <u>her workers</u> <u>to watch</u>.

Some verbs *must* be followed by a noun or pronoun before an infinitive: *advise, allow, cause, challenge, command, convince, encourage, forbid, force, hire, instruct, order, permit, persuade, remind, require, teach, tell, warn.*

> She instructed <u>her workers</u> <u>to watch</u>.

Do not use *to* before the infinitive when it comes after one of the following verbs and a noun or pronoun: *feel, have, hear, let, make* ("force"), *see, watch.*

> She let her workers <u>learn</u> by observation.

EXERCISE 1.5.8   Revising: Verbs Plus Gerunds or Infinitives

Revise the following sentences so that gerunds or infinitives are used correctly with verbs. Circle the number preceding any sentence that is already correct.

Example

A politician cannot avoid to alienate some voters.

A politician cannot avoid <u>alienating</u> some voters.

1. A program called *Boostup.org* encourages students to finish high school.
2. People supporting this program hope that students will at least postpone to drop out of school.
3. Adults who want to help can promise mentoring a student.
4. Because of *Boostup.org*, many students who might have dropped out now plan going to college.
5. The organization persuades volunteers signing up via its Web site, *Facebook* page, and *Twitter* feed.

1.5f Use the appropriate particles with two-word verbs.

Some verbs consist of two words: the verb itself and a **particle,** a preposition or adverb that affects the meaning of the verb.

> <u>Look up</u> the answer. [Research the answer.]

> <u>Look over</u> the answer. [Examine the answer.]

The meanings of these two-word verbs are often quite different from the meanings of the individual words that make them up. (There are some three-word verbs, too, such as *put up with* and *run out of.*) A dictionary of English as a second language will define two-word verbs and say whether the verbs may be separated in a sentence, as explained in this section. (See p. 124 for a list of ESL dictionaries.)

1 Inseparable Two-Word Verbs

Verbs and particles that may not be separated by any other words include the following: *catch on, get along, give in, go out, grow up, keep on, look into, run into, run out of, speak up, stay away, take care of.*

> Faulty   Children <u>grow</u> quickly <u>up</u>.

> Revised   Children <u>grow</u> up quickly.

2 Separable Two-Word Verbs

Most two-word verbs that take direct objects may be separated by the object.

> Parents <u>help out</u> their children.

> Parents <u>help</u> their children <u>out</u>.

If the direct object is a pronoun, the pronoun *must* separate the verb from the particle.

> Faulty   Parents <u>help out</u> them.

> Revised   Parents <u>help</u> them <u>out</u>.

The separable two-word verbs include the following: *call off, call up, fill out, fill up, give away, give back, hand in, help out, look over, look up, pick up, point out, put away, put back, put off, take out, take over, try on, try out, turn down.*

EXERCISE 1.5.9   Revising: Verbs Plus Particles   ⟨CULTURE LANGUAGE⟩

The two- and three-word verbs in the sentences below are underlined. Some are correct as given, and some are not because they should or should not be separated by other words. Revise the verbs and other words that are incorrect. Consult the lists on these pages or an ESL dictionary if necessary to determine which verbs are separable.

Example

Hollywood producers never seem to come up with entirely new plots, but they also never run new ways out of to present old ones.

Hollywood producers never seem to come up with [correct] entirely new plots, but they also never run out of new ways to present old ones.

1. American movies treat everything from going out with someone to making up an ethnic identity, but few people look their significance into.
2. While some viewers stay away from topical films, others turn at the theater up simply because a movie has sparked debate.
3. Some movies attracted rowdy spectators, and the theaters had to throw out them.
4. Filmmakers have always been eager to point their influence out to the public.
5. Everyone agrees that filmmakers will keep creating controversy on, if only because it can fill up theaters.

1.6 VERB TENSES

> *Successful writers . . .*
>
> - Know the forms and uses of the verb tenses (below and next page).
> - Observe the special uses of the present tense (*sing*) (p. 41).
> - Observe the uses of the perfect tenses (*have/had/will have sung*) (p. 41).
> - Keep tenses consistent (p. 42).

Tense shows the time of a verb's action. It shows whether the action is occurring now, occurred in the past, or will occur in the future. The following box illustrates the tense forms for a regular verb. (Irregular verbs have different forms. See pp. 26–29.)

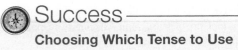

Success

Choosing Which Tense to Use

If the action . . .	Use This Tense	Example
. . . is occurring now		
. . . is happening now or occurs regularly	**Simple present**	The chef cooks huge meals.
. . . is happening (is in progress) now	**Present progressive**	The chef is cooking a huge meal.
. . . began in the past and continues in the present	**Present perfect**	The chef has cooked in this restaurant for two years.
. . . began in the past and is in progress now	**Present perfect progressive**	The chef has been cooking a huge meal since this morning.
. . . occurred in the past		
. . . began and ended in the past	**Simple past**	The chef cooked a huge meal.
. . . was happening in the past when another action happened	**Past progressive**	The chef was cooking a huge meal when she ran out of butter.
. . . occurred sometime in the past	**Present perfect**	The chef has designed new kitchens.
. . . occurred in the past		
. . . began and ended before another action occurred	**Past perfect**	The chef had cooked a huge meal when the guests canceled their reservation.
. . . was happening over time when another past action occurred	**Past perfect progressive**	The chef had been cooking a huge meal before the electricity went off.
. . . will occur in the future		
. . . will take place in the future	**Simple future**	The chef will cook a huge meal.
. . . will be happening over time in the future when another action occurs	**Future progressive**	The chef will be cooking a huge meal until sunset.
. . . will be completed by a certain time or event in the future	**Future perfect**	The chef will have cooked a huge meal by the time guests arrive.
. . . will continue until a certain time or event in the future	**Future perfect progressive**	The chef will have been cooking for the whole day when the waiters arrive.

In standard American English, a verb conveys time through its form. In some other languages and English dialects, various markers besides verb form may indicate the time of a verb. For instance, in African American Vernacular English, *I be attending class on Friday* means that the speaker attends class every Friday. But to someone who doesn't know the dialect, the sentence could mean last Friday, this Friday, or every Friday. In standard American English, the intended meaning is indicated by verb tense: *I attended class on Friday. I will attend class on Friday. I attend class on Friday.*

1.6a Learn the special uses of the present tense (*sing*).

In most academic, business, and career writing, you will use the past tense (*the rebellion occurred*). However, the present tense has several distinctive uses.

Action occurring now

She understands the problem.

Habitual or recurring action

Banks regularly undergo audits.

A general truth

The earth is round.

Discussion of literature, film, and so on

Huckleberry Finn has adventures we all envy.

Future time

Funding ends in less than a year.

1.6b Learn the uses of the perfect tenses (*have/had/will have sung*).

The **perfect tenses** consist of a form of *have* plus the verb's past participle (*closed, hidden*). They indicate an action completed before another specific time or action. The present perfect tense can also indicate action begun in the past and continued into the present.

present perfect
The dancer has performed here only once.

past perfect
The dancer had trained in Asia before his performance here ten years ago.

future perfect
He will have danced here again by the end of the month.

⬭ CULTURE LANGUAGE   In English sentences with the present perfect tense, the words *since* and *for* are followed by different information. After *since,* give a specific point in time: *The play has run since 1999.* After *for,* give a span of time: *In London it has run for decades.*

1.6c Keep tenses consistent.

Within a sentence, the tenses of verbs and verb forms need not be identical as long as they reflect actual changes in time: *Ramon will graduate from college thirty years after his father arrived in America.* But needless shifts in tense will confuse or distract readers:

Inconsistent tense	Immediately after Booth shot Lincoln, Major Rathbone threw himself upon the assassin. But Booth pulls a knife and plunges it into the major's arm.
Revised	Immediately after Booth shot Lincoln, Major Rathbone threw himself upon the assassin. But Booth pulled a knife and plunged it into the major's arm.
Inconsistent tense	The main character in the novel suffers psychologically because he has a clubfoot, but eventually he triumphed over his disability.
Revised	The main character in the novel suffers psychologically because he has a clubfoot, but eventually he triumphs over his disability. [Use the present tense to discuss the content of literature, film, and so on.]

EXERCISE 1.6.1   Revising: Verb Form and Tense

In the sentences below, correct any errors in verb form or tense. If a sentence is correct as given, circle the number preceding it.

Example

You is next in line.
You are next in line.

1. Carlos called and ask Jen if she wanted a ride to the basketball game.
2. Eric went to a party last week and meets a girl he knew in high school.
3. I cook spaghetti every Wednesday, and my family always enjoys it.
4. A package come in yesterday's mail for my office mate.
5. Fatima wears a beautiful red dress to her sister's wedding last week.
6. Marni answered a letter she receive from her former employer.
7. James waited until he was introduced, and then he run on stage.
8. The audience laughed loudly at the comedian's jokes and applauds at the funniest ones.
9. The group had ordered chicken wings, and it was not disappointed when the meal arrived.
10. Kayley spends the afternoon answering e-mail when sales were slow.

EXERCISE 1.6.2   Revising: Consistent Past Tense

In the paragraph below, change the tenses of the verbs as needed to maintain consistent simple past tense. If a sentence is correct as given, mark the number preceding it.

Example

Adria broke her ankle when she trips while she was practicing the broad jump.

Adria broke her ankle when she tripped while she was practicing the broad jump.

1 The 1960 presidential race between Richard Nixon and John F. Kennedy was the first to feature a televised debate. **2** Despite his extensive political experience, Nixon perspires heavily and looks haggard and uneasy in front of the camera. **3** By contrast, Kennedy was projecting cool poise and providing crisp answers that made him seem fit for the office of President. **4** The public responded positively to Kennedy's image. **5** His poll ratings shoot up immediately, while Nixon's take a corresponding drop. **6** The popular vote was close, but Kennedy won the election.

EXERCISE 1.6.3   Revising: Consistent Present Tense

In the following paragraph, change the tenses of the verbs as needed to maintain consistent simple present tense. If a sentence is correct as given, mark the number preceding it.

Example

The boy in the story wins the prize but lost it in a bet.

The boy in the story wins the prize but loses it in a bet.

1 E. B. White's famous children's novel *Charlotte's Web* is a wonderful story of friendship and loyalty. **2** Charlotte, the wise and motherly spider, decided to save her friend Wilbur, the young and childlike pig, from being butchered by his owner. **3** She made a plan to weave words into her web that described Wilbur. **4** She first weaves "Some Pig" and later presented "Terrific," "Radiant," and "Humble." **5** Her plan succeeded beautifully. **6** She fools the humans into believing that Wilbur was a pig unlike any other, and Wilbur lived.

1.7 VERB MOOD

Successful writers . . .

- Use the subjunctive forms appropriately: *I wish I were* (next page).
- Keep mood consistent (next page).

The **mood** of a verb indicates whether a sentence is a statement or a question (*The theater needs help. Can you help the theater?*), a command (*Help the theater*), or a nonfactual expression (*I wish I were an actor*).

1.7a Use the subjunctive verb forms appropriately: *I wish I were.*

The **subjunctive mood** expresses a suggestion, requirement, or desire, or it states a condition that is contrary to fact (that is, imaginary or hypothetical).

- **Verbs such as *ask, insist, urge, require, recommend,* and *suggest* indicate request or requirement.** They often precede a dependent clause beginning with *that* and containing the substance of the request or requirement. For all subjects, the verb in the *that* clause is the plain form:

  plain form
  Rules require that every donation be mailed.

- **Contrary-to-fact clauses state imaginary or hypothetical conditions. They usually begin with *if* or *unless,* or they follow *wish.*** For present contrary-to-fact clauses, use the verb's past-tense form (for *be,* use the past-tense form *were* for all subjects):

  past   past
  If the theater were in better shape and had more money, its future would be assured.

  past
  I wish I were able to donate money.

  For past contrary-to-fact clauses, use *had* plus the verb's past participle:

  past perfect
  The theater would be better funded if it had been better managed.

Note Do not use the helping verb *would* or *could* in a contrary-to-fact clause beginning with *if:*

Not   Many people would have helped if they would have known.

But   Many people would have helped if they had known.

1.7b Keep mood consistent.

Shifts in mood within a sentence or among related sentences can be confusing. Such shifts occur most frequently in directions.

Inconsistent mood	Cook the mixture slowly, and you should stir it until the sugar is dissolved. [Shifts from command to statement.]
Revised	Cook the mixture slowly, and stir it until the sugar is dissolved. [Consistent command.]

EXERCISE 1.7.1   Revising: Subjunctive Mood

Revise the following sentences with appropriate subjunctive verb forms.

Example

I would help the old man if there was a way I could reach him.
I would help the old man if there <u>were</u> a way I could reach him.

1. The letter requests that we are patient.
2. If I was rich, I'd still clip coupons from the paper.
3. The syllabus requires that each student writes three papers and takes two essay tests.
4. They treat me as if I was their son.
5. I wish the lighting in the office was better because my eyes are strained.

EXERCISE 1.7.2   Revising: Subjunctive Mood

Revise the following paragraph with appropriate subjunctive verb forms. If a sentence is correct as given, circle the number preceding it.

Example

If Natalie would have looked harder, she would have found her keys.
If Natalie <u>had</u> looked harder, she would have found her keys.

1 If John Hawkins had known of all the dangerous side effects of smoking tobacco, would he have introduced the plant to England in 1565? **2** In promoting tobacco, Hawkins noted that if a Florida Indian man was to travel for several days, he would have smoked tobacco to satisfy his hunger and thirst. **3** Early tobacco growers in the United States feared that their product would not gain acceptance unless it was perceived as healthful, so they spread Hawkins's story. **4** But local governments, more concerned about public safety and morality than health, passed laws requiring that colonists smoked tobacco only if they were five miles from any town. **5** To prevent decadence, in 1647 Connecticut passed a law mandating that one's smoking of tobacco was limited to once a day in one's own home.

1.8 VERB VOICE

Successful writers . . .

- Distinguish between active voice and passive voice, preferring active (next page).
- Keep voice consistent (p. 47).

The **voice** of a verb tells whether the subject of the sentence performs the action (**active**) or is acted upon (**passive**).

CULTURE LANGUAGE In standard American English, a passive verb always consists of a form of *be* plus the past participle of the main verb: *Rents are controlled*. If the *be* form is *be, being,* or *been,* then other helping verbs must also be used: *Rents will be controlled. Rents are being controlled. Rents should have been controlled.* Only a transitive verb (one that takes an object) may be used in the passive voice. (See pp. 13–14.)

Active and Passive Voice

Active voice   The subject performs the action.

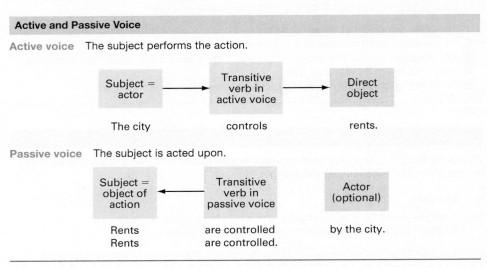

Subject = actor	Transitive verb in active voice	Direct object
The city	controls	rents.

Passive voice   The subject is acted upon.

Subject = object of action	Transitive verb in passive voice	Actor (optional)
Rents	are controlled	by the city.
Rents	are controlled.	

1.8a Distinguish between active voice and passive voice.

The active voice always names the performer of the verb's action. The passive voice often does not name the performer of the action, or it names the actor in a *by* phrase.

Active   Students use the Internet for research.

Passive   The Internet is used for research.

Passive   The Internet is used for research by students.

Use these guidelines for choosing active or passive voice:

- **Generally, prefer the active voice.** The active voice is usually more clear, concise, and emphatic than the passive voice.

  Active   Runoff from lawn fertilizers encourages algae growth.

  Passive   Algae growth is encouraged by runoff from lawn fertilizers.

- **Use the passive voice when the performer of the action is unknown.**

  The broken window had been wiped clean of fingerprints. [The person who wiped the window clean is unknown.]

- **Use the passive voice when the performer of the action is unimportant or less important than the object of the action.**

  The poem "Kitchenette Building" by Gwendolyn Brooks was discussed in class. [Who discussed the poem is less important than the poem.]

1.8b Keep voice consistent.

A shift in voice (and subject) within or between sentences can be awkward and even confusing.

Inconsistent voice	Two <u>police officers</u> <u>walked</u> toward me, and I <u>was asked</u> for identification.
Revised	Two <u>police officers</u> <u>walked</u> toward me and <u>asked</u> me for identification.

EXERCISE 1.8.1   Converting between Active and Passive Voices

Convert the verbs in the following sentences from active to passive or from passive to active. (In converting from passive to active, you may need to add a subject.) Which version of the sentence seems more effective and why?

Example

The building was demolished last spring.
The <u>city</u> <u>demolished</u> the building last spring.

1. Volunteers built the new school.
2. The aspiring actor was discovered by a talk-show host.
3. When the Eiffel Tower was built in 1889, it was thought by the French to be ugly.
4. Drugs are often prescribed to relieve depression.
5. Whales are still being killed by foreign fishing fleets.

1.9 SUBJECT-VERB AGREEMENT

Successful writers . . .

- Use *-s* or *-es* for the subject or the verb, but not both (p. 48).
- Make the subject and verb agree even when other words come between them (p. 49).
- Make the verb agree with a subject joined by *and, or,* or *nor* (pp. 49–50).
- Make the verb agree when the subject is an indefinite pronoun or collective noun (p. 50).
- Make the verb agree with the antecedents of *who, which,* or *that* (p. 51).
- Use a singular verb for a singular noun ending in *-s* (p. 51).
- Make the verb and subject agree even when the verb comes first (p. 52).
- Make a linking verb agree with its subject (p. 52).

The subject and verb in a sentence must agree. *Agree* means that they must be consistent, or fit together correctly, just as your clothing must agree with the occasion for which you are wearing it.

The subject of a sentence is either singular or plural. *Singular* means "one"; *plural* means "more than one." The subject determines what verb ending is used in the sentence. Singular subjects use singular verbs, and plural subjects use plural verbs. Singular verbs usually end in *-s* or *-es*. Plural verbs do not.

Singular subject and singular verb

The teenager acts sophisticated.

Plural subject and plural verb

The teenagers act sophisticated.

Some subject-verb agreement errors occur when endings are omitted. Other errors occur when the relationship between the sentence parts is unclear.

1.9a Use an *-s* or *-es* ending for the subject or the verb, but not both.

An *-s* or *-es* ending does opposite things to nouns and verbs: it usually makes a noun *plural*, and it always makes a present-tense verb *singular*. If the subject noun is plural, it will probably end in *-s*. The verb will not. If the subject is singular, it will *not* end in *-s*. The verb will end in *-s*.

Noun with *-s* = plural	Verb without *-s* = plural
The plants	grow quickly.
Dogs	eat kibble.

Noun without *-s* = singular	Verb with *-s* = singular
The plant	grows quickly.
The dog	eats kibble.

 If your first language or dialect is not standard American English, subject-verb agreement may be difficult for the following reasons:

• **Some English dialects omit the *-s* ending for singular verbs or use the *-s* ending for plural verbs:**

Nonstandard	The voter resist change.
Standard	The voter resists change.
Standard	The voters resist change.

The verb *be* changes spelling for singular and plural in both present and past tense. (See also p. 26.)

| Nonstandard | Taxes is high. They was raised just last year. |
| Standard | Taxes are high. They were raised just last year. |

Have also has a distinctive *-s* form, *has*:

Nonstandard   The new tax <u>have</u> little chance of passing.

Standard   The new tax <u>has</u> little chance of passing.

- **Some other languages change all parts of verb phrases to match their subjects,** but in English verb phrases only the helping verbs *be, have,* and *do* change for different subjects. The modal helping verbs—*can, may, should, will,* and others— do not change.

Nonstandard   The tax <u>mays</u> pass next year.

Standard   The tax <u>may</u> pass next year.

The main verb in a verb phrase also does not change for different subjects.

Nonstandard   The tax may <u>passes</u> next year.

Standard   The tax may <u>pass</u> next year.

1.9b Subject and verb should agree even when other words come between them.

The survival of hibernating frogs in freezing temperatures <u>is</u> [not <u>are</u>] fascinating.

A chemical reaction inside the cells of the frogs <u>stops</u> [not <u>stop</u>] the formation of ice crystals.

Note Phrases beginning with *as well as, together with, along with,* and *in addition to* do not change a singular subject to plural:

singular subject   singular verb
The president, together with the deans, <u>has</u> [not <u>have</u>] agreed.

1.9c Subjects joined by *and* usually take plural verbs.

Brandon and Andrew <u>were</u> roommates.

Exceptions When the parts of the subject form a single idea or refer to a single person or thing, they take a singular verb:

Avocado and bean sprouts <u>is</u> a California sandwich.

When a compound subject is preceded by the adjective *each* or *every*, the verb is usually singular:

Each man, woman, and child <u>has</u> a right to be heard.

1.9d When parts of a subject are joined by *or* or *nor*, the verb agrees with the nearer part.

Either the painter or the carpenter <u>knows</u> the cost.

The cabinets or the bookcases <u>are</u> too expensive.

When one part of the subject is singular and the other plural, avoid awkwardness by placing the plural part closer to the verb so that the verb is plural:

Awkward   Neither the owners nor the contractor <u>agrees</u>.

Revised   Neither the contractor nor the owners <u>agree</u>.

1.9e With *everyone* and other indefinite pronouns, use a singular or plural verb as appropriate.

Indefinite pronouns include *anyone, anybody, each, everyone, everybody, nobody, no one, nothing*, and *some one*. Most indefinite pronouns are singular in meaning (they refer to a single unspecified person or thing), and they take a singular verb:

Something <u>smells</u>.   Neither <u>is</u> right.

The indefinite pronouns *all, any, more, most, none*, and *some* take a singular or a plural verb depending on whether the word they refer to is singular or plural:

All of the money <u>is</u> reserved for emergencies.

All of the funds <u>are</u> reserved for emergencies.

1.9f Collective nouns such as *team* take singular or plural verbs depending on meaning.

A collective noun has singular form and names a group of persons or things: *army, audience, crowd, family, group, team*. Use a singular verb with a collective noun when the group acts as a unit:

The group <u>agrees</u> that action is necessary.

But when the group's members act separately, not together, use a plural verb:

The old group <u>have gone</u> their separate ways.

If a combination such as *group have* seems awkward, reword the sentence: *The <u>members</u> of the old group have gone their separate ways.*

CULTURE LANGUAGE   In standard American English, some noncount nouns (nouns that don't form plurals) are collective nouns because they name groups—for instance, *furniture, clothing, information, mail, machinery, equipment, military, police, vocabulary*. These noncount nouns usually take singular verbs:

Mail <u>*arrives*</u> *daily.* But some of these nouns take plural verbs, including *clergy, military, people, police,* and any collective noun that comes from an adjective, such as *the poor, the rich, the young, the elderly.* If you mean one representative of the group, use a singular noun such as *police officer* or *poor person.*

1.9g *Who, which,* and *that* take verbs that agree with their antecedents.

When used as subjects, *who, which,* and *that* refer to another word in the sentence, called the **antecedent**. The verb agrees with the antecedent:

> Mayor Garber ought to listen to people who <u>work</u> for her. [*Who* refers to *people.* The verb must agree with *people.*]

> Dr. Bardini is the only professor who <u>has</u> an assistant. [*Who* refers to *professor.* The verb must agree with *professor.*]

Agreement problems often occur with *who* and *that* when the sentence includes *one of the* or *the only one of the:*

> Emily is one of the aides who <u>work</u> unpaid. [Of the aides who work unpaid, Emily is one.]

> Emily is the only one of the aides who <u>knows</u> the community. [Of the aides, only one, Emily, knows the community.]

> **CULTURE LANGUAGE** In standard American English, a phrase beginning with *one of the* always includes a plural noun: *Emily is one of the* <u>*aides*</u> [not <u>*aide*</u>] *who work unpaid.*

1.9h *News* and other singular nouns ending in *-s* take singular verbs.

Singular nouns ending in *-s* include *athletics, economics, linguistics, mathematics, measles, mumps, news, physics, politics,* and *statistics* as well as place names such as *Athens, Wales,* and *United States.*

> After so long a wait, the news <u>has</u> to be good.

> Statistics <u>is</u> required of psychology majors.

A few of these words also take plural verbs, but only when they describe individual items rather than whole bodies of activity or knowledge: *The statistics* <u>*prove*</u> *him wrong.*

Measurements and figures ending in *-s* may also be singular when the quantity they refer to is a unit.

> Three years <u>is</u> a long time to wait.

> Three-fourths of the library <u>consists</u> of reference books.

1.9i The verb agrees with the subject even when it precedes the subject.

The verb precedes the subject mainly in questions and in constructions beginning with *there* or *here* and a form of *be*.

Is voting a right or a privilege?
verb subject

There are differences between rights and privileges.
      verb   subject

1.9j *Is, are,* and other linking verbs agree with their subjects.

Make a linking verb agree with its subject, usually the first element in the sentence, not with other words that rename or describe the subject.

The child's sole support is her court-appointed guardians.

Her court-appointed guardians are the child's sole support.

1.9k Use singular verbs with titles and with words being defined.

Hakada Associates is a new firm.

Dream Days remains a favorite book.

Folks is a down-home word for *people*.

EXERCISE 1.9.1   Revising: Subject-Verb Agreement

Revise the verbs in the following sentences as needed to make subjects and verbs agree. If the sentence is correct as given, circle the number preceding it.

Example
Each of the job applicants type sixty words per minute.
Each of the job applicants types sixty words per minute.

1. Neither of the options are likely to receive support.
2. The number of students at the demonstration was disappointing.
3. Neither the won ton soup nor the chicken wings appeals to me.
4. The library owns the only one of the copies that are in good condition.
5. The idea that people their age still bite their nails are funny.
6. Some members of the chorus are going on the European tour.

7. Only some of the rooms in the house needs painting.
8. Physics are the only subject she feels competent in.
9. Is there enough handouts to go around?
10. The printer, along with two software programs and a user's manual, are included in the package.
11. Either his brother or his sister are responsible for that prank.
12. Every man, woman, and child seems to have an opinion on how the federal dollar should be spent.
13. The police claimed that the crowd were endangering public safety.
14. He is one of those persons who breaks promises easily.
15. *Two Brothers* is the title of his newest novel.

EXERCISE 1.9.2   Revising: Subject-Verb Agreement

Revise the verbs in the following sentences as needed to make subjects and verbs agree. If a sentence is correct as given, circle the number preceding it.

Example

Olivia is the only member of the sales team who travel to four states.
Olivia is the only member of the sales team who <u>travels</u> to four states.

1 Results from recent research shows that humor in the workplace relieves job-related stress. **2** Reduced stress in the workplace in turn reduce illness and absenteeism. **3** It can also reduce friction within an employee group, which then work together more productively.

4 Weinstein Associates is a consulting firm that hold workshops designed to make businesspeople laugh. **5** In sessions held by one consultant, each of the participants practice making others laugh. **6** "Isn't there enough laughs within you to spread the wealth?" the consultant asks the students. **7** She quotes Casey Stengel's rule that the best way to keep your management job is to separate the underlings who hate you from the ones who have not decided how they feel. **8** Such self-deprecating comments in public is uncommon among business managers, the consultant says. **9** Each of the managers in a typical firm takes the work much too seriously. **10** The humorous boss often feels like the only one of the managers who have other things in mind besides profits.

11 Another consultant from Weinstein Associates suggest cultivating office humor with practical jokes and cartoons. **12** When a manager or employees drops a rubber fish in the water cooler or posts cartoons on the bulletin board, office spirit usually picks up. **13** If the job of updating the cartoons is entrusted to an employee who has seemed easily distracted, the employee's concentration often improves. **14** Even the former sourpuss becomes one of those who hides a bad temper. **15** Every one of the consultants caution, however, that humor has no place in life-affecting corporate situations such as employee layoffs.

Pronouns

Pronouns are words such as *she* and *who* that refer to nouns. They deserve special care because their meaning always comes from the other words they refer to. This section discusses pronoun case, matching pronouns and the words they refer to, and making sure pronouns refer clearly to the right nouns.

1.10 PRONOUN CASE

Successful writers . . .

- Distinguish between compound subjects and compound objects (facing page).
- Use the subjective case for subject complements (facing page).
- Use *who* or *whom* depending on the pronoun's function (p. 56).
- Choose between *we* or *us* before a noun (p. 58).
- Use the appropriate case after *than* or *as* (p. 58).

Case is the form of a pronoun that shows the reader how it functions in a sentence.

- **The subjective case** indicates that the pronoun is a subject or subject complement.
- **The objective case** indicates that the pronoun is an object of a verb or preposition.
- **The possessive case** indicates possession or ownership.

Pronouns change case as shown in the following chart.

Subjective	Objective	Possessive
I	me	my, mine
you	you	your, yours
he	him	his
she	her	her, hers
it	it	its
we	us	our, ours
you	you	your, yours
they	them	their, theirs
who	whom	whose
whoever	whomever	—

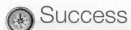 In standard American English, *-self* pronouns do not change form to show function. Their only forms are *myself, yourself, himself, herself, itself, ourselves, yourselves, themselves.* Avoid nonstandard forms such as *hisself, ourself,* and *theirselves.*

Faulty   Novick presented the proposal hisself.

Revised   Novick presented the proposal himself.

1.10a Distinguish between compound subjects and compound objects: *she and I* vs. *her and me.*

Subjects and objects consisting of two or more nouns or pronouns have the same case forms as they would if one pronoun stood alone:

compound
subject
She and Nick discussed the proposal.

compound
object
The proposal disappointed her and him.

If you are in doubt about the correct form, try this test:

Success

Testing for Case Forms in Compound Subjects or Objects

Steps	Examples
1. **Identify a compound construction** (one connected by *and, but, or, nor*).	[He, Him] and [I, me] won the prize.
2. **Write a separate sentence for each part of the compound.**	[He, Him] won the prize. [I, Me] won the prize.
3. **Choose pronouns that sound correct.**	He won the prize. I won the prize.
4. **Put the separate sentences back together.**	He and I won the prize.

1.10b Use the subjective case for subject complements: *It was she.*

After a linking verb, a pronoun renaming the subject (a subject complement) should be in the subjective case:

linking   subject
verb   complement
The ones who care most are she and Nick.

linking subject
verb complement
It was they whom the mayor appointed.

These constructions can sound stilted, especially when spoken. You can avoid stiffness by using the more natural order: *She and Nick are the ones who care most. The mayor appointed them.*

EXERCISE 1.10.1   Using Subjective and Objective Pronouns

From the pairs in brackets, select the appropriate subjective or objective pronoun(s) for each of the following sentences.

Example

"Between you and [I, me]," the salesman said, "this deal is the chance of a lifetime."

"Between you and me," the salesman said, "this deal is the chance of a lifetime."

1. Lisa and [I, me] were competing for places on the relay team.
2. The fastest runners at our school were [she, her] and [I, me], so [we, us] expected to make the team.
3. [She, Her] and [I, me] were friends but also intense rivals.
4. The time trials went badly, excluding both [she, her] and [I, me] from the team.
5. Next season [she, her] and [I, me] are determined to earn places on the team.

EXERCISE 1.10.2   Using Subjective and Objective Pronouns

In the following paragraph, select the appropriate subjective or objective pronoun from the pairs in brackets.

Example

The cat ran away from David and [I, me].
The cat ran away from David and me.

1 Jody and [I, me] had been hunting for jobs. **2** The best employees at our old company were [she, her] and [I, me], so [we, us] expected to find jobs quickly. **3** Between [she, her] and [I, me] the job search had lasted two months, and still it had barely begun. **4** Slowly, [she, her] and [I, me] stopped sharing leads. **5** It was obvious that Jody and [I, me] could not be as friendly as [we, us] had been.

1.10c The use of *who* vs. *whom* depends on the pronoun's function.

Use *who* where you would use *he* or *she*—all ending in vowels. Use *whom* where you would use *him* or *her*—all ending in consonants.

1 Questions

At the beginning of a question, use *who* for a subject and *whom* for an object:

subject
Who wrote the policy?

object
Whom does it affect?

Success

Testing for *Who* vs. *Whom* in Questions

Steps	Examples
1. **Ask the question, using *who* and *whom*.**	[Who, Whom] makes that decision? [Who, Whom] do I ask?
2. **Answer the question, using a personal pronoun.** Choose the pronoun that sounds correct, and note its case.	[She, Her] makes that decision. <u>She</u> makes that decision. [Subjective.] I ask [she, her]. I ask <u>her</u>. [Objective.]
3. **Use the same case (*who* or *whom*) in the question.**	<u>Who</u> makes that decision? [Subjective.] <u>Whom</u> do I ask? [Objective.]

2 Dependent Clauses

In a dependent clause, use *who* or *whoever* for a subject, *whom* or *whomever* for an object.

subject
Give old clothes to <u>whoever</u> needs them.

object
I don't know <u>whom</u> the mayor appointed.

 Success

Testing for *Who* vs. *Whom* in Dependent Clauses

Steps	Examples
1. **Locate the dependent clause.**	Few people know [who, whom] they should ask. People are unsure [who, whom] makes the decision.
2. **Rewrite the dependent clause as a separate sentence, substituting a personal pronoun for *who* or *whom*.** Choose the pronoun that sounds correct, and note its case.	They should ask [she, her]. They should ask <u>her</u>. [Objective.] [She, Her] usually makes the decision. She usually makes the decision. [Subjective.]
3. **Use the same case (*who* or *whom*) in the dependent clause.**	Few people know <u>whom</u> they should ask. [Objective.] They are unsure <u>who</u> makes the decision. [Subjective.]

Note Words such as *I think* and *she says* between subject and verb do not make the subject into an object: *She is the one* <u>who</u> [not <u>whom</u>] *we think will win.*

From the pairs in brackets, select the appropriate form of the pronoun in each of the following sentences.

Example

My mother asked me [who, whom] I was going with to the antique car exhibit.

My mother asked me whom I was going with to the antique car exhibit.

1. [Who, Whom] is next in line for the throne?
2. The author [who, whom] you are less familiar with may be the better of the two.
3. I went to the hairstylist [who, whom] Jack said was good.
4. There is always hard work for [whoever, whomever] wants it.
5. The owner of the pool, [whoever, whomever] it is, should invite us all for a swim.

1.10d Use the appropriate case in other constructions.

1 *We* or *us* with a Noun

The choice of *we* or *us* before a noun depends on whether the noun serves as a subject or an object.

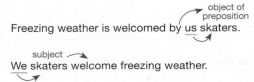

object of
preposition
Freezing weather is welcomed by us skaters.

subject
We skaters welcome freezing weather.

2 Pronoun after *than* or *as*

When a pronoun follows *than* or *as* in a comparison, the case of the pronoun indicates what words may have been omitted. A subjective pronoun must be the subject of an omitted verb.

subject
Some critics like Glass more than he [does].

An objective pronoun must be the object of an omitted verb:

object
Some critics like Glass more than [they like] him.

EXERCISE 1.10.4   Choosing the Appropriate Pronoun

From the pairs in brackets, select the appropriate subjective or objective pronoun for each of the following sentences.

Example

Convincing [we, us] veterans to vote yes on this issue will be difficult.
Convincing us veterans to vote yes on this issue will be difficult.

1. Obtaining enough protein is important to [we, us] vegetarians.
2. Zach is heavier than [I, me].
3. [We, Us] students appreciate clear directions on tests.
4. The two most shy people, [he, him] and Lucy, turned out to be the best actors.
5. My sister watches television more than [I, me].

EXERCISE 1.10.5   Revising: Pronoun Case

Revise all inappropriate case forms in the following paragraph. If a sentence is correct as given, circle the number preceding it.

Example

Her and Emma carpool to campus every day.
She and Emma carpool to campus every day.

1 Mike and I arrived at the campground just after sunset. **2** The manager, whom we thought looked like a movie star, was naturally reluctant to let we ruffians in, but eventually she showed us to a tiny campsite. **3** When we unpacked the tent, Mike and me discovered that we were missing two tent pegs. **4** Searching in the dark, Mike managed to find some sturdy sticks to use as pegs, and between he and I we managed to set up the tent. **5** But Mike was apparently more tired than me, because he didn't drive his pegs deeply enough into the ground. **6** Several hours later, when him and me had finally dozed off, the tent collapsed on top of us. **7** We piled everything into the car as fast as possible and took off down the road for a motel.

1.11 PRONOUN-ANTECEDENT AGREEMENT

Successful writers . . .

- Make a pronoun agree with an antecedent joined by *and, or,* or *nor* (next page).
- Make a pronoun agree when the antecedent is an indefinite pronoun (p. 61).
- Make a pronoun agree when the antecedent is a collective noun (p. 61).

A **pronoun** is a word used in place of a noun. The word a pronoun refers to is its **antecedent**. The antecedent is a noun or other pronoun elsewhere in the sentence or in a nearby sentence.

antecedent ⟵ pronoun
Jennifer brought her son to the party.

A singular pronoun is used to refer to a singular noun:

antecedent ⟵ pronoun
Juanita scolded Simon and then hugged him.

A plural pronoun is used to refer to a plural noun:

antecedent ⟵ pronoun
The weight of the bottles collapsed the shelves they were on.

For clarity, a pronoun should agree with its antecedent in person, number, and gender.

CULTURE LANGUAGE   The gender of a pronoun should match that of its antecedent, not of a noun that the pronoun may modify: *Sara Young invited her* [not *his*] *son to join the company's staff.* Also, nouns in English have only neuter gender unless they specifically refer to males or females. Thus nouns such as *book, table, sun,* and *earth* take the pronoun *it: I am reading a new book. It is inspiring.*

1.11a Antecedents joined by *and* usually take plural pronouns.

Mr. Bartos and I cannot settle our dispute.

The dean and my adviser have offered their help.

Exception When a compound antecedent follows *each* or *every,* the pronoun is singular.

Every girl and woman took her seat.

1.11b When parts of an antecedent are joined by *or* or *nor,* the pronoun agrees with the nearer part.

Tenants or owners must present their grievances.

Either the tenant or the owner will have her way.

When one subject is plural and the other singular, the sentence will be awkward unless you put the plural subject second:

Neither the owner nor the tenants have yet made their case.

1.11c With *everyone, person,* and other indefinite words, use a singular or plural pronoun as appropriate.

Indefinite words do not refer to a specific person or thing. Indefinite pronouns include *anyone, each, everybody, nobody, no one, nothing, somebody,* and *someone.* Generic nouns include *person, individual, and student.* Most indefinite pronouns and all generic nouns are singular in meaning. When they serve as antecedents of pronouns, the pronouns should be singular:

> Everyone on the women's team now has her own locker.
> indefinite
> pronoun

> Every person on the women's team now has her own locker.
> generic noun

The singular indefinite words can cause agreement problems. We often use these words to mean "many" or "all" rather than "one" and then refer to them with plural pronouns, as in *Everyone has their own locker.* Often, too, we mean indefinite words to include both masculine and feminine genders and thus resort to *they* instead of the **generic he**—the masculine pronoun referring to both genders, as in *Everyone deserves his privacy.* (For more on the generic he, which many readers view as sexist, see p. 120.) To achieve agreement in such cases, you have the options listed in the following box.

⊛ Success

Correcting Agreement with Indefinite Words

Incorrect Examples	Revision Methods	Revised Examples
Every athlete deserves their privacy.	Change the indefinite word to a plural, and use a plural pronoun to match.	Athletes deserve their privacy.
Everyone is entitled to their own locker.	Rewrite the sentence to omit the pronoun.	Everyone is entitled to a locker.
Now everyone has their private space.	Use *he or she* (*him or her, his or her*) to refer to the indefinite word.	Now everyone has his or her private space.

1.11d Collective nouns such as *team* take singular or plural pronouns depending on meaning.

A collective noun has singular form and names a group of persons or things: *army, audience, family, group, team.* Use a singular pronoun with a collective noun when referring to the group as a unit:

> The committee voted to disband itself.

When referring to the individual members of the group, use a plural pronoun:

The old group have gone their separate ways.

If a combination such as *group have . . . their* seems awkward, reword the sentence: *The members of the old group have gone their separate ways.*

CULTURE LANGUAGE In standard American English, collective nouns that are noncount nouns (they don't form plurals) usually take singular pronouns: *The mail sits in its own basket.* The noncount nouns that take plural pronouns include *clergy, military, people, police, and any collective noun that comes from an adjective, such as the rich and the poor: The police support their unions.*

EXERCISE 1.11.1 Revising: Pronoun-Antecedent Agreement

Revise the following sentences so that pronouns and their antecedents agree in person and number. Try to avoid the generic *he* (see opposite). Some items have more than one possible answer. If a sentence is correct as given, circle the number preceding it.

Example

Each of the Boudreaus' children brought their laundry home at Thanksgiving.

Each of the Boudreaus' children brought his or her laundry home at Thanksgiving.
Or: Each of the Boudreaus' children brought laundry home at Thanksgiving.
Or: All of the Boudreaus' children brought their laundry home at Thanksgiving.

1. Neither my brother nor my parents have made their vacation plans.
2. Everyone had to fill out a questionnaire describing their job.
3. The coalition launched a campaign to publicize their cause.
4. They asked each of the senators for their opinion.
5. No taxpayer will welcome an increase in their taxes.
6. Will either Hannah or Lucy send in their application?
7. Neither of the two candidates is well known for her honesty.
8. The team had never won on their home court.
9. The town offers few opportunities for someone to let out their tensions.
10. Did any of the boys believe they would get away with cheating?

EXERCISE 1.11.2 Revising: Pronoun-Antecedent Agreement

Revise the following paragraph so that pronouns and their antecedents agree in person and number. Try to avoid the generic *he* (see p. 303). If you change the subject of a sentence, be sure to change the verb as necessary for agreement. If a sentence is correct as given, circle the number preceding it.

Example

Every one of the students studies for their exams.

Every one of the students studies for his or her exams. *Or:* All of the students study for their exams.

1 Each girl raised in a Mexican American family in the Rio Grande Valley of Texas hopes that one day they will be given a *quinceañera* party for their fifteenth birthday. **2** Such celebrations are very expensive because it entails a religious service followed by a huge party. **3** A girl's immediate family, unless they are wealthy, cannot afford the party by themselves. **4** The parents will ask each close friend or relative if they can help with the preparations. **5** Surrounded by her family and attended by her friends and their escorts, the *quinceañera* is introduced as a young woman eligible for Mexican American society.

1.12 PRONOUN REFERENCE

Successful writers . . .

- Make a pronoun refer clearly to one antecedent (below).
- Place a pronoun close enough to its antecedent to ensure clarity (next page).
- Make a pronoun refer to a specific—not implied—antecedent (next page).
- Use *you* only to mean "you, the reader" (p. 66).
- Keep pronouns consistent (p. 66).

A pronoun should refer clearly to its **antecedent,** the noun it substitutes for. Otherwise, readers will have difficulty grasping the pronoun's meaning.

CULTURE·LANGUAGE In standard American English, a pronoun needs a clear antecedent nearby. But don't use both a pronoun and its antecedent as the subject of the same clause: *Bob* [not *Bob he*] *told Mark to go alone.* (See also p. 100.)

1.12a Make a pronoun refer clearly to one antecedent.

When either of two nouns can be a pronoun's antecedent, the reference will not be clear.

Confusing Juanita is sometimes confused with Alice, but she is much taller. [Who is taller?]

Revise such a sentence in one of two ways:

- **Replace the pronoun with the appropriate noun.** This revision will eliminate confusion, but the repeated nouns can be awkward.

Clear Juanita is sometimes confused with Alice, but Juanita [or Alice] is much taller.

- **Avoid repetition by rewriting the sentence.** If you use the pronoun, make sure it has only one possible antecedent.

Clear	Although they are sometimes confused with each other, Juanita is much taller than Alice.
Clear	Though sometimes confused with her, Juanita is much taller than Alice. ◄────────

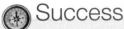 ## Success ──•

Revising Unclear Pronoun Reference

- **More than one possible antecedent:**

Confusing	To keep birds from eating seeds, soak them in blue food coloring.
Clear	To keep birds from eating seeds, soak the seeds in blue food coloring.

- **Antecedent too far away:**

Confusing	Employees should consult with their supervisor who require personal time.
Clear	Employees who require personal time should consult with their supervisor.

- **Antecedent only implied:**

Confusing	Many children begin reading on their own by watching television, but this should probably be discounted in government policy.
Clear	Many children begin reading on their own by watching television, but such self-instruction should probably be discounted in government policy.

1.12b Place a pronoun close enough to its antecedent to ensure clarity.

A clause beginning with *who, which,* or *that* should generally fall immediately after the word to which it refers.

Confusing	Jody found a vintage dress in the attic that her aunt had worn.
Clear	In the attic Jody found a vintage dress that her aunt had worn.

1.12c Make a pronoun refer to a specific antecedent, not an implied one.

A pronoun should refer to a specific noun or other pronoun.

1 Vague *this, that, which,* or *it*

This, that, which, or *it* should refer to a specific noun, not to a whole word group expressing an idea or situation.

Confusing	Jared has a good work history and large credit card balances. ⓐ This has made him unable to get a new student loan.
Clear	Jared has a good work history and large credit card balances. The debts have made him unable to get a new student loan.

2 Indefinite Antecedents with *it* and *they*

It and *they* should have definite noun antecedents. Rewrite a sentence if an antecedent is missing.

Confusing	In Chapter 4 of this book it describes the early flights of the Wright brothers.
Clear	Chapter 4 of this book describes the early flights of the Wright brothers.

Confusing	Even in reality TV shows, they present a false picture of life.
Clear	Even reality TV shows present a false picture of life.

3 Implied Nouns

A noun may be implied in some other word or phrase, as *happiness* is implied in *happy*, *driver* is implied in *drive*, and *mother* is implied in *mother's*. But a pronoun cannot refer clearly to an implied noun, only to a specific, stated one.

Confusing	In Cohen's report she made claims that led to a lawsuit.
Clear	In her report Cohen made claims that led to a lawsuit.
Confusing	Her reports on psychological development generally go unnoticed outside it.
Clear	Her reports on psychological development generally go unnoticed outside the field.

EXERCISE 1.12.1   Revising: Pronoun Reference

Rewrite the following sentences to eliminate unclear pronoun reference. If you use a pronoun in your revision, be sure that it refers to only one antecedent and that it falls close enough to its antecedent to ensure clarity.

Example

Saul found an old gun in the rotting shed that was just as his grandfather had left it.

In the rotting shed Saul found an old gun that was just as his grandfather had left it.

1. Lee played a piece on the piano that dated from the seventeenth century.
2. Two brothers had built the town's oldest barn, which over the years had served as a cow barn, a blacksmith shop, and a studio for artisans. However, no one could remember their names.
3. In impressionist paintings they used color to imitate reflected light.
4. The play was supposed to open in March and then had casting problems, but this changed.
5. Six or seven bearskin rugs decorated the rooms of the house, and Sam claimed to have killed them.

> EXERCISE 1.12.2   Revising: Pronoun Reference

Rewrite the following paragraph to eliminate unclear pronoun reference. If you use pronouns in your revision, be sure that each refers to only one antecedent and that it falls close enough to its antecedent to ensure clarity.

Example

On page 47 of the textbook, it summarizes the stages of child development.

Page 47 of the textbook summarizes the stages of child development.

1 There is a difference between the heroes of modern times and the heroes of earlier times: they have flaws in their characters. **2** Despite their imperfections, sports fans still admire Pete Rose, Babe Ruth, and Joe Namath. **3** Fans liked Rose for having his young son serve as batboy when he was in Cincinnati. **4** The reputation Rose earned as a gambler and tax evader may overshadow his reputation as a ballplayer, but it will survive. **5** He amassed an unequaled record as a hitter, using his bat to do things no one has ever done, and it remains even though Rose was banned from baseball.

1.12d Use *you* to mean only "you, the reader."

You should clearly mean "you, the reader." The context must be appropriate for such a meaning:

Inappropriate	In the fourteenth century you had to struggle simply to survive.
Revised	In the fourteenth century one [or a person] had to struggle simply to survive.

1.12e Keep pronouns consistent.

Within a sentence or a group of related sentences, pronouns should match each other.

Inconsistent pronouns	One finds when reading that your concentration improves with practice, so that I now comprehend more in less time.
Revised	I find when reading that my concentration improves with practice, so that I now comprehend more in less time.

EXERCISE 1.12.3   Revising: Consistency in Rronouns

Revise the following sentences to make them consistent in person and number.

Example

A plumber will fix burst pipes, but they won't repair waterlogged
appliances.

Plumbers will fix burst pipes, but they won't repair waterlogged
appliances.

1. When a student is waiting to hear from college admissions committees, you begin to notice what time the mail carrier arrives.
2. If tourists cannot find the Arts Center, one should ask for directions.
3. When taxpayers do not file their return on time, they may pay a penalty.
4. If a student misses too many classes, you may fail a course.
5. One should not judge other people's actions unless they know the circumstances.

EXERCISE 1.12.4   Revising: Pronoun Reference

Revise the following paragraph as needed so that pronouns are consistent and refer to specific, appropriate antecedents.

Example

In Grand Teton National Park they have moose, elk, and trumpeter
swans.

Moose, elk, and trumpeter swans live in Grand Teton National Park.

  1 "Life begins at forty" is a cliché many people live by, and this may or may not be true. **2** Whether one agrees or not with the cliché, you can cite many examples of people whose public lives began at forty. **3** For instance, when she was forty, Pearl Buck's novel *The Good Earth* won the Pulitzer Prize. **4** Kenneth Kanuda, past president of Zambia, was elected to it in 1964, when he was forty. **5** Catherine I became empress of Russia at age forty, more feared than loved by them. **6** Paul Revere at forty made his famous ride to warn American revolutionary leaders that the British were going to arrest them, which gave the colonists time to prepare for battle. **7** Forty-year-old Nancy Astor joined the British House of Commons in 1919 as its first female member, though they did not welcome her. **8** In 610 CE, Muhammad, age forty, began to have visions that became the foundation of the Muslim faith and have inspired millions of people to become one.

Modifiers

Modifiers describe or limit other words in a sentence. They are adjectives, adverbs, or word groups serving as adjectives or adverbs. This section shows how to solve problems in the forms of modifiers and in their relation to the rest of the sentence.

1.13 ADJECTIVES AND ADVERBS

Successful writers . . .

- Use adjectives only to modify nouns and pronouns, including after linking verbs (facing page).
- Use adverbs to modify verbs (facing page).
- Use comparative and superlative forms appropriately (p. 70).
- Avoid most double negatives (p. 73).
- Distinguish between present and past participles as adjectives (p. 74).
- Use *a, an, the,* and other noun markers appropriately (p. 75).

Adjectives and **adverbs** are modifiers that describe, restrict, or otherwise qualify the words to which they relate.

Functions of Adjectives and Adverbs

Adjectives modify nouns:	serious student
pronouns:	ordinary one
Adverbs modify verbs:	warmly greet
adjectives:	only three people
adverbs:	quite seriously
phrases:	nearly to the edge of the cliff
clauses:	just when we arrived
sentences:	Fortunately, she is employed.

Most adverbs are formed by adding *-ly* to adjectives: *badly, strangely, largely, beautifully.* But note that we cannot depend on *-ly* to identify adverbs because some adjectives also end in *-ly* (*fatherly, lonely*) and because some common adverbs do not end in *-ly* (*always, here, not, now, often, there*). Thus the only sure way to distinguish between adjectives and adverbs is to determine what they modify.

CULTURE LANGUAGE In standard American English, an adjective does not change along with the noun it modifies to show plural number: *square* [not *squares*] *spaces.* Only nouns form plurals.

1.13a Use adjectives only to modify nouns and pronouns.

Adjectives modify only nouns and pronouns. Use only adverbs, not adjectives, to modify verbs, adverbs, or other adjectives.

> **Faulty**   Some children suffer bad.
>
> **Revised**   Some children suffer badly.

 In standard American English, choosing between *not* and *no* can be a challenge. *Not* is an adverb, so it makes a verb or an adjective negative:

> They do <u>not</u> learn. They are <u>not</u> happy. They have <u>not</u> been in class.

(See p. 73 for where to place *not* in relation to verbs and adjectives.) *No* is an adjective, so it makes a noun negative:

> <u>No</u> child likes to fail. <u>No</u> good school fails children.

Place *no* before the noun or any other modifier.

1.13b Use an adjective after a linking verb to modify the subject. Use an adverb to modify a verb.

A modifier after a verb should be an adverb only if it describes the verb. If the modifier follows a linking verb and describes the subject, it should be an adjective.

Two word pairs are especially tricky. One is *bad* and *badly*:

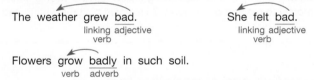

The other word pair is *good* and *well*. *Good* serves only as an adjective. *Well* may serve as an adverb with a host of meanings or as an adjective meaning only "fit" or "healthy."

EXERCISE 1.13.1   Revising: Adjectives and Adverbs

Revise the following sentences to make adjectives modify nouns and pronouns and to make adverbs modify verbs, adjectives, and other adverbs. If a sentence is correct as given, circle the number preceding it.

Example

The announcer warned that traffic was moving very slow.
The announcer warned that traffic was moving very <u>slowly</u>.

1. People who take their health serious often believe that movie-theater popcorn is a healthy snack.
2. Nutrition information about movie popcorn may make these people feel different.
3. One large tub of movie popcorn has twelve hundred calories and sixty grams of saturated fat—both surprisingly high numbers.
4. Once people are aware of the calories and fat, they may feel badly about indulging in this classic snack.
5. People who want to eat good should think twice before ordering popcorn at the movies.

EXERCISE 1.13.2   Revising: Adjectives and Adverbs

Revise the following paragraph to use adjectives and adverbs appropriately. If a sentence is correct as given, circle the number preceding it.

Example

Kayla sang the song as good as she could.
Kayla sang the song as <u>well</u> as she could.

1 The eighteenth-century essayist Samuel Johnson fared bad in his early life. **2** His family was poor, his hearing was weak, and he received little formal education. **3** After failing as a schoolmaster, Johnson moved to London, where he was finally taken serious as a critic and dictionary maker. **4** Johnson was real surprised when he received a pension from King George III. **5** Thinking about his meeting with the king, Johnson felt proudly that he had not behaved badly in the presence of the king. **6** Now, after living cheap for over twenty years, Johnson finally had enough money to eat and dress good. **7** He spent his time writing and living stylish.

1.13c Use the comparative and superlative forms of adjectives and adverbs appropriately.

Adjectives and adverbs can show degrees of quality or amount with the endings -*er* and -*est* or with the words *more* and *most* or *less* and *least*. Most modifiers have three forms: positive, comparative, and superlative. The **positive** form is the basic form listed in the dictionary: *My dog is quiet*. The **comparative** form is used to compare *two* persons, places, or things: *My dog is quieter than my neighbor's dog*. The **superlative** form is used to compare *more than two* persons, places, or things: *My dog is the quietest in the town*.

Positive	Comparative	Superlative
Adjectives		
red	redder	reddest
awful	more/less awful	most/least awful
Adverbs		
soon	sooner	soonest
quickly	more/less quickly	most/least quickly

Follow these rules for comparative and superlative forms:

- **For one-syllable adjectives or adverbs, add *-er* or *-est.*** Use the ending as well for some two-syllable modifiers.

  cold, colder, coldest   slow, slower, slowest
  narrow, narrower, narrowest

- **For most modifiers with two or more syllables, use the comparative word *more* or *less* or the superlative word *most* or *least.*** Do not add the *-er* or *-est* ending.

  reasonable, less reasonable, least reasonable
  interestingly, more interestingly, most interestingly

- **For two-syllable adjectives ending in *-y*, change the *-y* to *-i* and add *-er* or *-est.***

  drowsy, drowsier, drowsiest   lazy, lazier, laziest

Consult a dictionary if you are unsure of the forms of a particular adjective or adverb.

     Note Use the superlative form only for comparing *more than two* persons, places, or things.

     Faulty   Michael is the <u>tallest</u> of the two brothers.

     Revised   Michael is the <u>taller</u> of the two brothers.

1 Irregular Adjectives and Adverbs

Irregular modifiers change the spelling of their positive form to show comparative and superlative.

Irregular Adjectives and Adverbs		
Positive	**Comparative**	**Superlative**
Adjectives		
good	better	best
bad	worse	worst
little	littler, less	littlest, least
many		
some	more	most
much		
Adverbs		
well	better	best
badly	worse	worst

2 Double Comparisons

A double comparative or double superlative combines the *-er* or *-est* ending with the word *more* or *most*. It is redundant.

     Chang was the <u>wisest</u> [not <u>most wisest</u>] person in town.

     He was <u>smarter</u> [not <u>more smarter</u>] than anyone else.

3 Logical Comparisons

Absolute Modifiers

Some adjectives and adverbs cannot logically be compared—for instance, *perfect, unique, dead, impossible, infinite.* These absolute words can be preceded by adverbs like *nearly* or *almost* that mean "approaching," but they cannot logically be modified by *more* or *most* (as in *most perfect*).

Not	He was the most unique teacher we had.
But	He was a unique teacher.

Complete Comparisons

A comparison should be complete in the following ways:

- **The comparison must state a relation fully enough to be clear.**

Unclear	Carmakers worry about their industry more than environmentalists.
Clear	Carmakers worry about their industry more than environmentalists do.

- **The items being compared should in fact be comparable.**

Illogical	The cost of an electric car is greater than a gasoline-powered car. [Illogically compares a cost and a car.]
Revised	The cost of an electric car is greater than the cost of [or that of] a gasoline-powered car.

EXERCISE 1.13.3 Revising: Comparisons

Revise the following sentences so that the comparative and superlative forms of adjectives and adverbs are appropriate for formal usage.

> **Example**
>
> Attending classes full-time and working at two jobs was the most impossible thing I ever did.
>
> Attending classes full-time and working at two jobs was impossible [or the hardest thing I ever did].

1. I read the longest of the two books first.
2. That is the most saddest story I have ever heard.
3. Of the two major problems with nuclear power plants—waste disposal and radiation leakage—radiation leakage is the most terrifying.
4. If I study hard, I should be able to do more better on the next economics test.
5. Working last summer as an assistant to my teacher was one of the more unique experiences I have ever had.

EXERCISE 1.13.4   Using Comparatives and Superlatives

Write the comparative and superlative forms of each adjective or adverb below. Then use all three forms in your own sentences.

Example

heavy: heavier (comparative), heaviest (superlative)

The barbells were too <u>heavy</u> for me. The trunk was <u>heavier</u> than I expected. Joe Clark was the <u>heaviest</u> person on the team.

1. badly   **3.** understanding   **5.** well
2. good   **4.** steady

1.13d Watch for double negatives.

In a **double negative,** two negative words (such as *no, not, none, neither, barely, hardly,* or *scarcely*) cancel each other out. Some double negatives are intentional: for instance, *She was <u>not unhappy</u>* indicates with understatement that she was indeed happy. But most double negatives say the opposite of what is intended: *Jenny did <u>not</u> feel <u>nothing</u>* asserts that Jenny felt other than nothing, or something. For the opposite meaning, one of the negatives must be eliminated (*She felt <u>nothing</u>*) or one of them must be changed to a positive (*She did not feel <u>anything</u>*).

Faulty   The IRS <u>cannot hardly</u> audit all tax returns. <u>None</u> of its audits <u>never</u> touch many cheaters.

Revised   The IRS <u>cannot</u> audit all tax returns. Its audits <u>never</u> touch many cheaters.

EXERCISE 1.13.5   Revising: Double Negatives

Identify and revise the double negatives in the following sentences. Each error may have more than one correct revision. Circle the number preceding any sentence that is correct as given.

Example

My legs were so sore after the race that I couldn't hardly stand.
My legs were so sore after the race that I <u>could</u> hardly stand.

1. Interest in books about the founding of the United States is not hardly consistent among Americans: it seems to vary with the national mood.
2. Americans show barely any interest in books about the founders when things are going well in the United States.
3. However, when Americans can't hardly agree on major issues, sales of books about the Revolutionary War era increase.
4. During such periods, one cannot go to no bookstore without seeing several new volumes about John Adams, Thomas Jefferson, and other founders.
5. When Americans feel they don't have nothing in common, their increased interest in the early leaders may reflect a desire for unity.

1.13e Distinguish between present and past participles as adjectives.

Both present participles and past participles may serve as adjectives: *a burning building (present), a burned building (past).* As in the examples, the two participles usually differ in the time they indicate.

But some present and past participles—those derived from verbs expressing feeling—can have altogether different meanings. The present participle modifies something that causes the feeling: *That was a frightening storm* (the storm frightens). The past participle modifies something that experiences the feeling: *They quieted the frightened horses* (the horses feel fright).

The following participles are among those likely to be confused:

amazing/amazed	fascinating/fascinated
amusing/amused	frightening/frightened
annoying/annoyed	frustrating/frustrated
astonishing/astonished	interesting/interested
boring/bored	pleasing/pleased
confusing/confused	satisfying/satisfied
depressing/depressed	shocking/shocked
embarrassing/embarrassed	surprising/surprised
exciting/excited	tiring/tired
exhausting/exhausted	worrying/worried

EXERCISE 1.13.6 Revising: Present and Past Participles

Revise the adjectives in the following sentences as needed to distinguish between present and past participles. If a sentence is correct as given, circle the number preceding it.

Example

The subject was embarrassed to many people.
The subject was embarrassing to many people.

1. Several critics found Alice Walker's *The Color Purple* to be a fascinated book.
2. One confused critic wished that Walker had deleted the scenes set in Africa.
3. Another critic argued that although the book contained many depressed episodes, the overall effect was excited.
4. Since other readers found the book annoyed, this critic pointed out its many surprising qualities.
5. In the end most critics agreed that the book was a satisfied novel about the struggles of an African American woman.

1.13f Use *a, an, the,* and other noun markers appropriately.

Certain adjectives mark nouns because they always precede nouns. These **noun markers** include *a, an,* and *the* (next page) as well as *my, this, some,* and similar words (pp. 77–78).

In standard American English, the use of noun markers depends on the context they appear in and the kind of noun they precede:

- **A** *proper noun* **names a particular person, place, or thing and begins with a capital letter:** *February, Joe Allen, Red River.* Most proper nouns are not preceded by noun markers.

- **A** *count noun* **names something that is countable in English and can form a plural:** *girl/girls, apple/apples, child/children.* A singular count noun is always preceded by a noun marker; a plural count noun sometimes is.

- **A** *noncount noun* **names something not usually considered countable in English, and so it does not form a plural.** A noncount noun is sometimes preceded by a noun marker. Here is a sample of noncount nouns, sorted into groups by meaning:

  Abstractions: confidence, democracy, education, equality, evidence, health, information, intelligence, knowledge, luxury, peace, pollution, research, success, supervision, truth, wealth, work

  Food and drink: bread, candy, cereal, flour, meat, milk, salt, water, wine

  Emotions: anger, courage, happiness, hate, joy, love, respect, satisfaction

  Natural events and substances: air, blood, dirt, gasoline, gold, hair, heat, ice, oil, oxygen, rain, silver, smoke, weather, wood

  Groups: clergy, clothing, equipment, furniture, garbage, jewelry, junk, legislation, machinery, mail, military, money, police, vocabulary

  Fields of study: architecture, accounting, biology, business, chemistry, engineering, literature, psychology, science

A dictionary of English as a second language will tell you whether a noun is a count noun, a noncount noun, or both. (See pp. 123–24 for recommended dictionaries.)

1 *A, an,* and *the*

With Singular Count Nouns

A or *an* precedes a singular count noun when the reader does not already know its identity, usually because you have not mentioned it before:

> A scientist in our chemistry department developed a process to strengthen metals. [*Scientist* and *process* are being mentioned for the first time.]

The precedes a singular count noun that has a specific identity for the reader, for one of the following reasons:

- **You have mentioned the noun before.**

  A scientist in our chemistry department developed a process to strengthen metals. The scientist patented the process. [*Scientist* and *process* were presented in the preceding sentence.]

- **You identify the noun immediately before or after you state it.**

  The most productive laboratory is the research center in the chemistry department. [*Most productive* identifies *laboratory*. *In the chemistry department* identifies *research center*. And *chemistry department* is a shared facility—see below.]

- **The noun names something unique—the only one in existence.**

  The sun rises in the east. [*Sun* and *east* are unique.]

- **The noun names an institution or facility that is shared by the community of readers.**

  Many men and women aspire to the presidency. [*Presidency* is a shared institution.]

The is not used before a singular noun that names a general category:

  Wordsworth's poetry shows his love of nature [not the nature].

  General Sherman said that war is hell. [*War* names a general category.]

  The war in Iraq has left many wounded. [*War* names a specific war.]

With Plural Count Nouns

A or *an* never precedes a plural noun. *The* does not precede a plural noun that names a general category. *The* does precede a plural noun that names specific representatives of a category.

  Men and women are different. [*Men* and *women* name general categories.]

  The women formed a team. [*Women* refers to specific people.]

With Noncount Nouns

A or *an* never precedes a noncount noun. *The* does precede a noncount noun that names specific representatives of a general category.

  Vegetation suffers from drought. [*Vegetation* names a general category.]

  The vegetation in the park withered or died. [*Vegetation* refers to specific plants.]

With Proper Nouns

A or *an* never precedes a proper noun. *The* generally does not precede proper nouns.

> <u>Garcia</u> lives in <u>Boulder</u>.

There are exceptions, however. For instance, we generally use *the* before plural proper nouns (<u>the</u> *Boston Celtics*) and before the names of groups and organizations (<u>the</u> *Department of Justice*), ships (<u>the</u> *Lusitania*), oceans (<u>the</u> *Pacific*), mountain ranges (<u>the</u> *Alps*), regions (<u>the</u> *Middle East*), rivers (<u>the</u> *Mississippi*), and some countries (<u>the</u> *Netherlands*).

EXERCISE 1.13.7   Revising: Noun Markers   (CULTURE LANGUAGE)

For each blank in the following paragraphs, indicate whether a, an, the, or no noun marker should be inserted.

Example

On our bicycle trip across _____ country, we carried _____ map and plenty of _____ food and _____ water.

On our bicycle trip across <u>the</u> country, we carried <u>a</u> map and plenty of food and water.

1 From _____ native American Indians who migrated from _____ Asia 20,000 years ago to _____ new arrivals who now come by _____ planes, _____ United States is _____ nation of foreigners. **2** It is _____ country of immigrants who are all living under _____ single flag.

3 Back in _____ seventeenth and eighteenth centuries, at least 75 percent of the population came from _____ England. **4** However, between 1820 and 1975 more than 38 million immigrants came to this country from elsewhere in _____ Europe. **5** Many children of _____ immigrants were self-conscious and denied their heritage; many even refused to learn _____ native language of their parents and grandparents. **6** They tried to "Americanize" themselves. **7** The so-called Melting Pot theory of _____ social change stressed _____ importance of blending everyone together into _____ kind of stew. **8** Each nationality would contribute its own flavor, but _____ final stew would be something called "American."

9 This Melting Pot theory was never completely successful. In the last half of the twentieth century, _____ ethnic revival changed _____ metaphor. **10** Many people now see _____ American society as _____ mosaic. **11** Americans are once again proud of their heritage, and _____ ethnic differences make _____ mosaic colorful and interesting.

---

2 Other Noun Markers

The following noun markers may be used as indicated with singular count nouns, plural count nouns, or noncount nouns.

With Any Kind of Noun (Singular Count, Plural Count, Noncount)

my, our, your, his, her, its, their, possessive nouns *(boy's, boys')*
whose, which(ever), what(ever)
some, any, the other
no

Their account is overdrawn. [Singular count.]
Their funds are low. [Plural count.]
Their money is running out. [Noncount.]

Only with Singular Nouns (Count and Noncount)

this, that

This account has some money. [Count.]
That information may help. [Noncount.]

Only with Noncount Nouns and Plural Count Nouns

most, enough, other, such, all, all of the, a lot of

Most funds are committed. [Plural count.]
Most money is needed elsewhere. [Noncount.]

Only with Singular Count Nouns

one, every, each, either, neither, another

One car must be sold. [Singular count.]

Only with Plural Count Nouns

these, those
both, many, few, a few, fewer, fewest, several
two, three, and so forth

Two cars are unnecessary. [Plural count.]

Note *Few* means "not many" or "not enough." *A few* means "some" or "a small but sufficient quantity."

Few committee members came to the meeting.
A few members can keep the committee going.

Do not use *much* with a plural count noun.

Many [not Much] members want to help.

Only with Noncount Nouns

much, more, little, a little, less, least, a large amount of

Less luxury is in order. [Noncount.]

Note *Little* means "not many" or "not enough." *A little* means "some" or "a small but sufficient quantity."

> <u>Little</u> time remains before the conference.
> The members need <u>a little</u> help from their colleagues.

Do not use *many* with a noncount noun.

> <u>Much</u> [not <u>Many</u>] work remains.

EXERCISE 1.13.8   Revising: Noun Markers

In the following sentences, identify and revise missing or incorrect noun markers. Circle the number preceding any sentence that is correct as given.

Example

> Much people love to swim for exercise or just plain fun.
> <u>Many</u> people love to swim for exercise or just plain fun.

1. Few swimmers are aware of the possible danger of sharing their swimming spot with others.
2. These danger has increased in recent years because of dramatic rise in outbreaks of the parasite cryptosporidium.
3. Swallowing even little water containing cryptosporidium can make anyone sick.
4. Chlorine is used in nearly every public pools to kill parasites, but the chlorine takes six or seven days to kill cryptosporidium.
5. Most health authorities advise people to limit their swimming in public pools and to drink as little of the pool water as possible.

EXERCISE 1.13.9   Revising: Adjectives and Adverbs

Revise the paragraph below to correct errors in the use of adjectives and adverbs.

Example

> Sports fans feel happily when their team wins.
> Sports fans feel <u>happy</u> when their team wins.

   1 Americans often argue about which professional sport is better: basketball, football, or baseball. **2** Basketball fans contend that their sport offers more action because the players are constant running and shooting. **3** Because it is played indoors in relative small arenas, basketball allows fans to be more closer to the action than the other sports. **4** Football fanatics say they don't hardly stop yelling once the game begins. **5** They cheer when their team executes a complicated play good. **6** They roar more louder when the defense stops the opponents in a goal-line stand. **7** They yell loudest when a fullback crashes in for a score. **8** In contrast, the supporters of baseball believe that it is the better sport. **9** It combines the one-on-one duel of pitcher and batter struggling valiant with the tight teamwork of double and triple plays. **10** Because the game is played slow and careful, fans can analyze and discuss the manager's strategy.

1.14 MISPLACED AND DANGLING MODIFIERS

Successful writers . . .

- Place modifiers clearly (below).
- Place adverbs to avoid awkwardness or error (facing page).
- Arrange adjectives correctly (p. 82).
- Identify dangling modifiers, and connect them to their sentences (p. 83).

A modifier needs to relate clearly to the word it describes, and that need limits its possible positions in a sentence. A misplaced modifier does not relate to the intended word (see below). A dangling modifier does not relate sensibly to anything in the sentence (see pp. 83–84).

1.14a Avoid misplaced modifiers.

A **misplaced modifier** falls in the wrong place in a sentence. Readers may think it modifies the wrong word or won't know which word it is supposed to modify. Misplaced modifiers are usually awkward or confusing. They may even be unintentionally funny.

Confusing	This is the only cookie in a bag that tastes like Mom's. [Actual advertisement.]
Clear	This is the only bagged cookie that tastes like Mom's.

1 Clear Placement

Readers tend to link a modifier to the nearest word it could modify. Any other placement can link the modifier to the wrong word.

Confusing	He served steak to the men on paper plates.
Clear	He served the men steak on paper plates.
Confusing	According to the police, many dogs are killed by automobiles and trucks roaming unleashed.
Clear	According to the police, many dogs roaming unleashed are killed by automobiles and trucks.

2 *Only* and Other Limiting Modifiers

Limiting modifiers include *almost, even, exactly, hardly, just, merely, nearly, only, scarcely,* and *simply.* They should fall immediately before the words or word groups they modify.

Unclear	They only saw each other during meals.
Revised	They saw only each other during meals.
Revised	They saw each other only during meals.

3 Adverbs with Grammatical Units

Adverbs can often be moved around in sentences, but some will be awkward if they interrupt certain grammatical units.

* **A long adverb stops the flow from subject to verb.**

	subject — adverb — verb
Awkward	The city, after the deadly hurricane, began massive rebuilding.

	— adverb — subject verb
Revised	After the deadly hurricane, the city began massive rebuilding.

* **A *split infinitive*—an adverb placed between *to* and the verb—can be awkward.**

	infinitive
Awkward	The weather service expected temperatures to not rise.
Revised	The weather service expected temperatures not to rise.

A split infinitive may sometimes be unavoidable without rewriting, but it may still bother some readers.

infinitive
Several US industries expect to more than triple their use of robots.

4 Other Adverb Positions (CULTURE LANGUAGE)

Placements of a few adverbs can be difficult for nonnative speakers of English.

* **Adverbs of frequency** include *always, never, often, rarely, seldom, sometimes,* and *usually.* They generally appear at the beginning of a sentence, before a one-word verb, or after a helping verb.

  helping   adverb
  main verb verb
  Robots have sometimes put humans out of work.

  adverb   verb phrase
  Sometimes robots have put humans out of work.

  Adverbs of frequency always follow the verb *be.*

  verb adverb
  Robots are often helpful to workers.

When *rarely*, *seldom*, and other negative adverbs of frequency begin a sentence, the normal subject-verb order changes. (See also p. 115.)

adverb verb subject
Rarely are robots simple machines.

- **Adverbs of degree** include *absolutely, almost, certainly, completely, definitely, especially, extremely, hardly,* and *only.* They fall just before the word modified (an adjective, another adverb, sometimes a verb).

  adverb   adjective
  Robots have been especially useful in making cars.

- **Adverbs of manner** include *badly, beautifully, openly, sweetly, tightly, well,* and others that describe how something is done. They usually fall after the verb.

  verb   adverb
  Robots work smoothly on assembly lines.

- **The adverb *not*** changes position depending on what it modifies. When it modifies a verb, place it after the helping verb (or the first helping verb if more than one).

  helping   main
  verb   verb
  Robots do not think.

  When *not* modifies another adverb or an adjective, place it before the other modifier.

  adjective
  Robots are not sleek machines.

- **A one-word adverb in a question** falls after the first helping verb and subject.

  helping   rest of
  verb   subject   adverb   verb phrase
  Will spacecraft ever be able to leave the solar system?

5 Order of Adjectives (CULTURE LANGUAGE)

English follows distinctive rules for arranging two or three adjectives before a noun. (A string of more than three adjectives before a noun is rare.) The order is shown in the following chart.

Noun marker	Opinion	Size or shape	Color	Origin	Material	Noun used as adjective	Noun
many						state	laws
	lovely		green	Thai			birds
a	fine			German			camera
a		square			wooden		table
all						business	reports
the			blue		litmus		paper

See pp. 147–48 on punctuating adjectives before a noun.

EXERCISE 1.14.1   Revising: Misplaced Modifiers

Revise the following paragraph so that modifiers clearly and appropriately describe the intended words.

Example

Although at first I feared the sensation of flight, I came to enjoy flying over time.

Although at first I feared the sensation of flight, <u>over time</u> I came to enjoy flying.

1 People dominate in our society who are right-handed. **2** Hand tools, machines, and doors even are designed for right-handed people. **3** However, nearly 15% may be left-handed of the population. **4** Children when they enter kindergarten generally prefer one hand or the other. **5** Parents and teachers should not try to deliberately change a child's preference for the left hand.

EXERCISE 1.14.2   Arranging Adjectives   (CULTURE LANGUAGE)

A group of adjectives follows each sentence below. Arrange the adjectives as needed for appropriate order in English, and place them in the sentence.

Example

Programs for computer graphics perform _____ chores. (*drafting, many, tedious*)

Programs for computer graphics perform <u>many tedious drafting</u> chores.

1. _____ researchers are studying image controls for computer graphics. (*several, university*)
2. The controls depend on _____ object connected by wires to the computer. (*T-shaped, hand-sized, a*)
3. The image allows a biochemist to walk into _____ display of a molecule. (*three-dimensional, gigantic, a*)
4. Using _____ gestures, the biochemist can rotate and change the entire image. (*simple, hand*)
5. _____ games also depend on computer graphics. (*computer, all, video*)
6. Even _____ games operate this way. (*sophisticated, flight, simulated*)

1.14b Connect dangling modifiers to their sentences.

A **dangling modifier** does not sensibly modify anything in its sentence.

Dangling   Passing the building, the vandalism became visible.

Like most dangling modifiers, the preceding one introduces a sentence, contains a verb form (*passing*), and implies but does not name a subject (whoever is passing). Readers assume that the subject is the someone passing the building and that this implied subject is the same as the subject of the sentence (*vandalism* in the example).

When it is not, the modifier "dangles" unconnected to the rest of the sentence. Here is another example:

Dangling   Although intact, graffiti covered every inch of the walls and windows. [The walls and windows, not the graffiti, were intact.]

To revise a dangling modifier, you have to rewrite the sentence it appears in. (Trying to revise just by moving the modifier will still leave it dangling: *The vandalism became visible passing the building.*) Choose a revision method depending on what you want to emphasize in the sentence.

- **Rewrite the dangling modifier as a complete clause with its own stated subject and verb.** Readers can accept that the new subject and the sentence subject are different.

  Dangling   Passing the building, the vandalism became visible.

  Revised   As we passed the building, the vandalism became visible.

- **Change the subject of the sentence to a word the modifier properly describes.**

  Dangling   Trying to understand the causes, vandalism has been extensively studied.

  Revised   Trying to understand the causes, researchers have extensively studied vandalism.

 Success ─────────────────────────────

Identifying and Revising Dangling Modifiers

1. **Find a subject.** If the modifier lacks a subject of its own (e.g., *when in diapers*), identify what it describes.

2. **Connect the subject and modifier.** Verify that what the modifier describes is in fact the subject of the independent clause. If it is not, the modifier is probably dangling:

   ┌── modifier ──┐   subject
   Dangling   When in diapers, my mother remarried.

3. **Revise as needed.** Revise a dangling modifier (*a*) by recasting it with a subject of its own or (*b*) by changing the subject of the independent clause:

   Revision a   When I was in diapers, my mother remarried.

   Revision b   When in diapers, I attended my mother's second wedding.

EXERCISE 1.14.3   Revising: Dangling Modifiers

Revise the following sentences to eliminate any dangling modifiers. Each item has more than one possible answer.

Example

Driving north, the vegetation became increasingly sparse.

Driving north, <u>we noticed</u> that the vegetation became increasingly sparse.
Or: <u>As we drove north</u>, the vegetation became increasingly sparse.

1. By turning the lights down, the room looked less dingy.
2. To file a formal complaint, a statement must be submitted.
3. Having prepared thoroughly, the exam was easy for me.
4. Though usually energetic, emotional problems had sapped her strength.
5. Staring at the ceiling, the idea became clear.
6. Sagging and needing a new coat of paint, Mr. Preston called the house painter.
7. Monday passed me by without accomplishing anything.
8. To obtain disability income, a doctor must certify that an employee cannot work.
9. When only a ninth grader, my grandmother tried to teach me double-entry bookkeeping.
10. After weighing the alternatives, his decision became clear.

EXERCISE 1.14.4   Revising: Dangling Modifiers

Revise the sentences in the following paragraph to eliminate any dangling modifiers. Each item has more than one possible answer. Circle the number preceding any sentence that is correct as given.

Example

Looking for mates, the croaking of frogs can also attract predators.

<u>Croaking to look</u> for mates, <u>frogs</u> can also attract predators. *Or::* <u>A way of looking for mates</u>, the croaking of frogs can also attract predators.

1 Andrew Jackson's career was legendary in his day. **2** Starting with the American Revolution, service as a mounted courier was Jackson's choice. **3** Though not well educated, a successful career as a lawyer and judge proved Jackson's ability. **4** Earning the nicknames "Old Hickory" and "Sharp Knife," Jackson established his military prowess in the War of 1812. **5** Losing only six dead and ten wounded, the triumph of the Battle of New Orleans burnished Jackson's reputation. **6** After putting down raiding parties from Florida, Jackson's victories helped pressure Spain to cede that territory. **7** While Jackson was briefly governor of Florida, the US presidency became his goal. **8** With so many skills and deeds of valor, Jackson's fame led to his election to the presidency in 1828 and 1832.

Revise the following paragraph to eliminate any misplaced or dangling modifiers.

1 Central American tungara frogs silence several nights a week their mating croaks. **2** When not croaking, the chance that the frogs will be eaten by predators is reduced. **3** The frogs seem to fully believe in "safety in numbers." **4** They more than likely will croak along with a large group rather than by themselves. **5** By forgoing croaking on some nights, the frogs' behavior prevents the species from "croaking."

Sentence Errors

A word group punctuated as a sentence will confuse or annoy readers if it lacks needed parts, has too many parts, or has parts that don't fit together.

1.15 SENTENCE FRAGMENTS

Successful writers . . .

- Test sentences for completeness (facing page).
- Revise sentence fragments (p. 88).
- Recognize the acceptable uses of incomplete sentences (p. 89).

The word *fragment* means "incomplete part." A **sentence fragment** is an incomplete sentence: it does not express a complete thought. For example, *Going to the supermarket* is not a complete thought because it does not tell who or what goes to the supermarket. The phrase *The clerk during the morning shift* is not a complete thought because it does not tell what the clerk is doing.

 ## Success

Is It a Fragment or a Complete Sentence?

A complete sentence or independent clause

1. contains a subject and a verb (*The wind blows*)

2. and is not a dependent clause (beginning with a word such as *because* or *who*).

A sentence fragment

1. lacks a verb (*The wind blowing*),

2. or lacks a subject (*And blows*),

3. or is a dependent clause not attached to a complete sentence (*Because the wind blows*).

1.15a Test your sentences for fragments.

A word group punctuated as a sentence should pass *all three* of the following tests. If the word group fails any test, it is a fragment and needs revision.

Test 1: Does the word group have a verb?

Look for a verb in the group of words.

Fragment	Uncountable numbers of sites on the Web.
Revised	Uncountable numbers of sites make up the Web.

The verb in a complete sentence must be able to change form as indicated below. A verb form that cannot change in this way cannot serve as a sentence verb.

	Complete Sentences	Sentence Fragments
Singular	The network grows.	The network growing.
Plural	Networks grow.	Networks growing.
Present	The network grows.	
Past	The network grew.	The network growing.
Future	The network will grow.	

CULTURE LANGUAGE Some languages allow forms of *be* to be omitted as helping verbs or linking verbs. But English requires stating forms of *be*, as shown in the following revised example.

Fragment	The network taking a primary role in communication and commerce.
Revised	The network is taking a primary role in communication and commerce.

Test 2: Does the word group have a subject?

To find the subject, ask who or what performs the action of the verb. Usually, the subject will come before the verb. If there is no subject, the word group is probably a fragment.

Fragment	And has enormous popular appeal.
Revised	And the Web has enormous popular appeal.

In one kind of complete sentence, a command, the subject *you* is understood: [*You*] *try this recipe.*

CULTURE LANGUAGE Some languages allow the omission of the sentence subject, especially when it is a pronoun. But in English, except in commands, the subject is always stated.

Fragment	Internet sales are expanding dramatically. Are threatening traditional stores.
Revised	Internet sales are expanding dramatically. They are threatening traditional stores.

Test 3: Does the word group begin with a word that makes it a
dependent clause?

A dependent clause usually begins with a subordinating word, such as one of the
following:

Subordinating Conjunctions			Relative Pronouns	
after	once	until	that	who/whom
although	since	when	which	whoever/whomever
as	than	where		
because	that	whereas		
if	unless	while		

Dependent clauses serve as parts of sentences (nouns or modifiers), not as whole
sentences.

Fragment When the government devised the Internet.

Revised The government devised the Internet.

Revised When the government devised the Internet, <u>no expansive
computer network existed</u>.

Fragment The reason that the government devised the Internet.

Revised The reason that the government devised the Internet <u>was to
link agencies, departments, and defense contractors</u>.

Note Questions beginning with *how, what, when, where, which, who, whom, whose,*
and *why* are not sentence fragments: *Who was responsible? When did it happen?*

1.15b Revise sentence fragments.

You can revise most fragments by combining them with independent clauses or
by making them into independent clauses with subjects, verbs, and no subordinating words. These methods are illustrated in the following box.

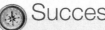 Success ───────────────────────────

Revising a Sentence Fragment

1. Combine the fragment with an independent clause.

                       dependent clause   independent clause

Fragment <u>While my boss was on the phone.</u> She began to eat
her lunch.

                     dependent clause   independent clause

Revised While my boss was on the phone**,** she began to eat her lunch.

           independent clause   phrase

Fragment We asked friends to come. As well as relatives.

           independent clause   phrase

Revised We asked friends to come as well as relatives.

Revising a Sentence Fragment *(continued)*

2. **Add any missing subject or verb or both.** Make sure your revision can stand alone as a complete sentence.

Fragment	The customer refused to pay her bill. <u>Then started to complain loudly.</u>
Revised	The customer refused to pay her bill. Then <u>she</u> started to complain loudly.

subject
added

Fragment	The Winter Olympics were held in Turin. <u>Snowing every day.</u>
Revised	The Winter Olympics were held in Turin. <u>It snowed</u> every day.

subject   verb
added   added

3. **Remove or replace the subordinating word.** Create a complete sentence by removing a subordinating conjunction or by replacing a relative pronoun with a new subject. Be sure the word group can stand alone as a complete sentence.

dependent clause

Fragment	I did not finish the mystery novel. <u>Because its predictable plot bored me.</u>
Revised	I did not finish the mystery novel. <u>Its predictable plot bored me.</u>

conjunction
removed

dependent clause

Fragment	The Web uses hyperlinks. <u>Which allow users to move easily among sites.</u>
Revised	The Web uses hyperlinks. <u>They</u> allow users to move easily among sites.

new subject

1.15c Be aware of the acceptable uses of incomplete sentences.

A few word groups lacking the usual subject-predicate combination are incomplete sentences, but they are considered acceptable. They include commands (*Shut the window.*); exclamations (*Oh no!*); questions and answers (*Where next? To Kansas.*); and descriptions in employment résumés (*Weekly volunteer in soup kitchen.*).

Experienced writers sometimes use sentence fragments when they want to achieve a special effect. Such fragments appear more in informal than in formal writing. However, unless you are experienced and thoroughly secure in your own writing, you should avoid all fragments and concentrate on writing complete sentences.

EXERCISE 1.15.1   Identifying and Revising Sentence Fragments

Apply the tests for completeness to each of the following word groups. If a word group is a complete sentence, circle the number preceding it. If it is a sentence fragment, revise it in two ways: by making it a complete sentence and by combining it with an independent clause of your own.

Example

And could not find his money.

The word group has a verb (*could . . . find*) but no subject.

Revised into a complete sentence: And <u>he</u> could not find his money.

Combined with a new main clause: <u>He was confused</u> and could not find his money.

1. The water spilling onto the floor.
2. A big black cat with piercing blue eyes.
3. Whoever burned the painting should be ashamed.
4. But kept it a secret.
5. After the drinking age was raised.
6. The books displayed were rare.
7. Whom the child feared.
8. Using newspaper and string to wrap the package.
9. Because of the drought, watering plants was forbidden.
10. Whenever I hear that song.

EXERCISE 1.15.2   Revising: Sentence Fragments

Correct any sentence fragment in the following word groups either by combining it with an independent clause or by making it a complete sentence. If an item contains no sentence fragment, circle the number preceding it.

Example

Jujitsu is good for self-protection. Because it enables one to overcome an opponent without the use of weapons.

Jujitsu is good for self-protection because it enables one to overcome an opponent without the use of weapons. *Or:* Jujitsu is good for self-protection. <u>It</u> enables one to overcome an opponent without the use of weapons.

1. Human beings who perfume themselves. They are not much different from other animals.
2. Animals as varied as insects and dogs release pheromones. Chemicals that signal other animals.
3. Human beings have a diminished sense of smell. And do not consciously detect most of their own species' pheromones.
4. The human substitute for pheromones may be perfumes. Most common in ancient times were musk and other fragrances derived from animal oils.
5. Some sources say that people began using perfume to cover up the smell of burning flesh. During sacrifices to the gods.

6. Perfumes became religious offerings in their own right. Being expensive to make, they were highly prized.
7. The earliest historical documents from the Middle East record the use of fragrances. Not only in religious ceremonies but on the body.
8. In the nineteenth century, chemists began synthesizing perfume oils. Which previously could be made only from natural sources.
9. The most popular animal oil for perfume today is musk. Although some people dislike its heavy, sweet odor.
10. Synthetic musk oil would help conserve a certain species of deer. Whose gland is the source of musk.

EXERCISE 1.15.3   Revising: Sentence Fragments

Revise the following paragraph to eliminate sentence fragments by combining them with independent clauses or rewriting them as complete sentences.

Baby red-eared slider turtles are brightly colored. With bold patterns on their yellowish undershells. Which serve as a warning to predators. The bright colors of skunks and other animals. They signal that the animals will spray nasty chemicals. In contrast, the turtle's colors warn largemouth bass. That the baby turtle will actively defend itself. When a bass gulps down a turtle. The feisty baby claws and bites. Forcing the bass to spit it out. To avoid a similar painful experience. The bass will avoid other baby red-eared slider turtles. The turtle loses its bright colors as it grows too big. For a bass's afternoon snack.

1.16 COMMA SPLICES AND RUN-ON SENTENCES

Successful writers . . .

- Separate independent clauses not joined by *and, but*, or another coordinating conjunction (next page).
- Separate independent clauses that are related by *however, for example*, and so on (p. 95).

When a sentence contains two independent clauses in a row, readers need a signal that one independent clause is ending and another is beginning. The usual signal is a comma with a coordinating conjunction (*and, but, or,* etc.) or a semicolon:

The ship was huge**,** and its mast stood eighty feet high.

The ship was huge**;** its mast stood eighty feet high.

Two serious problems occur when readers are not given this signal:

- **In a *comma splice*, two independent clauses are joined (or spliced) *only* with a comma:**

    independent   comma
        clause   ↓   independent clause
    The ship was huge, its mast stood eighty feet high.

- **In a *run-on sentence* or *fused sentence*, no punctuation or conjunction is used between the clauses:**

    no punctuation
    or conjunction
          ▾
    The ship was huge its mast stood eighty feet high.

This chapter discusses the repairs for these errors.

(CULTURE LANGUAGE) In standard American English, two independent clauses in the same sentence must be separated by a comma and a coordinating conjunction or by a semicolon. If your native language does not have this rule or if you tend to write long sentences, consider editing especially for comma splices and run-on sentences.

1.16a Separate independent clauses not joined by *and*, *but,* or another coordinating conjunction.

If your readers point out comma splices or run-on sentences in your writing, you're not creating enough separation between independent clauses in your sentences. Use one of the following methods to repair the problem.

1 Separate Sentences

Make two independent clauses into separate sentences when the ideas expressed are only loosely related.

Complete sentence . **Complete sentence** .

Comma splice   Many students do not have a specific career goal, they come to college for a broad education.

Revised   Many students do not have a specific career goal. They come to college for a broad education.

(CULTURE LANGUAGE) Making separate sentences may be the best option if you are used to writing very long sentences in your native language but often write comma splices in English.

2 Coordinating Conjunction

Insert a coordinating conjunction in a comma splice when the ideas in the independent clauses are closely related and equally important.

Independent clause ,	**coordinating conjunction**	**independent clause** .
	and nor so	
	but for yet	
	or	

Comma splice	Some laboratory-grown foods taste good, they are nutritious.
Revised	Some laboratory-grown foods taste good , and they are nutritious.

In a run-on sentence, insert a comma and a coordinating conjunction.

Run-on sentence	Chemists have made much progress they still have a way to go.
Revised	Chemists have made much progress , but they still have a way to go.

Note Do not use a comma along with *also, plus,* or *then* to join independent clauses. These words are not coordinating conjunctions.

3 Semicolon

Insert a semicolon between two independent clauses when the relation between the ideas is very close and obvious without a conjunction.

Independent clause ;	**independent clause** .

Comma splice	Good taste is rare in laboratory-grown vegetables, they are usually bland.
Revised	Good taste is rare in laboratory-grown vegetables; they are usually bland.

4 Subordination

When one idea is less important than the other, express the less important idea in a dependent clause.

Dependent clause ,	**independent clause** .

Comma splice	The apartment size was adequate, the décor was tasteless.
Revised	Although the apartment size was adequate, the décor was tasteless.

✳ Success

Finding and Revising Comma Splices and Fused Sentences

The following steps can help you identify and revise comma splices and run-on sentences.

1. **Underline the independent clauses in your draft.**

   <u>Sailors trained on the ship</u>. <u>They learned about wind and sails</u>. <u>Trainees who took the course ranged from high school students to Navy officers</u>. <u>The ship was built in 1910</u>, <u>it had sailed ever since</u>. In almost a century, <u>it had circled the globe forty times</u>. <u>It burned in 2001</u> <u>its cabins and decks were destroyed</u>.

2. **Are consecutive independent clauses separated by periods?**

   If **yes**, OK.
   If **no**, go to question 3.

   Comma splice   The ship was built in 1910, it had sailed ever since.

   Run-on sentence   It burned in 2001 its cabins and decks were destroyed.

3. **Are consecutive independent clauses linked by a comma?**

   If **yes**, go to question 4.

   Comma splice   The ship was built in 1910, it had sailed ever since.

   If **no**, go to question 5.

   Run-on sentence   It burned in 2001 its cabins and decks were destroyed.

4. **Does a coordinating conjunction follow the comma between independent clauses?**

   If **yes**, OK.
   If **no**, add a coordinating conjunction: *and, but, or, nor for, so, yet*.

   Revised   The ship was built in 1910<u>**,** and</u> it had sailed ever since.

5. **Are consecutive independent clauses separated by a semicolon?**

   If **yes**, OK.
   If **no**, add a semicolon.

   Revised   It burned in 2001<u>**;**</u> its cabins and decks were destroyed.

As an alternative to these revision methods, you can also subordinate one clause to another:

   Revised   <u>When</u> it burned in 2001, its cabins and decks were destroyed.

1.16b Separate independent clauses that are related by *however, for example,* and so on.

Two groups of words that are not conjunctions describe how one independent clause relates to another: **conjunctive adverbs** and other **transitional words and phrases**. (See pp. 240–41 for a longer list of transitional words and phrases.)

Common Conjunctive Adverbs and Transitional Words and Phrases			
accordingly	for instance	instead	on the contrary
anyway	further	in the meantime	otherwise
as a result	furthermore	in the past	similarly
at last	hence	likewise	still
besides	however	meanwhile	that is
certainly	incidentally	moreover	then
consequently	in contrast	namely	thereafter
even so	indeed	nevertheless	therefore
finally	in fact	nonetheless	thus
for all that	in other words	now	undoubtedly
for example	in short	of course	until now

When two independent clauses are related by a conjunctive adverb or another transitional expression, they must be separated by a period or by a semicolon. The adverb or expression is also generally set off by a comma or commas.

Independent clause ; **conjunctive adverb or transitional expression ,** **independent clause .**

however
for example,
etc.

Comma splice   Healthcare costs are higher in the United States than in many other countries, <u>consequently</u> health insurance is also more costly.

Revised   Healthcare costs are higher in the United States than in many other countries. <u>Consequently</u>, health insurance is also more costly.

Revised   Healthcare costs are higher in the United States than in many other countries; <u>consequently</u>, health insurance is also more costly.

Unlike coordinating conjunctions (*and, but,* and so on) and subordinating conjunctions (*although, because,* and so on), conjunctive adverbs and transitional words and phrases can be moved within a clause. To test whether a word or phrase is a conjunctive adverb or transitional expression, try moving it around.

Healthcare costs are higher in the United States than in many other countries; health insurance, <u>consequently</u>, is also more costly.

EXERCISE 1.16.1   Identifying and Revising Comma Splices

Correct each comma splice in the following items in *two* of the following ways: make separate sentences of the independent clauses; insert an appropriate coordinating conjunction after the comma; substitute a semicolon for the incorrect comma; or subordinate one clause to another. If an item contains no comma splice, circle the number preceding it.

> **Example**
>
> Carolyn still had a headache, she could not get the child-proof cap off the aspirin bottle.
>
> Carolyn still had a headache because she could not get the child-proof cap off the aspirin bottle. [Subordination.]
>
> Carolyn still had a headache, for she could not get the child-proof cap off the aspirin bottle. [Coordinating conjunction.]

1. Tony's new apartment is well equipped, it has a flat-screen TV, a DVR, and an Internet connection.
2. Cecilia did not feel prepared for her concert, she had not yet memorized her solo.
3. She reached Wayne's voicemail each time she called his number, consequently, she stopped calling him.
4. The blender was very old, it still worked on some speeds.
5. Antonio began his career as a news reporter, now, however, he is a second-string film critic.
6. The student guards at the gym rarely ask to see identification, they are usually too busy doing their homework.
7. The election was held on a rainy day, the weather kept people away from the polls.
8. We lost the game against Colliersville, though we had been favored to win.
9. Sean bought a new suit for the interview, he didn't get the job.
10. Homeowners are rebelling against the property tax, many of them believing they should not have to bear the expense of local government.

EXERCISE 1.16.2   Identifying and Revising Run-on Sentences

Revise each of the run-on sentences in the following items in *two* of four ways: make separate sentences of the independent clauses; separate the clauses with a semicolon; insert an appropriate coordinating conjunction and a comma; or make one clause dependent on the other.

> **Example**
>
> Tim was shy he usually refused invitations.
> Tim was shy, so he usually refused invitations.
> Tim was shy; he usually refused invitations.

1. He did not finish work until midnight he was too tired to drive home.
2. The record Sarah bought was defective she returned it to the store.
3. The speaker is a well-known poet he teaches a poetry seminar at the university.
4. The skills center offers job training to people who need it it can't guarantee jobs, though.
5. The parking problem in the downtown area is getting out of hand the mayor suggests a new underground parking garage.

EXERCISE 1.16.3   Sentence Combining: Comma Splices and Run-on Sentences

Combine each pair of sentences below into one sentence without creating a comma splice or a run-on sentence. Use one of the following methods to combine the sentences: supply a comma and an appropriate coordinating conjunction; supply a semicolon; or subordinate one clause to the other. You will have to add, delete, or change words as well as punctuation.

Example

The sun sank lower in the sky. The colors gradually faded.

<u>As</u> the sun sank lower in the sky, the colors gradually faded. [The first clause is subordinated to the second.]

1. I once worked as a switchboard operator. However, after a week I was fired for hopeless incompetence.
2. The candidate's backers learned of his previous illegal activities. They withdrew their support.
3. College tuition remained stable for a long time. In recent decades it has risen sharply.
4. Teachers sometimes make unfair assignments. They don't take account of the workload in other courses.
5. I nearly froze trying to unlock the car door. I discovered I was standing next to the wrong red truck.
6. Many proud people restrict their activities. They are afraid to fail at something new.
7. We thought my seven-year-old brother was a genius. He read an entire encyclopedia.
8. The driver was lucky to escape uninjured. His car was destroyed, however.
9. Some walrus hunters found and nursed the sick explorer. He died two weeks later.
10. Two railroad lines cut through the town. They intersect a block from the main street.

EXERCISE 1.16.4   Revising: Comma Splices and Run-on Sentences

Revise each comma splice and run-on sentence in the following paragraph, using the technique that seems most appropriate for the meaning.

A good way to meet new people during the summer is to take evening courses, many colleges, high schools, and adult-education centers offer them. They attract different kinds of people who share common interests. Last summer in my woodworking class I met a woman who was also interested in colonial chairs we have been touring antique shows ever since. This summer in my singing class I met several people who enjoy country music as much as I do, we have gone to numerous concerts together, we are planning a trip to Nashville. If I had not attended evening classes, I would not have met these new friends, they have enriched my life.

1.17 MIXED SENTENCES

Successful writers . . .
- Match subjects and predicates in meaning (below).
- Match subjects and predicates in grammar (facing page).
- State parts of clauses, such as subjects, only once (p. 100).

A **mixed sentence** contains parts that do not fit together. The misfit may be in grammar or in meaning.

1.17a Match subjects and predicates in meaning.

In a sentence with mixed meaning, the subject seems to do or be something illogical. Such a mixture is sometimes called **faulty predication** because the predicate conflicts with the subject.

1 Illogical Equation with *be*

When a form of *be* connects a subject and a word that describes the subject (a subject complement), the two words must be logically related.

> Mixed   A compromise between the city and the country would be the ideal place to live. [A compromise cannot be a place to live.]

> Revised   A community that offered the best qualities of both city and country would be the ideal place to live.

2 *Is when, is where*

Definitions require nouns on both sides of *be*. Clauses that define and begin with *when* or *where* are common in speech but should be avoided in writing.

> Mixed   An examination is when you are tested on what you know.

> Revised   An examination is a test of what you know.

3 *Reason is because*

The commonly heard construction *reason is because* is redundant since *because* means "for the reason that":

> Mixed   The reason the temple requests donations is because the school needs to expand.

> Revised   The reason the temple requests donations is that the school needs to expand.

> Revised   The temple requests donations because the school needs to expand.

4 Other Mixed Meanings

Faulty predications are not confined to sentences with *be*.

Mixed	The use of emission controls was created to reduce air pollution.
Revised	Emission controls were created to reduce air pollution.

1.17b Match subjects and predicates in grammar.

Many mixed sentences start with one grammatical plan or construction but end with a different one:

	┌──────── modifier (prepositional phrase) ──────────┐ predicate
Mixed	By paying more attention to impressions than facts leads us to misjudge others.

This mixed sentence makes a prepositional phrase work as the subject of *leads,* but prepositional phrases cannot function as sentence subjects. The sentence needs a subject that works with the predicate.

	┌──────── modifier (prepositional phrase) ──────────┐subject
Revised	By paying more attention to impressions than facts, we
	predicate
	misjudge others.

A mixed sentence is especially likely when you are working on a computer and connect parts of two sentences or rewrite half a sentence but not the other half. A mixed sentence may also occur when the subject and predicate verb do not carry the principal meaning. (See pp. 104–05.)

EXERCISE 1.17.1   Revising: Mixed Sentences

Revise the following sentences so that their parts fit together both in grammar and in meaning. Each item has more than one possible answer.

Example

When they found out how expensive pianos are is why they were discouraged.
They were discouraged because they found out how expensive pianos are.
When they found out how expensive pianos are, they were discouraged.

1. A blend of healthy and appealing food would be a good place for lunch.
2. The different accents of students is in where they grew up.
3. An antique is when an object is one hundred or more years old.
4. Schizophrenia is when a person withdraws from reality and behaves in abnormal ways.
5. The reason many people don't accept the theory of evolution is because it goes contrary to their religious beliefs.

1.17c State parts of sentences, such as subjects, only once.

In some languages other than English, certain parts of sentences may be repeated. These include the subject in any kind of clause or an object or adverb in an adjective clause. In English, however, these parts are stated only once in a clause.

1 Repetition of Subject

You may be tempted to restate a subject as a pronoun before the verb. But the subject needs stating only once in its clause.

Faulty	The <u>liquid</u> it reached a boil.
Revised	The <u>liquid</u> reached a boil.
Faulty	<u>Gases</u> in the liquid they escaped.
Revised	<u>Gases</u> in the liquid escaped.

2 Repetition in an Adjective Clause

Adjective clauses begin with *who, whom, whose, which, that, where,* and *when*. The beginning word replaces another word: the subject (*He is the person who called*), an object of a verb or preposition (*He is the person whom I mentioned*), or a preposition and pronoun (*He knows the office where* [*in which*] *the conference will occur*).

Do not state the word being replaced in an adjective clause.

Faulty	The technician <u>whom</u> the test depended on <u>her</u> was burned. [*Whom* should replace *her*.]
Revised	The technician <u>whom</u> the test depended on was burned.

Adjective clauses beginning with *where* or *when* do not need an adverb such as *there* or *then*.

Faulty	Gases escaped at a moment <u>when</u> the technician was unprepared <u>then</u>.
Revised	Gases escaped at a moment <u>when</u> the technician was unprepared.

Note *Whom, which,* and similar words are sometimes omitted but are still understood by the reader. Thus the word being replaced should not be stated.

Faulty	Accidents rarely happen to technicians the lab has trained <u>them</u>. [*Whom* is understood: . . . *technicians* <u>whom</u> *the lab has trained*.]
Revised	Accidents rarely happen to technicians the lab has trained.

EXERCISE 1.17.2   Revising: Repeated Subjects and Other Parts

Revise the following paragraph to eliminate any unneeded words. If a sentence is correct as given, mark the number preceding it.

Example

Scientists they use special instruments for measuring the age of artifacts.

Scientists use special instruments for measuring the age of artifacts.

1 Archaeologists and other scientists they can often determine the age of their discoveries by means of radiocarbon dating. **2** This technique it can be used on any material that once was living. **3** This technique is based on the fact that all living organisms they contain carbon. **4** The most common isotope is carbon 12, which it contains six protons and six neutrons. **5** A few carbon atoms are classified as the isotope carbon 14, where the nucleus consists of six protons and eight neutrons there.

Kate Chopin's "The Story of an Hour" (1894) invites readers to experience the lack of freedom felt by women in her era. Rather than present a treatise on the issue, however, her literary narrative form allows her to open the issue more subtly, asking readers to interpret its social message. Visual texts, likewise, often function in these more subtle ways—and so must be "read" critically and rhetorically. What does the image suggest about this woman's life? What details create its mood and feel? If you were to create a story about this woman, how might you characterize her?

2

Clarity and Style

2.1 EMPHASIS

Successful writers . . .

- Use subjects and verbs for key actors and actions (next page).
- Use sentence beginnings and endings for emphasis (p. 105).
- Use coordination to signal that ideas are equally important (p. 107).
- Use subordination to emphasize important ideas (p. 108).

To emphasize an important message in speech, you may speak loudly or slowly. To emphasize the main ideas in your writing, you need to use different strategies. This chapter will show you how to arrange sentence parts so that readers will easily grasp your main ideas.

Taken from *The Successful Writer's Handbook,* Third Edition by Kathleen T. McWhorter and Jane E. Aaron.

2.1a Use subjects and verbs effectively.

Every sentence has two essential parts—the subject and the verb. The subject usually names the actor; the verb usually specifies the subject's action: *Children* [subject] *grow* [verb]. When the subject and verb do not identify the key actor and action, readers must find that information elsewhere, and the sentence may be wordy and unemphatic.

In the following sentences, the subjects and verbs are underlined.

Unemphatic	The intention of the company was to expand its workforce. A proposal was also made to hire more minority workers.

The preceding sentences are unemphatic because their key ideas do not appear in their subjects and verbs. In the following revision, the sentences are not only clearer but more concise.

Revised	The company intended to expand its workforce. It also proposed to hire more minority workers.

The constructions discussed below usually drain meaning from a sentence's subject and verb.

1 Nouns Made from Verbs

Nouns that come from verbs can make the key actions of sentences unclear and wordy. These nouns include *intention* (from *intend*), *proposal* (from *propose*), *decision* (from *decide*), *expectation* (from *expect*), and *inclusion* (from *include*).

Unemphatic	After the company made a decision to hire more workers with disabilities, its next step was the construction of wheelchair ramps and other facilities.
Revised	After the company decided to hire more workers with disabilities, it constructed wheelchair ramps and other facilities.

2 Weak Verbs

Weak verbs, such as *made* and *was* in the unemphatic sentence above, tend to stretch out sentences and often hide key actions.

Unemphatic	The company is the leader among businesses in complying with the 1990 disabilities act. Its officers make frequent speeches on its policies to business groups.
Revised	The company leads other businesses in complying with the 1990 disabilities act. Its officers frequently speak on its policies to business groups.

3 Passive Voice

A verb in the active voice states action *performed* by the subject:

Sam dropped a plate.

A verb in the passive voice states action *received* by the subject:

The plate was dropped.

The passive voice de-emphasizes the true actor of the sentence or even omits it entirely (as in the preceding example). The active voice is usually clearer and more emphatic:

Unemphatic	The 1990 law is seen by most businesses as fair, but the costs of complying have sometimes been objected to.
Revised	Most businesses see the 1990 law as fair, but some have objected to the costs of complying.

(See also pp. 45–47 for help with editing the passive voice.)

EXERCISE 2.1.1   Revising: Emphasis of Subjects and Verbs

Rewrite the following sentences so that their subjects and verbs identify their key actors and actions.

Example

The issue of students making a competition over grades is a reason why their focus on learning may be lost.

Students who compete over grades may lose their focus on learning.

1. The work of many heroes was crucial in helping to emancipate the slaves.
2. The contribution of Harriet Tubman, an escaped slave herself, included the guidance of hundreds of other slaves to freedom on the Underground Railroad.
3. A return to slavery was risked by Tubman or possibly death.
4. During the Civil War she was also a carrier of information from the South to the North.
5. After the war, needy former slaves were helped by Tubman's raising of money.

2.1b Use sentence beginnings and endings for emphasis.

You can call attention to information by placing it first or last in a sentence, reserving the middle for incidentals. Generally, the end is more emphatic than the beginning.

Unemphatic	Education remains the single best means of economic advancement, despite its shortcomings. [Emphasizes shortcomings.]
Revised	Despite its shortcomings, education remains the single best means of economic advancement. [Emphasizes advancement more than shortcomings.]
Revised	Education remains, despite its shortcomings, the single best means of economic advancement. [De-emphasizes shortcomings.]

Generally, readers expect the beginning of a sentence to contain information that they already know or that you have already introduced. They expect the ending to contain new information. In the unemphatic passage below, the second and third sentences both begin with new topics (value and means), while the old topics from the first sentence (controversy and education) appear at the ends of the sentences. The pattern of the passage is A→B. C→B. D→A.

> **Unemphatic**
> A B
> Education often means controversy these days, with rising
>
> costs and constant complaints about its inadequacies.
> C
> But the value of schooling should not be obscured by the
> B D
> controversy. The single best means of economic
>
> advancement, despite its shortcomings, remains
> A
> education.

In the following revision, education and controversy remain the sentence subjects, and thus the focus, throughout. The passage follows the pattern A→B. B→C. A→D.

> **Revised**
> A B
> Education often means controversy these days, with rising
>
> costs and constant complaints about its inadequacies.
> B C
> But the controversy should not obscure the value of
> A
> schooling. Education remains, despite its shortcomings,
> D
> the single best means of economic advancement.

EXERCISE 2.1.2 **Sentence Combining: Beginnings and Endings**

Locate the main idea in each group of sentences below. Then combine each group into a single sentence that emphasizes that idea by placing it at the beginning or the end.

Example

The storm blew roofs off buildings. It caused extensive damage. It knocked down many trees.

Main idea at beginning: The storm caused extensive damage, blowing roofs off buildings and knocking down many trees.

Main idea at end: Blowing roofs off buildings and knocking down many trees, the storm caused extensive damage.

1. The lead singer aroused the audience. He was spinning around the stage. He was dancing with the microphone stand.
2. Many writers now draft their papers online. Computers make both revising and editing easier and faster.
3. The swan took flight. Its wings beat against the water. Its neck stretched forward.
4. The abandoned car was a neighborhood eyesore. Its windows were smashed. Its body was rusted and dented.
5. Jason walked with his back straight. He held his head high. He stared straight ahead. He hid his shame.

2.1c Use coordination to signal equality among ideas.

To **coordinate** means to make two or more things work together. In writing, coordination shows that two or more parts of a sentence are equally important in meaning. Use coordination in sentences in one of four ways:

- **Link two independent clauses with a comma and a coordinating conjunction,** such as *and, but, nor,* or *or.*

  | Independent clause | , | coordinating conjunction | independent clause | . |

  ↞── equally important ──↠

  Independence Hall in Philadelphia is now restored, but fifty years ago it was in bad shape.

- **Link two independent clauses with a semicolon alone or with a semicolon and a conjunctive adverb,** such as *however, indeed, moreover, therefore,* or *thus.*

  | Independent clause | ; | independent clause | . |

  | Independent clause | ; | conjunctive adverb | , | independent clause | . |

  ↞── equally important ──↠

  The building was standing; however, it suffered from decay.

- **Within clauses, link words and phrases with a coordinating conjunction,** such as *and* or *or.*

  | word or phrase | coordinating conjunction | word or phrase |

  ↞── equally important ──↠

  Both the employees and the officers of the corporation were uninterested

  ↞── equally important ──↠

  in expanding market share or developing new products.

- **Link independent clauses, words, or phrases with a correlative conjunction,** such as *not only . . . but also* or *either . . . or.*

  | correlative conjunction | clause, word, phrase | correlative conjunction | clause, word, phrase |

  ↞── equally important ──↠

  Either the electricity was off or the bulb had burned out.

EXERCISE 2.1.3   Sentence Combining: Coordination

Combine sentences in the following paragraph to coordinate related ideas in the ways that seem most effective to you. You will have to supply coordinating conjunctions or conjunctive adverbs and the appropriate punctuation.

   Many chronic misspellers do not have the time to master spelling rules. They may not have the motivation. They may rely on dictionaries to catch misspellings. Most dictionaries list words under their correct spellings. One kind of dictionary is designed for chronic misspellers. It lists each word under its common misspellings. It then provides the correct spelling. It also provides the definition.

2.1d Use subordination to emphasize important ideas.

To **subordinate** means to lower in rank or importance. In writing, subordination shows that some sentence parts are less important than others. Usually, the main idea appears in the independent clause and supporting details appear in dependent parts. Following are two common ways to use subordination in sentences.

- **Use a dependent clause beginning with a subordinating word,** such as *although, because, if, who, whom, that,* or *which.*

| Dependent clause | , | independent clause | . |

— less important — ┌—more important —┐
When I follow a study schedule, I accomplish more.

| Beginning of independent clause | , | dependent clause | , | end of independent clause | . |

———— less important ————
The choir, which includes members of all ages, won the award.
————more important ————

- **Use a phrase.**

| Phrase | , | independent clause | . |

— less important — ┌——— more important ———┐
Despite the weather, the horticulture class met outdoors.

| Beginning of independent clause | , | phrase | , | end of independent clause | . |

——— less important ———
Expenses, including travel and housing, are difficult to estimate.
——— more important ———

EXERCISE 2.1.4 Sentence Combining: Subordination

Combine each of the following pairs of sentences twice, each time using one of the subordinate structures in parentheses to make a single sentence. You will have to add, delete, change, and rearrange words.

Example

During the late eighteenth century, workers carried beverages in brightly colored bottles. The bottles had cork stoppers. (*Clause beginning that. Phrase beginning with.*)

During the late eighteenth century, workers carried beverages in brightly colored bottles that had cork stoppers.

During the late eighteenth century, workers carried beverages in brightly colored bottles with cork stoppers.

1. Shinsegae Centum City Department Store in South Korea is the largest department store in the world. It covers more than 3 million square feet. (*Phrase beginning covering. Phrase beginning with.*)
2. Route 93 is the most direct route to school. It is under construction. (*Clause beginning although. Phrase beginning the most.*)
3. Frances Perkins was the first female cabinet member in the United States. She was dedicated to social reform. (*Phrase beginning dedicated. Phrase beginning the first.*)
4. Computer-scored multiple-choice tests speed up grading. They are favored by many instructors. (*Clause beginning because. Phrase beginning favored.*)
5. Andrew Bradford began the American magazine industry. He first published *American Magazine* in 1741. (*Clause beginning who. Clause beginning when.*)

EXERCISE 2.1.5   Sentence Combining: Subordination

Rewrite the following paragraph in the way you think most effective to subordinate the less important ideas to the more important ones. Use dependent clauses or other subordinate constructions as appropriate.

    Many students today are no longer majoring in the liberal arts. I mean by "liberal arts" such subjects as history, English, and the social sciences. Students think a liberal arts degree will not help them get jobs. They are wrong. They may not get practical, job-related experience from the liberal arts, but they will get a broad education, and it will never again be available to them. Many employers look for more than a technical, professional education. They think such an education can make an employee's views too narrow. The employers want open-minded employees. They want employees to think about problems from many angles. The liberal arts curriculum instills such flexibility. The flexibility is vital to the health of our society.

2.2 PARALLELISM

Successful writers . . .

- Use parallelism with *and, but, or, nor,* and *yet* (next page).
- Use parallelism with *both . . . and, not . . . but,* or another correlative conjunction (next page).
- Use parallelism in comparisons, lists, headings, and outlines (p. 111).

Parallelism is a similarity of grammatical form for similar elements of meaning within a sentence or among sentences.

> The air is dirtied by <u>factories belching smoke</u>
> and
> <u>cars spewing exhaust.</u>

In this example the two underlined phrases have the same importance (both identify sources of air pollution), so they also have the same grammatical form. Parallelism thus clarifies the connection between the elements.

2.2a Use parallelism with *and, but, or, nor, yet.*

The coordinating conjunctions *and, but, or, nor,* and *yet* always signal a need for parallelism:

> <u>Thrilled</u> and <u>exhausted</u>, the runners crossed the finish line. [Parallel words.]
>
> Water poured <u>over the bulkheads</u> and <u>down the streets</u>. [Parallel phrases.]
>
> Workers were understandably disturbed <u>that they were losing their jobs</u> and <u>that no one seemed to care</u>. [Parallel clauses.]

When sentence parts that are linked by coordinating conjunctions are not parallel in structure, the sentence is awkward and distracting:

> Not parallel   The callers on the talk show included <u>a teenager</u>, <u>a man worked in construction</u>, and <u>a flight attendant</u>.
>
> Revised   The callers on the talk show included a teenager, a <u>construction worker</u>, and a flight attendant.
>
> Not parallel   The reasons steel companies kept losing money were <u>that their plants were inefficient</u>, <u>high labor costs</u>, and <u>foreign competition was increasing</u>.
>
> Revised   The reasons steel companies kept losing money were <u>inefficient plants</u>, high labor costs, and <u>increasing foreign competition</u>.

Be careful not to omit needed words in parallel items.

> Faulty   She's fortunate to have <u>skills</u> and <u>interest</u> in her job. [Idiom dictates different prepositions with *skills* and *interest*.]
>
> Revised   She's fortunate to have skills <u>for</u> and interest in her job.

2.2b Use parallelism with *both . . . and, not . . . but,* or another correlative conjunction.

Correlative conjunctions stress equal importance and balance between parts. Parallelism emphasizes this balance.

> It is not <u>a tax bill</u> but <u>a tax relief bill</u>, providing relief not <u>for the needy</u> but <u>for the greedy</u>.   —Franklin Delano Roosevelt

With correlative conjunctions, the element after the second connector must match the element after the first connector:

Not parallel	Huck Finn learns not only that human beings have an enormous capacity for folly but also enormous dignity. [The first part includes *that human beings have*; the second part does not.]
Revised	Huck Finn learns that human beings have not only an enormous capacity for folly but also enormous dignity. [Moving *that human beings have* makes the two parts parallel.]
Not parallel	The restaurant owner learned not only that customers have large expense accounts but also strong preferences. [The first part includes *that customers have*; the second part does not.]
Revised	The restaurant owner learned that customers have not only large expense accounts but also strong preferences. [Moving *that customers have* makes the two parts parallel.]

2.2c Use parallelism in comparisons.

Parallelism confirms the likeness or difference between two elements being compared using *than* or *as*:

Not parallel	Sometimes a sympathetic ear is more welcome than to receive an honest opinion.
Revised	Sometimes a sympathetic ear is more welcome than an honest opinion.

(See also p. 72 on making comparisons logical.)

2.2d Use parallelism in lists, headings, and outlines.

The items in a list or outline should be parallel. Parallelism is essential in a formal topic outline and in the headings that divide a paper into sections.

Not Parallel	Revised
Changes in Renaissance England	Changes in Renaissance England
1. Extension of trade routes	1. Extension of trade routes
2. Merchant class became more powerful	2. Increased power of the merchant class
3. The death of feudalism	3. Death of feudalism
4. Upsurging of the arts	4. Upsurge of the arts
5. Religious quarrels began	5. Rise of religious quarrels

EXERCISE 2.2.1 Revising: Parallelism

Revise the following sentences to make coordinate, compared, or listed elements parallel in structure. Add or delete words or rephrase as necessary to increase the effectiveness of each sentence.

Example

After emptying her bag, searching the apartment, and having called the library, Jennifer realized she had lost the book.

After emptying her bag, searching the apartment, and calling the library, Jennifer realized she had lost the book.

1. Her tennis coach taught her how to serve and rushing the net and winning the point.
2. The unprepared student wishes for either a blizzard or to have a blackout on exam day.
3. In moving from Vermont to California, I was bothered less by the distance than to experience the climate change and especially that Christmases are warm and snowless.
4. After a week on a construction job, Leon felt not so much exhausted as that he was invigorated by the physical labor.
5. Her generosity, sympathetic nature, and the fact that she is able to motivate employees make her an excellent supervisor.

EXERCISE 2.1.2 Sentence Combining: Parallelism

Combine each group of sentences below into one concise sentence in which parallel elements appear in parallel structures. You will have to add, delete, change, and rearrange words. Each item has more than one possible answer.

Example

Kristin sorted the books neatly into piles. She was efficient about it, too.
Kristin sorted the books neatly and efficiently into piles.

1. The professor spoke rapidly. Moreover, his voice was almost inaudible.
2. The cyclists finally arrived at their destination. They arrived after riding uphill most of the day. They had also endured a hailstorm.
3. Finding an apartment requires expenditures of time and energy. It requires paying close attention to *Craigslist* and other listings. It also requires that one learn the city's neighborhoods.
4. After making several costly mistakes, he stopped to consider the jobs available to him. He thought about his goals for a job.
5. We returned from camping very tired. We were dirty. Mosquito bites covered us.

EXERCISE 2.2.3 Revising: Parallelism

Revise the following paragraph to create parallelism wherever it is required for elements with parallel meaning.

The great white shark has an undeserved bad reputation. Many people consider the great white not only swift and powerful but also to be a cunning and cruel predator on humans. However, scientists claim that the great white attacks humans not by choice but as a result of chance. To a shark, our behavior in the water is similar to that of porpoises, seals, and sea lions—the shark's favorite foods. These sea mammals are both agile enough and can move fast enough to evade the shark. Thus the shark must attack with swiftness and noiselessly to surprise the prey and giving it little chance to escape. Humans become the shark's victims not because the shark has any preference or hatred of humans but because humans can neither outswim nor can they outmaneuver the shark. If the fish were truly a cruel human-eater, it would prolong the terror of its attacks, perhaps by circling or bumping into its intended victims before they were attacked.

2.3 VARIETY AND DETAILS

Successful writers . . .

- Vary sentence length (below).
- Vary sentence structure (below).
- Add relevant details (p. 115).

To make your writing clear and interesting, use sentences that vary in length and structure and that contain concrete details.

2.3a Vary the length of sentences.

In most contemporary writing, sentences tend to vary from about ten to about forty words. If your sentences are all at one extreme or the other, readers may have difficulty locating main ideas and seeing the connections among them.

- **Long sentences.** If most of your sentences contain thirty-five words or more, your main ideas may not stand out from the details that support them. Break some of the long sentences into shorter, simpler ones.

- **Short sentences.** If most of your sentences contain fewer than ten or fifteen words, all your ideas may seem equally important and the links between them may not be clear. Combine some sentences into longer ones that emphasize main ideas.

2.3b Vary the structure of sentences.

Your writing will be monotonous if all your sentences follow the same pattern, like soldiers marching in a parade. Try these techniques for varying structure.

1 Subordination

A string of independent clauses can be especially tiring.

> **Unvaried** The moon is now drifting away from the earth. It moves away at the rate of about one inch a year. This movement is lengthening our days. They increase a thousandth of a second every century. Forty-seven of our present days will someday make up a month. We might eventually lose the moon altogether. Such great planetary movement rightly concerns astronomers, but it need not worry us. It will take 50 million years.

Revise such writing by expressing the less important information in dependent clauses and phrases (underlined).

> **Revised** The moon is now drifting away from the earth about one inch a year. At a thousandth of a second every century, this movement is lengthening our days. Forty-seven of our present days will someday make up a month, if we don't eventually lose the moon altogether. Such great planetary movement rightly concerns astronomers, but it need not worry us. It will take 50 million years.

2 Varied Sentence Beginnings

An English sentence often begins with its subject, which generally refers back to old information from a preceding sentence (see pp. 105–06).

> The defendant's lawyer was determined to break the prosecution's witness. He relentlessly cross-examined the stubborn witness for a week.

However, an unbroken sequence of sentences beginning with the subject quickly becomes monotonous.

> **Monotonous** The defendant's lawyer was determined to break the prosecution's witness. He relentlessly cross-examined the witness for a week. The witness had expected to be dismissed within an hour and was visibly irritated. She did not cooperate. She was reprimanded by the judge.

Beginning some of these sentences with other expressions makes the paragraph clearer and more readable.

> **Revised** The defendant's lawyer was determined to break the prosecution's witness. For a week he relentlessly cross-examined the witness. Expecting to be dismissed within an hour, the witness was visibly irritated. She did not cooperate. Indeed, she was reprimanded by the judge.

The underlined expressions represent the most common choices for varying sentence beginnings:

- **Add a phrase that modifies the verb,** such as *For a week* (modifies the verb *cross-examined*).

- **Add a phrase that modifies a noun,** such as *Expecting to be dismissed within an hour* (modifies *witness*).

- **Use a transitional word or phrase,** such as *Indeed.* (See pp. 240–41 for a list.)

CULTURE LANGUAGE In standard American English, placing some negative adverb modifiers at the beginning of a sentence requires you to use the word order of a question, in which the verb or a part of it precedes the subject (see p. 73). These modifiers include *never, rarely, seldom,* and adverb phrases beginning in *no, not since,* and *not until.*

	adverb	subject	verb phrase

Faulty   Seldom a witness has held the stand so long.

	adverb	helping verb	subject	main verb

Revised   Seldom has a witness held the stand so long.

3 Varied Word Order

Occasionally you can vary a sentence by reversing the usual order of parts:

A dozen witnesses testified for the prosecution, and the defense attorney barely questioned eleven of them. The twelfth, however, he grilled. [Normal word order: *He grilled the twelfth, however.*]

Reverse-order sentences used without need are artificial. Use them only when you want to create special emphasis.

2.3c Add details.

Relevant details such as facts and examples add interest to keep your readers awake and help them grasp your meaning.

Flat   Constructed after World War II, Levittown, New York, consisted of thousands of houses in two basic styles. Over the decades, residents have altered the houses so dramatically that the original styles are often unrecognizable.

Detailed   Constructed on potato fields after World War II, Levittown, New York, consisted of more than seventeen thousand houses in Cape Cod and ranch styles. Over the decades, residents have added expansive front porches, punched dormer windows through roofs, converted garages to sun porches, and otherwise altered the houses so dramatically that the original styles are often unrecognizable.

EXERCISE 2.3.1   Revising: Varied Sentence Beginnings

Each item below contains a pair of simple sentences that begin with their subjects. Follow the instructions in parentheses for each item: either create a single sentence that begins with a modifier, or make one sentence begin with an appropriate transitional word or phrase.

Example

At first the *Seabird* was gaining position in the race. It finished in last place. (*Two sentences with transitional word or phrase*.)

At first the *Seabird* was gaining position in the race. However, it finished in last place.

1. The loan application was denied by the bank. The business had to close its doors. (*Two sentences with transitional word or phrase*.)
2. The school may build a new athletic complex. It will tear down the old field house. (*One sentence beginning with If*.)
3. Voting rights for women seemed a possibility in the 1860s. Women were not actually given the vote for nearly sixty years. (*Two sentences with transitional word or phrase*.)
4. College tuition has risen astronomically in recent years. A state university that once cost $5,500 per semester now costs $10,000. (*Two sentences with a transitional word or phrase*.)
5. William had orders to stay in bed. He returned to work immediately. (*One sentence beginning with Although*.)

EXERCISE 2.3.2   Revising: Variety

The following paragraph consists entirely of simple sentences that begin with their subjects. Use the techniques discussed in this chapter to vary the sentences. Delete, add, change, and rearrange words to make the paragraph more readable and to make important ideas stand out clearly.

The instructor found himself in class alone. He waited patiently for his students to arrive. He went over his lecture notes. He read yesterday's newspaper. No one arrived. He noticed an article on the front page of the paper. It instructed readers to turn their clocks back one hour. He realized his mistake. He smiled.

2.4 APPROPRIATE WORDS

Successful writers . . .

- Avoid nonstandard dialect in academic writing (facing page).
- Avoid slang, most colloquial language, and unnecessary technical words (facing page and p. 118).
- Avoid indirect and pretentious writing (p. 118).
- Avoid sexist and other biased language (p. 119).

Appropriate words are those that suit your writing situation—your subject, purpose, and audience. In most college and career writing you should rely on what's called **standard American English,** the dialect of English normally expected and used in school, business, the professions, government, and the communications media. (For more on its role in academic writing, see pp. 205–07.)

The vocabulary of standard American English is huge, allowing the expression of a wide range of ideas and feelings; but it does exclude words that only some groups of people use, understand, or find inoffensive. Some of these more limited vocabularies should be avoided altogether; others should be used cautiously and in appropriate situations, as when aiming for a special effect with an audience you know will appreciate it. Whenever you doubt a word's status, consult a dictionary (see p. 123). A label such as *nonstandard, slang,* or *colloquial* tells you that the word is generally not appropriate in academic or career writing.

2.4a Avoid nonstandard dialect in academic writing.

Like many countries, the United States includes scores of regional, social, and ethnic groups with their own distinct **dialects,** or versions of English. Standard American English is one of those dialects, and so are African American Vernacular English, Appalachian English, Creole, and the English of coastal Maine. All the dialects of English share many features, but each also has its own vocabulary, pronunciation, and grammar.

If you speak a dialect of English besides standard American English, be careful about using your dialect in situations where standard English is the norm, such as in academic and business writing. Dialects are not wrong in themselves, but when you use one dialect where another is expected, your writing may be perceived as unclear or incorrect. When you know standard English is expected in your writing, edit to eliminate expressions in your dialect that you know (or have been told) differ from standard English. These expressions may include *theirselves, hisn, them books,* and others labeled *nonstandard* by a dictionary. They may also include nonstandard verb forms, as discussed on p. 33. For help identifying and editing such language, see the Guide just before the back endpapers of this book.

You do not need to abandon your own dialect. You may want to use it in writing you do for yourself, such as journals, notes, and drafts, which should be composed as freely as possible. You may want to quote it in an academic paper, as when analyzing or reporting conversation in dialect. And, of course, you will want to use it with others who speak it.

2.4b Avoid slang.

Slang is the language used by a group, such as musicians or computer programmers, to reflect common experiences and to make technical references efficient. The following example is from an essay on the slang of "skaters" (skateboarders):

> Curtis slashed ultra-punk crunchers on his longboard, while the Rube-man flailed his usual Gumbyness on tweaked frontsides and lofty fakie ollies.
> —Miles Orkin, "Mucho Slingage by the Pool"

Among those who understand it, slang may be vivid and forceful. It often occurs in dialog, but most slang is too flippant and imprecise for effective communication, and it is generally inappropriate for college and career writing.

| Slang | Many students start out <u>pretty together</u> but then <u>get weird</u>. |
| Revised | Many students start out <u>with clear goals</u> but then <u>lose their direction</u>. |

2.4c Avoid most colloquial language.

Colloquial language is the everyday spoken language, including expressions such as *get together, go nuts, chill out,* and *get along.*

When you write informally, colloquial language may be appropriate to achieve the casual, relaxed effect of conversation. An occasional colloquial word dropped into otherwise more formal writing can also help you achieve a desired emphasis. But most colloquial language is not precise enough for college or career writing. In such writing you should generally avoid any words and expressions labeled *informal* or *colloquial* in your dictionary.

| Colloquial | According to a Native American myth, the Great Creator <u>had a dog hanging around with him</u> when he created the earth. |
| Revised | According to a Native American myth, the Great Creator <u>was accompanied by a dog</u> when he created the earth. |

Note See also pages 205–06 for a discussion of formal and informal language in academic writing.

2.4d Avoid unnecessary technical words.

All disciplines and professions rely on specialized language that allows their members to communicate precisely and efficiently with each other. Chemists, for instance, have their *phosphatides,* and literary critics have their *motifs* and *subtexts.* Without explanation, technical words are meaningless to nonspecialists. When you are writing for nonspecialists, avoid unnecessary technical terms and carefully define any terms you must use.

2.4e Avoid indirect and pretentious writing.

Small, plain, and direct words are almost always preferable to big, showy, or evasive words. Take special care to avoid the following:

- *Euphemisms* **substitute for language that the writer thinks may be unpleasant, offensive, or too blunt,** such as *passed away* for *died* or *misspeak* for *lie.* Use euphemisms only when you know that blunt, truthful words would needlessly hurt or offend members of your audience.

- *Double talk* **(at times called *doublespeak* or *weasel words*) is language intended to confuse or to be misunderstood:** the *revenue enhancement* that is really a tax, the *biodegradable* bags that will last for decades. Double talk has no place in honest writing.

- *Pretentious writing* **is fancy language that is more elaborate than its subject requires.** Choose your words for their exactness and economy. The big, ornate word may be tempting, but pass it up. Your readers will be grateful.

Pretentious	To perpetuate our endeavor of providing funds for our elderly citizens as we do at the present moment, we will face the exigency of enhanced contributions from all our citizens.
Revised	We cannot continue to fund Social Security and Medicare for the elderly unless we raise taxes.

2.4f Avoid sexist and other biased language.

Even when we do not mean it to, our language can express hurtful prejudices toward groups of people. Such biased language can be obvious—words such as *nigger, cracker, mick, kike, fag, dyke,* and *broad.* But it can also be subtle, making statements about groups in ways that may be familiar but that are also inaccurate or unfair.

Biased language reflects poorly on the user, not on the person or persons whom it mischaracterizes or insults. Be sure to use language that treats people respectfully as individuals and labels groups as they wish to be labeled.

1 Stereotypes of Race, Ethnicity, Religion, Age, and Other Characteristics

A **stereotype** characterizes and judges people on the basis of their membership in a group:

Men are uncommunicative.

Women are emotional.

Liberals want to raise taxes.

Conservatives are affluent.

In your writing, avoid statements about traits of whole groups that may be true of only some members.

Stereotype	Elderly drivers should have their licenses limited to daytime driving only. [Asserts that all elderly people are poor night drivers.]
Revised	Drivers with impaired night vision should have their licenses limited to daytime driving only.

Some stereotypes have become part of the language, but they are still potentially offensive.

Stereotype	The administrators are too blind to see the need for a new gymnasium. [Equates vision loss and lack of understanding.]
Revised	The administrators do not understand the need for a new gymnasium.

2 Sexist Language

Among the most subtle and persistent biased language is that expressing narrow ideas about men's and women's roles, position, and value in society. Like other stereotypes, **sexist language** can hurt or irritate readers, and it reveals the writer's thoughtlessness or unfairness. The following box suggests ways of eliminating sexist language.

 Success ―――――――――――――――――――――――――――――――――――――

Eliminating Sexist Language

- **Avoid demeaning and patronizing language.**

  Sexist   Dr. Keith Kim and Lydia Hawkins coauthored the article.

  Revised   Dr. Keith Kim and Dr. Lydia Hawkins coauthored the article.

  Revised   Keith Kim and Lydia Hawkins coauthored the article.

- **Avoid occupational or social stereotypes.**

  Sexist   The considerate doctor praises a nurse when she provides his patients with good care.

  Revised   The considerate doctor praises a nurse who provides good care for patients.

- **Avoid referring needlessly to gender.**

  Sexist   Marie Curie, a woman chemist, discovered radium.

  Revised   Marie Curie, a chemist, discovered radium.

- **Avoid using *man* or words containing *man* to refer to all human beings.**
  Here are a few alternatives:

businessman	businessperson
chairman	chair, chairperson
congressman	representative, congressperson, legislator
craftsman	craftsperson, artisan
layman	layperson
mankind	humankind, humanity, human beings, humans
manmade	handmade, manufactured, synthetic, artificial
manpower	personnel, human resources
policeman	police officer
salesman	salesperson

  Sexist   Man has not reached the limits of kindness.

  Revised   Humankind [or Humanity] has not reached the limits of kindness.

Eliminating Sexist Language *(continued)*

- **Avoid the generic *he,*** the male pronoun used to refer to both
  genders. (See also p. 61.)

Sexist	The newborn <u>child</u> explores <u>his</u> world.
Revised	Newborn <u>children</u> explore <u>their</u> world. [Use the plural for the pronoun and the word it refers to.]
Revised	The newborn <u>child</u> explores <u>the</u> world. [Avoid the pronoun altogether.]
Revised	The newborn <u>child</u> explores <u>his or her</u> world. [Substitute male and female pronouns.]

  Use the last option sparingly—only once in a group of sentences and only to stress
  the singular individual.

CULTURE LANGUAGE   Forms of address vary widely from culture to culture. In some cultures, for instance, one shows respect by referring to all older women as if they were married, using the equivalent of *Mrs.* Usage in the United States is changing toward making no assumptions about marital status, rank, or other characteristics—for instance, addressing a woman as *Ms.* unless she is known to prefer *Mrs.* or *Miss.*

3 Inappropriate Labels

Labels for groups of people can be shorthand stereotypes and can ignore readers' preferences. Although sometimes dismissed as "political correctness," sensitivity in applying labels hurts no one and helps gain your readers' trust and respect.

- **Avoid labels that (intentionally or not) insult the person or group you refer to.** A person with emotional problems is not a *mental patient.* A person using a wheelchair is not *wheelchair-bound.*

- **Use names for racial, ethnic, and other groups that reflect the preferences of each group's members,** or at least many of them. Examples of current preferences include *African American* or *black* and *people with disabilities* (rather than *the disabled* or *the handicapped*). But labels change often. To learn how a group's members wish to be labeled, ask them directly, attend to usage in reputable periodicals, or check a recent dictionary.

- **Identify a person's group only when it is relevant to the point you're making.** Consider the context of the label: Is it a necessary piece of information? If not, don't use it.

EXERCISE 2.4.1   Revising: Appropriate Words

Rewrite the following sentences as needed for standard American English, focusing on inappropriate slang, technical or pretentious language, and biased language. Consult a dictionary as needed.

Example

Cancer victims have the necessity for all the medical care due to those who are in the extremity of illness.

Cancer patients need all the medical care due to those who are extremely ill.

1. Acquired immune deficiency syndrome (AIDS) is a major deal all over the world, and those who think the disease is limited to homos, mainliners, and foreigners are quite mistaken.
2. A doctor may help his patients by obtaining social services for them as well as by providing medical care.
3. Whenever a soldier is killed by friendly fire, authorities investigate his death.
4. My female sibling went on a caloric reduction program two seasons prior to her nuptials.
5. The food shortages in some parts of Africa are so severe that tens of thousands of people have met their demise.
6. A social worker may visit someone displaced by severe weather and determine whether he qualifies for public assistance, since many victims don't have the dough for new abodes.
7. The most stubborn members of the administration still will not hearken to our pleas for a voice in college doings.
8. They bought a beaut of a Victorian house in a ritzy neighborhood.
9. I almost failed physics because some jerk stole my notes.
10. Her arm often aches, but she says it doesn't bother her none.

EXERCISE 2.4.2   Revising: Sexist Language

Revise the following sentences to eliminate sexist language. If you change a singular noun or pronoun to plural, be sure to make any needed changes in verbs or other pronouns.

1. When a student applies for a job, he should prepare the best possible résumé, because the businessman who is scanning a stack of résumés will read them all quickly.
2. The person who wants his résumé to stand out will make sure it highlights his best points.
3. A person applying for a job as a mailman should emphasize his honesty and responsibility.
4. A girl applying for a position as a home-care nurse should also emphasize her honesty and responsibility as well as her background of capable nursing.
5. Someone seeking work as a computer programmer will highlight his experience with programming languages.
6. A student without extensive job experience should highlight his volunteer work.
7. For instance, a student may have been chairman of a campus organization or secretary of her church's youth group.
8. If everyone writing a résumé considers what the man who will read it is looking for, the applicant will know better what he should include and how he should format that information.

2.5 EXACT WORDS

Successful writers . . .

- Use a dictionary and a thesaurus for help in writing exactly (below).
- Choose the right word for the meaning (next page).
- Use concrete and specific words (p. 126).
- Take care with idioms, including those with prepositions (p. 127).
- Use figurative language when appropriate (p. 129).
- Avoid trite expressions, or clichés (p.130).

To write clearly and effectively, be sure to find the words that fit your meaning exactly and convey your attitude accurately.

2.5a Use a dictionary and a thesaurus.

For writing exactly, a dictionary is essential and a thesaurus can be helpful.

Dictionaries

A dictionary defines words and provides pronunciation, grammatical functions, history, and other information. The following sample is from *Merriam-Webster Online* (*merriam-webster.com*):

PARTIAL ONLINE DICTIONARY ENTRY

reck·on 🔊 *verb* \re-kən\

reck·oned | reck·on·ing 🔊

Definition of RECKON

transitive verb

1 a : COUNT <*reckon* the days till Christmas>

   b : ESTIMATE, COMPUTE <*reckon* the height of a building>

   c : to determine by reference to a fixed basis <the existence of the United States is *reckoned* from the Declaration of Independence>

2 : to regard or think of as : CONSIDER

3 *chiefly dialect* : THINK, SUPPOSE <I *reckon* I've outlived my time — Ellen Glasgow>

By permission. From *Merriam-Webster's Collegiate® Dictionary,* 11th edition ©2014 by Merriam-Webster Inc. (www.Merriam-Webster.com).

Other useful online sites are *Dictionary.com* (*dictionary.com*) and *The Free Dictionary* (*the freedictionary.com*), which provide entries from several dictionaries at once. *Dictionary.com* also offers a translator that converts text between languages, such as English to

Spanish. *The Free Dictionary* offers dictionaries in more than a dozen languages besides English.

If you prefer a print dictionary, good ones, in addition to *Merriam-Webster's Collegiate,* include *American Heritage College Dictionary, Random House Webster's College Dictionary,* and *Webster's New World College Dictionary.* Some of these books come with CD versions as well.

(CULTURE LANGUAGE) If English is not your native language, you probably should have a dictionary prepared especially for students using English as a second language (ESL). Such a dictionary contains special information on prepositions, count versus noncount nouns, and many other matters. The following are reliable print ESL dictionaries, each with an online version at the URL in parentheses: *Longman Dictionary of Contemporary English (ldoceonline.com), Oxford Advanced Learner's Dictionary (oxfordadvancedlearnersdictionary.com), Merriam-Webster Advanced Learner's English Dictionary (learnersdictionary.com).*

Thesauruses

To find a word with the exact shade of meaning you intend, you may want to consult a thesaurus, or book of **synonyms**—words with approximately the same meaning. A print or online thesaurus lists most imaginable synonyms for thousand of words. For instance, on the site *Thesaurus.com* the word *reckon* has nearly fifty synonyms, including *account, evaluate,* and *judge.*

Because a thesaurus aims to open up possibilities, its lists of synonyms include approximate as well as precise matches. The thesaurus does not define synonyms or distinguish among them, however, so you need a dictionary to discover exact meanings. In general, don't use a word from a thesaurus—even one you like the sound of—until you are sure of its appropriateness for your meaning.

2.5b Use the right word for your meaning.

All words have one or more basic meanings, called **denotations**—the meanings in the dictionary. To make sure your readers understand you, use words correctly, according to their established denotations.

- **Consult a dictionary whenever you are unsure of a word's meaning.**

- **Distinguish between similar-sounding words that have widely different meanings:**

  Incorrect Older people often suffer <u>infirmaries</u> [places for the sick].

  Correct   Older people often suffer <u>infirmities</u> [disabilities].

  Some words, called **homonyms,** sound exactly alike but differ in meaning: for example, *principal/principle* and *rain/reign/rein.* (See pp. 180–81 for a list of commonly confused homonyms.)

- **Distinguish between words with related but distinct meanings:**

  Incorrect Commercials <u>continuously</u> [unceasingly] interrupt many television shows.

  Correct   Commercials <u>continually</u> [regularly] interrupt many television shows.

In addition to their emotion-free meanings, many words also carry related meanings that evoke specific feelings. These **connotations** can shape readers' responses and are thus a powerful tool for writers. In the following example pairs, the words have related denotations but very different connotations:

pride: sense of self-worth
vanity: excessive regard for oneself

firm: steady, unchanging, unyielding
stubborn: unreasonable, bullheaded

enthusiasm: excitement, strong interest
mania: excessive interest or desire

A dictionary can help you track down words with the exact connotations you want. Besides providing meanings, your dictionary may also list and distinguish synonyms to guide your choices. A thesaurus can also help if you use it carefully, as discussed on the previous page.

EXERCISE 2.5.1   Revising: Denotation

Revise the following sentences to replace any underlined word that is used incorrectly. If an underlined word is used correctly, circle the number preceding the sentence. Consult a dictionary if you are uncertain of a word's meaning.

Example

Sam and Dave are going to Bermuda and Hauppauge, <u>respectfully</u>, for spring vacation.

Sam and Dave are going to Bermuda and Hauppauge, <u>respectively</u>, for spring vacation.

1. The <u>enormity</u> of the beached whale—and its horrible stench—both amazed and repelled us.
2. Hospital personnel must wear protective clothing when tending a patient with a highly <u>communicative</u> disease.
3. The writer was <u>rewarded</u> many prizes for his books.
4. One <u>affect</u> of the report is that doctors are less willing to order expensive tests for their patients.
5. Having been <u>deferred</u> from acting on impulse, she felt paralyzed by indecision.

EXERCISE 2.5.2   Considering the Connotation of Words

Fill in the blank in each sentence below with the most appropriate word from the list in parentheses. Consult a dictionary to be sure of your choice.

1. Infection with the AIDS virus, HIV, is a serious health _____. (*problem, worry, difficulty, plight*)
2. Once the virus has entered the blood system, it _____ T-cells. (*murders, destroys, slaughters, executes*)
3. The _____ of T-cells is to combat infections. (*ambition, function, aim, goal*)
4. Without enough T-cells, the body is nearly _____ against infections. (*defenseless, hopeless, desperate*)
5. To prevent exposure to the virus, one should be especially _____ in sexual relationships. (*chary, circumspect, cautious, calculating*)

2.5c Use concrete and specific words.

Clear, exact writing balances abstract and general words, which outline ideas and objects, with concrete and specific words, which sharpen and add detail.

- **Abstract words** name qualities and ideas: *beauty, inflation, management, culture, liberal.* **Concrete words** name things we can know by our five senses of sight, hearing, touch, taste, and smell: *sleek, humming, brick, bitter, musty.*

- **General words** name classes or groups of things, such as *birds, weather,* or *buildings,* and include all the varieties of the class. **Specific words** limit a general class, such as *buildings,* by naming a variety, such as *skyscraper, Victorian courthouse,* or *hut.*

Abstract and general words are useful in the broad statements that announce your main points.

The wild horse in America has a <u>romantic</u> history.

Relations between the sexes today are more <u>relaxed</u> than they were in the past.

But such statements need development with concrete and specific details that help readers perceive what you're describing. *Crumbly bread, soft velvet,* the *wine-dark sea* of the poet Homer—these phrases evoke images and trigger memories. Details can turn a vague sentence into an exact one:

Vague   The size of his hands made his smallness real. [How big were his hands? How small was he?]

Exact   Not until I saw his delicate, doll-like hands did I realize that he stood a full head shorter than most other men.

Look for places in your drafts where you can substitute a sense word for a cliché or an abstract noun.

EXERCISE 2.5.3   Revising: Concrete and Specific Words

Make the following paragraph vivid by expanding the sentences with appropriate details of your own choosing. Substitute concrete and specific words for the abstract and general ones that are underlined.

1 I remember <u>clearly</u> how <u>awful</u> I felt the first time I <u>attended</u> Mrs. Murphy's second-grade class. **2** I had <u>recently</u> moved from a <u>small</u> town in Missouri to a <u>crowded</u> suburb of Chicago. **3** My new school looked <u>big</u> from the outside and seemed <u>dark</u> inside as I <u>walked</u> down the <u>long</u> corridor toward the classroom. **4** The class was <u>noisy</u> as I neared the door; but when I <u>entered, everyone</u> became <u>quiet</u> and <u>looked</u> at me. **5** I felt <u>uncomfortable</u> and <u>wanted</u> a place to hide. **6** However, in a <u>loud</u> voice Mrs. Murphy <u>directed</u> me to the front of the room to introduce myself.

EXERCISE 2.5.4   Using Concrete and Specific Words

For each of the following abstract or general words, give at least two other words or phrases that are increasingly specific or concrete. Consult a diction-ary as needed. Use the most specific or concrete word from each group in a sentence of your own.

Example

awake, watchful, vigilant
Vigilant guards patrol the buildings.

1. fabric	**5.** reach (*verb*)	**9.** serious	**13.** virtue
2. delicious	**6.** green	**10.** pretty	**14.** angry
3. car	**7.** walk (*verb*)	**11.** teacher	**15.** crime
4. narrow-minded	**8.** flower	**12.** nice	

2.5d Take care with idioms.

Idioms are expressions in any language that do not fit the rules for meaning or grammar—for instance, *put up with, plug away at, make off with.*

Idiomatic combinations of verbs or adjectives and prepositions can be confusing for both native and nonnative speakers of English. Some of these pairings are listed in the following box. (More appear on pp. 38–39.)

Idioms with Prepositions

abide by a rule
    in a place or state
according to
accuse of a crime
accustomed to
adapt from a source
    to a situation
afraid of
agree on a plan as a group
    to someone else's plan
    with a person
angry with
aware of
based on
belong in or on a place
    to a group
capable of
certain of
charge for a purchase
    with a crime

concur in an opinion
    with a person
consist of
contend for a principle
    with a person
dependent on
differ about or over a question
    from in some quality
    with a person
disappointed by or in a person
    in or with a thing
familiar with
identical with or to
impatient for a raise
    with a person
independent of
infer from
inferior to
involved in a task
    with a person

(continued)

Idioms with Prepositions (continued)

oblivious of or to surroundings	rewarded by the judge
of something forgotten	for something done
occupied by a person	with a gift
in study	similar to
with a thing	sorry about an error
opposed to	for a person
part from a person	superior to
with a possession	wait at a place
prior to	for a train, a person
proud of	in a room
related to	on a customer
responsible for	

CULTURE · LANGUAGE If you are learning standard American English, you may find its prepositions difficult: their meanings can shift depending on context, and they have many idiomatic uses. In mastering the prepositions of standard English, you probably can't avoid memorization. But you can help yourself by memorizing related groups, such as *at/in/on* and *for/since*.

At, *in*, or *on* in expressions of time

- Use *at* before actual clock time: <u>at</u> *8:30.*
- Use *in* before a month, year, century, or period: <u>in</u> *April,* <u>in</u> *2014,* <u>in</u> *the twenty-first century,* <u>in</u> *the next month.*
- Use *on* before a day or date: <u>on</u> *Tuesday,* <u>on</u> *August 3,* <u>on</u> *Labor Day.*

At, *in*, or *on* in expressions of place

- Use *at* before a specific place or address: <u>at</u> *the school,* <u>at</u> *511 Iris Street.*
- Use *in* before a place with limits or before a city, state, country, or continent: <u>in</u> *the house,* <u>in</u> *a box,* <u>in</u> *Oklahoma City,* <u>in</u> *China,* <u>in</u> *Asia.*
- Use *on* to mean "supported by" or "touching the surface of": <u>on</u> *the table,* <u>on</u> *Iris Street,* <u>on</u> *page 150.*

For or *since* in expressions of time

- Use *for* before a period of time: <u>for</u> *an hour,* <u>for</u> *two years.*
- Use *since* before a specific point in time: <u>since</u> *1999,* <u>since</u> *Friday.*

A dictionary of English as a second language is the best source for the meanings of prepositions. See the suggestions on pp. 123–24.

> EXERCISE 2.5.5   Using Prepositions in Idioms

Insert the preposition that correctly completes each idiom in the following sentences. Consult the preceding list or a dictionary as needed.

Example

I disagree _____ many feminists who say women should not be homemakers.

I disagree <u>with</u> many feminists who say women should not be homemakers.

1. He had waited for years, growing impatient _____ her demands and _____ the money that she would leave to him.
2. The writer compared gorilla society _____ human society.
3. They agreed _____ most things, but they differed consistently _____ how to raise their child.
4. I was rewarded _____ my persistence _____ an opportunity to meet the senator.
5. He would sooner part _____ his friends than part _____ his Corvette.

2.5e Use figurative language when appropriate.

Figurative language (or a **figure of speech**) departs from the literal meanings of words, usually by comparing very different ideas or objects.

Literal   As I try to write, I can think of nothing to say.

Figurative   As I try to write, <u>my mind is a slab of black slate</u>.

Figurative language can often capture meaning more precisely and emotionally than literal language. When the poet Carl Sandburg writes, "The fog comes in on little cat feet," we can *see* the fog approaching as a cat does, silently. Here is a figure of speech at work in technical writing (paraphrasing the physicist Edward Andrade):

The molecules in a liquid move continuously like couples on an overcrowded dance floor, jostling each other.

The two most common figures of speech are the simile and the metaphor. Both compare two things of different classes, often one abstract and the other concrete. A **simile** makes the comparison explicit and usually begins with *like* or *as*:

Whenever we grow, we tend to feel it, <u>as</u> a young seed must feel the weight and inertia of the earth when it seeks to break out of its shell on its way to becoming a plant.
                                                                    —Alice Walker

A **metaphor** claims that the two things are identical, omitting such words as *like* and *as*:

A school is a hopper into which children are heaved while they are young and tender; therein they are pressed into certain standard shapes and covered from head to heels with official rubber stamps.

                                                    —H. L. Mencken

Be sure to use fresh, unique figurative expressions; avoid the tired, overused ones you've heard before. (See the next page.)

> EXERCISE 2.5.6   Using Figurative Language

Invent appropriate similes or metaphors of your own to describe each of the following scenes or qualities, and use the figure in a sentence.

Example

The attraction of a lake on a hot day
The small waves <u>like fingers beckoned</u> us irresistibly.

1. The sound of a kindergarten classroom
2. People waiting in line for something, such as boarding a bus or a plane.
3. The politeness of strangers meeting for the first time
4. A streetlight seen through dense fog
5. The effect of watching television for ten hours straight

2.5f Avoid trite expressions.

Trite expressions, or **clichés**, are phrases so old and so often repeated that they have become stale. They include the following:

add insult to injury	a needle in a haystack
better late than never	point with pride
crushing blow	pride and joy
easier said than done	ripe old age
face the music	rude awakening
few and far between	shoulder the burden
green with envy	shoulder to cry on
hard as a rock	sneaking suspicion
heavy as lead	stand in awe
hit the nail on the head	strong as an ox
hour of need	thin as a rail
ladder of success	tried and true
moving experience	wise as an owl

To edit clichés, listen to your writing for any expressions that you have heard or used before. You can also supplement your efforts with a style checker, which may include a cliché detector. When you find a cliché, substitute fresh words of your own or restate the idea in plain language.

> EXERCISE 2.5.7   Revising: Trite Expressions

Revise the following sentences to eliminate trite expressions.

Example

The basketball team had almost seized victory, but it faced the test of truth in the last quarter of the game.

The basketball team <u>seemed about to win</u>, but the <u>real test</u> came in the last quarter of the game.

1. These disastrous consequences of the war have shaken the small nation to its roots.
2. Some say that liberal arts majors face an uphill climb getting jobs in business; others observe that corporations have been looking high and low for liberal arts students.
3. When my father retired from the gas company after thirty long years, he was honored to receive a large clock in recognition of his valued service.
4. Sam shouldered his way through the crowd, hoping to catch a glimpse of the actress who had become the woman of his dreams.
5. My new car was supposed to be a technological triumph, but the catalytic converter started smelling to high heaven after only 500 miles.

2.6 CONCISENESS

Successful writers . . .

- Focus on the subject and verb (below).
- Cut or shorten empty words and unneeded repetition (p. 133).
- Reduce modifiers (p. 134).
- Revise *there is* and *it is* constructions (p. 134).
- Combine sentences (p. 135).

Concise writing makes every word count. Being concise is not the same as being brief. Rather, the length of an expression should be appropriate to the thought.

CULTURE ▸ LANGUAGE As this chapter's examples show, wordiness is not a matter of incorrect grammar. An English sentence may be grammatical and still contain unneeded words that make it unclear or awkward.

2.6a Focus on the subject and verb.

Using the subjects and verbs of your sentences for the key actors and actions will reduce words and emphasize important ideas. (See pp. 104–06 for more on this topic.)

Wordy   The <u>reason</u> why most of the country shifts to daylight time <u>is</u> that summer days are much longer than winter days.

Concise   Most of the <u>country shifts</u> to daylight time because summer days are much longer than winter days.

Focusing on subjects and verbs will also help you avoid the following other causes of wordiness.

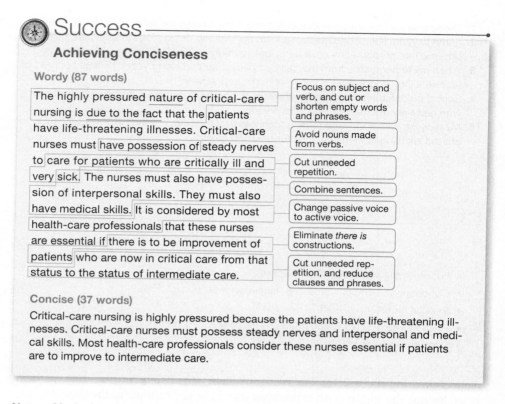

Success ─────────────────────────────────

Achieving Conciseness

Wordy (87 words)

The highly pressured nature of critical-care nursing is due to the fact that the patients have life-threatening illnesses. Critical-care nurses must have possession of steady nerves to care for patients who are critically ill and very sick. The nurses must also have possession of interpersonal skills. They must also have medical skills. It is considered by most health-care professionals that these nurses are essential if there is to be improvement of patients who are now in critical care from that status to the status of intermediate care.

Focus on subject and verb, and cut or shorten empty words and phrases.

Avoid nouns made from verbs.

Cut unneeded repetition.

Combine sentences.

Change passive voice to active voice.

Eliminate *there is* constructions.

Cut unneeded repetition, and reduce clauses and phrases.

Concise (37 words)

Critical-care nursing is highly pressured because the patients have life-threatening illnesses. Critical-care nurses must possess steady nerves and interpersonal and medical skills. Most health-care professionals consider these nurses essential if patients are to improve to intermediate care.

Nouns Made from Verbs

Wordy   The <u>occurrence</u> of the winter solstice, the shortest day of the year, <u>is</u> an event occurring about December 22.

Concise   The winter <u>solstice</u>, the shortest day of the year, <u>occurs</u> about December 22.

Weak Verbs

Wordy   The earth's axis <u>has</u> a tilt as the planet <u>is in orbit</u> around the sun so that the northern and southern hemispheres <u>are</u> alternately in alignment toward the sun.

Concise   The earth's axis <u>tilts</u> as the planet <u>orbits</u> the sun so that the northern and southern hemispheres alternately <u>align</u> toward the sun.

Passive Voice

Wordy   During its winter the northern hemisphere <u>is tilted</u> farthest away from the sun, so the nights <u>are made</u> longer and the days <u>are made</u> shorter.

Concise   During its winter the northern hemisphere <u>tilts</u> away from the sun, <u>making</u> the nights longer and the days shorter.

See also pp. 45–47 on changing the passive voice to the active voice.

2.6b Cut or shorten empty words.

Empty words contribute little or nothing to meaning. Many can be cut entirely. The following are just a few examples:

all things considered	in a manner of speaking
as far as I'm concerned	in my opinion
for all intents and purposes	last but not least
for the most part	more or less

Other empty words can also be cut, usually along with some of the words around them.

area	kind
aspect	manner
case	nature
element	situation
factor	thing
field	type

Still others can be reduced from several words to a single word:

For	Substitute
at all times	always
at the present time	now, yet
because of the fact that	because
by virtue of the fact that	because
due to the fact that	because
for the purpose of	for
in order to	to
in the event that	if
in the final analysis	finally

Cutting or reducing such words and phrases will make your writing move faster and work harder.

Wordy As far as I am concerned, because of the fact that a situation of discrimination still exists in the field of medicine, women have not at the present time achieved equality with men.

Concise Because discrimination still exists in medicine, women have not yet achieved equality with men.

2.6c Cut unneeded repetition.

Unnecessary repetition weakens sentences.

Wordy Many unskilled workers without training in a particular job are unemployed and do not have any work.

Concise Many unskilled workers are unemployed.

Be especially alert to phrases that say the same thing twice. In the examples below, the unneeded words are underlined:

circle <u>around</u>	important [<u>basic</u>] essentials
consensus <u>of opinion</u>	puzzling <u>in nature</u>
cooperate <u>together</u>	repeat <u>again</u>
final completion	return <u>again</u>
frank <u>and honest</u> exchange	square [<u>round</u>] <u>in shape</u>
the future <u>to come</u>	surrounding circumstances

CULTURE LANGUAGE   The preceding phrases are redundant because the main word already implies the underlined word or words. An English dictionary will tell you what meanings a word implies. *Assassinate,* for instance, means "murder someone well known," so the following sentence is redundant: *Julius Caesar was assassinated <u>and killed</u>.*

2.6d Reduce modifiers.

Modifiers can be shortened or lengthened depending on the emphasis you want to achieve. When editing sentences, consider whether you can reduce any modifiers without loss of emphasis or clarity.

Wordy   The weight-loss industry faces new competition from lipolysis, <u>which is a cosmetic procedure that is relatively</u> <u>noninvasive.</u>

Concise   The weight-loss industry faces new competition from lipolysis, <u>a relatively noninvasive cosmetic procedure.</u>

2.6e Revise *there is* and *it is* constructions.

You can postpone the sentence subject with the words *there is* (*there are, there was, there were*) and *it is* (*it was*): *There is reason for voting. It is your vote that counts.* These **expletive constructions** can be useful to emphasize the subject (as when introducing it for the first time) or to indicate a change in direction. But often they just add words and create limp substitutes for more vigorous sentences:

Wordy   <u>There is</u> a completely noninvasive laser treatment <u>that</u> makes people thinner by rupturing fat cells and releasing the fat into the spaces between cells. <u>It is the expectation of some doctors</u> that the procedure will replace liposuction.

Concise   A completely noninvasive laser treatment makes people thinner by rupturing fat cells and releasing the fat into the spaces between cells. <u>Some doctors expect</u> that the procedure will replace liposuction.

CULTURE LANGUAGE   When you must use an expletive construction in an English sentence, be careful to include *there* or *it.* Only commands and some questions can begin with verbs.

2.6f Combine sentences.

Often the information in two or more sentences can be combined into one tight sentence:

Wordy	People who receive fat-releasing laser treatments can lose inches from their waists. They can also lose inches from their hips and thighs. They do not lose weight. The released fat remains in their bodies.
Concise	People who receive fat-releasing laser treatments can lose inches from their waists, hips, and thighs; but they do not lose weight because the released fat remains in their bodies.

EXERCISE 2.6.1   Revising: Writing Concisely

Revise the following sentences to make them more concise by converting passive voice to active voice, cutting empty words, eliminating repetition, reducing modifiers, and revising *there is* or *it is* constructions.

Example

The problem in this particular situation is that we owe more money than we can afford under present circumstances.
The problem is that we owe more money than we can afford.

1. As far as I am concerned, the major weakness of the restaurant in question is that the service is surly, in a manner of speaking.
2. The contestant was seated behind a screen so that she could not be seen by the judges while her performance was heard.
3. After all these years there is still something calling me back to the town where I lived as a child.
4. The protesters were ordered by the police to clear the sidewalk when the motorcade was approaching.
5. There must have been some reason why he acted as he did, whether conscious or unconscious.

EXERCISE 2.6.2   Revising: Writing Concisely

Make the following paragraph more concise. Combine sentences when doing so reduces wordiness.

If sore muscles after exercising are a problem for you, there are some measures that can be taken by you to ease the discomfort. It is advisable to avoid heat for the first day of soreness. The application of heat within the first twenty-four hours can cause an increase in muscle soreness and stiffness. In contrast, the immediate application of cold will help to reduce inflammation. Blood vessels are constricted by cold. Blood is kept away from the injured muscles. There are two ways the application of cold can be made: you can take a cold shower or use an ice pack. Inflammation of muscles can also be reduced with aspirin, ibuprofen, or another anti-inflammatory medication. When healing is occurring, you need to take it easy. A day or two after overdoing exercise, it is advisable for you to get some light exercise and gentle massage.

Chu Ta was a 17th century Chinese painter, known for works that exhibit a seemingly spontaneous and free-form style. This simple effectiveness usually comes from many years of regular practice and discipline and it applies to writing as well as painting.

3

Punctuation

3.1 END PUNCTUATION

Successful writers . . .

- Use a period after most sentences and with some abbreviations (next page).
- Use a question mark after a direct question and sometimes to indicate doubt (p. 139).
- Use an exclamation point after a strong statement, interjection, or command (p. 140).

The period (.), exclamation point (!), and question mark (?) each has distinctive uses.

Taken from *The Successful Writer's Handbook,* Third Edition by Kathleen T. McWhorter and Jane E. Aaron.

3.1a Use a period after most sentences and with some abbreviations.

1 Statements, Mild Commands, and Indirect Questions

Statement

The airline went bankrupt.   It no longer flies.

Mild command

Think of the possibilities.   Please consider others.

Indirect question

An **indirect question** reports what someone asked but not in the exact form or words of the original question:

The judge asked why I had been driving with my lights off.

No one asked how we got home.

CULTURE LANGUAGE   In standard American English, an indirect question uses the wording and subject-verb order of a statement: *The reporter asked why the bank failed* [not *why did the bank fail*].

2 Abbreviations

Use periods with abbreviations that consist of or end in small letters. Otherwise, omit periods from abbreviations.

Dr.	Mr., Mrs.	e.g.	Feb.	ft.
St.	Ms.	i.e.	p.	a.m., p.m.
PhD	BC, BCE	USA	IBM	AM, PM
BA	AD, CE	US	USMC	AIDS

Note When a sentence ends in an abbreviation with a period, don't add a second period: *My first class is at 8 a.m.*

EXERCISE 3.1.1   Revising: Periods

Revise the following sentences so that periods are used correctly. If a sentence is correct as given, circle the number preceding it.

Example

Several times I wrote to ask when my subscription ended?
Several times I wrote to ask when my subscription ended.

1. Cut the flowers and put them in the vase
2. The office manager asked whose computer was broken?
3. The championship game begins at 7:30 PM sharp.
4. The area of the new athletic complex is almost 8200 sq ft.
5. Plato wrote *Republic* in about 370 BC.

3.1b Use a question mark after a direct question and sometimes to indicate doubt.

1 Direct Questions

Who will follow her**?**

What is the difference between these two people**?**

After indirect questions, use a period: *We wondered who would follow her.* (See the preceding page.)

Questions in a series are each followed by a question mark:

The officer asked how many times the suspect had been arrested.
Three times**?** Four times**?** More than that**?**

Note Do not combine question marks with other question marks, periods, commas, or other punctuation.

2 Doubt

A question mark within parentheses can indicate doubt about a number or date.

The Greek philosopher Socrates was born in 470 (**?**) BC and died in 399 BC from drinking poison. [Socrates's birthdate is not known for sure.]

Use sentence structure and words, not a question mark, to express sarcasm or irony.

Not   Stern's friendliness (?) bothered Crane.

But   Stern's <u>insincerity</u> bothered Crane.

EXERCISE 3.1.2   Revising: Question Marks

Add, delete, or replace question marks as needed in the following sentences. If a sentence is correct as given, circle the number preceding it.

Example

"When will it end?," cried the man dressed in rags.
"When will it end**?**" cried the man dressed in rags.

1. I often wonder whether I will remember any of my French when I'm sitting in a café in Paris?
2. Why does the poem end with the question "How long?"
3. "What does *ontogeny* mean?" the biology instructor asked?
4. The candidate for Congress asked whether there was anything he could do to help us?
5. Ulysses and his mariners took seven years to travel from Troy to Ithaca. Or was it six. Or eight?

3.1c Use an exclamation point after a strong statement, interjection, or command.

No! We must not lose this election!

Come here immediately!

Note Do not combine exclamation points with periods, commas, or other punctuation marks. And use exclamation points sparingly, even in informal writing. Overused, they'll fail to impress readers, and they may make you sound overemphatic.

EXERCISE 3.1.3   Revising: Exclamation Points

Add or replace exclamation points as needed in the following sentences. If a sentence is correct as given, circle the number preceding it.

Example

What a shock it was to hear her scream "Stop"
What a shock it was to hear her scream "Stop!"

1. I was so late returning from lunch that I missed the three o'clock meeting!
2. Look both ways before you cross the street.
3. "Well, now!" he said loudly.
4. The child's cries could be heard next door: "Don't go. Don't go."
5. As the firefighters moved their equipment into place, police walked through the crowd shouting, "Move back."

EXERCISE 3.1.4   Revising: End Punctuation

Insert appropriate end punctuation (periods, question marks, or exclamation points) where needed in the following paragraph.

When Maureen approached Jesse with her idea for a class gift to the school, he asked if she knew how much it would cost "Forget it if it's over $500," he said "Do you think the class can come up with even that much" Both of them knew the committee treasury contained only the $200 given by Dr Wheeler Maureen said that she thought they could raise the rest with a talent show "That's ridiculous" exclaimed Jesse "What talent Dr Wheeler's Whose" But he softened when Maureen asked him if he would perform his animal imitations Jesse loved to do animal imitations.

3.2 THE COMMA

Successful writers . . .

- Use a comma between independent clauses linked by *and, but, or, nor, for, so,* or *yet* (p. 142).
- Use a comma after most introductory elements (p. 143).
- Use commas to set off nonessential interrupting and concluding elements (p. 145).
- Use commas between items in a series and between some adjectives (pp. 147–48).
- Use commas with dates, addresses, place names, and long numbers (p. 149).
- Use commas with most quotations (p. 150).
- Avoid unnecessary commas (p. 151).

The comma (**,**) is the most common punctuation mark within sentences. It is also the most misused punctuation mark. If you omit a needed comma or add an unnecessary one, your sentences will be confusing. This sentence is confusing at first because it lacks an important comma:

Confusing   While very tall Abraham Lincoln was not an overbearing man.

Clear   While very tall**,** Abraham Lincoln was not an overbearing man.

Overall, the comma is used to separate parts of a sentence from one another, as shown in the box below.

 Success

Using the Comma

- **Separate independent clauses linked by a coordinating conjunction** (next page).

    Main clause **,** { for and or / so but nor / yet } **main clause** .

    The building is finished**,** but it has no tenants.

- **Set off most introductory elements** (p. 143).

    Introductory element **,** **main clause** .

    Unfortunately**,** the only tenant pulled out.

(continued)

Using the Comma *(continued)*

- **Set off nonessential elements** (p. 145).

| Main clause | , | nonessential element | . |

The empty building symbolizes a weak local economy , which affects everyone.

| Beginning of main clause | , | nonessential element | , | end of main clause | . |

The primary cause , the decline of local industry , is not news.

- **Separate items in a series** (p. 147).

... item 1 , item 2 , {and/or} item 3 ...

The city needs healthier businesses , new schools , and improved housing.

- **Separate adjectives that equally modify the same word** (p. 148).

... first adjective , second adjective word modified ...

A tall , sleek skyscraper is not needed.

Other uses of the comma:
Separate parts of dates, addresses, place names, and long numbers (p. 149).
Separate quotations and signal phrases (p. 150).
See also pp. 151–52 for when *not* to use the comma.

3.2a Use a comma with independent clauses linked by *and, but, or, nor, for, so, yet.*

When a coordinating conjunction links words or phrases, do not use a comma: *Dugain plays and sings Irish and English folk songs.* However, *do* use a comma when a coordinating conjunction joins independent clauses, as in the next examples.

Caffeine can keep coffee drinkers alert , and it may elevate their mood.

Caffeine was once thought to be safe , but now researchers warn of harmful effects.

Coffee drinkers may suffer sleeplessness , for the drug acts as a stimulant to the nervous system.

Note The comma goes before, not after, the coordinating conjunction.

EXERCISE 3.2.1   Revising: Comma with Linked Independent Clauses

Insert a comma before each coordinating conjunction that links independent clauses in the following sentences.

> **Example**
>
> I would have attended the concert but I had to baby-sit for my niece and nephew.
>
> I would have attended the concert, but I had to baby-sit for my niece and nephew.

1. I have auditioned for many lead roles but I have been offered only one minor speaking part and two walk-on parts.
2. Smartphones continue to come down in price so more people are buying them.
3. Kampala is Uganda's capital and largest city and it serves as the nation's social and economic center.
4. He wanted to wear his black leather jacket but his roommate had borrowed it.
5. We had driven all night and all day to get to the town and we were too tired to sightsee or search for a cozy inn.

EXERCISE 3.2.2   Sentence Combining: Linked Independent Clauses

Combine each of the following pairs of sentences into one sentence by using the coordinating conjunction in parentheses. Then insert a comma between the clauses.

> **Example**
>
> The circus had just come to town. Everyone wanted to see it. (*and*)
> The circus had just come to town, and everyone wanted to see it.

1. The police must have based the accusation on the polygraph test. They would not have made it at all. (*or*)
2. We once thought cell phones were a faultless invention. Now we know they can create problems. (*but*)
3. We caught Sam in his lie. He refused to tell the truth. (*yet*)
4. Parents sometimes combine their last names. Their children bear both their names. (*so*)
5. In many bird species the female builds the nest. The male defends it. (*and*)

3.2b Use a comma after most introductory elements.

An introductory element begins a sentence and modifies something in the independent clause. The element is usually followed by a comma.

> **Word**
>
> Fortunately, the news was good.

> **Phrase**
>
> As predicted, the rain began at 4:00 PM.

Dependent Clause

Even when they are raised apart, identical twins grow up very alike.

Transitional Word or Phrase

After a while, the child became bored with the expensive toy.

Note The subject of a sentence is not an introductory element but a part of the independent clause. Thus, do not use a comma to separate the subject and its verb.

Not Some tourists, may be disappointed.

But Some tourists may be disappointed.

EXERCISE 3.2.3   Revising: Commas with Introductory Elements

Insert commas where needed after introductory elements in the following sentences. If a sentence is punctuated correctly as given, circle the number preceding it.

Example

After the new library opened the old one became a student union.
After the new library opened, the old one became a student union.

1. Giggling to themselves the children ran behind the barn.
2. Before you proceed to your argument state your thesis.
3. Running water is a luxury in some of the distant villages.
4. Even when employees have been laid off they may still be entitled to health insurance from the company.
5. Predictably the lawyer was late for the meeting.

EXERCISE 3.2.4   Sentence Combining: Introductory Elements

Combine each pair of sentences below into one sentence that begins with an introductory phrase or clause as specified in parentheses. Follow the introductory element with a comma. You will have to add, delete, change, and rearrange words.

Example

The girl was humming to herself. She walked up the stairs. (*Phrase beginning Humming*.)

Humming to herself, the girl walked up the stairs.

1. The government cut back on its student loan program. Students and their parents have had to rely more on banks. (*Clause beginning Since*.)
2. More than five hundred people signed the petition. The mayor did not respond. (*Clause beginning Although*.)
3. One needs information to vote wisely. One needs objective information about the candidates' backgrounds and opinions. (*Phrase beginning To*.)
4. The flags were snapping in the wind. They made the speaker's message seem even more urgent. (*Phrase beginning Snapping*.)
5. Rhode Island has approximately 1200 square miles. It is the smallest state in the country. (*Phrase beginning With*.)

3.2c Use a comma or commas to set off many interrupting and concluding elements.

Commas around part of a sentence often signal that the element is not necessary to the meaning. This **nonessential element** may modify or rename the word it refers to, but it does not limit the word to a particular individual or group. The meaning of the word would still be clear if the element were deleted:

Nonessential Element

The company **,** <u>which is located in Oklahoma</u> **,** has a good reputation.

(Because it does not restrict meaning, a nonessential element is also called a **nonrestrictive element**.)

In contrast, an **essential** (or **restrictive**) **element** *does* limit the word it refers to: the element cannot be omitted without leaving the meaning too general. Because it is essential, such an element is *not* set off with a comma or commas.

Essential Element

The company rewards employees <u>who work hard</u>.

Omitting the underlined words would distort the meaning: the company doesn't necessarily reward *all* employees, only the hardworking ones.

Note When optional information falls in the middle of the sentence, be sure to use one comma *before* it and one *after* it.

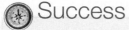 Success

Testing for Nonessential and Essential Elements

Steps	Examples
1. **Identify the element.**	Hai Nguyen <u>who lives in Denver</u> was born in Vietnam. The teacher gives awards to students <u>who work hard</u>.
2. **Remove the element. Does the basic meaning of the sentence change?**	**No.** Hai Nguyen was born in Vietnam. **Yes.** The teacher gives awards to students.
3. If *no*, the element is *nonessential* and should be set off with punctuation. If *yes*, the element is *essential* and should not be set off with punctuation.	Hai Nguyen **,** who lives in Denver **,** was born in Vietnam. The teacher gives awards to students who work hard.

1 Commas with Nonessential Modifiers and Appositives

Nonessential modifiers and appositives may add detail to sentences, but they can be omitted with no loss of clarity.

Nonessential Modifiers

Hai Nguyen, who emigrated from Vietnam, lives in Denver.

His company, which is ten years old, studies the pollution of air and water.

Nguyen's family lives in Chicago, even though he lives in Denver.

Nonessential Appositives

Hai Nguyen's work, research into air pollution, keeps him in Denver.

His wife, Tina Nguyen, writes stories for a newspaper in Chicago.

2 Commas with Transitional Words or Phrases or with Parenthetical Expressions

A transitional word or phrase such as *however, for example,* and *of course* forms a link between ideas. (See pp. 240–41 for a list.) The word or phrase is nonessential and is usually set off with a comma or commas.

Many students, for example, had no health insurance.

A parenthetical expression provides additional information not essential for meaning—for instance, *fortunately, all things considered,* and *published in 1990.* It can be enclosed in parentheses (see p. 172) or, with more emphasis, in commas.

Recycling, it seems, must be convenient to be successful.

3 Commas with Phrases of Contrast

Many recyclers focus on the environmental benefits, not the inconvenience.

4 Commas with *Yes* and *No*

Almost everyone agrees that, yes, the advantages outweigh the disadvantages.

5 Commas with Words of Direct Address

Do you agree, readers?

EXERCISE 3.2.5   Revising: Punctuation of Nonessential and Essential Elements

Insert commas in the following sentences to set off nonessential elements, and delete any commas that incorrectly set off essential elements. If a sentence is correct as given, circle the number preceding it.

Example

Elizabeth Blackwell who attended medical school in the 1840s was the first American woman to receive a medical degree.

Elizabeth Blackwell **,** who attended medical school in the 1840s **,** was the first American woman to receive a medical degree.

1. *The Time Machine* a novel by H. G. Wells is a haunting portrayal of Darwin's evolutionary theory carried to a terrible conclusion.
2. The report concluded that Americans who pay property taxes are the most disgruntled citizens.
3. All people, over six feet tall, can join the Boston Beanstalks Club.
4. Jarratt studies the eating disorder bulimia researching its causes and treatment.
5. Those of us, who hadn't seen the concert, felt we had missed something.

3.2d Use commas between items in a series.

A **series** consists of three or more items of equal importance. Separate series items with commas. Do not use commas around series.

The names Belial **,** Beelzebub **,** and Lucifer sound ominous.

I plan to take math **,** psychology **,** and biology next semester.

The comma before the last item in a series (before *and*) is optional, but it is never wrong and it is usually clearer.

EXERCISE 3.2.6   Revising: Commas within a Series

Insert commas in the following sentences to separate elements in a series. If a sentence is correct as given, circle the number preceding it.

Example

Anna Spingle worked as an assistant a baby-sitter and a crossing guard.
Anna Spingle worked as an assistant **,** a baby-sitter **,** and a crossing guard.

1. The tedious work absence of people her own age and low salary de-pressed Debra.
2. She was a Miamian by birth a farmer by temperament and a worker to the day she died.
3. For his second birthday I'd like to buy my son a plastic hammer a punching bag and a stuffed animal.
4. Television newscasters rarely work full-time as reporters investigate only light stories if any and rarely write the copy they read on the air.
5. Commuting by bus gives me time to do the reading for my courses and saves me money on gas and car upkeep.

3.2e Use commas between some adjectives.

Use a comma between two or more adjectives when each one modifies the same word equally. As a test, such adjectives could be joined by *and*.

The book had a worn_, cracked binding.

The beach had a desolate_, windswept atmosphere.

Do not use a comma between adjectives when the second one forms a unit with the modified word. As a test, the two adjectives could not sensibly be joined by *and*.

The house overflowed with ornate electric fixtures.

Among the junk in the attic was one lovely vase.

 ## Success

Testing for Commas with Adjectives

Step	Examples
1. **Identify the adjectives.**	She was a faithful sincere friend.
	They are dedicated medical students.
2. **Can the two adjectives be sensibly joined by the word *and*?**	**Yes.** She was a faithful and sincere friend.
	No. They are dedicated and medical students.
3. **If *yes*, use a comma to separate the adjectives.**	She was a faithful, sincere friend.
If *no*, do not use a comma to separate the adjectives.	They are dedicated medical students.

EXERCISE 3.2.7   Revising: Commas between Adjectives

Insert commas in the following sentences as needed to separate adjectives. If a sentence is correct as given, circle the number preceding it.

Example

Automakers need to offer more small fuel-efficient cars.
Automakers need to offer more small, fuel-efficient cars.

1. The manager bought new pine bar stools for the restaurant.
2. The first boats were probably crude heavy canoes made from hollowed-out logs.
3. We bought a heavy waterproof tarp to cover the campsite.
4. The comedian's outrageous offensive monologue was not broadcast.
5. I called the police when I received a third crank phone call.

EXERCISE 3.2.8   Revising: Punctuation of Series and Adjectives

Insert commas as needed in the following paragraph to separate series items or adjectives. If a sentence is correct as given, circle the number preceding it.

Example

The daring provocative groundbreaking performance earned an Oscar.
The daring, provocative, groundbreaking performance earned an Oscar.

1 Shoes with high heels were originally designed to protect the wearer's feet from mud garbage and animal waste in the streets. **2** The first high heels worn strictly for fashion, however, appeared in the sixteenth century. **3** They were made popular when the short powerful King Louis XIV of France began wearing them. **4** At first, high heels were worn by men and were made of colorful silk fabrics soft suedes or smooth leathers. **5** But Louis's influence was so strong that men and women of the court priests and cardinals and even household servants wore high heels. **6** By the seventeenth and eighteenth centuries, only wealthy fashionable French women wore high heels. **7** At that time, French culture represented the one true standard of elegance and refinement. **8** High-heeled shoes for women spread to other courts of Europe among the Europeans of North America and to all social classes. **9** Now high heels are common, though depending on the fashion they range from short squat thick heels to tall skinny spikes. **10** A New York boutique recently showed a pair of purple satin pumps with tiny jeweled bows and four-inch stiletto heels.

3.2f Use commas with dates, addresses, place names, and long numbers.

When they appear within sentences, elements punctuated with commas are also ended with commas.

Dates

July 4, 1776, was the day the Declaration was signed. [Note that commas appear before *and* after the year.]

The United States entered World War II in December 1941. [No comma is needed between a month or season and a year.]

Addresses and place names

Use the address 806 Ogden Avenue, Swarthmore, PA 19081, for all correspondence. [No comma is needed between a state abbreviation or name and a zip code.]

Numbers

The new assembly plant cost $7,525,000.

A kilometer is 3,281 feet [*or* 3281 feet].

EXERCISE 3.2.9 Revising: Punctuation of Dates, Addresses, Place Names, and Numbers

Insert commas as needed in the following sentences.

Example

The house cost $87000 fifteen years ago.
The house cost $87,000 fifteen years ago.

1. The novel opens on February 18 2054 in Montana.
2. The world's population exceeds 7100000000.
3. Boulder Colorado sits at the base of the Rocky Mountains.
4. Whoever writes PO Box 725 Asheville NC 28803 will get a quick response.
5. The police discovered that the call was made on September 28 2007 from Ames Iowa.

3.2g Use commas with most quotations.

A comma or commas usually separate a quotation from a signal phrase that identifies the source, such as *she said* or *he replied*.

Eleanor Roosevelt said, "You must do the thing you think you cannot do."

"Knowledge is power," wrote Francis Bacon.

Do not use a comma when the signal phrase interrupts the quotation between independent clauses. Instead, follow the signal phrase with a semicolon or a period, depending on the punctuation used in the source.

"That part of my life was over," she wrote; "his words had sealed it shut."

"That part of my life was over," she wrote. "His words had sealed it shut."

EXERCISE 3.2.10 Revising: Punctuation of Quotations

Insert commas or semicolons in the following sentences to correct punctuation with quotations.

Example

When asked to open her bag, the shoplifter said "I didn't steal anything."
When asked to open her bag, the shoplifter said, "I didn't steal anything."

1. "Having chicken pox as an adult" the doctor explained "is much more serious than having it as a child."
2. "We are not only a Latin-American nation" Fidel Castro said in 1977 "we are also an Afro-American nation."
3. "The mass of men lead lives of quiet desperation" Henry David Thoreau wrote in *Walden*.
4. "I'll be on the next bus for Cleveland" the woman promised.
5. "I think of the open-ended writing process as a voyage in two stages" Peter Elbow says.

3.2h Delete commas where they are not required.

Commas can make sentences choppy and even confusing if they are used more often than needed.

1 No Comma between Subject and Verb, Verb and Object, or Preposition and Object

Faulty	The returning <u>soldiers, received</u> a warm welcome. [Separated subject and verb.]
Revised	The returning <u>soldiers received</u> a warm welcome.
Faulty	They had <u>chosen, to fight</u> for their country <u>despite, the risks.</u> [Separated verb *chosen* and its object; separated preposition *despite* and its object.]
Revised	They had <u>chosen to fight</u> for their country <u>despite the risks.</u>

2 No Comma in Most Compound Constructions

Compound constructions consisting of two elements almost never require a comma. The only exception is the sentence consisting of two independent clauses linked by a coordinating conjunction: *The computer network failed, but employees kept working* (see p. 142).

Faulty	┌──── compound subject ────┐ <u>Banks, and other financial institutions</u> have helped older ┌── compound object of preposition ──┐ people with <u>money management, and investment.</u>
Revised	<u>Banks and other financial institutions</u> have helped older people with <u>money management and investment.</u>
Faulty	┌──── compound predicate ────┐ One bank <u>created</u> special accounts for older people, <u>and held</u> ┌─ compound object of verb ─┐ <u>classes, and workshops.</u>
Revised	One bank <u>created</u> special accounts for older people <u>and held</u> <u>classes and workshops.</u>

3 No Comma After a Conjunction

Faulty	Parents of adolescents notice increased conflict at puberty, <u>and,</u> they complain of bickering.
Revised	Parents of adolescents notice increased conflict at puberty, <u>and</u> they complain of bickering.
Faulty	<u>Although,</u> other primates leave the family at adolescence, humans do not.
Revised	<u>Although</u> other primates leave the family at adolescence, humans do not.

4 No Commas Around Essential Elements

Faulty	Hawthorne's work, *The Scarlet Letter,* was the first major American novel. [The title is essential to distinguish the novel from the rest of Hawthorne's work.]
Revised	Hawthorne's work *The Scarlet Letter* was the first major American novel.
Faulty	The symbols, that Hawthorne uses, have influenced other novelists. [The clause identifies which symbols have been influential.]
Revised	The symbols that Hawthorne uses have influenced other novelists.
Faulty	Published in 1850, *The Scarlet Letter* still resonates today, because of its theme of secret sin. [The clause is essential to explain why the novel resonates.]
Revised	Published in 1850, *The Scarlet Letter* still resonates today because of its theme of secret sin.

Note Like the *because* clause in the preceding example, most adverb clauses are essential because they describe conditions necessary to the main clause.

5 No Commas Around a Series

Commas separate the items *within* a series (p. 147) but do not separate the series from the rest of the sentence.

Faulty	The skills of, hunting, herding, and agriculture, sustained the Native Americans.
Revised	The skills of hunting, herding, and agriculture sustained the Native Americans.

6 No Comma Before an Indirect Quotation

Faulty	The report concluded, that dieting could be more dangerous than overeating.
Revised	The report concluded that dieting could be more dangerous than overeating.

EXERCISE 3.2.11   Revising: Needless and Misused Commas

Revise the following sentences to eliminate needless or misused commas. If a sentence is correct as given, circle the number preceding it.

Example

The portrait of the founder, that hung in the dining hall, was stolen.
The portrait of the founder that hung in the dining hall was stolen.

1. Classes were canceled for five days because, of the heat.
2. My sister was furious, when I dragged her out of bed.
3. The students, having finished their exams, drove home for the holidays.
4. The guidebook suggested a visit to the Smithsonian, and to the Kennedy Center.

5. The 5 percent rent decrease for all rent-controlled units, reflects this year's lower property taxes.
6. Of all the novels by Charles Dickens, his tale, *David Copperfield*, is still a favorite of readers.
7. The coach said, that next year the team would have a winning season.
8. Mary bought some of her books used, and borrowed the rest.
9. Forest fires are destructive, but they can benefit the woods they burn.
10. One Internet provider created special accounts for senior citizens and, offered workshops.

EXERCISE 3.2.12   Revising: Commas

Insert commas as needed in the following paragraphs, and delete any misused commas. If a sentence is correct as given, circle the number preceding it.

1 Ellis Island New York reopened for business in 1990 but now the visitors are tourists not immigrants. **2** This spot which lies in New York Harbor was the first American soil seen, or touched by many of the nation's immigrants. **3** Though other places also served as ports of entry for foreigners none has the symbolic power of, Ellis Island. **4** Between its opening in 1892 and its closing in 1954, over 20 million people about two-thirds of all immigrants were detained there before taking up their new lives in the United States. **5** Ellis Island processed over 2000 newcomers a day when immigration was at its peak between 1900 and 1920.

6 As the end of a long voyage and the introduction to the New World Ellis Island must have left something to be desired. **7** The "huddled masses" as the Statue of Liberty calls them indeed were huddled. **8** New arrivals were herded about kept standing in lines for hours or days yelled at and abused. **9** Assigned numbers they submitted their bodies to the pokings and proddings of the silent nurses and doctors, who were charged with ferreting out the slightest sign, of sickness disability or insanity. **10** That test having been passed, the immigrants faced interrogation by an official through an interpreter. **11** Those, with names deemed inconveniently long or difficult to pronounce, often found themselves permanently labeled with abbreviations, of their names, or with the names, of their hometowns. **12** But, millions survived the examination humiliation and confusion, to take the last short boat ride to New York City. **13** For many of them and especially for their descendants Ellis Island eventually became not a nightmare but the place where a new life began.

3.3 THE SEMICOLON

Successful writers . . .

- Use a semicolon between independent clauses not joined by *and, but, or, nor, for, so,* or *yet* (next page).
- Use a semicolon between independent clauses related by *however, for example,* and so on (p. 155).
- Use semicolons between series items containing commas (p. 156).
- Avoid unnecessary semicolons (p. 156).

The semicolon (;) separates equal and balanced sentence elements, as the following box shows.

 Success

Using the Semicolon

Use a Semicolon	Examples
. . . to separate two related independent clauses not joined by a comma and a coordinating conjunction.	Yolanda had a 99 average in math; she earned an A in the course.
. . . to separate two independent clauses joined by a conjunctive adverb or a transitional word or phrase.	Marguerite earned an A on her term paper; consequently, she was exempt from the final exam.
. . . to separate items in a series when they contain commas.	The play's characters included Marianne Loundsberry, the heroine; Ellen and Sarah, her children; Barry, her ex-husband; and Louise, Marianne's best friend.

3.3a Use a semicolon between independent clauses not joined by *and, but, or, nor, for, so,* or *yet.*

Use a semicolon between independent clauses when they are not connected by one of the coordinating conjunctions: *and, but, or, nor, for, so,* or *yet.* The semicolon signals that one clause is ending and another is beginning.

> Recycling trash is one way to help the environment; conserving energy is another.

> People who recycle rarely complain about the extra work; they believe they have a responsibility to the earth.

EXERCISE 3.3.1   Revising: Semicolons between Independent Clauses

Insert semicolons or substitute them for commas to separate independent clauses in the following sentences.

Example

One man at the auction bid prudently another did not.
One man at the auction bid prudently; another did not.

1. Steve spent an evening writing the paper he spent an entire day typing it.
2. Pet rocks and bongo boards were once immensely popular today they are forgotten objects.
3. Karate is not just a technique for self-defense, like a religion, it teaches inner calm.
4. The Himalayas are the world's loftiest mountain range, they culminate in the world's highest mountain, Mount Everest.
5. Subways in New York City are noisy, dirty, and sometimes dangerous they are also a superbly efficient means of transportation.

3.3b Use a semicolon between independent clauses related by *however, for example*, and so on.

Use a semicolon between independent clauses that are related by two kinds of words and phrases:

- **Conjunctive adverbs,** such as *however, indeed, therefore,* and *thus.* (For a list of conjunctive adverbs, see p. 95.)

conjunctive
adverb

Blue jeans have become fashionable all over the world**;** however, the American originators still wear more jeans than anyone else.

- **Transitional words and phrases,** such as *after all, for example, in fact,* and *of course.* (For a list of transitional words and phrases, see pp. 240–41.)

transitional
phrase

Blue jeans are very popular**;** in fact, more than half a billion pairs were sold in North America last year.

A conjunctive adverb or transitional word or phrase may move around within its clause, so the semicolon will not always come just before the adverb or transitional expression. The adverb or transitional expression itself is usually set off with a comma or commas.

Blue jeans have become fashionable all over the world**;** the American originators**,** however**,** still wear more jeans than anyone else.

EXERCISE 3.3.2   Revising: Semicolons between Independent Clauses with Conjunctive Adverbs and Transitional Words or Phrases

Insert a semicolon in each sentence below to separate independent clauses related by a conjunctive adverb or a transitional word or phrase, and insert a comma or commas to set off the adverb or transitional word or phrase.

Example

He knew that tickets for the concert would sell quickly therefore he arrived at the box office hours before it opened.

He knew that tickets for the concert would sell quickly**;** therefore**,** he arrived at the box office hours before it opened.

1. Door-to-door salespeople are less common than they once were even so they still turn up from time to time.
2. It was 11 PM on his twentieth birthday still his family had not acknowledged the day.
3. The music suddenly went quiet consequently everyone could hear their argument.
4. The elevator shakes when it goes down the inspector says it is safe however.
5. We must cut down on our fuel consumption otherwise we'll find ourselves with *no* fuel, not just less.

> **EXERCISE 3.3.3   Sentence Combining: Related Independent Clauses**
>
> Combine each numbered set of sentences into one sentence containing only two independent clauses. Connect the clauses with a semicolon plus the word given in parentheses, setting off the added word with a comma or commas. You will have to add, delete, change, and rearrange words. Each item has more than one possible answer.
>
> **Example**
>
> The Albanians censored their news. We got little news from them. And what we got was unreliable. (*therefore*)
>
> The Albanians censored their news; therefore, the little news we got from them was unreliable.
>
> 1. She was disappointed with the conclusion of the novel. It seemed anticlimactic. She went on to read the author's other two books. (*nonetheless*)
> 2. Most young children did not enjoy the movie. The jokes went over their heads. The characters' adventures frightened them. (*furthermore*)
> 3. My grandfather grew up in Italy. But he never spoke Italian in the United States. He always spoke English. (*instead*)
> 4. Peanuts thrive in light, sandy soil. They are an ideal crop for the South. In the South such soil is common. (*thus*)
> 5. The speaker's nervousness showed in his damp brow. His trembling voice also indicated nervousness. His hands shook so badly that he could barely hold his notes. (*moreover*)

3.3c Use semicolons between series items containing commas.

Use semicolons (rather than commas) to separate items in a series when the items contain commas.

> The custody case involved Amy Dalton, the child; Ellen and Mark Dalton, the parents; and Ruth and Hal Blum, the grandparents.

3.3d Delete or replace unneeded semicolons.

Too many semicolons can make writing choppy. And semicolons are often misused in certain constructions that call for other punctuation or no punctuation.

1 **No Semicolon between an Independent Clause and a Dependent Clause or Phrase**

The semicolon does not separate unequal parts, such as independent clauses and dependent clauses or phrases.

> **Faulty**   Pygmies are in danger of extinction; because of encroaching development.
>
> **Revised**   Pygmies are in danger of extinction because of encroaching development.

Faulty	According to African authorities; only about 35,000 Pygmies exist today.
Revised	According to African authorities, only about 35,000 Pygmies exist today.

2 No Semicolon Before a Series or Explanation

Colons and dashes, not semicolons, introduce series, explanations, and so forth.

Faulty	Teachers have heard all sorts of reasons why students do poorly; psychological problems, family illness, too much work, too little time.
Revised	Teachers have heard all sorts of reasons why students do poorly: psychological problems, family illness, too much work, too little time.

EXERCISE 3.3.4   Revising: Semicolons

In the following paragraph, insert semicolons as needed and eliminate any misused semicolons, substituting other punctuation as appropriate. If a sentence is correct as given, circle the number preceding it.

1 The set, sounds, and actors in the movie captured the essence of horror films. **2** The set was ideal; dark, deserted streets, trees dipping their branches over the sidewalks, mist hugging the ground and creeping up to meet the trees, looming shadows of unlighted, turreted houses. **3** The sounds, too, were appropriate, especially terrifying was the hard, hollow sound of footsteps echoing throughout the film. **4** But the best feature of the movie was its actors; all of them tall, pale, and thin to the point of emaciation. **5** With one exception, they were dressed uniformly in gray and had gray hair. **6** The exception was an actress who dressed only in black as if to set off her pale yellow, nearly white, long hair; the only color in the film. **7** The glinting black eyes of another actor stole almost every scene, indeed, they were the source of the film's mischief.

3.4 THE COLON

Successful writers . . .

- Use a colon to introduce a concluding explanation, series, appositive, or quotation (next page).
- Use colons with salutations of business letters, titles and subtitles, and divisions of time (p. 159).
- Avoid unnecessary colons (p. 159).

The colon (:) is mainly a mark of introduction. It signals that the words following will explain or add information. The colon also has several conventional uses, such as in expressions of time.

Success

Using the Colon

Use a Colon . . .	Examples
. . . **to introduce an explanation.**	Mathematics is enjoyable: it requires concentration and accuracy.
. . . **to introduce items in a series.**	The purposes of speeches vary: to inform, to persuade, or to entertain.
. . . **to introduce an appositive.**	Judo has another name: jujitsu.
. . . **after an independent clause that introduces a quotation.**	My brother stated his point loudly: "Never borrow my car without asking first!"
. . . **to separate titles and subtitles and divisions of time and to set off the salutation of a business letter.**	*Biology: The Study of Life* 5:47 PM Dear Dr. Rodriguez:

3.4a Use a colon for introduction.

As an introducer, a colon always ends an independent clause. It may or may not be followed by an independent clause.

Concluding Explanation

Soul food has a deceptively simple definition: the ethnic cooking of African Americans.

Concluding Series

At least three soul food dishes are familiar to most Americans: fried chicken, barbecued spareribs, and sweet potatoes.

Concluding Appositive

Soul food has one disadvantage: fat.

Concluding Quotation After an Independent Clause

One soul food chef has a solution: "Instead of using ham hocks to flavor beans, I use smoked turkey wings. The soulful, smoky taste remains, but without all the fat of pork."

3.4b Use colons with salutations of business letters, titles and subtitles, and divisions of time.

Salutation of a Business Letter

Dear Ms. Burak**:**

Title and Subtitle

*Anna Freud***:** *Her Life and Work*

Time

12**:**26   6**:**00

3.4c Delete or replace unneeded colons.

Use the colon only at the end of an independent clause, not in the following situations:

- **Delete a colon after a verb:**

  Faulty   The best-known soul food dish <u>is</u>: fried chicken.

  Revised   The best-known soul food dish <u>is</u> fried chicken.

- **Delete a colon after a preposition:**

  Faulty   Soul food recipes can be found <u>in</u>: mainstream cookbooks as well as specialized references.

  Revised   Soul food recipes can be found <u>in</u> mainstream cookbooks as well as specialized references.

- **Delete a colon after *such as* or *including*:**

  Faulty   Many Americans have not tasted delicacies <u>such as</u>: chitlins and black-eyed peas.

  Revised   Many Americans have not tasted delicacies <u>such as</u> chitlins and black-eyed peas.

EXERCISE 3.4.1   Revising: Colons

Insert colons as needed in the following sentences, or delete colons that are misused.

Example

Mix the ingredients as follows sift the flour and salt together, add the milk, and slowly beat in the egg yolk.

Mix the ingredients as follows**:** sift the flour and salt together, add the milk, and slowly beat in the egg yolk.

1. During the interview she detailed: her impressions of the job, her own qualifications, and her career hopes.
2. He concluded with a threat "Either rehire me, or I will go to the labor board."

3. Three breeds of dogs are very popular collies, poodles, and golden retrievers.
4. She left her cottage at 8:00 in the morning with only one goal in mind to murder the man who was blackmailing her.
5. The pilgrims had one major reason for coming to the New World they sought religious freedom.

EXERCISE 3.4.2   Revising: Colons and Semicolons

In the following paragraph, insert colons and semicolons as needed and delete or replace them where they are misused. If a sentence is correct as given, circle the number preceding it.

1 Sunlight is made up of three kinds of radiation: visible rays; infrared rays, which we cannot see; and ultraviolet rays, which are also invisible. **2** Infrared rays are the longest; measuring 700 nanometers and longer; while ultraviolet rays are the shortest; measuring 400 nanometers and shorter. **3** Especially in the ultraviolet range; sunlight is harmful to the eyes. **4** Ultraviolet rays can damage the retina: furthermore, they can cause cataracts on the lens. **5** The lens protects the eye by: absorbing much of the ultraviolet radiation and thus protecting the retina. **6** Protecting the retina, however, the lens becomes a victim; growing cloudy and blocking vision. **7** The best way to protect your eyes is: to wear hats that shade the face and sunglasses that screen out ultraviolet rays. **8** Many sunglass lenses have been designed as ultraviolet screens; many others are extremely ineffective. **9** People who spend much time outside in the sun; owe it to themselves to buy and wear high-quality sunglasses that shield their eyes.

3.5 THE APOSTROPHE

Successful writers . . .

- Use the apostrophe to show possession (next page).
- Do not use the apostrophe to form a plural noun, a singular verb, or a possessive personal or relative pronoun (p. 163).
- Use the apostrophe to form contractions (p. 165).

The apostrophe (') is used as part of a word mainly to indicate possession and the omission of one or more letters.

3.5a Use the apostrophe to show possession.

A noun or indefinite pronoun shows possession with an apostrophe and, usually, -*s*: *the dog's hair, everyone's hope.* Only personal pronouns and relative pronouns do not use apostrophes for possession: *mine, yours, his, hers, its, ours, theirs,* and *whose.*

   Note   Remember that the apostrophe or apostrophe-plus-*s* is an *addition.* Before this addition, always spell the name of the owner or owners without dropping or adding letters.

> ## ✳ Success
>
> ### Using and Not Using the Apostrophe
>
> | Use the Apostrophe | Examples | |
> |---|---|---|
> | **. . . to show possession for nouns and indefinite pronouns.** | *Singular* | *Plural* |
> | | Ms. Park's | the Parks' |
> | | lawyer's | lawyers' |
> | | everyone's | two weeks' |
> | **. . . to form contractions.** | It's a girl. [It is a girl.] | |
> | | you're [you are] | |
> | | won't [will not] | |
>
> | Do Not Use an Apostrophe | | |
> |---|---|---|
> | **. . . to form plurals of nouns.** | *Incorrect::* book's are | |
> | | *Correct:* books are | |
> | | *Incorrect:* the Freed's | |
> | | *Correct:* the Freeds | |
> | **. . . with verbs ending in -s.** | *Incorrect::* swim's | |
> | | *Correct:* swims | |
> | **. . . to form the possessives of personal and relative pronouns.** | *Incorrect:* it's toes | |
> | | *Correct:* its toes | |
> | | *Incorrect::* who's car | |
> | | *Correct::* whose car | |

1 For singular words, add -'s.

Bill Boughton's skillful card tricks amaze children.

Some of the earth's forests are regenerating.

Everyone's fitness can be improved through exercise.

When a singular word ends in -*s*, you should still add -'s:

Henry James's novels reward the patient reader.

The business's customers filed suit.

Exception An apostrophe alone may be added to a singular word ending in *-s* when another *s* would make the word difficult to say: *Moses' mother, Joan Rivers' jokes.* But the added *-s* is never wrong (*Moses's, Rivers's*).

2 **For plural words ending in -s, add only an apostrophe.**

Workers' incomes have fallen slightly.

Many students benefit from several years' work after they graduate from high school.

The Jameses' talents were extraordinary.

Notice the difference in the possessives of singular and plural words ending in *-s*. The singular form usually takes *-'s*: *James's*. The plural takes only the apostrophe: *Jameses'*.

3 **For plural words not ending in -s, add -'s.**

Children's educations are at stake.

We need to attract the media's attention.

4 **For compound words, add -'s only to the last word.**

The brother-in-law's business failed.

Taxes are always somebody else's fault.

5 **For two or more owners, add -'s depending on possession.**

Individual Possession

Bale's and Mason's styles are similar. [Each man has his own style.]

Joint Possession

The child recovered despite her mother and father's neglect. [The mother and father were jointly neglectful.]

EXERCISE 3.5.1   Forming Possessives

Form the possessive of each word or word group in brackets.

Example

The [men] blood pressures were higher than the [women].

The men's blood pressures were higher than the women's.

1. The [treasurer] resignation was expected.
2. My [brother-in-law] attitude was predictable.
3. The [Smiths] car alarm went off at midnight.
4. [Laura and Jane] landlord was totally unreasonable.
5. They visited [Keats] house on Hampstead Heath.

  6. An [hour] exercise was plenty.
  7. She studied the [goddesses] roles in Greek myths.
  8. Higher pay and three [weeks] vacation were the focus of the [sanitation workers] strike.
  9. John [Adams] letters to his wife illuminate his character.
 10. [Everyone] books were stolen from the gym.
 11. [Children] clothes are ridiculously expensive.
 12. [Emily and Sarah] husbands are both out of work.
 13. The [utility companies] recent price increases are unlawful.
 14. Sam [Prince] speech won special praise.
 15. The [Hickses] decision to move upset their children.

3.5b Do not use the apostrophe to form a plural noun, a singular verb, or a possessive pronoun.

1 Plural Nouns

The plurals of nouns are generally formed by adding *-s* or *-es,* never with an apostrophe: *boys, families, Joneses, Murphys.*

Faulty	The Jones' controlled the firm's until 2001.
Revised	The Joneses controlled the firms until 2001.

2 Singular Verbs

Verbs ending in *-s* never take an apostrophe:

Faulty	The subway break's down less often now.
Revised	The subway breaks down less often now.

3 Possessives of Personal and Relative Pronouns

His, hers, its, ours, yours, theirs, and *whose* are possessive forms of the personal pronouns *he, she, it, we, you,* and *they* and the relative pronoun *who.* They do not take apostrophes:

Faulty	Who's house is that? It's roof leaks.
Revised	Whose house is that? Its roof leaks.

Don't confuse possessive pronouns with contractions. See page 165.

EXERCISE 3.5.2   Revising: Apostrophes with Possessives

In the following paragraph, insert or reposition apostrophes as needed and delete any needless apostrophes. If a sentence is correct as given, circle the number preceding it.

Example

Its true that the companys policy left employees sick days unpaid.

It's true that the company's policy left employees' sick days unpaid.

1 The eastern coast of Belize was once a fishermans paradise, but overfishing caused the fishing industrys sharp decline in this Central American country. **2** The country's government is now showing the world that leaders' foresight can turn a problem into an opportunity. **3** Belize is capitalizing on something that can capture tourists interest: whale sharks. **4** Huge but harmless to people, whale sharks regularly visit Belizes coast to feed on smaller fishes eggs. **5** The predictable gatherings of the shark's attract large numbers of scuba diver's and snorkeler's, so that the fishs' fascinating beauty has become an economic treasure. **6** A tourists eagerness to spend money for an up-close view of whale sharks is Belizes renewable and reliable resource.

EXERCISE 3.5.3 Distinguishing between Plurals and Possessives

Revise the following sentences to correct mistakes in the formation of plurals or of the possessive case of pronouns. If a sentence is correct as given, circle the number preceding it.

> **Example**
>
> Was the raincoat her's?
>
> Was the raincoat hers?

1. Radio talk-show host's all sound the same.
2. Its unfairness was clear.
3. We could hear the shouts of the boys playing basketball down the street.
4. The designer bag's, each with it's own distinctive look, went on sale.
5. The responsibility was your's.
6. The Russian's high prices make our's seem reasonable.
7. Its shocking color made the car easy to spot.
8. Theirs was far messier.
9. Book's can be good friend's.
10. Street crime was a particular focus of their's.

EXERCISE 3.5.4 Revising: Misuses of the Apostrophe

Revise the following paragraph by deleting or repositioning apostrophes or by repairing incorrect possessive pronouns or contractions. If a sentence is correct as given, circle the number preceding it.

> **Example**
>
> The dog wagged it's tail.
>
> The dog wagged its tail.

1 Research is proving that athlete's who excel at distance running have physical characteristics that make them faster than most people. **2** For example, they're hearts are larger. **3** An average adult's heart pump's about fifteen liters of blood per minute, but a competitive distance runner's heart circulate's twice as much. **4** Elite runners are also more efficient: they're able to run with less effort than less talented runners must exert. **5** In addition, competitive runner's are able to keep running for long time's at high levels of exertion. **6** Although these abilities can be honed in training, they cannot be acquired by a runner: they are his' or her's from birth.

3.5c Use the apostrophe to form contractions.

A **contraction** replaces one or more letters, numbers, or words with an apostrophe, as in the following examples:

it is, it has	it's	you are	you're
they are	they're	who is, who has	who's
cannot	can't	were not	weren't
does not	doesn't	class of 2017	class of '17

Note Don't confuse contractions with personal pronouns:

Contractions	Personal Pronouns
It's a book.	Its cover is green.
They're coming.	Their car broke down.
You're right.	Your idea is good.
Who's coming?	Whose party is it?

EXERCISE 3.5.5   Forming Contractions

Form contractions from each set of words below. Use each contraction in a complete sentence.

Example

we are: we're

We're open to ideas.

1. she would	**5.** do not	**8.** is not
2. could not	**6.** she will	**9.** it is
3. they are	**7.** hurricane of 2010	**10.** will not
4. he is		

EXERCISE 3.5.6   Revising: Contractions and Personal Pronouns

Revise the following sentences to correct mistakes in the use of contractions and personal pronouns. Circle the number preceding any sentence that is correct as given.

Example

The company gives it's employees their birthdays off.

The company gives its employees their birthdays off.

1. They're reasons for the merger were questioned.
2. Its important to review you're notes before taking an exam.
3. I can begin work whenever your ready for me.
4. After spending two weeks on vacation, their now looking for jobs.
5. When it's team won the championship, the city celebrated.
6. The investigators wondered whose gun it was.
7. Its a wonder that any rivers remain unspoiled.

8. Business is a good major because it's certain that corporations will always need competent managers.
9. The Soltis, who's daughter was married last year, retired to Florida.
10. The only way of avoiding a fine is to pay you're taxes on time.

3.6 QUOTATION MARKS

Successful writers . . .

- Use quotation marks to enclose direct quotations, including dialog (below and facing page).
- Use quotation marks around the titles of works that are parts of other works (pp. 167–68).
- Use quotation marks to enclose words being used in a special sense (p. 168).
- Avoid unnecessary quotation marks (p. 169).
- Place quotation marks inside or outside other marks according to standard practice (p. 169).

Quotation marks—either double (" ") or single (' ')—mainly enclose direct quotations and certain titles. Additional information on using quotations appears elsewhere in this book:

- **Using commas with signal phrases such as *she said* to introduce quotations.** See p. 150.
- **Using the ellipsis mark and brackets to indicate changes in quotations.** See pp. 174–76.
- **Quoting sources versus paraphrasing or summarizing them.**
- **Integrating quotations into your text.**
- **Acknowledging the sources of quotations to avoid plagiarism.**
- **Formatting long prose quotations and poetry quotations.**

3.6a Use quotation marks with direct quotations.

A **direct quotation** reports what someone said or wrote, in the exact words of the original.

1 Double Quotation Marks

"Life," said the psychoanalyst Karen Horney, "remains a very efficient therapist."

Note Do not use quotation marks with an **indirect quotation**, which reports what someone said or wrote but not in the exact words of the original: *Karen Horney remarked that life is a good therapist.*

2 Single Quotation Marks

Use single quotation marks to enclose a quotation within a quotation.

> "In formulating any philosophy," Woody Allen writes, "the first consideration must always be: What can we know? Descartes hinted at the problem when he wrote, 'My mind can never know my body, although it has become quite friendly with my leg.'"

EXERCISE 3.6.1   Revising: Double and Single Quotation Marks

Insert double and single quotation marks as needed in the following sentences. Circle the number preceding any sentence that is correct.

Example

The bus driver always says Go get 'em, tiger! to my five-year-old.

The bus driver always says "Go get 'em, tiger!" to my five-year-old.

1. Why, the lecturer asked, do we say Bless you! or something else when people sneeze but not acknowledge coughs, hiccups, and other eruptions?
2. She said that sneezes have always been regarded differently.
3. Sneezes feel more uncontrollable than some other eruptions, she said.
4. Unlike coughs and hiccups, she explained, sneezes feel as if they come from inside the head.
5. She concluded, People thus wish to recognize a sneeze, if only with a Gosh.

3.6b Set off quotations of dialog according to standard practice.

When quoting conversations, begin a new paragraph for each speaker.

> "What shall I call you? Your name?" Andrews whispered rapidly, as with a high squeak the latch of the door rose.
> "Elizabeth," she said. "Elizabeth."
>
> —Graham Greene, *The Man Within*

When you quote a single speaker for more than one paragraph, put quotation marks at the beginning of each paragraph but at the end of only the last paragraph.

3.6c Use quotation marks around the titles of works that are parts of other works.

Use quotation marks to enclose the titles of works that are published or released within larger works. (See the following box.) Use single quotation marks for a quotation within a quoted title, as in the article title and essay title in the box. And enclose all punctuation in the title within the quotation marks, as in the article title.

Titles to Be Enclosed in Quotation Marks	
Titles	**Examples**
Song	"The Star-Spangled Banner"
Short story	"The Gift of the Magi"
Short poem	"Mending Wall"
Article in periodical	"Does 'Scaring' Work?"
Essay	"Joey: A 'Mechanical Boy'"
Page or document on a Web site	"Readers' Page" (on the site *Friends of Prufrock*)
Episode of a television or radio program	"The Mexican Connection" (on *60 Minutes*)
Subdivision of a book	"The Mast Head" (Chapter 35 of *Moby-Dick*)
Use italics or underlining for other titles. (See pp. 190–92.)	

Note Some academic disciplines do not require quotation marks for titles within source citations.

EXERCISE 3.6.2   Revising: Quotation Marks for Titles

Insert quotation marks as needed for titles and words in the following sentences. If quotation marks should be used instead of italics, insert them.

Example

In the movie *Dead Poets Society,* Whitman's poem O Captain! My Captain! is often recited.

In the movie *Dead Poets Society*, Whitman's poem "O Captain! My Captain!" is often recited.

1. In Chapter 8, titled *How to Be Interesting*, the author explains the art of conversation.
2. The Beatles' song Let It Be reminds Martin of his uncle.
3. The article that appeared in *Mental Health* was titled Children of Divorce Ask, "Why?"
4. In the encyclopedia the discussion under Modern Art fills less than a column.
5. One prizewinning essay, *Cowgirls on Wall Street*, first appeared in *Entrepreneur* magazine.

3.6d Use quotation marks to enclose words being used in a special sense.

On movie sets movable "wild walls" make a one-walled room seem four-walled on film.

Note Use italics or underlining for defined words.

3.6e Delete quotation marks where they are not required.

Title of Your Paper

Faulty   "The Death Wish in One Poem by Robert Frost"

Revised   The Death Wish in One Poem by Robert Frost

Or   The Death Wish in "Stopping by Woods on a Snowy Evening"

Common Nickname

Faulty   As President, "Jimmy" Carter preferred to use his nickname.

Revised   As President, Jimmy Carter preferred to use his nickname.

Slang or Trite Expression

Quotation marks will not excuse slang or a trite expression that is inappropriate to your writing. If slang is appropriate, use it without quotation marks.

Faulty   We should support the President in his "hour of need" rather
           than "wimp out on him."

Revised   We should give the President the support he needs rather
           than turn away like cowards.

3.6f Place other punctuation marks inside or outside quotation marks according to standard practice.

1 Commas and Periods: Inside Quotation Marks

Swift uses irony in his essay "A Modest Proposal."

Many first-time readers are shocked to see infants described
as "delicious."

"'A Modest Proposal,'" writes one critic, "is so outrageous that
it cannot be believed."

Exception When a parenthetical source citation immediately follows a quotation, place any period or comma *after* the citation.

One critic calls the essay "outrageous" (Olms 26).

Partly because of "the cool calculation of its delivery" (Olms 27),
Swift's satire still chills a modern reader.

2 Colons and Semicolons: Outside Quotation Marks

A few years ago the slogan in elementary education was "learning
by playing"; now educators are concerned with basic skills.

We all know what is meant by "inflation": more money buys less.

3 **Dashes, Question Marks, and Exclamation Points:**
Inside Quotation Marks Only if Part of the Quotation

When a dash, question mark, or exclamation point is part of the quotation, place it *inside* quotation marks. Don't use any other punctuation, such as a period or comma.

"But must you—" Maria hesitated, afraid of the answer.

"Go away!" I yelled.

Did you say, "Who is she?" [When both your sentence and the quotation would end in a question mark or exclamation point, use only the mark in the quotation.]

When a dash, question mark, or exclamation point applies only to the larger sentence, not to the quotation, place it *outside* quotation marks—again, with no other punctuation.

One evocative line in English poetry—"Now slides the silent meteor on"—comes from Alfred, Lord Tennyson.

Who said, "Now cracks a noble heart"?

The woman called me "stupid"!

EXERCISE 3.6.3   Revising: Quotation Marks

Revise the following sentences for the proper use of quotation marks. Insert quotation marks where they are needed, remove them where they are not needed, and be sure that other marks of punctuation are correctly placed inside or outside the quotation marks. If a sentence is correct as given, circle the number preceding it.

Example

The award-winning story was titled *How to Say I'm Sorry to a Child*.

The award-winning story was titled "How to Say 'I'm Sorry' to a Child."

1. The reading included Virginia Woolf's essay The Anatomy of Fiction.
2. "No smoking on this bus!" the driver shouted.
3. The commercial says, Lite Beer is a third less filling than your regular beer; but how do they measure that?
4. Wearing coveralls and work boots, she looked like a "hick."
5. How can we answer children who ask, Is there a Santa Claus?
6. In America the signs say, Keep off the grass; in England they say, Please refrain from stepping on the lawn.
7. In *King Richard II* Shakespeare called England "This precious stone set in the silver sea".
8. The doctors gave my father an "electrocardiogram."
9. Our forests—in Longfellow's words, The murmuring pines and the hemlocks—are slowly succumbing to land development.
10. Must we regard the future with what the philosopher Kierkegaard called fear and trembling?

Insert quotation marks as needed in the following paragraph. If a sentence is correct as given, circle the number preceding it.

1 In a history class we talked about a passage from the *Gettysburg Address,* the speech delivered by President Abraham Lincoln on November 19, 1863:

> **2** Four score and seven years ago our fathers brought forth on this continent, a new nation, conceived in Liberty, and dedicated to the proposition that all men are created equal. **3** Now we are engaged in a great civil war, testing whether that nation, or any nation so conceived and so dedicated, can long endure.

4 What was Lincoln referring to in the first sentence? the teacher asked. **5** Perhaps we should define *score* first. **6** Explaining that a score is twenty years, she said that Lincoln was referring to the document in which the colonies had declared independence from England eighty-seven years earlier, in 1776. **7** One student commented, Lincoln's decision to end slavery is implied in that first sentence. **8** The President was calling on the authority of the Founding Fathers. **9** Lincoln gave the speech at the dedication of the National Cemetery in Gettysburg, Pennsylvania, another student added. **10** It was the site of a very bloody Civil War battle. **11** A third student noted that in the second sentence Lincoln was posing the central question of the war: whether a nation founded on equality can long endure.

3.7 OTHER MARKS

Successful writers . . .

- Use the dash to indicate shifts and to set off some sentence elements (below).
- Use parentheses to enclose parenthetical expressions and labels for lists within sentences (p. 172–73).
- Use the ellipsis mark to indicate omissions from quotations (p. 174).
- Use brackets to indicate changes in quotations (p. 176).
- Use the slash between options and between lines of poetry run into the text (p. 176).

3.7a Use the dash or dashes to indicate shifts and to set off some sentence elements.

The dash (—) is mainly a mark of interruption: it signals a shift, insertion, or break. In your papers, form a dash with two hyphens (--) or use the character called an em dash on your word processor. Do not add extra space around or between the hyphens or around the em dash.

Note Be sure to use a pair of dashes when a shift or interruption falls in the middle of a sentence.

Shifts in Tone or Thought

The novel—if one can call it that—appeared in 2013.

Nonessential Elements

The qualities Monet painted—sunlight, rich shadows, deep colors—abounded near the rivers and gardens he used as subjects.

Though they are close together—separated by only a few blocks—the two neighborhoods could be in different countries.

Introductory Series

Shortness of breath, skin discoloration or the sudden appearance of moles, persistent indigestion, the presence of small lumps—all these symptoms may signify cancer.

Concluding Series or Explanations

The patient may undergo a battery of tests—imaging, blood work, perhaps even a biopsy.

Many patients are disturbed by the MRI tests—by the need to keep still for long periods in an exceedingly small space.

EXERCISE 3.7.1 Revising: Dashes

Insert dashes as needed in the following sentences.

Example

What would we do if someone like Adolf Hitler that monster appeared among us?

What would we do if someone like Adolf Hitler—that monster—appeared among us?

1. His exuberant I should say outlandish ravings electrified the crowd.
2. The two brothers one tall and thin, the other short and stocky look nothing alike.
3. The difficulties of city living they hardly need explaining can undermine the most cheerful spirit.
4. The movie theater business is undergoing dramatic changes changes that affect what movies are made and shown.
5. To feed, clothe, and shelter the needy these are real achievements.

3.7b Use parentheses to enclose parenthetical expressions and labels for lists within sentences.

Note Parentheses *always* come in pairs, one before and one after the punctuated material.

1 Parenthetical Expressions

Parenthetical expressions include explanations, facts, and examples that may be helpful or interesting but are not essential to meaning. Parentheses de-emphasize parenthetical expressions. (Commas emphasize them more than parentheses do, and dashes emphasize them still more.)

> The population of Philadelphia (now about 1.5 million) has declined since 1950.

Note Don't put a comma before a parenthetical expression enclosed in parentheses. Punctuation after the parenthetical expression should be placed outside the closing parenthesis.

> **Incorrect** The population of Philadelphia compares with that of Phoenix, (just under 1.5 million.)
>
> **Correct** The population of Philadelphia compares with that of Phoenix (just under 1.5 million)

When a complete sentence falls within parentheses, place the period *inside* the closing parenthesis.

> In general, coaches will tell you that scouts are just guys who can't coach. (But then, so are brain surgeons.) —Roy Blount

2 Labels for Lists within Sentences

> Outside the Middle East, the countries with the largest oil reserves are (1) Venezuela (63 billion barrels), (2) Russia (57 billion barrels), and (3) Mexico (51 billion barrels).

Do not enclose such labels in parentheses when you set a list off from your text.

EXERCISE 3.7.2   Revising: Parentheses

Insert parentheses as needed in the following sentences.

Example

Students can find good-quality, inexpensive furniture for example, desks, tables, chairs, sofas, even beds in junk stores.

Students can find good-quality, inexpensive furniture (for example, desks, tables, chairs, sofas, even beds) in junk stores.

1. T. S. Eliot's *The Waste Land* 1922 is one of the most analyzed poems in the English language.
2. The Golden Gate Bridge actually it's closer to red is a famous landmark of San Francisco.
3. Our present careless use of coal and oil will lead to a series of unpleasant events: 1 all of us will have to cut back drastically on our use of resources; 2 only the rich will have access to these resources; and 3 no one will have access to them, for they will be exhausted.
4. Some exotic pets monkeys and fragile breeds of dog require too much care to be enjoyable.
5. The Hundred Years' War 1337–1453 between England and France was actually a series of widely spaced battles, not a continuous war.

3.7c Use the ellipsis mark to indicate omissions from quotations.

The ellipsis mark, consisting of three periods separated by space (. . .), generally indicates an omission from a quotation. All the following examples quote from this passage about environmentalism:

Original Quotation

At the heart of the environmentalist world view is the conviction that human physical and spiritual health depends on sustaining the planet in a relatively unaltered state. Earth is our home in the full, genetic sense, where humanity and its ancestors existed for all the millions of years of their evolution. Natural ecosystems—forests, coral reefs, marine blue waters—maintain the world exactly as we would wish it to be maintained. When we debase the global environment and extinguish the variety of life, we are dismantling a support system that is too complex to understand, let alone replace, in the foreseeable future.

—Edward O. Wilson, "Is Humanity Suicidal?"

1. Omission of the middle of a sentence

"Natural ecosystems . . . maintain the world exactly as we would wish it to be maintained."

2. Omission of the end of a sentence, without source citation

"Earth is our home. . . ." [The sentence period, closed up to the last word, precedes the ellipsis mark.]

3. Omission of the end of a sentence, with source citation

"Earth is our home . . ." (Wilson 27). [The sentence period follows the source citation.]

4. Omission of parts of two or more sentences

Wilson writes, "At the heart of the environmentalist world view is the conviction that human physical and spiritual health depends on sustaining the planet . . . where humanity and its ancestors existed for all the millions of years of their evolution."

5. Omission of one or more sentences

As Wilson puts it, "At the heart of the environmentalist world view is the conviction that human physical and spiritual health depends on sustaining the planet in a relatively unaltered state. . . . When we debase the global environment and extinguish the variety of life, we are dismantling a support system that is too complex to understand, let alone replace, in the foreseeable future."

6. Omission from the middle of a sentence through the end of another sentence

"Earth is our home. . . . When we debase the global environment and extinguish the variety of life, we are dismantling a support system that is too complex to understand, let alone replace, in the foreseeable future."

7. Omission of the beginning of a sentence, leaving a complete sentence

a. Bracketed capital letter

"[H]uman physical and spiritual health," Wilson writes, "depends on sustaining the planet in a relatively unaltered state." [No ellipsis mark is needed because the bracketed *H* indicates that the letter was not capitalized originally and thus that the beginning of the sentence has been omitted.]

b. Small letter

According to Wilson, "human physical and spiritual health depends on sustaining the planet in a relatively unaltered state." [No ellipsis mark is needed because the small *h* indicates that the beginning of the sentence has been omitted.]

c. Capital letter from the original

One reviewer comments, ". . . Wilson argues eloquently for the environmentalist world view" (Ham 28). [An ellipsis mark is needed because the quoted part of the sentence begins with a capital letter and it's otherwise not clear that the beginning of the original sentence has been omitted.]

8. Use of a word or phrase

Wilson describes the earth as "our home." [No ellipsis mark needed.]

Note these features of the examples:

- **Use an ellipsis mark when it is not otherwise clear that you have left out material from the source,** as when you omit one or more sentences (examples 5 and 6) or when the words you quote form a complete sentence that is different in the original (examples 1–4 and 7c).

- **You don't need an ellipsis mark when it is obvious that you have omitted something,** such as when a bracketed or small letter indicates omission (examples 7a and 7b) or when a phrase clearly comes from a larger sentence (example 8).

- **Place an ellipsis mark after a sentence period** *except* **when a parenthetical source citation follows the quotation,** as in examples 3 and 7c. Then the sentence period comes after the citation.

When you omit one or more lines of poetry or paragraphs of prose from a displayed quotation, use a separate line of ellipsis marks across the full width of the quotation to show the omission.

In "Song: Love Armed" from 1676, Aphra Behn contrasts two lovers' experiences of a romance:

> Love in fantastic triumph sate,
>   Whilst bleeding hearts around him flowed,
> . . . .
> But my poor heart alone is harmed,
>   Whilst thine the victor is, and free. (lines 1-2, 15-16)

> **EXERCISE 3.7.3**   Using Ellipsis Marks

Use ellipsis marks and any other needed punctuation to follow the numbered instructions for quoting from the following paragraph.

Women in the sixteenth and seventeenth centuries were educated in the home and, in some cases, in boarding schools. Men were educated at home, in grammar schools, and at the universities. The universities were closed to female students. For women, "learning the Bible," as Elizabeth Joceline puts it, was an impetus to learning to read. To be able to read the Bible in the vernacular was a liberating experience that freed the reader from hearing only the set passages read in the church and interpreted by the church. A Protestant woman was expected to read the scriptures daily, to meditate on them, and to memorize portions of them. In addition, a woman was expected to instruct her entire household in "learning the Bible" by holding instructional and devotional times each day for all household members, including the servants.

—Charlotte F. Otten,
English Women's Voices, 1540–1700

1. Quote the fifth sentence, but omit everything from *that freed the reader* to the end.
2. Quote the fifth sentence, but omit *was a liberating experience that*.
3. Quote the first and sixth sentences.

3.7d Use brackets to indicate changes in quotations.

Brackets have specialized uses in mathematical equations, but their main use for all kinds of writing is to indicate that you have altered a quotation to explain, clarify, or correct it.

"That Chevron station [just outside Dallas] is one of the busiest in the nation," said a company spokesperson.

3.7e Use the slash between options and between lines of poetry run into the text.

Option

Some teachers oppose pass/fail courses.

Poetry

Many readers have sensed a reluctant turn away from death in Frost's lines "The woods are lovely, dark and deep, / But I have promises to keep" (13–14).

When separating lines of poetry in this way, leave a space before and after the slash.

EXERCISE 3.7.4 Revising: Other Punctuation Marks

Insert dashes, parentheses, brackets, ellipsis marks, or slashes as needed in the following sentences, or remove them where they are not needed. When different marks would be appropriate in the same place, be able to defend the choice you make. Circle the number preceding any sentence that is already correct.

Example

The residents of the neighborhood including many who grew up there signed a petition against further development.

The residents of the neighborhood—including many who grew up there—signed a petition against further development. [The dashes emphasize the parenthetical expression.]

1. I read about Emma Goldman (or Red Emma), an American anarchist who died in 1940.
2. From the reviewer's sentence "The acting is amazingly incompetent, given that these actors can be powerful," the advertisement extracted praise by using an ellipsis mark: "The acting is amazingly powerful."
3. The bikers—tattooed and draped in chains look more threatening than they really are.
4. James Joyce's *Ulysses* first published in 1922 is a beautiful, shocking novel.
5. Paying taxes one of life's certainties is only a little less painful than the other certainty.

This image from the 2014 film *Selma* depicts Dr. Martin Luther King (played by David Oyelowo) and fellow activists during the Montgomery voting rights marches. A review of this film praised the aesthetic qualities of the film, while downplaying claims that the film lacked historical accuracy. Can evaluative judgments change depending upon the criteria we use to judge them?

4

Spelling and Mechanics

4.1 SPELLING AND THE HYPHEN

Successful writers . . .

- Identify and correct typical spelling problems (below).
- Follow spelling rules (p. 181).
- Use the hyphen to form or divide words (p. 185).

You can train yourself to spell better, and this chapter will tell you how. But you can improve instantly by acquiring three habits:

- **Carefully proofread your writing.**
- **Be suspicious of your spellings.**
- **Check a dictionary *every time* you doubt a spelling.**

Taken from *The Successful Writer's Handbook,* Third Edition by Kathleen T. McWhorter and Jane E. Aaron.

Note A spelling checker can help you find errors, but its usefulness is limited.

4.1a Look for typical spelling problems.

1 Pronunciation

In English, the pronunciation of a word does not always indicate how it is spelled. Pronunciation is especially misleading with **homonyms,** words pronounced the same but spelled differently. Some homonyms and near-homonyms appear in the following box.

Words Commonly Confused	
accept (to receive) except (other than)	hear (to perceive by ear) here (in this place)
affect (to have an influence on) effect (a result)	heard (past tense of *hear*) herd (a group of animals)
all ready (prepared) already (by this time)	hole (an opening) whole (complete)
allusion (an indirect reference) illusion (an erroneous belief or perception)	its (possessive of *it*) it's (contraction of *it is* or *it has*)
ascent (a movement up) assent (to agree, or an agreement)	know (to be certain) no (the opposite of *yes*)
bare (unclothed) bear (to carry, or an animal)	lessen (to reduce) lesson (something learned)
board (a plane of wood) bored (uninterested)	loose (not attached) lose (to misplace)
brake (to stop) break (to smash)	meat (flesh) meet (to encounter, or a competition)
buy (to purchase) by (next to)	passed (past tense of *pass*) past (after, or a time gone by)
cite (to quote an authority) sight (the ability to see) site (a place)	patience (forbearance) patients (persons under medical care)
desert (to abandon) dessert (after-dinner course)	peace (the absence of war) piece (a portion of something)
discreet (reserved, respectful) discrete (individual, distinct)	plain (clear) plane (a carpenter's tool, or an airborne vehicle)
fair (average, or lovely) fare (a fee for transportation)	presence (the state of being at hand) presents (gifts)
forth (forward) fourth (after *third*)	principal (most important, or the head of a school) principle (a basic truth or law)

(continued)

Words Commonly Confused (continued)

rain (precipitation) reign (to rule) rein (a strap for an animal)	to (toward) too (also) two (following *one*)
raise (to lift up) raze (to tear down)	waist (the middle of the body) waste (discarded material)
right (correct) rite (a religious ceremony) write (to make letters)	weak (not strong) week (Sunday through Saturday) weather (climate) whether (*if*, or introducing a choice)
road (a surface for driving) rode (past tense of *ride*)	
scene (where an action occurs) seen (past participle of *see*)	which (one of a group) witch (a sorcerer)
stationary (unmoving) stationery (writing paper)	who's (contraction of *who is* or *who has*) whose (possessive of *who*)
their (possessive of *they*) there (opposite of *here*) they're (contraction of *they are*)	your (possessive of *you*) you're (contraction of *you are*)

2 Different Forms of the Same Word

Often, the noun form and the verb form of the same word are spelled differently: for example, *advice* (noun) and *advise* (verb). Sometimes the noun and the adjective forms of the same word differ: *height* and *high*; *generosity* and *generous*. Similar changes occur in the parts of some irregular verbs (*know, knew, known*) and the plurals of irregular nouns (*woman, women*).

4.1b Follow spelling rules.

1 *ie* vs. *ei*

To distinguish between *ie* and *ei*, use the familiar jingle:

I before *e,* except after *c,* or when the syllable is pronounced "ay" as in *neighbor* and *weigh.*

i before *e*	believe	thief	hygiene
ei after *c*	ceiling	conceive	perceive
ei sounded as "ay"	sleigh	eight	beige

Exceptions For some exceptions, remember this sentence:

The weird foreigner neither seizes leisure nor forfeits height.

EXERCISE 4.1.1   Distinguishing between *ie* and *ei*

Insert *ie* or *ei* in the words below. Check doubtful spellings in a dictionary.

Example

th__f
thief

1. br__f
2. dec__ve
3. rec__pt
4. s__ze

5. for__gn
6. pr__st
7. gr__vance
8. f__nd

9. l__surely
10. ach__ve
11. pat__nce
12. p__rce

13. h__ght
14. fr__ght
15. f__nt
16. s__ve

---

2 **Final *e***

When adding an ending to a word with a final *e*, drop the *e* if the ending begins with a vowel (*a, e, i, o, u,* and sometimes *y*):

advise + able = advisable   surprise + ing = surprising

Keep the *e* if the ending begins with a consonant (any letter that is not a vowel):

care + ful = careful   like + ly = likely

Exceptions Retain the *e* after a soft *c* or *g*, to keep the sound of the consonant soft rather than hard: *courageous, changeable.* And drop the *e* before a consonant when the *e* is preceded by another vowel: *argue + ment = argument, true + ly = truly.*

EXERCISE 4.1.2   Keeping or Dropping a Final *e*

Combine the following words and endings, keeping or dropping a final *e* as necessary to make correctly spelled words. Check doubtful spellings in a dictionary.

Example

use + ing
using

1. malice + ious
2. love + able
3. service + able

4. retire + ment
5. sue + ing
6. virtue + ous

7. note + able
8. battle + ing
9. suspense + ion

---

3 **Final *y***

When adding an ending to a word with a final *y*, change the *y* to *i* if it follows a consonant:

beauty, beauties   worry, worried   supply, supplies

But keep the *y* if it follows a vowel, if it ends a proper name, or if the ending is -*ing*:

day, da<u>y</u>s   Minsky, Minsky<u>s</u>   cry, cr<u>y</u>ing

EXERCISE 4.1.3 Keeping or Dropping a Final *y*

Combine the following words and endings, changing or keeping a final *y* as necessary to make correctly spelled words. Check doubtful spellings in a dictionary.

Example

try + ing
tr<u>y</u>ing

1. imply + s
2. messy + er
3. apply + ing

4. delay + ing
5. defy + ance
6. say + s

7. solidify + s
8. Murphy + s
9. supply + ed

4 Final Consonants

When adding an ending to a one-syllable word ending in a consonant, double the final consonant when it follows a single vowel. Otherwise, don't double the consonant.

slap, sla<u>pp</u>ing   park, par<u>k</u>ing   pair, pai<u>r</u>ed

In words of more than one syllable, double the final consonant when it follows a single vowel *and* when it ends a stressed syllable once the new ending is added. Otherwise, don't double the consonant.

refer, refer<u>r</u>ing   refer, refe<u>r</u>ence   relent, relen<u>t</u>ed

EXERCISE 4.1.4 Doubling Consonants

Combine the following words and endings, doubling final consonants as necessary to make correctly spelled words. Check doubtful spellings in a dictionary.

Example

commit + ed
commi<u>tt</u>ed

1. repair + ing
2. admit + ance
3. benefit + ed

4. shop + ed
5. conceal + ed
6. allot + ed

7. drip + ing
8. declaim + ed
9. parallel + ing

5 Prefixes

When adding a prefix, do not drop a letter from or add a letter to the original word:

<u>un</u>necessary   <u>dis</u>appoint   <u>mis</u>spell

EXERCISE 4.1.5 Attaching Prefixes

Combine the following prefixes and words to make correctly spelled words. Check doubtful spellings in a dictionary.

Example

mis + informed
<u>mis</u>informed

1. mis + place
2. non + essential
3. dis + service
4. pre + conception
5. in + appropriate
6. un + fold
7. dis + charge
8. mis + shape
9. under + run

---

6 Plurals

Most nouns form plurals by adding *s* to the singular form. Add *es* for the plural of nouns ending in *s*, *sh*, *ch*, or *x*.

boy, boy<u>s</u>   kiss, kisse<u>s</u>   church, churche<u>s</u>

Nouns ending in *o* preceded by a vowel usually form the plural with *s*. Those ending in *o* preceded by a consonant usually form the plural with *es*.

ratio, ratio<u>s</u>   hero, heroe<u>s</u>

Some very common nouns form irregular plurals.

child, childre<u>n</u>   woman, wome<u>n</u>   mouse, mic<u>e</u>

Some English nouns that were originally Italian, Greek, Latin, or French form the plural according to their original language.

analysis, analys<u>e</u>s   criterion, criteri<u>a</u>   piano, piano<u>s</u>

basis, base<u>s</u>   datum, dat<u>a</u>   thesis, these<u>s</u>

crisis, crise<u>s</u>   medium, medi<u>a</u>

A few such nouns may form irregular or regular plurals: for instance, *index*, *indic<u>e</u>s*, *index<u>e</u>s*; *curriculum*, *curricul<u>a</u>*, *curriculum<u>s</u>*. The regular plural is more contemporary.

With compound nouns, add *s* to the main word of the compound. Sometimes this main word is not the last word.

city-state<u>s</u>   father<u>s</u>-in-law   passer<u>s</u>by

(CULTURE LANGUAGE) In standard American English, noncount nouns do not form plurals, either regularly (with an added *s*) or irregularly. Examples of noncount nouns include *equipment*, *intelligence*, and *wealth*. See p. 75.

EXERCISE 4.1.6   **Forming Plurals**

Make correct plurals of the following singular words. Check doubtful spellings in a dictionary.

Example

city
cities

1. pile	**5.** mile per hour	**9.** Bales	**13.** thief
2. donkey	**6.** box	**10.** cupful	**14.** goose
3. beach	**7.** switch	**11.** libretto	**15.** hiss
4. summary	**8.** sister-in-law	**12.** video	**16.** appendix

---

EXERCISE 4.1.7   **Working with a Spelling Checker**

Try your computer's spelling checker on the following paragraph. Type the paragraph exactly as it appears below, and run it through your spelling checker. Then proofread it to correct the errors missed by the checker. (Hint: There are fourteen errors in all.)

1 The whether effects all of us, though it's affects are different for different people. **2** Some people love a fare day with warm temperatures and sunshine. **3** They revel in spending a hole day outside without the threat of rein. **4** Other people prefer dark, rainy daze. **5** They relish the opportunity to slow down and here they're inner thoughts. **6** Most people agree, however, that to much of one kind of whether—reign, sun, snow, or clouds—makes them board.

4.1c Use the hyphen to form words.

The hyphen is used mainly to form compound words, such as adjectives and numbers.

1 **Compound Adjectives**

When two or more words serve together as a single adjective before a noun, a hyphen forms the modifying words clearly into a unit.

She is a well-known actor.

Some Spanish-speaking students work as translators.

When such a compound adjective follows the noun, the hyphen is unnecessary.

The actor is well known.

Many students are Spanish speaking.

The hyphen is also unnecessary in a compound modifier beginning with an *-ly* word, even before the noun: *clearly defined* terms.

When part of a compound adjective appears only once in two or more parallel compound adjectives, hyphens indicate which words the reader should mentally join with the missing part.

> School-age children should have eight- or nine-o'clock bedtimes.

2 Fractions and Compound Numbers

Hyphens join the numerator and denominator of fractions: *one-half, three-fourths*. Hyphens also join the parts of the whole numbers *twenty-one* to *ninety-nine*.

When a hyphenated number is part of a compound adjective before a noun, join all parts of the modifier with hyphens: *sixty-three-foot wall*.

3 Prefixes and Suffixes

Do not use hyphens with prefixes except as follows:

- **With the prefixes *self-*, *all-*, and *ex-*:** *self-control, all-inclusive, ex-student*.
- **With a prefix before a capitalized word:** *un-American*.
- **With a capital letter before a word:** *T-shirt*.
- **To prevent misreading:** *de-emphasize, re-create a story*.

Only one suffix requires a hyphen: *-elect*, as in *president-elect*.

EXERCISE 4.1.8 Using Hyphens in Compound Words

Insert hyphens as needed in the following compounds, consulting a dictionary as needed. If a compound is correct as given, circle the number preceding it.

Example

pre Victorian
pre-Victorian

1. reimburse
2. deescalate
3. forty odd soldiers
4. little known bar
5. seven eighths

6. seventy eight
7. happy go lucky
8. preexisting
9. senator elect
10. postwar

11. two and six person cars
12. ex songwriter
13. V shaped
14. reeducate

4.2 CAPITAL LETTERS

Successful writers . . .

- Capitalize the first word of every sentence (below).
- Capitalize proper nouns, proper adjectives, and words used as essential parts of proper nouns (below).
- Capitalize most words in titles and subtitles of works (p. 189).

Generally, capitalize a word only when a dictionary or conventional use says you must.

4.2a Capitalize the first word of every sentence.

Every writer should own a good dictionary.

4.2b Capitalize proper nouns, proper adjectives, and words used as essential parts of proper nouns.

1 Proper Nouns and Proper Adjectives

Proper nouns name specific persons, places, and things: *Shakespeare, California, World War I.* **Proper adjectives** are formed from some proper nouns: *Shakespearean, Californian.* Capitalize all proper nouns and proper adjectives but not *a, an,* or *the* preceding them.

Proper Nouns and Adjectives to Be Capitalized

Specific persons and things

Stephen King	Boulder Dam
Napoleon Bonaparte	the Empire State Building

Specific places and geographical regions

New York City	the Mediterranean Sea
China	the Northeast, the South

But: northeast of the city, going south

Days of the week, months, holidays

Monday	Yom Kippur
May	Christmas

Historical events, documents, periods, movements

the Vietnam War	the Renaissance
the Constitution	the Romantic Movement

(continued)

Proper Nouns and Adjectives to Be Capitalized (continued)	

Government offices, departments, and institutions

House of Representatives Polk Municipal Court

Department of Defense El Camino Hospital

But: the court, the department, the hospital

Academic institutions and departments

Central Community College Department of Nursing

University of Kansas Haven High School

But: the university, college course, high school diploma

Political, social, athletic, and other organizations and associations and their members

Democratic Party, Democrats League of Women Voters

Sierra Club Boston Celtics

B'nai B'rith Chicago Symphony Orchestra

Races, nationalities, and their languages

Native American Germans

African American Swahili

Caucasian Italian

But: blacks, whites

Religions, their followers, and terms for the sacred

Christianity, Christians God

Catholicism, Catholics Allah

Judaism, Orthodox Jews the Bible [**but** biblical]

Islam, Muslims the Koran, the Qur'an

2 Common Nouns Used as Essential Parts of Proper Nouns

Capitalize the common nouns *street, avenue, park, river, ocean, lake, company, college, county,* and *memorial* when they are part of proper nouns naming specific places or institutions:

Main Street Lake Superior

Central Park Ford Motor Company

Missouri River Madison College

Pacific Ocean George Washington Memorial

3 Compass Directions

Capitalize compass directions only when they name a specific region instead of a general direction:

Students from the <u>West</u> often melt in <u>eastern</u> humidity.

4 Relationships

Capitalize the names of relationships only when they precede or replace proper names:

> Our <u>aunt</u> scolded us for disrespecting <u>Father</u> and <u>Uncle Jake</u>.

5 Titles with Persons' Names

Before a person's name, capitalize his or her title. After or apart from the name, do not capitalize the title.

> Professor Otto Osborne   Otto Osborne, a professor
>
> Doctor Jane Covington   Jane Covington, a doctor
>
> Governor Ella Moore   Ella Moore, the governor

Note Many writers capitalize a title denoting very high rank even when it follows a name or is used alone: *George W. Bush, past President of the United States.*

4.2c Capitalize most words in titles and subtitles of works.

Capitalize all the words in a title *except* the following: noun markers (*a, an, the*); *to* in infinitives; coordinating conjunctions (*and, but,* etc.); and prepositions (*with, between,* etc.). Capitalize even these words when they are the first or last word in a title or when they fall after a colon or semicolon.

> "Courtship through the Ages"   *Management: A New Theory*
>
> *A Diamond Is Forever*   "Once More to the Lake"
>
> "Knowing Whom to Ask"   *An End to Live For*
>
> *Learning from Las Vegas*   *File under Architecture*

EXERCISE 4.2.1   Revising: Capitals

Revise the following paragraph to correct errors in capitalization, consulting a dictionary as needed. If a sentence is correct as given, circle the number preceding it.

Example

> The Cities of Minneapolis–St. paul, also known as the twin cities, are located on the Mississippi river.
>
> The <u>c</u>ities of Minneapolis–St. <u>P</u>aul, also known as the <u>T</u>win <u>C</u>ities, are located on the Mississippi <u>R</u>iver.

1 San Antonio, texas, is a thriving city in the southwest that has always offered much to tourists interested in the roots of spanish settlement in the new world. **2** Most visitors stop at the Alamo, one of five Catholic Missions built by Priests to convert native americans and to maintain spain's claims in the area. **3** The Alamo is famous for being the site of an 1836 battle that helped to create the republic of Texas. **4** San Antonio has grown tremendously in recent years. **5** The Hemisfair plaza and the San Antonio river link tourist and convention facilities. **6** Restaurants, Hotels, and shops line the River. **7** the haunting melodies of "Una paloma blanca" and "malagueña" lure passing tourists into Casa rio and other mexican restaurants. **8** The university of Texas at San Antonio has expanded, and a Medical Center lies in the Northwest part of the city. **9** A marine attraction on the west side of San Antonio entertains grandparents, fathers and mothers, and children with the antics of dolphins and seals. **10** The City has attracted high-tech industry, creating a corridor between san antonio and austin.

4.3 ITALICS OR UNDERLINING

> *Successful writers . . .*
>
> - Italicize or underline the titles of works that appear independently (below).
> - Italicize or underline the names of ships, aircraft, spacecraft, and trains (next page).
> - Italicize or underline foreign words that are not part of the English language (p. 192).
> - Occasionally, use italics or underlining for emphasis (p. 192).

Italic type and <u>underlining</u> indicate the same thing: the word or words are being distinguished or emphasized. Italic type is now used almost universally in business and academic writing. Some instructors do recommend underlining, so ask your instructor for his or her preference.

Always use either italics or underlining consistently throughout a document in both text and source citations. If you are using italics, make sure that the italic characters are clearly distinct from the regular type. If you are using underlining and you underline two or more words in a row, underline the space between the words, too: <u>Criminal Statistics: Misuses of Numbers</u>.

4.3a Italicize or underline the titles of works that appear independently.

Italicize or underline the titles of works that are published, released, or produced separately from other works. (See the following box.) Use quotation marks for all other titles. (See pp. 167–68.)

Titles to Be Italicized or Underlined

Books	**Television and radio programs**
War and Peace	*Radio Lab*
And the Band Played On	*American Idol*
Plays	**Long poems**
Hamlet	*Beowulf*
The Phantom of the Opera	*Paradise Lost*
Computer software	**Periodicals**
Acrobat Reader	*Time*
Google	*Philadelphia Inquirer*
Web sites	**Published speeches**
YouTube	Lincoln's *Gettysburg Address*
Friends of Prufrock	**Movies, DVDs, and videos**
Pamphlets	*Schindler's List*
The Truth about Alcoholism	*How to Relax*
Long musical works	**Works of visual art**
Tchaikovsky's *Swan Lake*	Michelangelo's *David*
But: Symphony in C	Picasso's *Guernica*

Use quotation marks for other titles. (See pp. 167–68.)

Note Italicize or underline a mark of punctuation only when it is part of the title. In newspaper titles, highlight the name of the city only when it is part of the title. And for all periodical titles, do not capitalize or highlight *the,* even when it is part of the title.

Who is the publisher of the Manchester *Guardian*?

The national edition of the *New York Times* differs from the late edition.

Exceptions Legal documents, the Bible, the Koran, and their parts are generally not italicized or underlined:

Not They registered their *deed*.

But They registered their deed.

Not We studied the *Book of Revelation* in the *Bible*.

But We studied the Book of Revelation in the Bible.

4.3b Italicize or underline the names of ships, aircraft, spacecraft, and trains.

Challenger	*Orient Express*	*Queen Mary 2*
Apollo XI	*Montrealer*	*Spirit of St. Louis*

4.3c Italicize or underline foreign words that are not part of the English language.

Italicize or underline a foreign expression. A dictionary will say whether a word is still considered foreign to English.

> The scientific name for the brown trout is *Salmo trutta*. [The Latin scientific names for plants and animals are always italicized or underlined.]

> The Latin *De gustibus non est disputandum* translates roughly as "There's no accounting for taste."

4.3d Occasionally, italics or underlining may be used for emphasis.

Italics or underlining can stress an important word or phrase, especially in reporting how someone said something. But use such emphasis rarely, or your writing may sound immature or hysterical.

EXERCISE 4.3.1   Revising: Italics or Underlining

In the following sentences, mark (1) the words and phrases that need highlighting with italics or underlining and (2) the words and phrases that are highlighted unnecessarily.

Example

Of Hitchcock's movies, Psycho is the scariest.
Of Hitchcock's movies, *Psycho* is the scariest.

1. The essay contains many puns and jeux de mots.
2. The author's stories have appeared in Ebony, Vogue, and Ms., among other magazines.
3. The director warned the writer that the screenplay for Adam in Love had better be finished *tout de suite*.
4. I read all of Beowulf last semester, and then I saw the movie.
5. According to the magazine Publishers Weekly, Markosian's book is out of print.
6. San Francisco's major newspaper is the Chronicle.
7. Both the *Old Testament* and the *New Testament* of the *Bible* offer profound lessons in human nature.
8. Homo sapiens has evolved further than any other species.
9. Whether he's watching American Idol, a golf tournament, or The Daily Show, Jason is happy in front of the television.
10. My aunt was in kindergarten when the space shuttle Challenger exploded.

4.4 ABBREVIATIONS

> *Successful writers . . .*
>
> - Use familiar abbreviations (below).
> - Generally spell out units of measurement and names of places, calendar designations, people, and courses (below).

The following guidelines on abbreviations pertain to the text of a nontechnical document. All academic disciplines use abbreviations in source citations, and much technical writing, such as in the sciences and engineering, uses many abbreviations in the document text.

Usage varies, but writers increasingly omit periods from abbreviations that consist of or end in capital letters: *US, BA, PhD, USMC.* See p. 138 on punctuating abbreviations.

4.4a Use familiar abbreviations.

Titles before names	Dr., Mr., Mrs., Ms., Rev., Gen.
Titles after names	MD, DDS, DVM, PhD, Sr., Jr.
Institutions	LSU, UCLA, TCU, NASA
Organizations	CIA, FBI, YMCA, AFL-CIO
Corporations	IBM, CBS, ITT, GM
People	JFK, LBJ, FDR
Countries	USA, UK
Specific numbers	no. 36 *or* No. 36
Specific amounts	$7.41, $1 million
Specific times	11:26 AM (*or* a.m.), 2:00 PM (*or* p.m.)
Specific dates	44 BC, AD 1492, 44 BCE, 1492 CE

Note The abbreviations BC ("before Christ"), BCE ("before the common era"), and CE ("common era") always follow the date. In contrast, AD (*anno domini,* "in the year of the Lord") always precedes the date.

4.4b Generally spell out units of measurement and names of places, calendar designations, people, and courses.

In most academic, general, and business writing, the following types of words should always be spelled out. (In source citations and technical writing, however, these words are more often abbreviated.)

Units of measurement

The dog is thirty inches [not in.] high.

Geographical names

The publisher is in Massachusetts [not Mass. or MA].

Names of days, months, and holidays

The truce was signed on <u>Tuesday</u> [not <u>Tues.</u>], <u>April</u> [not <u>Apr.</u>] 16.

Names of people

<u>Robert</u> [not <u>Robt.</u>] Frost wrote accessible poems.

Courses of instruction

I'm majoring in <u>political science</u> [not poli. sci.].

EXERCISE 4.4.1   Revising: Abbreviations

Revise the following sentences as needed to correct faulty use of abbreviations for non-technical writing. Circle the number preceding any sentence in which abbreviations are correct as given.

Example

One prof. spent five class hrs. reading from the textbook.
One <u>professor</u> spent five class <u>hours</u> reading from the textbook.

1. The kite was flying at about a hundred ft. when the line snapped.
2. Old Louisville, a section of Louisville between Third and Fourth Sts., near Central Pk., has some beautiful Victorian houses.
3. Scientists say that a comet crashed into the earth about 6.5 mill. yrs. ago.
4. Upon his inauguration on Fri., Jan. 20, 1961, JFK became the first Roman Catholic president in American history.
5. Mount Vesuvius erupted in *anno Domini* 79 and buried Pompeii.
6. Mr. Harold Marsh, Jr., donated a new wing for the library.
7. The Lynch brothers, Wm. & Robt., went bankrupt in the same year.
8. They asked the rev. to marry them on horseback.
9. The television networks NBC, CBS, ABC, and Fox have been losing viewers to cable and satellite networks.
10. The impact of the comet would have created 400-ft. tidal waves across the Atl. Ocean, temps. higher than 20,000 degs., and powerful earthquakes.

4.5 NUMBERS

Successful writers . . .

- Use numerals and words according to convention (next page).
- Spell out numbers that begin sentences (next page).

This chapter addresses the use of numbers (numerals versus words) in the text of a nontechnical document. Numerals are more common in technical writing.

4.5a Use numerals or words according to convention.

1 Numerals, Not Words

Numbers requiring three or more words

366   36,500

Round numbers over a million

26 million   2.45 billion

Exact amounts of money

$3.5 million $4.50

Days and years

June 18, 1985   AD 12
456 BC   12 CE

The time of day

9:00 AM   3:45 PM

Addresses

355 Heckler Avenue
Washington, DC 20036

Decimals, percentages, and fractions

22.5   3½
48% (*or* 48 percent)

Scores and statistics

a ratio of 8 to 1   21 to 7
a mean of 26

Pages, chapters, volumes, acts, scenes, lines

Chapter 9, p. 123
Hamlet, act 5, scene 3

 In standard American English, a comma separates the numerals in long numbers (*26,000*), and a period functions as a decimal point (*2.06*).

2 Words, Not Numerals

In nontechnical academic writing, spell out numbers of one or two words. A hyphenated number may be considered one word.

> <u>sixty</u> days
> <u>forty-two</u> laps
> <u>one hundred</u> people

In business and technical writing, use numerals for numbers over ten and for all numbers that refer to exact measurements (*2 nanoseconds, 1 hour*).

4.5b Spell out numbers that begin sentences.

For clarity, spell out any number that begins a sentence. If the number requires more than two words to spell out, reword the sentence so that the number falls later and can be expressed as a numeral.

> **Faulty**   <u>4.3 billion</u> people live in Asia.
>
> **Revised**   The population of Asia is <u>4.3 billion</u>.

EXERCISE 4.5.1   Revising: Numbers

Revise the following sentences to correct the use of numbers for nontechnical academic writing. Circle the number preceding any sentence in which numbers are already used appropriately.

Example

Sara paid three hundred and forty-five dollars for a bridesmaid's dress she would never wear again.

Sara paid $345 for a bridesmaid's dress she would never wear again.

1. 1036 Colgate University students played Twister for three and one-half hours on May fifth, 1984, in the largest game on record.
2. I lost a trivia game because I forgot that sixteen hundred Pennsylvania Avenue is the White House.
3. Only 27 percent of the 350 consumers we polled preferred the new product to the old one.
4. The largest carousel in the United States is 100 feet tall and cost over a million and three-quarters dollars to build.
5. Covering four hundred and two acres, Angkor Wat in Cambodia is one of the largest religious buildings ever constructed.
6. A liter is equal to almost one and six-hundredths quarts.
7. Not until page ninety-nine, in the middle of Chapter five, does the author introduce the main character.
8. I was born on May fifteenth, six days after my dog.
9. Peter Minuit bought Manhattan Island from the Indians for twenty-four dollars.
10. Dominating the town's skyline was a sign that stood thirty feet off the ground and measured one hundred feet by thirty-seven feet.

Unit 2

The Writing Process

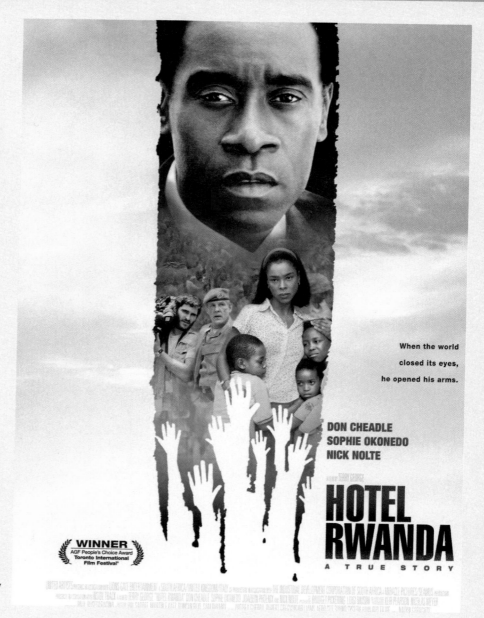

When the world closed its eyes, he opened his arms.

DON CHEADLE
SOPHIE OKONEDO
NICK NOLTE

A FILM BY TERRY GEORGE

HOTEL RWANDA
A TRUE STORY

WINNER
AGF People's Choice Award
Toronto International
Film Festival

The acclaimed 2004 movie *Hotel Rwanda* depicts the effects of the 1994 genocide in Rwanda that resulted in the deaths of 800,000 people. Research projects can examine whether films like this one accurately portray the genocide.

5

Writing in College

Successful writers . . .

- Become academic writers (next page).
- Understand the writing process and the assignment (next page).
- Find a subject, consider audience, and define a purpose (p. 201).
- Choose structure and content (p. 205).
- Use academic language (p. 205).

Writing, like many other skills, is not a single-step process. Players of competitive sports, for example, spend time trying out new plays, practicing, and reviewing previous games. Writing involves similar planning, preparation, and review. Writing usually does not proceed in a lockstep sequence. Instead, you might start over several times or circle back to change something that you have already written. Or you might uncover a new idea, explore it, and change the focus of your work.

Taken from *The Successful Writer's Handbook,* Third Edition by Kathleen T. McWhorter and Jane E. Aaron.

5.1 BECOMING AN ACADEMIC WRITER

As an academic writer, you will study a subject, acquire its vocabulary, and learn to express yourself as others in the discipline do. As you learn more about each discipline, you will learn to ask questions and communicate your answers. In any discipline, making the transition to academic writing will be easier if you practice the following strategies.

 Success

Becoming an Academic Writer

- **Study the syllabus for each course.** This outline lays out the instructor's expectations as well as the course topics, assignments, and deadlines.
- **Do the assigned reading.** You'll gain experience with the discipline's terms and ideas, and you'll become familiar with the kinds of writing expected of you.
- **Learn to read, speak, and write in the language of the discipline.** Use word mapping, keep a vocabulary log, and pay attention to common prefixes, roots, and suffixes used in the discipline.
- **Attend and participate in class.** Make class attendance a priority, whether or not the instructor checks the roll. Listen carefully, take notes, ask questions, and join in discussions.
- **Ask questions.** Instructors, advisers, tutors, other students—all can help you.
- **Understand the writing situation posed by each assignment.** Knowing your audience, purpose, options for subjects, and other elements of the situation will help you meet the assignment's expectations. (See below on analyzing assignments.)

5.2 UNDERSTANDING THE WRITING PROCESS

People have individual techniques for writing, but all writing involves the five basic steps described in the box below.

The Steps in the Writing Process	
Steps	**What They Involve**
1. **Generating ideas (invention)**	Finding ideas to write about
2. **Developing a thesis statement and organizing ideas**	Stating the main point of an essay in sentence form
	Discovering ways to arrange ideas logically and clearly
3. **Drafting**	Expressing ideas in sentences and paragraphs
4. **Revising**	Rethinking ideas and finding ways to make writing clearer, more complete, and more interesting through additions, deletions, and rearrangements
5. **Editing**	Correcting errors in grammar, spelling, punctuation, and the like

5.3 UNDERSTANDING YOUR WRITING ASSIGNMENT

Any writing assignment you do for a college course has requirements that determine how and what you will write.

Critical Thinking

Analyzing Writing Assignments

Here are questions to ask to make sure you understand each assignment fully:

- **What does your writing assignment ask you to write about?** If the assignment doesn't specify a subject, what subjects might be appropriate?
- **Who will read your writing?** What do your readers already know and think about your subject?
- **What is the purpose of your assignment?** For instance, does it ask you to explain something or to argue a point?
- **How much flexibility do you have for this writing?** What does the stated or implied assignment tell you?
- **How long should your writing be?** If no length is assigned, what seems appropriate for your topic, audience, and purpose?
- **What organization and format does the assignment require?** For instance, are you asked to write a letter, make a proposal, or report information?
- **When is the assignment due?** How will you apportion the work you have to do in the available time?

5.4 FINDING YOUR SUBJECT

A subject for writing has several basic requirements:

- **It should be suitable for the assignment.**
- **It should be neither too general nor too limited** for the length of the paper and the deadline assigned.
- **It should be something you care about.**

When you receive an assignment, study it to guide your choice of subject:

- **What is expected?** Many writing assignments contain words such as *discuss, describe, analyze, report, interpret, explain, define, argue,* and *evaluate.* These words specify the way you are to approach your subject and what your general purpose is. (See p. 204.)

- **For whom are you writing?** Many assignments will specify or imply who your readers are, but sometimes you will have to figure out for yourself who your audience is and what it expects of you. (For more on analyzing your audience, see the following section.)

- **What kind of research is required?** Sometimes an assignment specifies the kinds of sources you are expected to consult, and you can use such information to choose your subject. (If you are unsure whether research is required, check with your instructor.)

- **Does the subject need to be narrowed?** To handle the subject in the length and time required, you'll often need to limit it.

Be sure to narrow the subject so that you can cover it adequately within the space and time assigned. Federal aid to college students could be the subject of a book; the kinds of aid available or why the government should increase aid would be a more appropriate subject for a four-page paper due in a week. Here are guidelines for narrowing broad subjects:

- **Break your broad subject into as many specific subjects as you can think of.** Make a list.

- **For each specific subject that interests you and fits the assignment, roughly sketch out the main ideas.** Consider how many paragraphs or pages of specific facts, examples, and other details you would need to pin those ideas down. This thinking should give you at least a vague idea of how much work you'd have to do and how long the resulting paper might be.

- **Break a too-broad subject down further,** repeating the previous steps.

EXERCISE 5.4.1   Essay-In-Progress: Finding and Narrowing a Subject for Your Essay

As the first step in developing a two- to three-page essay for the instructor and the other students in your writing course, choose a subject and narrow it. Use the guidelines in the previous section to come up with a topic that is suitably interesting, appropriate, and specific.

5.5 CONSIDERING YOUR AUDIENCE

Some of your writing assignments may specify a certain group of readers—for instance, fellow students, the city council, or the editors of a newspaper. Such readers' needs and expectations vary widely.

Many assignments will specify or assume an educated audience or an academic audience. Still other assignments will specify or assume an audience of experts on your subject, readers who look for writing that meets the subject's requirements for claims and evidence, organization, language, format, and other qualities. Considering the needs and expectations of your audience can help you decide what to say and how to say it.

Critical Thinking

Questions to Ask	Factors to Consider
• Who are my readers?	• Age
• How will the audience react to my message?	• Gender and orientation
• What does my audience already know about my topic?	• Occupation
	• Level of education
• What does the audience need to know about the topic?	• Social and economic background
	• Ethnic and cultural background
• What ideas might interest, excite, or offend readers?	• Political point of view
	• Religious and moral beliefs
• What misconceptions might readers have about my topic?	• Hobbies and special interests

Much of your academic writing will have only one reader besides you: the instructor of the course for which you are writing. Instructors fill two main roles as readers:

- **They represent the audience you are addressing.** They are members of the audience, when you address academic readers or subject experts. Or they may imagine themselves as members of your audience—reading, for instance, as if they sat on the city council. In either case, they're interested in how effectively you write for the audience.

- **They serve as coaches,** guiding you toward achieving the goals of the course and, more broadly, toward the academic aims of building and communicating knowledge.

EXERCISE 5.5.1   Considering Audience

Choose one of the following subjects, and, for each audience specified, ask the questions in the box opposite. Decide on four points you would make that would be appropriate for each audience. Then write a paragraph for each audience based on your four points.

1. The effects of cell phone use: for elementary school students and for adults in the workplace.
2. Your opposition to a proposed law requiring adult bicyclists to wear helmets: for cyclists who oppose the law and for people who favor it.
3. Why your neighbors should remove the wrecked truck from their front yard: for your neighbors and for your town zoning board.

EXERCISE 5.5.2   Essay-In-Progress: Analyzing the Audience for Your Essay

Use the questions in the box opposite to determine as much as you can about the probable readers of your essay-in-progress (see Exercise 5.4.1). What does your analysis reveal about the specific information your readers need?

5.6 DEFINING YOUR PURPOSE

Your purpose is what you hope to accomplish through your writing. It is your answer to a potential reader's question, "So what?"

5.6a Understanding the General Purposes for Writing

For most academic writing, your general purpose will be mainly explanatory or mainly argumentative. In explanatory writing, you will aim to clarify your subject so that readers understand it as you do. In argumentative writing, you will aim to gain readers' agreement with a debatable idea about the subject.

These general purposes may overlap in a single piece of writing, but usually one is primary. Your primary purpose will influence your particular slant on your topic, the supporting details you choose, even the words you use.

5.6b Understanding Specific Purposes for Writing

You can think of your purpose very specifically by taking into account your topic and what you may want readers to do or think as a result of reading your writing. Here are examples:

> To explain why the county has been unable to attract new businesses so that readers better understand the local economic slump

> To persuade readers to support the college administration's plan for more required courses

With any writing assignment, try to define your specific purpose as soon as possible. Many instructors identify or suggest the purpose of an assignment by using a keyword, as shown in the following box.

Critical Thinking

Keyword	How to Complete the Assignment
Report	Study, organize, and objectively present information.
Summarize	Concisely state the main points.
Discuss	Examine the main points, competing views, or implications of the subject.
Compare and contrast	Explain similarities and differences between two subjects (see also pp. 245–46).
Define	Explain the meaning of a term or concept, giving distinctive characteristics, limitations, and so on (see also pp. 244–45).
Analyze	Identify the parts of the subject and discuss how they work together (see also p. 245).
Interpret	Infer the subject's meaning or implications.
Evaluate	Judge the quality or significance of the subject, considering the pros and cons.
Argue	Take a position on the subject and support your position with evidence.

EXERCISE 5.6.1   Essay-In-Progress: Defining a Purpose for Your Essay

For your essay-in-progress, use your thinking so far about topic (Exercise 5.4.1, p. 202) and audience (Exercise 5.5.2, p. 203) to define a general purpose and a specific purpose for your writing.

5.7 CHOOSING STRUCTURE AND CONTENT

Many academic writing assignments will suggest how you should organize your paper and even how you should develop your ideas. No matter what type of paper an assignment specifies, there are features that are common across disciplines. Follow these general guidelines for your academic writing.

- **Develop a main point or claim, called a *thesis*.** Everything in the paper should relate clearly to this claim.
- **State the thesis,** usually near the beginning of the paper.
- **Support the thesis with evidence,** drawn usually from research and sometimes from your own experience. The kinds of evidence will depend on the discipline you're writing in and the type of paper you're doing.
- **Interact with sources.** Do not merely summarize sources but evaluate and synthesize them from your own perspective.
- **Acknowledge sources fully,** using the documentation style appropriate to the discipline.
- **Balance your presentation.** Discuss evidence and opposing views fairly, and take a serious and impartial approach.
- **Organize clearly within the framework of the type of writing you're doing.** Develop your ideas as simply and directly as your purpose and content allow. Clearly relate sentences, paragraphs, and sections so that readers always know where they are in the paper's development.

5.8 USING ACADEMIC LANGUAGE

American academic writing uses standard American English. This form of English is also used in business, the professions, government, the media, and other sites of social and economic power. It is "standard" not because it is better than other forms of English, but because it is accepted as the common language, much as the dollar bill is accepted as the common currency.

In writing, standard American English varies a great deal, from the formality of an academic research report to the more relaxed language of this handbook.

Drawn-out phrasing, such as *widespread problem of obesity among Americans.*	**More Formal**

Responsibility for the widespread problem of obesity among Americans depends on the person or group describing the problem and proposing a solution. Some people believe the cause lies with individuals who make poor eating choices for themselves and parents who feed unhealthy foods to their children. Others take strong issue with the food industry, citing food manufacturers and fast-food chains that create and advertise food that is high in sugar, fat, and sodium. Still others place responsibility on American society as a whole for preferring a sedentary lifestyle centered on screen-based activities such as watching television and using computers for video games and social interaction.

More complicated sentence structures, such as *take strong issue with the food industry, citing food manufacturers and fast-food chains that create and advertise . . . .*

More formal vocabulary: *responsibility, children, television.*

Less Formal

More informal phrasing, such as *obesity epidemic.*

Less complicated sentence structures, such as *demonize food manufacturers and fast-food chains for creating and advertising. . . .*

More informal vocabulary: *blame, kids, TV.*

Who or what is to blame for the obesity epidemic depends on who is talking and what they want to do about the problem. Some people blame eaters for making bad choices and parents for feeding their kids unhealthy foods. Others demonize food manufacturers and fast-food chains for creating and advertising sugary, fatty, and sodium-loaded food. Still others point to Americans generally for spending too much time in front of screens watching TV, playing video games, or going on *Facebook.*

As different as they are, both examples illustrate the common features of academic language:

- **It follows the conventions of standard American English for grammar and usage,** presented in guides such as this handbook.

- **It uses a standard vocabulary,** not one that only some groups understand, such as slang, an ethnic or regional dialect, or another language. (See pp. 116–21 for more on specialized vocabularies.)

- **It avoids the informalities of everyday speech, texting, and instant messaging.** These informalities include incomplete sentences, slang, no capital letters, and shortened spellings (*u* for *you*, *b4* for *before*, *thru* for *through*, and so on).

- **It generally uses the third person (*he, she, it, they*).** The first person (*I, we*) is sometimes appropriate to express personal opinions or invite readers to think along (*I discovered that the problem of obesity . . .*), but don't use it with a strongly explanatory purpose. The second person (*you*) is appropriate only in addressing readers directly (as in this handbook), and even then it may seem too friendly or familiar (*You should know that obesity . . .*).

- **It is authoritative and neutral.** In the preceding examples, the writers express themselves confidently, not timidly (as in *Explaining the causes of obesity requires the reader's patience because . . .*). They also refrain from hostility (*The food industry's callous attitude toward health*) and enthusiasm (*The food industry's clever and appealing advertisements*).

At first, the diverse demands of academic writing may leave you searching for an appropriate voice. In an effort to sound fresh and confident, you may write too casually:

Too Casual

Getting the truth about the obesity epidemic in the US requires some heavy lifting. It turns out that everyone else is to blame for the problem—big eaters, reckless corporations, and all those Americans who think it's OK to be a couch potato.

In an effort to sound "academic," you may produce wordy and awkward sentences:

Wordy and Awkward

The responsibility for the problem of widespread obesity among Americans depends on the manner of defining the problem and the proposals for its solution. In some discussions, the cause of obesity is thought to be individuals who are unable or unwilling to make healthy choices in their own diets and parents who similarly make unhealthy choices for their children. [The passive voice in this example—*cause . . . is thought to be* instead of *people blame*—adds to its wordiness and indirection. See pp. 45–47 for more on verb voice.]

CULTURE LANGUAGE Learning to write standard American English in no way requires you to abandon your first language or dialect. Like most multilingual people, you are probably already skilled at switching between languages as the situation demands. You may speak one way with your relatives, for example, and another way with an employer. As you practice academic writing, you'll develop the same flexibility with it.

EXERCISE 5.8.1   Using Academic Language

Revise the following paragraph to make the language more academic while keeping the factual information the same.

If you buy into the stereotype of girls chatting away on their cell phones, you should think again. One of the major wireless companies surveyed 1021 cell phone owners for a period of five years and—surprise!—reported that guys talk on cell phones more than girls do. In fact, guys were way ahead of girls, using an average of 571 minutes a month compared to 424 for girls. That's 35 percent more time on the phone! The survey also asked about conversations on home phones, and while girls still beat the field, the guys are catching up.

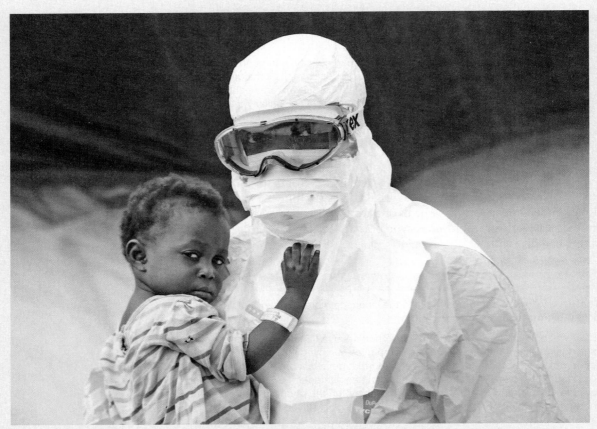

Investigating is a process that can answer questions, solve problems, and address fears that arise from a lack of solid information. The Ebola outbreak in Africa in 2014 made that point clear, as a great deal of investigation was needed to help save lives and stem Ebola's spread, as well as to fight misinformation. Writers, similarly, use investigation techniques to compose valid and effective work.

6

Prewriting

6.1 GENERATING IDEAS

Successful writers . . .

- Keep a writing journal (next page).
- Observe surroundings (p. 211).
- Discover ideas through freewriting (p. 211).
- Develop ideas through brainstorming and clustering (p. 212).
- Use questioning to see the possibilities of a topic (p. 213).

Writers use a variety of techniques to help generate or discover ideas and information about their subjects. **Whichever of the following techniques you use, do your work in writing, not just in your head.** You won't lose ideas, and the very act of writing will lead you to fresh insights.

Taken from *The Successful Writer's Handbook,* Third Edition by Kathleen T. McWhorter and Jane E. Aaron.

CULTURE
LANGUAGE
The process of discovering ideas explained here encourages rapid writing without a lot of thinking beforehand about what or how you will write. If your first language is not standard American English, you may find it helpful initially to do this exploratory writing in your native language or dialect. Then translate the worthwhile material for use in your drafts.

6.1a Keeping a Journal

A **journal** is a record of your ideas—a kind of diary, but one more concerned with ideas than with daily events. When you write in a journal, you can work out your ideas without the pressure of an audience "out there" who will evaluate your logic or organization or correctness. If you write every day, even just for a few minutes, the routine will loosen your writing muscles and improve your confidence.

You can use a journal for varied purposes: perhaps to confide your feelings, think critically about what you read, or pursue ideas from a course. One student, Katy Moreno, used her journal for the last purpose. Her composition instructor had distributed an essay by Thomas L. Friedman about globalization and the job market. The instructor then gave the following assignment, calling for a response to reading:

> In "It's a Flat World, after All," Thomas L. Friedman describes today's global job market, focusing not on manufacturing jobs that have been "outsourced" to overseas workers but on jobs that require a college degree and are no longer immune to outsourcing. Friedman argues that keeping jobs in the United States requires that US students, parents, and educators improve math and science education. As a college student, how do you respond to this analysis of the global market for jobs? What do you think today's college students should be learning?

On first reading the essay, Moreno had found it convincing because Friedman's description of the job market matched her family's experience: her mother had lost her job when it was outsourced to India. After rereading the essay, however, Moreno was not persuaded that more math and science would necessarily improve students' opportunities and preserve their future jobs. She compared Friedman's advice with details she recalled from her mother's experience, and she began to develop a response by writing in her journal:

> Friedman is certainly right that more jobs than we realize are going overseas—that's what happened to Mom's job and we were shocked! But he gives only one way for students like me to compete—take more math and science. At first I thought he's totally right. But then I thought that what he said didn't really explain what happened to Mom—she had lots of math + science + tons of experience, but it was her salary, not better training, that caused her job to be outsourced. An overseas worker would do her job for less money. So she lost her job because of money + because she wasn't a manager. Caught in the middle. I want to major in computer science, but I don't think it's smart to try for the kind of job Mom had—at least not as long as it's so much cheaper for companies to hire workers overseas.

(Further examples of Katy Moreno's writing appear in the following chapters.)

Your *Facebook* page is also a kind of journal in the sense that you are writing both to share and to explore ideas and responses. If you have a *Facebook* page, challenge yourself to write longer posts. And always remember that you can change your privacy settings on social-networking sites to restrict access to your writings. Never post *anything* to a social-networking site that you wouldn't want your professor, your coach, your children, or your employer to see.

CULTURE LANGUAGE   A journal can be especially helpful if your first language is not standard American English. You can practice writing to improve your fluency, try out sentence patterns, and experiment with vocabulary words.

Using Readings as Sources of Journal Topics

Everything you read can be a stimulus for ideas and an excellent source of journal writing topics. Whether you read course materials, newspapers, magazines, novels, blogs, or *Facebook* entries, you might

- React to an argument.
- Recollect a similar event that happened to you.
- Question a viewpoint, trend, or policy.
- Evaluate a writer's thesis.
- Describe a writer's technique.
- Compare two positions on an issue.

6.1b Observing Your Surroundings

Sometimes you can find a good subject or good ideas by looking around you with all your senses alert. To get the most from observation, you should have a notepad and pen, a handheld computer, or a camera phone handy. Take notes, draw sketches, or take photographs. Back at your desk, study the results for oddities or patterns that you'd like to explore further.

6.1c Freewriting

Freewriting is a process of discovering ideas by writing without stopping for a certain amount of time (say, ten minutes) or to a certain length (say, one page). Here is how it works:

- **Write about anything that comes to mind.** What you write about is not important; the act of writing is. If you have a subject, start by focusing on it and see where your writing takes you.
- **Keep writing; don't stop.** Repeat the same words or ideas until new ones come. Don't worry if your ideas seem dumb or unimportant.
- **Don't go back to reread.** Rereading will only distract you.

- **Don't stop to fix errors.** Grammar, spelling, and punctuation are not important at this stage.

- **If you write on a computer, darken the screen.** The computer will record your writing, but you won't be able to see it and you won't be tempted to tinker with it.

An example of freewriting can be found in Katy Moreno's journal entry on p. 210.

6.1d Brainstorming

Brainstorming is a way of developing ideas by making a list of everything you can think of about a subject. There is no need to write in sentences; instead, list words and phrases. Don't try to organize your ideas; just list them as you think of them. Give yourself a time limit. You'll find that ideas come faster that way.

Here is an example of brainstorming by a student, Johanna Abrams, on what a summer job can teach:

> summer work teaches—
> > how to avoid the sun in summer
> > seriously: discipline, budgeting money, value of money
> which job? Burger King cashier? baby-sitter? mail-room clerk?
> mail room: how to sort mail into boxes: this is learning??
> Mrs. King! the mail-room queen as learning experience
> the shock of getting fired: what to tell parents, friends?
> Mrs. K was so rigid—dumb procedures
> initials instead of names on the mail boxes—confusion!
> Mrs. K's anger, resentment: the disadvantages of being smarter than
> > your boss
> the odd thing about working in an office: its own rules for how to act
> what Mr. D said about the pecking order—big chick (Mrs. K) pecks on
> > little chick (me)
> a job can beat you down—make you be mean to other people

6.1e Clustering

Clustering, also called **branching**, is a visual way of discovering ideas. Here's how it works:

- **Write and circle your subject in the middle of a whole sheet of paper.** Think of this as the trunk of a tree.

- **Think of ideas about your subject, and write them near the circle.**

- **Connect each idea to the circle with a line.** Think of these connected ideas as the primary branches of the tree.

- **Create secondary branches.** Write ideas that further explain any of the primary ideas nearby, and connect them with lines.

The example below shows how a student used clustering for ten minutes to explore the topic of divorce.

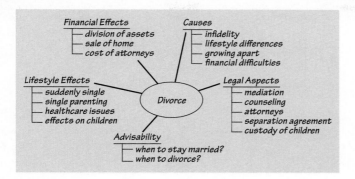

6.1f Questioning

Asking yourself a set of questions about your subject—and writing out the answers—can help you look at a topic objectively and see fresh possibilities in it. The questions that follow can also be useful in probing an essay subject, especially when you are telling a story or examining causes and effects.

- **Who was involved?**
- **What happened?**
- **What were the results?**
- **When did it happen?**
- **Where did it happen?**
- **Why did it happen?**
- **How did it happen?**

EXERCISE 6.1.1   Essay-in-Progress: Using Freewriting, Brainstorming, Clustering, or Questioning

If you haven't tried any of them before, experiment with freewriting, brainstorming, clustering, or questioning. Continue with the subject you selected in Exercise 5.1.1 (p. 202), or begin with a new subject. Write or draw for at least ten minutes without stopping to reread and edit. When you finish your experiment, examine what you have written for ideas and relationships that could help you develop the subject. What do you think of the technique you tried? Did you have any difficulties with it? Did it help you loosen up and generate ideas?

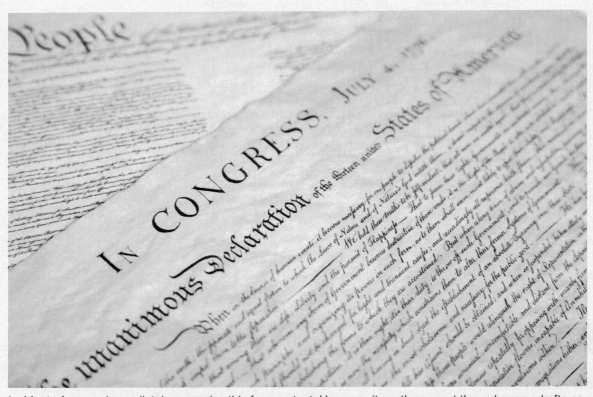

Most of us can immediately recognize this famous text. However, its authors went through many drafts as they debated how to "declare" their independence as rebels against a world power.

7

Drafting

7.1 DRAFTING

Successful writers . . .
- Write effective drafts (next page).
- Learn from a sample first draft (p. 217).

Writing a draft is a way of trying out ideas to see if and how they work. You may express ideas in several different ways and, after several drafts, settle on what works best.

Taken from *The Successful Writer's Handbook*, Third Edition by Kathleen T. McWhorter and Jane E. Aaron.

Managing Your Drafting Time

Use the following suggestions to plan your time for writing:

- **Begin when you have a fresh, clear mind.** Don't start a draft when you feel tired, pressured, or rushed.
- **Set aside enough time to get a substantial start.** For a brief essay, writing a first draft is likely to take an hour or two.
- **Before you stop writing, make a note of what you expect to do next.** Then you can easily pick up where you left off.

7.1a Starting Your Draft

The only correct drafting method is one that works for you. The following suggestions can help you write effective first drafts:

- **Review your outline and thesis statement.** They will help you get started.

- **Write in complete sentences, but don't worry about your style, grammar, spelling, punctuation, and the like.** These are very important matters, but save them for revision.

- **Concentrate on explaining your topic sentence or thesis statement, using ideas from your outline.** Focus first on those ideas that you think express your main point particularly well.

- **Think of a first draft as a chance to experiment with different ideas and ways of organizing them.** While you are writing, if you think of a better way to organize or express your ideas, or if you think of new ideas, make changes. Be flexible. Do not worry about getting your exact wording at this point.

- **As your draft develops, feel free to change your focus or even your subject, unless it has been assigned.** If your draft is not working out, don't hesitate to start over completely. Go back to generating ideas. Writers often make false starts before they produce a draft that satisfies them.

- **Keep going.** Skip over sticky spots; leave a blank if you can't find the right word; put alternative ideas or phrasings in brackets so that you can consider them later without bogging down. If an idea pops out of nowhere but doesn't seem to fit in, jot it down on a separate sheet or write it into the draft and bracket or boldface it for later attention.

- **Don't expect immediate success.** When you finish your first draft, you should feel that you have the *beginnings* of a paper you will be happy with. Now ask yourself if you have a sense of the direction your paper will take. Do you have a main idea? Do you have supporting details? Is the organization logical? If you can answer yes to these questions, you have something on paper to work with and revise.

7.1b Examining a Sample First Draft

Katy Moreno's first-draft response to Thomas L. Friedman's "It's a Flat World, after All" appears on these pages. (The first two paragraphs include the page numbers in Friedman's article that Moreno summarized material from.) As part of her assignment, Moreno showed the draft to four classmates whose suggestions for revision appear in the margin. They used the Comment function of *Microsoft Word*, which allows users to add comments without inserting words into the document's text. (Notice that the classmates ignore errors in grammar and punctuation, concentrating instead on larger issues such as thesis, clarity of ideas, and unity.)

Title?

In "It's a Flat World, after All," Thomas L. Friedman argues that, most US students are not preparing themselves as well as they should to compete in today's economy. Not like students in India, China, and other countries are (34-37). The outsourcing of my mother's job proves that Thomas L. Friedman's advice to improve students' technical training is too narrow.

> **Comment [Jared]:** Your mother's job being outsourced is interesting, but your introduction seems rushed.

> **Comment [Rabia]:** The end of your thesis statement is a little unclear—too narrow for what?

Friedman describes a "flat" world where recent technology like the Internet and wireless communication make it possible for college graduates all over the globe, in particular in India and China, to get jobs that once were gotten by graduates of US colleges and universities (37). He argues that US students need more math and science in order to compete (37).

> **Comment [Erin]:** Can you include the reasons Friedman gives for overseas students' success?

I came to college with first-hand knowledge of globalization and outsourcing. My mother, who worked for sixteen years in the field of information technology (IT), was laid off six months ago when the company she worked for decided to outsource much of its IT work to a company based in India. My mother majored in computer science, had sixteen years of experience, and her bosses always gave her good reviews. She never expected to be laid off and was surprised when she was. She wasn't laid off because of her background and performance. In fact, my mother had a very strong background in math and science and years of training and job experience. The reason was because her salary and benefits cost the company more than outsourcing her job did. Which hurt my family financially, as you can imagine.

> **Comment [Nathaniel]:** Tighten this paragraph to avoid repetition? Also, how does your mother's experience relate to Friedman and your thesis?

A number of well-paid people in the IT department where my mother worked, namely IT managers, were not laid off. As my mother explained at the time, they kept their jobs because they were better at planning and they communicated better, they were better writers and speakers than my mother.

> **Comment [Erin]:** What were the managers better at planning for?

Like my mother, I am more comfortable in front of a computer than I am in front of a group of people. I planned to major in computer science. Since my mother lost her job, though, I have decided to take courses in English and history too, where the classes will require me to do different kinds of work. When I enter the job market, my well-rounded education will make me a more attractive job candidate, and, will help me to be a versatile, productive employee.

> **Comment [Nathaniel]:** Can you be more specific about the kinds of work you'll need to do?

> **Comment [Rabia]:** Can you work this point into your thesis?

We know from our history that Americans have been innovative, hard-working people. We students have educational opportunities to compete in the global economy, but we must use our time in college wisely. As Thomas L. Friedman says, my classmates and I need to be ready for a rapidly changing future. We will have to work hard each day, which means being prepared for class, getting the best grades we can, and making the most of each class. Our futures depend on the decisions we make today.

> **Comment [Jared]:** Conclusion seems to go off in a new direction. Friedman mentions hard work, but it hasn't been your focus before.

> **Comment [Rabia]:** Don't forget your works cited.

Remembering Rwanda:
USING GENOCIDE FILMS MORE EFFECTIVELY IN THE CLASSROOM

About this Site: This site is designed for educators and students who want to go beyond the limited understanding of the Rwanda genocide offered by films to better understand the causes and effects of this horrific event. Read more

The Case for More Effective Methods: Read Carrie Gingrich's essay about the need for new and more effective methods for teaching about the Rwanda genocide. Full Essay

About the Author: Carrie Gingrich is a student majoring in English at York College of Pennsylvania. Full Bio

Resources for Teachers: Want to learn effective methods for using film to teach history and spur critical thinking? Links

Resources for Students: Go beyond the story told in the films to learn more about the Rwanda genocide. Links

Selected Bibliography: Many historians, survivors, and political figures have analyzed the events leading to the Rwanda genocide. This selected bibliography can help you find credible articles and books on this topic. Bibliography

Blog: These blogs can help connect you with other teachers and students interested in this topic. Teacher Blog

Beginning in April, 1994, and continuing for 100 days, more than 800,000 Rwandans were slaughtered, an average of 10,000 people per day.

" **Will the world remember? Will we say never again?**

Educators and their students have a responsibility to help correct misconceived understandings.

Links to Film Clips about the Rwanda Genocide

One of the most effective and powerful ways students learn about the past is through film. Films about this genocide were meant to portray and preserve what happened; the stated goal of many of these filmmakers was to help viewers learn from its cruel mistakes. **In the end, though, films like these squeeze into one drop the ocean of what happened.** They focus on one story. In doing so, they lose the fact that the genocide was more than just one story, more than one drop. This site can help teachers and students learn the full story.

This site provides resources for teachers to go beyond the emotional impact of film and help students think more deeply about the past—and so help to create a less violent future.
Site Created and Maintained by Carrie Gingrich. She is interested in working with others who share this goal. **Contact her**

Research can be used to produce many different genres of writing that address diverse audiences. Carrie Gingrich, who researched the causes and media presentation of the Rwanda genocide, created this web page and wrote a research paper. What audiences does each genre allow her to reach?

8

Organization

Chapter essential . . .
- Organize your ideas (next page).

Finding your main idea gives you focus and direction. Organizing your raw material helps you clear away unneeded ideas, spot possible gaps, and energize your subject.

Taken from *The Little, Brown Compact Handbook*, Ninth Edition by Jane E. Aaron.

8.1 ORGANIZING YOUR IDEAS

Most essays share a basic pattern of introduction (states the subject), body (develops the subject), and conclusion (pulls the essay's ideas together). Within the body, every paragraph develops some aspect of the essay's main idea, or thesis. See pp. 260–61 for Katy Moreno's essay, with annotations highlighting the body's pattern of support for the thesis statement.

(CULTURE LANGUAGE) If you are not used to reading and writing American academic prose, its pattern of introduction-body-conclusion and the organization schemes discussed on the next page may seem unfamiliar. For instance, instead of introductions that focus quickly on the topic and thesis, you may be used to openings that establish personal connections with readers. And instead of body paragraphs that stress general points and support those points with evidence, you may be used to general statements without support (because writers can assume that readers will supply the evidence themselves) or to evidence without explanation (because writers can assume that readers will infer the general points). When writing American academic prose, you need to take into account readers' expectations for directness and for the statement and support of general points.

8.1a The General and the Specific

To organize material for an essay, you need to distinguish general and specific ideas and see the relations between ideas. General and specific refer to the number of instances or objects included in a group signified by a word. The following "ladder" illustrates a general-to-specific hierarchy:

Most general

life form
plant
rose
Uncle Dan's prize-winning American Beauty rose

Most specific

As you arrange your material, pick out the general ideas and then the specific points that support them. Set aside points that seem irrelevant to your key ideas. On a computer you can easily experiment with various arrangements of general ideas and supporting information: save your master list of ideas to a new file, and then move material around.

8.1b Schemes for Organizing Essays

An essay's body paragraphs may be arranged in many ways that are familiar to readers. The choice depends on your subject, purpose, and audience.

- **Spatial:** In describing a person, place, or thing, move through space systematically from a starting point to other features—for instance, top to bottom, near to far, left to right.
- **Chronological:** In recounting a sequence of events, arrange the events as they actually occurred in time, first to last.
- **General to specific:** Begin with an overall discussion of the subject; then fill in details, facts, examples, and other support.
- **Specific to general:** First provide the support; then draw a conclusion from it.
- **Climactic:** Arrange ideas in order of increasing importance to your thesis or increasing interest to the reader.
- **Problem-solution:** First outline a problem that needs solving; then propose a solution.

8.1c Outlines

It's not essential to craft a detailed outline before you begin drafting an essay; in fact, too detailed a plan could prevent you from discovering ideas while you draft. Still, even a rough scheme can show you patterns of general and specific, suggest proportions, and highlight gaps or overlaps in coverage.

There are several kinds of outlines, some more flexible than others.

Scratch or Informal Outline

A scratch or informal outline includes key general points in the order they will be covered. It may also list evidence for the points.

Here is Katy Moreno's scratch outline for her essay on the global job market:

Thesis Statement

My mother's experience of having her job outsourced taught a lesson that
Friedman overlooks: technical training by itself can be too narrow to produce
the communicators and problem solvers needed by contemporary businesses.

Scratch Outline

Mom's outsourcing experience
    Excellent tech skills
    Salary too high compared to overseas tech workers
    Lack of planning + communication skills, unlike managers who kept jobs
Well-rounded education to protect vs. outsourcing
    Tech training, as Friedman says
    Also, communication, problem solving, other management skills

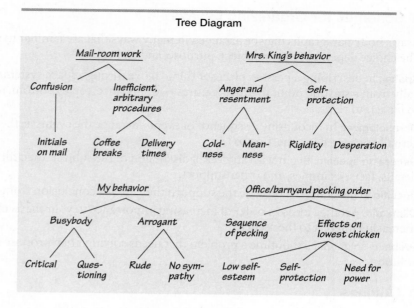

Tree Diagram

Tree Diagram

In a tree diagram, ideas and details branch out in increasing specificity. Unlike more linear outlines, this diagram can be supplemented and extended indefinitely, so it is easy to alter. From her brainstorming about a summer job, Johanna Abrams created the tree diagram on the facing page to develop this thesis statement:

Thesis Statement
Two months working in a large agency taught me that an office's pecking order should be respected.

Formal Outline

A formal outline not only lays out main ideas and their support but also shows the relative importance of all the essay's elements. On the basis of her scratch outline above, Katy Moreno prepared the formal outline on the next page for her essay on the global job market.

Thesis Statement
My mother's experience of having her job outsourced taught a lesson that Friedman overlooks: technical training by itself can be too narrow to produce the communicators and problem solvers needed by contemporary businesses.

Formal Outline

I. Summary of Friedman's article
   A. Reasons for outsourcing
      1. Improved technology and access
      2. Well-educated workers
      3. Productive workers
      4. Lower wages
   B. Need for improved technical training in US
II. Experience of my mother
   A. Outsourcing of job
      1. Mother's education, experience, performance
      2. Employer's cost savings
   B. Retention of managers' jobs
      1. Planning skills
      2. Communication skills
III. Conclusions about ideal education
   A. Needs of US businesses
      1. Technical skills
      2. Management skills
         a. Communication
         b. Problem solving
         c. Versatility
   B. Consideration of personal goals
      1. Technical training
      2. English and history courses for management skills

This example illustrates several principles of outlining that can ensure completeness, balance, and clear relationships:

- **All parts are systematically indented and labeled:** Roman numerals (I, II) for primary divisions; indented capital letters (A, B) for secondary divisions; further indented Arabic numerals (1, 2) for supporting examples; and still further indented small letters (a, b) for details.

- **The outline divides the material into several groups.** A long list of points at the same level should be broken up into groups.

- **Topics of equal generality appear in parallel headings,** with the same indention and numbering or lettering.

- **All subdivided headings break into at least two parts.** A topic cannot logically be divided into only one part.

- **All headings are expressed in parallel grammatical form**—in the example, as phrases using a noun plus modifiers. This is a topic outline; in a sentence outline all headings are expressed as full sentences.

8.1d Unity and Coherence

Two qualities of effective writing relate to organization: unity and coherence. When you perceive that someone's writing "flows well," you are probably appreciating these qualities.

To check an outline or draft for **unity**, ask these questions:

- **Is each section relevant to the main idea (thesis) of the essay?**
- **Within main sections, does each example or detail support the principal idea of that section?**

To check your outline or draft for **coherence,** ask the following questions:

- **Do the ideas follow a clear sequence?**
- **Are the parts of the essay logically connected?**
- **Are the connections clear and smooth?**

The following informative essay illustrates some ways of achieving unity and coherence (highlighted in the annotations).

Who Benefits from the Money in College Football?

Introduction establishing subject of essay

Anyone who follows Division 1-A college football cannot fail to notice the money that pours into every aspect of the sport—the lavish stadiums, corporate sponsorships, televised games, and long post-season playoff tournament series. The money may seem to flow to everyone, but in reality it doesn't.

Thesis statement

Although college football is a multimillion-dollar industry for the schools, conferences, and television networks, the benefits do not extend to the players.

Paragraph idea, linked to thesis statement

Colleges and universities are major players in the for-profit football industry.

Paragraph developed with evidence supporting its idea

A vibrant football program attracts not only skilled coaches and talented players but also wealthy, sports-minded donors who give money for state-of-the art stadiums and facilities. These great facilities in turn attract fans, some of whom are willing to pay high ticket prices to watch games in luxurious sky boxes and thus generate more profits for the schools' athletic departments.

Paragraph idea, linked to thesis statement

The athletic conferences to which the schools belong—such as the Big Ten, the Atlantic Coast Conference, and the Pac-12—reap financial rewards from college football.

Paragraph developed with evidence supporting its idea

Each conference maintains a Web site to post schedules and scores, sell tickets and merchandise, and promote interest in its teams. However, the proceeds from ticket and merchandise sales surely pale in comparison to the money generated by the annual College Football Playoff—the three-week-long post-season football extravaganza. Each game is not only televised but also carries the name of a corporate sponsor that pays for the privilege of having its name attached to a bowl game.

Paragraph idea, linked to thesis statement

Like the schools and athletic conferences, the television networks profit from football.

Paragraph developed with evidence supporting its idea

Networks sell advertising slots to the highest bidders for every televised game during the regular season and the College Football Playoff, and they work to sustain fans' interest in football by cultivating viewers on the Web. For instance, one network generates interest in up-and-coming high school players through *Scout.com*, a Web site that posts profiles of boys being recruited by colleges and universities and that is supported, at least in part, through advertising and paid subscriptions.

Amid these money-making players are the actual football players, the young men who are bound by NCAA rules to play as amateurs and to receive no direct compensation for their hours of practice and field time. They may receive scholarships that cover tuition, room and board, uniforms, medical care, and travel. Yet these payments are a small fraction of the millions of dollars spent on and earned from football.

Many critics have pointed out the disparity between players' rewards and the industry's profits. Recent efforts to unionize the players and file lawsuits on their behalf have caused schools, conferences, and the NCAA to make some concessions in scholarship packages and rules. However, these changes do not fundamentally alter a system in which the big benefits go to everyone but the players.

—Terrence MacDonald (student)

> Transition and new paragraph idea, linked to thesis statement

> Paragraph developed with evidence supporting its idea

> Conclusion echoing thesis statement and summarizing

EXERCISE 8.1.1   Organizing Ideas

The following list of ideas was extracted by a student from freewriting he did for a brief paper on soccer in the United States. Using his thesis statement as a guide, pick out the general ideas and arrange the relevant specific points under them. In some cases you may have to infer general ideas to cover specific points in the list.

Thesis Statement

Although its growth in the United States has been slow and halting, professional soccer may finally be poised to become a major American sport.

List of Ideas

In countries of South and Latin America, soccer is the favorite sport.

In the United States the success of a sport depends largely on its ability to attract huge TV audiences.

Soccer was not often presented on US television.

In 2010 and 2014 the World Cup final was broadcast on ABC and on Spanish-language Univision.

In the past, professional soccer could not get a foothold in the United States because of poor TV coverage and lack of financial backing.

The growing Hispanic population in the United States could help soccer grow as well.

Investors have poured hundreds of millions of dollars into the top US professional league.

Potential fans did not have a chance to see soccer games.

Failures of early start-up leagues made potential backers wary of new ventures.

Recently, the outlook for professional soccer has changed dramatically.

The US television audience for the 2014 US–Ghana match was larger than the average US television audience for baseball's World Series.

The second dimension that Friedman misses is that a number of well-paid people in my mother's IT department, namely IT managers, were not laid off. As my mother explained at the time, they kept their jobs because they were experienced at figuring out the company's IT needs, planning for changes, researching and proposing solutions, and communicating in writing and speech—skills that her more narrow training and experience had missed. Friedman misses these skills by focusing only on technical training. Without the ability to solve problems creatively and to communicate, people with technical expertise alone may not have enough to save their jobs, as my mother learned.

— Topic sentence

— Examples to support the main idea

— Final comment

Main idea
The ancient Egyptians were masters of preserving dead people's bodies by making mummies of them. Basically, mummification consisted of removing the internal organs, applying natural preservatives inside and out, and then wrapping the body in layers of bandages. And the process was remarkably effective. Indeed, mummies several thousand years old have been discovered nearly intact. Their skin, hair, teeth, finger- and toenails, and facial features are still evident. Their diseases in life, such as smallpox, arthritis, and nutritional deficiencies, are still diagnosable. Even their fatal afflictions are still apparent: a middle-aged king died from a blow on the head; a child king died from polio.

Explanation

Explanation

Specific examples

Jill's story is typical for "recruits" to religious cults. She was very lonely in college and appreciated the attention of the nice young men and women who lived in a house near campus. They persuaded her to share their meals and then to move in with them. Between intense bombardments of "love," they deprived her of sleep and sometimes threatened to throw her out. Jill became increasingly confused and dependent, losing touch with any reality besides the one in the group. She dropped out of school and refused to see or communicate with her family. Before long she, too, was preying on lonely college students.

— Topic sentence

Important events in chronological order

9

Paragraph Development

9.1 PARAGRAPHS

Successful writers . . .
- Write complete paragraphs (next page).
- Maintain paragraph unity (p. 229).
- Achieve paragraph coherence (p. 233).
- Use patterns to develop paragraphs (p. 239).
- Write effective introductory and concluding paragraphs (p. 244).

A **paragraph** is a group of related sentences set off by a beginning indention or, sometimes, by extra space. Paragraphs organize your ideas and show the development of your thesis.

Taken from *The Successful Writer's Handbook,* Third Edition by Kathleen T. McWhorter and Jane E. Aaron.

This chapter discusses four qualities of an effective body paragraph: completeness, unity, coherence, and development. In addition, the chapter discusses two special kinds of paragraphs: introductions and conclusions.

CULTURE LANGUAGE If your native language is not English and you have difficulty with paragraphs, don't worry about paragraphing during drafting. Instead, during a separate step of revision, divide your text into parts that develop your main points. Mark those parts with indentions.

Critical Thinking

Checklist: Revising Paragraphs

☐ **Is the paragraph complete?** Does it state a main idea, provide supporting details, and connect the main idea and supporting details with transitions and possibly a concluding sentence? (See opposite.)

☐ **Is the paragraph unified?** Does it focus on one main idea that is either stated in a topic sentence or otherwise apparent? (See opposite.)

☐ **Is the paragraph coherent?** Do the sentences follow a clear sequence? Are the sentences linked as needed by parallelism, repetition or restatement, consistency, and transitional words and phrases? (See p. 233.)

☐ **Is the paragraph developed?** Is the general idea of the paragraph well supported with specific evidence such as details, facts, examples, and reasons? (See p. 239.)

9.1a Writing Complete Paragraphs

Like essays, paragraphs need certain parts to be complete. The parts of paragraphs are similar to the parts of essays, as shown in the diagram below. Paragraphs focus on a main idea that is often, but not always, stated at the beginning of the paragraph in a topic sentence (see below). Paragraphs contain supporting information that explains the main idea and that is linked to the main idea through transitional words and phrases (see pp. 236–37). And paragraphs often end with a concluding sentence that connects the supporting information back to the main idea.

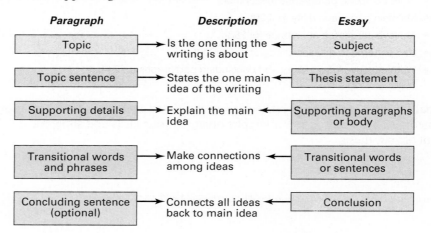

Paragraph	Description	Essay
Topic	Is the one thing the writing is about	Subject
Topic sentence	States the one main idea of the writing	Thesis statement
Supporting details	Explain the main idea	Supporting paragraphs or body
Transitional words and phrases	Make connections among ideas	Transitional words or sentences
Concluding sentence (optional)	Connects all ideas back to main idea	Conclusion

9.1b Maintaining Paragraph Unity

1 Stating the Main Idea

An effective paragraph develops one main idea—in other words, it is **unified.** That main idea is often expressed in a **topic sentence** at the beginning of the paragraph. The rest of the sentences in the paragraph explain or support the topic sentence.

> The second dimension that Friedman misses is that a number of well-paid people in my mother's IT department, namely IT managers, were not laid off. As my mother explained at the time, they kept their jobs because they were experienced at figuring out the company's IT needs, planning for changes, researching and proposing solutions, and communicating in writing and speech—skills that her more narrow training and experience had missed. Friedman misses these skills by focusing only on technical training. Without the ability to solve problems creatively and to communicate, people with technical expertise alone may not have enough to save their jobs, as my mother learned.
> —Katy Moreno, student

Topic sentence

Examples to support the main idea

Final comment

Moreno's paragraph works because it states the main idea in the first sentence and supports it in the remainder of the paragraph.

What if Moreno had written this paragraph instead?

> The second dimension that Friedman misses is that a number of well-paid people in my mother's IT department, namely IT managers, were not laid off. As my mother explained at the time, they kept their jobs because they were experienced at figuring out the company's IT needs, planning for changes, researching and proposing solutions, and communicating in writing. Like my mother, these managers had families to support, so they were lucky to keep their jobs. Our family still struggles with the financial and emotional effects of my mother's unemployment.

Topic sentence

Examples supporting the main idea

Digression

The digression wanders from the topic of why some managers kept their jobs, so the paragraph fails to deliver on the commitment of its topic sentence.

2 Placing the Topic Sentence

The topic sentence of a paragraph may be placed anywhere in the paragraph, depending on how you want to direct readers' attention and how complex your main idea is.

In the most common arrangements, the topic sentence comes at the beginning of the paragraph, comes at the end, or is not stated at all but is nonetheless apparent.

Topic Sentence at the Beginning

When your topic sentence appears first in a paragraph, it can help you select the details that follow. For readers, the topic-first model establishes a framework in which all the supporting details can be understood. Reading Moreno's paragraph on p. 229, we easily relate each detail or example back to the point made in the first sentence. Here is another example:

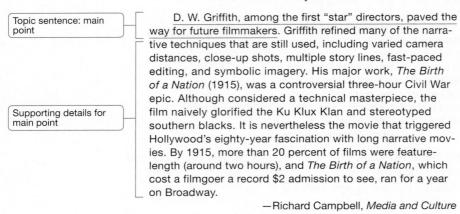

D. W. Griffith, among the first "star" directors, paved the way for future filmmakers. Griffith refined many of the narrative techniques that are still used, including varied camera distances, close-up shots, multiple story lines, fast-paced editing, and symbolic imagery. His major work, *The Birth of a Nation* (1915), was a controversial three-hour Civil War epic. Although considered a technical masterpiece, the film naively glorified the Ku Klux Klan and stereotyped southern blacks. It is nevertheless the movie that triggered Hollywood's eighty-year fascination with long narrative movies. By 1915, more than 20 percent of films were feature-length (around two hours), and *The Birth of a Nation*, which cost a filmgoer a record $2 admission to see, ran for a year on Broadway.

—Richard Campbell, *Media and Culture*

Topic Sentence at the End

In some paragraphs the main idea may be stated at the end, after supporting sentences have made a case for the general statement. Because this model leads the reader to a conclusion by presenting all the evidence first, it can prove effective in argument.

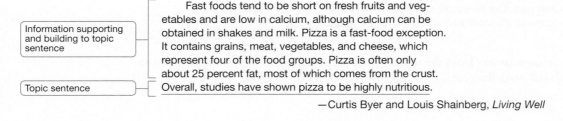

Fast foods tend to be short on fresh fruits and vegetables and are low in calcium, although calcium can be obtained in shakes and milk. Pizza is a fast-food exception. It contains grains, meat, vegetables, and cheese, which represent four of the food groups. Pizza is often only about 25 percent fat, most of which comes from the crust. Overall, studies have shown pizza to be highly nutritious.

—Curtis Byer and Louis Shainberg, *Living Well*

Expressing the main idea at the end of the paragraph does not eliminate the need to unify the paragraph. The idea in the topic sentence must still govern the selection of all the preceding details.

Main Idea Not Stated

Occasionally, a paragraph's main idea will be so obvious that it need not be stated at all, even in the previous paragraph.

> Workers in the *primary sector* of an economy extract resources directly from Earth. Most workers in this sector are usually in agriculture, but the sector also includes fishing, forestry, and mining. Workers in the *secondary sector* transform raw materials produced by the primary sector into manufactured goods. Construction is included in this sector. All other jobs in an economy are within the *tertiary sector*, sometimes called the *service sector*. The tertiary sector includes a great range of occupations, from a store clerk to a surgeon, from a movie ticket seller to a nuclear physicist, from a dancer to a political leader.
>
> Details adding up to the unstated idea that economic activities are divided into three sectors
>
> —Edward Bergman and William Renwick, *Introduction to Geography*

A paragraph without a topic sentence should still have a main idea, and its details should develop that idea.

3 Using Topic Sentences to Guide Your Reading

Identifying the topic sentence enables you to organize a paragraph's ideas and details and to judge their relative importance. Organized sets of ideas are easier to recall than unrelated facts. Identifying topic sentences is also useful when highlighting textbooks, outlining, writing summaries, and paraphrasing.

EXERCISE 9.1.1 **Revising a Paragraph for Unity**

The following paragraph contains ideas or details that do not support its main idea. Identify the topic sentence and delete the unrelated material.

In the southern part of the state, some people still live much as they did a century ago. They use coal- or wood-burning stoves for heating and cooking. Their homes do not have electricity or indoor bathrooms or running water. The towns they live in don't receive adequate funding from the state and federal governments, so the schools are poor and in bad shape. Beside most homes there is a garden where fresh vegetables are gathered for canning. Small pastures nearby support livestock, including cattle, pigs, horses, and chickens. Most of the people have cars or trucks, but the vehicles are old and beat-up from traveling on unpaved roads.

EXERCISE 9.1.2 **Essay-in-Progress: Evaluating Paragraph Unity**

Choose an essay you are working on in class, and examine the body paragraphs for unity. Do they have clear topic sentences? If not, are the paragraphs' main ideas still clear? Are the paragraphs unified around their main ideas? Should any details be deleted for unity? Should other, more relevant details be added in their stead?

> ### EXERCISE 9.1.3   Writing a Unified Paragraph
>
> Each of the following topic sentences states the main idea of a paragraph. Develop each topic sentence into a unified paragraph by using the relevant information in the supporting statements. Delete each statement that does not relate directly to the topic, and then rewrite and combine sentences as appropriate. Place the topic sentence in the position that seems most effective to you.
>
> 1. **Topic sentence:** The development of speech in infants follows a definite sequence or pattern of development.
>
>   **Supporting information:**
>   By the time an infant is six months old, he or she can make twelve different speech sounds.
>   Mindy, who is only three months old, is unable to produce any recognizable syllables.
>   During the first year, the number of vowel sounds a child can produce is greater than the number of consonant sounds he or she can make.
>   Between six and twelve months, the number of consonant sounds a child can produce continues to increase.
>   Parents often reward the first recognizable word a child produces by smiling or speaking to the child.
>
> 2. **Topic sentence:** An oligopoly is a market structure in which only a few companies sell a certain product.
>
>   **Supporting information:**
>   The automobile industry is a good example of an oligopoly, even though it gives the appearance of being highly competitive.
>   The breakfast cereal, soap, and cigarette industries, although basic to our economy, operate as oligopolies.
>   Monopolies refer to market structures in which only one industry produces a particular product.
>   Monopolies are able to exert more control and price fixing than oligopolies.
>   In the oil industry there are only a few producers, so each producer has a fairly large share of the sales.

> ### EXERCISE 9.1.4   Turning Topic Sentences into Unified Paragraphs
>
> Develop three of the following topic sentences into detailed and unified paragraphs.
>
> 1. Men and women are different in at least one important respect.
> 2. The best Web search engine is [*name*].
> 3. Fans of _____ music [*country, classical, rock, rap, jazz, or another kind*] come in [*number*] varieties.
> 4. Professional sports have [*or* have not] been helped by extending the regular season with championship playoffs.
> 5. The ideal job is _____.

9.1c Achieving Paragraph Coherence

When a paragraph is **coherent**, readers can see how it holds together: the sentences seem to flow logically and smoothly into one another. Exactly the opposite happens with this paragraph:

> The ancient Egyptians were masters of preserving dead people's bodies by making mummies of them. Mummies several thousand years old have been discovered nearly intact. The skin, hair, teeth, finger- and toenails, and facial features of the mummies were evident. One can diagnose the diseases they suffered in life, such as smallpox, arthritis, and nutritional deficiencies. The process was remarkably effective. Sometimes apparent were the fatal afflictions of the dead people: a middle-aged king died from a blow on the head, and polio killed a child king. Mummification consisted of removing the internal organs, applying natural preservatives inside and out, and then wrapping the body in layers of bandages.

The paragraph is hard to read. The sentences lurch rather than glide from point to point.

The paragraph as it was actually written appears below. This original version is much clearer because the writer arranged information differently and built links into his sentences so that they would flow smoothly:

- After stating the main idea in a topic sentence, the writer moves to two more specific explanations and illustrates the second with four sentences of examples.
- (Circled words) repeat or restate key terms or concepts.
- [Boxed words] link sentences and clarify relationships.
- Underlined phrases are in parallel grammatical form to reflect their parallel content.

> Main idea
> The ancient Egyptians were masters of preserving dead people's
> Explanation
> bodies by (making (mummies) of them. [Basically,] (mummification) con-
> sisted of removing the internal organs, applying natural preservatives inside
> Explanation
> and out, and then wrapping the body in layers of bandages. [And] (the process)
> was remarkably effective. [Indeed,] (mummies) several thousand years old
> Specific examples
> have been discovered nearly intact. (Their) skin, hair, teeth, finger- and
> toenails, and facial features are [still] evident. (Their) diseases in life, such
> as smallpox, arthritis, and nutritional deficiencies, are [still] diagnosable.
> [Even] (their) fatal afflictions are [still] apparent: a middle-aged king died from
> a blow on the head; a child king died from polio.
>
> —Mitchell Rosenbaum (student), "Lost Arts of the Egyptians"

1 Organizing Paragraphs

A coherent paragraph organizes information so that readers can easily follow along. These are common paragraph arrangements:

- **General to specific:** Sentences move from general statements to more specific ones. In the paragraph by Rosenbaum on the previous page, the writer moves from general procedures for whole-body mummification to specific details about skin, hair, teeth, nails, features, diseases, and means of death.
- **Climactic:** Sentences increase in drama or interest, ending in a climax. In the paragraph opposite about sleep, the writer begins with basic information about sleep and moves to more startling cases.
- **Spatial:** Sentences scan a person, place, or object from top to bottom, from side to side, or in some other way that approximates the way people look at things. In the paragraph by Woolf on p. 239, the writer moves from a description of the walls and the windows to objects, the rug, cabinets, and bookcases.
- **Chronological:** Sentences present events as they occurred in time, earlier to later. The paragraph by LaFrank on p. 236 describes how cold viruses are transmitted in the order in which events happen.

2 Using Parallelism

Parallelism helps tie sentences together. In the next paragraph the underlined parallel structures link all sentences after the first one, and parallelism also appears within many of the sentences (as in *He served . . . , survived . . . , and earned* in sentence 8). The paragraph comes from a student's profile of President Ronald Reagan.

> Ronald Reagan holds a particularly interesting place in American history, combining successful careers in show business and in politics. After graduating from college in 1932, he worked as a radio sports announcer with an affinity for describing game details. He then launched a successful film career, starring in dozens of movies. After a stint in the US Army, he assumed the role of host for *General Electric Theater*, a weekly TV program that ran from 1953 to 1962. He first entered politics by supporting candidates and making speeches in the 1950s and early 1960s. He became governor of California in 1966 and served for eight years. He ran unsuccessfully for the US presidency in 1976 and then won the job in 1980, when he became the fortieth President. He served two terms, survived an assassination attempt, and earned a popularity that most politicians can only envy.
>
> —William Brooks (student),
> "Ronald Reagan, the Actor President"

3 Using Repetition and Restatement

Repeating or restating key words helps make a paragraph coherent and also reminds readers what the topic is. In the following paragraph note the circled repetition of *sleep* and the restatement of *adults*.

> Perhaps the simplest fact about (sleep) is that individual needs for it vary widely. Most (adults sleep) between seven and nine hours, but occasionally (people) turn up who need twelve hours or so, while some (rare types) can get by on three or four. Rarest of all are those (legendary types) who require almost no (sleep) at all; respected researchers have recently studied three (such people.) One of them—a healthy, happy woman in her seventies—(sleeps) about an hour every two or three days. The other two are men in early middle age, who get by on a few minutes a night. One of them complains about the daily fifteen minutes or so he's forced to "waste" in (sleeping.)
>
> —Lawrence A. Mayer,
> "The Confounding Enemy of Sleep"

4 Maintaining Consistency

Consistency (or the lack of it) occurs primarily in the person and number of nouns and pronouns and in the tense of verbs. Any inconsistencies not required by meaning will interfere with a reader's ability to follow the development of ideas.

Note the underlined inconsistencies in the next paragraphs:

Shifts in Tense

In the Hopi religion, water is the driving force. Since the Hopi lived in the Arizona desert, they needed water urgently for drinking, cooking, and irrigating crops. Their complex beliefs are focused in part on gaining the assistance of supernatural forces in obtaining water. Many of the Hopi kachinas, or spirit essences, were directly concerned with clouds, rain, and snow.

> Shifts between present and past tense

Shifts in Number

Kachinas represent the things and events of the real world, such as clouds, mischief, cornmeal, and even death. A kachina is not worshiped as a god but regarded as an interested friend. They visit the Hopi from December through July in the form of men who dress in kachina costumes and perform dances and other rituals.

> Shifts between plural and singular number

Shifts in Person

Unlike the man, the Hopi woman does not keep contact with kachinas through costumes and dancing. Instead, one receives a small likeness of a kachina, called a *tihu,* from the man impersonating the kachina. You are more likely to receive a tihu as a girl approaching marriage, though a child or older woman may receive one, too.

> Shifts from *woman* to *one* and from third to second person

5 Using Transitional Words and Phrases

Transitional words and phrases such as *therefore, in contrast,* and *meanwhile* make connections between sentences, as do the underlined expressions in this paragraph:

> Medical science has thus succeeded in identifying the hundreds of viruses that can cause the common cold. It has also discovered the most effective means of prevention. One person transmits the cold viruses to another most often by hand. For instance, an infected person covers his mouth to cough. He then picks up the telephone. Half an hour later, his daughter picks up the same telephone. Immediately afterward, she rubs her eyes. Within a few days, she, too, has a cold. And thus it spreads. To avoid colds, therefore, people should wash their hands often and keep their hands away from their faces.
>
> —Kathleen LaFrank (student),
> "Colds: Myth and Science"

Note that you can use transitional words and phrases to link paragraphs as well as sentences. In the first sentence of LaFrank's paragraph, the word *thus* signals that the sentence refers to an effect discussed in the preceding paragraph. The list in the following box groups many transitional words and phrases by the functions they perform. Use these words and phrases carefully because the ones in each group are not interchangeable. For instance, *besides, finally,* and *second* may all be used to add information, but each has its own distinct meaning.

Transitional Words and Phrases

To Add or Show Sequence

again, also, and, and then, besides, finally, first, further, furthermore, in addition, last, moreover, next, second, still, too

To Compare

also, in the same way, likewise, similarly

To Contrast

although, and yet, but, but at the same time, despite, even so, even though, for all that, however, in contrast, in spite of, nevertheless, notwithstanding, on the contrary, on the other hand, regardless, still, though, yet

To Give Examples or Intensify

after all, an illustration of, even, for example, for instance, indeed, in fact, it is true, of course, specifically, that is, to illustrate, truly

To Indicate Place

above, adjacent to, below, elsewhere, farther on, here, near, nearby, on the other side, opposite to, there, to the east, to the left

To Indicate Time

after a while, afterward, as long as, as soon as, at last, at length, at that time, before, earlier, formerly, immediately, in the meantime, in the past, lately, later, meanwhile, now, presently, shortly, simultaneously, since, so far, soon, subsequently, then, thereafter, until, until now, when

Transitional Words and Phrases (continued)

To Repeat, Summarize, or Conclude

all in all, altogether, as has been said, in brief, in conclusion, in other words, in particular, in short, in simpler terms, in summary, on the whole, that is, therefore, to put it differently, to summarize

To Show Cause or Effect

accordingly, as a result, because, consequently, hence, otherwise, since, then, therefore, thereupon, thus, to this end, with this object

---

Letting Transitional Words and Phrases Guide Your Reading

Transitional words and phrases:

- **Help you follow an author's train of thought.** Transitional words and phrases are signposts that tell you what is coming next in the sentence or paragraph.
- **Show you how ideas are related to one another.** For example, the transitional phrase *as a result* tells you that a cause-effect relationship is being explained.
- **Hint when to speed up or slow down.** For example, the phrase *in contrast* tells you that a new idea is coming and you should slow down. The phrase *in other words* tells you that the author is continuing with the same thought, so if you've grasped the idea you may be able to speed up a bit.

CULTURE LANGUAGE If transitional words and phrases are not common in your native language, you may be tempted to compensate when writing in English by adding them to the beginnings of most sentences. But too many can be intrusive and awkward. When using transitional words and phrases, consider the reader's need for a signal: often the connection from sentence to sentence is already clear from the context or can be made clear by relating the content of sentences more closely. When you do need transitional words and phrases, try varying their positions in your sentences, as illustrated in LaFrank's paragraph on p. 236.

EXERCISE 9.1.5   Arranging Sentences Coherently

After the topic sentence (the first sentence), the sentences in the student paragraph below have been deliberately scrambled to make the paragraph incoherent. Using the topic sentence and other clues as guides, rearrange the sentences in the paragraph to form a well-organized, coherent unit.

   We hear complaints about the Postal Service all the time, but we should not forget what it does *right*. The total volume of mail delivered by the Postal Service each year makes up almost half the total delivered in all the world. Its 70,000 employees handle 140,000,000,000 pieces of mail each year. And when was the last time they failed to deliver yours? In fact, on any given day the Postal Service delivers almost as much mail as the rest of the world combined. That huge number means over 2,000,000 pieces per employee and over 560 pieces per man, woman, and child in the country.

EXERCISE 9.1.6 Eliminating Inconsistencies

The following paragraph is incoherent because of inconsistencies in person, number, and tense. Identify the inconsistencies and revise the paragraph to give it coherence.

The Hopi tihu, or kachina likeness, is often called a "doll," but its owner, usually a girl or woman, does not regard them as a plaything. Instead, you treated them as a valued possession and hung them out of the way on a wall. For its owner the tihu represents a connection with the kachina's spirit. They are considered part of the kachina, carrying a portion of the kachina's power.

EXERCISE 9.1.7 Using Transitional Words and Phrases

Transitional words and phrases have been removed from the following paragraph at the numbered blanks. Fill in each blank with an appropriate transitional word or phrase (1) to contrast, (2) to intensify, and (3) to show effect. Consult the box on pp. 236–37 if necessary.

All over the country, people are swimming, jogging, weight lifting, dancing, walking, playing tennis—doing anything to keep fit. ___(1)___ this school has consistently refused to construct and equip a fitness center. The school has ___(2)___ refused to open existing athletic facilities to all students, not just those playing organized sports. ___(3)___ students have no place to exercise except in their rooms and on dangerous public roads.

EXERCISE 9.1.8 Essay-in-Progress: Evaluating Paragraph Coherence

Choose an essay you are working on in class, and examine the body paragraphs of your essay to see how coherent they are and how their coherence could be improved. Do the paragraphs have a clear organization? Do you use repetition and restatement, parallelism, and transitional words and phrases to signal relationships? Are the paragraphs consistent in person, number, and tense? Revise two or three paragraphs in ways you think will improve their coherence.

EXERCISE 9.1.9 Turning Topic Sentences into Coherent Paragraphs

Develop three of the following topic sentences into coherent paragraphs. Organize your information by space, by time, or for emphasis, as seems most appropriate. Use repetition and restatement, parallelism, consistency, and transitional words and phrases to link sentences.

1. The most interesting character in the book [or movie] was _____.
2. Of all my courses, _____ is the one that I think will serve me best throughout life.
3. Although we in the United States face many problems, the one we should concentrate on solving first is _____.
4. The most dramatic building in town is the _____.
5. Cell phones have made our lives _____.

9.1d Developing Paragraphs Using Patterns

An effective, well-developed paragraph always provides the specific information that readers need and expect in order to understand you and to stay interested in what you say. To develop or shape an idea in a paragraph, one or more of the following patterns may help.

1 Narration (How did it happen?)

Narration tells a story. It presents a sequence of events, usually in the order in which they happened (that is, chronologically). A narrative is concerned not just with the sequence of events but also with their importance to the essay as a whole.

> Jill's story is typical for "recruits" to religious cults. She was very lonely in college and appreciated the attention of the nice young men and women who lived in a house near campus. They persuaded her to share their meals and then to move in with them. Between intense bombardments of "love," they deprived her of sleep and sometimes threatened to throw her out. Jill became increasingly confused and dependent, losing touch with any reality besides the one in the group. She dropped out of school and refused to see or communicate with her family. Before long she, too, was preying on lonely college students.

Topic sentence

Important events in chronological order

—Hillary Begas (student), "The Love Bombers"

2 Description (How does it look, sound, smell, taste, or feel?)

Description presents the details of a person, place, thing, or feeling, using concrete and specific words that appeal to the five senses: sight, sound, taste, touch, and smell. Together the details convey a dominant mood, illustrate an idea, or achieve some other purpose. Note that this paragraph does not include a topic sentence:

> The sun struck straight upon the house, making the white walls glare between the dark windows. Their panes, woven thickly with green branches, held circles of impenetrable darkness. Sharp-edged wedges of light lay upon the window-sill and showed inside the room plates with blue rings, cups with curved handles, the bulge of a great bowl, the crisscross pattern in the rug, and the formidable corners and lines of cabinets and bookcases. Behind their conglomeration hung a zone of shadow in which might be a further shape to be disencumbered of shadow or still denser depths of darkness.

Many sensory details adding up to a picture of a house

—Virginia Woolf, *The Waves*

3 Illustration (What are examples of it?)

Illustration uses examples to explain an idea. Katy Moreno on p. 229 uses several specific examples. A single extended example, as in the next paragraph, may also be used.

Topic sentence

Single detailed example

The language problem that I was attacking loomed larger and larger as I began to learn more. When I would describe in English certain concepts and objects enmeshed in Korean emotion and imagination, I became slowly aware of nuances, of differences between two languages even in simple expression. The remark "Kim entered the house" seems to be simple enough, yet, unless a reader has a clear visual image of a Korean house, his understanding of the sentence is not complete. When a Korean says he is "in the house," he may be in his courtyard, or on his porch, or in his small room! If I wanted to give a specific picture of entering the house in the Western sense, I had to say "room" instead of house—sometimes. I say "sometimes" because many Koreans entertain their guests on their porches and still are considered to be hospitable, and in the Korean sense, going into the "room" may be a more intimate act than it would be in the English sense. Such problems!

—Kim Yong Ik, "A Book-Writing Venture"

4 Listing (What reasons or information support it?)

Sometimes you can develop a paragraph by listing your reasons for stating a main idea or the information that supports it. For instance:

Topic sentence

Three reasons arranged in order of increasing importance

There are three reasons, quite apart from scientific considerations, that mankind needs to travel in space. The first reason is the need for garbage disposal: we need to transfer industrial processes into space, so that the earth may remain a green and pleasant place for our grandchildren to live in. The second reason is the need to escape material impoverishment: the resources of this planet are finite, and we shall not forgo forever the abundant solar energy and minerals and living space that are spread out all around us. The third reason is our spiritual need for an open frontier: the ultimate purpose of space travel is to bring to humanity not only scientific discoveries and an occasional spectacular show on television but a real expansion of our spirit.

—Freeman Dyson, "Disturbing the Universe"

5 Definition (What is it?)

A definition is an explanation of what something is. Complicated, abstract, or controversial terms often require detailed explanation. The following definition comes from a biology textbook.

Topic sentence providing brief definition

Expanded definition, including importance

Genetics is the scientific study of heredity, the transmission of characteristics from parents to offspring. Genetics explains why offspring resemble their parents and also why they are not identical to them. Genetics is a subject that has considerable economic, medical, and social significance and is partly the basis for the modern theory of evolution. Because of its importance, genetics has been a topic of central interest in the study of life for centuries. Modern concepts in genetics are fundamentally different, however, from earlier ones.

Lead-in to comparison with earlier definition

> —Michael C. Mix et al., *Biology: The Network of Life*

6 Division or Analysis (What are its parts?)

With division or analysis, you separate something into its parts. You may approach the elements critically, interpreting their meaning and significance. Or you may simply identify and explain them:

> A typical daily newspaper compresses considerable information into the top of the first page, above the headlines. The most prominent feature of this space, the newspaper's name, is called the *logo* or *nameplate*. Under the logo and set off by rules is a line of small type called the *folio line*, which contains the date of the issue, the volume and issue numbers, copyright information, and the price. To the right of the logo is a block of small type called a *weather ear*, a summary of the day's forecast. And above the logo is a *skyline*, a kind of advertisement in which the paper's editors highlight a special feature of the issue.

Topic sentence

Four parts of the subject, arranged spatially

> —Kansha Stone (student), "Anatomy of a Paper"

7 Classification (What groups or categories can it be sorted into?)

When you classify items, you sort them into groups. The classification allows you to see and explain the relations among the items. The following paragraph identifies three groups, or classes, of parents:

> In my experience, the parents who hire daytime sitters for their school-age children tend to fall into one of three groups. The first group includes parents who work and want someone to be at home when the children return from school. These parents are looking for an extension of themselves, someone who will give the care they would give if they were at home. The second group includes parents who may be home all day themselves but are too disorganized or too frazzled by their children's demands to handle child care alone. They are looking for an organizer and helpmate. The third and final group includes parents who do not want to be bothered by their children, whether they are home all day or not. Unlike the parents in the first two groups, who care for their children however they can, these parents seek a permanent substitute for themselves.

Topic sentence

Three groups of parents

> —Nancy Whittle (student), "Modern Parenting"

8 Comparison and Contrast (How is it like, or different from, other things?)

Comparison and contrast may be used separately or together to develop an idea. Comparison focuses on similarities between two or more items; contrast focuses on differences. The following paragraph illustrates one of two common ways of organizing a comparison and contrast: **subject by subject.** The paragraph considers first one subject and then the other.

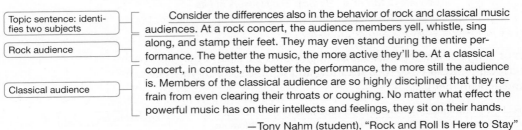

Topic sentence: identifies two subjects	Consider the differences also in the behavior of rock and classical music audiences. At a rock concert, the audience members yell, whistle, sing
Rock audience	along, and stamp their feet. They may even stand during the entire performance. The better the music, the more active they'll be. At a classical
Classical audience	concert, in contrast, the better the performance, the more still the audience is. Members of the classical audience are so highly disciplined that they refrain from even clearing their throats or coughing. No matter what effect the powerful music has on their intellects and feelings, they sit on their hands.

—Tony Nahm (student), "Rock and Roll Is Here to Stay"

The next paragraph illustrates the other common organization: **point by point,** with the two subjects discussed side by side and matched feature for feature:

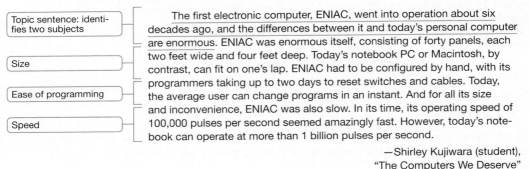

Topic sentence: identifies two subjects	The first electronic computer, ENIAC, went into operation about six decades ago, and the differences between it and today's personal computer are enormous. ENIAC was enormous itself, consisting of forty panels, each
Size	two feet wide and four feet deep. Today's notebook PC or Macintosh, by contrast, can fit on one's lap. ENIAC had to be configured by hand, with its
Ease of programming	programmers taking up to two days to reset switches and cables. Today, the average user can change programs in an instant. And for all its size
Speed	and inconvenience, ENIAC was also slow. In its time, its operating speed of 100,000 pulses per second seemed amazingly fast. However, today's notebook can operate at more than 1 billion pulses per second.

—Shirley Kujiwara (student),
"The Computers We Deserve"

9 Cause and Effect (Why did it happen, or what results did it have?)

We use cause and effect to explain why something happened (causes) or what happened as a result of an action (effects). In the following paragraph the author looks at the cause of an effect:

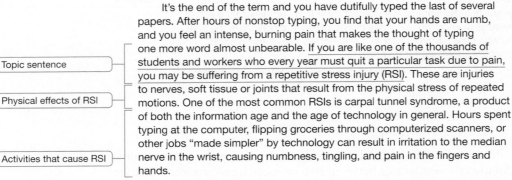

	It's the end of the term and you have dutifully typed the last of several papers. After hours of nonstop typing, you find that your hands are numb, and you feel an intense, burning pain that makes the thought of typing one more word almost unbearable. If you are like one of the thousands of
Topic sentence	students and workers who every year must quit a particular task due to pain, you may be suffering from a repetitive stress injury (RSI). These are injuries
Physical effects of RSI	to nerves, soft tissue or joints that result from the physical stress of repeated motions. One of the most common RSIs is carpal tunnel syndrome, a product of both the information age and the age of technology in general. Hours spent typing at the computer, flipping groceries through computerized scanners, or
Activities that cause RSI	other jobs "made simpler" by technology can result in irritation to the median nerve in the wrist, causing numbness, tingling, and pain in the fingers and hands.

—Rebecca Donatelle, *Access to Health*

🔟 Process (How does one do it, or how does it work?)

When you analyze how to do something or how something works, you explain a process. The following example identifies the process, describes the equipment needed, and details the steps in the process:

> As a car owner, you waste money when you pay a mechanic to change the engine oil. The job is not difficult, even if you know little about cars. All you need is a wrench to remove the drain plug, a large, flat pan to collect the draining oil, plastic bottles to dispose of the used oil, and fresh oil. First, warm up the car's engine so that the oil will flow more easily. When the engine is warm, shut it off and remove its oil-filler cap (the owner's manual shows where this cap is). Then locate the drain plug under the engine (again consulting the owner's manual for its location) and place the flat pan under the plug. Remove the plug with the wrench, letting the oil flow into the pan. When the oil stops flowing, replace the plug and, at the engine's filler hole, add the amount and kind of fresh oil specified by the owner's manual. Pour the used oil into the plastic bottles and take it to a waste-oil collector, which any garage mechanic can recommend.

Topic sentence: identifies process

Equipment needed

Steps in the process

> —Anthony Andreas (student), "Do-It-Yourself Car Care"

EXERCISE 9.1.10 Essay-in-Progress: Evaluating Paragraphs

Choose an essay you are working on in class, and examine the development of the body paragraphs in your writing. Where does specific information seem adequate to support your general statements? Where does support seem skimpy? Try using appropriate patterns of development to fill out skimpy paragraphs. Revise the paragraphs as necessary to make your ideas clearer and more interesting. It may help you to pose the questions on pp. 239–43.

EXERCISE 9.1.11 Writing with the Patterns of Development

Write at least three complete, unified, coherent, and well-developed paragraphs, each one developed with a different pattern. Draw on the topics provided here, or choose your own topics.

1. **Narration**
   A disappointment
   Leaving home
   Waking up

2. **Description (objective or subjective)**
   A crowded or an empty place
   A food
   An intimidating person

3. **Illustration**
   Why study
   Having a headache
   The best sports event

4. **Listing**
   Annoying habits of coworkers
     or classmates
   Factors to consider when
     creating a *Facebook* profile
   Characteristics of the ideal job

5. **Definition**
   Humor
   An adult
   Fear

6. **Division or analysis**
   A television news show
   A barn
   A piece of music

7. **Classification**
Factions in a dispute
Types of Web sites
Kinds of teachers

8. **Comparison and contrast**
Surfing the Web and watching TV
High school and college football
Movies on TV and in a theater

9. **Cause and effect**
Connection between tension and anger
Connection between credit cards and debt
Causes of a serious accident

10. **Process**
Preparing for a job interview
Protecting your home from burglars
Making a jump shot

9.1e Writing Introductory and Concluding Paragraphs

1 Introductions

An introduction draws readers from their world into yours:

- **It focuses readers' attention on the topic and arouses their curiosity about what you have to say.**
- **It specifies your subject and implies your attitude toward it.**
- **It often includes your thesis statement.**
- **It is concise and sincere.**

Several options for focusing readers' attention are listed in the box below.

Writing Effective Introductions	
Strategy	**Example**
Ask a provocative or controversial question.	How would you feel if the job you had counted on getting suddenly fell through?
State a startling fact or statistic.	Last year, the United States government spent a whopping one billion dollars a day on interest on the national debt.
Begin with a story or an anecdote.	The day Liam Blake left his parka on the bus was the first day of what would become the worst snowstorm the city had ever seen.
Use a quotation.	Robert Frost wrote, "Two roads diverged in a wood, and I— / I took the one less traveled by, / And that has made all the difference."
State a little-known fact, a myth, or a misconception.	What was Harry S. Truman's middle name? Stephen? Samuel? Simpson? Actually, it's just plain "S." There was a family dispute over whether to name him for his paternal or his maternal grandfather, an argument that was settled by simply using the common initial "S."

 These options for an introduction may not be what you are used to if your native language is not English. In other cultures, readers may seek familiarity or reassurance from an author's introduction, or they may pre-

fer an indirect approach to the subject. In academic and business English, however, writers and readers prefer concise, direct expression.

Effective Openings

A very common introduction opens with a statement or question about the essay's general subject, clarifies or limits the subject in one or more sentences, and then presents the point of the essay in the thesis statement. You can visualize this type of introduction as a funnel, as shown in the following diagram:

Here is an example of the funnel introduction:

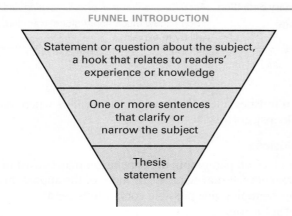

FUNNEL INTRODUCTION

Statement or question about the subject, a hook that relates to readers' experience or knowledge

One or more sentences that clarify or narrow the subject

Thesis statement

In this moment there is a man standing at a stop light with a cardboard sign that reads "ANYTHING HELPS" in the dark, thick letters of a Sharpie. In this same moment there is a woman entering a shelter with her two children- a single mother unable to pay the rent. There is a man who gets a job at a restaurant and leaves the streets for good. There is a woman who dies- she spent too many cold nights sleeping with her face pressed to concrete. There are homeless individuals in every community, city, village, town, and corner of this world. Homelessness, in its most basic definition, is to be without a home. However, the term "homeless" has come to be associated with many stereotypes such as poverty, destitution, drug addiction, alcohol addiction, violence, apathy, criminality, etc. These stereotypes are destructive to the humanity and dignity of homeless people and restrict their true identity as neighbors and friends.

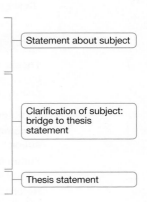

Statement about subject

Clarification of subject: bridge to thesis statement

Thesis statement

—Amanda Keithly (student), "Breaking Down Barriers with Stories"

In much business writing, it's more important to tell readers immediately what your point is than to try to engage them. This introduction to a brief memo quickly outlines a problem and (in the thesis statement) suggests a way to solve it:

Starting next month, the holiday rush and staff vacations will leave our department short-handed. We need to hire two or perhaps three temporary keyboarders to maintain our schedules for the month.

Openings to Avoid

When writing and revising your introduction, avoid approaches that are likely to bore or confuse readers:

Avoiding Ineffective Openings	
Strategy to Avoid	**Example**
Using a vague generality or truth	Throughout human history, people have always been concerned about . . .
Making a direct announcement	The purpose of this essay is to . . .
Referring to the essay's title	"The History of the Guitar" is an interesting topic because . . .
Quoting a dictionary definition	According to Webster, *global warming* can be defined as . . .
Making an apology	I don't know much about global warming, but in this essay I will try to explain . . .

2 Conclusions

Your conclusion finishes off your essay and tells readers where you think you have brought them. It answers the question, "So what?"

Effective Conclusions

Usually set off in its own paragraph, the conclusion may consist of a single sentence or a group of sentences. It may take one or more of the approaches listed in the following box. The examples give possible conclusions for an essay that develops the thesis statement at the top.

Writing Effective Conclusions	
Thesis statement: Americans are overly concerned with physical appearance, as evidenced by our national obsession with diet to achieve thinness, plastic surgery to enhance natural beauty, and tattoos and piercings to embellish the body.	
Strategy	**Example**
Recommend a course of action.	Americans should focus on character and personality rather than on physical appearance.
Summarize the essay.	Overall, the trend toward an emphasis on personal appearance is superficial and detrimental to personal growth and happiness.
Refer to an idea mentioned in the introduction.	The next time Christie looks in the mirror, let's hope she sees a beautiful teenager with a full life ahead of her instead of what she has been seeing—a never-thin-enough girl who needs body art to make her attractive.
Restate your thesis and reflect on its implications.	Americans' obsession with physical appearance is a symptom of a larger problem in American society: materialism.

Writing Effective Conclusions (continued)	
Strike a note of hope or despair.	No doubt another million people will go under a plastic surgeon's knife in the next year in the fruitless effort to turn back their biological clocks.
Give a compelling fact, detail, or example.	The latest fad is a piercing above the upper lip in honor of Marilyn Monroe's mole. What could possibly be next?
Use a quotation.	As Shakespeare wrote in *The Taming of the Shrew,* "Kindness in women, not their beauteous looks / Shall win my love."

In the following paragraph the author concludes an essay on environmental protection with a call for action:

Until we get the answers, I think we had better keep on building power plants and growing food with the help of fertilizers and such insect-controlling chemicals as we now have. The risks are well known, thanks to the environmentalists. If they had not created a widespread public awareness of the ecological crisis, we wouldn't stand a chance. But such awareness by itself is not enough. Flaming manifestos and prophecies of doom are no longer much help, and a search for scapegoats can only make matters worse. The time for sensations and manifestos is about over. Now we need rigorous analysis, united effort and very hard work.

—Peter F. Drucker, "How Best to Protect the Environment"

[Summary and opinion]

[Call for action]

Conclusions to Avoid

Several kinds of conclusions usually do not work well:

- **A repeat of the introduction.** Don't simply replay your introduction. The conclusion should capture what the paragraphs of the body have added to the introduction.

- **A new direction.** Don't introduce a subject different from the one your essay has been about.

- **A sweeping generalization.** Don't conclude more than you reasonably can from the evidence you have presented. If your essay is about your frustrating experience trying to clear a parking ticket, you cannot reasonably conclude that all local police forces are too tied up in red tape to be of service to the people.

- **An apology.** Don't cast doubt on your essay. Don't say, *Even though I'm no expert* or anything similar. Rather, to win your readers' confidence, display confidence.

EXERCISE 9.1.12 **Essay-In-Progress: Evaluating Introductions and Conclusions**

Choose an essay you are working on in class. Do the paragraphs fulfill the requirements and avoid the pitfalls outlined on pp. 244–47? Revise them as needed for clarity, conciseness, focus, and interest.

Critical Thinking

Checklist: Revising Effectively

What to evaluate	How to evaluate
☐ **Purpose of the essay** (see p. 204)	Write a sentence stating your purpose in writing. Ask: • Does the purpose fulfill the assignment? • Is it consistent throughout the paper?
☐ **Thesis statement**	Highlight your thesis statement. Ask: • Does it identify the subject? • Does it express the main point of your essay?
☐ **Organization**	Underline the main points of your paper. Ask: • How well does each support the thesis? • Are the points arranged effectively?

> **Revisions condense long example of mother's experience.**

> **Paragraph's concluding sentences reinforce the point and connect to thesis statement.**

science, rose within the information technology (IT) department of a large company, ~~had sixteen years of experience,~~ and her bosses always gave her good performance reviews. Still, when her employer decided to outsource most of its IT work, my mother lost her job. ~~She never expected to be laid off and was surprised when she was. She wasn't laid off because of her background and performance. In fact, my mother had a very strong background in math and science and years of training and job experience.~~ The reason wasn't because her technical skills were inadequate. Instead, her salary and benefits cost the company more than outsourcing her job did. Until wages rise around the globe, jobs like my mother's will be vulnerable. No matter how well you are trained. ~~Which hurt my family financially, as you can imagine.~~

10

Revising

10.1 REVISING

> *Successful writers . . .*
>
> - Read drafts critically and revise to improve meaning and organization (next page).
> - Learn from a sample revision (p. 251).

Revising is an essential step that involves looking again at all the ideas and sentences you have written and often making major changes to them. You may add, delete, or rewrite sentences, paragraphs, and even complete sections. It's wise to revise in at least two stages, one devoted to basic meaning and organization (here called **revising**) and one devoted to word choice, grammar, punctuation, and other features of

Taken from *The Successful Writer's Handbook*, Third Edition by Kathleen T. McWhorter and Jane E. Aaron.

the surface (here called **editing**). Knowing that you will edit later gives you the freedom at first to look beyond the confines of the page or screen to the whole paper.

10.1a Revising the Whole Essay

To revise your writing, you have to read it critically, and that means you have to create some distance between your draft and yourself. One or more of the following techniques may help you see your work objectively.

- **Ask someone to read and react to your draft.**
- **Outline or draw a map of your draft.** Then examine the outline you've made for logical order, gaps, and digressions. A formal outline can be especially helpful because of its careful structure.
- **Listen to your draft.** Read the draft out loud to yourself or a friend, record and listen to it, or have someone read the draft to you.
- **Ease the pressure.** Don't try to re-see everything in your draft at once. Use the list in the following box, making a separate pass through the draft for each item.

Managing Your Time When Revising and Editing

Use the following suggestions to plan time for revising:

- **Do not try to revise immediately after finishing your draft.** Let the draft sit at least overnight if possible. The time will give you distance from the project and enable you to see it from a fresh perspective.
- **Allow time between revisions** so that, again, you come fresh to the work.
- **Don't try to revise and edit at the same time.** First make certain your draft says what you want it to say. Once it does, then work on polishing the essay, focusing on correctness.

Critical Thinking

Checklist: Revising Effectively

What to evaluate	How to evaluate
☐ **Purpose of the essay** (see p. 204)	Write a sentence stating your purpose in writing. Ask: • Does the purpose fulfill the assignment? • Is it consistent throughout the paper?
☐ **Thesis statement**	Highlight your thesis statement. Ask: • Does it identify the subject? • Does it express the main point of your essay?
☐ **Organization**	Underline the main points of your paper. Ask: • How well does each support the thesis? • Are the points arranged effectively?

Checklist: Revising Effectively (continued)

☐ **Support and development** (see pp. 239–43)	Place a check mark before each piece of supporting evidence. Ask: • Is each main point well supported? • Where might readers get confused or have problems understanding the content?
☐ **Unity** (see pp. 229–31)	Bracket any sentences or paragraphs that do not directly support the thesis. Ask: • Should these be cut, or can they be rewritten to support the thesis?
☐ **Coherence** (see pp. 233–37)	Read your essay aloud. Ask: • How clearly and smoothly does the essay flow? • Where does it seem rough, awkward, or unconnected? • Where can transitions be added?
☐ **Title, introduction** (see pp. 244–47), and conclusion (see pp. 246–47)	Reread the title, introduction, and conclusion. Ask: • Does the title identify the topic of the essay in an interesting way? • How well does the introduction capture readers' attention? • How effective is the conclusion in drawing the essay to a close?

10.1b Examining a Sample Revision

Katy Moreno was satisfied with her first draft: she had her ideas down, and the arrangement seemed logical. Still, from the revision checklist she knew the draft needed work, and her classmates' comments (p. 217) highlighted what she needed to focus on. Following is the first half of her revised draft, with marginal annotations highlighting the changes. Moreno used the Track Changes function on her word processor, so that deletions are crossed out and additions are in blue.

Can We Compete?

College Education for the Global Economy

~~Title?~~

> Descriptive title names topic and forecasts approach.

Today's students cannot miss news stories about globalization of the economy and outsourcing of jobs, but are students aware of how these trends are affecting the job market? In "It's a Flat World, after All," Thomas L. Friedman argues that most US students are not preparing themselves as well as ~~they should to compete in today's economy. Not like~~ students in India, China, and other countries ~~are~~ to compete in today's economy, which requires hard-working, productive scientists and engineers (34-37). Friedman's argument speaks to me because my mother recently lost her job when it was outsourced to India. But her experience taught a lesson that Friedman overlooks: technical training by itself can be too narrow to produce the

> Expanded introduction draws readers into Moreno's topic, clarifies her point of agreement with Friedman, and states her revised thesis.

communicators and problem solvers needed by contemporary businesses. ~~The outsourcing of my mother's job proves that Thomas L. Friedman's advice to improve students' technical training is too narrow.~~

Friedman describes a "flat" world where recent technology like the Internet and wireless communication makes it possible for college graduates all over the globe~~, in particular~~ to compete for high paying jobs that once belonged to graduates of US colleges and universities (34). He focuses on workers in India and China~~,~~ who graduate from college with excellent educations in math and science, who are eager for new opportunities, and who are willing to work exceptionally hard, often harder than their American counterparts and, for less money ~~to get jobs that once were gotten by graduates of US colleges and universities~~ (37). ~~He~~ Friedman argues that US students must be better prepared academically, especially in ~~need more~~ math and science, so that they can get and keep jobs that will otherwise go overseas ~~in order to compete~~ (37).

~~I came to college with first hand knowledge of globalization and outsourcing. My mother, who worked for sixteen years in the field of information technology (IT), was laid off six months ago when the company she worked for decided to outsource much of its IT work to a company based in India. My mother~~ At first glance, my mother's experience of losing her job might seem to support the argument of Friedman that better training in math and science is the key to competing in the global job market. Her experience, however, adds dimensions to the globalization story, which Friedman misses. First my mother had the kind of strong background in math and science that Friedman says, today's workers need. She majored in computer science, rose within the information technology (IT) department of a large company, ~~had sixteen years of experience,~~ and her bosses always gave her good performance reviews. Still, when her employer decided to outsource most of its IT work, my mother lost her job. ~~She never expected to be laid off and was surprised when she was. She wasn't laid off because of her background and performance. In fact, my mother had a very strong background in math and science and years of training and job experience.~~ The reason wasn't because her technical skills were inadequate. Instead, her salary and benefits cost the company more than outsourcing her job did. Until wages rise around the globe, jobs like my mother's will be vulnerable. No matter how well you are trained. ~~Which hurt my family financially, as you can imagine.~~

Expanded summary of Friedman's article specifies qualities of overseas workers.

New opening sentences connect to introduction and thesis statement, restating points of agreement and disagreement with Friedman.

Revisions condense long example of mother's experience.

Paragraph's concluding sentences reinforce the point and connect to thesis statement.

EXERCISE 10.1.1   Analyzing a Revised Draft

Compare Moreno's revised draft with her first draft on p. 217. Can you see the reasons for most of her changes? Where would you suggest further revisions, and why?

EXERCISE 10.1.2   Essay-in-Progress: Revising Your Own Draft

Revise your own first draft from Exercise 7.1.1 (p. 216). Use the revision checklist on pp. 250–51 as a guide. Concentrate on purpose, content, and organization, leaving smaller problems for the next draft.

∧̇	Insert comma
∧	Insert letter or word
∨̇	Insert quotation marks
⌒	Close up
¶	Begin a new paragraph
NO¶	Do not begin a new paragraph
⊙	Add period
#	Add space
⌐⌐	Transpose letters
⌐⌐	Transpose words
℘	Delete words
℘	Delete punctuation
ℳ	Use lower case
m̲	Capitalize

11

Proofreading

11.1 EDITING, FORMATTING, AND PROOFREADING

Chapter Essentials

- Edit the revised draft (next page).
- Use an editing checklist (p. 257).
- Format and proofread the final draft (p. 259).

After you have revised your essay so that you are satisfied with the content, turn to the work of editing your sentences to correct them and clarify your ideas.

Taken from *The Little, Brown Compact Handbook*, Ninth Edition by Jane E. Aaron.

11.1a Editing the Revised Draft

In your editing, work first for clear and effective sentences that flow smoothly from one to the next. Then check your sentences for correctness. Use the questions in the checklist on the next page to guide your editing.

1 Discovering What Needs Editing

Try these approaches to gain distance from your work:

- **Take a break.** Even fifteen minutes can clear your head.
- **Read the draft slowly, and read what you actually see.** Otherwise, you're likely to read what you intended to write but didn't. (If you have trouble slowing down, try reading your draft from back to front, sentence by sentence.)
- **Read as if you are encountering the draft for the first time.** Put yourself in the reader's place.
- **Have a classmate, friend, or relative read your work.** Make sure you understand and consider the reader's suggestions, even if eventually you decide not to take them.
- **Read the draft aloud or, even better, record it.** Listen for awkward rhythms, repetitive sentence patterns, and missing or clumsy transitions.
- **Learn from your own experience.** Keep a record of the problems that others have pointed out in your writing. When editing, check your work against this record.

2 A Sample Edited Paragraph

The third paragraph of Katy Moreno's edited draft appears below. Among other changes, she tightened wording, improved parallelism (with *consistently received*), corrected several comma errors, and repaired the final sentence fragment.

> At first glance, my mother's experience of losing her job might seem to support ~~the~~ Friedman's argument ~~of Friedman~~ that better training in math and science is the key to competing in the global job market. However, ~~Hh~~er experience~~, however,~~ adds dimensions to the globalization story~~, which~~ that Friedman misses. First, my mother had the kind of strong background in math and science that Friedman says~~,~~ today's workers need. She majored in computer science, rose within the information technology (IT) department of a large company, and consistently received ~~her bosses always gave her~~ good performance reviews. Still, when her employer decided to outsource most of its IT work, my mother lost her job. The reason wasn't ~~because~~ that her technical skills were inadequate. Instead, her salary and benefits cost the company more than outsourcing her job did. Until wages rise around the globe, jobs like my mother's will be vulnerable,~~. Nn~~o matter how well ~~you are~~ a person is trained.

Checklist for Editing

Are my sentences clear?

Do my words and sentences mean what I Intend them to mean? Is anything confusing? Check especially for these:

Exact language
Parallelism
Clear modifiers
Clear reference of pronouns
Complete sentences
Sentences separated correctly

Are my sentences effective?

How well do words and sentences engage and hold readers' attention? Where does the writing seem wordy, choppy, or dull? Check especially for these:

Emphasis of main ideas
Smooth and informative transitions
Variety in sentence length and structure
Appropriate language
Concise sentences

Do my sentences contain errors?

Where do surface errors interfere with the clarity and effectiveness of my sentences? Check especially for these:

- **Spelling errors**
- **Sentence fragments**
- **Comma splices**
- **Verb errors**
  Verb forms, especially -*s* and -*ed* endings, correct forms of irregular verbs, and appropriate helping verbs
  Verb tenses, especially consistency
  Agreement between subjects and verbs, especially when words come between them or the subject is *each, everyone,* or a similar word

- **Pronoun errors**
  Pronoun forms, especially subjective (*he, she, they, who*) vs. objective (*him, her, them, whom*)
  Agreement between pronouns and antecedents, especially when the antecedent contains *or* or the antecedent is *each, everyone, person,* or a similar word

- **Punctuation errors**
  Commas, especially with comma splices and with *and* or *but,* with introductory elements, with nonessential elements, and with series
  Apostrophes in possessives but not plural nouns (*Dave's/witches*) and in contractions but not possessive personal pronouns (*it's/its*)

3 Working with Spelling and Grammar/Style Checkers

A spelling checker and grammar/style checker can be helpful *if* you work within their limitations. The programs miss many problems and may even flag items that are actually correct. Further, they know nothing of your purpose and your audience, so they cannot make important decisions about your writing. Always use these tools critically:

- **Read your work yourself to ensure that it's clear and error-free.**
- **Consider a checker's suggestions carefully against your intentions.** If you aren't sure whether to accept a checker's suggestion, consult a dictionary, writing handbook, or other source. Your version may be fine.

Using a Spelling Checker

Your word processor's spelling checker can be a great ally: it will flag words that are spelled incorrectly and will usually suggest alternative spellings that resemble what you've typed. However, this ally can also undermine you because of its limitations:

- **The checker may flag a word that you've spelled correctly** just because the word does not appear in its dictionary.
- **The checker may suggest incorrect alternatives.** In providing a list of alternative spellings for your word, the checker may highlight the one it considers most likely to be correct. For example, if you misspell *definitely* by typing *definately*, your checker may highlight *defiantly* as the correct option. You need to verify that the alternative suggested by the checker is actually what you intend before selecting it. Consult an online or printed dictionary when you aren't sure about the checker's recommendations.
- **Most important, a spelling checker will not flag words that appear in its dictionary but you have misused.** The paragraph in the screen shot on the facing page contains eleven errors that a spelling checker overlooked. Can you spot them?

Using a Grammar/Style Checker

Grammar/style checkers can flag incorrect grammar or punctuation and wordy or awkward sentences. However, these programs can call your attention only to passages that *may* be faulty. They miss many errors because they are not yet capable of analyzing language in all its complexity. (For instance, they can't accurately distinguish a word's part of speech when there are different possibilities, as *light* can be a noun, a verb, or an adjective.) And they often question passages that don't need editing, such as an appropriate passive verb or a deliberate and emphatic use of repetition.

You can customize a grammar/style checker to suit your needs and habits as a writer. Most checkers allow you to specify whether to check grammar only or grammar and style. Some style checkers can be set to the level of writing you intend, such as formal, standard, and informal. (For academic writing choose formal.) You can

---

Spelling Checker

The whether effects all of us, though it's affects are different for different people. Some people love a fare day with warm temperatures and sunshine. They revel in spending a hole day outside. Other people enjoy dark, rainy daze. They like to slow down and here they're inner thoughts. Most people agree, however, that to much of one kind of weather makes them board.

A spelling checker failed to catch any of the eleven errors in this paragraph.

also instruct the checker to flag specific grammar and style problems that tend to occur in your writing, such as mismatched subjects and verbs, overused passive voice, or a confusion between *its* and *it's*.

11.1b Formatting and Proofreading the Final Draft

After editing your essay, format and proofread it before you submit it to your instructor. Follow any required format for your paper, such as MLA and APA.

Be sure to proofread the final essay several times to spot and correct errors. To increase the accuracy of your proofreading, you may need to experiment with ways to keep yourself from relaxing into the rhythm and the content of your prose. Here are a few tricks, including some used by professional proofreaders:

- **Read printed copy,** even if you will eventually submit the paper electronically. Most people proofread more accurately when reading type on paper than when reading it on a computer screen. (At the same time, don't view the printed copy as error-free just because it's clean. Clean-looking copy may still harbor errors.)
- **Read the paper aloud,** very slowly, and distinctly pronounce exactly what you see.
- **Place a ruler under each line as you read it.**
- **Read "against copy,"** comparing your final draft one sentence at a time against the edited draft.
- **Ignore content.** To keep the content of your writing from distracting you, read the essay backward sentence by sentence. Or use your word processor to isolate each paragraph from its context by printing it on a separate page. (Of course, reassemble the paragraphs before submitting the paper.)

11.1c Examining a Sample Final Draft

Katy Moreno's final essay appears on the following pages, presented in MLA format except for page numbers. Comments in the margins point out key features of the essay's content.

Katy Moreno

Professor Lacourse

English 110

14 February 2014

Descriptive title

Can We Compete?

College Education for the Global Economy

Introduction

Today's students cannot miss news stories about globalization of the economy and outsourcing of jobs, but are students aware of how these trends are affecting the job market? In "It's a Flat World, after All," Thomas L. Friedman argues that most US students are not preparing themselves as well as students in India, China, and other countries to compete in today's economy, which requires hard-working, productive scientists and engineers (34-37).

Summaries of Friedman cited with parenthetical page numbers using MLA style

Friedman's argument speaks to me because my mother lost her job when it was outsourced to India. But her experience taught a lesson that Friedman overlooks: technical training by itself can be too narrow to produce the communicators and problem solvers needed by contemporary businesses.

Thesis statement: basic disagreement with Friedman

Summary of Friedman's article

Friedman describes a "flat" world where technology like the Internet and wireless communication makes it possible for college graduates all over the globe to compete for high-paying jobs that once belonged to graduates of US colleges and universities (34). He focuses on workers in India and China who graduate from college with excellent educations in math and science, who are eager for new opportunities, and who are willing to work exceptionally hard, often harder than their American counterparts, and for less money (37). Friedman argues that US students must be better prepared academically, especially in math and science, so that they can get and keep jobs that will otherwise go overseas (37).

Transition to disagreements with Friedman

At first glance, my mother's experience of losing her job might seem to support Friedman's argument that better training in math and science is the key to competing in the global job market. However, her experience adds dimensions to the globalization story that Friedman misses. First, my mother had the kind of strong background in math and science that Friedman says today's workers need. She majored in computer science, rose within the information technology (IT) department of a large company, and consistently received good performance reviews. Still, when her employer decided to outsource most of its IT work, my mother lost her job. The reason wasn't that her technical skills

First disagreement with Friedman

Examples to support first disagreement

were inadequate; instead, her salary and benefits cost the company more than outsourcing her job did. Until wages rise around the globe, jobs like my mother's will be vulnerable, no matter how well a person is trained.

| Clarification of first disagreement

The second dimension that Friedman misses is that a number of well-paid people in my mother's IT department, namely IT managers, were not laid off. As my mother explained at the time, they kept their jobs because they were experienced at figuring out the company's IT needs, planning for changes, researching and proposing solutions, and communicating in writing and speech—skills that her more narrow training and experience had missed. Friedman misses these skills by focusing only on technical training. Without the ability to solve problems creatively and to communicate, people with technical expertise alone may not have enough to save their jobs, as my mother learned.

| Second disagreement with Friedman

| Explanation of second disagreement

| Conclusion summarizing both disagreements with Friedman

Like my mother, I am more comfortable in front of a computer than I am in front of a group of people, and I had planned to major in computer science. Since my mother lost her job, however, I have decided to take courses in English and history as well. Classes in these subjects will require me to read broadly, think critically, research, and communicate ideas in writing—in short, to develop skills that make managers. When I enter the job market, my well-rounded education will make me a more attractive job candidate and will help me to become the kind of forward-thinking manager that US companies will always need to employ here in the United States.

| Final point: business needs and author's personal goals

| Explanation of final point

Many jobs that require a college degree are indeed going overseas, as Thomas L. Friedman says, and my classmates and I need to be ready for a rapidly changing future. But rather than focus only on math and science, we need to broaden our academic experiences so that the skills we develop make us not only employable but also indispensable.

| Conclusion recapping points of agreement and disagreement with Friedman and summarizing essay

[New page.]

Work Cited

Friedman, Thomas L. "It's a Flat World, after All." *New York Times Magazine* 3 Apr. 2005: 32-37. Print.

| Work cited in MLA style

11.1d Preparing a Writing Portfolio

Your instructor may ask you to assemble samples of your writing into a portfolio once or more during the course. A portfolio gives you a chance to consider all your writing over a period and to choose the work that best represents you as a writer.

The purposes and requirements for portfolios vary. As you consider what work to include in your portfolio, answer the following questions:

- **What is the purpose of the portfolio?** A portfolio may be intended to showcase your best work, demonstrate progress you have made, or provide examples of your versatility as a writer.

- **What are the requirements of the portfolio?** You may be asked to submit final drafts of your best work; journal entries, notes, early drafts, and a final draft of one or more essays; or projects representing different types of writing—say, one narrative, one critical analysis, one argument, and so on.

- **Is a reflective essay or letter required as part of the portfolio?** Many teachers require an opening essay or letter in which you discuss the portfolio selections, explain why you chose each one, and perhaps evaluate your development as a writer. If a reflective essay is required, be sure you understand its purpose and scope.

- **Should the portfolio be print or electronic, or can you choose the medium?** If you plan to submit your portfolio electronically, be sure you know how to upload your files before the deadline.

- **How will the portfolio be evaluated?** Will it be read by peers, your instructor, or a committee of teachers? Will it be graded?

Unless the guidelines specify otherwise, provide error-free copies of your final drafts and label all your samples with your name before you place them in a folder or upload them as files.

Unit 3

Reading Comprehension, Analysis, and Evaluation

While the word *rhetoric* is sometimes used to mean "empty words," nothing could be further from the truth. Human language—which can be presented orally, in writing, and visually—is what gets things done. This image portrays the delivery of a famous speech by Elizabeth Cady Stanton that helped to persuade America's leaders to grant new rights to women. In this chapter, you'll have the chance to read and analyze that speech, and you'll learn more about how language can be used to persuade others and to inspire action.

Elizabeth Cady Stanton and Women's Rights

12

Active Reading

READING and responding to texts is a crucial part of many college-level writing courses. Because most writing—in any field—exists in a context of ongoing conversation, writing, and debate, college writers need to be effective critical readers. To understand critical and rhetorical reading, we have to define two key terms: *texts* and *reading*. A *text* can be any graphic matter—a textbook, an essay, a blog, a poem, an editorial, a photograph, an advertisement. Some people expand the definition of text to include any phenomenon in the world. In this widest sense, the layout of a restaurant, the behavior of children on a playground, and the clouds in the sky are all "texts" that can be read.

Similarly, the term *reading* has both narrow and broad senses. In the narrow sense, reading is simply understanding the words on a page. But reading has a variety of wider meanings as well. Reading can mean analyzing, as when an architect "reads" the blueprints and knows how to construct a building. Reading can also mean interpreting, as when a sailor "reads" the sky and knows that the day will bring winds and rough seas. And reading can mean examining texts or cultural artifacts and perceiving messages of racism, gender bias, or cultural exploitation. All these "readings" require a close critical and rhetorical attention to the text that involves analyzing, probing, and responding.

> ❝ Reading is not a passive process by which we soak up words and information from the page, but an active process by which we predict, sample, and confirm or correct our hypotheses about the written text. ❞
>
> —Constance Weaver,
> Author of *Reading Process and Practice*

Taken from *The Prentice Hall Guide for College Writers*, Eleventh Edition by Stephen P. Reid and Dominic DelliCarpini.

In this chapter, you will practice critical and rhetorical reading and responding to written texts (Chapter 13 will help you to analyze multimedia texts.) Active, critical reading requires multiple readings, asking questions, taking notes, and discussing ideas with other readers. Writing an accurate and objective summary is a key first step to responding to any text. Once you've written an accurate and objective summary, you are prepared to write a response to the text, analyzing it, agreeing or disagreeing with its ideas, offering your own interpretations of it.

This chapter will also introduce you to a specific kind of critical reading: rhetorical reading. In *rhetorical reading,* you read critically for specific persuasive strategies that writers use. How does the writer get the reader's attention? How, and how effectively, does the writer set forth a thesis, organize key ideas, lead from one point to the next, and conclude an argument? Does the writer use effective appeals to logic, emotion, or character? How do the writer's style, tone, and vocabulary contribute to her or his rhetorical appeals?

Techniques for Reading Critically and Responding to Texts

The critical reading of texts requires several techniques to ensure both comprehension and intelligent response. Although the strategies below are listed in an order typical for most critical reading assignments, remember that the critical reading process is just like any writing process. You may need to circle back and reread, summarize a second time, research key terms, or doublecheck on the author's background or publication context as you work.

Techniques for Reading Critically and Responding to Texts

Technique	Tips on How to Do It
Using active and responsive reading, writing, and discussing strategies.	Preview the author's background and the writing context. Prewrite about your own experiences with the subject. Read initially for information but then reread, make annotations, ask questions, research on the Internet, or do a double-entry log. Discuss the text with other readers in class or online.
Summarizing the main ideas or features of the text.	A summary should accurately and objectively represent the key ideas. Cite the author and title, accurately represent the main ideas, directly quote key phrases or sentences, and describe the main ideas or features of the text.
Responding to or critiquing the ideas in the text.	Responses may *agree or disagree* with the argument in the text; they may *analyze* the argument, organization, or quality of evidence in the text; and/or they may *reflect* on assumptions or implications.

Supporting the response with evidence.	Evidence should cite examples of strengths or weaknesses in the argument, evidence from other texts or outside reading, and/or examples from one's personal experience.
Combining summary and response into a coherent essay.	Usually the summary appears first, followed by the reader's response, but be sure to integrate the two parts. Your response should focus quickly on your main idea. Use a transition between the summary and response or integrate the summary and response throughout.

As you work on these techniques, don't simply read the text; listen to a class discussion and write out your critique. Use the interactive powers of reading, writing, and discussing to help you throughout your writing process. Annotate text by circling key ideas and writing your questions and responses in the margin. Continue reading and discussing your ideas after you have written out a draft.

CRITICAL READING STRATEGIES

12.1
Understand techniques for critical reading

Critical reading does not mean that you always criticize something or find fault. *Critical reading simply means questioning what you read.* You begin your critical reading by asking questions about every element in the rhetorical situation. Who is the *author,* and what is his or her background or potential bias? What was the *occasion,* and who was the intended *audience?* Is the writer's *purpose* achieved for that occasion and audience? Did the writer understand and fairly represent other writers' positions? Did the writer understand the *genre* and use it to achieve the purpose? How did the *cultural context* affect the author and the text? How did the context affect you as a reader?

Throughout the process, you will be asking about the writer's claim or argument, the representation of the background information, the organization, the logical use of evidence, and the effectiveness of the style, tone, and word choice. You will accomplish this by reading and then rereading, by probing key passages, by looking for gaps or ideas not included, by discussing the text with other readers, by assessing your position as a reader, and by continually making notes and asking questions.

Double-Entry Log

One of the most effective strategies to promote critical reading is a double-entry log. On the left-hand side, keep a running summary of the main ideas and features that you notice in the text. On the right-hand side, write your questions and reactions.

"Reading involves a fair measure of push and shove. You make your mark on a book and it makes its mark on you. Reading is not simply a matter of hanging back and waiting for a piece, or its author, to tell you what the writing has to say."

—David Bartholomae and Anthony Petrosky, Authors of *Ways of Reading*

Double-Entry Reading Log Format

Author and Title: _____

Summary

Main ideas, key features

Response

Your reactions, comments, and questions

Critical Rereading Guide

If your double-entry log does not yield useful ideas, try the ideas and suggestions in this rereading guide. First, read the text in its entirety. Then, let the following set of questions guide your rereading. The questions on the left-hand side will help you summarize and analyze the text; the questions on the right-hand side will start your critical reading and help focus your response.

Critical Rereading Guide

Summary and Analysis of Text	Critical Response
Purpose	
• Describe the author's overall *purpose* (to inform, explain, explore, evaluate, argue, negotiate, or other purpose). • How does the author/text want to affect or change the reader?	• Is the overall purpose clear or muddled? • Was the actual purpose different from the stated purpose? • How did the text affect you?
Audience/Reader	
• Who is the *intended* audience? • What *assumptions* does the author make about the reader's knowledge or beliefs? • From what *point of view* or in what *context* is the author writing?	• Are you part of the intended audience? • Does the author misjudge the reader's knowledge or beliefs? • Examine your own personal or cultural bias or point of view. How does that hinder you from being a critical reader of this text?
Occasion, Genre, Context	
• What was the *occasion* for this text? • What *genre* is this text? • What is the *cultural* or *historical context* for this text?	• What conversation was taking place on this topic? • Does the author's chosen genre help achieve the purpose for the audience? • What passages show the cultural forces at work on the author and the text?

Thesis and Main Ideas

- What key *question* or *problem* does the author/text address?

- What is the author's *thesis*?

- What *main ideas* support the thesis?

- What are the key passages or key moments in the text?

- Where is the thesis stated?

- Are the main ideas related to the thesis?

- Where do you agree or disagree?

- Does the text have contradictions or errors in logic?

- What ideas or arguments does the essay omit or ignore?

- What experience or prior knowledge do you have about the topic?

- What are the implications or consequences of the essay's ideas?

Organization and Evidence

- Where does the author *preview* the essay's organization?

- How does the author *signal* new sections of the essay?

- What kinds of *evidence* does the author use (personal experience, descriptions, statistics, interviews, other authorities, analytical reasoning, or other)?

- At what point could you accurately predict the organization of the essay?

- At what points were you confused about the organization?

- What evidence was most or least effective?

- Where did the author rely on assertions rather than on evidence?

- Which of your own personal experiences did you recall as you read the essay?

Language and Style

- What is the author's *tone* (casual, humorous, ironic, angry, preachy, academic, or other)?

- Are *sentences* and *vocabulary* easy, average, or difficult?

- What key *words* or *images* recur throughout the text?

- Did the tone support or distract from the author's purpose or meaning?

- Did the sentences and vocabulary support or distract from the purpose or meaning?

- Did recurring words or images relate to or support the purpose or meaning?

Remember that not all these questions will be relevant to a given text, but one or two of these questions may suggest a direction or give a *focus* to your overall response. When one of these questions does suggest a focus for your response to the essay, go back to the text, to other texts, and to your experience to gather *evidence* and *examples* to support your response.

SUMMARIZING AND RESPONDING TO AN ESSAY

12.2

Use critical reading techniques to summarize and respond to a text

Before you read the following essay by Casey Cavanaugh, "Why We Still Need Feminism." write for five minutes on the suggested Prereading Journal Entry that precedes the essay. You will be a much more responsive reader if you reflect on your own experiences and articulate your opinions *before* you are influenced by the author and her text. If possible, discuss your experiences and opinions with your classmates after you write your entry—but before you read the essay. Next, read the introductory note about Cavanaugh and *Huffington Post*, where this piece was published, to get background and context. Finally, practice active reading techniques as you read: Read first for information and enjoyment. Then reread and annotate the essay. Either write your comments and questions directly in the text or in a double-entry log.

Prereading Journal Entry

Describe your personal understanding of the term "feminist" and the kinds of reactions the word seems to bring out in others. Do the reactions seem to vary by gender, age, experience, or social class? Do you think feminism is something that still exists, or something that mostly describes a past movement? How would you define the term "feminism"? Finally, describe one personal experience that taught you something about how people tend to react to the word. What was the experience and how did you react?

Why We Still Need Feminism

Casey Cavanaugh

Casey Cavanaugh is a freelance writer and blogger who holds a bachelor's degree in writing with a minor in psychology. She is a freelance writer as well as a content manager for an advertising agency. Her work, which focuses on healthy lifestyles, relationships, and humor has appeared in online publications such as *Elite Daily* and the *Huffington Post*, where this essay first appeared in 2014. The *Huffington Post*, founded by journalist and businesswoman Ariana Huffington, is a largely left-leaning online news aggregator and blog site which is at once extremely popular and often criticized by conservatives.

Feminists are not angry lesbians who hate men. Feminists do not believe women are better than men, or that women deserve special privileges. They do not believe women are victims. 1

In order to be considered a feminist, you only need to be on board with one idea: All humans, male and female, should have equal political, economic and social rights. 2

Although more and more people are beginning to understand the true definition of feminism and openly identifying with it, there has always been a negative stigma attached to it. Part of this problem is the way our media sensationalizes things, trying to pass the most radical and extreme versions as the standard which, in this case, depicts a feminist as a man-hater who hates lipstick, crinkles her nose at stay-at-home moms, and unapologetically supports abortions on demand. 3

(Continued)

It's these false assumptions that cause anti-feminist campaigns, such as the   4
recent "Women Against Feminism," which consists of people posting photos of
themselves with statements such as: "I don't need feminism because I don't
choose to ignore the fact that men have issues too" and "I don't need feminism
because I already have equal rights." Reading through the majority of these
posts quickly brings forth a glaringly obvious problem: how misguided too
many people still are about what being a feminist actually means.

As Lena Dunham pointed out, "Feminism isn't a dirty word. It's not like   5
we're a deranged group who think women should take over the planet, raise our
young on our own and eliminate men from the picture."

Being a feminist has nothing to do with how you look, what you wear, who   6
you date, or how often you have sex. Being a feminist doesn't mean you think
women deserve special rights; it means you know we deserve equal ones.

While a primary purpose of feminism is to empower women, it does not   7
mean feminists view all women as weak and oppressed. Feminists are not aiming to make women stronger; they already know they're strong. They just want
society to see that too.

Empowering women does not mean belittling or punishing men. Men, too,   8
suffer from gender role assumptions that place expectations upon them to live
and act a certain way. Feminists believe each person should be viewed based on
their individual strengths and capabilities as a human being, not the strengths
and capabilities assumed of their gender. They believe every person should be
treated equally—not because of gender, but in spite of it.

Why We Still Need Feminism

There are some people who believe that feminism is a thing of the past—   9
that we don't need it anymore because the patriarchal system no longer exists.
After all, we can vote, right? That's true. In fact, in all demographics, females vote
more than men do. Yet, women still hold less than 20 percent of seats in Congress,
even though they make up more than half the population. Some believe the patriarchal system doesn't exist because we have equal employment opportunities.
But if this were really the case would there still be a 23 percent pay gap?

It is great so many women today feel like they have equal opportunities as   10
men. If it wasn't for past feminist movements, who knows where we would be
today. But we still need feminism, and will continue to need it, until every other
woman in the world feels this way as well.

We still need feminism because when people get married it is assumed the   11
woman will take the man's last name. Because when women are assaulted, they
are often the ones who feel ashamed.

We still need feminism because we teach women how to prevent rape, in-   12
stead of teaching people to not view women as objects. Because women are told
that walking alone at night makes them "an easy target." Because, sometimes, a

(Continued)

...*continued* Why We Still Need Feminism, **Casey Cavanaugh**

movie's rating (PG-13 versus R) depends on how much a female appears to be enjoying sex in a certain scene.

We still need feminism because our bodies are still being legislated, be- 13 cause McDonald's still asks us if we want a girl or boy toy, because we use terms like "bitch" and "pussy" to imply weakness.

We need feminism because FGM (Female Genital Mutilation), the act of 14 cutting off and restitching female genitals to prevent pleasurable sex—and can happen to girls as young as 5 months old—is still practiced in 29 countries. Because more than 120 countries don't have laws against marital rape, and still allow child brides—some as young as 6 years old.

We need feminism because infanticides, the act of killing children within a 15 year of birth, can be attributed to millions of fewer females than males in Middle Eastern countries, and because in Afghanistan women going to college can be considered justifiable grounds for disfiguring.

Being a feminist does not mean you think women can't speak for them- 16 selves, it means you realize that, even though some may be lucky enough to, there's still many who can't.

It Is Not a Gender Issue—It Is a Humanity Issue

It isn't about telling women what to do, it is giving them the ability and freedom 17 to be able to choose to do whatever they want to do—whether that be a stay at home mom, electrical engineer, or business CEO. The purpose is to create a so-ciety of equal say, to provide people with the freedom of choice, rather than limited choices of assumption.

Feminists don't believe women should look or behave a certain way, it 18 means they want women have to have the freedom to look and behave however they want—unapologetically. It is not about telling women what they need.

While reading through Women Against Feminism posts that say things 19 such as, "I don't need it because I already feel equal" and "I don't want feminism because I don't need special treatment, and don't support sleeping around," I can't help but think it isn't about our personal wants and needs, though they are all relevant, but rather what we—as a society—need.

If you are a feminist, you believe women should be treated the same as men, 20 not because we're better, but because we're human.

As Joseph Gordon-Levitt so eloquently worded it, "I'm a believer that if 21 everyone has a fair chance to be what they want to be and do what they want to do, it's better for everyone. It benefits society as a whole."

The idea that there are still people, let alone women, proudly declaring they 22 don't need feminism is alarming and frightening—at best.

We need feminism because people are still blindly agreeing that women 23 don't need to be paid for the same work as men, that they are okay with the in-difference and injustices so ingrained in society that they have accepted it as a way of life. That they are not only looking the other way to these issues, but they

(Continued)

are also entirely and genuinely convinced they are doing the world a favor by hushing feminist attempts.

Some people don't feel the need to voice their thoughts on the matter at all, and that's okay. But there is a big difference between being indifferent and being ignorant. And that difference is speaking out about an issue when your opinion is based on misguided information and false assumptions. 24

Why do we need feminism? For the same reason screenwriter John Whedon gave when asked why he writes such strong female characters, "Because you're still asking me that question." 25

Summarizing

The purpose of a summary is to provide a condensed and objective account of the main ideas and features of a text. Typically, a summary will do the following:

- *Cite the author and title of the text.* In some cases, the place of publication or the context for the essay may also be included.
- *Indicate the main ideas of the text.* Accurately representing the main ideas (while omitting the details) is the major goal of a summary.
- *Use direct quotation of key words, phrases, or sentences.* *Quote* the text directly for a few key ideas; *paraphrase* the other important ideas (that is, express the ideas in your own words).
- *Include author tags.* "According to Cavanaugh" or "as Cavanaugh explains" reminds the reader that you are summarizing the author and the text, not giving your own ideas. *Note:* Instead of repeating "Cavanaugh says," choose verbs that more accurately represent the purpose or tone of the original passage: "Cavanaugh argues," "Cavanaugh explains," "Cavanaugh warns," "Cavanaugh advises."
- *Avoid summarizing specific examples or data* unless they help illustrate the thesis or main idea of the text.
- *Report the main ideas as objectively as possible.* Represent the author and text accurately and faithfully. Do not include your reactions; save them for your response.

Summary of "Why We Still Need Feminism"

Following is a summary of Cavanaugh's essay. Do *not* read this summary, however, until you have tried to write your own. After you have made notes and written a draft for your own summary, you will more clearly understand the key features of a summary. *Note:* There are many ways to write a good summary. If your summary conveys the main ideas and has the features described above, it may be just as good as the following example. (Key features of a summary are annotated in the margin.)

> "Inferences about the writer's intentions appear to be an essential building block—one that readers actively use to construct a meaningful text. "
>
> —Linda Flower, Author of "The Construction of Purpose"

Title and author

Context for the essay

Use of direct
quotations

Author tag
Main idea paraphrase

In "Why We Still Need Feminism," journalist and blogger Casey Cavanaugh argues that feminism is still necessary by showing its true definition. Her argument is contrasted to current attitudes in the media toward feminism. More specifically, the ways that "media sensationalizes things, trying to pass the most radical and extreme versions as the standard which, in this case, depicts a feminist as a man-hater who hates lipstick, crinkles her nose at stay-at-home moms, and unapologetically supports abortions on demand." Cavanaugh explains the reasons why what she calls "anti-feminist campaigns" begin from false assumptions and work from "misguided" understandings of what feminism really is. Cavanaugh's central argument is that we need feminism because the same reasons that this movement began still exist: women still hold less than 20% of the seats in Congress, they are still expected to take their husband's last name, they still get less pay for equal work, and they are still treated as sexual objects—which is one of the causes for rape. She also uses examples from other cultures that demonstrate that while some countries have made progress, many still have practices like female genital mutilation and infanticide of girls. In the end, Cavanaugh asserts that feminism is most accurately not just pro-women, but pro-humanity—not because women are "better, but because we're human."

Author tag and main
idea paraphrases

Direct quotation

Responding

> **Reading the world always precedes reading the word, and reading the word implies continually reading the world.**
>
> —Paulo Freire,
> Author of
> *Literacy: Reading the Word and the World*

A response, unlike pure summary, requires a reaction and interpretation guided by your experiences, beliefs, and attitudes. Good responses say what you think, but then they *show why* you think so. They show the relationships between your opinions and the text, between the text and your experience, and between this text and other texts. That is why you need to first do a summary—to be sure you know the text well before you respond.

Types of Responses   Depending on its purpose and intended audience, a response to a text can take any of several directions. Responses may focus on one or more of the following strategies. Consider your purpose and audience or check your assignment to see which type(s) you should emphasize.

- *Analyzing the effectiveness of the text.* This response analyzes key features such as the clarity of the main idea, the rhetorical situation, the organization of the argument, the logic of the reasoning, the quality of the supporting evidence, and/or the effectiveness of the author's style, tone, and voice.
- *Agreeing and/or disagreeing with the ideas in the text.* Often responders react to the ideas or the argument of the essay. In this case, the responders show why they agree and/or disagree with what the author or the text says.
- *Interpreting and reflecting on the text.* The responder explains key passages or examines the underlying assumptions or the implications of the ideas. Often, the responder reflects on how his or her own experiences, attitudes, and observations relate to the text.

Kinds of Evidence Regardless of the direction they take, all responses must be supported by evidence, examples, facts, and details. Good responses draw on several kinds of supporting evidence.

- *Personal experience.* Responders may use *examples* from their personal experiences to show why they interpreted the text as they did, why they agreed or disagreed, or why they reacted as they did.
- *Evidence from the text.* Responders should cite *specific phrases or sentences* from the text to support their explanation of a section, their analysis of the effectiveness of a passage, or their agreement or disagreement with a key point.
- *Evidence from other texts.* Responders may bring in ideas and information from other relevant essays, articles, books, or graphic material.

Not all responses use all three kinds of supporting evidence, but all responses *must* have sufficient examples to support the responder's ideas, reactions, and opinions. Responders should not merely state their opinions. They must give evidence to *show* how and why they read the text as they did.

One final—and crucial—note about responses: A response should make a coherent, overall main point. It should not be just a laundry list of reactions, likes, and dislikes. Sometimes the main point is that the text is not convincing because it lacks evidence. Sometimes the point is that the text makes an original statement even though it is difficult to read. Perhaps the point will be that the author or the text stimulates the reader to reflect on his or her experience. Every response should focus on a coherent main idea.

Response to "Why We Still Need Feminism"

One possible response to Cavanaugh's essay follows. Before you read this response, however, write out your own reactions. There will be many different but valid responses to any given essay. For this response, marginal annotations indicate the different types of responses and the different kinds of evidence the writer uses.

Casey Cavanaugh's article is effective because she presents vivid examples of why feminism is still necessary. I like the way that she distinguishes the common understanding of a feminist—as a "man-hater" or one who "unapologetically supports abortions on demand" from the definition of feminism that she wants to present—as someone who believes that women deserve equal rights. She supports that idea nicely by quoting a male voice, Joseph Gordon-Levitt, who notes that feminism "benefits society as a whole."

Cavanaugh illustrates her point that it is "still necessary" by reminding us of the many situations in which women are still not treated equal—such as the

Central reason for effectiveness

Illustrates some of the best lines

Author tag

(Continued)

...*continued* Why We Still Need Feminism, **Casey Cavanaugh**

Personal reflections on the text

Quotation supports response

Supports point with evidence from another article

Evidence from the text

A minor critique

Responder's main point, which shows personal reaction

gender/wage gap and the lack of adequate representation in Congress. At the same time, I like the way that she avoids the "man-hater" definition by noting that "men, too, suffer from gender role assumptions." Indeed, the *Denver Post* has recently reported that the gender/wage gap has widened; now women make just 74.6 percent of what men make for the same job—down from the 84 percent that was seen in 2002.

Cavanaugh is also able to show why feminism is so important by including the most serious examples—rape, infanticide, and genital mutilation. This is able to overcome any sense that women are just whiners, but really a matter of life and death.

She may be a bit too critical of those who have alternative views of feminism in spots, such as when she talks about those who "blindly" agree that women don't deserve equal pay or those who are "hushing feminist attempts." But in the end, she seems reasonable and inclusive, which makes me feel—even as a man—able to support feminism.

RHETORICAL READING AND ANALYSIS

12.3
Understand techniques for rhetorical reading and analysis

If *rhetoric* is defined as the "art of persuasion," then rhetorical reading is the analysis of the strategies a speaker or writer employs to persuade her audience or readers. Although *rhetoric* sometimes has negative connotations—we may refer to a political speech or blog as being "empty rhetoric"—rhetoric typically refers to the study of the most effective ways to communicate a message to a specific audience.

Learning the skills required by a rhetorical analysis is important for improving your ability to read and write a variety of academic and public texts. Understanding how to read a text rhetorically and write a rhetorical analysis will help you in three important ways. First, you will become more familiar with the language and the key terms you will use extensively in this writing course. Second, you will acquire the vocabulary and analytical skills to provide helpful and constructive feedback during peer review. Finally—and most important—you will become more proficient at analyzing the strengths and weaknesses of texts you read in your other courses or in your own research. With these skills, you will be able to contribute to any academic or public conversation you encounter.

The Rhetorical Triangle

Here is an example of a contemporary version of the rhetorical triangle (sometimes called a "communication triangle"). This triangle presents the key features of any rhetorical situation: the author or writer, the text, the audience or readers, and the context—the place of publication and the occasion for which the text was written.

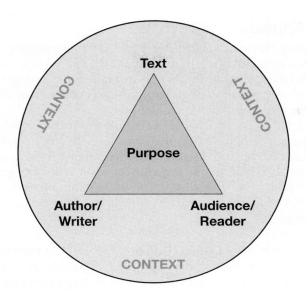

Rhetorical Analysis vs. Critical Reading

Rhetorical analysis relies on the critical reading processes you practiced earlier in this chapter, but here the emphasis is on identifying the key rhetorical strategies used by a writer and judging whether those strategies are effective, given the writer's purpose, occasion, audience, and genre. The emphasis is less on *what* the writer says—or whether you agree or disagree—and more on *how*, and *how effectively,* the writer constructs the essay or argument.

As the "Wh" Questions chart indicates, critical reading begins with asking *who, what, when, where,* and *why* questions about a text. Rhetorical reading asks—and answers—those questions, but in addition it focuses on the *how* questions: How does the writer construct the essay or text? How effective are the writer's chosen rhetorical strategies in achieving the purpose for the intended audience?

Rhetorical analysis requires knowing and using such key rhetorical terms as the writer's rhetorical occasion and situation; the writer's appeals to logic (logos), emotion (pathos), and character (ethos); and the writer's use of style to connect with readers and support the appeals to logos, pathos, and ethos.

Reminder: In rhetorical analysis, you will *not* explain why you agree or disagree with what the writer says. You will analyze only the rhetorical strategies and explain which strategies are most or least effective for the writer's purpose and audience.

"Wh" Questions

Critical Reading

Who is the writer?

Who is the intended reader?

When was it written?

Where does it appear?

Why is the writer writing on this topic?

What is the writer saying or arguing?

Rhetorical Analysis

How does the writer construct the essay or text?

What rhetorical strategies does the writer use?

How effective is each of those strategies?

Rhetorical Appeals

Like critical reading, rhetorical reading begins with an understanding of the key elements in the rhetorical situation. Who is the *author*, and what is his or her background? Why did the author write this text—what was the *occasion*? Who was the writer's *audience*? What was the writer's *purpose*? In what cultural or disciplinary *context* was the writer working? What *genre* did the writer use?

After identifying these elements of the rhetorical situation, you're ready to describe the key rhetorical strategies that the writer uses. The most important of them are the *rhetorical appeals to the writer's audience*. Writers appeal to an audience by using reasonable and reliable evidence and logic (logos), by demonstrating their character through their credibility and reliability (ethos), and by appealing effectively to emotions (pathos). For additional information on rhetorical appeals, see Chapter 18, Persuasive Writing (pages 562–565).

Appeal to Reason and Logic (Logos) Especially in formal and academic writing, writers convince their readers by being reasonable and logical. Effective writers construct a strong logos appeal by clearly stating their claims and offering sufficient supporting evidence. Evidence can include citations from accepted authorities, statistics or conclusions from scientific or peer-reviewed studies, and appropriate personal experience. A logos appeal can be strengthened by clear organization, a logical order or sequence to reasons and evidence, and a clear, logical, and grammatically appropriate style.

Problems in logical reasoning—the so-called fallacies of logic—can seriously weaken a writer's logos appeal. Fallacies such as "either-or" reasoning, hasty generalizations, "red herring" arguments, faulty analogies, "post hoc" arguments, "begging the question," circular arguments, "straw man" arguments, and other errors in reasoning will weaken any writer's logos appeal. For a full explanation of these fallacies in logic, see Chapter 18, Persuasive Writing (pages 610–612).

Appeal to Character and Credibility (Ethos) Writers are believable and convincing not only when they use good logos appeals but also when they establish their good character, credibility, and trustworthiness. We trust writers who are known experts or authorities, but we also trust writers who present all the relevant information, who give both sides of an argument, who do thorough research and present that research accurately and clearly, and who show fairness and reasonableness in their arguments. Ethos appeals can be undermined by writers who exaggerate, use emotional or loaded language, distort facts and figures, misrepresent alternative arguments, or omit key evidence.

Appeal to Emotion (Pathos) Appeals to emotion can be effective when the emotional content is genuine, appropriate for the subject, and not exaggerated. Often, writers use emotional appeals because they think that if they show they are passionate about the subject, they will win over their readers. However, emotional

Techniques for Rhetorical Analysis and Response

Technique	Tips on How to Do It
Using active reading, writing, and discussing strategies.	*Identify* the author's audience, purpose, genre, main arguments, and key rhetorical strategies.
Summarizing the author's audience, purpose, and main ideas and then noting the author's main rhetorical strategies.	Indicate the author's purpose, audience, occasion, context, and main arguments and *objectively* describe the key rhetorical strategies, including appeals to logos, pathos, and ethos as well as stylistic strategies.
Responding by analyzing the rhetorical effectiveness (strengths and weaknesses) of the text.	Consider clarity of writer's purpose, use of occasion, connection with audience, effectiveness of rhetorical appeals, clarity of organization, and appropriateness of style. *Focus* on the particular strategies you intend to analyze.
Citing evidence from the text to support your analysis of both the rhetorical strengths and weaknesses of the text.	Support your claims of effectiveness and ineffectiveness with *specific examples* from the text. What rhetorical strategies and appeals were most effective/ineffective for the purpose, audience, and context? Note any *gaps* or *missed opportunities* for making the argument more effective for its audience and context.
Combining summary and response into a coherent essay containing your thesis about the rhetorical effectiveness of the text.	Begin with the summary, followed by your rhetorical analysis of the text. Present your thesis about the overall effectiveness first, then develop your points and supporting evidence of both effectiveness and ineffectiveness.

appeals can backfire because the slightest overuse or exaggeration may negate the writer's logos or ethos appeals.

Combined Appeals Appeals to logos, ethos, and pathos are interconnected and interrelated. An effective logos appeal usually strengthens the author's ethos appeal. A strong ethos appeal makes readers expect a credible and logical argument. An appropriate use of pathos often makes the writer seem more human and credible, which supports the ethos appeal. On the negative side, an excessive use of pathos appeals can undermine a writer's credibility, and a writer's failure to cite logical supporting evidence or authorities will damage the ethos appeal.

In July, 1848, a small group of women who also had been involved in other social reform movements such as abolition of slavery and temperance gathered in what was to be the first full-scale women's rights movement in the United States. Organized by Elizabeth Cady Stanton and Lucretia Mott, the Convention resulted in the ratification of *The Declaration of Sentiments and Resolutions* (authored largely by Stanton), which made the case for women's equality and for rights that would recognize that equality. A version of the address that follows was delivered by Stanton on the morning of July 19, 1848. It was then slightly revised based on audience comments. The text below is the final version read by Stanton and then adopted on the morning of July 20, 1848. Speaking at a time when women were not afforded credibility as equally-capable citizens, Stanton builds the argument that "all men *and women* are created equal." The notes in the margin illustrate how Stanton combines the rhetorical appeals in order to make this case to both genders. The student essay at the end of this chapter provides an example of a full rhetorical analysis of this piece.

Declaration of Sentiments and Resolutions (Seneca Falls Resolution)

Elizabeth Cady Stanton et al.

Elizabeth Cady Stanton, the primary author of this famous Declaration, was an activist who used her rhetorical skills toward abolishing slavery and establishing the rights of women. Born in Johnstown, New York in 1815, Stanton was the daughter of a lawyer. She married a prominent reformer (though, the story goes, she omitted the word "obey" from the marriage vows at her wedding), and went on to become a central figure in the women's suffrage movement.

Introduction uses logos to explain the purpose and demonstrate her reasonable approach to a solution

1   When, in the course of human events, it becomes necessary for one portion of the family of man to assume among the people of the earth a position different from that which they have hitherto occupied, but one to which the laws of nature and of nature's God entitle them, a decent respect to the opinions of mankind requires that they should declare the causes that impel them to such a course.

Reference to the *Declaration of Independence* establishes the author's ethos

2   We hold these truths to be self-evident: that all men and women are created equal; that they are endowed by their Creator with certain inalienable rights; that among these are life, liberty, and the pursuit of happiness; that to secure these rights governments are instituted, deriving their just powers from the consent of the governed. Whenever any form of government becomes destructive of these ends, it is the right of those who suffer from it to refuse allegiance to it, and to insist upon the institution of a new government, laying its foundation on such principles, and organizing its powers in such form, as to them shall seem most likely to effect their safety and happiness. Prudence, indeed, will dictate that governments long established should not be changed for light and transient causes; and accordingly all experience hath shown that mankind are

(Continued)

more disposed to suffer, while evils are sufferable, than to right themselves by abolishing the forms to which they were accustomed. But when a long train of abuses and usurpations, pursuing invariably the same object evinces a design to reduce them under absolute despotism, it is their duty to throw off such government, and to provide new guards for their future security. Such has been the patient sufferance of the women under this government, and such is now the necessity which constrains them to demand the equal station to which they are entitled.

The history of mankind is a history of repeated injuries and usurpations on the part of man toward woman, having in direct object the establishment of an absolute tyranny over her. To prove this, let facts be submitted to a candid world.   3

He has never permitted her to exercise her inalienable right to the elective franchise.   4

He has compelled her to submit to laws, in the formation of which she had no voice.   5

He has withheld from her rights which are given to the most ignorant and degraded men—both natives and foreigners.   6

Having deprived her of this first right of a citizen, the elective franchise, thereby leaving her without representation in the halls of legislation, he has oppressed her on all sides.   7

He has made her, if married, in the eye of the law, civilly dead.   8

He has taken from her all right in property, even to the wages she earns.   9

He has made her, morally, an irresponsible being, as she can commit many crimes with impunity, provided they be done in the presence of her husband. In the covenant of marriage, she is compelled to promise obedience to her husband, he becoming, to all intents and purposes, her master—the law giving him power to deprive her of her liberty, and to administer chastisement.   10

He has so framed the laws of divorce, as to what shall be the proper causes, and in case of separation, to whom the guardianship of the children shall be given, as to be wholly regardless of the happiness of women—the law, in all cases, going upon a false supposition of the supremacy of man, and giving all power into his hands.   11

After depriving her of all rights as a married woman, if single, and the owner of property, he has taxed her to support a government which recognizes her only when her property can be made profitable to it.   12

He has monopolized nearly all the profitable employments, and from those she is permitted to follow, she receives but a scanty remuneration. He closes against her all the avenues to wealth and distinction which he considers most honorable to himself. As a teacher of theology, medicine, or law, she is not known.   13

He has denied her the facilities for obtaining a thorough education, all colleges being closed against her.   14

The logos appeal continues, drawing upon the same logical argument of the Declaration of Independence

Logos appeal is combined with an appeal to pathos through the plight of women

The pathos appeals become stronger as the Declaration continues, adding new examples, but never losing the logos- and ethos-based voice.

(Continued)

...continued Declaration of Sentiments and Resolutions, **Elizabeth Cady Stanton et al.**

He allows her in Church, as well as the State, but a subordinate position, *15* claiming Apostolic authority for her exclusion from the ministry, and, with some exceptions, from any public participation in the affairs of the Church.

He has created a false public sentiment by giving to the world of a different *16* code of morals for men and women, by which moral delinquencies which exclude women from society, are not only tolerated, but deemed of little account in man.

He has usurped the prerogative of Jehovah himself, claiming it as his right to as- *17* sign for her a sphere of action, when that belongs to her conscience and to her God.

He has endeavored, in every way that he could, to destroy her confidence in *18* her own powers, to lessen her self-respect, and to make her willing to lead a dependent and abject life.

Now, in view of this entire disfranchisement of one-half the people of this *19* country, their social and religious degradation—in view of the unjust laws above mentioned, and because women do feel themselves aggrieved, oppressed, and fraudulently deprived of their most sacred rights, we insist that they have immediate admission to all the rights and privileges which belong to them as citizens of the United States.

In entering upon the great work before us, we anticipate no small amount of *20* misconception, misrepresentation, and ridicule; but we shall use every instrumentality within our power to effect our object. We shall employ agents, circulate tracts, petition the State and National legislatures, and endeavor to enlist the pulpit and the press in our behalf. We hope this Convention will be followed by a series of Conventions embracing every part of the country.

Resolutions

WHEREAS, The great precept of nature is conceded to be, that "man shall pursue *21* his own true and substantial happiness." Blackstone in his Commentaries remarks, that this law of Nature being coeval with mankind, and dictated by God himself, is of course superior in obligation to any other. It is binding over all the globe, in all countries and at all times; no human laws are of any validity if contrary to this, and such of them as are valid, derive all their force, and all their validity, and all their authority, mediately and immediately, from this original; therefore,

RESOLVED, That such laws as conflict, in any way, with the true and sub- *22* stantial happiness of woman, are contrary to the great precept of nature and of no validity, for this is "superior in obligation to any other."

RESOLVED, That all laws which prevent woman from occupying such a *23* station in society as her conscience shall dictate, or which place her in a position inferior to that of man, are contrary to the great precept of nature, and therefore of no force or authority.

The claims based on Christian beliefs combine ethos and logos. The tone is reasonable, and the authority comes from God's word.

Here, the impassioned word choices add pathos to the argument

Referencing the process of petitioning for rights develops the ethos and logos of the author.

The resolution combine strong reasoning (logos) with appeals to the authority of reason and God (ethos)

(Continued)

RESOLVED, That woman is man's equal—was intended to be so by the   *24*
Creator, and the highest good of the race demands that she should be recognized as such.

RESOLVED, That the women of this country ought to be enlightened in   *25*
regard to the laws under which they live, that they may no longer publish their degradation by declaring themselves satisfied with their present position, nor their ignorance, by asserting that they have all the rights they want.

RESOLVED, That inasmuch as man, while claiming for himself intellectual   *26*
superiority, does accord to woman moral superiority, it is pre-eminently his duty to encourage her to speak and teach, as she has an opportunity, in all religious assemblies.

Stanton's logic builds upon the claims made by men about women's "moral superiority"

RESOLVED, That the same amount of virtue, delicacy, and refinement of   *27*
behavior that is required of woman in the social state, should also be required of man, and the same transgressions should be visited with equal severity on both man and woman.

RESOLVED, That the objection of indelicacy and impropriety, which is so   *28*
often brought against woman when she addresses a public audience, comes with a very ill-grace from those who encourage, by their attendance, her appearance on the stage, in the concert, or in feats of the circus.

RESOLVED, That woman has too long rested satisfied in the circumscribed   *29*
limits which corrupt customs and a perverted application of the Scriptures have marked out for her, and that it is time she should move in the enlarged sphere which her great Creator has assigned her.

The ethos appeal to God's authority continues

RESOLVED, That it is the duty of the women of this country to secure to   *30*
themselves their sacred right to the elective franchise.

RESOLVED, That the equality of human rights results necessarily from the   *31*
fact of the identity of the race in capabilities and responsibilities.

RESOLVED, therefore, That, being invested by the Creator with the same   *32*
capabilities, and the same consciousness of responsibility of their exercise, it is demonstrably the right and duty of woman, equally with man, to promote every righteous cause by every righteous means; and especially in regard to the great subjects of morals and religion, it is self-evidently her right to participate with her brother in teaching them, both in private and in public, by writing and by speaking, by any instrumentalities proper to be used, and in any assemblies proper to be held; and this being a self-evident truth growing out of the divinely implanted principles of human nature, any custom or authority adverse to it,

This long resolution asserts the ethos of women by demonstrating their right to participate in the freedoms afforded to all citizens

(Continued)

> *...continued* Declaration of Sentiments and Resolutions, **Elizabeth Cady Stanton et al.**
>
> whether modern or wearing the hoary sanction of antiquity, is to be regarded as a self-evident falsehood, and at war with mankind.
>
> [At the last session Lucretia Mott offered and spoke to the following resolution:]
>
> RESOLVED, That the speedy success of our cause depends upon the zeal- 33
> ous and untiring efforts of both men and women, for the overthrow of the monopoly of the pulpit, and for the securing to woman an equal participation with men in the various trades, professions, and commerce.

This added resolution widens the appeal to invite all members of the audience—men and women—into the cause.

Questions for Writing and Discussion

1. What affect does the blatant and obvious use of phrases from the *Declaration of Independence* have? Which of the appeals does this seem to employ most?

2. In the final version, Lucretia Mott added the resolution noting that "the speedy success of our cause depends upon the zealous and untiring efforts of both men and women." What does this add to the rest of the document? Rhetorically, what does it accomplish, and for what audience? Does it in any way undermine the overall purpose of the *Declaration*?

3. What parts of this document are especially effective in terms of the pathos appeal? Why? Describe the likely effect upon the audience of each gender.

4. What is the rhetorical effect of the pronouns "he" and "she" as used in this document? Try to systematically describe these uses by analyzing each one and drawing conclusions about their cumulative effect.

Rhetorical Analysis Guide

The following questions are intended to help you develop a rhetorical summary and response. As you read a text, you should analyze all the rhetorical features described below. In your response, address primarily the most effective and the least effective rhetorical choices. *Remember:* Writers make rhetorical choices throughout an essay or text. Your analytical task is to determine whether they made the most effective choices, given their occasion, purpose, and audience.

Guide to Rhetorical Analysis

Rhetorical Summary of Text	Rhetorical Analysis/Response
Purpose	
• Describe the author's overall purpose (to inform, explain, explore, evaluate, argue, negotiate, or other purpose).	• Is the author's purpose stated or unstated? • Was the actual purpose different from the stated purpose?

Audience/Reader

- Who is the intended audience?
- What assumptions does the author make about the reader's knowledge or beliefs?
- Where does the author effectively address the intended audience?
- Is the intended audience a likely audience for this purpose and thesis?

Occasion, Genre, Context

- What was the occasion for this text?
- What is the cultural or historical context?
- Of what genre is this text?
- Was the purpose appropriate for the occasion and context?
- Considering the author's purpose and audience, did the author choose an appropriate genre for this occasion?

Appeals to Logos, Ethos, and Pathos

- Where does the writer appeal to logos?
- Where does the writer appeal to ethos?
- Where does the writer appeal to pathos?
- What strategies make the logos appeals effective or ineffective?
- What strategies make the ethos appeals effective or ineffective?
- What strategies make the pathos appeals effective or ineffective?

Thesis and Main Ideas (a clear thesis helps support both logos and ethos appeals)

- What key question or problem does the author address?
- What is the author's thesis?
- What main ideas or reasons support the thesis?
- Is the writer's focus on a key question or problem effective?
- Is the thesis clearly stated?
- Are the supporting reasons clearly identifiable and related to the thesis?

Organization (a clear organization helps support both logos and ethos appeals)

- Where does the author preview the organization of the text?
- Where does the author signal new ideas or sections of the text?
- Is the organization clear and effective for the intended audience? Why or why not?
- Is the argument easy or difficult to follow? Where is the organization clear or confusing?

Style, Tone, Vocabulary (stylistic elements can support or detract from the appeals)

- Are sentences formal and academic or informal and colloquial?
- What is the author's tone (casual, humorous, ironic, preachy, academic, or other)?
- Is the vocabulary academic, technical, mainstream, informal, colloquial?
- Which sentences are or are not effective for the purpose and the intended audience?
- Where is the author's tone effective or ineffective for the audience?
- Where are word choices effective or ineffective for the audience?

Warming Up: Journal Exercises

The following topics will help you practice reading and responding.

1 **Community Service Learning Project.** Go to a local nonprofit organization and collect texts, images, and brochures that advertise the organization or explain its mission. Choose one or two documents and write a summary and response addressed both to your classmates and to the organization itself. Consider the rhetorical context of these documents (author, purpose, audience, occasion, genre, and cultural context) as you explain why they are or are not effective or appropriate and/or how you interpret the assumptions and implications contained in the texts or images. Your goal is to provide constructive suggestions about ways to revise or improve the texts.

2 **Visual Rhetoric.** Study the image on the first page of this chapter that portrays a famous drawing of the Seneca Falls Convention. In what ways does the image portray the character of a woman orator? What details of the image stand out to you, and what rhetorical appeals might they make? What rhetorical and cultural message does Cady Stanton's style of dress send? What does the caption add to our understanding of the image?

3 **Writing Across the Curriculum.** Because previewing material is an important part of active reading, most recent textbooks use previewing or prereading strategies at the beginning of each chapter. Find one chapter in a textbook that uses these previewing techniques. How does the author preview the material? Does the preview help you understand the material in the chapter?

4 **Collaborating with Peers.** Choose something that you have written recently, whether for a class, for personal reasons, or on social media, and ask a classmate to do the same. Share your writing with each other, explaining to your peer the purpose and audience of your piece. Then use the techniques of rhetorical analysis to evaluate each other's work, focusing on whether the purpose and audience have been adequately addressed, what parts of the piece use logos, pathos, or ethos appeals, and what revisions you might suggest to make the piece more persuasive.

Tips for Transferring Skills

The writing techniques discussed in this chapter can be used in many other situations you will face as a college writer and beyond. To reinforce these techniques, and to really put them to use, you should find ways to apply and practice them on other occasions and in other classes. Here are tips for using these techniques in a variety of writing situations.

1. One of the best ways to become a proficient and versatile writer is to read rhetorically. But when you read for other classes, you are likely paying attention to the content of the material, not the style. As you read material for other classes, use the skills learned in this chapter to analyze the use of logos, ethos, or pathos in that field, and whether one approach seems to be dominant in that style of writing. Also note other techniques that writers in, say, history or biology tend to use.

2. As you see advertisements on television or the Web, consider why they use the rhetorical appeals they do. Why do charities use pathos appeals? Why do some car adds use logos (mileage figures or engine type) while others use ethos (reputation) or pathos (Subaru's "love" campaign). This analytical approach might also help you in marketing or other business classes.

3. The rhetoric of science seems to be wholly based on logos appeals, but it also offers many appeals to ethos. As you read something for a science class, pay attention to how ethos (credibility) is enhanced by the author.

4. Usually we treat poetry and fiction purely as works of art. But are they also persuasive. As you read a work of literature for an English class, think about what parts of the piece seem to be trying to change your views or persuade you.

Reading Critically: Reading and Writing Processes

Using Critical Reading in Your Writing Processes

Critical reading can help you to summarize, analyze, and respond to all kinds of texts. Your reading and writing processes can help you, first, to fairly and accurately summarize a text, and then to provide commentary and analysis. Your analyses need to be based on solid evidence and examples, and they should demonstrate your knowledge of the rhetorical appeals and other techniques writers use. Taken together, a summary and critical reading response can help your audience to understand a text's purposes and how it attempts to accomplish those purposes. And using these processes to analyze the writing of others will also make you better at analyzing—and thereby improving—your own writing.

Writing that is based on the skills of critical reading can take many forms, as illustrated by this list of audiences and genres.

Audience	Possible Genres
Personal Audience	Class or laboratory notes, journal entry, blog, scrapbook, multimedia document
Academic Audience	Academic summary, summary and response, rhetorical analysis, synopsis, critique, review, journal entry, forum entry on class site, multimedia document
Public Audience	Column, editorial, letter to the editor, article in a magazine or newspaper, online site, newsletter, multimedia document

CHOOSING A SUBJECT

12.4
Use critical reading skills to select a text for analysis

"Plagiarism in America," an essay by Dudley Erskine Devlin, illustrates the various processes, activities, and strategies for reading and writing when summarizing, analyzing, and responding. As you read Devlin's essay, note how he summarizes and analyzes the problem before responding with possible solutions. How would you critically read and respond to Devlin's essay? Do you find his analysis adequate? What might you add, or where might you agree or disagree?

Prereading Journal Entry

In your journal, write what you already know about the subject of the essay. The following questions will help you recall your prior experiences and consider your own opinions. The purpose of this entry is to make you aware of your own experiences and opinions before you are influenced by the arguments of the essay.

- Did you or a friend in another writing class ever plagiarize part or all of a paper? What were the circumstances and what was the outcome?
- In your previous writing classes, what were you told about plagiarism? Did you sign an honor code? Did you learn how to paraphrase and use quotations? What were the penalties for plagiarism?
- Did your other writing teachers use plagiarism detection services such as Turnitin.com? Did knowing that help you avoid plagiarizing?

Plagiarism in America

Dudley Erskine Devlin

Dudley Erskine Devlin is a former English instructor at Colorado State University who has written editorials and blogs on contemporary issues. The targets for his columns are often controversial issues such as high-stakes testing in schools, texting while driving, and cyberbullying. This piece on plagiarism first appeared as an entry in one of Devlin's blogs.

Vice President Joe Biden lost his bid for the presidency in 1987 when it was 1 discovered that he had plagiarized a law review article in his first year at law school. Even some well-known authors, such as historians Doris Kearns and Stephen Ambrose, have been found guilty of plagiarism. So perhaps it's not surprising that high school and college students across the nation are also being found guilty of plagiarism. This epidemic of plagiarism, caused largely by students' ease of Internet access to millions of documents, needs to be met head-on with the most direct and effective surveillance and punishment measures possible.

Although cheating in schools has always been a problem, today's Wikipedia 2 generation is committing plagiarism in dramatically increased numbers. Recently, a Pew Internet & American Life Project survey showed that cheating and plagiarism have become epidemic—nearly one half of high school students reported that they or their friends cheated, even though the great majority said that cheating was definitely wrong. Researcher Donald McCabe reported in *Education Digest* that in a survey of 22 public high schools, 74% of the surveyed students reported one or more instances of test cheating in the past year and nearly 60% reported an incident involving plagiarism. McCabe also reported in *Liberal Education* that one out of every five or six college papers is plagiarized, and of the 51% of college students who self-reported that they cheated, four out of five indicated that they had bought a paper from the Internet or had cut and pasted material that they found on the Web. According to McCabe, students say, "I got it off the Internet so it's public information." They don't consider it to be a big deal. What's wrong with plagiarism, anyway? The information on the Internet—on Wikipedia, Spark Notes, or Gradesaver—is public, so why not just paste it in your paper?

Plagiarism in schools across America has definitely reached an epidemic 3 stage, but students, teachers, and administrators are divided about how to solve the problem. Some say plagiarism has always existed and because of the ease of technological access, we need increased surveillance. Others argue that students need more education in order to understand what plagiarism is and how to avoid it. Although both camps raise good points, rates of plagiarism will keep increasing until teachers and schools introduce zero tolerance rules.

(Continued)

Teachers must be more vigilant, and students who plagiarize must be punished swiftly and severely.

Some teachers argue that instead of surveillance and punishment, we 4 need to understand *why* students plagiarize, and then address the cause of the problem and educate everyone. When researchers ask students why they plagiarize, they uncover a variety of excuses. Frequently, students rationalize that they cheat because they see other students cheating or buying papers online, because they are in a large lecture class, or because they are taking a boring, required course. Students also blame outside forces— pressure from parents and pressure to get into college and maintain scholarships. Researcher Timothy Dodd of Duke University says that students often feel that they are "scrambling from assignment to assignment just trying to keep their heads above water. Students literally go on a scavenger hunt for information on the Internet, which they throw [into] a word file. Suddenly they think they have a paper." With all this pressure, Dodd says that "we shouldn't be surprised that these students are resorting to plagiarism to 'manage' their time."

Those who favor educational solutions point out that honor codes and on- 5 line tutorials do help explain what plagiarism is, why it is unethical, and how to write a paper that credits all the sources used. Research has shown that educating students about honor codes, especially in very small schools, can have a positive effect. For example, Mountain Lakes High School in New Jersey has an honor code that outlines "pro-active/preventative measures," such as student involvement in creating the honor code and assemblies to explain the code, instead of the punitive approach used in most high schools. Another solution sometimes touted by educators is a tutorial for all students about academic honesty and plagiarism. According to Trip Gabriel, writing in the *New York Times*, students at a selective college who completed a Web tutorial on plagiarism cheated 65% less than students who did not take the tutorial. However, these tutorials did not work as well with the hard core cheaters, students with lower SAT scores, male students, and student athletes.

Honor codes and tutorials for students about plagiarism are not, how- 6 ever, really effective solutions. Students already know what plagiarism is. They know they shouldn't copy someone else's work or buy a paper online. They know that they cannot just cut and paste from the Internet without using quotation marks and citing the author. They know they shouldn't have their parents or roommates write, revise, or edit their papers. So having teachers spend time in class or in tutorials or assemblies talking about plagiarism is not going to lessen this tidal wave of cheating. Teachers and administrators just need to adopt a zero tolerance policy and vigilantly monitor writing and test taking. And students who are caught plagiarizing need to fail the course and be placed on academic probation.

(Continued)

Supervising any test taking or writing situation is really the only solution. *7* Trip Gabriel describes a very effective system used at the University of Central Florida. The testing center does not allow gum chewing (this could disguise a student speaking into a hands-free cell phone to another student outside), the students are not allowed to wear hats (students can hide their eyes or they can write answers on the underside of the brim), and the center has eye-in-the-sky video cameras that record what each student is writing or doing on his computer. In this environment, cheating at UCF dropped significantly, to only 14 suspected students out of 64,000 exams administered. Another effective surveillance system is a plagiarism detection service such as Turnitin.com. This service, which is now used by 9,500 high schools and colleges, checks its ever expanding database for plagiarized essays and undocumented paragraphs, sentences, and phrases. Turnitin needs to be used by every teacher who assigns writing, and students caught plagiarizing should fail the course and be expelled from school, no questions asked.

Although some studies show that teaching students how to do legiti- *8* mate research, having school honor codes, and practicing citing Internet sources may help to reduce some cases of plagiarism or cheating, basically all students instinctively know what plagiarism is and that it is wrong to steal someone else's ideas, words, or facts. Therefore, high schools and colleges should focus their attention on surveillance and swift punishment. Just like drunk driving, no one quit drinking and driving just because someone else said that it was dangerous. Traffic fatalities began to drop only when increased enforcement and stricter DUI penalties were enforced. Schools and teachers need to increase surveillance, use plagiarism detection services such as Turnitin, and have committees composed of both faculty and students review each case. The minimum punishment should be failure of the paper and failure of the course, and subsequent cases of plagiarism should face academic probation. Maybe, just maybe, students would then learn that plagiarism in school could jeopardize their careers or cost them an election later in life.

COLLECTING

Text Annotation

12.5
Use collecting strategies to analyze a text

Most experts on reading and writing agree that you will learn and remember more if you write out your comments, questions, and reactions in the margins rather than just highlight sentences. Writing your responses helps you begin a conversation with the text. Reproduced below are one reader's marginal responses to paragraph 6 of Devlin's essay.

Clearly, not all students DO know what plagiarism is.

I had to learn how to cite authors to give them credit.

We can get help from students in our class and in the writing center, so why can't roommates help?

Honor codes and tutorials for students about plagiarism are not, however, really effective solutions. Students already know what plagiarism is. They know they shouldn't copy someone else's work or buy a paper online. They know that they cannot just cut and paste from the Internet without using quotation marks and citing the author. They know they shouldn't have their parents or roommates write, revise, or edit their papers. So having teachers spend time in class or in tutorials or assemblies talking about plagiarism is not going to lessen this tidal wave of cheating. Teachers and administrators just need to adopt a zero tolerance policy and vigilantly monitor writing and test taking. And students who are caught plagiarizing need to fail the course and be placed on academic probation.

Reading Log

A reading log, like text annotations, encourages you to interact with the author and the text and to record your comments and questions as you read. Just open a Word file and write down your thoughts as you read the text. Freewriting in a Word file allows you to develop more of your thoughts than simply writing in the margins of the text. Often these freewriting responses help you focus on ideas you will want to develop later in your analysis or response.

Here is one reading log response to Devlin's ideas about plagiarism.

In studies about childhood development, results show that kids follow behaviors they are shown. It is a conditioned response, and if a candidate for President is plagiarizing or an individual's favorite author is plagiarizing, it is logical that kids would do the same thing. From experience, I have had a lot of friends who have copied and pasted entire papers and gotten full credit on them because teachers don't have the proper resources to catch students when they decide to plagiarize. I know a lot of my friends continue to plagiarize because they never got caught so a feeling of invincibility arises and a habit is formed. Plagiarizing is wrong, and I can't say that I have never copied and pasted something because that would be a lie. I know it isn't something anyone should do, but when everyone else is doing it, it is easy to rationalize. Because of the ease of Internet access and the lack of consequences, a lot of students ignore what's wrong and what's right.

SHAPING AND DRAFTING

12.6

Use shaping and drafting strategies to develop a thesis and structure

As you think about ways to organize and develop your essay, be sure to reread your assignment and consider your purpose and audience. Each of the strategies described below will help you develop and organize specific parts of your summary or response. Even after you have written a first draft, look back and review these strategies to see whether one of them will make your response essay more effective.

Shaping Strategies

Do you want to . . .	Consider using this rhetorical strategy:
briefly summarize a text?	paraphrasing and quoting (pp. 293–294)
avoid plagiarizing?	avoiding plagiarism (p. 294)
organize a summary/response/analysis?	sample organizations for summary/response/analysis essays (pp. 294–299)
understand options for your response?	response-shaping options (pp. 296–298)

Paraphrasing, Quoting, and Avoiding Plagiarism

A summary should convey the main ideas, the essential argument, or the key features of a text. Its purpose should be to represent the text's ideas as concisely and objectively as possible. Paraphrases help you condense key ideas into fewer sentences; direct quotations help you convey the author's ideas accurately by citing key phrases. You avoid plagiarism by converting the author's ideas into your own language and by using quotation marks whenever you use a phrase or sentence written by the author.

Paraphrase

The purpose of a paraphrase is to restate concisely the author's ideas in your own language. A good paraphrase retains the original meaning without plagiarizing from the original text.

> *Original:* Those who favor educational solutions point out that honor codes and online tutorials do help explain what plagiarism is, why it is unethical, and how to write a paper that credits all the sources used.
> *Acceptable Paraphrase:* Student honor codes and tutorials do, according to some educators, teach students about plagiarism, how to avoid it, and the ethics of accurately citing resources.
> *Plagiarism:* Some educators argue that tutorials and honor codes actually do help explain what plagiarism is, why it is unethical, and how to credit sources. [This is plagiarism because the writer repeats the exact words (see highlighting) from the source without using quotation marks. The writer needs to put this information in his or her own language.]

Direct Quotation

Often summaries directly quote key phrases or sentences from the source. *Remember: any words or phrases within the quotation marks must be accurate, word-for-word transcriptions of the original.* Use direct quotations sparingly to convey key ideas in the essay:

> Devlin acknowledges that education can help reduce plagiarism through honor codes and tutorials that "help explain what plagiarism is, why it is unethical, and how to write a paper that credits all the sources used."

Use direct quotation of key words or phrases to express the author's thesis or claim:

> In "Plagiarism in America," Devlin argues that our "epidemic of plagiarism" must be "met head-on with the most forceful and effective surveillance and punishment measures possible."

Avoid the direct quotation of long sentences. Instead, use an ellipsis (three spaced points: . . .) to indicate words that you have omitted.

> *Original:* Another solution sometimes touted by educators is a tutorial for all students about academic honesty and plagiarism.
>
> *Condensed Quotation:* Devlin explains that "another solution . . . is a tutorial for all students" about avoiding plagiarism.

Avoiding Plagiarism

As you work with your sources, paraphrasing key ideas and quoting key phrases or sentences, keep in mind that in order to avoid plagiarizing, you need to document any ideas, facts, statistics, or actual language you use—both in your text and in a Works Cited or References page. *Plagiarism* is using the language, ideas, or visual materials of another person or source without acknowledging that person or source. Use the following guidelines to avoid plagiarism.

- Do not use language, ideas, or graphics from any essay, text, or visual image that you find online, in the library, or from commercial sources without acknowledging the source.
- Do not use language, ideas, or visual images from any other student's essay without acknowledging the source.

Sometimes students will plagiarize out of carelessness by inadequately citing words, specific language, ideas, or visual images. You can avoid this inadvertent plagiarism by learning how to quote accurately from your sources, how to paraphrase using your own words, and how to cite your sources accurately.

The best way to avoid inadvertent plagiarism is to ask your instructor how to document a source you are using. Your instructor will help you with the conventions of direct quotation, paraphrasing, and in-text reference or citation.

Sample Summaries

Here are two summaries of Devlin's essay on plagiarism, written by different writers. Notice that while both summaries convey the main ideas of the essay by using paraphrase and direct quotation, they are not identical. Check each summary to see how well it meets the guidelines for an effective summary.

Summary 1

Plagiarism. It is the dreaded word that every high school and college student fears. Although every student knows the consequences and fears getting caught, still many students continue to cheat. In "Plagiarism in America," Dudley Erskine Devlin argues that educators need to adopt zero tolerance policies about plagiarism. According to Devlin, plagiarism has reached epidemic proportions because of the Internet's ease of access as well as pressures that students feel to get good grades or earn scholarships. Devlin's main question is simple: How can we put an end to this epidemic? While Devlin notes that some educators believe that plagiarism would be reduced if students were better educated about plagiarism through online tutorials and honor codes, he believes educators should respond with surveillance and harsh punishments. The minimum punishment, Devlin argues, "should be failure of the paper and failure of the course," and repeat offenders should be put on academic probation or even be expelled from school. Devlin cites researchers who show that tutorials and honor codes can lessen the frequency of plagiarism, but he believes that increased surveillance, use of plagiarism detection devices such as Turnitin, and serious punishments are necessary to put an end to this epidemic.

Summary 2

In "Plagiarism in America," Dudley Erskine Devlin argues that plagiarism has become an epidemic in high schools and colleges, largely due to students' increased dependence on the Internet for research. Devlin supports his claim that cheating has become epidemic by citing statistics from researchers who show that approximately 20% of all college papers are plagiarized and that nearly two-thirds of surveyed high school students reported that they or their friends plagiarized an assignment. Devlin argues that although some educators believe this epidemic of plagiarism can be reduced by teaching students what plagiarism is and by encouraging students to sign honor codes, he believes that plagiarism rates will continue to increase until schools and teachers use "the most forceful and effective surveillance and punishment measures possible." Devlin cites statistics that show that educational tutorials and honor codes work for some schools, but he recommends that both cheating on tests and plagiarism be met by careful supervision of test taking environments and by using plagiarism detection devices such as Turnitin.com. According to Devlin, the current epidemic of plagiarism will be reduced only when "the minimum punishment" is failure of both the paper and the course, and when students who are caught more than once should face academic probation or be "immediately expelled from school, no questions asked."

Response Shaping

Strategies for organizing a response depend on the purpose of the response. Typically, responses have one or more of four purposes:

- Analyzing the effectiveness of the text
- Agreeing and/or disagreeing with the ideas in the text
- Interpreting and reflecting on the text
- Rhetorically analyzing the effectiveness of the text

As the explanations that follow illustrate, each type of response requires supporting evidence from the text, from other texts, and/or from the writer's own experience.

Analyzing Analysis divides a whole into its parts in order to better understand the whole. To analyze a text for its effectiveness, start by examining key parts or features of the text, such as the purpose, the intended audience, the thesis and main ideas, the organization and evidence, and the language and style. Notice how the following paragraph analyzes Devlin's illogical argument.

In addition, Devlin's argument in "Plagiarism in America" has clear problems in its logic and the support for his claims. Devlin acknowledges that "students, teachers, and administrators are divided" about how to solve the problem, but after citing two studies that show the statistical importance of educational approaches, he dismisses this evidence by saying "honor codes and tutorials for students" are not effective solutions because "students already know what plagiarism is." His only support for this claim is a series of assertions without any support from surveys or studies. Having dismissed these educational solutions, Devlin seems to commit an either/or fallacy by assuming that we should use either educational solutions or increased surveillance, but not both. And to add to this problem, Devlin cites the example of the surveillance system at the University of Central Florida's testing center. Devlin here confuses monitoring of tests with monitoring for plagiarism. Cheating on tests is not the same as plagiarizing papers or essays, and the two forms of cheating require different solutions. Devlin's problems with logic and lack of support continue into his final paragraph, where he uses the claim that plagiarism is just like drunk driving. He asserts that "traffic fatalities began to drop only when increased enforcement and stricter DUI penalties were enforced." Devlin cites no support for this claim and does not explain how or why the two situations require similar solutions.

Agreeing/Disagreeing Often a response to a text focuses on agreeing and/or disagreeing with its major ideas. Responses may agree completely, disagree completely, or agree with some points but disagree with others. Responses that agree with some ideas but disagree with others are often the most effective because they show that the responder sees both the strengths and weaknesses of an argument. In the following paragraph, notice how the responder agrees and disagrees and then supports each judgment with evidence.

In "Plagiarism in America," Dudley Erskine Devlin identifies an important problem that definitely needs fixing, but I can't agree with many of his recommended solutions. The statistics he cites from the Pew Internet and American Life project and from the Donald McCabe study appear to be accurate and do fit with my own experiences in high school. My school used Turnitin.com, a plagiarism detection system, in all my writing courses. I was required to turn in my essays to this Web site database, and I discovered the checking system is fairly successful. The majority of my friends who plagiarized essays were caught. However, I don't agree that these detection systems should be the only approach. Students in my class did need to learn about some of the technical aspects of citing sources. Most of us knew that we shouldn't turn in someone else's paper or copy and paste material from the Internet, but we still needed to know how to cite our sources and quote accurately. In addition, Devlin says that we shouldn't accept any help with our papers when he says that students "shouldn't have their parents or roommates write, revise, or edit their papers." In class, we regularly assisted each other with papers in peer review groups. These sessions always helped you see what you missed, what you did wrong, and how to do better. I don't see the difference between getting help from a roommate or the writing center and getting help from peers in your class, as long as no one is writing the paper for you. Finally, Devlin says that if you're caught plagiarizing you should "fail the course and be immediately expelled from school, no questions asked." This "zero tolerance" policy seems much too harsh. Students need a chance to learn from their mistakes, and receiving an F on the paper should be enough to ensure that the student won't do it again.

Interpreting and Reflecting   Many responses contain interpretations of passages that might be read differently depending on one's assumptions or the implications of an idea. An interpretation says, "Here is what the text says, but let me explain what it means, what assumptions the argument carries, or what the implications might be." Here is a paragraph from an interpretive response to Devlin's essay.

> In "Plagiarism in America," Devlin spends time talking about surveillance and punishment for plagiarism, but not much time thoughtfully considering his assumptions about what plagiarism is. He says, "Students already know what plagiarism is," and then he gives a few examples of a conventional definition. But the idea of plagiarism is dependent on culture and context. One context he mentions is the Internet. On the Internet, the idea of ownership of language and ideas is regularly challenged. On Wikipedia, for example, it would be extremely difficult to track down the writer of any given sentence or any idea. All of the comments have been posted, taken down, revised, and edited many times. So who is the author who "owns" these words and ideas? To whom should we give credit? Or do we need to give credit at all, since it may be "common knowledge" that we all share, knowledge that does not need documentation. Ideas and language on a wiki site are like a conversation, with many people offering contributions. Similarly, if I have a conversation with a classmate about my topic, and she gives me a suggestion about a different angle or idea, am I plagiarizing if I incorporate her idea without direct quotation marks and a footnote? What about when I use ideas from another course or even from a paper I wrote several years ago? We really cannot write anything without the ideas and contributions of many people's thoughts and contributions, and it would be impractical and even foolish to try to track down and document the source of every idea that springs to mind.

Analyzing Rhetorically   Rhetorical analysis of a passage uses the analyzing strategies described above, but in addition it uses the language of rhetoric and rhetorical appeals to identify an author's key strategies and to comment on their effectiveness. A rhetorical analysis identifies the author, publication context, intended audience and purpose, and then analyzes the writer's logos, ethos, and pathos appeals. In the next paragraph, the writer focuses on the effectiveness of Devlin's ethos appeals.

Related to his problems with using logos appeals, Devlin's ethos appeal at the beginning of his essay seems strong, but it weakens as the essay proceeds. Although Devlin himself is not a known expert on the topic, he gains early credibility by citing compelling statistics from both the Pew Internet study and Donald McCabe's research. He adds to this credibility and sense of fairness by acknowledging that there are two sides or "camps" to the issue—one that favors increased surveillance and one that favors increased education. At this point, he represents the educational solutions fairly, describing research on both honor codes and tutorial that demonstrate effectiveness. However, his ethos appeal begins to slide when he dismisses the educational solutions out of hand. In paragraph 6, Devlin's ethos continues to deteriorate when he seems to attack students by saying, "they know . . . , they know . . . , they know . . . ," and his language becomes more extreme, recommending "zero tolerance," "vigilantly" monitoring, and "academic probation." He begins paragraph 7 by saying that supervision "is really the only solution," then concludes the paragraph by dramatically increasing the punishment that students caught plagiarizing should receive: "Turnitin needs to be used by every teacher . . . and students caught plagiarizing should fail the course and be immediately expelled . . . no questions asked." Suddenly, instead of seeming credible and fair, Devlin's character has become judgmental, intolerant, and unreasonable. Overall, Devlin's ethos appeal is strong at the beginning of his essay, but by the end, the reader has lost confidence in his credibility because of his extreme and judgmental language and recommendations.

Organizing Summary/Response and Rhetorical Analysis Essays

There are four common ways to organize summary/response and rhetorical analysis essays. Select or modify one of them to fit your audience, purpose, and kind of response. Typically, a summary/response takes the following form.

Shaping Your Points: Summary/Response with Focus on the Text

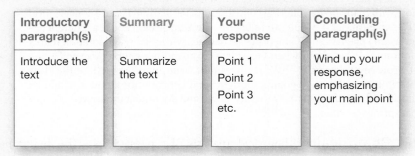

Introductory paragraph(s)	Summary	Your response	Concluding paragraph(s)
Introduce the text	Summarize the text	Point 1 Point 2 Point 3 etc.	Wind up your response, emphasizing your main point

A second kind of organization focuses initially on key ideas or issues and then examines the text or texts for their contributions to these key ideas. This form begins with the issues, then summarizes the text(s), and finally moves to the reader's responses.

Shaping Your Points: Summary/Response with Focus on the Issues

Introductory paragraph(s)	Summary	Your response	Concluding paragraph(s)
Introduce key issues	Summarize the text	Point 1 Point 2 Point 3 etc.	Wind up your response, emphasizing your main point

A third organization integrates the summary and the response. It begins by introducing the issue and/or the text, gives a brief overall idea of the text, and then summarizes and responds point by point.

Shaping Your Points: Integrated Summary/Response

Introductory paragraph(s)	Point 1	Point 2	Point 3, etc.	Concluding paragraph(s)
Introduce key issues and/or texts	Summarize the text's Point 1 Respond to the text's Point 1	Summarize the text's Point 2 Respond to the text's Point 2	Summarize the text's Point 3 Respond to the text's Point 3	Wind up your esponse, emphasizing your main point

A fourth organization is especially appropriate for the rhetorical analysis of a text.

Shaping Your Points: Rhetorical Analysis

Introductory paragraph(s)	Summary	Thesis statement	Rhetorical feature/ appeal 1	Rhetorical feature/appeal 2, etc.	Concluding paragraph(s)
Introduce text and purpose for the analysis	Summarize the text's rhetorical features and appeals	State the effectiveness of the text for its audience, context, purpose	Analyze effectiveness of rhetorical feature 1	Analyze effectiveness of rhetorical feature 2, etc.	Wind up your analysis, emphasizing your main point

If you have been reading actively, you have been writing throughout the shaping process. At some point, however, you will gather your best ideas into a working thesis that captures your central point of analysis and begin writing a draft. Even if your focus changes somewhat along the way, having a working thesis as you draft can keep you from drifting from your central point. Some writers like to have their examples and evidence ready when they begin drafting. Many writers have outlines in their heads or on paper. Perhaps you like to put your rough outline on the computer and then expand each section as you write. Finally, most writers like to skim the text and *reread their notes* immediately before they start their drafts.

Once you begin drafting, keep interruptions to a minimum. Because focus and concentration are important to good writing, try to keep writing for as long as possible. If you come to a spot where you need an example that you don't have at your fingertips, just make an insert in parentheses—(put the example about cosmetics and animal abuse here)—and keep on writing. Concentrate on having all your separate responses add up to one focused, overall response.

REVISING

12.7

Use revision strategies to assure a clear thesis and adequate examples

Revision means *reseeing*. Revising requires rereading the text and rewriting your summary and response as needed. While revision begins as you read and reread the text, it continues until—and sometimes after—you turn in a paper or send it to its intended audience.

A major step in your revision is receiving responses from peer readers and deciding on a revision plan based on the feedback. Use the following guidelines as you read your peers' papers and respond to their advice.

Guidelines for Revision

- **Review the purpose and audience for your assignment.** Is your draft addressed to the appropriate audience? Does it fulfill its intended purpose?
- **Reconsider the genre you selected.** Does the genre you selected (essay, letter, letter to the editor) still work for your audience and purpose? Are there multigenre elements you could add to make your summary and response more effective?
- **Continue to use your active reading/writing/discussing activities as you revise.** If you are uncertain about parts of your summary or response, reread the text, check your notes, or discuss your draft with a classmate.
- **Reread your summary for key features.** Make sure your summary indicates author and title, cites main ideas, uses an occasional direct quotation for key ideas, and includes author tags. Check your summary for

accuracy and objectivity. For rhetorical summaries, make sure you identify each of the key features: author, title, publishing information, context, and genre—as well as the key rhetorical appeals used.

- **Check paraphrases and direct quotations.** When you are paraphrasing you need to put the author's ideas into your own language. If you are quoting directly, make sure the words within quotation marks are accurate, word-for-word transcriptions.
- **Review the purpose of your response.** Are you analyzing, agreeing/disagreeing, interpreting, doing a rhetorical analysis, or writing some combination of the four? Do your types of responses fit the assignment, meet your purpose, and address your intended audience?
- **Amplify your supporting evidence.** Summary/response drafts often need additional, relevant evidence. Be sure you use sufficient personal experience, evidence from the text, or examples from other texts to support your response.
- **Collaborate with peers.** In order to check that your thesis is clear, ask peers to read your analysis and tell you what they take to be main point. If their response doesn't match your intention, delete or revise passages that do not maintain your focus.
- **Revise sentences to improve clarity, conciseness, emphasis, and variety.**
- **Edit your final version.** Use the spell check on your computer. Have a friend help proofread.

Using Rhetorical Analysis for Critical Reading

Throughout this chapter, you have learned how paying attention to the rhetorical situation and the techniques writers use to respond to it can make you a better critical reader—and a better writer. To understand the decisions made by any given author, we must first think about the surrounding circumstances, the likely reactions of the audience, and what Aristotle called "the available means of persuasion" used within those circumstances.

Emily Kuhl's essay uses the tools of rhetorical analysis to do just that. In order to expose the persuasive techniques used by Elizabeth Cady Stanton, she provides some background on the historical circumstances she faced. She also then reads closely and critically enough to understand not only *what* Stanton is arguing, but *how* she makes those arguments. As you read, note how Kuhl demonstrates ways that the various rhetorical appeals work together, and how she illustrates each claim with specific examples from the *Declaration*. Note also how her transitions help the reader to see the connections among the various pieces of Stanton's argument. After reading Kuhl's essay, you might go back to read Stanton's "Declaration" again, noting how your own understanding of it is enriched by this critical analysis.

Student Writing

The Rhetoric of the Seneca Falls Convention: Elizabeth Cady Stanton's Use of Appeals in Her Keynote Address and the Declaration of Sentiments

Emily Kuhl

The first paragraph provides some social and historical context for the piece being analyzed.

Kuhl lays out her thesis, which points out the dominant rhetorical appeal.

Specific examples illustrate the appeal.

During the nineteenth century, the United States saw the rise of political tensions, economic ones, the largest national conflict to ever occur in the country, and the Reconstruction Era. Within the first half of this period, though, there were several significant strides in social activism, with orators and writers working to advocate the rights of disenfranchised groups. Within the realm of women's rights, one very significant was the Seneca Falls Convention of 1848, the first organized event specifically orchestrated to address women's rights. 1

That Convention featured Elizabeth Cady Stanton's Keynote Address and resulted in the Declaration of Sentiments and Resolutions. This Declaration presents a sampling of the rhetorical strategies utilized in the early women's rights movement. Being primarily or completely authored by Cady Stanton, they also offer a lens through which to view her personal style and delivery. While the Keynote Address mainly employed pathetic appeals through Cady Stanton's use of imagery, the Declaration and Resolutions are formatted to show the logical angle of Cady Stanton's arguments. In this essay, I demonstrate the ways in which the dominant use of the logos appeal in the *Declaration and Resolutions* is enhanced by underlying pathos appeals. 2

Elizabeth Cady Stanton's Keynote Address, delivered on the opening day of the Convention on July 19, 1848, provided an introduction to the Convention's overall purpose. To make the most of the passionate emotional atmosphere and to set the tone for the remainder of the sessions, Cady Stanton heavily employed pathetic appeals. She opened by speaking about how those assembled do not wish "to seat every man at the head of a cradle, and to clothe every woman in male attire," undercutting the idea that they were radically attempting to subvert the social order through their actions (Cady Stanton, "Seneca," par. 1). 3

She also set the stage for the eventual form of the Declaration, arguing "against a form of government existing without the consent of the governed," which is "a shame and a disgrace to a Christian republic" (Cady Stanton, "Seneca," par. 4). 4

She goes on to build the emotional appeals by noting how "grossly insulting to the dignity of woman" it is that "drunkards, idiots, horse-racing, rum-selling rowdies, ignorant foreigners, and silly boys" are recognized in the eyes of the law, but women, regardless of their position or prowess, are consistently relegated to an automatic inferiority (Cady Stanton, "Seneca," par. 6). And in closing, she rebukes the degradation of women and empowers her cause by declaring, "We do 5

(Continued)

not expect our path will be strewn with the flowers of popular applause, but over the thorns of bigotry and prejudice will be our way, and on our banners will beat the dark storm clouds of opposition from those who have entrenched themselves behind stormy bulwarks of custom and authority. . ." (Cady Stanton, "Seneca," par. 15). By using strong language and vivid imagery, Cady Stanton effectively prepares the audience to receive the *Declaration of Sentiments and Resolutions*, which were presented later in the Convention's schedule.

The Declaration of Sentiments and Resolutions clarifies and substantiates the fervent tone from her Keynote Address, layering *logos* over the *pathos*-based appeals of the address. The Declaration of Sentiments is immediately striking because of its logic, which mirrors the Declaration of Independence written and signed by representatives of the American colonies to signify the dissolving of recognizing England as their higher authority. The Declaration of Sentiments acts in the same capacity, substituting the monarchy with the male-dominated society of the time. A list of grievances against this corrupt entity is also included. 6

This document begins with "When in the course of human events. . ." and copies several portions of the first part of the Declaration of Independence verbatim. Other phrases, "We hold these truths to be self-evident, that all men are created equal," are restructured into "We hold these truths to be self-evident, that all men and women are created equal" (Cady Stanton, "Declaration," par. 2). As the document continues past the introductory phase, of course, it becomes more specifically tailored to convey the grievances more relevant to the circumstances and audience and lists the various ways in which women have been oppressed and discriminated against. 7

The strong and forceful language, similar to that used in Cady Stanton's Keynote Address, is made to fit with the very formal tone of the pre-existing template instead of a newly generated speech. After describing how a woman is made "civilly dead" in the eyes of the law after marriage, is forced to submit to legislature in which she has no input or representation, and is treated unfairly in terms of property ownership, she reiterates how career and educational paths are deliberately made unavailable to women and these limitations are compounded by social barriers. All of these grievances have created the atmosphere in which the Convention was originally conceived. The women of the United States have reached the point where they, like the disenfranchised colonists of the eighteenth century, must petition for "all the rights and privileges which belong to them as citizens of the United States," (Cady Stanton, "Declaration," par. 18). 8

The Resolutions of the Seneca Falls Convention maintain a similar approach. They are not modelled after a specific historical document, but are presented more like a piece of legislation, listing each resolution in its own section and giving a brief reason as to why it is being proposed. It addresses women in a church or religious setting, their perceptions in society, and the general principle of having equal capabilities as men. 9

Provides an analysis of the effects of the appeal

Transition to a second part of Kuhl's analysis

Attention to the specific audience of the speech

The use of brief quotations captures the tone of the speech.

Kuhl combines the analysis of the text with the cultural and historical background.

Draws attention to specific elements of Cady Stanton's speech

(Continued)

...continued The Rhetoric of the Seneca Falls, **Emily Kuhl**

Asserts the technique then provides specific examples to illustrate it

Interwoven into these assertions is Cady Stanton's persistent dynamic language. For example, she offsets the dispassionate tone of resolutions like "That the same amount of virtue, delicacy, and refinement of behavior that is required of woman in the social state, should also be required of man, and the same transgression should be visited with equal severity on both man and woman," with later emotional appeals toward "righteous causes" and how "the hoary sanction of antiquity, is to be regarded as self-evident falsehood, and at war with mankind," (Cady Stanton, "Declaration," pars. 6–11). By combining logos with ethos, she plainly illustrates the movement's logic while also moving readers through her pathos appeals to morality and righteousness. 10

These two works reinforce Cady Stanton's cleverness with utilizing different appeals or stylistic choices toward one overarching persuasive goal. Her effective use of logos appeals could be due in large part to Cady Stanton's upbringing and background. On both her maternal and paternal sides, Cady Stanton had family members involved in the American Revolution, military service, and legislative positions. Beth Marie Waggenspack notes that Cady Stanton's autobiography mentions the influence of her family background: 11

> With several generations of vigorous enterprising ancestors behind me, I commenced the struggle of life under favourable circumstances . . . the same year that my father was elected to Congress. Perhaps the excitement of a political campaign, in which my mother took the deepest interest, may have had an influence on my life and given me the strong desire that I have always felt to participate in the rights and duties of government (Waggenspack 7). 12

Another reading of the text provides further detail and support for the analysis.

Kuhl extends the ideas of Waggenspack with her own analysis.

However, her family's background and opinions might have had another effect on Cady Stanton's career as well. Waggenspack explains that, although her father initially did not mind Cady Stanton's inquisitiveness and propensity to spend time in his law office, once he realized the depth of her interest, he began to rebuke her for it. Instead of discouraging her, though, she found inspiration and motivation in this reproach. Perhaps, from an early age, Cady Stanton was cultivating her tendency to form her own opinions apart from those issued by authoritative figures (if necessary) and grow her knowledge of pressing societal and legal issues. This cultivation of knowledge and interest, of course, led to her involvement in organizing the Seneca Falls Convention, creating these pieces of rhetoric, and continuing her career as an orator and social activist. 13

Demonstrates why the logos appeal was chosen

Her knowledge of the legal process and legal writing most likely helped Cady Stanton to realize the necessity of organizing the Declaration of Sentiments and the Resolutions of the Seneca Falls Convention in a highly logical and rational way rather than on a purely emotional foundation. The emotional charge of her language still exists, and the *pathos* in this document could appeal to a sense of American patriotism or Christian morality, but Cady Stanton is more concerned with proving the legitimacy and legal standing of these issues. Waggenspack brings in the historical 14

(Continued)

context, writing that at this time, "Women's sphere was separate because its domain was the home, where the demands for logical behavior and financial success that men faced were peripheral; thus, the domestic sphere began to be seen as the antithesis of an occupation, and therefore of lesser value" (Waggenspack 41).

Given that this declaration was meant to be shown to individuals, such as politicians, legislators, and the male population in general, it makes sense that Cady Stanton was concerned about showing this use of *logos* to outside audiences and not just those involved with the Convention and its goals. Stanton displayed a keen awareness of the specific points of the affairs that she wished to address and change. This knowledge then provided a steady foundation for her rhetorical moves. 15

Returns to one of the key claims of the analysis

Overall, Elizabeth Cady Stanton's Keynote Address, the Declaration of Sentiments, and the Resolutions of the Seneca Falls Convention all offer perspectives on rhetoric at a personal level, exclusive to Cady Stanton, as well as the context of the early women's rights movement. Her use of *pathos* and *logos*, both separately and in terms of one another, speak to her astute rhetorical moves and ability to analyze and contextualize her audience and purpose. They are not identical in these works, nor should they be; crafting one's argument to fit with the rhetorical situation is needed if a rhetor or orator wishes to make progress. She seems to navigate the social reform paradox and draw on personal experience to cultivate her reputation and create complementary rhetorical works for the Seneca Falls Convention. 16

The concluding statement draws together the rhetorical and cultural facets of the text.

Works Cited

Cady Stanton, Elizabeth. "Declaration of Sentiments and Resolutions." 1848. *City U of New York*. College of Staten Island Lib. Web. 5 Dec. 2013.

Cady Stanton, Elizabeth. "Seneca Falls Keynote Address." 1848. *Great American Documents*. Peacock Data, 2008. Web. 5 Dec. 2013.

Waggenspack, Beth Marie. *The Search for Self-sovereignty: The Oratory of Elizabeth Cady Stanton*. Westport: Greenwood, 1989. Print.

Questions for Writing and Discussion

1 Do your own double-entry log for the Seneca Falls Resolution. On the left-hand side, record your reactions and analyses of the speech. On the right-hand side, write your own questions and reactions. What appeals or techniques might you focus on? Compare your notes to Kuhl's analysis. How is your analysis different?

2 Kuhl's essay uses examples to illustrate the analyses she makes. Which examples do you think are most effective? Why? Go back to the speech and see if you can find other examples that either support or contradict Kuhl's main point.

3 While pathos and logos are at the center of this analysis, there are clearly other techniques at work in Stanton's speech. What other kinds of stylistic techniques does she use? Are there metaphors or similes? Does she use hyperbole (exaggeration) to support her point?

④ How does the use of Waggenspack's analysis, a secondary source, support Kuhl's essay? To practice incorporating secondary sources into your own rhetorical reading, find other rhetorical analyses of Stanton's speeches (there are many), and draw on them to further support or to critique Kuhl's analysis.

Applying What You Have Learned

① Many forms of writing follow certain conventions. For example, graduation speakers use a particular set of techniques. Likewise, movie or restaurant reviews share similar techniques, as do résumés and job application letters. Write an essay that discusses the common features of one type of communication. Begin by choosing a number of texts that share a style and a purpose and then, using your skills of critical reading, write an analysis that describes and illustrates (with examples and analysis) the key features of this kind of text. Formulate a thesis that summarizes the reasons why certain rhetorical techniques fit the particular audience and purpose for that kind of writing.

Using multimedia. As you choose a topic for your analysis, consider multimedia texts. Some online restaurant reviews include not only opinions of experts but also ratings by customers. Speeches can be analyzed not only in their text form but in video, allowing you to comment on the delivery style and voice as well as the words. Even job applications have electronic versions with hyperlinks, embedded video, electronic portfolios, and images. As you complete your analysis, be sure to consider examples from a variety of media and to comment on the difference between paper and media versions.

② Though rhetoric is most often used ethically, on occasion rhetoric *can* be used deceptively. Emotional appeals are sometimes used to cover the facts, statistics are presented in deceptive ways, or people claim to have credibility on a topic without real knowledge. Use your critical reading skills to expose the deceptive use of the appeals to pathos, logos, and/or ethos in a text that you find to be deceptive. For example, you might expose the false rhetoric in an advertising campaign that you deem sexist or racist, the embellishment of "facts" to create fear, or the false claims of credibility by an organization or an individual. Using examples, show your audience how they could be duped if they don't paying attention to deceptive uses of rhetorical appeals.

Multimedia options. Create a PowerPoint or Prezi version of your rhetorical analysis to accompany an oral presentation or to stand alone as a slideshow with audio narration. Remember that slideshow presentations should use few words and take advantage of visuals. How would you capture the main points from your analysis in that form? What kinds of examples would best illustrate the deceptive use of rhetoric? Consider analyzing texts that are themselves multimedia, illustrating the appeals in a video or a visual text—and providing examples in your own multimedia analysis.

③ Works of visual or literary art are often used in subtle or not-so-subtle ways to change people's minds about an issue or perspective. Choose a story, poem, or work of visual art, and after summarizing its key aesthetic features—the things that make it a work of art—demonstrate an underlying rhetorical appeal that others may not have seen. For example, you could show how a story embeds a subtle message about gender or a critique of a political party; you could demonstrate how a set of sculptures or paintings creates emotional reactions likely to change viewers' attitudes about an issue, or how a poem which seems to be purely about nature is also a commentary on a particular class of people. Your goal will be to help your readers see how art can be used to persuade.

Using multimedia. This assignment lends itself to a variety of multimedia possibilities. If you are analyzing a work of visual art, you can include images, including details or close-ups that show particular elements. Captions or text boxes can point out key features of an image or a written text; formatting, font elements, and commenting tools can highlight its main features and key examples. If you wish to illustrate these features at a glance, you could even create a large, single-page poster to point out key elements using arrows and textboxes.

This iconic photograph by Associated Press photographer Slava "Val" Veder portrayed a joyous moment to a country conflicted by the Vietnam War. But as Carolyn Kleiner Butler's essay "Coming Home" (included in this chapter) makes clear, the visual masks a much more complex story. This chapter considers ways to analyze the effects of multimedia on audience and how to use images and other media effectively and ethically.

13

In this chapter, you will learn to:

Analyzing and Evaluating

FOR 21st century writers, communication is increasingly a multimedia craft. Written texts are interwoven with pictures, photographs, works of art, charts, diagrams, and other graphics. Websites and other forms of digital communication put sound recordings, still images, video, music, podcasts, and video clips only a mouse click away. And the communication methods of the digital revolution continue to evolve rapidly from fixed, one-way communication to the instantaneous and interactive elements of "social" media. With all these tools at our disposal, writing might more accurately be described as multimedia *composing*.

For this reason, we now use the word *text* to refer to any object—written, visual, digital, and so forth—that serves a communication or rhetorical purpose. Keep that wider definition in mind as we discuss *texts* throughout this chapter. Another key term we'll use is *media* (and its singular form, *medium*.) A *medium* is the form of a communication. (See the diagram on page 310). To create *multimedia* texts, 21st century writers draw on more than one form.

Even as digital-age technologies continue to evolve, the rhetorical questions you learned in Chapter 12 remain useful: What are the purpose and audience for a text? What appeals to logic and reason, to emotion and feelings, to reliability and character is the writer making? How effective are those appeals?

> **❝** Graphic design creates visual logic and seeks an optimal balance between visual sensation and graphic information. Without the visual impact of shape, color, and contrast, pages are graphically boring and will not motivate the viewer. **❞**
>
> —Patrick Lynch and Sarah Horton, Authors of *Web Style Guide*

Taken from *The Prentice Hall Guide for College Writers*, Eleventh Edition by Stephen P. Reid and Dominic DelliCarpini.

However, to analyze multimedia texts, we also need new questions: What is the purpose of an embedded image or video clip, and how does it interact with the words? Who is the intended audience, and what media are most effective for reaching that audience? What author or group of authors constructed the pieces of a multimedia text, and what are the ethical boundaries in borrowing or remixing texts? What appeals to logic, emotion, or character does one text make, and how are those appeals enhanced by still or moving images, sound, or interactivity?

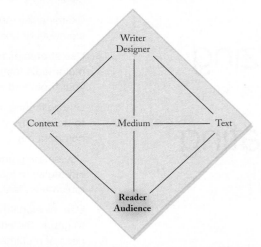

Key elements in the effects of new media on audiences and the relationship between text and context

After you have practiced analyzing the rhetorical effects of various types of media, you will be better prepared to switch roles from reader/audience to writer/designer of multimedia texts. In the second half of this chapter, you will practice some processes for thoughtfully designing multimedia texts. To do this, you will need analysis techniques for selecting the media forms that best support your purpose for your specific audience.

Techniques for Analyzing and Composing Multimedia Texts

The techniques for analyzing multimedia texts—as well as the surrounding context—are the same techniques you will need to compose with multimedia. As with all communication, you must first consider the rhetorical situation, and then go on to develop your composition to suit the needs of that situation. What are the purpose and the intended audience? What is the occasion for the communication, the surrounding context, the chosen genre and/or forms of *media*? The techniques explained

Techniques for Analyzing Multimedia Texts

Technique	Tips on How to Do It
Analyzing the rhetorical appeals made by multimedia elements of a text	Describe the purpose of this text and the most likely target audience. Note the *appeals to reason, to emotion,* or *to credibility* that are made. Then describe ways that the multimedia elements enhance those appeals.
Analyzing the media choices used in the text	Note the various media elements that have been included. Note the use of images or other visual features (including fonts, colors, page design), video, or audio elements. What purpose(s) does the use of each medium seem to have? What features of that medium make it an effective, or ineffective choice for the audience and purpose? What examples might you point out to illustrate the value of that medium?
Analyzing the multimedia text in context	Is the text a one-way text such as a magazine, essay, newspaper, or static website? Or does it rely on interactive features such as blogs, Facebook, and Twitter do? What does this publication site tell you about the purpose and desired relationship with the audience? What types of media can it accommodate, or not accommodate? What types of audiences are likely to be reached through this type of medium or site?
Analyzing the relationship between words and other media	Even when other media are used, words play a central role that should be noted. How do the *accompanying written words* complement the media employed? What do the written words in the text help you notice in the other media? (Or what do the words distract you from noticing?)
Synthesizing your analyses into a claim about the overall effectiveness of the text	Your goal is to combine or *synthesize* your analyses of the persuasive appeals of a text into a claim about the visual's *overall rhetorical effectiveness.* Try to develop a thesis that focuses on a specific media effect and makes a claim about how the chosen media and its features affects the success of the text for a particular audience.

here help you **analyze**—that is, look at each part of the multimedia text separately. They can also help you to **synthesize**—to put the pieces together in a way that helps you and others see how the parts work together (or do not work together) to achieve a rhetorical purpose for an intended audience. And finally, they can help you learn further techniques for **composing** multimedia documents yourself. In all cases, analysis should be aimed at the claim or claims that a text makes, the media and methods used to achieve those goals, and how effectively those goals are achieved through those media and methods.

RHETORICAL APPEALS IN MULTIMEDIA ENVIRONMENTS

13.1
Understand how multimedia elements support a text's rhetorical appeals

Like all texts, multimedia compositions usually have persuasive aims. And like those other texts, they employ rhetorical appeals to reason and logic (logos), to emotion (pathos), and to character and credibility (ethos). However, since the forms used to communicate go beyond words alone, a full analysis requires more specialized techniques. Your task when analyzing multimedia elements of a text is to consider the contributions made by *forms of persuasion that go beyond words alone.* How do those multimedia elements enhance, reinforce, or detract from achieving the rhetorical purpose? Below are suggestions for expanding the basic rhetorical appeals discussed in Chapter 12 to analyze how multimedia texts can enhance, reinforce, or detract from those appeals to reason, emotion, and character.

Appeal to Reason (Logos)

While a written argument can succeed because of its use of logic and evidence, multimedia enhancements often reinforce—or even supersede—the logos appeals of writing alone. Charts, graphs, and diagrams appeal to reason and logic by presenting data that demonstrate powerful evidence at a glance. The visual diagram on the following page, "Storing the Power of the Wind," which accompanied a newspaper story about alternative sources of energy, illustrates such an appeal to reason. Visually portraying a sequence of logical steps, it explains through text and images how wind could be used to generate hydrogen for powering electric grids as well as automobiles—and it does this in ways that would have been much more difficult to accomplish with words alone. Other examples of how graphs, charts, and diagrams can be used in this way appear on pages 317 and 318.

As you think about composing in multimedia, imagine how other media could enhance a logical sequence of steps. A video could walk us through the steps using moving images that demonstrate the processes. Audio voiceover could reinforce the images by pointing out key elements and connections; zoom features available on video or in Prezi presentations could point us to more specific elements of each visual. As you analyze the appeals to logic in a multimedia text, consider how the combination of words and other media elements contributes to the logic of the ideas, their careful organization, and the effective presentation of evidence. Concentrate especially on the parts of the text that would not have been as effective with words alone.

Appeal to Emotion (Pathos)

Writing can breed strong emotions, and that can accomplish our rhetorical purpose and move others to new beliefs or actions. With multimedia, we can not only quote song lyrics, we can embed audio clips that include the accompanying instrumentation.

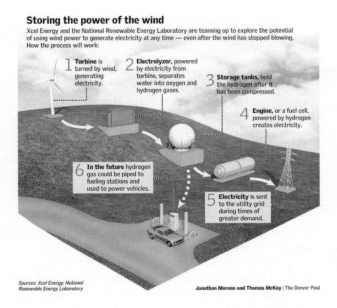

Storing the power of the wind

Xcel Energy and the National Renewable Energy Laboratory are teaming up to explore the potential of using wind power to generate electricity at any time — even after the wind has stopped blowing. How the process will work:

1 **Turbine** is turned by wind, generating electricity.

2 **Electrolyzer,** powered by electricity from turbine, separates water into oxygen and hydrogen gases.

3 **Storage tanks,** hold the hydrogen after it has been compressed.

4 **Engine,** or a fuel cell, powered by hydrogen creates electricity.

6 **In the future** hydrogen gas could be piped to fueling stations and used to power vehicles.

5 **Electricity** is sent to the utility grid during times of greater demand.

Sources: Xcel Energy; National Renewable Energy Laboratory

Jonathan Moreno and Thomas McKay | The Denver Post

We can not only describe a moving moment, we can depict it with video. And we can not only tell others about the glow on the face of our child at Christmas, but we can show it in a still or moving image that is transported across the world instantly. For the writer, the key is to use these emotional appeals artfully and thoughtfully—and in ways that do not undermine one's logic or credibility.

Similarly, as we analyze and employ emotional appeals, we should consider not only whether the media chosen are effective, but how and why they are—or are not—appropriate to the situation. Is a parody effective, or does sarcasm reflect badly on our credibility? Is an image of poverty likely to make our case to a group of potential donors, or would they prefer to see a spreadsheet or graph that shows the effect of charitable giving? As with all forms of communication, matching the form with the purpose and audience is crucial. So as you analyze the media elements in a text, try to gauge how they are likely to affect the emotional response of the audience. Are they appropriate or inappropriate, effective or detrimental to the overall purpose of the text?

Appeal to Character and Credibility (Ethos)

Appeals to character and credibility (*ethos*) can likewise be enhanced through multimedia. The iconic voice of James Earl Jones in the "This is CNN" voiceover gives the news channel an air of gravity (and helped win Jones a Voice Icon Award). The Apple icon on the back of a Macintosh Computer is now a sign of one's computer alliances. And the great seal of the United States is nearly always displayed on the podium

when the President makes an address. Even a type font can speak to one's integrity and image.

When an audience senses that the visual or sound matter conveys a sense of integrity and authenticity, that the maker of an image is sincere and is not relying on cheap emotional appeals, or that the visual communicates a sense of humanity and goodwill, the appeal to character is successful. Look at Dorothea Lange's images of a migrant mother on page 316. These pictures have an emotional appeal, to be sure, but they are composed with an integrity and a credibility that lend a strong character appeal to the photographer as well. Because Lange's pictures give the mother and her children dignity at the same time that they call attention to their plight, they reinforce Lange's own ethos. Again, your analytical task is to identify the kinds of multimedia enhancements that work either independently or with the written word to gain the trust of the intended audience. Keep in mind, though, that different audiences' trust may be based on different standards—so be sure to link any appeal to the intended audience and purpose.

Combined Appeals in Multimedia Texts

While analyzing or composing a text requires us to consider its various elements and their effects, in the end a successful effort usually combines appeals to logic, emotion, and character (whether in equal or unequal measure). So, after you have identified, described, and collected examples of appeals to logic, emotion, and character or credibility, you can then consider how the appeals work together— and whether their combination creates a unified overall purpose. This holds true both as you analyze the texts others have created and as you create your own. The goal is always to find or create a unified purpose in which all elements work together.

THE COMPONENTS OF MULTIMEDIA TEXTS

13.2

Examine the multimedia elements of texts

Since 21st century texts are often made up of more than words, these multimedia texts require that we have techniques for understanding and using their various components. There basic three types of media we will likely encounter as readers and writer/designers are "still" visuals (photos and other two-dimensional images), sounds (audio), and video (moving images often combined with sound). Each medium has elements that require our attention.

Analyzing Visual Components

When we analyze or use still images (two dimensional images without movement), whether they stand alone or are embedded in a larger text, we need to pay particular attention to details of composition, focus, narrative, and theme. Use the following sets of questions to guide your analysis and to help generate ideas and descriptions for use in your own compositions. Depending on the particular image, some questions will be more important than others.

- **Composition.** How are key images arranged or organized on the page? What use of color, contrasts of light and shade, or repeated figures are present? For example, an analysis might note that "the wall of books in the background of the photograph lend an air of learnedness and gravity to his character."
- **Focal Point.** What point or image first draws your attention? Do background figures or diagonal lines draw your attention to or away from the focal point? For example, an analysis might note that "our eyes are drawn quickly to the wide and bright eyes of the child as she first sees her long-absent mother."
- **Narrative.** What story or narrative does the image or visual suggest? How do these story elements support (or not support) the purpose or message for the intended audience? For example, an analysis might note that "depictions of the electric car riding through one of our national parks tell a story that makes the vehicle an environmental hero like Captain Planet."
- **Theme.** What message does this image want to promote? If the image is embedded in a larger text, does it serve or clash with its main purposes? For example, an analysis might note that "a photograph of a child looking at his electronic tablet while surrounded by others engaged in conversation takes on new significance within the context of an argument about the negative impact of technology on youth."

Now practice applying these questions to two photographs on the following page taken by Dorothea Lange, one of America's most famous documentary photographers of migrant workers and sharecroppers. Lange took these images during the Great Depression of the 1930s, near Berkeley, California. What message do the images, without words, portray?

In the first picture, the composition focuses on two women and three children. The makeshift tarp helps to frame these figures, and the diagonal lines from the chair and the woman on the left bring the viewer's focus to the children standing in the center and then to the mother on the right. The background helps establish the rural, agricultural setting.

In contrast, the second picture has much a much stronger **composition**. The main figure is the woman, with her two children, looking away from the camera, leaving the **focal point** on the mother. Even the angle of the mother's arm, with her chin in her hand, leads the eye to the woman's face. Her expression is determined, but without much hope. These compositional features all support the purpose and message of the photograph: A migrant mother is caring for her family, as best as she can, in the most primitive of environments.

As viewers, we construct our own **narrative** based on the information presented in the picture. This woman is caring for her children in a migrant worker environment. She has no apparent support. This shelter appears to be where she is living. Other family members may be working in the area, but we can only guess at their whereabouts.

We put all these analytical pieces together to understand better the purpose and meaning of this photograph. For its **theme**, the photograph brings something hidden (a human story of poverty and exploitation) out into the open and gives it dignity. Lange's purpose was to call attention to the predicament of migrant workers in order to gather support for governmental reform. Her purpose was thus persuasive: she hoped to change public awareness as a first step to improving governmental assistance programs.

While images like these can tell a story without words, you as a writer and a reader will need to analyze how images can work together with words to produce a single effect. Imagine, for example, how embedding the Lange images in a written text might serve an author who was making a case about poverty. How might the photos be used in an argument about current income equality or the growing incidence of children in poverty? In each case, because the images support a different purpose, they are likely to be "read" differently by the audience because of the surrounding context. Ideally, image and text should each contribute something of its own so that the combined effect is more powerful, appealing, and persuasive than either the written text or the image by itself. As you analyze an image, part of your job is to judge how well that effect is created.

> ❝ There can be no words without images. ❞
>
> —Aristotle, Author of *Rhetoric*

Information Graphics

One class of still images that can be effective in making a case are graphs and charts. While these images contain words and numbers, like other forms of written texts, they are carefully designed to produce the effects of an image by means of their composition, focal point, theme, and even the story they tell. Note, for example, how each of the graphs and charts that follow builds an argument on its own, yet could be part of a larger argument in which it is embedded.

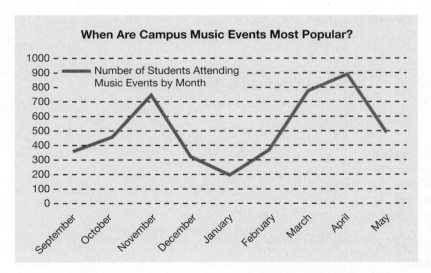

A line graph is useful for tracing phenomena across time as well as other instances in which you want to trace change. This line graph, produced by the Campus Activities Director of a student senate, depicts graphically the most popular months for music events on this campus. What conclusions might the senate draw from this?

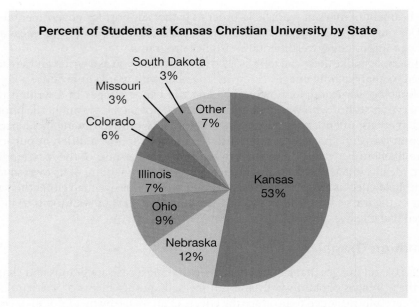

The pie chart is used to depict the percentage of students at this campus from its home and neighboring states. Pie charts allow us to quickly visualize the largest or most important elements in a situation. This pie chart, for example, allows viewers to quickly determine the states with the largest percentage of students, and to judge the relative percentage visually.

By grouping data by the relationship of two variables, scatter charts can shows graphically the correlation between the variables. While the general statement this chart makes is that higher tuition seems to provide higher quality, you might also note that some high quality institutions are not at the top of the tuition scale. What conclusions might a viewer make from this scatter chart?

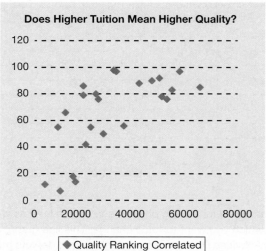

Analyzing Audio Components

As with the analysis of visuals, you will need to consider the individual elements of audio and develop a vocabulary to describe them. The most crucial elements are tone or pitch, timbre, loudness or volume, and duration.

- **Tone or Pitch.** Describe the tone of the voice or other sound elements you hear. Is it high or low? Deep or screechy? If it is a human voice, is its tone likely to inspire emotional reactions, breed confidence, or reinforce the logic of the argument? Does it seem to fit or clash with the overall purpose and audience? For example, an analysis might note that "the somber pitch of her voice portrayed her sorrow at the loss of the environmental protections that had long been in place."

- **Timbre.** Timbre refers to that which distinguishes one sound from another. Is one voice louder or sharper than another? Is there a discord or harmony between sounds? What sounds stand out in engaging emotions, or signal a change in the emotions or situation depicted? For example, you might read that "the change in timbre of the music each time the villain arrived on scene announced the inner evil of this devious character" or "the quiet, confident timbre of the candidate's voice supported the logic of her ideas more than the vehement yelling of her opponent."

- **Volume or Loudness.** The perception of loudness is often influenced by context: Sounds introduced after a period of silence may jar us more than others. In the case of human speech, is there a range of volume that is tied to the content or message? Are there whispers that carry appeals to emotion or credibility? Do pauses suggest thoughtfulness (and thus support an appeal to logos or ethos)? For example, an analysis of an audio tape might note that "his near whisper as he spoke of his fallen comrades-in-arms demonstrated the character of a true soldier."

- **Duration.** Our perception of sound (and thereby its rhetorical effect) is also influenced by its duration. Do some sounds in the text you are analyzing persist more than others? In the case of human speech, does a monologue or dialogue go on for an extended time? Or are statements short and pithy? For example, an analysis of a concert might note that the "applause continued well beyond its normal duration, reminding us that this was not merely a polite response to the performance."

As you analyze sound elements, then, you demonstrate how they contribute to the overall appeals of a multimedia text.

Analyzing Video Components

As with critical reading, analyzing and incorporating video requires that you break down the components and then synthesize them to show how the parts work together. Here are features of video to consider that can help focus your attention and provide the vocabulary for describing what you see and hear. (You will want to use vocabulary from the two previous sections as well.)

- **Format.** What is the format or genre of the video? Just as writing genres can be labeled (an essay, a story, a set of instructions), a video can be described as an interview, a documentary, a magazine, a parody, a news story, or a "talking head," to name a few. What audience expectations does each format bring? What does an audience expect from a news story—facts? objectivity?—or from a talking head—bias? criticism? What does an audience expect from a story format—characters? plot? setting? For example, you might note that "the documentary format lent an air of credibility to the story, especially given the deep background that was provided on the topic."

- **Style.** The style of a video is often related to its format, but it can be productive to analyze style separately. Would you describe a certain video as formal or informal, as polished or raw? Does it present a professional style or a more personal one? For example, a reviewer might note that "the polished style of the music video signaled that these once edgy artists had become sanitized by success."

- **Camera Angle and Perspective.** A video presentation is dependent not only on the visual elements described above but on how those elements are captured by the camera's point of view. What angles on the action portrayed are you given? Which shots are close-up? Which are wider? What happens when the camera moves your perspective from one to the other, zooming in and zooming out, either slowly or quickly? For example, an analysis of a political debate might note that "while the long shots favored the democrat, the close-ups showed his disdain for his opponent, undermining his character."

- **Sound.** Sound can be included in a video in two ways. One way is to record sound and visuals together, leaving them as they were—happening simultaneously and presented simultaneously. Sounds can also be—and often are—edited in after the fact. Which method seems to be the case with the video you are analyzing? Do sounds seem to be in their naturally occurring state? Has voiceover been added to tell us what to notice about the visuals? For example, a video analysis might suggest that "the clear and confident voice of the narrator helped the audience to understand the complex graph and to accept its reliability."

In the end, the key is to demonstrate how the various media elements work together to achieve an overall effect.

Synthesizing

The ultimate goal of a text is to serve a unified purpose for a specific audience. So, while your analysis and your choices as a writer rely on a variety of separate elements, you should always be aiming at *synthesis*, at showing how the parts work together. You examine the parts of a multimedia text in order to see how they work together, effectively or ineffectively, to convey a message to an audience. And you create multimedia texts in the same way—to make the parts work together to serve your purpose. Like written texts, multimedia texts need to be carefully edited to achieve that unified purpose. As you practice analyzing multimedia texts, consider how the techniques you find can serve you as you design your own texts.

Warming Up: Journal Exercises

The following exercises can help you to see connections between analysis and composing in multimedia. Using techniques learned in this chapter, respond to these exercises individually, in groups, or on your class website.

1. Imagine that you want to develop a video or narrate a PowerPoint or Prezi presentation about the processes by which wind power can be harnessed, based on the visual on page 313. How would you use the elements of sound and moving images to enhance it further?

2. Go to the Internet and find a video advertisement that you think is effective. Then experience it in four ways, making informal notes each time. First, watch it all the way through without stopping. Freewrite your initial reactions. Then watch it again, pausing each time you see a significant shift in the scene. Use techniques for analyzing still visuals to comment about the composition, focal point, narrative elements, and theme of the shots. Third, play the video all the way through, but don't watch it—just listen. What sound components do you notice? Finally, repeat the first step and then freewrite on additional insights that you might have had after completing the other forms of analysis. Keep these discoveries in mind as you create your own multimedia elements.

3. Find three advertisements for the same product (or the same kind of product, such as cars, jeans, or technology) that use three different media (magazines, a website, a video, an audio ad). Analyze each ad for its use of the media components discussed in this chapter. Describe how you might have made similar or different choices. Why? Go on to write a description of the ad that *you* would produce, and the media *you* would choose to use or embed. Pitch that ad to your classmates.

4. **Collaborate with peers.** One way to test the effect of multimedia elements is to try them out on various audiences. Choose or create three visuals to supplement a piece of writing or presentation that you are working on. Show each of the visuals to a variety of people who fall within your likely audience, and ask for their reactions. Keeping those reactions in mind, and then decide which visual best serves your purpose.

Analyzing Multimedia in Context

Multimedia texts can be powerful ways to communicate. Because they combine many senses, and because, as the old saying goes, "a picture is a worth a thousand words" (at least in some cases), it is important that we consider the larger context of any multimedia composition. Like all texts, multimedia texts have circumstances into which they enter. For us to be thoughtful analysts and creators of such a text, we need to consider its larger context. The essay that follows shows how the circumstances surrounding a powerful image can help us to better appreciate the ways that "text" and "context" work together—and how one can sometimes, obscure the other. Carolyn Kleiner Butler, in her analysis of an iconic photograph, examines its history and the personal story of the key figures in it. Her writing demonstrates how a media analysis can focus on social and historical context. Before you read the essay, examine this famous photograph, which appears on the first page of this chapter, and write down your own initial reactions to it. Then go on to read Butler's essay to see if the back story of this shot and the persons in it meshes with your first interpretations.

Coming Home

Carolyn Kleiner Butler

Carolyn Kleiner Butler has worked as a contributing editor to publications such as *U.S. News and World Report* and *Smithsonian*, where this essay first appeared in 2003. At this time, many families in the United States had loved ones serving in Iraq or Afghanistan. Butler analyzes a famous Vietnam-era photograph by Sal Veder, *Burst of Joy*, to show how the reality behind the photograph contrasts sharply with the appearance in the photograph.

Sitting in the back seat of a station wagon on the tarmac at Travis Air Force Base,   1
in California, clad in her favorite fuchsia miniskirt, 15-year-old Lorrie Stirm felt that she was in a dream. It was March 17, 1973, and it had been six long years since she had last seen her father, Lt. Col. Robert L. Stirm, an Air Force fighter pilot who was shot down over Hanoi in 1967 and had been missing or imprisoned ever since. She simply couldn't believe they were about to be reunited. The teenager waited while her father stood in front of a jubilant crowd and made a brief speech on behalf of himself and other POW's who had arrived from Vietnam as part of "Operation Homecoming."

The minutes crept by like hours, she recalls, and then, all at once, the car   2
door opened. "I just wanted to get to Dad as fast as I could," Lorrie says. She tore down the runway toward him with open arms, her spirits—and feet—flying. Her mother, Loretta, and three younger siblings—Robert Jr., Roger and Cindy— were only steps behind. "We didn't know if he would ever come home," Lorrie says. "That moment was all our prayers answered, all our wishes come true."

(Continued)

Associated Press photographer Slava "Sal" Veder, who'd been standing in a 3
crowded bullpen with dozens of other journalists, noticed the sprinting family
and started taking pictures. "You could feel the energy and the raw emotion in
the air," says Veder, then 46, who had spent much of the Vietnam era covering
antiwar demonstrations in San Francisco and Berkeley. The day was overcast,
meaning no shadows and near-perfect light. He rushed to a makeshift dark-
room in a ladies' bathroom on the base (United Press International had com-
mandeered the men's). In less than half an hour, Veder and his AP colleague
Walt Zeboski had developed six remarkable images of that singular moment.
Veder's pick, which he instantly titled *Burst of Joy*, was sent out over the news-
service wires, published in newspapers around the nation and went on to win a
Pulitzer Prize in 1974.

It remains the quintessential homecoming photograph of the time. Stirm, 4
39, who had endured gunshot wounds, torture, illness, starvation and despair
in North Vietnamese prison camps, including the infamous Hanoi Hilton, is
pictured in a crisp new uniform. Because his back is to the camera, as Veder
points out, the officer seems anonymous, an everyman who represented not
only the hundreds of POW's released that spring but all the troops in Vietnam
who would return home to the mothers, fathers, wives, daughters and sons
they'd left behind. "It's a hero's welcome for guys who weren't always seen or
treated as heroes," says Donald Goldstein, a retired Air Force lieutenant colonel
and a coauthor of *The Vietnam War: The Stories and the Photographs,* of the Stirm
family reunion picture. "After years of fighting a war we couldn't win, a war that
tore us apart, it was finally over, and the country could start healing."

But there was more to the story than was captured on film. Three days before 5
Stirm landed at Travis, a chaplain had handed him a Dear John letter from his
wife. "I can't help but feel ambivalent about it," Stirm says today of the photograph. "I was very pleased to see my children—I loved them all and still do, and I
know they had a difficult time—but there was a lot to deal with." Lorrie says, "So
much had happened—there was so much that my dad missed out on—and it
took a while to let him back into our lives and accept his authority." Her parents
were divorced within a year of his return. Her mother remarried in 1974 and lives
in Texas with her husband. Robert retired from the Air Force as a colonel in 1977
and worked as a corporate pilot and businessman. He married and was divorced
again. Now 72 and retired, he lives in Foster City, California.

As for the rest of the family, Robert Jr. is a dentist in Walnut Creek, California; 6
he and his wife have four children, the oldest of whom is a marine. Roger, a major in the Air Force, lives outside Seattle. Cindy Pierson, a waitress, resides in
Walnut Creek with her husband and has a daughter in college. And Lorrie Stirm
Kitching, now 47, is an executive administrator and mother of two sons. She
lives in Mountain View, California, with her husband. All four of Robert Stirm
Sr.'s children have a copy of *Burst of Joy* hanging in a place of honor on their
walls. But he says he can't bring himself to display the picture.

(Continued)

...continued Coming Home, **Carolyn Kleiner Butler**

Three decades after the Stirm reunion, the scene, having appeared in count- 7
less books, anthologies and exhibitions, remains part of the nation's collective
consciousness, often serving as an uplifting postscript to Vietnam. That the moment was considerably more fraught than we first assumed makes it all the more
poignant and reminds us that not all war casualties occur on the battlefield.

"We have this very nice picture of a very happy moment," Lorrie says, "but 8
every time I look at it, I remember the families that weren't reunited, and the
ones that aren't being reunited today—many, many families—and I think, I'm
one of the lucky ones."

Questions for Writing and Discussion

❶ While Butler provides the historical context for this photograph, because her
essay was published in 2003, it also had another context for readers: The war in
Iraq. How does that later context affect the way readers experience both the
photo and the essay?

❷ What does the information about the photographer and his words add to this
analysis? How does it change your understanding of the photograph?

❸ While Butler does not comment directly on the contrast between the "burst of
joy" in this photograph and the divorce that soon followed, is an implicit point
being made here? What is that point?

❹ **Collaborate with peers.** After viewing and reacting to the photograph and
reading Butler's essay, discuss your reactions with classmates. Begin your
discussion with each member of the group writing out, then sharing, what each
one takes to be Butler's main point or thesis. Since she does not state one
directly, you will need to decide whether there is an "implied thesis"—a point
that comes out indirectly.

Tips for Transferring Skills

The writing techniques discussed in this chapter can be used in many other
situations you will face as a college writer and beyond. To reinforce these techniques, and to really put them to use, you should find ways to apply and practice them on other occasions and in other classes. Here are tips for using these
techniques in a variety of writing situations.

1. Some of the skills for analyzing multimedia texts can be applied to the
study of the arts and humanities. As you study film or video, or as you
write analyses in an art history class, use those skills to help train your
eye and ear.

2. Business-related fields use the rhetorical appeals constantly. Marketing campaigns are deeply dependent on multimedia presentations. As you consider various theories and methods for attracting customers, consider how different media—including social media—draw on the rhetorical appeals.
3. As you complete writing assignments in other courses, consider the kinds of multimedia enhancements that could supplement your writing. Considering the discussion of various forms of media from this chapter, think about how you might use multimedia in the form of images, graphs, video, or audio within the writing you do.
4. Multimedia is used frequently to enhance oral presentation. As you plan a presentation for class, at work, or as a member of an organization, consider what kinds of media might be most appropriate. Use the skills for the analysis of media to inform your own use of it as well.

Composing with Multimedia: Writing Processes

The techniques for analyzing multimedia components should also inform the ways that you design your own media-enhanced texts. When you embed a graph, chart, or image in your essay, or create sound or video elements, be sure to pay attention to their rhetorical effect. Does this media component serve the writer's (or my) purpose? Will the writer's (or my) audience benefit by—or even expect—embedded elements such as graphs, charts, images, or visuals? Do these elements enhance the writer's (or my) credibility? The processes described below can help you both to analyze multimedia components you find in other texts and to create your own.

Using Multimedia Composing in Your Writing Processes

By analyzing a variety of media—words, audio, images, graphs and charts, video—you can learn a great deal about how a 21st century writer uses multimedia. For example, you might examine a video that is building an argument or selling a product, a website that is promoting a cause or an organization, or a digital essay with embedded visuals, sounds, or video. As you do so, use the skills of critical reading discussed in Chapter 12 to identify and describe the rhetorical situation—its purpose, audience, and social or political context. Use the techniques learned in this chapter to identify and analyze the effectiveness of its various media components. Pay special attention to the interaction of words and other media.

If you were completing an analysis essay, you would go on to formulate your claim or thesis, and use the findings of your analysis to illustrate why you are making this claim. For example, you might claim that the audio features of a video ad are central to achieving its purpose, or that the visuals or color choices on a website undermine its purpose—or are very effective for a particular audience. You would also consider the wider social contexts of the piece, and its use of the rhetorical appeals to reason, emotion, and character/credibility.

Audience	Possible Genres for Analyzing Multimedia
Personal Audience	Class notes, journal entry, scrapbook that constructs your family history, social networking page or blog that analyzes media phenomena
Academic Audience	Academic analysis of a historical phenomenon through artifacts, media critique, review, journal entry, forum entry on class site
Public Audience	Column, editorial, review, or critique in a magazine, newspaper, online site, newsletter, or multigenre document

You can also use your analytical skills to create your own multimedia text, enhancing a piece of writing that you are currently working on or have already written. You could add visual elements (images, charts or graphs, embedded audio or video, document design) to your writing that will support the message for your particular audience. You could even create a new version of your piece that uses media components—audio, video, PowerPoint or Prezi. As with all kinds of writing, first articulate the audience, purpose, genre, and context for this particular piece, then look for opportunities to provide multimedia elements that would help achieve your purpose for your audience.

Audience	Possible Multimedia Genres
Personal Audience	Photographs, art, digitized scrapbook images, collage, video, blog or personal website, comics
Academic Audience	Graphs, charts, diagrams, flow charts, organizational diagrams, photographs, digital images, art, embedded audio or video, oral presentation with visual aids
Public Audience	Graphs, charts, diagrams, flow charts, organizational diagrams, photographs, digital images, art, comics, website, graphic novel, audio or video essay or narrative, oral presentation with visual aids

CHOOSING A SUBJECT

Whether analyzing or creating in multimedia, you should choose a subject relevant to one of your other classes, your job, or an area of personal interest. If you are incorporating other media, be sure to consider what kinds of enhancements fit the audience and purpose. If you are analyzing a multimedia text, look for one that incorporates several forms of media. Remember that you can incorporate media from the original as examples in your essay. In either case, the key is to learn more about how multimedia can serve a writer's purpose.

As you look for subjects, and consider how multimedia can enhance your approach to that subject, don't forget our expanded definition of texts. You could, for example, analyze or create

- paper-based texts with embedded images or hyperlinks
- websites
- advertisements
- articles or textbooks in your field of study, noting the use of multimedia
- billboards or posters
- video or audio texts, including music and speeches

To choose an appropriate topic, look for texts in which multimedia is used to inform and/or persuade.

You could also compare or create a variety of media that may be used to address a topic, considering the advantages and disadvantages of each. As you do so, *remember that when you incorporate in your own work images or other materials from the Internet, you must give credit to the photographer, artist, or designer of the visual.*

13.3
Use strategies to match multimedia features with your topic and purpose

COLLECTING

The collecting process for an assignment can take many forms. If you are planning to do an analysis, your first task will be to locate a text (or texts) to study. You might begin with your subject; for example, if you are interested in studying images of female athletes, you could start with a depiction of a female athlete that you encountered and that got you thinking about such depictions in the media.

Whatever your subject, given the wealth of images, podcasts, and videos available on the Internet, you should limit any search as soon as the topic starts to come into focus. Once you locate several appropriate multimedia texts, begin analyzing and making notes, looking for key components of the images, audio, and video. Ask yourself:

- What specific elements of this topic most interest me and will most interest my audience?
- What search terms will help me to find the specific items (or the specific media) I am seeking?

13.4
Use collecting strategies to develop multimedia components

- What kinds of evidence am I looking for? Examples? Other analyses? Evidence of changes over time? Evidence of the effects of media depictions?
- What biases might I have coming into this analysis? How might I be sure that I am keeping an open mind?

Keep track of the themes and rhetorical appeals that seem to be common to the texts you find. Here are further tips for the collection process:

- Collect and analyze any accompanying written text or evidence that illustrates the social or historical context.
- Collect visuals belonging to the same genre (historical photographs, advertising campaigns, political photographs, Internet images); this can provide evidence helpful for your analysis.
- Research the background, context, origin, or maker or designer of the image, and look for other commentaries and analyses of that type or genre of visual. Use your *critical reading skills* to understand key points in these commentaries. And be sure to use your *observing skills* to help your analysis.
- Try closing your eyes and creating the piece you are analyzing for yourself— what details did you remember and reproduce and what details did you forget? If you have particular *memories* of this image or of the first time you saw this visual, you may want to add this to your notes.

The collecting process also allows you to gather bits of media that will serve as examples that

- support your analysis
- you can use (and cite!) to support a multimedia argument or tell a story
- can give you ideas for the kinds of multimedia texts you might create on your own

You might also think about how you can remix those elements to create a parody, an imitation, or a response to another multimedia text. If you pay close attention, you will also learn more about the available technologies that others used to develop their multimedia texts.

An index of software packages to which you or your school might have access to follows on page 329. Some packages offer free software use or free trials. (And there are many more!) These media can be worth playing with and trying out—and trying them out can also give you insight on analyzing the media.

SHAPING AND DRAFTING

13.5

Use shaping and drafting strategies to incorporate multimedia features

In the past, *publication* largely meant a printed book, newspaper, or journal. Today the possibilities for making our work public are much wider. Even academic papers have new possibilities and new expectations, now that we can embed images in an art history paper, and charts and graphs to a math or social science paper, and include video or audio in an oral presentation. And because "papers" are now often presented to

Multimedia Software and Sites

Media	Purposes	Software and Sites
Still images	Edit and insert photos and other images to build or support an argument, tell a story, or use as examples in an analysis.	Photoshop, Camtasia, Gimp, Paint.NET, PhoXO, Funny Photo Maker
Graphs and charts	Present quantitative or factual information in easily digestible form; support appeals to reason; can also support appeals to emotion and credibility.	Microsoft Word, Excel, ClickCharts, Chartgo
Websites	House a wide array of media; can be used for word-based presentations as well as a launchpad for audio, video, blogs, wikis, and other media.	Dreamweaver, Wix, Drupal, WordPress, Websitebuilder, Sitey
Audio	Edited sound clips can be used for analyses; to supply background music or voices from interviews; to illustrate the delivery of speeches; and to narrate a presentation on PowerPoint or Prezi	Audacity, Wavosaur, Wavepad, WaveShop, Power Sound Editor
Video	These packages help you to edit video shot on your phone or other devices (or videos you download) to make them fit more precisely your subject, purpose, and audience.	Camtasia, Videopad, Full Motion Video, Moviestorm, Avidemux
Wikis and blogs	Blogs are public online journals. Keeping a blog lets you put your thoughts out into the wider world, helps you gather feedback, and (like Websites) they incorporate multimedia. Wikis have this capability, but they also allow users to edit postings.	Blogger, Tumblr, Wordpress, MediaWiki, DokuWiki, Zoho Wiki, Tiki Wiki
Mashups and remixes	Mashups and remixes have a number of definitions; basically, they are comprised of recorded materials (audio, video, visual) from other uses. They are useful in extending, parodying, or changing the purposes of the original version. They can thus be useful in making an argument or analyzing how media sources build upon and respond to one another.	MindTouch Deki, Mixpad, ALShow, One True Media
Presentation software	Originally designed to create a slide show to accompany oral presentations, presentation software can be used as stand-alone media when you add written text or audio voiceover. You can also embed video or audio recordings to make them multimedia. In some cases, you can use presentation software to give a video-like feel to still images.	PowerPoint, Prezi, Fuze, SlideDog, SlideRocket
Text sharing and editing	Document or text sharing sites allow you to share written and other media, and they allow multiple editors to work together on a project remotely. Crowdsourcing extends editing to a wide group, similar to the way a wiki works.	Google.docs, Dropbox, Ares, BitTorrent

teachers electronically, they can include embedded media and even hyperlinks to additional evidence or examples.

With that in mind, your choices for shaping and drafting must necessarily take into account the appropriate media for achieving your purpose with your target audience. You should ask:

- What is my focused topic, and what media can best portray it?
- What am I trying to accomplish, and what media can help achieve that purpose?
- What audiences are likely to be most interested in this topic, and what media would they expect or benefit by?
- How will I deliver or publish my text, and what capabilities for multimedia does that provide?

Here's an example: You plan to analyze the famous wartime photograph included on the first page of this chapter, with the goal of helping other history students to better understand its implications and its historical and social contexts. Your notes might look like this:

My **topic** is a famous 1973 photograph of a returning POW and its reception by the public near the end of a very long and very controversial war in Vietnam. To discuss this photograph, I will need to show the visual itself. I can imagine also including newspaper clippings, still and moving images of the war and protests, antiwar music from the period, and audio clips from famous speeches or interviews. That would help to put the famous photograph in context.

My **purpose** is to illustrate not only the reception of this one photograph, but to show how media depictions of war can influence the public's view of a war— sometimes in ways that are not fully accurate. To do this, I will need to research and display other visual depictions of wars. It would be helpful to present them in the way they first appeared, maybe with the surrounding stories or advertisements from the original publication.

My **audience** is other history students, and since they are used to a wide variety of ways to get information and opinions, I should include more than just word-based texts and try to use visuals, audio, and video.

I would like to make this text available to others beyond my class, so I'll create **an electronic text with embedded multimedia examples** that I can place on my personal blog site after my teacher makes suggestions for revision. I'll ask my teacher if she prefers a paper version or an electronic one, so I will know what media I can include.

Before you begin drafting, collect all your notes, your visuals, and your research. Based on these materials, determine what you want the *focus* of your piece to be. Will you analyze a visual to demonstrate its internal characteristics and meaning or its relation to other images in its genre? Or will you analyze a media artifact to examine its relationship to social contexts (as in the example of the war photo) and the rhetorical appeals that the visual makes within those contexts? After you answer these questions, you will want to state the unifying point of the elements by formulating your thesis. **The thesis for an analytical essay should clearly state the specific argument that you are trying to make about the text's purpose and audience, and it should indicate how a specific set of multimedia features will attempt to achieve that purpose for that audience.**

The techniques described will be useful when you are analyzing a text. On other occasions, you are the writer/designer of a multimedia text. On those occasions, the rhetorical situation looks more like this:

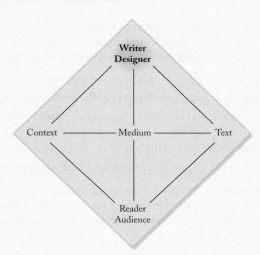

In the role of writer/designer, you still use traditional writing skills to shape and draft. But as you outline or use other shaping techniques, you should also note where you plan to embed other media, as the student writer Tanner Fox does in his notes:

My **topic** is problems that exist in the Transportation Security Administration. Since I am trying to demonstrate that there are alternatives to this system, I can use a brochure to illustrate a different kind of security system.

My **purpose** is not only to illustrate the problems with TSA, but also to show alternatives. To do this, I could create a visual depiction of both the problems and one possible solution through an Independent Security Firm.

My **audience** is both the decision makers in government agencies who address homeland security and entrepreneurs who might consider developing private companies that are more effective in providing security. I need to illustrate the viability of such a private firm by presenting examples.

While my academic paper detailing the problems will be useful for some audiences, the brochure I create can visually depict the advantages of considering privatization of the security systems we use at airports, and provide a graphic example of what this could look like.

Tanner Fox's paper and brochure, which appear on pages 334–338, show how a writer/designer can use visual images to build on an argument in words by experimenting with the placement of text, images, graphs, and embedded media—how arranging and rearranging chunks of text and visuals on a page can accomplish a purpose for different kinds of audiences.

Be sure to obtain feedback or peer response to help you as you make choices, draft, and revise. You might even have alternatives that you can test with peers to see which forms of media seem most effective; that is what professional designers do.

Visuals, illustrations, graphics, photographs, and document design all have a rhetorical effect. When you are composing a paper-based text, you have many possible ways of enhancing the words on the page. For example, you could add:

- Charts or graphs that illustrate quantitative information or a process
- Photographs or drawings that support or illustrate your argument
- Diagrams that show the relationship among the parts of an organization or machine
- Font choices that allow you to highlight or distinguish key points
- Text boxes that set off important examples or other elements

As you add visual elements to a paper-based text, consider their proper placement (ask yourself when you want the reader to encounter each visual), the design elements discussed above, and the kinds of visuals most likely to be effective with your audience.

When composing within a digital platform such as a website or a social media site, you will have many more options to consider. The words will still be important, but they can be enhanced through any of the following procedures:

- Imbed a sound file to capture a speaker's actual voice or a musical selection that adds an emotional element
- Link a video from YouTube to your website as an example of a point you are making, to illustrate a process or phenomenon, or to show a cultural trend.
- Add voiceover to a PowerPoint or Prezi presentation that will guide your audience through the presentation
- Choose web design templates—or create your own—that are appropriate to your topic and purpose and will enhance your ethos.

REVISING

13.6

Use revision strategies to gauge the effectiveness of multimedia components

As you revise your visual analysis or visual design project, consider your peer-response feedback. Some of it will be helpful, some of it may not be. You must decide what changes to make.

Guidelines for Revision

- **Review the purpose and audience.** If your purpose is to analyze the key parts of a multimedia text, have you identified the forms of media involved and then considered the conventions and effects of those media? Is there a clear, synthesizing claim that you make about a key element of the media used?

If you are designing a multimedia text, give a draft to a member of your intended audience or someone who might understand the needs of that audience. Does your reader seem to come away with the message you intended? Does the reader find the media helpful or distracting?

- **Check your text for its attention to rhetorical appeals.** If you are doing an analysis, make sure your draft comments on or makes use of the appropriate rhetorical appeals to logic, character, and emotion. Are the appeals effective for the purpose and audience of your draft? Do the appeals work together or conflict with one another? Have you embedded examples, including (when possible) multimedia examples?

If you are designing a multimedia text, what appeals do you rely on to move or inform your audience? Where do you use appeals to logic or emotion? Do the two ever clash? And what type of ethos (character) is the audience likely to assume by viewing or listening to your multimedia text? Will that ethos serve your purpose?

- **Collaborating with peers.** To help you reconsider the media components you have chosen, do what designers call a "user test." Present your composition to several peers, asking them to point out the multimedia elements that are most effective and the effect those elements had on them. Considering this feedback, decide whether your purpose would be better served by including (or excluding) specific forms of media.

- **Reconsider relationships between the chosen media and parts of the written text.** Much of the meaning and impact of embedded media depends on the accompanying text and on the social, political, and cultural contexts your audience will bring to it. Look again at the possible relationships, and be sure that the elements all work together without distracting the audience from your message. If you are doing an analysis, be sure you have considered those relationships in the text you are studying.

- **Reconsider the delivery format of your visual or your document.** If you are embedding multimedia as examples either to illustrate your analysis or to build your own story or argument, consider whether your delivery format is the best choice. What would happen if you changed from a paper-based to an electronic document (or vice versa)? What if you used a website or blog format? What if you used a narrated Prezi presentation? How would each change or affect your ability to embed multimedia? How would they affect the readers' progress through your text?

- **Organize your analysis.** Check your draft, considering how the audience will proceed through it and whether they are likely to be distracted from its flow by embedded media or page design. What will assure that the flow of ideas will help readers see your overall message, thesis, or claim?

Using Multimedia to Enhance Your Writing

Throughout this chapter, you have studied and practiced techniques and processes to help you use multimedia to enhance the written word. These techniques can be embedded into the writing you do, or can even stand alone as arguments made with visuals, sound, and snippets of writing that support those media. Student writer Tanner Fox used some of those methods to build his argument about improving homeland security. He first studied the security methods used at US airports that are regulated by a government agency. He then compared these methods with those used at Israeli airports. As you read his essay, note how he builds his argument from a variety of sources. Then note how Fox draws upon the research built into his essay to create a multimedia text in the brochure that follows. As you do your own writing, it is worthwhile to consider, as Fox did, how it could translate into other media representations through images, text boxes, and font changes. What other multimedia might Fox have used in his essay or brochure?

Student Writing

The Effectiveness of the Transportation Security Administration

Tanner Fox

Student writer Tanner Fox studied the security methods used at US airports that are regulated by a government agency. He compares these methods with those used at Israeli airports. As you read his essay, note how he builds his argument from a variety of sources. Note also how Fox uses research from his essay to create a multimedia text in the brochure that follows. As you do your own writing, it is worthwhile to consider, as Fox did, how it could be enhanced by images, text boxes, and font changes. What other multimedia might Fox have used in his essay or brochure?

From the beginning, the Transportation Security Administration, commonly referred to as the TSA, has been faced with scrutiny and doubt. Be it their controversial pat-down procedures, their large budget, or their constantly debated scanning techniques, the TSA has been the subject of much concern among the American people. Created with the intent to keep American aircraft safe from all manner of

(Continued)

danger, the administration has been closely monitored to make sure that it is performing the duties it was originally intended to execute. However, in recent years, accusations of everything from mistreatment of passengers to petty theft have plagued the TSA. It is clear that the Transportation Security Administration needs to be modified or eliminated.

One of the major operations of most Transportation Security Administration personnel is to identify deceptive behavior based on behavioral cues or indicators. The Department of Homeland Security and the United States Global Accountability Office conducted studies to identify how well TSA agents detect deceptive behavior. The findings indicate that the Transportation Security Administration could only identify deceptive behavior fifty-four percent of the time (Johanson). These studies point out that there has been a twenty-six percent rise in TSA employee misconduct over the past three years (McGregor) and that the annual number of misconduct cases has risen in the past three years, from 2,691 cases in 2010 to 3,408 cases in 2012 (De Rugy). The offenses are reported to include "everything from sleeping on the job, to failing to follow screening procedures, to even theft" (De Rugy). The Global Accountability Office suggests "TSA managers establish a process for conducting review of violations, better record misconduct cases in a central database, and develop procedures for following up on completed misconduct investigations" (De Rugy).

In an effort to locate some of the problems Americans have with the TSA, studies conducted in 2013 by IDEO, an international design firm, have attempted to pinpoint the areas of the TSA that American citizens find to be the most disagreeable. According to these case studies, the agency "faced the challenge of redefining its public face, which centered around poor perceptions of the checkpoint experience" ("Checkpoint"). The findings also suggest that the TSA might gain a more favorable public opinion if they introduce a human element into their workings.

Rafi Sela, the president of A.R. Challenges, an Israeli-based design consultant firm, is no proponent of the American style of airport security. "Checking luggage is very nice, it looks great, taking away the breast milk of the mother of a one month old baby, that looks great . . . it does nothing for security, it's just a show" (Berman). Sela has been pushing for the TSA to adopt more "Israeli-ized" airport security. This movement stems from the idea that Israeli airports handle security with greater ease than American airports. Sela summarizes this idea by claiming that Israeli airports are ". . . safer and less of a hassle than in America" (Berman). The A.R. Challenges president goes on to state that ". . . today even the stupidest terrorist can circumvent the [American] airport security in two seconds" (Berman).

Rafi Sela is not the only critic of the Transportation Security Administration's techniques. Bruce Schneier, a computer security and privacy specialist, also takes issue with the way airport security is handled in the United States. Bruce refers to TSA checkpoints as "security theaters," due to the fact that they put on a show, but do very little else to keep passengers safe (Carden). Bruce also suggests that the

Sets up the thesis as an alternative to the status quo.

Experts are cited to demonstrate need.

Direct quotations use the authority of the agency to support the writer's claim.

Note how the brochure that Fox created stresses this human element.

Note how this point is used as a pull-quote in the brochure below.

The visuals in Fox's brochure stress the "visual theatre" that exists at many checkpoints.

(Continued)

...continued The Effectiveness of the Transportation, **Tanner Fox**

reactionary tactics utilized by the TSA are effectively "doing the terrorists' jobs for them" (Carden).

The TSA has attempted to rectify the situation, stating that "the Transportation Security Administration is working to find and implement new ways to make travel not only more secure, but also more efficient" (Wanger). This bold affirmation comes from TSA spokesperson Ross Feinstein. He goes on to state that "these efforts are part of a system-wide shift away from the one-size-fits-all security model following the 9/11 attacks, and toward a transportation security system shaped by risk, and driven by the latest intelligence" (Wanger).

The *Huffington Post* agrees that learning from Israel's airport security could drastically improve how things are done in the states. Daniel Wanger, CEO of Country Risk Solutions, notes that Tel Aviv's Ben Gurion Airport "sets the gold standard for establishing and maintaining security in all its forms" (Wanger). He claims that Ben Gurion Airport achieves this accomplishment via a combination of comprehensive due diligence, common sense, and consistency (Wanger). Security at Ben Gurion includes questioning by highly trained personnel as they enter the airport. These interview sessions last anywhere from a few minutes to a few hours. Although this type of security may seem overly aggressive, the introduction of a human element is what sets Israeli security above all else.

How does this point find its way into the visuals that Fox uses in his brochure?

Ben Gurion Airport also utilizes the most effective technology available. Luggage passes through a pressure chamber designed to safely trigger any harmful explosive devices or weapons. High-tech x-ray scanners are nowhere to be seen in most Israeli airports. Instead, highly trained personnel patrol the security checkpoint. These agents are skilled in detecting suspicious behavior, and they are constantly on the lookout for anyone who may be out to cause trouble. If a passenger is discovered to be acting abnormally, he or she is then extensively monitored, and subjected to more questioning if need be (Wanger).

This helps build a transition to the next point.

Even the Transportation Security Administration itself recognizes the need to change. On its Website, the TSA indicates that innovation and technology are at the forefront of their efforts to create a safe environment. The administration states that it "is constantly moving forward its technology usage." The security administration also acknowledges that "there's no silver bullet technology, no cure all, no end-all-be-all . . ." ("Innovation"). The article states that employing a myriad of security devices is essential in maintaining the safety of all passengers. It is also important to note that the administration's Website features an "IdeaFactory." This section of the site focuses on "engaging employees to improve security" ("IdeaFactory"). Here, TSA employees are given the ability to "submit ideas, provide comments on new concepts, and rate ideas that should be recommended for implementation." ("IdeaFactory").

(Continued)

Although the Transportation Security Administration is not perceived as a model of security and efficiency, the Israeli method does not go without complaints, either. Many argue that passing through Ben Gurion is difficult if you come from an uncommon ethnic background. The Israeli airport security method may also be a bit too extreme at times, as it requires some travelers to endure incredibly long questioning sessions. These interviews can be uncomfortable, and they may lead to an unpleasant airport experience. Some may find this ultra-personal method to be as difficult and ineffective as the TSA's controversial pat-down procedures, and to be difficult to scale to much larger U.S. airports.

Perhaps combining the pseudo-security of the TSA with the intense human element of Ben Gurion will provide an efficient solution to this dilemma. The U.S. airport security method involves debated technology and showy yet ineffective tactics, and the Israeli security strategy involves an overly thorough interview process and a watchful eye on everyone at all times. Merging these two tactics may provide the best of both worlds. The "security theater" aspect of the TSA will be advantageous in deterring potential threats, while Israeli security will be reliable in detecting and eliminating those who have the potential to create problems in the airport. While these two types of security are vastly different, and they focus on totally separate aspects of security, they both strive to achieve the same goal. Employing the best features of both of these security methods may lead to a more pleasurable and secure airport experience. Hopefully, these two separate forms of security will one day be combined in some way to improve airport security for everyone.

Note how the writer tries to find a compromise position in this argument.

Works Cited

Berman, Jillian. "U.S. Airport Security Is 'Just a Show,' Expert Says." *Huffington Post*. TheHuffingtonPost.com, 23 Dec. 2013. Web. 21 Apr. 2014.

Carden, Art. "Time to Close the Security Theater." *Forbes*. N.p., 30 June 2011. Web. 22 Apr. 2014.

"Checkpoint Evolution for Transport Security Administration." *Ideo*. Ideo, 2009. Web. 5 Dec. 2013.

De Rugy, Veronique. "GAO's Report: The TSA Wasted $900 Million of Your Money." *National Review Online*. National Review Online, 14 Nov. 2013. Web. 5 Dec. 2013.

"IdeaFactory: Engaging Employees to Improve Security." *Transportation Security Administration*. U.S. Dept. of Homeland Security, n.d. Web. 22 Apr. 2014.

"Innovation and Technology." *Transportation Security Administration*. U.S. Dept. of Homeland Security, n.d. Web. 22 Apr. 2014.

(Continued)

...*continued* The Effectiveness of the Transportation, **Tanner Fox**

Johanson, Mark. "TSA Behavioral Detection Officers 'Not Effective' Waste of 200 Million Annually: Report." *International Business Times.* IBT Media, 14 Nov. 2013. Web. 5 Dec. 2013.

McGregor, Jena. "Report: TSA Employees Misconduct Up 26 Percent over the Past Three Years." *Washington Post*: n. p. Washington Post. Web. 5 Dec. 2013.

Wanger, Daniel. "What Israeli Airport Security Can Teach the World." *Huffington Post*. TheHuffingtonPost.com, 17 Mar. 2014. Web. 21 Apr. 2014.

Tanner Fox's essay makes the case for rethinking the ways that we do airport security. In order to make that case in a different way to an audience of possible airport clients, he created this brochure as a separate project. How does it draw on the research that he did for this essay? How do the words and visuals work together to "sell" this idea to his audience?

Independent Security Inc.

Shortened waiting periods, a quick, friendly interview with some of our staff, and you're on your way! It really is that simple!

What We Are All About

Our mission is to provide you with the most effective, secure experience possible. We pride ourselves on our ability to provide our customers with a short wait, and a secure, helpful security experience. Instead of pushing you through scanners and X-ray machines, we'll just interview you! No hassle, and no degrading procedures!

Frequently Asked Questions:

Q: What sort of questions will be asked in the interview?

A: We just want to get an idea of what you're doing and why you're flying. You will be asked to provide a reason for flying, as well as information like your family, friends, cultural background, and religion.

Q: Why doesn't Independent Security use the technology that other companies do?

A: Typically, "high-tech" security equipment is only used to provide a false sense of security. Although these machines may make you feel secure, you really aren't. It takes a one-on-one encounter to truly discover if someone poses a threat.

What Do the Experts Have to Say?

Bruce Schneier, a computer security and privacy specialist, has never been a fan of the TSA's methods. He puts and emphasis into engaging with customers, instead of pushing them through scanners.

"Independent Security brings the ultra-safe Israeli methods to the United States." — Rafi Sela

Safety and Security At Its Finest

Rafi Sela is the president of A.R. Challenges, an Israeli security firm. For years, she has stressed the need to "Israeli-ize" American airport security. Vehemently campaign against the use of "high-tech" security equipment, she has stated that things like body scanners and pat down procedures do "nothing for security, it is just a show."

Bringing the Security of Tel Aviv's Ben Gurion Airport to the States

Daniel Wanger, CEO of Country Risk Solutions, has called Tel Aviv's Ben Gurion airport "the gold standard for establishing and maintaining security in all its forms." Independent Security Inc. has modeled its operations off of the Israeli airport, and attempts to closely emulate it..

Suffer under the tyrannical rule of the TSA no longer! Independent Security Inc. does not utilize any kind of body scanners!

Introducing a Personal Touch to Airport Security!

Transforming the Way You Think About Airport Security...

At Independent Security, we strive to keep the customers satisfaction in mind. We understand that our customers have places to be! Nobody wants to stand in ridiculous lines, or be hassled by inefficient security methods. Independent Security, Inc. is about providing the customer with a convenient experience, all while maintaining an excellent level of security and complying with all government requirements. We'll focus on you, instead of you focusing on all of our methods and techniques. With one simple interview, you'll be on your way to your destination, no hassle necessary!

Questions for Writing and Discussion

1 In his researched essay, Tanner Fox addresses the problems associated with the TSA's handling of airport security. What seem to be his strongest arguments that a problem exists? What kinds of evidence does he present?

2 In the brochure that Fox created, he builds an argument for an alternative way to handle airport security. How does he use the information collected in his research essay to enhance the brochure?

3 Using techniques discussed in this chapter, analyze Fox's use of multimedia techniques in his brochure. How do the images and text boxes address problems with the current system? What kinds of layout and design features are most effective? Do any detract from the overall purpose?

4 Think about the genre of the brochure and its goals. Is this an appropriate choice for Fox's purpose? Are there other media that he might have chosen to make his case, and if so, what ones might be effective? If this argument were presented as a website, for example, what other media might have been used?

Applying What You Have Learned

1 You are deeply concerned about the effects of an advertising campaign on stereotypes about gender, ethnicity, social class, your generation, or some other group. Using the techniques presented in this chapter, write an analysis that demonstrates how subtle elements of an advertising campaign are damaging to a particular group or to our culture more generally. Begin by using the analytical skills of this chapter to go below the surface. Consider the visual elements of the advertisements, the sound and video, and other techniques that may be missed by someone who is experiencing those advertisements with less attention to detail. Your purpose is to help your audience be more aware of the subtle messages embedded in ads. Be sure to use examples from several media in order to show the effects of each.

Using multimedia. Since this assignment asks you to analyze the effects of multimedia components on an audience, it provides an excellent opportunity for you to embed those elements into your analysis. You could use images from the advertisements in a paper text, hyperlinks to visuals, audio, or video in an electronic one, or even create parodies that demonstrate your point. In any case, showing instead of just telling can drive home your analysis.

2 Choose a social issue or problem that concerns you. For example, you might be suspicious of the environmental effects of hydrolic fracturing of the earth ("fracking") to obtain natural gas. Or you might be concerned that your neighborhood no longer has adequate space for children to play. Or you might worry about voter apathy or government overreach. Start with serious academic research, making sure that you gather the facts about the situation first by using authoritative sources, talking to experts, and doing other forms of information collection. Then go on to analyze the multimedia depictions surrounding this issue. What public information is out there? Does it match the deeper investigations you've done? Analyze the relationship between the "facts" you've discovered and the media presentations of the topic, and write an analysis of the two sets of perspectives.

Using multimedia. After you've written your analysis of the issue and its public media presentation, use what you learned to inform other college students. Create a multimedia presentation to inform and/or persuade that audience in a compelling way. For example, you could develop a campaign with posters, flyers, or brochures if you prefer paper texts. Or you could create video, a website, a blog, or Facebook pages on the issue. Be sure to use the facts you have found in ethical and accurate ways, while employing a method of delivery that is likely to appeal to college-age students.

③ One compelling aspect of new media is how new it really is. Its newness has created serious generational and economic divides on how we experience the world. Those who still rely on reading newspapers see the world differently from those who get their news from web feeds, cable news, or infotainment. Do an analysis of a divide—generational, economic, racial, gender—that you suspect occurs because of the types of multimedia that are used by different groups. Start by reading on the topic, then use interviews, focus groups, or another form of field research to better inform yourself. Write an analysis of the effects of new forms of media (or a single new form) on various groups of people.

Using multimedia. Since this assignment asks you to do interviews or other forms of field research, you will have the opportunity to include multiple forms of media. You could videotape or audiotape the interviews and include the voices or images in your presentation via an electronic document, website, or hyperlink to YouTube or other share sites. You could use photographs of those you interview interacting with various types of media. You could embed graphs, charts, or tables to illustrate key differences among groups. You could even create a short documentary film on the topic, embedding your research into the video.

> ❝When we evaluate, we have in mind . . . an ideal of what a good thing—pianist, painting, or professor—should be and do, and we apply that ideal to the individual instance before us.❞
>
> —Jeanne Fahnestock and Marie Secor, Authors of *A Rhetoric of Argument*

> ❝Purpose and craftsmanship—ends and means—these are the keys to your judgment.❞
>
> —Marya Mannes, Journalist and social commentator

WE constantly pass judgment on people, places, objects, events, ideas, and policies. "Sue is a wonderful person." "The food in this cafeteria is horrible." "That movie ought to get an Oscar nomination for best picture." "That candidate should be re-elected." In addition to our own reactions, we are constantly exposed to the opinions of our friends, family members, teachers, and business associates. The media also barrage us with claims about products, famous personalities, and candidates for political office.

A claim or opinion, however, is not an *evaluation*. Your reaction to a person, a sports event, a meal, a movie, or a public policy becomes an evaluation *only* when you support your value judgment with clear standards and specific evidence. Your goal in evaluating something is not only to express your viewpoint, but also to *persuade* others to accept your judgment. You convince your readers by indicating the standards for your judgment and then supporting it with evidence: "The food in this cafeteria is horrible [your claim]. I know that not all cafeteria food tastes great, but it should at least be sanitary [one standard of judgment]. Yesterday, I had to dig a piece of green mold out of the meat loaf, and just as I stuck my fork into the green salad, a large black roach ran out [evidence]."

Most people interested in a subject will agree that certain standards are important; for example, that a cafeteria be clean and pest-free. The standards that you share with your audience are the *criteria* for your evaluation. You convince your readers that something is good or bad, ugly or beautiful, tasty or nauseating, by analyzing your subject in terms of your criteria. For each criterion, you support your judgment with specific *evidence*: descriptions, statistics, testimony, or examples from your personal experience. If your readers agree that your standards or criteria are appropriate, and if you supply sufficient evidence, your readers should be convinced. They will take your evaluation seriously—and think twice about eating at that roach-infested cafeteria.

Techniques for Writing Evaluations

There are many rhetorical situations within which you are asked to evaluate—to make and defend judgments about—something. The goal of these evaluations is often to help others make informed judgments based on an agreed-upon set of criteria. In other cases, evaluations are simply meant to help us better appreciate our experiences. We encounter evaluations constantly—reviews of films, books, restaurants, commercial products, public performances, and works of art. Some of them are little more than thinly disguised promotions; other reviews are thorough, complex, and highly critical. For any substantive evaluation, the review must set standards of judgment, rely on fair criteria, balance the positive and the negative, and provide sufficient evidence to persuade its readers. In this chapter, you will learn techniques for composing many forms of evaluation.

Taken from *The Prentice Hall Guide for College Writers*, Eleventh Edition by Stephen P. Reid and Dominic DelliCarpini.

Techniques for Evaluating

Technique	Tips on How to Do It
Assessing the rhetorical situation	Determine the occasion and context for your evaluation. Find examples of the genre in which you propose to write—where are the reviews or critiques typically published? Who is the audience, and what do they already believe or know about the topic?
Stating an *overall claim* about your subject	The overall claim is your *thesis* for your evaluation. It sums up the positive and negative judgments you make for each criterion.
Clarifying the *criteria* for your evaluation	A criterion is a standard of judgment that most people who are knowledgeable about your subject agree is important. A criterion serves as a yardstick against which you measure your subject.
Stating a *judgment* for each criterion	The overall claim is based on your *judgment* of each criterion. Avoid being too critical or too enthusiastic by including both positive and negative judgments.
Supporting each judgment with *evidence*	Evidence should include detailed observations, facts, examples, testimonials, quotations from experts, or statistics.
Balancing your evaluation with both *positive* and *negative* judgments about your subject	Evaluations that are all positive are merely advertisements; evaluations that are entirely negative may seem too harsh or mean-spirited.

EVALUATING COMMERCIAL PRODUCTS AND SERVICES

13.7
Understand techniques for evaluating commercial products and services

One frequent form of evaluation is the review of a commercial product or service. We rarely buy a car, hire a plumber, or book a hotel without first consulting the many online reviews now at our disposal. Learning to write evaluations that go beyond personal taste, however, requires important skills—skills that will also carry over to the evaluative writing you will do in future classes and on the job. The following evaluation of a Chinese restaurant in Washington, D.C., by journalist and critic Phyllis C. Richman, illustrates the main features of a restaurant review.

Hunan Dynasty

Phyllis C. Richman

Phyllis C. Richman, the author of several murder mysteries set in the restaurant industry, is best known as a food critic. She wrote for the *Washington Post* for 23 years after beginning her career as a critic for the *Baltimore Jewish times*, and she has appeared on several NPR radio shows and the *Oprah Winfrey Show*.

(Continued)

...*continued* Hunan Dynasty, **Phyllis C. Richman**

215 Pennsylvania Ave. SE, 546–6161
Open daily 11 A.M. to 3 P.M. for lunch, 3 P.M. to 10 P.M.
for dinner, until 11 P.M. on Friday and Saturday.
Reservations suggested for large parties.

1 Chinese restaurants in America were once places one went just to eat. Now one goes to dine. There are now waiters in black tie, cloths on the tables and space between those tables, art on the walls and decoratively carved vegetables on the plate—elegance has become routine in Chinese restaurants. What's more, in Chinese restaurants the ingredients are fresh (have you ever found frozen broccoli in a Chinese kitchen?), and the cooking almost never sinks below decent. . . . And it is usually moderately priced. In other words, if you're among unfamiliar restaurants and looking for good value, Chinese restaurants now are routinely better than ever.

2 The Hunan Dynasty is an example of what makes Chinese restaurants such reliable choices. A great restaurant? It is not. A good value? Definitely. A restaurant to fit nearly any diner's need? Probably.

3 First, it is attractive. There are no silk tassels, blaring red lacquer or Formica tables; instead there are white tablecloths and subtle glass etchings. It is a dining room—or dining rooms, for the vastness has been carved into smaller spaces—of gracefulness and lavish space.

4 Second, service is a strong priority. The waiters look and act polished, and serve with flourishes from the carving of a Peking duck to the portioning of dishes among the diners. I have found some glitches—a forgotten appetizer, a recommendation of two dishes that turned out nearly identical—but most often the service has been expert. . . .

5 As for the main dishes, don't take the "hot and spicy" asterisks too seriously, for this kitchen is not out to offer you a test of fire. The peppers are there, but not in great number. And, like the appetizers, the main dishes are generally good but not often memorable. Fried dishes—and an inordinate number of them seem to be fried—are crunchy and not greasy. Vegetables are bright and crisp. Eggplant with hot garlic sauce is properly unctuous; Peking duck is as fat-free and crackly-skinned as you could hope (though pancakes were rubbery). . . .

6 I have found only one dismal main dish in a fairly broad sampling: lemon chicken had no redeeming feature in its doughy, greasy, overcooked and underseasoned presentation. Otherwise, not much goes wrong. Crispy shrimp with walnuts might be preferable stir-fried rather than batter-fried, but the tomato-red sauce and crunchy walnuts made a good dish. Orange beef could use more seasoning but the coating was nicely crusty and the meat tender. . . .

7 So with the opening of the Hunan Dynasty, Washington did not add a stellar Chinese restaurant to its repertoire, but that is not necessarily what the city needed anyway. Hunan Dynasty is a top-flight neighborhood restaurant—with good food, caring service and very fair prices—that is attractive enough to set a mood for celebration and easygoing enough for an uncomplicated dinner with the family after work.

Reviews of commercial products or services vary in purpose and quality. To qualify as evaluation—and not just advertising—the authors and the publishers must maintain an independent status, uninfluenced by the manufacturers of the products or services they are judging.

An examination of two popular lines of cell phone, Android phones and iPhones, provides such a substantive evaluation. In this comparative evaluation, the editors at *Consumer Reports* judge the cell phones in terms of display, navigation, Web browsing, 4G compatibility, shopping, apps, cloud computing, and voice assistance. Notice that the editors comment on both the strengths and the weaknesses of each phone.

> ❝It is as hard to find a neutral critic as it is a neutral country in a time of war.❞
>
> —Katherine Anne Porter,
> Novelist and short story writer

Android vs. iPhone

Consumer Reports editors

Consumer Reports, where this review was first published, is an independent, nonprofit organization that has been testing products since 1936. Its product reviews are published anonymously, suggesting that they represent an organizational, not individual, evaluation of their subjects.

1   The most important determinant of what a smart phone can do, and how well it can do it, is its operating system. While Windows Phone and, even more so, BlackBerry have a significant presence, two rivals dominate the OS market: Apple, with its three models of iPhone (the new 4s along with the 4 and 3G S), and Google's Android, with dozens of phones from a host of manufacturers. Here's how those two titans compare on key attributes:

Advantage: Android

2   **Large displays.** Back in 2007, iPhone's 3.5-inch display was one of the largest, brightest, and sharpest you could get, and its recent color and resolution upgrades have been impressive. But the larger (4.3 inches and up) and equally dazzling screens on Android phones from HTC, Motorola, Samsung, and other makers seem better suited to the Web pages, games, and videos that users are increasingly accessing from their phones.

3   **Navigation.** Android phones offer free, spoken, turn-by-turn directions and traffic updates out of the box via Google Maps Navigation software. To get comparable performance and convenience, iPhone users have to shell out $40 to $50 for a navigation app from TomTom, Navigon, and others. But those aftermarket iPhone apps have an advantage: Their maps are stored on the phone, so you can navigate even when you lack good cellular reception. (Next month's issue will include Ratings of the newest versions of those apps.)

4   **Web browsing.** Apple has its pluses here, including a "reader" mode built into the Safari browser of the new iOS 5 operating system. You can tap it to read articles without the clutter of ads and other graphics and to save articles to read later.

(Continued)

Customization of the interface. Apple's interface is fairly fixed, albeit in a 5
highly intuitive manner, but the Android platform can be customized. Phone makers
can tweak the interface, carriers can install apps, and users can customize a phone's
look and feel using widgets and other tools. For example, some blend updates from
friends on Facebook, Twitter, and other social networks, and others manage all of
your phone's wireless connections.

4G compatibility. More than a dozen Android smart phones support this tech- 6
nology, far more than any other platform. Technically, only the AT&T version of the
iPhone 4S supports 4G; it runs on the carrier's HSPA+ network.

Shopping by phone. Android and Apple have apps that allow you to check the 7
prices of products and other details by scanning bar codes or QR codes (those square
blotches you might have seen in ads) using the phone's camera and a connection to
the Web.

However, only Android has the Google Wallet app, which allows you to make a 8
purchase using your smart phone as though it were a digital credit card. Use of that app
is limited to a handful of phones with near-field communications (NFC) capability.
Phones in our Ratings with that feature include the Sprint version of the Samsung
Nexus S 4G, the HTCAmaze 4G, and the T-Mobile Samsung Galaxy S II. The carrier
must offer the service (now only Sprint does), and merchants must be in the MasterCard
PayPass network, which operates in 150,000 U.S. locations.

Advantage: iPhone

Selection of apps and entertainment. No contest. Not only does Apple have 9
the most apps, games, songs, movies, and other forms of entertainment for download
but its platform also makes it very easy to pay for them—via your iTunes account. On
Android phones, payment arrangements are often between you and the individual
app seller, which means you're giving your credit-card number to multiple sources
instead of to just one.

Cloud computing. Android is the true pioneer when it comes to syncing contacts, 10
calendars, apps, and other phone-based elements via the Web and intelligently linking
them with Web-based data such as maps, social networks such as Facebook and Twitter,
photos, search-engine results, and more. Apple's iCloud feature takes the game to a
whole new level, giving users 5 gigabytes of free storage on its servers, to which they can
upload photos, music, documents created with apps from Apple or third parties that support iCloud, and more that can be accessed by up to 10 devices on one iTunes account.
Ditto for most apps and content, including videos and books bought from Apple, which
don't count against your limit. To get more storage for non-Apple files, you'll have to pay
up to $100 a year for 50GB. Both Google and Apple have new services that use the cloud
to stream music, but it's premature to compare them, because Google's app is still in beta.

Consistent and intuitive interface and "ecosystem." Apple sustains a famil- 11
iar, highly intuitive interface across its various devices and programs. That aids in the
sharing and integration of tasks across your digital life, especially if you own various
Apple devices.

(Continued)

Voice assistance. While Android efficiently allows users to perform universal   12
searches, launch apps, and even dictate and send messages through voice commands,
Apple now offers all that and more with its built-in Siri voice-activated assistant.
Currently available only on the iPhone 4S, Siri not only understands and executes requests but speaks back to you, in a female voice. Tell Siri to remind you about an appointment, and she'll set it up in the calendar after confirming with you that she got it right.

Siri sometimes demurs from speaking when you ask her questions involving calcu-   13
lations, such as, "Convert 42 pounds into ounces." But she's smart enough to show you
the correct answer—in this case, 672 ounces—on her display.

EVALUATING WORKS OF ART

13.8
Learn techniques for
evaluating visual and
performing arts

Evaluations of commercial products and services tend to emphasize usefulness,
practicality, convenience, and cost. On the other hand, evaluations of works of art
(or *aesthetic* evaluations) focus on the quality of the experience. With visual art, we
evaluate form, color, texture, design, balance, image, or theme. With the performing
arts, we evaluate the work of the authors as well as the performers and technical
teams. Principles of aesthetic evaluation also apply to novels, short stories, essays,
and poems.

Evaluating Visual Art

In the following selection, Paul Richard, former art critic for the *Washington Post,* evaluates the painting *American Gothic* by Grant Wood. (Grant Wood's painting, *American
Gothic,* can be accessed quickly through Google images.) Although the painting was
completed in 1930, the occasion for Richard's review was the Grant Wood exhibition
at the Renwick Gallery of the Smithsonian American Art Museum in 2006. Richard's
overall claim is that *American Gothic* is a famous and even iconic example of American
art—as well known as Andy Warhol's Campbell's, soup can or Norman Rockwell's
Thanksgiving turkey. The fact that *American Gothic* has so often been the subject of
parody (search Google images, "American Gothic Parodies") is further evidence of
the painting's iconic status.

"American Gothic," Pitchfork Perfect

Paul Richard

Paul Richard was an art critic for the *Washington Post* for over 40 years. His perspectives on
the works displayed at the National Gallery were widely respected.

Is "American Gothic" America's best-known painting? Certainly it's one of them. Grant   1
Wood's dual portrait—with its churchy evocations, its stiffness and its pitchfork—
pierced us long ago, and got stuck into our minds. Now, finally, it's here.

(Continued)

...continued "American Gothic," Pitchfork Perfect, **Paul Richard**

"American Gothic," which hasn't been in Washington in 40 years, goes on view today at the Renwick Gallery of the Smithsonian American Art Museum. By all means, take it in—although, of course, you have already. 2

It should have gone all fuzzy—it's been parodied so often, and parsed so many ways—but the 1930 canvas at the Renwick is as sharp as ever. Its details are finer than its travesties suggest, its image more absorbing. It's also smaller than one might have imagined, at only two feet wide. Wood painted it in his home town of Cedar Rapids, Iowa, showed it only once and then sold it, with relief, to the Art Institute of Chicago—for $300. 3

The picture with a pitchfork is an American unforgettable. Few paintings, very few, have its recognizability. Maybe Whistler's mother. Maybe Warhol's soup can. Maybe Rockwell's Thanksgiving turkey. They're national emblems, all of them, visual manifestations of the American dream. 4

Whistler's figure, stiff and dark, looks half-enthroned and half—embalmed; what she evokes is Mom. Family and food are the twin themes of the Rockwell. And with his Campbell's can, fluorescent-lit, Warhol nails shopping. 5

"American Gothic," too, hits the psychic bull's-eye. Wood's sly painting gives us the bedrock Christian values, the sober rural rectitude and the gnawing fear of sex that have made this country great. 6

The dangers of the dirty deed might not be depicted, but they're present nonetheless. The sinful is suggested by the serpent made of hair that slithers up the woman's neck to whisper in her ear, by the lightning rod atop the house and, of course, by the Devil's pitchfork. Wood's painting has a wink in it. No wonder it has been so frequently cartooned. 7

"The couple in front of the house have become preppies, yuppies, hippies," writes critic Robert Hughes, "Weathermen, pot growers, Ku Kluxers, jocks, operagoers, the Johnsons, the Reagans, the Carters, the Fords, the Nixons, the Clintons, and George Wallace with an elderly black lady." 8

But cartoons tend toward the slapdash, and Wood's calculated image is not at all haphazard. Nothing's out of place. The bright tines of the fork have been echoed one, two, three, by, at the left, the distant steeple, the window's pointed arch and the sharp roof at the right. The pitchfork rhymes as well with the seams of the man's overalls. When Wood painted "American Gothic," he fit its symmetries together as if he were making a watch. . . . 9

The picture takes its title from an architectural fashion. In its higher manifestations, American Gothic gave us the Washington Cathedral and the colleges at Yale. Far out in the sticks (in, for instance, rural Iowa), the style left its mark on the factory-made windows, porch columns and pattern books that in the 19th century were shipped in by train. 10

"American Gothic's" farmhouse, with its pointed gable window, is another local artifact. Wood discovered that wooden building in nearby Eldon, Iowa. It's still there. His figures were local, too. The bald man is his dentist, B. H. McKeeby. The woman is Wood's sister, Nan. (She was 30 at the time, McKeeby, 62.) Their 11

(Continued)

eyes are cold, their mouths are prim. They wear period clothes. He stares the viewer down, she averts her gaze. They understand their roles.

Modern art, this isn't. Wood's painting is behind its times, rather than ahead 12 of them. What gives the work its punch is its slippery ambiguities. These haven't aged at all.

Try asking it a question. Is the woman the farmer's wife, or might she be 13 (nudge, nudge) the famous farmer's daughter of countless naughty jokes?

What does this painting mean to do, celebrate or satirize? Do its figures 14 dwell in paradise, where the pioneering Protestant verities still hold, or is their rural neighborhood not so far from Hell? . . .

I don't know whether Wood expected "American Gothic" to become an 15 American icon, but he wouldn't have been surprised. In the early 1930s, mythic American icons were very much on his mind.

Had you asked him to identify America's best-known paintings, you can 16 bet he would have named two pictures of George Washington: Gilbert Stuart's likeness, the so-called Atheneum Portrait of 1796, the one that's on the dollar; and "Washington Crossing the Delaware" (1851), Emanuel Leutze's famous river scene with ice floes. In fact, both of these chestnuts can be found in Wood's own art. . . .

What is remarkable about "American Gothic" is its famousness. What is 17 equally remarkable is that the picture's fame was not achieved by accident. The Renwick's show suggests that's what Grant Wood had in mind.

Evaluating Performances

Evaluating live, recorded, or filmed performances of people in sports, dance, drama, debate, public meetings or lectures, and music may involve practical criteria such as the price of tickets to sports events or rock concerts. However, aesthetic criteria also apply. In film evaluations, for example, the usual criteria are good acting and directing, an entertaining or believable story or plot, memorable characters, dramatic special effects, and so forth.

As you read the review of the film *Selma* that appears on page 351, look for the writer's judgments about specific criteria (acting, directing, the effectiveness of certain scenes, the use of dialect) and her overall claim about the film.

Warming Up: Journal Exercises

The following exercises ask you to write evaluations. Read all of the exercises and then write on the three that interest you most. If another idea occurs to you, write about it.

1. **Writing Across the Curriculum.** Choose the best of the courses that you are currently taking. To persuade a friend to take it, evaluate the course, the teacher, or both. What criteria and evidence would you select to persuade your friend?

2. To gather information for yourself about a possible job or career, interview a person in your prospective field about his or her job or profession. Focus your questions on the person's opinions and judgments about this career. What criteria does this person use to judge it? What other jobs would serve as a good basis for comparison? What details from this person's daily routine support his or her judgments?

3. At your place of work, evaluate one of your products or services. Write down the criteria and evidence that your business might use to determine whether it is a "good" product or service. Then list the criteria and evidence that your customers or patrons probably use. Are the two sets of criteria and evidence identical? Explain.

4. **Collaborating with peers.** In a group, pick a current film that all or most of you have seen. Start by discussing whether most of you thought this was a "good" film or not. As you talk, try to identify the criteria that members of the group are using to make their judgment. Compare those criteria with the criteria used by Ann Hornaday in her review of the film *Selma*.

What elements of composition and individual details from this image from the film *Selma* make it effective? How does it help you better understand Ann Hornaday's review of the film?

"Selma": Humanizing Rev. Martin Luther King Jr.

Ann Hornaday

Ann Hornaday holds a degree in Government and has worked as a researcher and editorial assistant at *Ms.* magazine. She has published movie reviews for the *New York Times, Austin American-Statesman, Baltimore Sun*, and *Washington Post*.

In her review of *Selma*, for the *Washington Post*, December 23, 2014, Ann Hornaday, begins by praising this film about Dr. Martin Luther King and then provides the reasoning for her judgment. Note how Hornaday implicitly establishes her criteria for a "good" film, how she describes the artistic techniques of the filmmaker and actors, and how she places the film in a historical context. Because this film was criticized for being inaccurate in some of its history, you might also read other reviews of the film in order to compare judgments and criteria.

1 One of the most vexing facts of cinematic life the past 50 years is that the Rev. Martin Luther King Jr. and the civil rights movement he led have not been given their rightful place in the feature-film canon. Often relegated to the shadows of ancillary plots, atmospheric background and blurry historical context, what were arguably the most pivotal events in American life during the 20th century never found their rightful place—front, center and spotlit—in the dominant narrative art form of that era.

2 Until now.

3 And it was worth the wait.

4 With "Selma," director Ava DuVernay has created a stirring, often thrilling, uncannily timely drama that works on several levels at once. Yes, it's an impressive historic pageant, and one that will no doubt break the ice for similar-themed movies to come. But DuVernay, whose roots are in the indie world, having directed the films "I Will Follow" and "Middle of Nowhere," has also rescued King from his role as a worshiped—and sentimentalized—secular saint. Here, she presents him as a dynamic figure of human-scale contradictions, flaws and supremely shrewd political skills.

5 Indeed, the most riveting passages of "Selma," which chronicles three marches King planned and finally led from Selma to Montgomery, Alabama, in 1965, aren't the speeches and ground-level skirmishes that led up to the marches. Rather, the most pulse-quickening material can be found in the meetings between King (David Oyelowo) and President Lyndon B. Johnson (Tom Wilkinson) as they argued the issue of voting rights. Early in "Selma," King travels to the White House to implore the president to pass a voting rights bill, while a weary LBJ—who had signed the Civil Rights Act just a year before—asks King to be patient, and support his War on Poverty in the meantime. Watching these redoubtable figures spar, cajole, strong-arm and size each other up winds up

(Continued)

being enormously entertaining. Much like the backroom machinations that propelled Steven Spielberg's "Lincoln," King's push-me-pull-you pas de deux with Johnson reveals talents as a political operator that were every bit as spectacular as his soaring oratory.

Anyone who is familiar with those speeches will realize that they're not 6 reproduced note-for-note in "Selma," which was written by Paul Webb. The filmmakers didn't have access to the rights to King's speeches, so in a brilliant workaround, DuVernay approximates his words, allowing viewers to focus on their meaning rather than on how literally Oyelowo reproduces them. For his part, Oyelowo doesn't mimic King so much as channel him: His voice, devoid of King's familiar church-bell timbre, is his own, and he has used it to create a bona fide character rather than a superficial impersonation.

Exquisitely shot by cinematographer Bradford Young, "Selma" plunges the 7 audience into 1960s Alabama, where we see Annie Lee Cooper (Oprah Winfrey, who also helped produce) try once again to register to vote. She's prepared when the registrar demands that she recite the preamble to the U.S. Constitution, and she even knows how many county judges reside in Alabama. Asked to name them, however, she falters.

Later, Cooper would figure prominently in King's strategy of drawing atten- 8 tion to the fight he led against injustice and racism; among the many things "Selma" does brilliantly is giving the lie to nonviolence as a merely passive, benign form of protest. Instead, we see King using it not just as a moral force, but also as a battle of images, in which searing footage and photographs of protesters being brutalized by local terrorists and law enforcement officials would, with luck, electrify the nation in support of his cause.

Like any historical drama, "Selma" contains its share of compressions and 9 the stiff, declarative rhythms of "important" billboard scenes. But for the most part, DuVernay makes sweeping, smooth work of a challenging collection of events, which spanned the murder of a young marcher named Jimmie Lee Jackson; White House huddles with King and Alabama Gov. George Wallace (Tim Roth); the savage beatings of Annie Lee Cooper and a Boston clergyman named James Reeb; King's imprisonment with fellow civil rights leader Ralph Abernathy; the arrival on the scene of Malcolm X; a tense conversation between King and his wife, Coretta (beautifully played by Carmen Ejogo); arguments between King, the Student Nonviolent Coordinating Committee and the Southern Christian Leadership Conference; a court case countermanding Wallace's order to stop the march; and, finally, the three demonstrations that culminated in the passage of the Voting Rights Act of 1965.

DuVernay stages all of this with economy, grace and skillful, authoritative 10 aplomb. "Selma" carries viewers along on a tide of breathtaking events so assuredly that they never drown in the details or the despair, but instead are left buoyed: The civil rights movement and its heroes aren't artifacts from the distant past, but messengers sent on an urgent mission for today. There are several

(Continued)

reasons to see "Selma" —for its virtuosity and scale, scope and sheer beauty. But then there are its lessons, which have to do with history, but also today: "Selma" invites viewers to heed its story, meditate on its implications and allow those images once again to change our hearts and minds.

Questions for Writing and Discussion

1 What implicit or explicit criteria does Hornaday use to suggest the quality of this film? That is, what seems to be the most important elements of a film for this critic? What examples illustrate those criteria or values?

2 In order to make her case, Hornaday uses vivid description. What passages are most effective in helping us to see, hear, and feel the effects of this film? What word choices are particularly striking?

3 While this is a favorable review, Hornaday also offers critique. How does she manage to find fault while still presenting strongly positive conclusions about the film?

4 How would this review be read differently by those who have already seen the film as opposed to those who are considering seeing it? What parts in particular might cause different reactions? How would it affect someone who went to see the film after reading the review?

Tips for Transferring Skills

The writing techniques discussed in this chapter can be used in many other situations you will face as a college writer and beyond. To reinforce these techniques, and to really put them to use, you should find ways to apply and practice them on other occasions and in other classes. Here are tips for using these techniques in a variety of writing situations.

1. In this chapter you learned methods for evaluating both commercial and artistic objects. Similar methods can be applied to the judgments you will need to make about the methodologies used in the sciences. The "Methods" section in science papers is designed to show why the design of an experiment is valid and reliable. As you read journal articles in the sciences, pay attention to the explicit and implicit criteria used to show that an experiment's method is well designed.

2. If you are enrolled in business classes, you will often use evaluation methods to judge whether a business plan, marketing strategy, or management technique is effective. As you conduct those evaluations while reading business case studies, consider the ways in which this field judges success or effectiveness. Identifying those underlying principles can help you understand better the values of the field.

(Continued)

3. You likely refer frequently to both aesthetic and commercial reviews online. Before seeing a film, you may look at reviews on *Rotten Tomatoes*. Before buying a new phone, you check out both *Consumer Reports* and social media chat about the latest versions. And you may even check Rate My Professor to choose classes. As you consult those services, use the techniques in this chapter to help you decide how valid their reviews are.

4. College campuses are usually rife with opportunities to view the arts—student art shows, campus exhibitions and galleries, musical performances, and so on. As you attend performances or visit exhibitions, try out the skills you have learned in this chapter to help you better appreciate and understand the arts on your campus.

Evaluating: Writing Processes

Using Evaluating in Your Writing Processes

> ❝I love criticism so long as it's unqualified praise.❞
>
> —Noel Coward, Playwright, songwriter, novelist, director, and performer

Depending on the audience and genre, the techniques of evaluating can help you to review a product or service, a work of art, or a performance. Evaluation works best when you can revisit or review the subject of your essay as you write, since details are very important. Be sure to select criteria for judgment that your audience will also accept—or that you can help them to accept. The evidence you collect should support your judgment for each criterion. *Remember: In order to remain objective and credible, evaluations should contain both positive and negative judgments.*

As the grid below indicates, the review is the most common genre for evaluating, but "reviews" cover a wide range of documents. Some film reviews, for example, are academic and critical whereas others merely indicate the major plot line without much critical evaluation. As you choose a topic, be sure to consider the expectations of your audience. Are they expecting merely to be informed or entertained, or do they want the thorough and critical evaluation described in this chapter?

Audience	Possible Genres for Evaluating
Personal Audience	Class notes, journal entry, blog, scrapbook, or social networking page
Academic Audience	Academic critique, media critique, review, journal entry, forum entry on class site, multimedia document
Public Audience	Column, article, or critique in a magazine, newspaper, newsletter, online site, or multimedia document

CHOOSING A SUBJECT

13.9
Use strategies to choose a topic for evaluation

If you have already settled on a possible subject, go on to the collecting and shaping strategies. If you have not found a subject, consider these ideas.

- Comparing and contrasting lead naturally to evaluation. For example, compare two places you've lived in, two friends, or two jobs. Compare two famous people from the same profession. Compare your expectations about a person, place, or event with the reality. The purpose of your comparison is to determine, for a specific audience, which is "better," based on the criteria you select and the evidence you find.

- Evaluating a career choice can help you choose appropriate courses, think about summer jobs, and prepare for job interviews. Begin by describing several jobs that fit your career goals. Then go to the following websites and gather information.

  http://www.monster.com   http://www.bestjobsusa.com
  http://www.careers.com   money.cnn.com/services/careerbuilder
  http://careers.yahoo.com   http://www.getthatgig.com

     Choose the career criteria that are most important for you, such as job satisfaction, location, benefits, salary, or education requirements. Is job satisfaction more important than pay or location? Rank your criteria in order of importance. Then write an evaluation of one or two jobs that you find described on the Internet or in your local newspaper.

- **Community Service Learning.** Community service-learning projects often require an assessment at the end of the period of service. These reflective evaluations start with the goals of the agency, the goals of your class project, and your goals as a learner as the major criteria. Then you gather evidence to see how well the actual experiences and projects met the overall project goals. Sometimes participants use short evaluation questionnaires to get feedback at the midpoint and then again at the end of the project. If you are participating in a community service-learning project, check with your teacher or coordinator about how to write this assessment.

COLLECTING

13.10
Use collecting strategies to develop criteria and gather examples

Once you have a tentative subject and audience in mind, ask the following questions to focus your collecting activities.

- Can you *narrow, restrict,* or *define* your subject to focus your paper?
- What *criteria* will you use to evaluate your subject?
- What *evidence* might you gather? As you collect evidence, focus on three questions:
  What *comparisons* can you make between your subject and similar subjects?

What are the *uses* or *consequences* of this subject?

What *experiments* or *authorities* might you cite for support?

- What initial *judgments* are you going to make?

Observing

Observation and description of your subject are crucial to a clear evaluation. In most cases, your audience will need to know *what* your subject is before they can understand your evaluation.

- Examine a place or object repeatedly, looking at it from different points of view. Take notes. Describe it. Draw it, if appropriate. Analyze its component parts. List its uses. To which senses does it appeal—sight, sound, touch, smell, taste? If you are comparing your subject to similar subjects, observe them carefully. Remember: Each time you observe your subject, you will see more key details.

- If you are evaluating a person, collect information about this person's life, interests, abilities, accomplishments, and plans for the future. If you are able to observe the person directly, describe his or her physical features, write down what he or she says, and describe the person's environment.

- If you are evaluating a performance or an event, a recording or video can be extremely useful. If possible, choose a concert, film, or play on tape that you can stop and review as necessary. If a recording or video is not available, attend the performance or event twice.

Making notes in a *three-column log* is an excellent collecting strategy for evaluations. Using the following example from Phyllis Richman's evaluation of the Hunan Dynasty restaurant, list the criteria, evidence, and judgments for your subject.

Subject: Hunan Dynasty Restaurant		
Criteria	**Evidence**	**Judgment**
Attractive setting	No blaring red-lacquer tables	Graceful
	White tablecloths	
	Subtle glass etchings	
Good service	Waiters serve with flourishes	Often expert
	Some glitches, such as forgotten appetizer	

Remembering

You are already an authority on many subjects, and your personal experiences may help you evaluate your subject. Try *freewriting, looping, branching,* or *clustering* your subject to help you remember relevant events, impressions, and information. In evaluating appliances for consumer magazines, for example, reporters often use products over a period of months, recording data, impressions, and experiences. Those experiences and memories are then used to support criteria and judgments. Evaluating a film often requires remembering similar films; a vivid narrative of your memories, when making comparisons, can help convince an audience that a performance is good or bad.

Reading

Ideas and evidence for your evaluation may come from reading descriptions of your subject, other evaluations of your subject, or the testimony of experts. Be sure you read such texts critically: Who is the intended audience for the text? What evidence does the text give? What is the author's bias? What are other points of view?

Investigating

All evaluations involve some degree of formal or informal investigation as you probe the characteristics of your subject and seek evidence to support your judgments.

Use the Library or the Internet   Check the library and Internet resources for information on your subject, for ideas about how to design and conduct an evaluation of that subject, for possible criteria, for data in evaluations already performed, and for a sense of different audiences. In an evaluation of chocolate chip cookies, for example, *Consumer Reports* suggests criteria and outlines procedures. The magazine rated some two dozen popular store-bought brands, as well as four "boutique" or freshly baked varieties, on "strength of chocolate flavor and aroma, cookie and chip texture, and freedom from sensory defects." Compare these reviews to the more crowdsourced reviews like those on Angie's List. How are they different?

Gather Field Data   you may want to supplement your personal evaluation with a sample of other people's opinions by using *questionnaires* or *interviews*. If you are rating a film, you might give people leaving the theater a brief *questionnaire,* asking for their responses on key criteria relating to the movie they just saw. If you are rating a class, you might want to *interview* several students to support your claim that the class was either effective or ineffective. The interviews might also give you specific examples that you can then use as evidence to support your own judgments.

SHAPING AND DRAFTING

As you think about how to organize and develop your essay, be sure to reread your assignment and reconsider your purpose and audience. For your evaluating essay, you can use shaping strategies from your previous essays, but be sure to consider the following strategies designed for evaluative essays.

13.11
Use techniques for organizing an evaluation

Shaping Strategies

Do you want to . . .	Consider using these rhetorical modes or strategies:
write for a particular audience or publication?	possible audiences and genres (p. 358)
organize your evaluation by specific criteria?	analysis by criteria (p. 358)
compare two subjects for your evaluative essay?	comparison and contrast (p. 359)
evaluate the effect of the subject on your audience?	causal analysis (p. 360)
get your reader's attention and make your overall claim clear?	title, introduction, and conclusion (p. 361)

Audience and Genre

As you consider ways to organize and shape your explaining essay, think about your probable audience and genre. Reviews vary greatly in length, critical depth, complexity, and reader appeal. Think about your own purpose and goal; find several magazines, newspapers, or websites that publish the kind of review you would like to write, and use the best ones as genre models—not as blueprints—to guide your own writing.

Analysis by Criteria

Evaluations are often organized by criteria. You decide which criteria are appropriate for the subject and audience, and then you use those criteria to outline the essay. Your paragraph(s) of introduction establish your thesis or overall claim and then give background information: what the subject is, why you are evaluating it, what the competition is, and how you gathered your data. Then you order the criteria according to some plan: chronological order, spatial order, order of importance, or another logical sequence. Phyllis Richman's evaluation of the Hunan Dynasty restaurant follows the criteria pattern:

Shaping Your Points: Analysis by Division or Criteria

Introductory paragraphs	Criterion 1: Setting and atmosphere	Criterion 2: Service	Criterion 3: Quality of food	Concluding paragraphs
Information about the Hunan Dynasty, etc.	**Judgment:** Hunan Dynasty is attractive	**Judgment:** Hunan Dynasty has expert service despite an occassional glitch	**Judgment:** Main dishes are good but not memorable	Hunan Dynasty is a top-flight neighborhood restaurant

Comparison and Contrast

Many evaluations compare two subjects in order to demonstrate why one is preferable to the other. Books, films, restaurants, courses, music, writers, scientists, historical events, sports—all can be evaluated by means of comparison and contrast. In evaluating two Asian restaurants, for example, student writer Chris Cameron uses a comparison-and-contrast structure to shape her essay. In the following body paragraph from that essay, Cameron compares two restaurants, the Unicorn and the Yakitori, on the basis of her first criterion—an atmosphere that seems authentically Asian.

> Of the two restaurants, we preferred the authentic atmosphere of the Unicorn to the cultural confusion at the Yakitori. On first impression, the Yakitori looked like a converted truck stop, sparsely decorated with a few bamboo slats and Japanese print fabric hanging in slices as Bruce Springsteen wailed loudly in the ears of the customers. The feeling at the Unicorn was quite the opposite as we entered a room that seemed transported from Chinatown. The whole room had a red tint from the light shining through the flowered curtains, and the place looked truly authentic, from the Chinese patterned rug on the wall to the elaborate dragon on the ceiling. Soft oriental music played as the customers sipped tea from small porcelain cups and ate fortune cookies.

Cameron used the following *alternating* comparison-and-contrast shape for her entire essay.

Shaping Your Points: Alternating Comparison and Contrast of Two Subjects

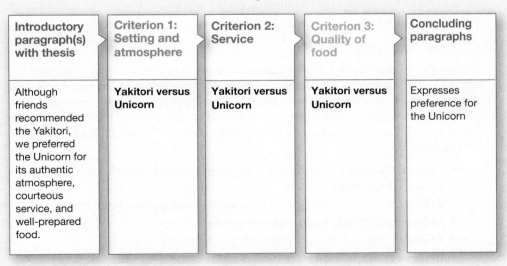

Introductory paragraph(s) with thesis	Criterion 1: Setting and atmosphere	Criterion 2: Service	Criterion 3: Quality of food	Concluding paragraphs
Although friends recommended the Yakitori, we preferred the Unicorn for its authentic atmosphere, courteous service, and well-prepared food.	Yakitori versus Unicorn	Yakitori versus Unicorn	Yakitori versus Unicorn	Expresses preference for the Unicorn

On the other hand, Cameron might have used a *block* comparison-and-contrast structure an organizational pattern that would take this shape.

Shaping Your Points: Block Comparison/Contrast of Two Subjects

Introductory paragraph(s) with thesis	Yakitori Restaurant	Unicorn Restaurant	Concluding paragraphs
Although friends recommended the Yakitori, we preferred the Unicorn for its authentic atmosphere, courteous service, and well-prepared food.	Atmosphere, service, and food	Atmosphere, service, and food as compared to the Yakitori's	Expresses preference for the Unicorn

Chronological Order

Writers often use chronological order, especially in reviewing a book or a film, to shape parts of their evaluations. Film reviewers rely on chronological order to sketch an outline of the plot as they comment on the quality of the acting, directing, or cinematography.

Causal Analysis

Evaluations of works of art, performances, or consumer products often measure the effect on the audience. While the *Consumer Report*'s evaluation of the Apple and Android smart phones included earlier in this chapter is largely organized as a comparison/contrast, a closer look will demonstrate that many of the evaluations are based upon criteria related to the effect features have on the usability of the devices for the readers.

- **Criteria:** A good smart phone's navigation system is reliable even when the signal is not strong.
- **Evidence:** "You can navigate even when you lack good cellular reception."
- **Judgement:** IPhone has the advantage of reliability.
- **Criteria:** A good smart phone is adaptable to user needs.
- **Evidence:** "Apple's interface is fairly fixed . . . . but [Android] users can customize a phone's look and feel using widgets and other tools."

Research Tips

Before you draft your evaluating essay, stop for a moment and *evaluate your sources* of information and opinion. If you are citing ideas or information from library articles—or especially from the Internet—be skeptical. How reliable is your source? What do you know about your source's reliability or editorial slant? Does the author have a particular bias? Be sure to *qualify* any biased or absolute statements you use from your sources.

If you cite observations or field sources (interviews, surveys), evaluate the information you collected. Does it reflect only one point of view? How is it biased? Are your responses limited in number or point of view? Remember: You may use sources that reflect a limited perspective, but *be sure to alert your readers to those limitations*. For example, you might say, "Of course, the administrator wanted to defend this student program when he said...."

- **Judgment:** Android is more adaptable.
- **Criteria:** A smart phone should provide information and convenience for consumers.
- **Evidence:** "Android and Apple have apps that allow you to check the price of products and other details by scanning bar codes," and "However, only Android has the Google Wallet app, which allows you to make a purchase using your smart phone as though it were a digital credit card."
- **Judgment:** Though both provide consumer information, the Android is superior because of the added convenience of the Google wallet app.
- **Criteria:** A good smart phone should be cost-effective.
- **Evidence:** "To get more storage for non-Apple files, you'll have to pay up to $100 a year for 50 GB."
- **Judgment:** The Android is superior because it is less likely to need memory upgrades.

Title, Introduction, and Conclusion

Titles of evaluative writing tend to be short and succinct, stating what product, service, work of art, or performance you are evaluating ("'American Gothic,' Pitchfork Perfect").

Introductory paragraphs provide background information and description and usually give an overall claim or thesis. In some cases, however, the overall claim comes last, in a Recommendations section or in a summary paragraph. If the overall claim appears in the opening paragraphs, the concluding paragraph may simply review the strengths or weaknesses or advise the reader: This *is* or *is not* worth seeing, reading, watching, doing, or buying.

> ❝ I have to stop being afraid of being wrong; I can't wait until everything is perfect before the work comes out. I don't have that kind of time. ❞
>
> —Sherley Anne Williams, Novelist and critic

> **❝** I have rewritten—often several times— every word I have ever published. My pencils outlast their erasers. **❞**
>
> —Vladimir Nabokov, Novelist

As you begin to draft, have your criteria in front of you, your data or evidence at hand, and a general plan or sketch outline in mind. As you write, focus on your audience. If your evaluation needs to be short, you may have to use only those criteria that will appeal most effectively to your audience. As you write, check occasionally to be sure that you are including your key criteria. While some parts of the essay may seem forced, other parts will grow and expand as you get your thoughts on paper. As in other papers, don't stop to check spelling or worry about an occasional awkward sentence. If you stop and can't get going, reread what you have written, look over your notes or sketch outline, and pick up the thread again.

REVISING

13.12
Use revision techniques to support and organize your evaluation

Remember that revision is not just changing a word here and there or correcting occasional spelling errors. Make your evaluation more effective for your reader by including more specific evidence, changing the order of your paragraphs to make them clearer, cutting out an unimportant point, or adding a point that one of your readers suggests.

Guidelines for Revision

- **Review your purpose, audience, and genre.** Is your purpose clear to your target audience? Should you modify your chosen genre to appeal to your audience?
- **Review possibilities for visuals or graphics.** What additions or changes to images might be appropriate for your purpose, genre, or audience?
- **Collaborating with peers.** Criteria are *standards of value* that contain categories and judgments. Criteria such as "good fuel economy," "good reliability," and "powerful use of light and shade in a painting" all suggest what the person making a judgment most values. As you revise your essay, ask peers to review your implied and explicit criteria to see whether your standards match those that are generally agreed upon—or whether they are too idiosyncratic.
- **Examine your criteria from your audience's point of view.** Which criteria are most important in evaluating your subject? Will your readers agree that the criteria you select are indeed the most important ones? Will changing the order in which you present your criteria make your evaluation more convincing?
- **Include both positive and negative evaluations of your subject.** If all of your judgments are positive, your evaluation will sound like an advertisement.

If all of your judgments are negative, your readers may think you are too critical.

- **Be sure to include supporting evidence for each criterion.** Without data or support, your evaluation will be just an opinion that will not persuade your reader.

- **Avoid overgeneralizing in your claim.** If you are evaluating only three cell phones, for example, you cannot claim that one of them is the best cell phone available. You can only say it is the best of the three you evaluated.

- **Unless your goal is humor or irony, compare subjects that belong in the same class.** Comparing a Ford Focus to a BMW is absurd because they are not similar in terms of cost, design, or purpose.

- **If you need additional evidence to persuade your readers, review the questions at the beginning of the Collecting section of this chapter.** Have you addressed all the key questions listed there?

- **If you are citing other people's data or quoting sources, check to make sure your summaries and data are accurate.**

- *Signal* **the major divisions in your evaluation to your reader using clear transitions, key words, and paragraph hooks.** At the beginning of new paragraphs or sections in your essay, let your reader know where you are going.

- **Revise sentences for directness and clarity.**

- **Edit your evaluation for correct spelling, appropriate word choice, punctuation, usage, and grammar.**

USING EVALUATING TO MAKE A JUDGMENT

This chapter focuses on the ways that techniques of evaluation can help us to not only make judgments, but also to move our audience toward accepting those judgments. In order to accomplish this purpose, writers first establish a shared set of criteria—standards that the writer and the audience both accept. Once those standards are established, then agreeing upon the conclusions can be accomplished by analyzing the degree to which the evidence suggests that those standards have been met.

For her evaluative essay, education major Stefanie Fuchs wrote about an Italian progressive educational method known as the Reggio approach. Her essay first sets up the key criteria for successful education based upon creativity and students' ongoing interest in learning. Then, she compares the American focus on standardized tests with the Reggio Emilia schools, and provides specific examples of student achievement to help readers share her belief in the superiority of these progressive schools. As you read this evaluation, note the various techniques discussed in this chapter that the author uses to move her readers toward her conclusion about these schools.

Student Writing

Reggio Emilia's Advanced Educational System

Stefanie Fuchs

The writer begins by establishing common criteria.

Evaluative claim

The author previews the shape of the essay

Comparison and contrast supports the evaluation

Implicit criteria suggest that individualism is a key criterion

Demonstrates the importance of the evaluation for choices made in our system of education

Description supports the main idea of individualized education

Supports the main idea of localized, rather than corporate, education

The criteria are reinforced

Every school has its own philosophy. Some focus on creativity, others focus on preparing for the workforce. Most say they focus on independence and individuality, but none do so like the schools of Reggio Emilia. This is where the most advanced early childhood education system was first created and is still used today. The Reggio approach has impacted countless teachers and their ability to utilize it in their classrooms. Loris Malaguzzi, founder of the Reggio approach, says, "Our task, regarding creativity, is to help children climb their own mountains, as high as possible" (LeBlanc). The first thing to learn about Reggio Emilia is the background of the schools and how they came to be. Following that, it is important to understand the similarities and differences between Reggio Emilia and similar schools such as Montessori schools. Finally, the most important thing to be taken from the Reggio Emilia approach to teaching is the impact it has on its students and the change it would bring to American schools if applied. The Reggio Emilia approach is an adventurous and risky idea that proves to have a lifelong impact on children. American schools focus strongly on the core curriculum and standardized testing and not enough on the individual student's wants and interests. If the Reggio approach was adopted into American education I feel that students would have a more positive attitude toward education, would be more likely to pursue higher education, and would become successful members of society.

Reggio Emilia is a quaint city located in the northern hills of Italy. It is well known for its "vintage basil vinegars, Parmigianino cheese, and Lambrusco wine" (LeBlanc). The city is also known for its advanced early childhood education system. The Reggio Emilia schools were first created after World War II by local parents who wanted their children to receive a better education than they were receiving in the public schools. "Family is important in Italian culture, and parents were determined to keep it that way" (LeBlanc). The first school was established in 1945 and was available for children from birth to six regardless of social status, income, and disabilities (LeBlanc). The first school was built using scrap material from the war and the conjoined effort of local people. The founding members chose Loris Malaguzzi to create and enforce the school's ideals. After leaving his teaching job in the public school systems of Italy, Loris Malaguzzi studied psychology in Rome, where he was influenced by people like Vygotsky, Dewey, Piaget, and Bruner (LeBlanc). Malaguzzi wanted people to realize that children were competent, resourceful, curious, imaginative, inventive, and possess a desire to communicate and interact with others (Loh). Everything in these schools would be child led. The projects, whether short term or long term, would be based on the interests of the children and not controlled by the teachers. The

(Continued)

children would have the freedom to observe and interact with nature and their environment and other adults and peers. This freedom was believed to help the children to achieve better communication skills and have a better ability to express one's emotions and feelings. Most Reggio teachers strongly believe that "children learn through interaction with others, including parents, staff and peers in a friendly learning environment" (Loh).

These schools not only give the students responsibility and freedom with expressing their emotions but also help with skills needed throughout life. "Reggio approach articulates children to acquire skills of critical thinking and collaboration" (Loh). Because of the independence, the children cannot rely on teachers to fix a problem. The students are expected to figure out a solution and work through the problem on their own. Reggio Emilia schools focus on independence and responsibility and have shown the world that even the youngest of people can handle and surprise you with their abilities.

Reggio Emilia schools are drastically different from most American schools. However, there are schools in America that share some of the same ideas and philosophical values. A counterpart to Reggio schools in America are Montessori schools. Montessori schools, like Reggio Emilia, "believe children to be competent, resourceful, and independent" (Irinyi). Both schools focus on the responsibility and independence of the students. Founders of both schools utilized the teachings from influential doctors like Piaget and Vygotsky ("Montessori"). However, Montessori schools encourage individual work and give children the freedom to work without checking in with teachers or being interrupted.

Montessori is also different in the way they collect data. Montessori schools focus on "observing the children, carefully recording the work and progress of the children" (Irinyi). Reggio uses documentation by recording not only the work of the student but also the words of a child. Michelle Irinyi describes some other differences between the two schools:

Montessori	Reggio Emilia
Created *for* parents	Created *by* parents
Believes in the Universal child	Believes in particular cultures
Prepared environment	Grounds/building form environment
Teachers as link between children and environment	Teacher as co-teacher
Focus on autonomy and independence	Focus on connection between child and environment

These schools both utilize the freedom and the openness of their schools to give their students the most enjoyable and child-focused learning.

The Reggio schools have made a significant impact on learning for Italy, as the parent is strongly influential in both the schools and their child's life. Parents are aware that both home and school life correspond with education and are

Margin notes:

Criterion based on self-efficacy

Counters the possible criticism that these schools do not teach important skills

The criteria of student responsibility is reinforced

Contrast is used to evaluate

Comparison based on key criteria

Note how the chart is used to compare key criteria

Key point of comparison

(Continued)

...*continued* Reggio Emilia's Advanced Educational System, **Stefanie Fuchs**

Another evaluative criterion: teacher's role as mentor

closely linked (LeBlanc). Children, teachers, parents, and community are interactive and work together, building a community of inquiry between adults and children (Loh). In Reggio Emilia, the role of the teacher is first and foremost to be a learner alongside the children. The teacher is a resource and a guide as he or she lends expertise to children (Loh). Teachers work in pairs and stay with a certain group of students for up to three years so that they can create a strong connection with the children (Natoli). Teachers also organize the environments with possibilities for children to explore and problem solve, often in small groups (Loh). The schools feature areas where the children can go inside and outside as they please and quiet areas where children can rest and sleep whenever desired.

Establishes key evidence

Example illustrates how the schools fulfill the criteria for excellence

One way to judge the effectiveness of these schools is through the accounts of projects and experiences from the children themselves. One teacher's journal entry, for example, described her students as they created a water park for birds. The students used materials they could find around the school like umbrellas and cups and other recyclable materials. Working and communicating together, and with no help from the teachers, they built a four-foot tall water park which included a ferris wheel and waterfall (North). Howard Gardner, who believes in the notion of schools of multiple intelligence, noted that "what Reggio teaches us is that even if we knew everything in the world about the brain and about the mind, we couldn't really tell what children could do" (Building). This is evident in the examples of the work the Reggio students have completed.

Expert voice helps to establish ethos

Criteria reinforced as conclusion is established

If we seek to give students the opportunity to flourish and open up, these techniques are clearly superior to more standardized methods. Giving students the opportunity to show independence not only helps their learning capabilities but also has been shown to help with confidence and the students' future mental states. If this approach were incorporated into American schools, it would help future generations to be more knowledgeable and more open to communication. It would give the American public school system the tools it needs to be successful.

Final return to key criteria

The Reggio Emilia schools focus significantly on independence, creativity, communication and connections. The children have shown us that this approach is extremely successful and truly impacts their lives. They receive an education that is based on them and their interests. As Malaguzzi asserted, "each child is unique and the protagonist of his or her own growth. Children desire to acquire knowledge, have much capacity for curiosity and amazement, and yearn to create relationships with others and communicate" (Scandinavian).

Direct evaluative statement

Establishes the ethos of the writer

I believe that the Reggio Emilia approach is the best in the world and that it empowers the student and teaches students more than any curriculum can try to teach. It teaches the students right and wrong and independence. It teaches them to problem solve without depending on others. It teaches students how to work with others and how to make their own lives prosper. As a future educator, I hope to be able to use this approach in my classroom. I hope one day to be able to teach

(Continued)

my students how to be independent and to make my classroom environment more like those of Reggio Emilia. The teachers who influenced me the most were the ones who understood my personality and let me be independent and challenged me and didn't give me the answers. I know that I learned more from the teachers who challenged me than those who gave me the answers. Nothing would make me more proud than to watch my students flourish in this type of environment and not have to teach a curriculum focused on standardized test scores.

An appeal to both pathos and logos

Key point of contrast shows the superiority of the Reggio Emilia schools by the established criteria

Works Cited

Building Blocks Preschool Learning Center. "CNN News Report on Reggio Emilia Italy Early Childhood Schools in the US." Online video clip. *Youtube.* Youtube, 18 Mar. 2013. Web. 6 Oct. 2014. http://www.youtube.com/watch?v=XVv5ZL9nlgs

Irinyi, Michelle. "Comparing Educational Philosophies: Montessori and Reggio Emilia." NAMC Montessori Teacher Training. 2 Aug. 2013. Web. 6 Oct. 2014. http://montessoritraining.blogspot.com/2013/08/comparing-montessori-reggio-emilia.html

LeBlanc, Miriam. "Reggio Emilia: An Innovative Approach to Education." Community Playthings. N.d. Web. 6 Oct. 2014. http://www.communityplaythings.co.uk/learning-library/articles/reggio-emilia

Loh, Andrew. "Reggio Emilia Approach." Bartholomew Consolidated School Corporation. Dec. 2006. Web. 6 Oct. 2014. http://download.cmclre.com/r/reggio-emilia-approach-bartholomew-consolidated-school-corporation-w11808.html

"Montessori Materials & Learning Environments." The International Montessori Index. N.d. Web. 6 Oct. 2014. http://www.montessori.edu/prod.html

Natoli, Carol. "Reggio Emilia Model Approach Philosophy of Education Early Childhood Education Helicopter Parent." Education Space. 12 Aug. 2009. Web. 6 Oct. 2014. http://www.educationspace360.com/index.php/reggio-emilia-model-approach-philosophy-of-education-early-childhood-education-helicopter-paren-15770/

North American Reggio Emilia Alliance. N.d. Web. 6 Oct. 2014. http://reggioalliance.org/

"Reggio Emilia Approach." *Wikipedia.* Wikipedia Foundation. 4 Nov. 2014. Web. 6 Oct. 2014. http://en.wikipedia.org/wiki/Reggio_Emilia_approach

The Scandinavian School of San Francisco. "Reggio Emilia Philosophy." Education.com. 17 July 2013. Web. 6 Oct. 2014. http://www.education.com/reference/article/Ref_Reggio_Emilia/

"What Is Reggio Emilia? Reggio Emilia: Defining a New Generation." Children's Garden of Learning. N.d. Web. 6 Oct. 2014. http://www.childrensgarden-vail.com/what-reggio-emilia

Questions for Writing and Discussion

1. In her evaluative essay, Stefanie Fuchs argues strongly for the Reggio Emilia schools. Is her argument based mostly on logos, ethos, or pathos? What examples might you use to illustrate the appeals she uses?

2. Reread Fuchs's essay and then write out a three-column log (criteria, evidence, judgments) that she might have used to organize her evaluation. List the evidence for each of her criteria. Does she have sufficient evidence to support her judgment of each criterion? Are her sources reliable? Explain.

3. Throughout her essay, Fuchs implicitly argues against standardized testing. In what ways does standardized testing not meet the criteria for judging academic achievement? Does Fuchs make that case adequately? How might that case be strengthened?

4. Who are the most likely audiences for an evaluation like this? After you have identified two or three likely audiences, go on to make a list of the criteria they might most care about. Where does Fuchs address, or fail to address, those criteria adequately?

Applying What You Have Learned

1. While we tend to make personal judgments about every product and service we purchase, each of us also has more expertise on some topics than others. Write an essay that helps others with less knowledge about a topic than you have to better understand why a particular product or service is, or is not, up to standard. Your goal is twofold: (1) to educate your audience enough so that they understand the important criteria, and (2) to help them see why a product or service does or does not fulfill those criteria. The key is to choose a topic about which you have studied enough (formally or informally) to speak confidently about it, and to collect enough information about that topic to illustrate well your judgment. As you shape and draft, be sure that you keep both purposes in mind, and that you write at a level that will be understood by your intended audience.

Using multimedia. While there are many criteria by which we make judgments about a product or service, at least some of those criteria are visual. We want a phone to function well, but how it looks also matters. We want to stay at a hotel that has great service, but its location and physical space is also important. In order to make your case about quality, adding visual media—photographs, video, and so forth—can make both your judgment and your explanations about criteria more effective. Use captions and other drawing tools to point out key features within the visual representations.

② Write an in-depth review of a film, play, gallery show, or other artwork or performance. While this type of evaluation has similarities with the evaluation of other products, judgments about art are less about monetary value and more about aesthetic value. If you were reviewing a film, how much money it made might be one thing to consider, but that is not enough to call it a great film; you would also need to consider plot, acting, costuming, its underlying message, and so forth. Choose an art form about which you have some knowledge or experience, but also read reviews and study the criteria that others generally use for judging that kind of art. Shape and draft your essay so that it helps your reader understand the criteria you are using to make your judgments, and then provides examples of how the artwork meets, or fails to meet, those criteria. Be sure to use vivid description and plenty of examples to illustrate your point.

Using multimedia. Aesthetic evaluations can be enhanced by helping readers to experience a work of art. Embedding images or video into your analysis is one way to help your audience better understand your evaluations. To do this effectively, however, choose carefully the images or clips you will use, and edit them in ways that illustrate precisely the point you are making. It is useful to show details of an artwork close up, to illustrate technique or style, or to edit just the right clip of a video so that is demonstrates precisely the point you want to make. Your goal is to use the multimedia element to illustrate a facet of the artwork, and thereby the degree to which the piece meets the criteria for a positive review.

③ With the great number of news outlets today, it can be difficult to gauge what sources are most objective, reliable, or useful. Write an evaluation of one or a small group of news sources, and make an argument for one type of news source being best for a particular audience. You'll need first to set up criteria for what you and your audience would agree are the most important elements of an effective news source. Is it about accuracy? Thoroughness? Objectivity? Depth of reporting? Availability? After establishing criteria, go on to make an argument as to which new source/sources meet and/or fail to meet the criteria. Collect examples that illustrate how the criteria is or is not met, perhaps using comparison and contrast as well as analytical techniques. As you shape and draft your essay, make sure that your thesis is clear from the start and that you lay out the criteria you will use to defend that thesis.

Using multimedia. Depending on the kind of news source that you will evaluate, using video or audio clips or including screen shots from a website can help to illustrate the points that you are raising. One possible approach to this assignment is to compare the presentation of news across media outlets, showing how one news story is covered in several media—print, network television, cable television, websites, blogs, Twitter, etc. As you look at the various presentations of a news story, evaluate the effectiveness of each medium and its ability to meet the criteria for best news outlet.

MEMORANDUM

DATE: March 24, 2013

TO: Professor Mary Ann Evans, Ph.D.

FROM: George Eliot, Student

SUBJECT: Summary

In fulfillment of the "summary" assignment in English 110, Workplace Communications, here is a memo report. I have summarized a NASA news release, "NASA Opens New Era in Measuring Western U.S. Snowpack." A copy of the release is attached.

NASA Opens New Era in Measuring Western U.S. Snowpack

For the purpose of better water management, NASA's new Airborne Snow Observatory mission has mapped two major mountain watersheds in California and Colorado to predict the volume of runoff that will result from melting snow.

"Changes in and pressure on snowmelt-dependent water systems are motivating water managers, governments and others to improve understanding of snow and its melt," said Tom Painter of NASA's Jet Propulsion Laboratory, which is jointly coordinating the effort with the California Department of Water Resources.

14

Summaries

Learning Objective

When you complete this chapter, you'll be able to write clear, concise, and complete summaries that convey the content and emphasis of the original sources.

I N the broadest sense, *all* writing is a form of summary. Whenever we put words on paper or computer screen, we condense ideas and information to make them coherent to the reader. Ordinarily, however, the term *summary* refers to a brief statement of the essential content of something heard, seen, or read. For any kind of summary, the writer reduces a body of material to its bare essentials. Creating a summary is therefore an exercise in *compression*, requiring logical organization, clear and concrete terminology, and sensitivity to the reader's needs. By that definition, a summary is the same as any other kind of workplace communication. Summary writing, however, demands an especially keen sense of not only what to include but also of

Taken from *Workplace Communications: The Basics*, Sixth Edition by George J. Searles.

what to *leave out*. The goal is to highlight the key points and not burden the reader with unnecessary details. In the workplace context, the most common summary application is in the abstracts and executive summaries that accompany long reports. This chapter explores the main principles governing the writing of summaries—a valuable skill in many work settings.

TYPES OF SUMMARIES: DESCRIPTIVE, INFORMATIVE, AND EVALUATIVE

In general, summaries can be classified into three categories: descriptive, informative, and evaluative.

A **descriptive summary** states what the original document is about but does not convey any of the document's specific information. It is much like a table of contents in paragraph form. Its main purpose is to help a reader determine whether the document summarized is of any potential use in a given situation. For example, a pamphlet providing descriptive summaries of federal publications on workplace safety may be quite helpful to a personnel director wishing to educate employees about a particular job-related hazard. Similarly, a purchasing agent might consult descriptive summaries to determine the potential relevance of outside studies on needed equipment or supplies. A descriptive summary might look something like this:

> This report discusses a series of tests conducted on industrial-strength coil springs at the TopTech Laboratories in Northton, Minnesota, in January 2013. Three kinds of springs were evaluated for flexibility, durability, and heat resistance to determine their relative suitability for several specific manufacturing applications at Northton Industries.

After reading this summary, someone seeking to become better informed about the broad topic of coil springs might decide to read the report.

An **informative summary,** on the other hand, goes considerably further and presents the document's content, although in greatly compressed form. A good informative summary that includes the document's conclusions and recommendations (if any) can actually enable a busy reader to *skip* the original altogether. Here's an informative version of the previous descriptive summary:

> This report discusses a series of tests conducted on industrial-strength coil springs at the TopTech Laboratories in Northton, Minnesota, in January 2013. Three kinds of springs—all manufactured by the Mathers Spring Co. of Marietta, Ohio—were tested: serial numbers 423, 424, and 425. The springs were evaluated for flexibility, durability, and heat resistance to determine their relative suitability for several specific manufacturing applications at Northton Industries. In 15 tests using a Flexor Meter, #423 was found to be the most flexible, followed by #425 and #424, respectively. In 15 tests using a Duro Meter, #425 proved the most durable, followed by #423 and #424, respectively. In 15 tests using a Thermal Chamber, #423 was the most heat-resistant, followed by #424 and #425, respectively. Although #423

compiled the best overall performance rating, #425 is the preferred choice because the applications in question require considerable durability and involve relatively few high-temperature operations.

The **evaluative summary** is even more fully developed and includes the writer's personal assessment of the original document. The following is an evaluative version of the same summary. Notice that the writer inserts subjective value judgments throughout.

> This rather poorly written and finally unreliable report discusses a series of flawed experiments conducted on industrial-strength coil springs at the TopTech Laboratories in Northton, Minnesota, in January 2013. Three kinds of springs—all manufactured by the Mathers Spring Co. of Marietta, Ohio—were tested: serial numbers 423, 424, and 425. The springs were evaluated for flexibility, durability, and heat resistance to determine their relative suitability for several specific manufacturing applications at Northton Industries. In 15 tests using the notoriously unreliable Flexor Meter, #423 was rated the most flexible, followed by #425 and #424, respectively. In 15 tests using the equally outdated Duro Meter, #425 scored highest, followed by #423 and #424, respectively. In 15 tests using a state-of-the-art Thermal Chamber, #423 was found to be the most heat-resistant, followed by #424 and #425, respectively. Although #423 compiled the best overall performance rating, the report recommends #425 on the grounds that the specific applications in question require considerable durability and involve relatively few high-temperature operations. However, these conclusions are questionable at best. TopTech Laboratories has since shut down after revelations of improper procedures. Two of the three test sequences involved obsolete instruments, and #425 proved markedly inferior to #423 and #424 in the only test sequence that can be considered reliable.

Of the three categories, the informative summary is by far the most common. As in a *Reader's Digest* condensed version of a longer original article, the purpose of an informative summary is to convey the main ideas of the original in shorter form. To make an informative summary concrete and to the point rather than vague and rambling, be sure to include hard data—such as names, dates, and statistics—as well as the original document's conclusions and recommendations, if any. Sometimes including a good, well-focused quotation from the original can also be very helpful to the reader. Avoid lengthy examples and sidetracks, however, because a summary must always be *brief*—usually no more than a quarter of the original document's length.

In addition, a summary should retain the *emphasis* of the original. For example, a relatively minor point in the source should not take on disproportionate significance in the summary (and perhaps should be omitted altogether). However, crucial information in the original should be equally prominent in the summary, and all information in the summary should spring directly from something in the source. Unless the summary's purpose is to evaluate, no new or additional information should appear, nor should personal opinion or comments be included.

For clarity, all workplace writing should be worded in the simplest possible terms. This is especially important in a summary, which is meant to stand alone. If the reader must go back to the original to understand, the summary is a failure. Therefore, the summary should be coherently organized and written in complete sentences with unmistakably clear meaning. As mentioned before, active verbs are best. They are especially helpful in a summary because they enable you to express ideas in fewer words than passive constructions do.

Depending on its nature, a summary that accompanies a long report is called an *abstract* or *executive summary*. If the summary is intended simply to provide a general overview of the report, it appears near the beginning of the report and is called an *abstract*. If the summary is intended to assist management in making decisions without having to read the report it precedes, it is called an *executive summary*.

Summarizing Print Sources

To summarize information that already exists in a written document, follow these simple steps:

1. Read the entire document straight through to get a general sense of its content. Pay particular attention to the introduction and the conclusion.
2. Watch for context clues (title, subheadings, visuals, boldface print, etc.) to ensure that you have an accurate understanding of the document.
3. Go back and underline or highlight the most important sentences in each paragraph. Write down all those sentences.
4. Now edit the sentences you selected, compressing, combining, and streamlining. When producing a summary of something you've written yourself, it's permissable to *abridge* the material, retaining some of the original wording. This is strictly prohibited, however, when summarizing someone else's work. Instead, you must rephrase the content in your own words. Otherwise, you're guilty of *plagiarism*—a serious offense for which you can incur severe penalties.
5. Reread your summary to check that it flows smoothly. Insert transitions— such as *therefore, however,* and *nevertheless*—where necessary to eliminate any abrupt jump from one idea to another.
6. Include concrete facts such as names, dates, statistics, conclusions, and recommendations. This is especially important in a summary, which is typically written as one long paragraph incorporating many ideas.
7. Correct all typos and mechanical errors in spelling, capitalization, punctuation, and grammar.

Figures 14.1 through 14.4 depict the major steps in the creation of an effective summary from an existing text—in this case, a NASA press release about new data-gathering technology, which provides accurate measurement of snow melt in the Western United States.

May 02, 2013

Steve Cole
Headquarters, Washington
202-358-0918
stephen.e.cole@nasa.gov

Alan Buis
Jet Propulsion Laboratory, Pasadena, Calif.
818-354-0474
alan.buis@jpl.nasa.gov

RELEASE: 13-131

NASA OPENS NEW ERA IN MEASURING WESTERN U.S. SNOWPACK

WASHINGTON—A new NASA airborne mission has created the first maps of the entire snowpack of two major mountain watersheds in California and Colorado, producing the most accurate measurements to date of how much water they hold.

The data from NASA's Airborne Snow Observatory mission will be used to estimate how much water will flow out of the basins when the snow melts. The data-gathering technology could improve water management for 1.5 billion people worldwide who rely on snowmelt for their water supply.

"The Airborne Snow Observatory is on the cutting edge of snow remote-sensing science," said Jared Entin, a program manager in the Earth Science Division at NASA Headquarters in Washington. "Decision makers like power companies and water managers now are receiving these data, which may have immediate economic benefits."

The mission is a collaboration between NASA's Jet Propulsion Laboratory (JPL) in Pasadena, Calif., and the California Department of Water Resources in Sacramento.

A Twin Otter aircraft carrying NASA's Airborne Snow Observatory began a three-year demonstration mission in April that includes weekly flights over the Tuolumne River Basin in California's Sierra Nevada and monthly flights over Colorado's Uncompahgre River Basin. The flights will run through the end of the snowmelt season, which typically occurs in July. The Tuolumne watershed and its Hetch Hetchy Reservoir are the primary water supply for San Francisco. The Uncompahgre watershed is part of the Upper Colorado River Basin that supplies water to much of the western United States.

The mission's principal investigator, Tom Painter of JPL, said the mission fills a critical need in an increasingly thirsty world, initially focusing on the western United States, where snowmelt provides more than 75 percent of the total freshwater supply.

"Changes in and pressure on snowmelt-dependent water systems are motivating water managers, governments and others to improve understanding of snow and its melt," Painter said. "The western United States and other regions face significant water resource challenges because of population growth and faster melt and runoff of snowpacks caused by climate change. NASA's Airborne Snow Observatory combines the best available technologies to provide precise, timely information for assessing snowpack volume and melt." The observatory's two instruments measure two properties most critical to understanding snowmelt runoff and timing. Those two properties have been mostly unmeasured until now.

A scanning lidar system from the Canadian firm Optech Inc. of Vaughan, Ontario, measures snow depth to determine the first property, snow water equivalent with lasers. Snow water equivalent represents the amount of water in the snow on a mountain. It is used to calculate the amount of water that will run off.

An imaging spectrometer built by another Canadian concern, ITRES of Calgary, Alberta, measures the second property, snow albedo. Snow albedo represents the amount of sunlight reflected and absorbed by snow. Snow albedo controls the speed of snowmelt and timing of its runoff.

By combining these data, scientists can tell how changes in the absorption of sunlight cause snowmelt rates to increase. The Airborne Snow Observatory flies at an altitude of 17,500 feet–22,000 feet (5,334 to 6,705 meters) to produce frequent maps that scientists can use to monitor changes over time. It can calculate snow depth to within about 4 inches (10 centimeters) and snow water equivalent to within 5 percent. Data are processed on the ground and made available to participating water managers within 24 hours. Before now, Sierra Nevada snow water equivalent estimates have been extrapolated from monthly manual ground snow surveys conducted from January through April. These survey sites are sparsely located, primarily in lower to middle elevations that melt free of snow each spring, while snow remains at higher elevations. Water managers use these survey data to forecast annual water supplies. The information affects decisions by local water districts, agricultural interests and others. The sparse sampling can lead to large errors. In contrast, the NASA observatory can map all the snow throughout the entire snowmelt season.

"The Airborne Snow Observatory is providing California water managers the first near-real-time, comprehensive determination of basin-wide snow water equivalent," said Frank Gehrke, mission co-investigator and chief of the California Cooperative Snow Surveys Program for the California Department of Water Resources. "Integrated into models, these data will enhance the state's reservoir operations, permitting more efficient flood control, water supply management and hydroelectric power generation."

Gehrke said the state will continue to conduct manual surveys while it incorporates the Airborne Snow Observatory data. "The snow surveys are relatively inexpensive, help validate observatory data and provide snow density measurements that are key to reducing errors in estimating snow water equivalent," he said.

Painter plans to expand the airborne mapping program to the entire Upper Colorado River Basin and Sierra Nevada. "We believe this is the future of water management in the western United States," he said.

For more information about the Airborne Snow Observatory, visit:

http://aso.jpl.nasa.gov/

-end-

FIGURE 14.1 • News Release with Most Important Sentences Underlined

Source: http://www.nasa.gov/topics/earth/features/earth20130502.html

A new NASA airborne mission has created the first maps of the entire snowpack of two major mountain watersheds in California and Colorado.

The data from NASA's Airborne Snow Observatory mission will be used to estimate how much water will flow out of the basins when the snow melts. The data-gathering technology could improve water management.

The mission is a collaboration between NASA's Jet Propulsion Laboratory (JPL) in Pasadena, Calif., and the California Department of Water Resources in Sacramento.

"Changes in and pressure on snowmelt-dependent water systems are motivating water managers, governments and others to improve understanding of snow and its melt," Painter said. "The western United States and other regions face significant water resource challenges because of population growth and faster melt and runoff of snowpacks caused by climate change.

A scanning lidar system . . . measures . . . snow water equivalent . . . to calculate the amount of water that will run off.

An imaging spectrometer . . . measures . . . snow albedo . . . the amount of sunlight reflected and absorbed by snow. Snow albedo controls the speed of snowmelt and . . . runoff.

By combining these data, scientists can tell how changes in the absorption of sunlight cause snowmelt rates to increase.

Before now, Sierra Nevada snow water equivalent estimates have been extrapolated . . . .

The sparse sampling can lead to large errors.

these data will enhance the state's reservoir operations, permitting more efficient flood control, water supply management and hydroelectric power generation.

Painter plans to expand the airborne mapping program to the entire Upper Colorado River Basin and Sierra Nevada.

FIGURE 14.2 • Compilation of Release's Most Important Sentences

For the purpose of better water management, NASA's new Airborne Snow Observatory mission has mapped two major mountain watersheds in California and Colorado to predict the volume of runoff that will result from melting snow.

"Changes in and pressure on snowmelt-dependent water systems are motivating water managers, governments and others to improve understanding of snow and its melt," said Tom Painter of NASA's Jet Propulsion Laboratory, which is jointly coordinating the effort with the California Department of Water Resources.

"The western United States and other regions face significant water resource challenges because of population growth and faster melt and runoff of snowpacks caused by climate change," Painter added.

A laser scanner measures the snow's depth to estimate the amount of water runoff, while an imaging spectrometer calculates the role of sunlight in speeding up the rate of snowmelt and ensuing runoff.

By combining these data, scientists can tell how changes in the absorption of sunlight cause snowmelt rates to increase.

In the past, such predictions were based on extrapolation from small data samples, resulting in major miscalculations.

But these new, more reliable data will lead to better reservoir operations, flood control, water supply management, and power generation.

Painter said that this program will be expanded to include the whole Upper Colorado River Basin and Sierra Nevada.

FIGURE 14.3 • Release's Most Important Sentences, Edited and Revised

MEMORANDUM

DATE: March 24, 2013

TO: Professor Mary Ann Evans, Ph.D.

FROM: George Eliot, Student

SUBJECT: Summary

In fulfillment of the "summary" assignment in English 110, Workplace Communications, here is a memo report. I have summarized a NASA news release, "NASA Opens New Era in Measuring Western U.S. Snowpack." A copy of the release is attached.

NASA Opens New Era in Measuring Western U.S. Snowpack

For the purpose of better water management, NASA's new Airborne Snow Observatory mission has mapped two major mountain watersheds in California and Colorado to predict the volume of runoff that will result from melting snow.

"Changes in and pressure on snowmelt-dependent water systems are motivating water managers, governments and others to improve understanding of snow and its melt," said Tom Painter of NASA's Jet Propulsion Laboratory, which is jointly coordinating the effort with the California Department of Water Resources.

"The western United States and other regions face significant water resource challenges because of population growth and faster melt and runoff of snowpacks caused by climate change," Painter added.

A laser scanner measures the snow's depth to estimate the amount of water runoff, while an imaging spectrometer calculates the role of sunlight in speeding up the rate of snowmelt and ensuing runoff.

By combining these data, scientists can tell how changes in the absorption of sunlight cause snowmelt rates to increase.

In the past, such predictions were based on extrapolation from small data samples, resulting in major miscalculations.

But these new, more reliable data will lead to better reservoir operations, flood control, water supply management, and power generation.

Painter said that this program will be expanded to include the whole Upper Colorado River Basin and Sierra Nevada.

FIGURE 14.4 • Summary (Memo Report Format)

Summarizing Nonprint Sources

To summarize a speech, briefing, broadcast, or another oral presentation for which no transcript exists, you must rely on your own notes. Therefore, you should develop some sort of personal system of shortcuts, incorporating abbreviations, symbols, and other notations, to enable you to take notes quickly without missing anything important. Figure 14.5 lists 20 such shortcuts. You will likely develop others of your

Notation	Meaning	Explanation
=	Is	Symbol instead of word
#	Number	Symbol instead of word
&	And	Symbol instead of word
∴	Therefore	Symbol instead of word
2	To, too, two	Numeral instead of word
4	For, four	Numeral instead of word
B	Be, bee	Letter instead of word
C	See, sea	Letter instead of word
U	You	Letter instead of word
Y\	Why	Letter instead of word
R	Are	Letter instead of word
R̷	Are not	Slash to express negation
w.	With	Abbreviation
w̷.	Without	Slash to express negation
bcs	Because	Elimination of vowels
2B	To be	Blend of numeral and letter
B4	Before	Blend of letter and numeral
rathan	Rather than	Blend of two words
rite	Right	Phonetic spelling
turn handle	Turn the handle	Elimination of obvious

FIGURE 14.5 • **Note-Taking Shortcuts**

own. However, this strategy is no help if you have to *think* about it. To serve its purpose, your shortcuts have to become instinctive. Furthermore, you must be able to translate your shortcuts back into regular English as you review your notes. Like anything, this process becomes easier with practice.

To facilitate summarizing from nonprint sources, you can use a handheld microcassette recorder or download the material to your computer via digital recorder. This will allow you to listen more attentively afterward, at your own pace, under more conducive conditions. But this is a good strategy only if there's no rush or if exact quotation is crucial. And even if recording, it's still important to take good notes—both to maximize understanding through attentive listening and to guard against mechanical failure. Of course, your notes should always highlight the most important points so you can review them later. But searching for those sections on the tape or in audio files can be very time-consuming unless your notes provide orientation. Helpfully, the better cassette recorders are equipped with a counter similar to an automobile's mileage odometer. You can save yourself a lot of frustration by including counter numbers in your notes. If your notes indicate, for example, that Point A was discussed when the counter was at 075, Point B was discussed at 190, and Point C at 250, locating the desired sections of the tape will now be much easier. You can achieve an even higher level of efficiency by using a digital recorder. Even the least expensive ones are available with DSS Player Pro software, which helps you manage and locate recorded files.

Checklist

Evaluating a Summary

A good summary

- ☐ Is no more than 25 percent as long as the original;
- ☐ Accurately reports the main points of the original;
- ☐ Includes no minor or unnecessary details;
- ☐ Includes nothing extraneous to the original;
- ☐ Preserves the proportion and emphasis of the original;
- ☐ Is well-organized, providing transitions to smooth the jumps between ideas;
- ☐ Maintains an objective tone;
- ☐ Uses clear, simple language;
- ☐ Contains no typos or mechanical errors in spelling, capitalization, punctuation, or grammar.

Higher-end models enable you to navigate through the menu to assign contact points and then easily find and make selections. Some even use voice activation to access specific texts.

Exercises

EXERCISE 14.1

Here are three summaries of the same article, Stephen Kelly's "Resurrection of a Garden" in the April 2007 issue of *Landscape Superintendent and Maintenance Professional,* a trade magazine aimed at institutional groundskeeping managers. Identify each of the three as descriptive, informative, or evaluative.

Summary A

The 1500-acre City Park in New Orleans was originally home to Native Americans but was acquired by the French after the city's founding in 1718 and became a park in 1854. Its attractions include the world's largest collection of mature oak trees, an art museum and sculpture garden, a 12-acre botanical garden, an arboretum, an amusement park, and many sporting facilities, including a 26,500-seat stadium and three golf courses. After Hurricane Katrina in 2005, however, 90% of the park was under water. Trees, grass, plants, buildings, and equipment were destroyed. Damages totaled $43 million, and all but 23 of 260 employees were laid off. Thanks to donors and thousands of volunteers, the botanical garden was reopened in March 2006, and by the end of the summer, over $5.6 million had been raised. But park officials are fearful that state insurance coverage and FEMA support will be inadequate—mere "pennies on the dollar."

Summary B

In general, this article seems quite optimistic and upbeat. Even its title reinforces that impression. And the opening paragraphs focus on the park's role as the site of many European-style pistol and saber duels, a grim but colorful feature of the park's history. Photo captions provide horticultural details that will interest the target readership, and much of the text celebrates the park's many outstanding features. But this congratulatory tone belies the facts. Of $43 million in damages caused by Hurricane Katrina in 2005, only $5.6 million in donations had been raised by the end of summer 2006, plus a mere $216,000 in FEMA reimbursements, despite an agency pledge to pay 90%. A park official has noted that "eligible expenses" is a term open to interpretation and has expressed fears that state insurance payments "will be pennies on the dollar." Interestingly, the magazine's Table of Contents page includes a section of fine print identifying two New Orleans park officials as "editorial contributors" to the article. Their presence lends credibility to the technical details but raises questions about the article's intentions. Given those individuals' vested interest in drawing attention to the dire challenges facing City Park, one would expect a more urgent tone.

Summary C

This illustrated three-page article summarizes the history and many attractions of City Park in New Orleans. It then details the park's devastation by Hurricane Katrina in August of 2005 and discusses current efforts to repair that damage and continue restoration projects. The article praises the generosity of philanthropists and other donors and acknowledges the help of volunteer workers. However, it does express doubts about the adequacy of promised financial assistance from state insurance coverage and FEMA reimbursement.

EXERCISE 14.2

Write a 100-word descriptive summary of a recent article from a reputable periodical or Web site in your field of study or employment. Submit the article along with the summary.

EXERCISE 14.3

Write a 250-word informative summary of the same article mentioned in Exercise 14.2. Submit the article along with the summary.

EXERCISE 14.4

Write a 300-word evaluative summary of the same article mentioned in Exercises 14.2 and 14.3. Submit the article along with the summary.

EXERCISE 14.5

Write a 200-word informative summary of the plot of a recent episode of your favorite television show.

EXERCISE 14.6

Write a 250-word informative abstract of a term paper you've completed in the past for another course. Submit the term paper along with the abstract.

EXERCISE 14.7

Write an informative summary of an article from a popular periodical (for example, *Time, Rolling Stone,* or *Sports Illustrated*). Make the summary no more than 20 percent as long as the article, and submit the article along with the summary.

EXERCISE 14.8

Summarize a lecture given by the instructor of one of your other classes. Limit the summary to roughly 500 words.

EXERCISE 14.9

Write a 75-word informative summary of an article from your local newspaper. Select an article at least 300 words long. Submit the article along with your summary.

Described by Robert F. Kennedy as "one of the heroic figures of our time," César Chávez (1927–1993) spent his lifetime improving the conditions of agricultural workers in America. In 1994, President Clinton posthumously awarded Chávez the Presidential Medal of Freedom, the nation's highest and most prestigious civilian award. In his essay in this chapter, "César Chávez Saved My Life," Daniel Alejandrez remembers Chávez's influence on his life.

15

Reflective Writing

BOTH observing and remembering are essential to good writing in a variety of genres. Good observing skills come in handy when you are writing up a science experiment, making notes during a field trip, or describing something for a friend. In addition, the strategies that you learn from careful observation and description will help you write about your memories of particular people, places, and events. Observing and remembering are remarkably interrelated skills: observing certain places or events often brings back memories of other experiences; likewise, remembering a person or a place will often bring up specific observed details—the color of someone's hair, the aroma of bacon and eggs for breakfast, or the sounds of the city or country. In this chapter, you will practice key observing techniques and then use them as you write an essay about a personal memory.

Observing is essential to both learning and communicating. Good writers draw on all their senses: sight, smell, touch, taste, and hearing. In addition, experienced writers notice what is *not* there: a friend who is usually present but is now absent; the absolute quiet in the air that precedes an impending storm. Writers of description also look for *changes* in their subjects—from light to dark or from noise to sudden silence. Good writers of description use their *experiences* to help see and describe a

> **My task . . . is, by the power of the written word, to make you hear, to make you feel— it is, before all, to make you see.**
> —Joseph Conrad, Author of *Heart of Darkness* and other novels

> **. . . Not that it's raining, but the feel of being rained upon.**
> —E. L. Doctorow, Author of *Ragtime* and other novels

Taken from *The Prentice Hall Guide for College Writers*, Eleventh Edition by Stephen P. Reid and Dominic DelliCarpini.

place or event: How is this room or building or neighborhood similar to or different from other places you have been? Finally, writers of effective description are good *researchers*: if you're not sure exactly when it happened or what it means, searching a database or Google can help you—and your readers—identify what something is, where it occurs, or why it is important.

Good description follows the advice of experienced writers: *Show, don't tell.* Showing through vivid detail allows readers to reach the conclusions that you may be tempted to tell them; you will need to use specific details to communicate the look, the feel, the weight, the sounds, and the smells.

Remembering also has a set of strategies and techniques that effective writers use. The first and most important strategy is to focus on specific scenes set at a particular time and place. Just as good description *shows* rather than tells, an effective narrative tells a story; it picks key scenes, sets them in time and place, and then recreates them by using description, dialogue, and important incidents. In addition, effective remembering requires describing key *changes* and *conflicts*. Finally, effective remembering essays emphasize a single key idea, leaving the reader with the impressions the writer wishes to convey.

Techniques for Observing and Remembering

TECHNIQUES FOR OBSERVING

15.1
Understand the observing techniques writers use to develop details

This chapter will help you to develop the kinds of writing that rely upon observation skills, skills that will help you put into words the details that make writing vivid and memorable. You can use the skills discussed and the examples provided to practice your own writing. To make the most of what follows, try out the techniques described.

Observing People

Observing people—their dress, body language, facial features, behavior, eating habits, and conversation—is a pastime that we all share. In a *Rolling Stone* article, Brian Hiatt describes U2 lead singer Bono in his native Dublin. Notice how the descriptive details and images work together to create the dominant impression of Bono as a high-energy rock star, conversationalist, and global philanthropist.

> Bono rounds a corner onto a narrow Dublin street, boots crunching on old cobblestone, sleek, black double-breasted overcoat flapping in the January breeze. . . . He's running late for his next appointment, which is not unusual in what must be one of the most overstuffed lives on the planet: "part-time" rock stardom; global advocacy for Africa's poor that's won him nominations for the Nobel Peace Prize; various multinational business and charitable ventures; an op-ed column for

Techniques for Writing About Observations

Technique	Tips on How to Do It
Giving sensory details (sight, sound, smell, touch, taste)	Use *sensory descriptions, comparisons,* and *images.* "Zoom in" on crucial details. Include *actual dialogue* and *names of things* where appropriate.
Describing what is *not* there	Sometimes keen observation requires stepping back and noticing what is *absent*, what is *not* happening, or who is *not* present.
Noting changes in the subject's form or condition	Even when the subject appears static—a landscape, a flower, a building—look for evidence of change: a tree being enveloped by tent worms, a six-inch purple-and-white iris that eight hours earlier was just a green bud, a sandstone exterior of a church being eroded by acid rain.
Learning about your subject	The observant eye requires a critical, inquiring mind. Read about your subject. Google key ideas or terms. Ask other people or experts on the subject. Probe to find what is *unusual*, *surprising*, or *controversial* about your subject.
Focusing on a dominant idea	Focus on those details and images that clarify the main ideas or discoveries. Discovery often depends on the *contrast* between the writer's expectations and the reality.

the *New York Times*; and four kids with Ali Hewson, his wife of 26 years. "I find it very hard to leave home," he says, "because my house is full of laughter and songs and kids."

Interviewing Bono is like taking an Alaskan husky for a walk—you can only suggest a general direction, and then hold on for dear life. Over an 80-minute lunch at a favorite Dublin restaurant, Eden, he repeatedly goes off on wild, entertaining tangents, which tend to include names such as Bill Clinton, Microsoft co-founder Paul Allen, genomic researcher Craig Venter and Archbishop Desmond Tutu (Bono calls him "the Arch"). He tosses out one killer sound bite after another, blue eyes moving like tropical fish behind today's pinkish-purple shades.

He eats his chicken breast in big bites, avoiding the potatoes, talking with his mouth full—and when the chicken is gone, he dips a finger into the sauce and licks it off, more than once. "We began this decade well—I think we'll end it better," he says, sitting on a white chair at a white table in a restaurant that's otherwise empty—apparently because management has cleared it out for him. "Wouldn't it be great if, after all these years, U2 has their heyday? That could be true of a painter or a filmmaker at this stage."

Observing Places

In the following passage, John Muir describes California and the Yosemite Valley as it looked nearly 150 years ago. John Muir was the founder of the Sierra Club, whose first mission was to preserve the vision of Yosemite that Muir paints in these paragraphs. Notice how Muir uses all of the key techniques for observing as he vividly describes the California Sierra.

Arriving by the Panama steamer, I stopped one day in San Francisco and then inquired for the nearest way out of town. "But where do you want to go?" asked the man to whom I had applied for this important information. "To any place that is wild," I said. This reply startled him. He seemed to fear I might be crazy and therefore the sooner I was out of town the better, so he directed me to the Oakland ferry.

So on the first of April, 1868, I set out afoot for Yosemite. It was the bloom-time of the year over the lowlands and coast ranges; the landscapes of the Santa Clara Valley were fairly drenched with sunshine, all the air was quivering with the songs of the meadow-larks, and the hills were so covered with flowers that they seemed to be painted. Slow indeed was my progress through these glorious gardens, the first of the California flora I had seen. Cattle and cultivation were making few scars as yet, and I wandered enchanted in long wavering curves, knowing by my pocket map that Yosemite Valley lay to the east and that I should surely find it.

Looking eastward from the summit of the Pacheco Pass one shining morning, a landscape was displayed that after all my wanderings still appears as the most beautiful I have ever beheld. At my feet lay the Great Central Valley of California, level and flowery, like a lake of pure sunshine, forty or fifty miles wide, five hundred miles long, one rich furred garden of yellow *Compositae*. And from the eastern boundary of this vast golden flower-bed rose the mighty Sierra, miles in height, and so gloriously colored and so radiant, it seemed not clothed with light, but wholly composed of it, like the wall of some celestial city. Along the top and extending a good way down, was a rich pearl-gray belt of snow; below it a belt of blue and dark purple, marking the extension of the forests; and stretching along the base of the range a broad belt of rose-purple; all these colors, from the blue sky to the yellow valley smoothly blending as they do in a rainbow, making a wall of light ineffably fine. Then it seemed to me that the Sierra should be called, not the Nevada or Snowy Range, but the Range of Light.

In general views no mark of man is visible upon it, nor anything to suggest the wonderful depth and grandeur of its sculpture. None of its magnificent forest-crowned ridges seems to rise much above the general level to publish its wealth. No great valley or river is seen, or group of well-marked features of any kind standing out as distinct pictures. Even the summit peaks, marshaled in glorious array so high in the sky, seem comparatively regular in form. Nevertheless the whole range five hundred miles long is furrowed with canyons 2,000 to 5,000 feet deep, in which once flowed majestic glaciers, and in which now flow and sing the bright rejoicing rivers.

TECHNIQUES FOR WRITING ABOUT MEMORIES

Writing vividly about memories includes all the skills of careful observing, but it adds several narrative strategies. Listed below are six techniques that writers use to compose effective remembering essays. As you read the essays that follow, notice how each writer uses these techniques. Then use the techniques when you write your own remembering essay. Not all writing about memories will use all the techniques, but using one or two of them may transform a lifeless account into an effective narrative.

15.2
Understand the remembering techniques writers use to develop details

Techniques for Writing About Memories

Technique	Tips on How to Do It
Using *detailed observation* of people, places, and events	• Writing vividly about memories requires many of the skills of careful observation. Use *sensory descriptions*, *comparisons*, and *images*. Include *actual dialogue* where appropriate.
Focusing on *occasion and cultural context*	• Think about the personal occasion that motivated you to write about your experience. You may want to set your experiences in a larger cultural context.
Creating *specific scenes* set in time and space	• Show your reader the actual events—don't just tell about them. Narrate or recreate specific incidents as they actually happened. Avoid summarizing events or presenting just the conclusions (for instance, "Those experiences really changed my life").
Noting *changes*, *contrasts*, or *conflicts*	• Describe changes in people or places. Show contrasts between two memories or between memories of expectations and the subsequent realities. Narrate conflicts between people or ideas. Resolving (or sometimes not resolving) these changes, contrasts, or conflicts can even be the point of your memoir.
Making *connections* between *past* events, people, or places and the *present*	• The main idea or focus of your narrative may grow out of the connections you make between the past and the present: what you felt then and how you feel now; what you thought you knew and what you know now.
Discovering and focusing on a *main idea*	• Your narrative should not be a random account of your favorite memories. It should have a clear main point—something you learned or discovered or realized—without stating a "moral" to your story.

> **❝Time passes and the past becomes the present. . . . These presences of the past are there in the center of your life today. You thought . . . they had died, but they have just been waiting their chance. ❞**
>
> —Carlos Fuentes, Mexican essayist and novelist, author of *The Crystal Frontier*

Beyond these techniques, you should keep several points in mind. Normally, you will write in the *first person,* using *I* or *we.* Although you will usually write in the *past tense,* sometimes you may wish to lend immediacy to the events by retelling them in the *present tense.* Finally, you may choose straightforward *chronological order,* or you may begin near the end and use a *flashback* to tell the beginning of the story.

The key to effective remembering is to go beyond *generalities* and *conclusions* about your experiences ("I had a lot of fun—those days really changed my life"). Recall specific incidents set in time and place that *show* how and why those days changed your life. The specific incidents should show your *main point* or *dominant idea.*

The following passage by Andrea Lee began as a journal entry in 1978 when she lived in Moscow and Leningrad after her graduation from college. She later combined those firsthand observations with her memories and published them in a collection called *Russian Journal.* She uses first person and, frequently, present tense as she describes her reactions to the sights of Moscow. In these paragraphs she weaves observations and memories together to show her main idea: The contrast between American and Soviet Union–style advertising helped her understand both the virtues and the faults of American commercialism. (The annotations in the margin illustrate how Lee uses all five remembering techniques.)

Specific scene

In Mayakovsky Square, not far from the Tchaikovsky Concert Hall, a big computerized electric sign sends various messages flashing out into the night. An outline of a taxi in green dots is accompanied by the words: "Take Taxis—All Streets Are Near." This is replaced by multicolored human figures and a sentence urging Soviet citizens to save in State banks. The bright patterns and messages come and go, making this one of the most sophisticated examples of advertising in Moscow.

Detailed observation

Even on chilly nights when I pass through the square, there is often a little group of Russians standing in front of the sign, watching in fascination for five and ten minutes as the colored dots go through their magical changes. The first few times I saw this, I chuckled and recalled an old joke about an American town so boring that people went out on weekends to watch the Esso sign.

Connects past and present

Advertising, of course, is the glamorous offspring of capitalism and art: Why advertise in a country where there is only one brand, the State brand, of anything, and often not enough even of that? There is nothing here comparable to the glittering overlay of commercialism that Americans, at least, take for granted as part of our cities; nothing like the myriad small seductions of the marketplace, which have led us to expect to be enticed. The Soviet political propaganda posters that fill up a small part of the Moscow landscape with their uniformly cold red color schemes and monumental robot-faced figures are so unappealing that they are dismissable.

Contrast

Detailed observation

I realize now, looking back, that for at least my first month in Moscow, I was filled with an unconscious and devastating disappointment. Hardly realizing it, as I walked around the city, I was looking for the constant sensory distractions I was accustomed to in America. Like many others my age, I grew up reading billboards and singing advertising jingles; my idea of beauty was shaped—perniciously, I think—by the models with the painted eyes and pounds of shining hair whose beauty was accessible on every television set and street corner.

Connects past and present

Contrast and change
Main idea

Remembering People

In the following passage from his introduction to *The Way to Rainy Mountain*, N. Scott Momaday remembers his grandmother. While details of place and event are also recreated, the primary focus is on the character of his grandmother as revealed in several *specific*, recurring actions. Momaday does not give us generalities about his feelings (for instance, "I miss my grandmother a lot, especially now that she's gone"). Instead, he begins with specific memories of scenes that *show* how he felt.

> Now that I can have her only in memory, I see my grandmother in the several postures that were peculiar to her: standing at the wood stove on a winter morning and turning meat in a great iron skillet; sitting at the south window, bent above her beadwork, and afterwards, when her vision failed, looking down for a long time into the fold of her hands; going out upon a cane, very slowly as she did when the weight of age came upon her; praying. I remember her most often at prayer. She made long, rambling prayers out of suffering and hope, having seen many things. I was never sure that I had the right to hear, so exclusive were they of all mere custom and company. The last time I saw her she prayed standing by the side of her bed at night, naked to the waist, the light of a kerosene lamp moving upon her dark skin. Her long, black hair, always drawn and braided in the day, lay upon her shoulders and against her breasts like a shawl. I do not speak Kiowa, and I never understood her prayers, but there was something inherently sad in the sound, some merest hesitation upon the syllables of sorrow. She began in a high and descending pitch, exhausting her breath to silence; then again and again—and always the same intensity of effort, of something that is, and is not, like urgency in the human voice. Transported so in the dancing light among the shadows of her room, she seemed beyond the reach of time. But that was illusion; I think I knew then that I should not see her again.

Remembering Places

In this passage from *Farewell to Manzanar*, Jeanne Wakatsuke Houston recalls the place in California where, as Japanese-Americans, her family was imprisoned during World War II. As you read, look for specific details and bits of description that convey her main idea.

> In Spanish, *Manzanar* means "apple orchard." Great stretches of Owens Valley were once green with orchards and alfalfa fields. It has been a desert ever since its water started flowing south into Los Angeles, sometime during the twenties. But a few rows of untended pear and apple trees were still growing there when the camp opened, where a shallow water table had kept them alive. In the spring of 1943 we moved to block 28, right up next to one of the old pear orchards. That's where we stayed until the end of the war, and those trees stand in my memory for the turning of our life in camp, from the outrageous to the tolerable.
>
> Papa pruned and cared for the nearest trees. Late that summer we picked the fruit green and stored it in a root cellar he had dug under our new barracks. At night the wind through the leaves would sound like the surf had sounded in Ocean Park, and while drifting off to sleep, I could almost imagine we were still living by the beach.

> **"** A writer is a reader moved to emulation. **"**
>
> —Saul Bellow, Author of *Henderson the Rain King*

> **"** There are two ways to live. One is as though nothing is a miracle, the other is as though everything is. **"**
>
> —Albert Einstein, Author of *What I Believe*

> **"** Some very small incident that takes place today may be the most important event that happens to you this year, but you don't know that when it happens. You don't know it until much later. **"**
>
> —Toni Morrison, Nobel Prize–winning author of *Beloved* and *Song of Solomon*

Remembering Events

Techniques for remembering an event are illustrated in the following paragraphs by Karen Blixen, who wrote *Out of Africa* under the pen name Isak Dinesen. In this excerpt from her journals, Blixen describes a startling change that occurred when she shot a large iguana. The annotations in the margin identify the use of observed details to construct from memories a story that has a central purpose or main idea.

Sensory description

Comparisons, images, and sensory details

Changes in condition

Learning about the subject

What is not there
Dominant idea: Now colorless and dead

In the Reserve I have sometimes come upon the Iguana, the big lizards, as they were sunning themselves upon a flat stone in a riverbed. They are not pretty in shape, but nothing can be imagined more beautiful than their coloring. They shine like a heap of precious stones or like a pane cut out of an old church window. When, as you approach, they swish away, there is a flash of azure, green and purple over the stones, the color seems to be standing behind them in the air, like a comet's luminous tail.

Once I shot an Iguana. I thought that I should be able to make some pretty things from his skin. A strange thing happened then, that I have never afterwards forgotten. As I went up to him, where he was lying dead upon his stone, and actually while I was walking the few steps, he faded and grew pale, all color died out of him as in one long sigh, and by the time that I touched him he was grey and dull like a lump of concrete. It was the live impetuous blood pulsating within the animal, which had radiated out all that glow and splendor. Now that the flame was put out, and the soul had flown, the Iguana was as dead as a sandbag.

Warming Up: Journal Exercises

To practice writing about your memories, read the following exercises and write on the three that interest you most. If another idea occurs to you, write about it.

1. Go through old family photographs and find one of yourself, taken at least five years ago. Describe the person in the photograph—what he or she did, thought, said, or hoped. How is that person like or unlike the person you are now?

2. What are your earliest memories? Choose one particular event. How old were you? What was the place? Who were the people around you? What happened? After you write down your own memories, call members of your family, if possible, and interview them for their memories of this incident. How does what you remember differ from what your family tells you? Revise your first memory to incorporate details provided by your family.

3. At some point in the past, you may have faced a conflict between what was expected of you—by parents, friends, family, coach, or employer—and your own personality or abilities. Describe one occasion when those expectations seemed unrealistic or unfair. Was the experience entirely negative, or was it, in the long run, positive?

4. **Collaborating with peers.** Ask two of your peers to read an early draft of a story about a past experience you had. Then ask them which details seem to be most vivid, and which they think were either not as important or could have been embellished. This can help you to make decisions about what kinds of details are effective.

⑤ Read the following short educational memories written by Michelle A. Rhee and Lisa Randall. Then write a few paragraphs for your classmates, narrating a special memory of a person or an event that had a positive impact on your own education or your life.

Calvin in Motion

Michelle A. Rhee

Michelle Rhee is the founder and chief executive of Students First

When I was teaching second grade in Baltimore, there was an adorable but disruptive boy in my class named Calvin. He talked over me, talked over his friends and couldn't participate in an appropriate way. I was constantly urging him to sit still and be quiet, and I even held one of those awfully serious what-do-we-do meetings with his father. Nothing worked. Until the day I put a dustpan in Calvin's hand. It all started when he threw a pile of pencil-sharpener shavings all over the room during story time. I gave Calvin the dustpan and a brush and told him to clean up the mess. Then, I proceeded with the story. As I read, I heard Calvin mumbling while he twirled around with that dustpan. After a few minutes, to my astonishment, I realized Calvin was answering my questions about the story. He sounded like a model student. Never before had I imagined that I would get Calvin on task by telling him to do an activity that was entirely unrelated to my lesson. Because Calvin was a kinesthetic kid, or a physical learner, he could only focus on school if he was up and moving. From that day on, Calvin would play with manipulative toys and sometimes even take a lap around the classroom while I was instructing. He taught me that all kids learn in wildly different ways and that all children are reachable and teachable.

Just Ask. Then Keep Asking.

Lisa Randall

Lisa Randall is a professor of physics at Harvard University and the author of *Knocking on Heaven's Door* and *Warped Passengers*

I was shy the way many geeky girls can be. Professors hardly noticed that they rarely answered girls' questions before some boy who didn't actually know the answer interrupted. But a professor who later became my adviser gave me the best advice I ever received,

(Continued)

...*continued* Just Ask. Then Keep Asking, **Lisa Randall**

which was to not be afraid to speak up and ask questions. Suddenly teachers were speaking directly to me, and my questions were usually good enough that I could detect the relief of other students who actually had the same ones, reassuring me I was doing the right thing. Now, as a professor, I know not to see classes as passive experiences. The occasional interruption keeps people engaged and illuminates subtle points, and in research even leads to new research directions. Just participating and questioning makes your mind work better. Don't you agree?

Combining Observing and Remembering Techniques

While writing based on observations and writing based on memories may differ somewhat—because what is being described is either right in front of us or in our minds—you have likely discerned that the techniques are quite similar. Both involve a careful use of detail and description, both attempt to help the reader envision something through words, and both rely upon our own perspectives on the subject through our tone and voice. Each of the excerpts above illustrates that.

In the essay that follows, you can see how elements of both remembering and observation are used by the author to describe a past event and an important leader. Labor and civil rights worker César Chávez (1927–1993) founded the National Farm Workers Association and used the nonviolent principles of Mahatma Gandhi and Dr. Martin Luther King, Jr. to gain dignity, fair wages, and humane working conditions for farm workers. The writer draws on vivid memories of Chávez's work and uses his skills of observation to describe the prison scenes he depicts. These skills are ones that you can practice to enrich your own writing.

César Chávez Saved My Life

Daniel "Nene" Alejandrez

Daniel Alejandrez, the founder of *Barrios Unidos*, has spent his life fighting poverty, drugs, and gangs in Latino communities. In this essay, written in 2005 for *Sojourners* magazine, he remembers how the principles and the voice of César Chávez inspired him to help others.

I'm the son of migrant farm workers, born out in a cotton field in Merigold, Mississippi. My family's from Texas. A migrant child goes to five or six different schools in one year, and you try to assimilate to whatever's going on at that time. I grew up not having shoes or only having one pair of pants to wear to

1

(Continued)

school all week. I always remembered my experience in Texas, where Mexicans and blacks couldn't go to certain restaurants. That leaves something in you.

I saw how my father would react when Immigration would come up to the fields or the boss man talked to him. I would see my father bow his head. I didn't know why my father wasn't standing up to this man. As a child working in the rows behind him, I said to myself, "I'll never do that." A deep anger was developing in me. [2]

But it was also developing in my father; the way that he dealt with it was alcohol. He would become violent when he drank on the weekends. I realized later that the reason he would bow his head to the boss is that he had seven kids to feed. He took that humiliation in order to feed me. [3]

I stabbed the first kid when I was 13 years old. I shot another guy when I was 15. I almost killed a guy when I was 17. On and on and on. Then, in the late 1960s, I found myself as a young man in the Vietnam War. I saw more violence, inflicted more violence, and then tried to deal with the violence. [4]

I came back from the war addicted to heroin, as many, many young men did. I came back to the street war, in the drug culture. Suddenly there were farm workers—who lost jobs because of the bringing of machines into the fields—who turned into drug dealers; it's easier money. [5]

But when I was still working in the fields, something happened. I was 17 years old, out in the fields of central California, and suddenly I hear this voice coming out of the radio, talking about how we must better our conditions and better our lives in the migrant camps. It was like this voice was talking just to me. [6]

The voice was César Chávez. He said, "You must organize. You must seek justice. You must ask for better wages." [7]

It's 1967. I'm busting my ass off pitching melons with six guys. Because we're the youngest, they put us on the hardest job, but we're getting paid $1.65 an hour. The guys working the harvesting machines are making $8 an hour. We said to ourselves, "Something's not right." [8]

Having the words of César Chávez, I organized the young men and called a strike. After lunch we just stopped working. We didn't go back on the fields. This was sort of a hard thing because my father was a foreman to this contractor, so I was going against him. He was concerned that we were rocking the boat—but I think he was proud of me. We shut down three of the melon machines, which forced the contractor to come, and then the landowner came. "What's going on?" he said. We said, "We're on strike, because we aren't getting our money." After about two hours, they said, "Okay, we're going to raise it to $1.95." [9]

But it wasn't the $1.95—it was the fact that six young men were being abused, and that this little short Indian guy, César Chávez, had an influence. I kept his words. [10]

When I wound up in Vietnam, I heard about Martin Luther King and his stand against the war. Somebody also told me about Mahatma Gandhi. I didn't know who he was, only that he was a bald-headed dude that had done this kind of stuff. [11]

(Continued)

In Vietnam I realized that there were people that I had never met before, that had never done nothing to me, never called me a dirty Mexican or a greaser or nothing, and all of sudden I had to be an enemy to them. *12*

I started looking at the words of César Chávez in terms of nonviolence. I looked at the violence in the community, in the fields, yet Chávez was still calling for peace. *13*

It has been an incredible journey since those days. For us this is a spiritual movement. In Barrios Unidos, that's the primary thing—our spirit comes first. How do we take care of ourselves? Whatever people believe in, no matter what faith or religion, how do we communicate to the youngsters who are spiritually bankrupt? Many of us were addicted to drugs or alcohol, and we have to find a spiritual connection. Working with gang members, there's a lot of pain, so you have to find ways for healing. As peacemakers, we are wounded peacemakers. *14*

This work has taken us into the prisons. Throughout the years, we've been talking about the high rate of incarceration among our people, and the drug laws. Many people are doing huge amounts of time for non-violent drug convictions; they did not need to be incarcerated—they need treatment. Currently in this country we deal with treatment by incarcerating people, which leads them to more violence and more negative ways of living. *15*

As community-based organizations, we have had to prove to the correctional institutions that we're not in there to create any revolution. We're there to try to help. I'm asking how I can change the men that have been violent. How do I help change their attitude toward society and toward their own relatives? We see them as our relatives—these are our relatives that are incarcerated. How can we support them? *16*

We go into the prison as a cultural and spiritual group helping men in prison to understand their own culture and those of different cultures. They come from great warrior societies. But the warrior tradition doesn't just mean going to war, but also fighting for peace. The prisoners who help organize the Cinco de Mayo, Juneteenth, and Native powwow ceremonies within the prison system are a true testament of courage to change the madness of violence that has unnecessarily claimed many lives. By providing those ceremonies, we allow them to see who they really are. They weren't born gang members, or drug addicts, or thieves. *17*

My best example of hope in the prisons is when we take the Aztec dancers into the institutions. They do a whole indigenous ceremony. At the end, they invite people to what's called a friendship dance. It's a big figure-eight dance. *18*

The first time that we were in prison in Tracy, California, out on the yard, there were 2,000 men out there. The ceremony was led by Laura Castro, founder of the Xochut Aztec dance group, a very petite woman, very keen to her culture. *19*

(Continued)

She says to me, "What do you think, Nane? Do you think that these guys will come out and dance?" I'm looking at those guys—tattoos all over them and swastikas and black dudes that are really big. It's incredible to be in the prison yard. I say to her, "I don't know."

But what ties all those guys together is the drumbeat. Every culture has   *20* some ceremonial drum you play. When the drumbeat started in the yard, the men just started coming. They divide themselves by race and then by gang. You got Norteños, Sureños, Hispanos, blacks, whites, Indians, and then "others" (mostly the Asian guys).

When the men were invited into the dance, those guys emptied out the   *21* bleachers. They came. They held hands. This tiny woman, Laura, led them through the ceremony of the friendship dance. They went round and round. There were black, white, and brown holding hands, which doesn't happen in prison. And they were laughing. For a few seconds, maybe a minute, there was hope. We saw the smiles of men being children, remembering something about their culture. The COs [correctional officers] came out of the tower wondering what the hell was going on with these men dancing in prison, holding hands. It was an incredible sight. That day, the Creator was present. I knew that God's presence was there. Everyone was given a feeling that something had happened that wasn't our doing.

Questions for Writing and Discussion

❶ One key strategy for writing successful narratives is setting and describing specific scenes. Alejandrez does an excellent job of setting two key scenes—one from his childhood and one from later in life. For each of these scenes, explain how Alejandrez (a) sets up the scene, (b) describes what happens using detailed observations, (c) uses dialogue to make the scene more vivid and dramatic, and (d) makes connections between the past and the present.

❷ One key theme or motif in Alejandrez's essay is the idea of a "spiritual connection." Drawing on your description from question 1, explain how the idea of a spiritual connection is important in both key scenes. How is this theme evoked in the final sentences of Alejandrez's essay? Explain.

❸ Using Alejandrez's essay as a guide, write a remembering essay about a person in your life who became a role model or was influential at a key point in your life. Include key scenes showing how, when, and why this person was influential and then tell what you were able to accomplish because of that influence. Be sure to use observing skills as well.

④ Go to the official websites for César Chávez and Barrios Unidos. What parallels are there between the lives of César Chávez and Daniel Alejandrez? How have civil rights movements changed because of new media such as Twitter, Facebook, and blogs? How are or were the goals of the United Farm Workers and Barrios Unidos different? Explain.

Tips for Transferring Skills

The writing techniques discussed in this chapter can be used in many situations you will face as a college writer and beyond. To reinforce these techniques and put them to use, you should look for ways to apply and practice them in other classes. Here are tips for using these techniques in a variety of writing situations.

1. The texts we read have many elements that require careful observation. To transfer the skills you have learned in this chapter to your reading in classes like history, philosophy, and literature, pay close attention to the details in a text. You can practice by annotating a text in the margins, pointing out the details you notice as you read closely.

2. Behavioral sciences such as psychology, sociology, and business often ask you to read case studies—narratives about human behaviors and actions. For example, a study of consumer habits can be offered to suggest effective marketing strategies. Or a case study about a foreign culture can be used to show subtle differences among the ways that different cultures or genders view the world. As you write case studies in those courses, you can use observation and recollection techniques to bring out the main points.

3. Though we usually think of metaphor and simile as literary techniques, they are common practices in the sciences. A scientist might call the nucleus of a cell its "control center" or describe nerves as "like a roadway for thought impulses." As you read and write in a science course, make notes of the use of figurative language by other writers, and adopt those techniques yourself.

4. When you write up a lab report or an experimental method, part of your job is to describe in detail the actions you have taken or will take in chronological order. As you write in one of your natural or behavioral science courses, you can use time-based transitions (after, next, before) to demonstrate the proper order for a process. You might also think about how you could use multimedia techniques to show the actual steps in a process.

Observing and Remembering: Writing Processes

Using Observing and Remembering in Your Writing Processes

Many writing occasions will ask you to recall and then use specific examples and scenes that recreate memories or detail observations. As you think about your audience and the genre most suited for that audience, use the chart that follows to help you develop your ideas and start your writing. Browsing specialty magazines, books, or websites may give you an idea of how writers adapt their writing to particular audiences and purposes. As you browse, make note of the observing and remembering techniques you find. You may even want to copy some striking examples in your journal.

> **“Memory is more indelible than ink.”**
>
> —Anita Loos, Author of *Kiss Hollywood Goodbye*

Audience	Possible Genres for Writing About Memories
Personal Audience	Autobiographical essay, memoir, journal entry, social networking site entry, blog, photo essay, scrapbook, multigenre document.
Academic Audience	Essay for humanities or social science class, journal entry, forum entry on class site, multigenre document, observations of lab experiment or field study.
Public Audience	Column, memoir, or essay in a magazine, newspaper, or newsletter; memoir or essay in an online site or blog; online memoir in a multigenre document; publicity piece for an organization.

CHOOSING A SUBJECT

If one of the journal exercises on pages 397–398 suggests a workable subject, try the collecting and shaping strategies described in the following pages. If none of the exercises leads to an interesting subject, consider these ideas:

15.3
Choose significant topics from remembered events

- Interview (in person or over the phone) a parent, a brother or sister, or a close friend. What events or experiences does your interviewee remember that were important to you?
- Look at a map of your town, city, state, or country and do an inventory of places you have been. Make a list of trips you have taken, with dates and years. Which of those places is the most memorable for you?

- Dig out a school yearbook or look through the pictures and comments on your friends' Facebook profiles. Whom do you remember most clearly? What events do you recall most vividly?
- Go to the library and look through news magazines or newspapers from five to ten years ago. What were the most important events of those years? What do you remember about them? Where were you and what were you doing when these events occurred? Which events had the largest impact on your life?

Note: Avoid choosing overly emotional topics such as the recent death of a close friend or family member. If you are too close to your subject, responding to your reader's revision suggestions may be difficult. Ask yourself if you can emotionally distance yourself from that subject. If you received a C for such an essay, would you feel devastated?

COLLECTING

15.4

Apply strategies for developing vivid details

When you have chosen a subject for your essay, try the following collecting strategies.

Brainstorming

Brainstorming is jotting down anything and everything that comes to mind that is remotely connected to your subject: words, phrases, images, or complete thoughts. You can brainstorm by yourself or in groups, with everyone contributing ideas and one person recording them.

Clustering

Clustering is a visual scheme for brainstorming and free-associating about your topic. It can be especially effective for remembering because it helps you sketch relationships among your topics and subtopics. As you can see from the sample sketch, the diagram you make should help you see relationships between ideas or get a rough idea about an order or shape you may wish to use.

Looping

Looping is a method of controlled freewriting that generates ideas and provides focus and direction. Begin by freewriting about your subject for eight to ten minutes. Then pause, reread what you have written, and *underline* the most interesting or important idea in what you've written so far. Then, using that sentence or idea as your starting point, write for eight to ten minutes more. Repeat this cycle, or "loop," one more time. Each loop should add ideas and details from some new angle or viewpoint, but overall you will be focusing on the most important ideas that you discover.

SHAPING AND DRAFTING

15.5

Organize details into a narrative with a central purpose

Begin by reconsidering your purpose; perhaps it has become clearer since you recorded it in your journal entry. In your journal, jot down tentative answers to the following questions. If you don't have an answer, go on to the next question.

- **Subject:** What is your general subject?
- **Specific topic:** What aspect of your subject interests you?
- **Purpose:** Why is this topic interesting or important to you or your readers?
- **Main idea:** What might your main idea be?
- **Audience:** For whom are you writing? Why might your reader or readers be interested in this topic? Consider possible audiences for this chapter's assignments for observing and remembering (pages 410–411).

- **Genre:** What genre might help you communicate your purpose and main idea most effectively to your audience? (Review genre options suggested with the chapter assignment.)

Shaping Strategies

Do you want to . . .	Consider using this rhetorical strategy:
use several images or graphics?	multigenre and multimedia possibilities (p. 402)
use chronological order or flashback?	chronological order (p. 402)
contrast the present to the past?	comparison/contrast (p. 403)
use figurative language?	simile and metaphor (p. 403)
create a narrator with a distinct voice?	voice and tone (p. 404)
use dialogue between characters?	dialogue (p. 405)
have a catchy title, introduction, or conclusion?	title, introduction, conclusion (p. 405)

As you think about ways to organize and shape your essay, reread your assignment and think about your purpose and possible audience. Review the strategies below for shaping ideas that might work for your topic. After you have written a draft, come back and review these shaping possibilities to see if one will make your essay more dramatic, vivid, or memorable.

Multigenre and Multimedia

As you collect ideas, draft passages, and discuss your assignment with your peers, think about appropriate genre possibilities. Start by reviewing the genre alternatives in the chapter assignment. You may choose to write in a traditional narrative format. Or you may want to use a multigenre or multimedia format with photographs, graphics, drawings, scrapbook materials, video, podcasts, or web links. Check with your instructor to see if a multigenre approach meets the assignment.

Chronological Order

If you are writing about remembered events, you will probably use some form of chronological order. Begin by making a list of the major scenes or events. Normally, you will be using a straightforward chronological order, but you may wish to use a flashback, starting in the middle or near the end and then returning to the beginning. In a paragraph about her struggles to break free from a controlling boyfriend, student writer Gabrielle Termini begins with the moment that she was first able to feel her own independence, then returns to an earlier moment in which such freedom seemed impossible. Note how the use of third person narration allows Termini to demonstrate the new perspective she had gained on her own situation–almost as if she was now able to see her situation from the outside.

> Somehow, not knowing what would come next in her life no longer seemed frightening. Instead, each decision was her own, and it all felt manageable, even joyful. What had happened to that woman that only a month ago had felt paralyzed when asked how she expected to support herself without him? For what seemed like the hundredth time, she had asked Jon to move out. And as always, he had started to pack his things while reciting the responsibilities that she would have to manage on her own, the difficulties she would face trying to support herself, and the lonely nights she was likely to spend without him. Sometimes she would stop him before he left, panicked by the thought of fending for herself. Once or twice, she had let him go for a day or two before begging him to return. And each time he did, it became clearer that his bursts of anger, his verbal abuse—and even the increasingly frequent threats of physical abuse—were simply part of her life. That was who she was. That was the way things were. Because the alternative seemed just too lonely, just too empty, just too hard to sustain. But now those memories had become cautionary tales, and the fears of an unknown future had become something else: the excitement of the new, thrillingly uncertain world before her.

Comparison/Contrast

Although you may be comparing or contrasting people, places, or events from the past, you will probably also be comparing or contrasting the past and the present. You may do that at the beginning, noting how something in the present reminds you of a past person, place, or event. You may do it at the end, as Andrea Lee does in *Russian Journal*. Or you may do it both at the beginning and at the end. Comparing or contrasting the past with the present will often clarify your dominant idea.

Simile and Metaphor

Similes and metaphors create vivid word pictures or images by making comparisons. This figurative language may take up only a sentence or two, or it may shape several paragraphs.

- A *simile* is a comparison using *like* or *as*: A is *like* B. In the passage earlier in this chapter from *Out of Africa*, Karen Blixen uses similes to describe the iguanas she comes across:

  > [The iguanas] shine *like* a heap of precious stones or *like* a pane cut out of an old church window. When, as you approach, they swish away, there is a flash of azure, green and purple over the stones, the color seems to be standing behind

them in the air, *like* a comet's luminous tail.... Now that the flame was put out, and the soul had flown, the Iguana was *as* dead *as* a sandbag.

- A *metaphor* is a direct or implied comparison suggesting that A *is* B. In a passage earlier in this chapter, John Muir uses both simile and metaphor when he compares the Great Central Valley of California first to a lake, and then to a garden. He uses simile when he says the valley is *like* a lake, and he uses metaphor when he equates (without using *like* or *as*) the valley to a "vast golden flower-bed":

> At my feet lay the Great Central Valley of California, level and flowery, *like* a lake of pure sunshine, forty or fifty miles wide, five hundred miles long, one rich furred garden of yellow *Compositae*. And from the eastern boundary of this *vast golden flower-bed* rose the mighty Sierra....

Voice and Tone

The term *voice* refers to a writer's personality as revealed through language. Writers may use emotional, colloquial, or conversational language to communicate a sense of personality. Or they may use abstract, impersonal language either to conceal their personalities or to create an air of scientific objectivity.

Tone is a writer's attitude toward the subject. The attitude may be positive or negative. It may be serious, humorous, honest, or ironic; it may be skeptical or accepting; it may be happy, frustrated, or angry. Often voice and tone overlap, and together they help us hear a writer talking to us. In the following passage, we can hear the voice of student writer Mason Potteiger as he describes his love of baseball.

> Look. I know that I am out of step with the trends. I know that the proclamation that I am about to make opens me up to ridicule from all sorts of folks. Fitness advocates, who believe sport should involve a serious cardiovascular workout. The younger crowd, who crave constant movement if not violent encounters on the field of play. And advertisers, who seek out the flashiest of athletes to hawk their products. I'll be tweeted into oblivion. But this proclamation I must make.
>
> I love baseball. Baseball is the most beautiful of sports.
>
> But, seeing its beauty takes a higher level of sensitivity than the average sports fan possesses these days. It takes a trained eye to appreciate from the highest seats in the bleachers how a cast of nine dancers scatter in unison to the "AHHHHH" of the crowd each time the ball is hit. Or to have the trained ear to listen to a radio broadcast and immediately recognize *that* sound, the sound that announces a baseball destined to clear the left centerfield wall. Baseball fans know it just from the tone of a wooden bat crashing through the leather, stitched casing of what was before a perfectly round orb. (And, by the way, what stark-raving-mad lunatic created the aluminum bat?) Baseball fans, at least sometimes, know how to appreciate the purity of *just listening* in a multimedia world. Radio broadcasts of baseball remain the soundtrack to my past, to whom the Phillies played back-up harmony.
>
> So yes, I admit it. Baseball has little of what has made sports into multi-billion dollar industries. But for that, too, I love the game. When I pass by the growing number of soccer fields in my neighborhood that exist alongside now-vacated ballparks, I find myself wanting to stop and remind those kids-in-shorts that the most difficult act in all of sports is still hitting a nasty slider.

Dialogue

Dialogue, which lets us hear the voices of people and events rather than be told about them, can be a strategy for shaping parts of your narrative. Even though you might not remember the exact words from a conversation, you can write dialogue that re-creates what you remember each person's saying during a scene. Dialogue can bring to life the tone and voice of the participants in a conversation, and so help the readers to experience a remembered or observed scene first hand. Dialogue can also be used to express the words that are in our minds as we think through a topic—an internal dialogue. In the excerpt that follows from Kate Chopin's "The Story of an Hour," we see both types of dialogue as the main character contemplates the life she faces after hearing about the death of her husband.

> And yet she had loved him—sometimes. Often she had not. What did it matter! What could love, the unsolved mystery, count for in face of this possession of self-assertion which she suddenly recognized as the strongest impulse of her being!
>
> "Free! Body and soul free!" she kept whispering.
>
> Josephine was kneeling before the closed door with her lips to the keyhole, imploring for admission. "Louise, open the door! I beg, open the door—you will make yourself ill. What are you doing Louise? For heaven's sake open the door."
>
> "Go away. I am not making myself ill." No; she was drinking in a very elixir of life through that open window.
>
> Her fancy was running riot along those days ahead of her. Spring days, and summer days, and all sorts of days that would be her own. She breathed a quick prayer that life might be long. It was only yesterday she had thought with a shudder that life might be long.

Title, Introduction, and Conclusion

In your journal, sketch out several titles you might use. You may want a title that is merely an accurate label, such as *Russian Journal*, or you may prefer something less direct that gets your reader's attention. For example, for her essay that appears later in this chapter, Kaitlynn Pick chooses the title "The Mean Reads," referring readers to the significance of a part of the story that is only made clear as the narrative unfolds.

Introductions or beginning paragraphs take several shapes. Some writers plunge the reader immediately into the action and later fill in the scene and context. Introductions or beginning paragraph take several shapes. Some writers plunge the reader immediately into the action–as Brian Hiatt does in his description of Bono as he "rounds a corner onto a narrow Dublin street"—and later fill in the scene and context. Others are more like Lisa Randall, announcing her subject—her shyness—and then telling a story that illustrates that subject. At some point, however, readers do need to know the context—the *who, what, when,* and *where* of your account.

Conclusions are also of several types. Some writers will return to the present and discuss what they have learned, as Andrea Lee does in *Russian Journal*. Some writers conclude with dramatic moments, or an emotional scene, such as N. Scott Momaday's recollection earlier in this chapter of the moment when he realized he would never see his grandmother again. But many writers will tie the conclusion back to the

> "I start at the beginning, go on to the end, then stop."
>
> —Gabriel García Márquez, Author of *One Hundred Years of Solitude*

> "I always know the ending; that's where I start."
>
> —Toni Morrison, Nobel Prize–winning novelist

"The difference between the right word and the nearly right word is the same as that between lightning and the lightning bug. "

—Mark Twain,
Author of
Adventures of Huckleberry Finn

beginning. In your journal, experiment with several possibilities until you find the one that works best for your subject.

When you have experimented with the shaping strategies, reconsider your purpose, audience, and main idea. Working from your journal material and from your collecting and shaping activities, draft your essay. It is important *not* to splice parts together or just recopy and connect segments, for they may not fit or flow together. Instead, reread what you have written, and start afresh.

Avoid interruptions by choosing a quiet place to work. Follow your own writing rituals. Try to write nonstop. If you cannot think of the right word, put a line or a dash, but keep on writing. When necessary, go back and reread what you have written.

REVISING

15.6

Apply revision techniques to address your purpose and your audience

Revising begins when you get your first idea and start collecting and shaping. It continues as you redraft sections of your essay and rework your organization. In many classes, you will give and receive advice from the other writers in your class. Use the guidelines below to give constructive advice about an observing and remembering essay draft.

Guidelines for Revision

- **Reexamine your purpose and audience.** Are you doing what you intended?
- **Reconsider the genre and medium you selected.** Is it working for your purpose and audience? Can you add multigenre or multimedia elements to make your narrative more effective? Could you tell your story in an image, video, or audio composition?
- **Revise to make the main idea of your account clearer.** You don't need a "moral" to the story or a bald statement saying, "This is why this person was important." The details themselves should help the reader know clearly why you wanted to write about the memory that you chose.
- **Provide close and detailed observation.** *Show*, don't just tell. Can you use any of the collecting and shaping strategies for observing discussed in this chapter?
- **Have you used straight chronological order?** If your order works, keep it. If not, should you begin in the middle and do a flashback? Would it be more effective to move back and forth from present to past or stay in the past until the end?

- **Cue your reader by occasionally using transitional words to signal changes.** Transitional words include *then, when, first, next, last, before, after, while, sooner, later, finally, yesterday, today.*
- **What are the key images in your account?** Should you add or delete an image to show the experience more vividly?
- **Collaborate with peers.** While we often think we know how our voice will be heard, its tone can sometimes be misunderstood. Ask a classmate to read your draft and to focus on voice and tone. Do they support your purpose? If you are using a persona, is it an appropriate one for your audience and purpose?
- **Revise sentences to improve clarity, conciseness, emphasis, and variety.**
- **Check your dialogue for proper punctuation and indentation.**
- **When you are relatively satisfied with your draft, edit for correct spelling, appropriate word choice, punctuation, and grammar.**

Using Observing and Remembering in Storytelling

Throughout this chapter, you have studied and practiced techniques and processes to help you embed observations and memories in your writing. While many forms of writing use these techniques, they are particularly useful to the creation of stories. Stories are sometimes told for their own sake, and sometimes they can be used to persuade or influence readers. Storytelling, called "narrative" writing, is also used to help give context or depth to scientific or business writing—to give the details surrounding an experiment or describe a business plan.

In her creative non-fiction narrative, student writer Kaitlynn Pick uses the skills of remembering and observing to tell a personal story. But is there also a rhetorical purpose? Is it meant to change readers, make them more aware, or to ask them to think or act differently? As you read what follows, analyze Pick's writing process and style to help you to consider the various ways the skills learned in this chapter can also be used to enrich your own use of narrative in a variety of rhetorical situations.

Student Writing

The Mean Reds

Kaitlynn Pick

As Kaitlynn Pick developed her story about a childhood memory, she collected details to help readers truly see the objects as she did. This process, illustrated below, is used by many writers as they construct words and phrases that will bring memories to life for their readers.

(Continued)

...continued The Mean Reds, **Kaitlynn Pick**

Observations and Memories	Specific Details	Phrasings
What I found in the box	Grandma's sayings Grandpa's sea shell	A worn lid; Grandma-In-Heaven's favorite fortune cookie sayings, and Grandpa's purple sea shell
A *Beauty and the Beast* playbill	The playbill was very worn, like someone looked at it often	tattered fold of paper, type faded gray and textured soft to touch by years of reflection
Memories of how I felt when I found the playbill	Memories that led to regrets	I hold the small parcel in my clenched fist, concentrate on the back of my eyelids, and scream.
The sight of her friend's signature	The signature seemed childlike	red juvenile scrawl of a signature
Memories of Russell's smile and hugs	Feelings of happiness and security	that impish grin of his, pulling me into one of those hugs that made the world feel right
Memories of younger days	Things I didn't fully understand then that I can see more clearly now as an adult	Those were the days when our childhoods were still intact— before we were torn away from each other in a cruel joke of ignorance.

Kaitlyn Pick's finished essay exhibits how her skills of observation enrich a story about a seemingly simple moment, allowing her readers to experience the memories and regrets that one object brought forth. The comments in the margin indicate how some of the techniques presented in this chapter are illustrated in Pick's narrative.

The modifiers (*gingerly* and *worn*) create the mournful tone of the story

Her happy memories are contrasted with the family history of her friend

This "tattered" paper becomes a metaphor for the tattered life it recalls

With a sigh, I slide the box off the shelf, gingerly remove the worn lid, and ease its contents across my vivid bed spread. A letter from Mema, Grandma-In-Heaven's favorite fortune cookie sayings, and Grandpa's purple sea shell, as well as many more memories and wishes, glance back at me as I survey the odd assortment. A tattered fold of paper, type faded gray and textured soft to touch by years of reflection, brings a sad smile to my face. His red juvenile scrawl of a signature stands bold against its reminiscent backdrop.

(Continued)

"I am going to be a star one day. Just you wait! That will be worth a billion dollars someday, Kate," he said with that impish grin of his, pulling me into one of those hugs that made the world feel right. Those were the days before he faded away, before an alcoholic father twisted his mind, before the life of drugs and booze seemed like his only escape. Those were the days when our childhoods were still intact—before we were torn away from each other in a cruel joke of ignorance. How was I supposed to function when I rushed to his locker only to find it cleared out and his name scrubbed from the rosters? How could they make the choice that I, at the age of thirteen, knew was the worst thing for him? It took me years to realize that he had never spoken up. His mother knew nothing about the cruelties he endured at his father's hand—knew nothing of how much my best friend, her son, was terrified of living with that awful man.

The boy who signed that *Beauty and the Beast* playbill in March of 2007 ceases to exist. In his place, a grey young man stumbles through life in a daze of forced repression as each pop, each hit, each swallow, smears away the nightmares. Tears burn in my eyes and my throat threatens to close as I slowly fold the paper. I hold the small parcel in my clenched fist, concentrate on the back of my eyelids, and scream. I scream at him for not speaking up. I scream at his father for breaking him. I scream at myself for not saving him. I scream that I will only ever see my Russell again scrawled in red ink on a battered piece of paper.

Dialogue makes the memory more immediate

Use of flashback to return to the memories spurred by finding the box of artifacts

Rhetorical questions heighten the tone of despair

Multiple phrasings used to describe the substance abuse

Returns to the object that spurred the memories and helps to reveal the meaning of the title

Questions for Writing and Discussion

1. Psychological research has shown that people remember traumatic events more vividly and with more detail than other events. Has that been true in your experience? Recall two experiences—one happy, one traumatic—and write about whether your experiences support or do not support the research.

2. While it may not seem that personal narratives have a thesis, they often at least imply a central point that can function much like a thesis. If you were to write a thesis that captures Kaitlynn Pick's main point in this essay, what would it be?

3. The notes in the margins of the essay indicate techniques that Kaitlynn Pick uses in her essay. Reread the essay and add your own annotations, pointing out other techniques that she uses to bring out key observations and memories.

4. Pick's essay draws on a simple observation to build a rich description of the memories that it brings forth. Using a similar technique, describe something that you have kept primarily for its sentimental value, and write an essay that helps us see the deeper memories embedded in a seemingly unimportant object.

Applying What You Have Learned

The assignments below provide you with opportunities to write on topics that are enriched by the skills of observing and remembering. Choose one of these tasks and, using the processes and techniques discussed in this chapter, narrow your topic, purpose, and audience, and then select a form of writing that best fits the situation. As you compose, remember that a 21st century "writer" can compose in more than words: We now have the ability to compose electronic texts (blogs, text messages, e-mails), visual texts (images, video), and audio texts (embedded dialogue, music, other sounds). We also create "multimedia" texts—compositions that include combinations of words, images, and sounds that affect many senses. So, following each suggested assignment, you will find suggestions on how your writing could be enhanced by multimedia elements.

1. Since communication is so central to being human, our most vivid memories often involve the moments or the people who helped us to attain new literacy skills—a parent, a teacher, a friend. Using the skills of observation and remembering you learned in this chapter, tell a story that helps your audience to experience with you a key moment in your literacy history. It could tell us about someone who was instrumental in your literacy learning, or it could relate a story about a particularly challenging communication moment. You could describe a key insight that helped drive your literacy forward, or even a moment (or person) who impeded that progress. Be sure to choose an appropriate audience for your narrative and articulate its purpose. Is it primarily to move your readers, to persuade them, or to inform them?

Using multimedia. You could enhance your literacy narrative with images (photographs of places or people from your story, scans of an early piece of your writing), with sounds (recorded interviews with people who helped you attain literacy or talking about literacy skills), or with video (of key places or people in your story). You could even tell the entire story using one of these media. Narrate your story with an audio recording, create a video performance, present pieces of your narrative with video interviews, or use a photographic essay that helps us see the key people, places, or moments in your literacy history. Imagine how a series of pictures—perhaps with captions—could show development over time better than words alone.

2. Too often we know little about what people in a specific career field do on a day-to-day basis. Write an essay that helps you, and others who are interested in a particular field, learn more. Begin by remembering the thoughts, expectations, and experiences that led you to consider this field of work—perhaps even in childhood. Express those memories as vividly as you can. Then, in order to compare those memories with the realities of the field, visit a workplace where people do the work you are considering. Observe the interactions of workers, the things that occupy their time, and how they talk and write. You could also interview workers to get a sense of why they chose the field, what they like best and least

about it, and their own memories of work. Having collected this information, write an essay that helps you and others have a richer understanding of this career field.

Using multimedia. This kind of assignment lends itself to collecting and presenting your observations and memories in many media. As you observe the workplace, you could take photographs, record the thoughts and memories of people on the job on audio or video, or demonstrate their work products via images. Each of these enhancements could be used to depict vividly what it is like to participate in this work. You could even create a type of documentary film that narrates a day in the life of a person in this field of work.

③ One reason for writing, discussed later in this book, is to propose solutions to problems. But before you demonstrate a problem and propose a solution, you need to fully understand its nature. That involves both observation and remembering. Start with a problem you have noticed on campus, in your community, in your workplace, or in an organization of which you are a member. At first you might rely on memories of when you perceived or encountered the problem— implicitly racist comments in your workplace, a lack of follow-through in your organization, infrastructure problems in a community park. Then use your skills of observation to dig into its causes and its effects. Spend time "on location," observing carefully to find details that could be at the root of the problem or at least help to describe it. Write an essay that uses these memories and observations to demonstrate the nature of the problem for an audience who you believe needs to pay more attention to it. Use techniques presented in this chapter to make your illustration of the problem as vivid as possible.

Using multimedia. Often problems are best illustrated through multiple media. Consider, for example, how charities portray poverty or other social problems through the voices and images of those affected. As you collect memories and details about the problem that you are investigating, use the capabilities of digital recording that are available on devices such as smart phones to do audio or video interviews with stakeholders, to take pictures of the disrepair in a county park, or to show the challenges faced by an organization. You could also use images or video clips that are available through Internet searches to show the history of the problem or its existence on a larger scale. Media can often help you make more of an impact than words alone.

Unit 4

The Information Literacy Cycle

16

Information Literacy

16.1 BEGINNING THE RESEARCH ASSIGNMENT

In this section, you will learn to:

- Use invention strategies to discover a topic for your project.
- Identify the characteristics of a strong research question, and apply a working knowledge of your topic to propose your initial research question.
- Apply genre knowledge to understand an academic article.
- Understand the elements of a research proposal, and apply them to your topic.

The Importance of Getting Curious

Despite what they say, curiosity is not dead. You know the obituary: At some point around the age of (fill in the blank), we stop wondering about things. We lose that childlike sense that the world is something to explore. Actually, we never stop being

Taken from *The Curious Researcher: A Guide to Writing Research Papers*, Eighth Edition by Bruce Ballenger.

curious, especially if we feel like there's a good reason for it. More than ever, we live in an information-rich environment, and the Internet makes information more accessible than ever before. Say you're having a conversation with a friend about deodorant. "I wonder what the first deodorant was?" asks she. "That's the kind of question that the Internet was made for," says you. And within a minute, you report that the first commercial deodorant was a product called "Mum," invented in the 1880s, though noncommercial deodorants were in use 5,000 years ago. This kind of short-term curiosity—sometimes called "situational curiosity"—is incredibly common in this Internet age.

On the other hand, genuine research relies on a sustained interest in something. It can begin with situational curiosity. For example, I once wrote an entire book on lobsters, an interest that was initially triggered by childhood memories of eating them during the holidays with my family and, many years later, reading a newspaper article that reported the lobster catch was down 30 percent and some believed the lobster fishery was on the verge of collapse. I wondered, will lobster go the way of caviar and become too expensive for people like me?

That was the question that triggered my research, and it soon led to more questions. What kept me going was my own curiosity. If your research assignment is going to be successful, you need to get curious, too. If you're bored by your research topic, your paper will almost certainly be boring as well. By chapter's end, you'll make a proposal about what you want to investigate. But begin by simply wondering a little.

Seeing the World with Wonder

Your curiosity must be the driving force behind your research paper. It's the most essential ingredient. The important thing, then, is this: *Choose your research topic carefully. If you lose interest in it, change your topic to one that does interest you, or find a different angle.*

In most cases, instructors give students great latitude in choosing their research topics. (Some instructors narrow the field, asking students to find a focus within some broad, assigned subject. When the subject has been assigned, it may be harder for you to discover what you are curious about, but it won't be impossible, as you'll see.) Some of the best research topics grow out of your own experience (though they certainly don't have to), as mine did when writing about lobster overfishing. Scholars tell us that a good way to sustain your curiosity in a topic is to find something to research that has some personal relevance. Begin searching for a topic by asking yourself this question: *What have I seen or experienced that raises questions that research can help answer?*

Getting the Pot Boiling

A subject might bubble up immediately. For example, I had a student who was having a terrible time adjusting to her parents' divorce. Janabeth started out wanting to know about the impact of divorce on children and later focused her paper on how divorce affects father-daughter relationships.

Kim remembered spending a rainy week on Cape Cod with her father, wandering through old graveyards, looking for the family's ancestors. She noticed patterns on the stones and wondered what they meant. She found her ancestors as well as a great research topic.

Manuel was a divorced father of two, and both of his sons had recently been diagnosed with attention deficit disorder (ADD). The boys' teachers strongly urged Manuel and his ex-wife to arrange drug therapy for their sons, but they wondered whether there might be any alternatives. Manuel wrote a moving and informative research essay about his gradual acceptance of drug treatment as the best solution for his sons.

For years, Wendy loved J. D. Salinger's work but never had the chance to read some of his short stories. She jumped at the opportunity to spend five weeks reading and thinking about her favorite author. She later decided to focus her research paper on Salinger's notion of the misfit hero.

Accidental topics, ideas that you seem to stumble on when you aren't looking, are often successful topics. My research on Maine lobsters was one of those. Sometimes one topic triggers another. Chris, ambling by Thompson Hall, one of the oldest buildings on his school's campus, wondered about its history. After a little initial digging, he found some 1970s news clips from the student newspaper describing a student strike that paralyzed the school. The controversy fascinated him more than the building did, and he pursued the topic. He wrote a great paper.

If you're still drawing a blank, try the following exercise in your notebook.

EXERCISE 16.1.1   Building an Interest Inventory

STEP 1: From time to time I'll hear a student say, "I'm just not interested in *anything* enough to write a paper about it." I don't believe it. The real problem is that the student simply hasn't taken the time to think about everything he knows and everything he might want to know. Try coaxing those things out of your head and onto paper by creating an "interest inventory."

Start with a blank journal page or word processing document. Create three columns per page with the words below:

PLACES, TRENDS, THINGS, TECHNOLOGIES,
PEOPLE, CONTROVERSIES, HISTORY,
JOBS, HABITS, HOBBIES

Under each title, brainstorm a list of words (or phrases) that come to mind when you think about *what you know and what you might want to know* about the category. For example, for TRENDS, you might be aware of the use of magnets for healing sore muscles, or you might know a lot about extreme sports. Put both down on the list. Don't censor yourself. Just write down whatever comes to mind, even if it makes sense only to you. This list is for your use only. You'll probably find that ideas come to you in waves—you'll jot down a few things and then draw a blank. Wait for the next wave to come and ride it. But if you're seriously becalmed, start a new column with a new word from the list above and brainstorm ideas in that category. Do this at least four times with different words. Feel free to return to any column to add new ideas as they come to you, and don't worry about repeated items. Some things simply straddle more than one category. For an idea of what this might look like, here's what one student did with the exercise (Figure 16.1.1).

Places

Freedom Tower (WTC)

Syria

Subway tunnels

Mines and caves

South Africa

Rural Western America (Wyoming, Idaho, Montana)

Galapagos

Venice (sinking?)

Guantanamo Bay

Controversies

Westboro Baptist Church

LDS and FLDS

Scientology

Racism—Trayvon Martin

Marriage equality

Paparazzi and celebrities (Kanye assault charge)

Teen suicide

The Millennial generation

Sugar addiction

Diversity in the fashion industry

Rights issues and copyright

NSA and security

Jobs

Police officer

Public office (mayor, comptroller, governor, borough president)

Wedding planner

Stylist

Nutritionist/personal trainer

Animal trainer

Computer hacker

Postal worker

Publisher

Schoolteacher

Marine biologist

Weapons manufacturer

Drug dealer

Soldier

Trends

3-D printing

Stupid baby names (North West, Blue Ivy)

Hip diets (paleo, gluten-free, intermittent fasting)

TV on the Internet vs. live TV

Cats on the Internet (Grumpy Cat, Lil' Bub)

Internet memes

Vampires/zombies

Mustaches

Micro-apartments

FIGURE 16.1.1   Interest Inventory: A Student Example

Allot a total of 20 minutes to do this step: 10 minutes to generate lists in four or more categories, a few minutes to walk away from it and think about something else, and the remaining time to return and add items to any column as they occur to you. (The exercise will also work well if you work on it over several days. You'll be amazed at how much information you can generate.)

STEP 2: Review your lists. Look for a single item in any column that seems promising. Ask yourself these questions: Is this something that raises questions that research can help answer? Are they potentially interesting questions? Does this item get at something I've always wondered about? Might it open doors to knowledge I think is important, fascinating, or relevant to my life?

Circle the item.

STEP 3: For the item you circled, generate a list of questions—as many as you can—that you'd love to explore about the subject. This student's interest inventory turned up a topic she didn't expect: teeth whitening. Here are some of her opening questions:

Are tooth whiteners safe?

What makes teeth turn browner over time?

How has society's definition of a perfect smile changed over time?

Are whiter teeth necessarily healthier than darker teeth?

Is it true that drinking coffee stains your teeth?

How much money is spent on advertising tooth-whitening products each year?

What percentage of Americans feel bad about the shade of their teeth?

Do dentists ever recommend that people whiten their teeth?

Is there any way to keep your teeth from getting darker over time?

Can teeth get too white?

Why do I feel bad that my teeth aren't perfect?

Do other cultures have the same emphasis on perfectly white teeth as Americans do?

Are there the same standards for men's teeth and women's teeth?

What judgments do we make about people based simply on the color of their teeth?

How does America's dental hygiene compare with that of other countries? Is the "Austin Powers" myth really true?

The kinds of questions she came up with on her tentative topic seem encouraging. Several already seem "researchable." What about you? Do any of your questions give you a hunger to learn more?

Other Ways to Find a Topic

If you're still stumped about a tentative topic for your paper, consider the following:

- *Surf the Net.* The Internet is like a crowded fair on the medieval village commons. It's filled with a range of characters—from the carnivalesque to the scholarly—all participating in a democratic exchange of ideas and information. There are promising research topics everywhere. For instance, you might even scour Tweets that you've received from a person or organization you're following. Follow the Tweets from news organizations and major magazines, which often provide summaries of their major articles.

- *Search a research database.* Visit your library's Web site and check a database in a subject area that interests you. For example, suppose you're a psychology major and would like to find a topic in the field. Try searching PsycINFO, a popular database of psychology articles. Most databases can be searched by author, subject, keyword, and so on. Think of a general area you're interested in—say, bipolar disorder—and do a subject or keyword search. That will produce a long list of articles, some of which may have abstracts or summaries that will pique your interest. Notice the "related subjects" button? Click that and see a long list of other areas in which you might branch off and find a great topic.

• *Browse Wikipedia.* While the online "free content" encyclopedia isn't a great source for an academic paper, Wikipedia is a warehouse of potential research topic ideas. Start with the main page, and take a look at the featured or newest articles. You can also browse articles by subject or category.

• *Consider essays you've already written.* Could the topics of any of these essays be further developed as research topics? For example, Diane wrote a personal essay about how she found the funeral of a classmate alienating—especially the wake. Her essay asked what purpose such a ritual could serve—a question, she decided, that would best be answered by research. Other students wrote essays on topics like the difficulty of living with a depressed brother and an alcoholic parent, which yielded wonderful research papers. A class assignment to read Ken Kesey's *One Flew Over the Cuckoo's Nest* inspired Li to research the author.

• *Pay attention to what you've read recently.* What articles or Web sites have sparked your curiosity and raised interesting questions? Rob, a hunter, encountered an article that reported the number of hunters was steadily declining in the United States. He wondered why. Karen read an account of a particularly violent professional hockey game. She decided to research the Boston Bruins, a team with a history of violent play, and examine how violence has affected the sport. Don't limit yourself to articles or Web sites. What else have you read recently—perhaps magazines or books—or seen on TV that has made you wonder?

• *Consider practical topics.* Perhaps some questions about your career choice might lead to a promising topic. Maybe you're thinking about teaching but wonder about current trends in teachers' salaries. One student, Anthony, was being recruited by a college to play basketball and researched the tactics coaches use to lure players. What he learned helped prepare him to make a good choice.

• *Think about issues, ideas, or materials you've encountered in other classes.* Have you come across anything that intrigued you, anything that you'd like to learn more about?

• *Look close to home.* An interesting research topic may be right under your nose. Does your hometown (or your campus community) suffer from a particular problem or have an intriguing history that would be worth exploring? Jackson, tired of dragging himself from his dorm room at 3:00 A.M. for fire alarms that always proved false, researched the readiness of the local fire department to respond to such calls. Ellen, whose grandfather worked in the aging woolen mills in her hometown, researched a crippling strike that took place there 60 years ago. Her grandfather was an obvious source for an interview.

• *Collaborate.* Work together in groups to come up with interesting topics. Try this idea with your instructor's help: Organize the class into small groups of five. Give each group 10 minutes to come up with specific questions about one general subject—for example, American families, recreation, media, race or gender, health, food, history of the local area, environment of the local area, education, and so forth. Post these questions on newsprint as each group comes up with them. Then rotate the groups so that each has a shot at generating questions for every subject. At the end of 40 minutes, the class will have generated perhaps 100 questions, some uninspired and some really interesting. You can also try this exercise on the class Web site using the discussion board or group features.

What Is a Good Topic?

A few minutes browsing the Internet convinces most of my students that the universe of good research topics is pretty limited: global warming, abortion rights, legalization of pot, same-sex marriage, and the like. These are usually the topics of the papers you can buy with your Visa card at sites like freeessays.com (yeah, right). These are also often topics with the potential to bore both reader and writer to death because they inspire essays that are so predictable.

But beginning with a good question, rather than a preconceived answer, changes everything. Suddenly subjects are everywhere: What is with our cultural obsession about good teeth? Is it true that lawnmowers are among the most polluting engines around? What's the deal with the devastation of banana crops, and how will that affect prices at Albertson's down the street? Are "green" automobiles really green? Even the old, tired topics get new life when you find the right question to ask. For example, what impact will the availability of medical marijuana vending machines in California have on the legal debate in that state?

What's a good topic? Initially, it's all about finding the right question and especially one that you are really interested in (see box below). Later, the challenge will be limiting the number of questions your paper tries to answer. For now, look for a topic that makes you at least a little hungry to learn more.

What Makes a Question "Researchable"?

• It's not too big or too small.
• It focuses on some aspect of a topic about which something has been said.
• It interests the researcher.
• Some people have a stake in the answer. It has something to do with how we live or might live, what we care about, or what might be important for people to know.
• It implies an approach or various means of answering it.
• It raises more questions. The answer might not be simple.

Where's Waldo? and the Organizing Power of Questions

For a long time, I thought school writing assignments were exclusively exercises in deduction. You start by coming up with a thesis and then try to find examples to support it. This kind of writing starts with an idea and supports it with evidence, moving from the general to the specific. There's nothing wrong with this. In a lot of writing situations—say, the essay exam or SAT writing test—this approach makes a great deal of sense. But much academic research, at least initially, works inductively. You look for patterns in information that raise interesting questions, and it is these questions that redirect the researcher's gaze back to the information, this time more selectively and purposefully.

In other words, you start with a lot of data, form a question or hypothesis about the patterns in what you see, and then return to the data again, this time focusing on what is relevant. In this way, you get control of the information by looking at less of it.

The visual puzzles in the *Where's Waldo?* series of children's books are a great example of the power of good questions to manage information. As you know, Waldo, with his red-and-white-striped stocking cap and jersey, is hidden in a picture among hundreds of other people, many of whom look a lot like him. The challenge, quite simply, is to find Waldo in all of this data. Imagine, though, if the game didn't ask, "Where's Waldo?" but "Where are the men?" or "Where are the women?" in the picture. Suddenly, much more information is relevant and the search isn't nearly as focused. A better question might be, "Where are the people wearing yellow?" That eliminates some of the data but still leaves a lot to work with. Obviously, "Where's Waldo?" is the best question because you know what you're looking for and what you can ignore.

Similarly, a good inquiry question will focus your investigation of any topic. Starting with an answer—a thesis or main point—before you do any research is efficient; it sets you on a steady march to a destination you already know. But beginning with questions, while sometimes a messier process, is a much more powerful way to see what you don't expect to see. Try the following exercise, and you'll see what I mean.

EXERCISE 16.1.2   The Myth of the Boring Topic

This exercise requires in-class collaboration. Your instructor will organize you into four or five small groups and give each group a commonplace object; it might be something as simple as a nail, an orange, a pencil, a can of dog food, or a water bottle. Whatever the object, it will not strike you as particularly interesting—at least not at first.

STEP 1: Each group's first task is to brainstorm a list of potentially interesting questions about its commonplace object. What questions do you have about this thing, or, even more importantly, this *category* of thing (i.e., not just this particular water bottle but water *bottles*)? Choose a recorder who will post the questions as you think of them on a large piece of newsprint taped to the wall. Inevitably, some of these questions will be pretty goofy ("Is it true that no word rhymes with orange?"), but work toward questions that might address the *history* of the object, its *uses,* its possible *impact on people,* or *the processes* that led to its creation in the form in which you now see it.

STEP 2: After 20 minutes, each group will shift to the adjacent group's newsprint and study the object that inspired that group's questions. Spend 5 minutes thinking up additional interesting questions about the object that didn't occur to the group before yours. Add these to the list on the wall.

STEP 3: Stay where you are or return to your group's original object and questions. Review the list of questions, and choose *one* you find both interesting and most "researchable" (see the box "What Makes a Question 'Researchable'?"). In other words, if you were an editorial team assigned to propose a researched article that focuses on this object for a general interest magazine, what might be the starting question for the investigation? The most interesting question and the most researchable question may or may not be the same.

In Idaho where I live, there are stones called geodes. These are remarkably plain-looking rocks on the outside, but with the rap of a hammer they easily break open to reveal glittering crystals in white and purple hues. The most commonplace subjects and objects are easy to ignore because we suspect there is nothing new to see or know about them. Sometimes it takes the sharp rap of a really good question to crack open even the most familiar subjects, and then suddenly we see that subject in a new light. What I'm saying is this: A good question is the tool that makes the world yield to wonder, and knowing this is the key to being a curious researcher. Any research topic—even if the instructor assigns it—can glitter for you if you discover the questions that make you wonder.

Making the Most of an Assigned Topic

Frequently, you'll be encouraged to choose your own topic for a research essay. But if your instructor either assigns a topic or asks you to choose one within a limited subject, recall that Exercise 16.1.2 "The Myth of the Boring Topic," suggests that writers can write about nearly any topic—assigned or not—if they can discover good questions. Alternatively, examine your assigned topic through the following "lenses." One might give you a view of your topic that seems interesting.

- *People.* Who has been influential in shaping the ideas in your topic area? Is there anyone who has views that are particularly intriguing to you? Could you profile that person and her contributions?

- *Trends.* What are the recent developments in this topic? Are any significant? Why?

- *Controversies.* What do experts in the field argue about? What aspect of the topic seems to generate the most heat? Which is most interesting to you? Why?

- *Places.* Can you ground a larger topic in the particulars of a specific location that is impacted by the issue? For example, controversies over wolf management in the West can find a focus in how the debate plays out in Challis, Idaho, where some of the stakeholders live.

- *Impact.* What about your topic currently has the most effect on the most people? What may have the most effect in the future? How? Why?

- *Relationships.* Can you put one thing in relationship to another? If the required subject is Renaissance art, might you ask, "What is the relationship between Renaissance art and the plague?"

Developing a Working Knowledge

In inquiry-based research, you often begin a project not knowing much about the topic. But in order to find the questions that will sustain your investigation, you have to quickly listen in to what other people have said about it. For example, take Jacky's interest in reality TV (see Figure 16.1.2). She certainly knows *something* about reality TV since she is addicted to the show "Hoarders." She knows enough to ask a preliminary question: Why do people watch programs like this? But Jacky needs to have working knowledge of her topic before she will be ready to pose an inquiry question that might work. But what kinds of things do you need to know in order to ask a good question?

Consider the follow example on the question, *Which theory of dog training works best?*

Case Study on Developing Working Knowledge: Theories of Dog Training

A few years ago, we took our Lab puppy, Stella, to eight weeks of dog training. We thought things went well: She learned a "down stay," she would come when we called, and she wouldn't pull on her leash. Recently, we took our new golden retriever, Ada,

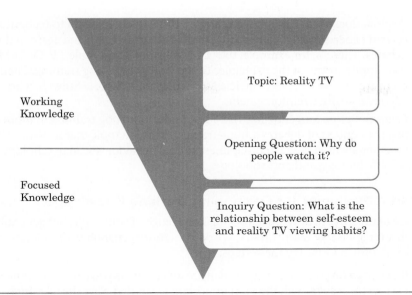

FIGURE 16.1.2 Steps for Developing an Inquiry Question. You need some background (or working) knowledge on your topic before you can settle on a researchable inquiry question. In this example, Jacky begins with a very general question, and after learning enough about her topic (focused knowledge), is able to craft the inquiry question that will guide her research for the next few weeks.

to a different trainer, and the first thing he said was that the method we used with Stella "simply wouldn't work" with Ada. It was clear that he disapproved of our first trainer's approach. "I don't know how she stays in business," he said. The experience confirmed the feeling I already had: that despite advances in the study of animal behavior, there is little agreement on the best way to make Fido sit on command. Dog trainers are a particularly contentious lot.

If I develop a working knowledge on theories of dog training, what might I discover?

1. *Definitions.* I quickly discover that there are competing definitions about things I thought were settled. What, for example, is a "well-behaved" dog? What do trainers mean when they use the term "correction"? What's the difference between "operant" and "classical" conditioning?

2. *Debates.* After just 10 minutes of searching online, it's obvious that there are fundamental disagreements among dog trainers on a whole range of issues. Should you reward dogs with food or simply with praise? Should disobedient dogs be punished with pain—say, a yank on a prong collar or a jolt from a shock collar—or with removing something they want—a treat or a ball? Should theories of dog training be based on the behavior of wild canines like wolves or based on the belief that there are fundamental differences between them?

3. *People.* It doesn't take much searching on this subject to begin to recognize certain experts or advocates whose names come up again and again in the debates. There is, for example, the "Dog Whisperer" on cable TV, Cesar Milan, who applies some of the principles of the wolf pack to dog training. Then there are behaviorists like Patricia McConnell and Victoria Stilwell, who advocate positive reinforcement.

4. *Contexts.* Before long, I realize that I can understand dog training in more than just the context of debates among trainers. This is a topic that leashes together a whole range of disciplines: animal behavior, social psychology, wildlife biology, and anthropology.

Research Strategies for Developing Working Knowledge

There are many ways to develop a working knowledge of your topic, but generally the research strategy is like many others: Work from more general information to more specialized information. Try these steps:

1. *Begin with a Google search.* Enter as many search terms as you can at one time to narrow the results, with the most important terms first. Save the relevant results.

2. *Search general and subject encyclopedias.* I know that Wikipedia is the first thing that comes to mind, but there are other, better encyclopedias. You'll find bound versions of the venerable *Encyclopaedia Britannica* in your library; your library might also provide free online access. There are online encyclopedias galore, including the *Columbia Encyclopedia* and *Encyclopedia.com*. Subject encyclopedias (see list on next page) are more focused references, and they are sadly underused by students. There are subject encyclopedias on hundreds of subjects: art history, war, African American literature, nutrition—you name it. (My favorite is the *Encyclopedia of Hell*.) You can find these online at your university library as well as at the Internet Public Library (http://www.ipl.org).

3. *Use the Internet Public Library.* The merger of the Internet Public Library and Librarians' Internet Index created a supersite that is a boon to online researchers. This is currently the most successful effort on the Web to bring some order to the chaos that is the Internet. Here you will find specialized encyclopedias, a search portal for finding additional reliable sources on your topic, and even special collections.

4. *Try Google Scholar.* Regular Google searches will turn up all kinds of results—mostly commercial sites—but Google Scholar will get you the kind of information that you know you can count on as reliable and authoritative—journal articles and scholarly books. These publications are often "peer reviewed," so everything that sees print, online or off, passes academic muster.

5. *Start building a bibliography.* Finally, conclude your working knowledge search by collecting the basic bibliographic information on the most useful sources you found. A convenient way to do this is to use a "citation machine," a Web-based program that automatically prompts you for the bibliographic information and then magically turns it into citations in whatever citation format you want. Don't trust one of these to generate references for your

Subject Encyclopedias	
Humanities	**Social Sciences**
Dictionary of Art	*African-American Encyclopedia*
International Dictionary of Films and Filmmakers	*Dictionary of Psychology*
Encyclopedia of World Art	*Encyclopedia of Marriage and the Family*
Encyclopedia of Religion	*Encyclopedia of Psychology*
Encyclopedia of Philosophy	*The Blackwell Encyclopedia of Social Psychology*
Encyclopedia of African American Culture and History	*Encyclopedia of Educational Research*
Encyclopedia of America	*Encyclopedia of Social Work*
Encyclopedia of Sociology Social History	*Encyclopedia of World Cultures*
	Encyclopedia of the Third World
	Encyclopedia of Democracy
	Guide to American Law: Everyone's Legal Encyclopedia
Science	**Other**
Dictionary of the History of Science	*Encyclopedia of the Modern Islamic World*
Dictionary of the History of Medicine	*The Baseball Encyclopedia*
Encyclopedia of the Environment	*Encyclopedia of Women and Sports*
Concise Encyclopedia of Biology	*Encyclopedia of World Sport*
Encyclopedia of Bioethics	*The World Encyclopedia of Soccer*
Encyclopedia of Science and Technology	*Worldmark Encyclopedia of the Nations*
Macmillan Encyclopedias of Chemistry and Physics	
Food and Nutrition Encyclopedia	

final essay—they can make mistakes—but they're great as a preliminary method for collecting a list of citations. Visit Citation Machine (http:// citationmachine.net), bibme (http://www.bibme.org), or another site and enter information about your best sources, choosing APA or MLA format.

Using Apps to Manage Your Research

There are a growing number of free applications you can use to keep track of your research. These programs will not only help you organize online sources but will also help you build a bibliography. See Table 16.1.1 below for some of the current options.

The Reference Librarian: A Living Source

There are compelling reasons to visit the library, even at this early stage in your research. First and foremost is that the reference desk is where reference librarians hang out, and these are people you should get to know. They can save you time by guiding you to the very best sources on your topic, and they often give great advice on how to

TABLE 16.1.1 Software for Managing Research

	Zotero	Mendeley	RefWorks	EndNote
Web-based or desktop?	Web-based	Web-based, but has desktop program that syncs with Web program	Web-based	Desktop only, but Web option, EndNote Web, is available after purchase
Available offline?	Yes	Yes	No	Yes
Available in app?	Third-party apps	iPhone and iPad apps	No	No, but has mobile capability
Cost	Free	Free	$100. May be available free through your university's library	$249.99. May be available free through your university's library
Import capabilities	Can import from databases and Web pages	Can import from databases and Web pages, with Mendeley browser plug-in	Can import from databases and Web pages	Can import from databases and Web pages
Citation capture from Web pages	Yes. Can archive page and annotate	Yes, from certain sites. Can archive page and annotate	Yes	Yes, with Ref-Grablt plug-in
Citation styles	Many available, difficult to modify	Many available, difficult to modify	Many available, and can modify and add styles	Many available. Can modify, but cannot add new styles
Storage size	Unlimited local storage. 100 MB available online (more for purchase)	Unlimited local storage. 1 GB available online (more for purchase)	Limited to 10,000 citations in Web program, but unlimited in desktop program	100 MB per user, but can be increased to 5 GB
Sharing options	Create groups, share references	Share references, create one three-member group free (more available for purchase)	Create groups, share references	Create groups, share references

narrow your research question. Reference specialists are invaluable to college researchers; without a doubt, they're the most important resource in the library.

Narrowing the Subject

Consider these two photographs. The first is a long shot of a school in my neighborhood. It's not particularly interesting. The shot is straight-on—the most obvious way of seeing—and while it's clear what the subject is in the photograph, there's isn't much that catches the eye.

The second image is a much closer shot of *a part of* the school—the same subject but much more narrowly focused. While it's hardly a great picture, the photo is far more visually interesting than the long shot, with the geometric shadows of the stair railings clashing with the orderly horizontal lines of the cement steps. This is what often happens in photography when you begin to look more closely at a larger subject that interests you, varying distance, angle, and light.

In writing, when we talk about narrowing your focus, this is what we mean: Maybe start with a long shot but then find some aspect of the topic to look at more closely. This is especially important with projects that involve research because they involve so much information. An investigation with too broad a focus is a hindrance to writers because it's hard to know what information *not* to include, and the result is usually a paper that is general and uninteresting. On the other hand, if you can move in for a closer shot, you'll see an *aspect* of your topic that's less obvious, more interesting, and more efficient to research. With a camera, narrowing a focus is easy: Get closer to your subject. In writing, it's a little more difficult. You have to find the right inquiry question to direct your gaze. In the exercise that follows, I'll prompt you to first generate a lot of questions about your topic to help you find your way to the inquiry questions that will drive your project.

Other Ways to Narrow Your Subject

1. **Time.** Limit the time frame of your project. Instead of researching the entire Civil War, limit your search to the month or year when the most decisive battles occurred.
2. **Place.** Anchor a larger subject to a particular location. Instead of exploring "senioritis" at American high schools, research the phenomenon at the local high school.
3. **Person.** Use the particulars of a person to reveal generalities about the group. Instead of writing about the homeless problem, write about a homeless man.
4. **Story.** Ground a larger story in the specifics of a "smaller" one. Don't write about dream interpretation, write about a dream *you* had and use the theories to analyze it.

EXERCISE 16.1.3   Finding the Questions

Although you can do this exercise on your own, your instructor will likely ask that you do it in class this week. That way, students can help one another. (If you do try this on your own, only do Steps 3 and 4 in your research notebook.)

STEP 1: Post a large piece of paper or newsprint on the wall. (In a classroom with computers, you can do this exercise in an open Word document.) At the very top of the paper, write the title of your tentative topic (e.g., "Plastics in the Ocean").

STEP 2: Take a few minutes to briefly describe why you chose the topic.

STEP 3: Spend 5 minutes or so briefly listing what you know about your topic already. This is information you harvested this week from your effort to develop working knowledge on your proposed topic. You might list any surprising facts or statistics, the extent of the problem, important people or institutions involved, key schools of thought, common misconceptions, observations you've made, important trends, major controversies, and so on.

STEP 4: Now spend 15 or 20 minutes brainstorming a list of questions *about your topic* that you'd like to answer through your research. Make this list as long as you can; try to see your topic in as many ways as possible. Push yourself on this; it's the most important step.

STEP 5: As you look around the room, you'll see a gallery of topics and questions on the walls. At this point in the research process, almost everyone will be struggling to find a focus. You can help one another. Move around the room, reviewing the topics and questions other students have generated. For each topic posted on the wall, do two things: Add a question *you* would like answered about that topic that's not on the list, and check the *one* question on the list you find most interesting. (It may or may not be the one you added.)

If you do this exercise in class, note the question about your topic that garnered the most interest. This may not be the one that interests you the most, and you may choose to ignore it altogether. But it is helpful to get some idea of what typical readers might want most to know about your topic.

You also might be surprised by the rich variety of topics other students have tentatively chosen for their research projects. The last time I did this exercise, I had students propose papers on controversial issues such as the use of dolphins in warfare, homelessness, the controversy over abolishment of fraternities, legalization of marijuana, and censorship of music. Other students proposed somewhat more personal issues, such as growing up with an alcoholic father, date rape, women in abusive relationships, and the effects of divorce on children. Still other students wanted to learn about historical subjects, including the role of Emperor Hirohito in World War II, the student movement in the 1960s, and the Lizzie Borden murder case. A few students chose topics that were local. For example, one student recently researched the plight of nineteenth-century Chinese miners digging for gold in the mountains just outside of Boise. Another did an investigation of skateboard culture in town, a project that involved field observation, interviews, and library research.

Crafting Your Opening Inquiry Question

What do you do with the gazillion questions you've generated on your research topic? Throw most of them away. But not yet! If you look carefully at the list of questions you (and your peers) generated in Exercise 16.1.3, you will likely see patterns. Some of your questions will clump together in more general categories. Perhaps a group of questions is related to the history of your topic, trends, processes, local relevance, and so on. Look for these patterns, and especially questions that might be combined or that inspire new questions.

Your work this week will culminate in the crafting of a tentative inquiry question and research proposal that will guide your research and writing next week. This question will constantly evolve as you learn more; but for now, create the one question around which you will launch your project. Remember, your inquiry question should be the kind of question that will ultimately lead you to make some judgment: a claim, thesis, interpretation, theory, or evaluation. But what kinds of questions are these? As I mentioned earlier, questions of fact or definition are great for developing working knowledge, but they often lead to reporting information rather than making a judgment about what you discovered. But there are questions that do lead you to claims, and these are the type of inquiry questions you're working to find. In Table 16.1.2, you can see six categories of questions that often do lead to judgment and can sustain inquiry over time.

In Exercise 16.1.3, you probably generated a whole raft of fact and definition questions. Now the challenge is to use those questions to develop some working knowledge of your topic, and then to craft a tentative inquiry question that will guide your research project. Don't rush the process. You need to know something about your topic before you will land on a good inquiry question.

TABLE 16.1.2 Types of Inquiry Questions

Type	Question	Example
Policy	What should be done about _____ ?	What might be ethical guidelines for how participants are treated in reality TV shows?
Hypothesis	What is the best explanation for _____ ?	Is the popularity of reality TV shows another manifestation of the breakdown of community in the United States?
Relationship	What is the relationship between _____ and _____ ? What might be the cause of _____ ?	Does watching reality crime shows affect viewers' attitudes toward the police?
Interpretation	What might _____ mean?	How might we interpret the politics of race relations on *Survivor*?
Value	How good is _____ ?	Which reality crime show provides the most realistic picture of police work?
Claim	What does the evidence about _____ suggest is true?	Is there evidence that shows like *Intervention* help viewers develop more sympathetic attitudes toward addiction?

Methods for Focusing Your Paper: An Example

A clear, narrow research question is the one thing that will give you the most traction when trying to get your research project moving. It's also one of the hardest steps in the process. Like gulping air after a dive into the deep end of a pool, our natural instinct at the beginning of a research project is to inhale too much of our subject. We go after the big question—why is poverty a problem?—and quickly wonder why we are submerged in information, struggling to find a direction. That's why I've spent so much time on giving you a range of methods to craft a workable research question.

In Table 16.1.2, I offered one approach to finding a strong inquiry question using policy, interpretation, hypothesis, claim, value, and relationship questions. Here's another approach based on time, person, place, and story, which is described in the "Other Ways to Narrow Your Subject" on page 430. Any one of these questions would be a good starting place for an inquiry into fad diets.

Topic: Fad Diets

Opening question: What is the basis for our culture's current obsession with fad diets?

1. Time—How does human gastronomic history play a role in the popularity of the "Paleo" diet?
2. Person—How did Dr. Atkins' low-carb diet launch the dieting industry, which is now so powerful today?
3. Place—Where is each diet the most popular? What do cost and accessibility have to do with popularity?
4. Story—What were the effects of the 1944–1945 Minnesota Starvation Experiment? How have these findings influenced dieting strategy and healthfulness today?

Possible Purposes for a Research Assignment

As you're considering your inquiry question, think a bit about the motive behind your project. Are you primarily interested in exploring what you think or making an argument? While any essay can have more than one purpose, which would you say is your *main* motive in writing your paper—at least at this moment?

1. *To explore.* You pose the question *because* you're unsure of the answer. This is what draws you to the topic. You're most interested in writing an essay, not a paper; that is, you want to write about what you found out in your research and what you've come to believe is the best or truest answer to the question you pose. Your essay will have a thesis, but it will probably surface toward the end of the paper rather than at the beginning. This is what I would call a *research essay* rather than a research paper, and it's the most open-ended form for academic inquiry. Exploratory essays often begin with sense-making or relationship-analyzing questions.

2. *To argue.* You know you have a lot to learn about your topic, but you have a very strong hunch about what the answer to your research question might be. In other words, you have a hypothesis you want to test by looking at the evidence. Inspired by a hypothesis question ("Is it true that . . . ?"), you report on your investigation. However, you may quickly move from a hunch to a conviction; and then you move immediately into arguing your claim, trying to influence what your readers think and even how they behave. Your thesis is a statement—for example, *Muslim religious schools in Pakistan are not to blame for Islamic extremism*—that you can probably roughly articulate at the beginning of your project. It may very well change as you learn more, but when you write your paper, your purpose is to state a central claim and make it convincing. Frequently, that claim is stated near the beginning of the paper.

EXERCISE 16.1.4   Research Proposal

This is an important moment in the research process. How well you've crafted your research question will significantly influence the success of your project. You can change your mind later, but for now, jot down a brief proposal that outlines your research plan in your research notebook or to turn in to your instructor. It should include the following:

1. Inquiry question
2. Primary purpose
   • Explore: What are additional questions that most interest you and might help you discover the answers to your research question?
   • Argue: What theory or hypothesis about your topic are you testing? What is your tentative main claim or thesis?
3. What, if any, prior beliefs, assumptions, preconceptions, ideas, or prejudices do you bring to this project? What personal experiences may have shaped the way you feel? Before you began developing working knowledge on the topic, what were you thinking about it? What are you thinking about it now?

Reading for Research

For this assignment, and many others in your other college classes, you will have to read things that you find difficult. Maybe they seem really boring or full of jargon or hard to follow, or perhaps they seem to be all of those things. Aside from procrastinating, how do you deal with that?

Researchers who study reading say that the best readers are guided by a strong sense of purpose—they know why they are reading something and what they hope to get from it. They also have some knowledge of the *type* of text they're reading. They know where to look for what they need to know. More than anything, though, the strongest readers are those who already have some prior knowledge about the subject. Yet even in situations where you have little prior knowledge of the subject you're reading about, you can still read effectively if you read "rhetorically."

Reading Rhetorically

When you're reading to write, three things will influence how you read:

1. Your motive for reading
2. Your prior knowledge of the topic
3. Your experience with the genres you read

When you're researching a topic for a college class, especially a topic about which you may know little, #2 becomes a problem immediately. Because you don't know much about your topic—the key arguments and people involved, the accepted facts and discredited claims, and so on—you're already at a disadvantage. Then there are the unfamiliar genres you're likely to confront, especially academic journal articles, with their sometimes dense language and formal conventions. These challenges prompt many students to change topics, sidestep scholarly sources, or lean on just a few sources that they *do* seem to understand, usually familiar genres like Web pages and popular articles.

And what's wrong with that? Mostly this: You'll end up with less interesting things to say. If you're always mining the surface for information, ignoring the deeper veins below, you'll discover pretty quickly that you're reading the same stuff over and over again about your subject.

Earlier in this chapter, you began developing your working knowledge of your topic, and that knowledge will help you immensely as you tackle more challenging reading. The other thing you need to develop is your genre knowledge. What does that mean? You become a *rhetorical reader* who is skilled at recognizing how certain kinds of texts are organized and where to look for the information you need. Rhetorical readers also know the intended audience for a certain kind of text and what kinds of evidence are most persuasive for that audience. They quickly make adjustments when they encounter unfamiliar genres and change their reading strategies to make the most of those genres.

How to Read an Academic Article

Recent studies on the research routines of college students are mostly unsurprising: Students rely heavily on Google and largely skim off the top of the search results. They also tend to avoid using library databases. Naturally, one explanation for this is that students simply don't know how to use them (see the next section for help with that). Another is that they simply don't want to deal with scholarly articles. Since these are genres that are often crucial to academic research, let's explore how they might be read by a nonexpert.

An article in the biological sciences is different from an article in political science, which is different from one in criminology. But there are some basic similarities. This describes the structure of a lot of academic articles:

1. This is the problem or question I propose to explore.
2. This is what people have already said about it.
3. This is my claim or hypothesis.

4. This is how I propose to test the hypothesis or argue the claim.
5. Here are my results or here are the reasons and evidence that support the claim.
6. This is what is significant about what I found.
7. Here are a few things that merit further study.

Knowing that this is roughly the structure of most academic articles, you know where to look for the things you want to know. For example, you know to look about a third of the way in an article to find the hypothesis or claim, and just before that you can often find a review of the literature. Unless the article is directly relevant to your research question, you probably won't actually read the whole article in most cases but will "skim and scan."

Rhetorical Reading Strategies

The table below offers suggestions about how to put your genre knowledge of academic articles to work.

First Look	Second Look
To determine relevance • Read the abstract, if there is one. • Skim the introductory material. Do the literature review and discussion of the research question seem to point in your chosen direction? • Check titles and subtitles. Do they include terms or concepts you've seen before?	Mining material in a relevant article • Subtitles, if present, are often signposts for content. • The "discussion" section in some articles provides a rich analysis of the findings. • Scan the first few sentences of every paragraph in relevant sections.
To glean the basic argument or hypothesis • The abstract, if present, will often state this. • Toward the end of the introductory material, you'll often find the phrase "this paper will argue" or "we predicted" or "we hypothesize."	Harvest key phrases and terms • The introductory material, particularly the literature review, will provide you with the terms and phrases experts typically use to discuss the topic. Collect these to use as keywords in subsequent searches.
Peruse the bibliography • The review of literature in the introduction will summarize other studies, books, or articles that address the topic. Harvest relevant citations for follow-up. • Scan the bibliography. Do any titles seem promising?	To find quotable material • Avoid the tendency to quote a statistical discussion (paraphrase instead). • Look for well-put explanations or summaries of the findings or argument. These can be found anywhere but are often in the final sections.

Reading Strategies for Research Writers

- First develop a working knowledge.
- Let your own purposes guide you: example, context, challenge.
- Anticipate your own resistance.
- Learn the organizing principles of articles.
- Read with a pen in your hand.

16.2 FINDING SOURCES

In this section, you will learn to:

- Identify your typical research routines and adapt them to college-level research.

- Apply keyword and index search techniques to find sufficient information.

- Understand different types of information and apply this knowledge to finding varied sources on your topic.

- Distinguish between sources that have more or less authority in academic writing, and practice a method of evaluating online sources.

- Illustrate a finding, process, trend, or argument relevant to your topic using an infographic.

What Are Your Research Routines?

Most of us have a research strategy, and it's simple: Google it. One scholar describes this as a kind of affliction. "Google dependence," she writes, has the following symptoms: The afflicted one "always returns to Google when confused; repeatedly asserts that 'Google is my friend'; demonstrates the belief that Google has everything; uses Google as an all-inclusive tool." I'm as addicted as anyone to Google's powerful search engine, and one of my purposes in this chapter is to help you use it better (see "Google Tips and Tricks" on page 443).

But even if you use it well, Google alone won't cut it for academic research. We'll explore other options. However, what databases you search is only part of the story; *what you do* with what you find is even more important. Let's begin by thinking about your current habits as an academic researcher. Look at the following table. Which of the terms—"fast surfer," "broad scanner," or "deep diver"—applies to your typical school research routines?[1]

---

[1]See Heinstrom, Jannica. "Fast Surfing, Broad Scanning, and Deep Diving: The Influence of Personality and Study Approach on Students' Information-seeking Behavior." *Journal of Documentation* 60.2 (2005): 228–47.

Fast surfer	• I'd prefer to read only the sources that are written so that I can understand them.
	• If I don't find much on my topic when I search, I usually assume that there isn't much written about it.
	• I always feel under a lot of time pressure when I do research.
	• I pretty much limit myself to searching for the kinds of sources that I'm familiar with.
	• I just look for what I need and little more.
Broad scanner	• I search for a range of sources on my topic, a process that I don't necessarily plan but that develops slowly as I work.
	• I often find my best sources accidentally.
	• I'm pretty careful about evaluating the reliability of the relevant sources I do find.
Deep diver	• I'm more interested in getting the highest-quality sources than in finding a lot of sources.
	• I'm very open to changing my mind about what I think on my topic.
	• I spend some time planning my research because I want to be thorough.

Depending on what and why we're researching—and for whom—any one of these profiles might apply. That doesn't make you a lousy researcher. But because academic research needs to be *authoritative*—presenting the strongest evidence and solid reasoning—and because, as a student, you need to be *efficient* with your time, it pays to be a "deep diver."

Deep divers possess a quality we've already talked about: *the willingness to suspend judgment.* I can't overstate how important this is to academic inquiry—and to maximizing your learning. But you also need to plan your research rather than proceed haphazardly, hoping for happy accidents.

Planning for the Dive

A research strategy is built from a good inquiry question. We spent considerable time on that last week. With a tentative question in place, a working knowledge of your topic, and perhaps a research proposal, you're ready to plunge more deeply into relevant sources. There's you and an ocean of information. What are you after?

1. Enough information to fully explore a narrowly focused topic
2. Varied sources
3. Quality sources

To accomplish these goals, you'll need to cast a wide net for information. Simply surfing the web won't be enough. Use a complementary research strategy that drills down into information from three sources: the internet, the library, and people (see Figure 16.2.1). The deeper you drill, the more specialized (and often authoritative) the sources you'll find.

Find Enough Information by Using the Best Search Terms

When my kids were small, the Harry Potter phenomenon had everyone muttering magic words. "Flipendo," said Julia, trying to turn the dog into a gerbil. "Wingardium leviosa," said Becca, who was determined to elevate her little sister six feet off the ground. Chopsticks substituted for magic wands. I knew this because we suddenly had too few when the take-out Chinese meal arrived; that was the only part of this magical revival that swept the household that I didn't much like.

Some writers foolishly think that there's magic involved in getting good words on the page when it's really much more simple and not at all mysterious: You have to have your seat in the chair and your fingers on the keyboard or curled around a pen. But there is a kind of magic you can perform as a researcher, and it also involves the right words uttered in the right order. *How* you phrase your search of a library database or the World Wide Web makes an enormous difference in the results. I've come to believe that this ability, almost more than any other, is the researcher's most important skill.

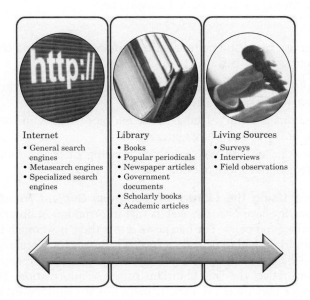

FIGURE 16.2.1 Maximize coverage of quality sources by investigating on three fronts.

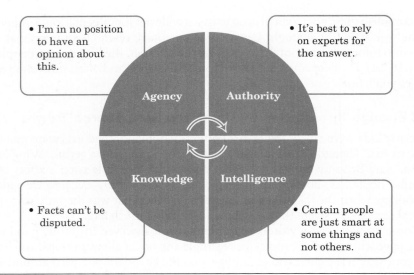

FIGURE 16.2.1A Our knowledge beliefs include how we feel about our agency, or ability to contribute, our attitude towards authority, our view about intelligence and learning, and most importantly, our ideas about the nature of knowledge. Is it certain or uncertain? When we do research, these beliefs figure into how we react to challenges and feel about our performance. For example, the person who agrees with the statements above would likely be comfortable writing a research report and very frustrated by the kind of academic research we're discussing here.

You can harvest more and better results by understanding and effectively using three search tactics:

- *Index searches* deploy the language that librarians use to catalog books and other materials in university libraries.
- *Keyword searches* in library databases use relevant terms with "connectors" like AND, OR, or NOT to produce better results.
- *Keyword searches* on the Web combine a string of terms, along with exact phrases, to generate more relevant hits.

Index Searches Using the *Library of Congress Subject Headings* An advantage that libraries have over the Web is that information in libraries is more organized. That's the good news. The bad news is that there is so much information to organize that librarians had to develop a special language for searching it. It's not an alien language—the words are familiar—but it is a language that requires that certain words be used to reflect the way librarians organize information. These searches, called *index searches,* may therefore initially seem less straightforward than the more familiar *keyword searches.*

More specifically, reference librarians use something called the *Library of Congress Subject Headings (LCSH),* which divides all knowledge into areas. These divisions are the *index terms* that you can use for index searches, which will almost always help you to find more relevant books on your topic. How do you find out these index terms? A couple ways: There is a four-volume book in your library's reference room—sometimes called the "Red Book." These volumes are the standard reference to index terms. You can also go online to search the *LCSH* (http://authorities. loc.gov/). There you can search by subject, name, or title, and the software will tell you what subject headings to use when searching for books in the library. But the easiest method to know what Library of Congress (LOC) terms to use is to go to your library's online book database and do an initial search with terms you *think* might work. When you find relevant books, you'll likely see the relevant LOC terms in your results. For example, I did a keyword search using the term *cyberterrorism* in my library's book database and found a great book: *Cyberterrorism: The Use of the Internet for Terrorist Purposes.* The results page also suggested the following index terms as active links that would help me narrow my search:

Cyberterrorism—Prevention

Computer networks—Security measures

Computer security—Law and legislation

Knowing these index terms is a huge help, particularly in the early stages of a research project. Just enter the suggested terms in your library online book index, and you'll be surprised by the quality of the results.

Keyword Searches in Library Databases   Compared to a Google search, library database searches (see a list of some of these databases on page 460) rely much more on coming up with keywords and trying them in different combinations. For example, searching for books using the word "wildfires" will produce an avalanche that will quickly bury you. Efficient research requires that you maximize the number of relevant results and minimize the number of irrelevant ones. That's why searches that use careful combinations of keywords are so important. Many libraries and Internet search engines use something called "Boolean" connectors to help you when you search databases. (These connectors were invented by George Boole, a British logician, more than 100 years ago.)

The system essentially requires the use of the words AND, OR, and NOT between the search terms or keywords. The word AND, say, between "animal" and "rights" will search a database for documents that include *both* of those terms. Just keying in *animal rights* without the AND connector will often get the same results because the AND is implied. If you want to search for *animal rights* as an exact phrase, library databases ask you to put the phrase in parentheses or quotation marks.

The use of the connector OR between search terms, obviously, will produce a list of documents that contain either of the terms. That can be a lot of results. In the early stages of your project, you might want to browse a heap of results; that way you can explore different angles on your topic, see the more common treatments, and discover some alternative search terms. The NOT connector is less frequently used but really can be quite helpful if you want to *exclude* certain documents. Suppose, for example, you were interested in researching the problem of homelessness in Washington State, where you live. To avoid getting information on Washington D.C., where it's also a problem, use the connector NOT.

> **Homeless AND Washington NOT D.C.**

As you can see from the example above, it's possible to use the connectors between a number of terms—not just two. In fact, the art of creating keyword searches is both using the right words (those used by librarians) and using them in the right combinations (those that in combination sufficiently narrow your search and give you the best results).

One final search technique that can be very useful, especially in library database searches, is something called "nesting." This involves the use of parentheses around two or more terms in a phrase. This prompts the computer to look for those terms first. For example, suppose you were searching for articles on the ethics of animal rights, but you were particularly interested in information in two states, Idaho and Montana. You might construct a search phrase like this one:

> **(Montana OR Idaho) AND animal AND rights AND ethics**

Putting the two states in parentheses tells the software to prioritize Montana or Idaho in the results, generating a much more focused list of sources related to animal rights and ethics.

Keyword Searches on the World Wide Web In the last chapter, you did a subject search on the Web using popular sites, such as the Internet Public Library (http://ipl.org), that specialize in those kinds of subject searches. Far more common are searches that use so-called search engines, such as Google. As you probably know, these are remarkable software programs that in a split second "crawl" the Web, searching for documents that contain the keywords you type in. Lately, the magic of these search engines has been tarnished a bit by commercialism, allowing advertisers to purchase priority listings in search engine results and not always making that fact obvious to the searcher. But these search engines are still essential and getting better all the time.

Keyword searches are the most common method of searching the Web, used much more than subject searches. Unfortunately, there isn't consistency in search languages. Some permit Boolean searching. Some use a variation on Boolean that involves symbols rather than words. But Google, the giant of search engines, has made all of this a bit simpler through the search form provided by its Advanced Search option. You can find this on Google's search page. Once in Advanced Search, you can use the boxes provided to perform all the usual Boolean tricks but without having to use the connector words like AND, OR, or NOT.

Google Tips and Tricks

If you want to . . .	Use . . .	For example . . .
Find related pages	**related:** followed by Web site address	**related:** www.epicurious .com
Automatically search within a specific site or type of site	**site:** followed by Web site or Web site type	microbiology **site: edu** or crime **site:** www.nytimes .com
Search for words or phrases in an open Web document	**Control-F (Windows)** or **Command-F (Mac)** and a search window opens	Search for the term "revision" in an article about writing
Search by file type	**file type:** followed by 3-letter abbreviation	Obamacare **file type: PDF**
Ignore words in your search	**minus sign (–)** followed by word to ignore	pet training **– cats**
Include words in your search	**quotation marks (" ")** around word to include	**"the" borrowers**
Include results with synonyms	**tilde sign (~)** before word	eggplant **~roasting**
Retain stop words in phrases without quotes	**plus sign (+)** in front of stop word to retain	fish **+and** chips
Search for two options	capitalized **OR** between two options	yellow **OR** black Labradors
Match any single word in a search	**asterisk (*)** to find matching word or words	"four score and *years ago" or "undergrad program pre*"
Search number range	**two dots (..)** between values	used laptops **$50..$1000**
Log and search your own search history	**Web history:** www.google .com/history	

Because of the mind-boggling amount of information on the Web, careful keyword searches are critical. Researchers waste more online time either not finding what they wanted or sifting through layers and layers of irrelevant documents because of thoughtless keyword searches. For example, notice in Figure 16.2.2 how the search on the relationship between social networks and friendship can be dramatically changed by adding terms. An initial search on Google simply using the keywords *social* and *network* produced a mind-boggling 334 million documents. Just adding *one more* keyword cut the number of hits by 6,000 percent! Finally, when combined with a phrase ("intimacy of friendship"), a search with the two terms *social* and *network* yielded significantly fewer and more focused results.

Find Varied Sources

One of the first things I notice when I'm reading research essay drafts is whether the writer leans too heavily on a single source. Does an author or article reappear again and again on page after page, like a pigeon at a favorite roost? This is not good. It typically means that the writer has too few sources and must keep turning to these few, or one source is especially relevant to the topic, and the writer can't resist repeatedly inviting the author to reappear.

Vary your sources. This means not only using a sufficient number so that your essay is informative but also using different *kinds* of sources whenever you can. In part, the kinds of sources you rely on in preparing your paper depend on your topic. Remember my research question on competing theories of dog training? That's a current topic. There's an ongoing debate online and on cable TV about which approach is best. In addition, the topic has a history in the published literature. I'll be checking both newspapers and magazines, along with Web sites, but I'll also search

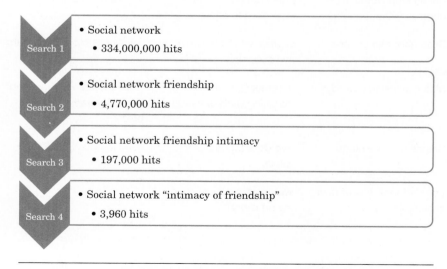

Search 1
- Social network
  - 334,000,000 hits

Search 2
- Social network friendship
  - 4,770,000 hits

Search 3
- Social network friendship intimacy
  - 197,000 hits

Search 4
- Social network "intimacy of friendship"
  - 3,960 hits

FIGURE 16.2.2 How Multiple Search Terms Narrow Results

the journals and books at the library. If you're writing about whether the release of secret documents by WikiLeaks endangers U.S. service members in Afghanistan, then much of your information will come from current sources; you're less likely to find books on this topic.

There are several ways to think about how sources can be distinguished from each other:

- Are they primary or secondary sources?
- Are they objective or subjective?
- Are they stable or unstable?

Primary vs. Secondary Sources   One way of looking at information is to determine whether it's a *primary* or a *secondary* source. A primary source presents the original words of a writer—his speech, poem, eyewitness account, letter, interview, or autobiography. A secondary source analyzes somebody else's work. Whenever possible, choose a primary source over a secondary one, because the primary source is likely to be more accurate and authoritative.

The subject you research will determine the kinds of primary sources you encounter. For example, if you're writing a paper on a novelist, then his novels, stories, letters, and interviews are primary sources. Research on the engineering of the Chicago River in 1900, a partly historical subject, might lead to a government report on the project or a firsthand account of its construction in a Chicago newspaper. Primary sources for a paper in the sciences might be findings from an experiment or observations. For a paper in business, marketing information or technical studies might be primary sources. A videotape of a theatrical performance is a primary source, while the reviews in the local newspaper are secondary sources.

Objective vs. Subjective   For now, I'm going to sidestep the debate over whether *any* source can be fully objective and simply point out that, generally speaking, we can divide all sources into those that attempt to report facts that have been gathered systematically, minimizing author bias, and those that don't pretend to be anything more than the author's opinion, perhaps supported by evidence gleaned from objective sources. You can probably guess some examples of objective sources: experiments, survey results, carefully designed studies of many kinds. The best of these are "peer reviewed" (see page 447) to double-check their accuracy. As you know, many academics prize these objective sources as the best evidence. Subjective sources are all over the map, from government propaganda to blogs to op-ed essays in the local newspaper. Of course, just because someone is pushing a point of view doesn't make a source useless. It just means that you need to consider how that point of view colors the source and read it more critically.

Stable or Unstable?   When information went digital, a new phenomenon emerged; sometimes information simply disappears. That Web page you cited in your draft, with the great statistics on scooter fatalities, is there one day and gone the next. One of the reasons you cite sources in academic writing is so readers can consult them, making a missing Web page a serious problem. Disappearing Web pages, of course, are hard to predict, but you can make some judgments about the stability of an online source. Has it been around for a long time? Is it routinely updated? Are print versions of an online document available? Is the site associated with a reputable institution? Unstable sources are a shaky foundation for any academic essay. It's best to avoid using them.

Find Quality Sources

The aim of your research strategy is not only to find interesting information on your topic but also to find it in *authoritative* sources. What are these? The highest-quality sources are those types found on the bottom of the upside-down pyramid in Figure 16.2.3. These are works that are most likely to be written by and then reviewed by experts in their fields (see the "What Does 'Peer Reviewed' Mean?" box on page 447). You find these "peer-reviewed" articles in scholarly journals, some of which are now available online as well as in the library. The downside of dealing with sources at the bottom of the authoritative pyramid is that they may be written in the *discourse* of the field; that may make the writing seem jargon-filled and hard to follow. Of course, as a nonspecialist you aren't the intended audience for the work. But the effort to make sense of an academic article really pays off. Your readers will

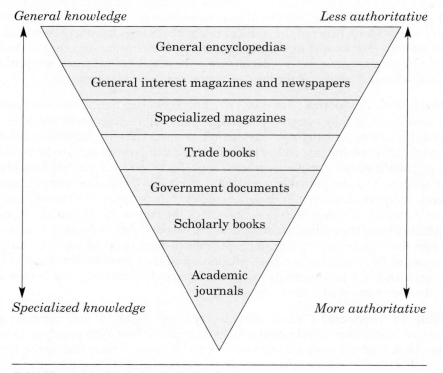

FIGURE 16.2.3 **Pyramid of Library Sources**

What Does "Peer Reviewed" Mean?

Broadly speaking, periodicals, books, Web sites, and magazines are one of two types: scholarly or popular. Popular publications include magazines like *Newsweek* or online sites like *Slate*, which are staff written, usually by nonexperts for a more general audience. Scholarly publications are written and edited by experts for others in their fields, and the best of these are "peer reviewed." This means that before an article is published online or in print, a group of fellow experts read and comment on its validity, argument, factual accuracy, and so on. The article doesn't appear in print until this review is completed and the journal editor is satisfied that the other scholars think the work is respectable.

What does this mean for you? It means that you can count on the authoritative muscle of a peer-reviewed source to help you make a strong point in your paper.

know that you're relying on the best information available; beyond that, you're more credible because it's clear that you're willing to dig deeply to explore your research question.

When Was It Published? If you're researching the treatment of slaves in nineteenth-century New Orleans, then currency is obviously less of an issue than it might be if your project were to explore the impact of the Toyota Prius on marketing practices for hybrid vehicles. Generally, in any project related to the social sciences, a recent publication date carries more weight, which is one reason APA citations emphasize date of publication. The currency of Web pages and online documents can also be important. A site that is regularly updated is obviously more likely to have the latest information on the topic.

Why Journal Articles Are Better Than Magazine Articles If your topic has been covered by academic journal articles, rely heavily on these sources if you can. An article on, say, suicide among college students in a magazine like *Time* is less valuable than one in the *American Journal of Psychology*. Granted, the latter may be harder to read, but you're much more likely to learn something from a journal article because it's written by an expert and is usually narrowly focused. Also, because academic articles are carefully documented, you may be able to mine bibliographies for additional sources. And, finally, scholarly work, such as that published in academic journals and books (usually published by university presses), is especially authoritative because it's often subject to peer review. Other authorities in the field have scrutinized the author's evidence, methods, and arguments; the published work has truly passed muster.

Look for Often-Cited Authors As you make your way through information on your topic, pay attention to the names of authors whose works you often encounter or who are frequently mentioned in bibliographies. These individuals are often the best scholars in the field, and it will be useful to become familiar with their work and use it, if possible, in your paper. If an author's name keeps turning up, use it as another term for searching the library databases or Google Scholar. Doing so might yield new sources you wouldn't necessarily encounter in other ways.

Not All Books Are Alike   When writing my high school research reports, I thought that books were always the best sources because, well, books are thick, and anyone who could write that much on any one subject probably knows what she's talking about. Naive, I know.

One of the things college teaches is *critical thinking*—the instinct to pause and consider before rushing to judgment. I've learned not to automatically believe in the validity of what an author is saying (as you shouldn't for me) even if she did write a thick book about it.

If your topic lends itself to using books as sources, then evaluate the authority of each before deciding to use it in your paper. This is especially important if your paper relies heavily on one or two books. Consider the following:

- Is the book written for a general audience or for more knowledgeable readers?
- Is the author an acknowledged expert in the field?
- Is there a bibliography? Is the information carefully documented?
- How was the book received by critics? To find out quickly, search the Web using the author's name and title of the book as search terms.

Evaluating Online Sources   Librarians help maintain the order, stability, and quality of information in the library. By comparison, the Internet is anarchy. Everyone knows that you have to be vigilant about trusting the accuracy, balance, and reliability of Web documents. Unfortunately, there's continuing evidence that student researchers still have a hard time assessing the quality of online sources. While the criteria for evaluating sources just mentioned apply to Web documents, Web documents also deserve special attention.

Here are some general guidelines to follow (later I'll suggest a more vigorous approach for evaluating online sources):

- *Always keep your purpose in mind.* For example, if you're exploring the lobbying methods of the National Rifle Association, then you will want to hear, and see, what this organization has to say on its Web site. In looking at the NRA Web pages, you'll know full well that they are not unbiased; however, for your purpose, they are both relevant and authoritative. After all, who knows more about the NRA than the NRA?

- *Favor governmental and educational sources over commercial ones.* There are plenty of exceptions to this, but in general you're wise to rely more heavily on material sponsored by groups without a commercial stake in your topic. How can you tell the institutional affiliation of sources? Sometimes it's obvious: They tell you. But when it's not obvious, the *domain name* provides a clue. The .com that follows a server name signifies a commercial site, while .edu, .org, or *.gov* usually signals an educational, nonprofit, or governmental entity. The absence of ads also implies that a site is noncommercial.

- *Favor authored documents over those without authors.* There's a simple reason for this: You can check the credentials of an author. You can do this by sending an e-mail message to him or her, a convenience often available as a link on a Web page, or you can do a quick search to see if that author has published other books or articles on your topic. If writers are willing to put their names on a document, they might be more careful about the accuracy and fairness of what they say.

- *Favor Web pages that have been recently updated over those that haven't been changed in a year or more.* Frequently, at the bottom of a Web page there is a line indicating when the information was posted to the Internet and/or when it was last updated. Look for it.

- *Favor Web sources that document their claims over those that don't.* Most Web documents won't feature a bibliography. That doesn't mean that they're useless to you, but be suspicious of a Web author who makes factual assertions without supporting evidence.

A Key to Evaluating Internet Sources.   As an undergraduate, I was a botany major. Among other things, I was drawn to plant taxonomy because the step-by-step taxonomic keys for discovering the names of unfamiliar plants gave the vegetative chaos of a Wisconsin meadow or upland forest a beautiful kind of logic and order. The key that follows is modeled after the ones I used in field taxonomy. This one is a modest attempt to make some sense of the chaos on the Web for the academic researcher, particularly when the usual approaches for establishing the authority of traditional scholarship and publications fail—for example, when documents are anonymous, their dates of publication aren't clear, or their authors' affiliations or credentials are not apparent.

If you're not sure whether a particular Web document will give your essay credibility, see Figure 16.2.4 and work through the following steps:

1. Does the document have an author or authors? If *yes*, go to Step 2. If *no*, go to Step 7.

Authored Documents

2. Does the document appear in an online journal or magazine that is "refereed"? In other words, is there any indication that every article submitted must be reviewed by other scholars in the field before it is accepted for publication? If *yes*, you've found a good source. If *no* (or you're unsure), go to Step 3.

3. Is the document from a government source? (Online, look for the .gov domain.) If *yes*, then it is likely a good source. If *no*, go to Step 4.

4. Does the document appear in an online publication affiliated with a reputable educational institution (e.g., a university) or nonprofit educational organization (e.g., the American Cancer Society)? (Online, look for the .edu or .org domain.) If *yes*, it's likely to be trustworthy. If *no*, go to Step 5.

5. If the author isn't clearly affiliated with a reputable institution, does he or she offer any credentials that help establish expertise on the topic? (For example, an advanced degree in the relevant discipline is encouraging.) If credentials

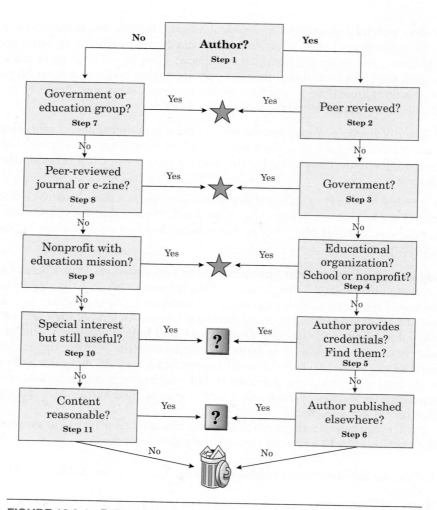

FIGURE 16.2.4 Follow the flowchart for a rigorous review of a Web document or page, beginning with whether the author is obvious or not. Sites that earn stars are generally more trustworthy. Those with question marks still may be useful, depending on the situation. Be particularly wary of information on commercial or special interest sites.

are missing, can you find an author's credentials by Googling the author's name? Is there an e-mail link to the author so you can inquire about affiliations or credentials? If *no,* go to Step 6.

6. Has the author published elsewhere on the topic in reputable journals or other publications? Check this at the library by searching under the author's name in the catalog or appropriate databases. If *no,* reconsider the value of the source. You could be dealing with a lone ranger who has no expertise on your topic and no relevant affiliations.

Unauthored Documents

7. If the online document has no author, is it from an institutional source like a university (.edu) or the state or federal government (.gov)? If *yes*, then chances are the document is useful. If *no*, go to Step 8.

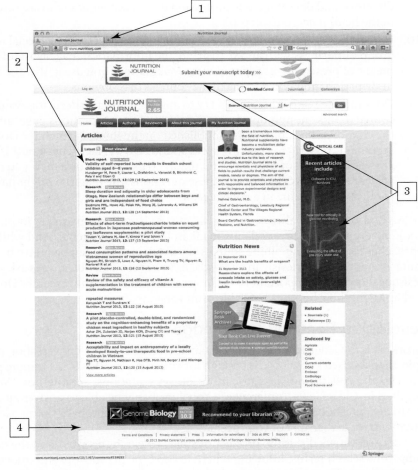

1. **Website URL:** Check the domain (.gov, .edu, .com, etc.) for type and reliability of source, though that isn't always revealing. In this case, though the site is from a commercial domain it's an educational journal.
2. **Authors:** Do articles and features have an author(s)?
3. **Advertisements:** The presence of ads on a web page, particularly if they're tied to content, might mean it has a commercial bias. Not the case here, though.
4. **Site and domain information:** The bottom of a web page might include invaluable information on who compiled the page, its currency, and background on the source (look for "About Us" or something similar).

FIGURE 16.2.5   Scanning a Web Site. For a cursory evaluation of a Web site, it helps to know where to look.

8. Is the anonymous document published in an online journal or magazine? Is it refereed? (See Step 2.) If *yes,* it's likely a good source. If *no,* go to Step 9.

9. Is the document part of a publication or Web page from a nongovernment source whose mission is described in the document, and does it suggest that the organization's goals include research and education? Is there a board of directors, and does it include professionals and academics who are respected in the field? If *no,* go to Step 10.

10. Even if the organization offering the information represents a special interest group or business with an axe to grind, the information may be useful as a means of presenting its point of view. Make sure, if you use it, that the information is qualified to make the source's bias obvious.

11. Does the site seem reasonable? Try to apply the usual criteria for evaluating a source to this anonymous document. Does it have a citations page, and do the citations check out? Was it published on the Internet recently? Does the argument the writer is making seem sound? Do the facts check out? If the answer is *no* to all of the above, then don't trust the document. If you can answer *yes* to more than one of these questions, the material might have some marginal value in a college paper.

A good researcher always takes a skeptical view of claims made in print; she should be even more wary of claims made in Internet documents. And while these approaches for evaluating online sources should help, it still can be pretty tricky deciding whom to take seriously in cyberspace. So to sort it all out, always ask yourself these questions: How important is this Internet document to my research? Do I really need it? Might there be a more reliable print version?

Developing Focused Knowledge

If working knowledge equips you to sustain a 1-minute dinner conversation on your topic, then focused knowledge is enough for you to make a 15- or 20-minute presentation to the rest of the class (for more on presentations, see the box "Working Together: In-Class News Conference"). You'll probably be able to answer all of your classmates' questions. You'll hardly be an expert, but you'll probably know a lot more about your topic than any of your peers.

Focused knowledge is the product of smart research this week and the next, refining your search terms, knowing where to look for the most useful information, and using your time efficiently. As you'll see later in this section, focused knowledge also depends on what you *do* with what you find. Most important, especially at this point, are these two questions:

1. Is this information relevant to my inquiry question?
2. Does it *change* my question?

At its most basic, relevance is simply deciding whether that article or book you found is on topic. Say you're researching the disappearance of the world's frogs, and you find a *Scientific American* article titled "Extinction Countdown: World's Frogs Are Disappearing." It obviously couldn't be more relevant. But, as you develop more

Working Together: In-Class News Conference

By the end of this week, you should be ready to make a presentation to your class on your topic. Imagine that it's a press conference similar to the ones shown on television. You will give a 15-minute talk on your topic to your classmates, who will later, like veteran newspaper reporters, follow up with questions. Your presentation will be carefully timed. It shouldn't be any longer than the allotted time limit; any less than the allotted time suggests that you haven't yet developed a focused knowledge of your topic.

Plan your presentation with the following things in mind:

- *Rather than simply report everything you've learned about your topic, try to give your talk some emphasis.* For example, focus on what you've learned so far that most surprised you and why. Or present the most common misconceptions about your topic and why they miss the mark. Or provide some background about why the question you're exploring is important and share some of the answers you've discovered so far. If your topic has a personal dimension, tell that story, and share how your research has helped you understand your experience differently.
- *Don't read a speech.* It's fine to have notes with you—in fact, it's a good idea—but try to avoid reading them. Make your presentation as interesting as you can. After all, this is a chance to discover what other people think about your topic—what interests them about it and what doesn't. This talk is a great chance to try out some approaches to your topic that you may later use to make your essay more compelling.
- *Consider visuals.* PowerPoint or Prezi (see http://prezi.com) presentations are great because they help you organize the talk. Also think about using photographs, graphs, charts, and other visuals to present your information.
- *Begin by stating your focusing question.* Every presentation should start by establishing what question is driving your investigation. You might even put this on the board when you begin.

While you listen to your peers' presentations, think about what questions they raise that interest you. These might be questions of clarification, questions about an assertion the presenters or one of their sources made, or areas that the speakers didn't cover but that you wonder about. Imagine that you're a hard-nosed reporter anxious to get the story right.

focused knowledge, you can make more focused judgments. *How* is a source relevant? With some traditional research papers, this question may simply mean, how does it support my point? But genuine academic inquiry is about discovery, and because it begins with questions, information isn't just used to line up ducks in the service of a preconceived point. The relevant sources you encounter online and in the library can help your project in many more ways:

- *Refine the inquiry question.* Last week your question was, "Why are the world's frog's disappearing?" But you read some articles and browse some books and you realize that a more focused and interesting question is this: "What is the relationship between climate change and the decline in amphibians?"

- *Help the literature review.* A very common move in most academic research is establishing what has already been said about the question you're posing. Which scientists have published on frogs and climate change? What do they agree on? What are their disagreements? What don't they know?

- *Reveal interesting patterns.* Scholars who study the differences between how experts and novices do research often notice this: Experienced researchers see patterns in data that novices don't notice. Experts *expect* patterns, and you should look for them, too. Does the information you find seem to tell a story? Does the most persuasive information suggest a particular answer to your research question? Are there relationships among facts, theories, or claims that surprise you? Are there any unexpected contradictions, causes, or connections? For example, in Figure 16.2.6, I've created a "word cloud" of the last 320 words you just read. A "word cloud" takes some text and creates an image that represents word frequency in the text. The visually bigger words are repeated more than the smaller ones. Note the pattern of emphasis on certain subjects and relationships—questions and information, relevance and research, change and focus. In a sense, when you develop focused knowledge on your topic, you gather a cloud of information much like this one, except richer and more complicated. Constantly analyze the relationships in what you're finding—what are the most frequent arguments, which ideas seem connected, what facts stick out?

FIGURE 16.2.6   Looking for Patterns

What About a Thesis?

Ultimately, you must have a thesis, something you are saying about your research question. But when should you know what that is?

Are You Suspending Judgment?   Should you have a thesis at this point? That depends on the purpose of your project. If it's exploratory, if your motive is to discover what you think, then it's too early to make any bold statements that answer the question you're researching. It might even be counterproductive. Inquiry-based investigations depend on your willingness to *suspend judgment* long enough to discover what you think.

Are You Testing Assumptions?   If, however, you feel that you have developed some ideas about what you want to say, now might be an excellent time to make a list of your theories, assumptions, or beliefs about your topic. They will be invaluable guides for your research this week because you can examine these beliefs against the evidence and potentially break through to new understandings about your research question.

What Are You Arguing?   In some cases, you know that what you think is the best answer to your research question even before you've done much investigation of the topic, and your motive is to build a convincing argument around that claim. For example, consider this claim: *Lawnmowers make a significant contribution to CO_2 emissions in the United States.* Maybe this is something you heard or read somewhere from a reputable source, and it's something you strongly suspect is true. Maybe your instructor asked you to make that argument, or you're writing an opinion piece for an assignment. Conventional research papers are frequently organized from the beginning around a thesis or claim. If that's the kind of project you're working on, now would be a good time to craft a sentence that states your most important assertion or main idea. This may well be refined or even discarded later on as you learn more, but it will help with your research this week.

To generate a *tentative* thesis statement at this point, try finishing one of the following sentences:

1. While most people think _____ about _____, I think _____.
2. The most convincing answer to my research question is _____.
3. The main reason that _____ is a problem is _____, and the best solution is _____.
4. Among the causes of _____, the least understood is _____.
5. Though much has been said about _____, very little attention has been paid to _____.
6. All of the evidence so far about _____ points to _____ as a significant cause/solution/effect/problem/interpretation/factor.

You'll be implementing your research strategy this week and next, looking at sources in the library and on the Web. The exercises that follow will help guide these searches, making sure that you don't overlook some key source or reference. Your instructor may ask you to hand in a photocopy of the exercise as a record of your journey.

Keeping Track of What You Find: Building a Bibliography

For the next two weeks, you're going to collect a lot of material on your research question: PDF copies of articles, books, bookmarked Web pages, images, and perhaps even audio and video files. You will make your life easier if you don't just collect but *record* what you find. Your options include the following:

- *Basic bibliography.* This is the minimalist approach. You simply keep a running list, using the appropriate citation method, of information on each source you think you'll use in your essay. If you're using MLA, for example, this will become your Works Cited page. An online citation machine, like bibme (http://www.bibme.org), can help you build it. You can, of course, wait until the last minute to do this but, trust me, you will regret it.

- *Working bibliography.* This is one step up from the basic bibliography (see Figure 16.2.7) and is the simplest form of what's called an "annotated bibliography." A working bibliography provides a brief *summary* of what the source says: what topics it covers and what the basic argument or main ideas are. If you're using a double-entry journal, then you can find the material you need for your summary there. Your annotation may be a brief paragraph or more, depending on the source.

- *Evaluative bibliography.* In some ways, this is the most useful annotated bibliography of all because it challenges you not only to "say back" what you understand sources to be saying but also to offer some judgments about whether you find them persuasive or relevant. You might comment on what you consider the strengths of the source or its weaknesses. Is writing an evaluative bibliography more work? You bet. But ultimately you are writing your paper as you go because much of the material you generate for the bibliography can be exported right into your essay. Your double-entry journal provides the raw material for these annotations.

Your instructor will tell you what kind of bibliography you should build for this project, but at the very least you should consider maintaining a basic bibliography as you go. Put it on a "cloud," like Google Docs or Evernote, that will store your draft bibliography on the Web and always be available wherever you find a new source—in the library, at home, or in the campus computer lab.

Searching Library Databases for Books and Articles

Despite the appeal of the Web, the campus library remains your most important source of information for academic research. Sure, it can be aggravating. There's that missing book or that article that isn't available in full text. You needed that article! Most of all, there's the sense of helplessness you might feel as a relative novice using a large, complicated, and unfamiliar reference system.

Topic: Theories of Dog Training
Focusing Question: Should dogs be trained using positive reinforcement exclusively?

1. Katz, Jon. "Why Dog Training Fails." *Slate Magazine.*
   N.p. 14 Jan. 2005. Web. 22 Dec. 2010.

   Katz argues that most theories of dog training fail to take into account the realities of raising an animal in a "split-level," not a training compound. He calls his own method the "Rational Theory," which he describes as an "amalgam" of techniques that takes into account the actual situation of both dog and owner.

2. Schilder, Matthijs B. H., and Joanne A. M. van der Borg. "Training Dogs with the Help of the Shock Collar: Short and Long Term Behavioural Effects." *Applied Animal Behaviour Science* 85 (2004): 319–34. Medline. Web. 23 Dec. 2010.

   Researchers had two groups of German shepherds, one training with shock collars and the other training without them. They then studied both "direct reactions" of dogs to the shock and their later behavior. Study found that dogs trained with shock collars consistently showed more signs of stress during and after training, including "lower ear positions." Finding "suggests that the welfare of these shocked dogs is at stake, at least in the presence of their owner."

3. Shore, Elise, Charles Burdsal, and Deanna Douglas. "Pet Owners' Views of Pet Behavior Problems and Willingness to Consult Experts for Assistance." *Journal of Applied Animal Welfare Science* 11.1 (2008): 63–73. Print.

   Study notes that 30 percent of dogs that are given to shelters are there because owners complained of behavior problems; yet only 24 percent of owners surveyed enrolled in obedience classes. Researchers surveyed 170 dog and cat owners and determined that the highest concern was about animals who threatened people, and those owners were most likely to ask for assistance and they mostly turned to the Web unless there was a charge.

FIGURE 16.2.7   Working Bibliography: An Example

In this chapter and the last one, you were introduced to basic library search strategies, knowledge that will help give you some mastery over the university library. Now you'll expand on that knowledge, and at the same time you'll move from a working knowledge of your topic to a deeper understanding, one that will crystallize by reading and writing about what you find.

It's hard for newcomers to the university to fully appreciate the revolution the last decade brought to how we do college research. All you need to know, really, is that finding sources is infinitely easier. And with the growing availability of full-text PDFs of articles and e-books, you can end a session of searching with not just a citation but also the printout of the article.

Because there are still relatively few digital versions of books, you should use the library the old-fashioned way: Journey into the "stacks," which at big schools can be cavernous, floor-to-ceiling aisles of books. The trip is well worth it because even if you discover that the book you want isn't right for your project, that book is surrounded by 100 others on your topic or related ones. Browse like you do on Amazon.

You will save time if you know *where* to look for the book you want, and so you must be familiar with how librarians organize books.

Finding Books

There are two systems for classifying books: the Dewey Decimal and the Library of Congress systems.

The Library of Congress system, which uses both letters and numbers, is much more common in college libraries. This is the system with which you should become most familiar. Each call number begins with one or two letters, signifying a category of knowledge, which is followed by a whole number between 1 and 9,999. A decimal and one or more Cutter numbers sometimes follow. The Library of Congress system is pretty complex, but it's not hard to use. As you get deeper in your research, you'll begin to recognize call numbers that consistently yield useful books. It is sometimes helpful to simply browse those shelves for other possibilities.

Understanding Call Numbers   The call number, that strange code on the spine of a library book, is something most of us want to understand just well enough to find that book on the shelf. How much do you need to know? First, you should know that there is more than just the alphabet at work in arranging books by their call numbers, and that the call numbers tell you more than merely where books are shelved. Take for example the call number for *The Curious Researcher*.

The call number shown in Figure 16.2.8 tells you the subject area of the book, a little something about its author, and when the book was published. This is useful to know not only because it will help you find the book, but it also might prompt you to find other, possibly more recent, books on the same subject on a nearby shelf. In Figure 16.2.9, you can see how Library of Congress call numbers determine the arrangement of books on the shelf.

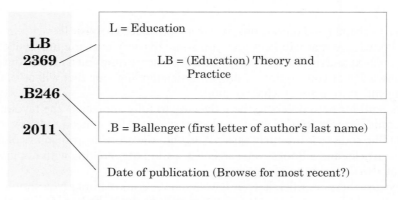

FIGURE 16.2.8   Deciphering the Call Number Code

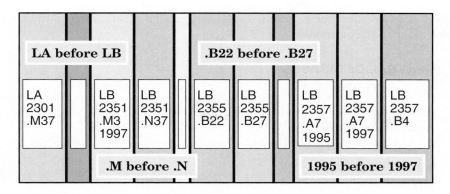

FIGURE 16.2.9   How Books Are Arranged on the Library Shelf

Coming Up Empty Handed?   In the unlikely event that you can't find any books by searching directly using the online catalog, there's another reference you can check that will help locate relevant articles and essays that are *a part* of a book whose title may otherwise seem unpromising. Check to see if your library has a database called the Essay and General Literature Index. Search that database with your keywords or subject and see if it produces something useful. List the relevant results as instructed previously. In addition, Google Book Search (http://books.google.com) allows users to do full-text searches of many titles. Those books in the public domain (i.e., the rights have lapsed) are available to any user in digital versions. This is a particularly rich resource for older texts, including some dating back hundreds of years.

Checking Bibliographies   One tactic that might lead to a mother lode of sources for your essay is to look at the bibliographies at the back of (mostly) scholarly books (and articles). Don't ever set aside a promising book until you've checked the bibliography! Jot down complete bibliographic information from citations you want to check out later. Keep a running list of these in your research notebook.

Interlibrary Loan   If your library doesn't have the book (or article) you really want, don't despair. Most college libraries have a wonderful low- or no-cost service to students called interlibrary loan. The library will search the collections of other libraries to find what you're looking for and have it sent, sometimes within a week or less. Use the service by checking with the reference desk or your library's Web site.

Article Databases

There are two kinds of article databases at your library: general databases that cover multiple disciplines and specialized databases that are discipline specific. The general databases cover multiple subjects, so their coverage is wide but shallow. The specialized databases are subject specific, so their coverage is deep but narrow. Of course,

I don't know which of these general databases you have at your library, but here are some of the most common:

GENERAL DATABASES
Academic OneFile
Academic Search
Academic Search Premier
ArticleFirst
IngentaConnect
JSTOR
ProQuest Central
Web of Science

Many of these multidisciplinary databases index popular magazines and some newspapers, and even some scholarly journals, which makes them very useful. For example, Academic Search Premier indexes nearly 14,000 magazines and journals. Increasingly, these databases include full-text articles, an extraordinary convenience for students working from home.

Common Specialized Databases		
Humanities	Science and Technology	Social Sciences
America, History and Life	AGRICOLA (Agriculture)	Anthropological Index
Arts and Humanities Citation Index	Applied Science & Technology Index	ComAbstracts (Communication)
Historical Abstracts	Biological Abstracts	Contemporary Women's Issues
Humanities Index	CINAHL (Nursing)	
Literature Resource Center	Computer Literature Index	Criminal Justice Abstracts
MLA International Bibliography (Literature and composition)	GeoRef Abstracts (Geology)	PAIS (Public Affairs)
	Health Reference Center	PsycINFO
	MathSciNet	Social Sciences Index
Music Index	Medline Web of Science (Medicine)	Social Work
Project Muse		Sociological Abstracts
Religion and Philosophical Collection		Worldwide Political Science Abstracts
Business	**Education**	
ABI/Inform	Education Full Text	
Business Source Elite	Education Index	
FreeEDGAR	ERIC	

Specialized databases are subject specific. These are usually listed by discipline on your library's Web pages. The advantage of using these databases is that they will produce many scholarly articles that might be relevant to your research question, though they may not all be full text. For a list of some of these, see the table on page 460.

Finally, certain article databases are focused on certain *types* of publications. The most important of these are indexes to newspapers (see following list, "Newspaper Databases"). They don't index the small-town papers, but they do provide citations to the so-called national newspapers such as the *New York Times,* the *Washington Post,* the *Los Angeles Times,* the *Wall Street Journal,* and the *Christian Science Monitor.* What's good about the national newspapers is that they're among the most authoritative journalistic sources; in other words, because of their large and experienced staffs, the information they provide is more trustworthy than that of smaller newspapers and online news outlets.

If you're looking for state or local newspapers, you have a couple of options. The larger papers (and many magazines, for that matter) also have their own Web sites, where you may be able to search their archives and retrieve full-text articles. Some sites charge for this service, though you can usually request them from your campus library for free. A convenient method for searching some of these sites is to use a news search engine, which will consult thousands of papers in a few seconds. Two of the best of these search engines are Google News (http://news.google.com) and Yahoo News (http://news.yahoo.com).

Occasionally, the local papers are also indexed online by the university library, and copies are available on microfilm. More and more frequently, however, local papers, like their larger counterparts in major cities, have their own Web sites, where you can use keyword searches to scour their archives.

NEWSPAPER DATABASES

Alternative Press Index

Ethnic Newswatch

LexisNexis Academic

National Newspaper Index

National Newspapers

Newspaper Source

ProQuest Central

Saving Search Results

Most online book indexes and article databases allow you to save your search results. Some of these databases allow you to mark the relevant results and then print them out. Some databases and most university libraries also allow you to create an account and a file for your search results. Through the Web page at my library, I can save searches, build a list of books I want to check out, and even publish my bibliographies so others can see them (and I can see theirs). Finally, you can always e-mail your search results page to yourself and organize a bibliography on your own computer.

Develop your focused knowledge by doing a thorough search using your library's book index and article databases. Unlike in Web and database searches, in book searches it often pays off to begin with broad subject terms. I got better results, for example, when I searched for books on theories of dog training with *animal behavior-canine* than I did with *dog training theories*. Searches that begin broadly might lead you to a relevant chapter in an otherwise irrelevant book.

Choose one of the bibliographies (see page 456) as a way of collecting relevant results. Your instructor may ask you to hand these in to gauge your progress. Remember that online citation machines like bibme.org can help you compile these results in the appropriate format (MLA or APA).

Advanced Internet Research Techniques

I love the word "portal." It summons images of a little window on some vast space-ship that frames the face of an open-mouthed observer looking in wonder at the vast reaches of the universe beyond. Researching on the Internet is a lot like peeping out of that window. There is just so much out there: billions of documents, gazillions of words, each a fragment of electronic data floating in cyberspace, like dust motes in some vast sunbeam. There's useful knowledge for academic writing out there, but it's hard to find and it's easy to get lost.

You're no stranger to the Web, of course, but now, more than ever, your research on the Internet needs to be *efficient*. You need fewer, more focused results and better-quality results. To get these, you need to amp up your Internet search skills by understanding the differences among search engines and what each can do to maximize your penetration of information on the Web.

Types of Search Engines

The most popular search engine is Google, a search engine with an enormous database that is relatively simple to use. It's easy to forget sometimes that Google is in good company; there are plenty of powerful alternatives that may generate some different results. In fact, studies in recent years consistently show that the major search engines turn up different results as much as 85 percent of the time! It obviously pays off for researchers to use more than one.

Here's a partial list of the best of these general research engines.

POPULAR GENERAL SEARCH ENGINES

AltaVista (http://www.altavista.com)

Ask.com (http://www.ask.com)

Bing (http://www.bing.com)

Google (http://www.google.com)

Lycos (http://www.lycos.com)

Yahoo! Search (http://search.yahoo.com)

Google and the others are really quite amazing, but they do have limitations. For one thing, they only index pages on the Web that have hyperlinks pointing to them elsewhere or whose creators have requested they be indexed by a particular search tool. In addition, these databases may not be current.

There are so-called metasearch tools such as Dogpile (http://www.dogpile.com/) that are able to deploy multiple general search engines in the service of a single search (see the following list). These are very useful, particularly at the beginning of an Internet search on your topic. However, metasearch engines aren't quite as good as they sound because they skim off the top results from each individual search tool, so you won't see the range of results you would get if you focused on one of the search engines with its own large database.

METASEARCH ENGINES

Dogpile (http://www.dogpile.com)

Mamma (http://www.mamma.com)

Search.com (http://www.search.com)

Yippy (http://yippy.com)

Finally, there are also specialized search engines (sometimes called "vertical" search engines) that focus on particular subjects such as education, politics, and psychology, as well as search engines that specialize in searching certain *kinds* of content, like finding people, images, blogs, and so on. You probably already use a specialized search engine (and might not know it) when you use a site like Pricegrabber (http://www.pricegrabber.com) to comparison shop online. In the last chapter, you were also introduced to Google Scholar, another example of a search portal that focuses on specialized content, in this case journal articles and books. There are so many of these that a list—even if it were selective—wouldn't do justice to these focused Web crawlers. One place to visit online to help you find a relevant specialized search engine for your project is Noodletools (http://www.noodletools.com/). Click on the link at the bottom of the site's page for "Choose the Best Search."

What are the keys to maximizing the efficiency of your Internet research? In the exercise that follows, you'll learn to do the following:

1. Increase your coverage by using multiple search engines, not just your favorite one.
2. If possible, exploit subject directories that allow you to drill down from general to more specific topic categories. These are often put together by people—not software—who are concerned with quality content.
3. Be thoughtful about what and how many keywords you use to search. Generally, the more words—and especially phrases—you use, the more likely you are to generate relevant hits. This contrasts with searching library databases, which respond better to more focused keywords and phrases.

EXERCISE 16.2.2 Academic Research on the Internet

STEP 1: You already searched on your topic on a general search engine—probably Google—and in the last chapter you tried Google Scholar. Now, using some of the keyword combinations you developed for your topic, try at least two more general search engines from the list on page 462. Remember to play around with keywords, and don't forget the search language you learned earlier in this chapter. The Help button on whatever metasearch tool you use will give you the specifics on what connectors—Boolean or others—it accepts.

STEP 2: Launch a search using one or more of the metasearch engines listed on page 463. Save your relevant results.

STEP 3: Finally, visit Noodletools (http://www.noodletools.com/) and find the link for "Choose the Best Search." Scroll down and find a search engine, perhaps a specialized one, that you haven't tried yet. As before, save relevant results.

STEP 4: Add to your bibliography (see "Keeping Track of What You Find" on page 456) by including Web pages that seem promising, and print copies of them for notetaking. A Web-based citation machine like bibme.org can help you with this.

Living Sources: Interviews and Surveys

Arranging Interviews

A few years ago, I researched a local turn-of-the-century writer named Sarah Orne Jewett for a magazine article. I dutifully read much of her work, studied critical articles and books on her writing, and visited her childhood home, which is open to the public in South Berwick, Maine. My research was going fairly well, but when I sat down to begin writing the draft, the material seemed flat and lifeless. A few days later, the curator of the Jewett house mentioned that there was an 88-year-old local woman, Elizabeth Goodwin, who had known the writer when she was alive. "As far as I know, she's the last living person who knew Sarah Orne Jewett," the curator told me. "And she lives just down the street."

The next week, I spent three hours with Elizabeth Goodwin, who told me of breakfasting with the famous author and eating strawberry jam and muffins. Elizabeth told me that many years after Jewett's death, the house seemed haunted by her friendly presence. One time, when Elizabeth lived in the Jewett house as a curator, some unseen hands pulled her back as she teetered at the top of the steep staircase in the back of the house. She likes to believe it was the author's ghost.

This interview transformed the piece by bringing the subject to life—first for me as the writer, and later for my readers. Ultimately, what makes almost any topic compelling is discovering why it matters to *people*—how it affects their lives. Doing interviews with people close to the subject, both experts and nonexperts, is often the best way to find that out.

If you'd like to do some interviews, now is the time to begin arranging them.

Finding Experts   You may be hesitant to consider finding authorities on your topic to talk to because, after all, you're just a lowly student who knows next to nothing. How could you possibly impose on that sociology professor who published the book on anti-Semitism you found in the library? If that's how you feel, keep this in mind: *Most people, no matter who they are, love the attention of an interviewer, no matter who she is, particularly if what's being discussed fascinates them both.* Time and again, I've found my own shyness creep up on me when I pick up the telephone to arrange an interview. But almost invariably, when I start talking with my interview subject, the experience is great for us both.

So, how do you find experts to interview?

- *Check your sources.* As you begin to collect books, articles, and Internet documents, note their authors and affiliations.

- *Check the phone book.* The familiar Yellow Pages can be a gold mine. Carin, who was writing a paper on solar energy, merely looked under that heading and found a local dealer who sold solar energy systems to homeowners. Mark, who was investigating the effects of sexual abuse on children, found a counselor who specialized in treating abuse victims.

- *Ask your friends and your instructors.* Your roommate's boyfriend's father may be a criminal attorney who has lots to say about the insanity defense for your paper on that topic. Your best friend may be taking a photography course with a professor who would be a great interview for your paper on the work of Edward Weston. One of your instructors may know other faculty working in your subject area who would do an interview.

- *Check the faculty directory.* Many universities publish an annual directory of faculty and their research interests. On my campus, it's called the *Directory of Research and Scholarly Activities.* From it, I know, for example, that two professors at my university have expertise in eating disorders, a popular topic with student researchers.

- *Check the* Encyclopedia of Associations; *the* Encyclopedia of Associations: Regional, State, and Local Organizations; *or the* Encyclopedia of Associations: International Organizations. These references (also available online through some libraries) list organizations with interests ranging from promoting tofu to preventing acid rain. Each listing includes the name of the group, its address and phone number, a list of its publications, and a short description of its purpose. Sometimes such organizations can direct you to experts in your area who are available for live interviews or to spokespeople who are happy to provide phone interviews.

- *Check the Internet.* You can use the Internet to find the e-mail addresses and phone numbers of many scholars and researchers, including those affiliated with your own university and ones nearby. Often, these experts are listed in online directories for their colleges or universities. Sometimes you can find knowledgeable people by subscribing to a listserv or Internet discussion group on your topic. Often an expert will have her own Web page, and her e-mail address will provide a hypertext link. (For more details, see "Finding People on the Internet," later in this chapter on page 469.)

Finding Nonexperts Affected by Your Topic   The distinction between *expert* and *nonexpert* is tricky. For example, someone who lived through 12 months of combat in Vietnam certainly has direct knowledge of the subject, though probably hasn't published an article about the war in *Foreign Affairs*. Similarly, a friend who experienced an abusive relationship with her boyfriend or overcame a drug addiction is, at least in a sense, an authority on abuse or addiction. Both individuals would likely provide invaluable interviews for papers on those topics. The voices and the stories of people who are affected by the topic you're writing about can do more than anything else to make the information come to life, even if they don't have PhDs.

You may already know people you can interview about your topic. Last semester, Amanda researched how mother-daughter relationships change when a daughter goes to college. She had no problem finding other women anxious to talk about how they get along with their mothers. A few years ago, Dan researched steroid use by student athletes. He discreetly asked his friends if they knew anyone who had taken the drugs. It turned out that an acquaintance of Dan's had used the drugs regularly and was happy to talk about his experience.

If you don't know people to interview, try posting notices on campus kiosks or bulletin boards. For example, "I'm doing a research project and interested in talking to people who grew up in single-parent households. Please call 555-9000." Also, poll other students in your class for ideas about people you might interview for your paper. Help each other out.

Making Contact   By the end of this week, you should have some people to contact for interviews. First, consider whether to ask for a face-to-face, telephone, or e-mail interview. Though I've never tried it for this purpose, Skype, the free online software that allows users to make a video call anywhere in the world, might be a great interview tool. The personal interview is almost always preferable; you not only can listen, but can also watch, observing your subject's gestures and the setting, both of which can be revealing. When I'm interviewing someone in her office or home, for example, one of the first things I may jot down are the titles of books on the bookshelf. Sometimes, details about gestures and settings can be worked into your paper. Most of all, the personal interview is preferable because it's more natural, more like a conversation.

Be prepared. You may have no choice in the type of interview. If your subject is off campus or out of state, your only options may be the telephone, e-mail, or regular mail.

When contacting a subject for an interview, first state your name and then briefly explain your research project. If you were referred to the subject by someone she may know, mention that. A comment like "I think you could be extremely helpful to me" or "I'm familiar with your work, and I'm anxious to talk to you about it" works well. When thinking about when to propose the interview with an expert on your topic, consider arranging it *after* you've done some research. You will not only be more informed, but you will also have a clearer sense of what you want to know and what questions to ask.

Conducting Interviews   You've already thought about whether interviews might contribute to your paper. If there's a chance that they will, build a list of possible interview subjects and contact several of them. By the end of this week, you should begin interviewing.

I know. You wouldn't mind putting it off. But once you start, it will get easier and easier. I used to dread interviewing strangers, but after making the first phone call, I got some momentum going, and I began to enjoy it. It's decidedly easier to interview friends, family, and acquaintances, but that's the wrong reason to limit yourself to people you know.

Whom to Interview?   Interview people who can provide you with what you want to know. That may change as your research develops. In your reading, you might have encountered the names of experts you'd like to contact, or you may have decided that what you really need is some anecdotal material from someone with experience in your topic. It's still not too late to contact interview subjects who didn't occur to you earlier, but do so immediately.

What Questions to Ask?   The first step in preparing for an interview is to ask yourself, What's the purpose of this interview? In your research notebook, make a list of *specific questions* for each person you're going to interview. Often, these questions are raised by your reading or other interviews. What theories or ideas encountered in your reading would you like to ask your subject about? What specific facts have you been unable to uncover that your interview subject may provide? What don't you understand that he could explain? Would you like to test one of your own impressions or ideas on your subject? What about the subject's work or experience would you like to learn? Interviews are wonderful tools for clearing up your own confusion and getting specific information that is unavailable anywhere else.

Now make a list of more *open-ended questions* you might ask some or all of the people you're going to talk to. Frankly, these questions are a lot more fun to ask because you're likely to be surprised by some of the answers. For example:

- In all your experience with _____, what has most surprised you?
- What has been the most difficult aspect of your work?
- If you had the chance to change something about how you approached _____, what would it be?
- Can you remember a significant moment in your work on _____? Is there an experience with _____ that stands out in your mind?
- What do you think is the most common misconception about _____? Why?
- What are significant current trends in _____?

- Who or what has most influenced you? Who are your heroes?
- If you had to summarize the most important thing you've learned about _____, what would it be?
- What is the most important thing other people should know or understand?

As you develop both specific and open-ended questions, keep in mind what you know about each person—his work in the field and personal experience with your topic. You may end up asking a lot of the same questions of everybody you interview, but try to familiarize yourself with any special qualifications a subject may have or experiences he may have had. That knowledge might come from your reading, from what other people tell you about your subject, or from your initial telephone call to set up the interview.

Also keep in mind the *kinds* of information an interview can provide better than other sources: anecdotes, strong quotes, and sometimes descriptive material. If you ask the right questions, a live subject can paint a picture of his experience with your topic, and you can capture that picture in your paper.

During the Interview. Once you've built a list of questions, be prepared to ignore it. Interviews are conversations, not surveys. They are about human interaction between two people who are both interested in the same thing.

I remember interviewing a lobsterman, Edward Heaphy, on his boat. I had a long list of questions in my notebook, which I dutifully asked, one after the other. My questions were mechanical and so were his answers. I finally stopped, put my notebook down, and talked informally with Edward for a few minutes. Offhandedly, I asked, "Would you want your sons or daughter to get in the business?" It was a totally unplanned question. Edward was silent for a moment, staring at his hands. I knew he was about to say something important because, for the first time, I was attentive to him, not my notepad. "Too much work for what they get out of it," he said quietly. It was a surprising remark after hearing for the last hour how much Edward loved lobstering. What's more, I felt I had broken through. The rest of the interview went much better.

Much of how to conduct an interview is common sense. At the outset, clarify the nature of your project—what your paper is on and where you're at with it. Briefly explain again why you thought this individual would be the perfect person to talk to about it. I find it often helps to begin with a specific question that I'm pretty sure my subject can help with. But there's no formula. Simply be a good conversationalist: Listen attentively, ask questions that your subject seems to find interesting, and enjoy sharing an interest with your subject. Also, don't be afraid to ask what you fear are obvious questions. Demonstrate to the subject that you *really* want to understand.

Always end an interview by making sure you have accurate background information on your subject: name (spelled correctly), position, affiliation, age (if applicable), phone number. Ask if you can call him with follow-up questions, should you have any. And always ask your subject if he can recommend any additional reading or other people you should talk to. Of course, mention that you're appreciative of the time he has spent with you.

Notetaking.   There are basically three ways to take notes during an interview: Use a digital recorder, a notepad, or both. I adhere to the third method, but it's a very individual choice. I like digital recorders (smartphones work great, by the way) because I don't panic during an interview that I'm losing information or quoting inaccurately. I don't want to spend hours transcribing interviews, so I also take notes on the information I think I want to use. If I miss anything, I consult the recording later. Sometimes, I find that there is no recording—the machine decided not to participate in the interview—but at least I have my notes.

Get some practice developing your own notetaking technique by interviewing your roommate or taking notes on the television news. Devise ways to shorten often-used words (e.g., *t* for *the, imp* for *important,* and *w/o* for *without*).

The E-Mail Interview

The Internet opens up new possibilities for interviews; increasingly, experts (as well as nonexperts interested in certain subjects) are accessible through e-mail and even Facebook. While electronic communication doesn't quite approach the conversational quality of the conventional, face-to-face interview, the spontaneous nature of e-mail exchanges can come pretty close. It's possible to send a message, get a response, respond to the response, and get a further response—all in a single day. And for shy interviewers and interviewees, an e-mail conversation is an attractive alternative.

Finding People on the Internet.   Finding people on the Internet doesn't have to involve a needle and hay if you have some information on the person for whom you're looking. If you know an expert's name and his organizational affiliation, several search tools may help you track down his e-mail address. You can, of course, Google the person. But there are other methods, too.

For example, an easy way to use the Internet to find someone to interview is through a Web document on your topic. These often include e-mail links to people associated with the site or document. You can also find academics by visiting the Web sites of the universities or colleges where they teach and using the online faculty/staff directories to find their addresses. If you don't know the institutions with which an academic is affiliated, you can often find these listed in their articles, books, or Web page. To find the home pages of hundreds of American universities and colleges, visit the following site: the Yahoo Education Directory (http://dir.yahoo.com/Education/). This search page allows you to find the home pages of universities in the United States. It includes links to a number of sites that also index colleges and universities, as well as their various programs.

Making Contact by E-Mail.   Once you find the e-mail address of someone who seems a likely interview subject, proceed courteously and cautiously. One of the Internet's haunting issues is its potential to violate privacy. Be especially careful if you've gone to great lengths in hunting down the e-mail address of someone involved with your research topic; she may not be keen on receiving unsolicited e-mail messages from strangers. It would be courteous to approach any potential interview subject with a short message that asks permission for an online interview. To do so, briefly describe your project and why you think this individual might be a good source for you. As always, you will be much more likely to get an enthusiastic response from someone if you can demonstrate your knowledge of her work on or experience with your topic.

Let's assume your initial contact has been successful and your subject has agreed to answer your questions. Your follow-up message should ask a *limited* number of questions—say, four or five—that are thoughtful and, if possible, specific. Keep in mind that while the e-mail interview is conducted in writing rather than through talking, many of the methods for handling conventional interviews still apply.

The Discussion Board and Listserv Interview. Discussion or message boards can be good places to find people—and sometimes experts—who are passionately interested in your research topic or question. How do you find one that might be relevant to your project? Try visiting one of the following directories, which list these sites by subject.

SEARCH ENGINES FOR DISCUSSION GROUPS

BoardReader (http://boardreader.com)

BoardTracker (http://www.boardtracker.com)

Google Groups (http://groups.google.com)

Yahoo! Groups (http://groups.yahoo.com)

A way to get some help with knowing what to ask—and what not to—is to spend some time following the discussion of list participants before you jump in yourself. You might find, for example, that it would be far better to interview one participant with interesting views than to post questions to the whole list.

But if you do want to query the discussion board, avoid posting a question that may have already received substantial attention from participants. You can find out what's been covered by consulting the list's FAQs (frequently asked questions). The issue you're interested in may be there, along with a range of responses from list participants, which will spare you the need to ask the question at all.

Planning Informal Surveys

Christine was interested in dream interpretation, especially exploring the significance of symbols or images that recur in many people's dreams. She could have simply examined her own dreams, but she thought it might be more interesting to survey a group of fellow students, asking how often they dream and what they remember. An informal survey, in which she would ask each person several standard questions, seemed worth trying.

You might consider it, too, if the responses of a group of people to some aspect of your topic could reveal a pattern of behavior, attitudes, or experiences worth analyzing. Informal surveys are decidedly unscientific. You probably won't get a large enough sample size, nor do you likely have the skills to design a poll that would produce statistically reliable results. But you probably won't actually base your paper on the survey results, anyway. Rather, you'll present specific, concrete information about some patterns in your survey group or, perhaps, use some of your findings to help support your assertions.

Defining Goals and Audience   Begin planning your informal survey by defining what you want to know and whom you want to know it from. Christine suspected that many students have dreams related to stress. She wondered if there were any similarities among students' dreams. She was also curious about how many people remember their dreams and how often and whether this might be related to gender. Finally, Christine wanted to find out whether people have recurring dreams and, if so, what those were about. There were other things she wanted to know, but she knew she had to keep the survey short.

If you're considering a survey, make a list in your research notebook of things you might want to find out and specify the group of people you plan to talk to. College students? Female college students? Attorneys? Guidance counselors? Be as specific as you can about your target group.

Paper or Electronic?   After you mull over the purpose of your survey, you need to decide whether you'll distribute it electronically or on paper. These days, free online software like the popular SurveyMonkey (see Figure 16.2.10) allows users to easily create basic digital surveys. You can distribute the survey to a targeted list of recipients by e-mail or post it on a blog, Web site, or even on social media like Facebook and Twitter. In addition, a program like SurveyMonkey helps you analyze the results and filter, compare, and summarize the data with charts and graphs. Web-based surveys are also cheaper than paper surveys.

Why *wouldn't* you want to go digital instead of using old-fashioned paper surveys? A couple of reasons:

- With paper, you can target an audience much more easily, particularly if you can actually *locate* those potential respondents in a specific time or place. For example, if you want to survey your school's football fans, distributing your survey on game day at the tailgate party will give you direct access to your survey audience.
- Not everyone has easy Internet access.
- The free versions of the online software may limit the number of responses you can gather.
- Response rates to electronic surveys can be lower than response rates to paper surveys.

Despite these drawbacks, a Web-based survey is often the best choice for an undergraduate research project, particularly if you can find ways to target your audience, make a personal appeal for a response, and send out a reminder or two.

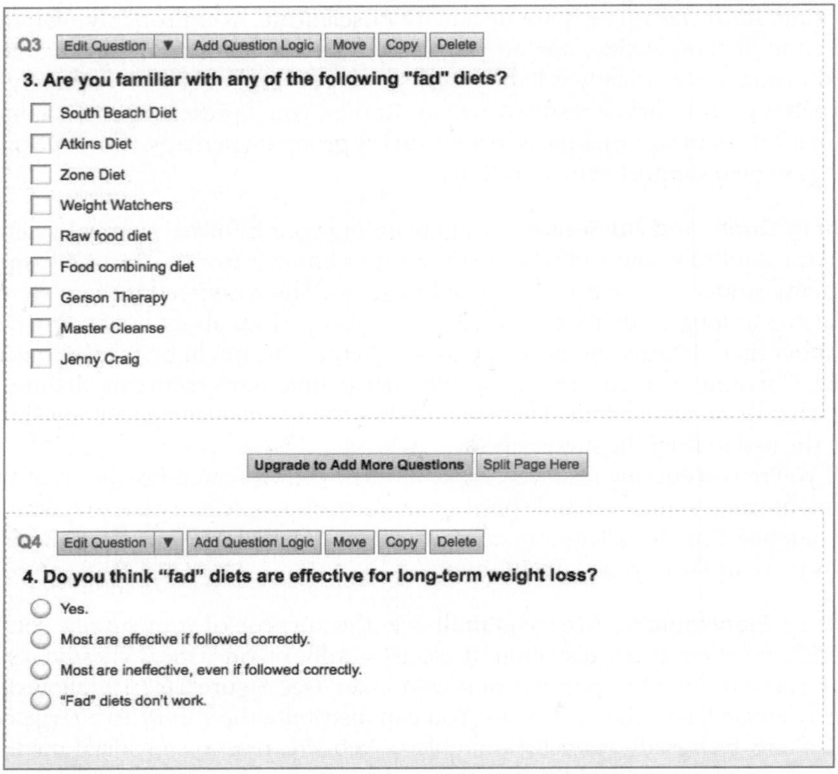

FIGURE 16.2.10 **A Sample Online Survey.** A student researching fad diets used SurveyMonkey to design and distribute her survey. This screen shot shows several of her questions, which are structured rather than open-ended. The key with structured questions like these is that you have to know enough about your subject to know the appropriate answers.

Types of Questions There are typically two broad categories of survey questions: open-ended and structured. Below you can see the advantages and disadvantages of each for your survey.

Question Type	Examples	Advantage	Disadvantage
Open-ended	Brief response, essay question	May get surprising answers. More insight into respondents' thoughts and ideas.	Take more time. Can't easily be measured.
Structured	Multiple choice, true/false, Likert, ranking	Easier to analyze responses. Don't take much time.	Must know enough to provide appropriate choices.

Generally speaking, you should limit the number of open-ended questions you use since they are more demanding on the respondents. But don't hesitate to use them if you hope to open a window on the thinking of your survey audience. These responses might not reveal a pattern, but they often provide interesting anecdotal evidence that you can use in your essay.

Crafting Questions   A survey shouldn't be too long (probably no more than six or seven questions, and fewer if you rely mostly on open-ended questions), it shouldn't be biased (questions shouldn't skew the answers), it should be easy to score (especially if you hope to survey a relatively large number of people), it should ask clear questions, and it should give clear instructions for how to answer.

As a rule, informal surveys should begin (or end) as polls often do: by getting vital information about the respondent. Depending on the purpose of your survey, you might also want to know whether respondents are registered to vote, whether they have political affiliations, what year of school they're in, or any number of other factors. Ask for information that provides different ways of breaking down your target group.

Avoid Loaded Questions.   Question design is tricky business. Biased questions should be avoided by altering language that is charged and presumptuous. Take, for example, the question *Do you think it's morally wrong to kill unborn babies through abortion?* This wording is charged and is also presumptuous (it is unlikely that all respondents believe that abortion is killing). One revision might be *Do you support or oppose providing women the option to abort a pregnancy during the first 20 weeks?* This is a direct and specific question, neutrally stated, that calls for a yes or no answer.

Controversial topics, like abortion, are most vulnerable to biased survey questions. If your topic is controversial, take great care to eliminate bias by avoiding charged language, especially if you have strong feelings yourself.

Avoid Vague Questions.   Another trap is asking vague questions. One such question is *Do you support or oppose the university's alcohol policy?* This wording assumes that respondents know what the policy is, and it ignores the fact that the policy has many elements. A revised question might ask about one part of the policy: *The university recently established a policy that states that underage students caught drinking in campus dormitories are subject to eviction. Do you support or oppose this policy?* Other equally specific questions might ask about other parts of the policy.

Drawbacks of Open-Ended Questions.   Open-ended questions often produce fascinating answers, but they can be difficult to tabulate. Christine's survey on dream interpretation asked, *Please briefly describe the dream you best remember or one that sticks out in your mind.* She got a wide range of answers—or sometimes no answer at all—but it was hard to quantify the results. Almost everyone had different dreams, which made it difficult to discern much of a pattern. However, she was still able to use some of the material as anecdotes in her paper, so it turned out to be a question worth asking.

Designing Your Multiple-Choice Questions.   As you've seen, the multiple-choice question is an alternative to the open-ended question, leaving room for a number of *limited* responses, which are easier to quantify.

The challenge in designing multiple-choice questions is to provide choices that will likely produce results. For example, from her reading and talking to friends, a student studying fad diets came up with a comprehensive list of the most popular diets (see Figure 16.2.10). Design choices you think your audience will respond to, but consider giving them room to say your choices weren't theirs by including a "none of the above" option or an open-ended "other" selection that allows respondents to insert their own answers.

Using Scaled Responses.   The best-known of these types of questions is the Likert scale, which provides respondents with the chance to express their levels of agreement or disagreement with a statement. Typically, you'd provide a related group of statements. For example, suppose you wanted to collect some data on how students feel about rider traffic on campus. Using a Likert's scale, you might develop a series of questions like those below.

	Strongly Agree	Agree	Undecided	Disagree	Strongly Disagree
1. Speeding bicyclists are a problem on the quad.	1	2	3	4	5
2. Speeding skateboarders are a problem on the quad.	1	2	3	4	5
3. The university should consider a policy that requires bicyclists to dismount when on the quad.	1	2	3	4	5
4. . . .	1	2	3	4	5

Conducting Surveys   Once you have finalized your questions, you can make plans to distribute the survey to the target group you defined earlier. Though surveys can be distributed by phone and mail (remember that?), it's far more likely that you'll distribute your survey online or in person. We'll concentrate on those two methods.

In-Person Surveys.   The university community, where large numbers of people are available in a confined area, lends itself to administering surveys this way. A survey can be distributed in dormitories, dining halls, classes, or anywhere else the people you want to talk to gather. You can stand outside the student union and stop people as they come and go, or you can hand out your survey to groups of people and collect them when the participants have finished. Your instructor may be able to help distribute your survey to classes.

Although an exclusively university audience won't always be relevant, for some research questions it is exactly what's needed. Anna, writing a paper on date rape, surveyed exclusively women on campus, many of whom she found in women's dormitories. For his paper on the future of the fraternity system, David surveyed local "Greeks" at their annual awards banquet.

How large a sample should you shoot for? Because yours won't be a scientific survey, don't bother worrying about statistical reliability; just try to survey as many people as you can. Certainly, a large (say, more than 100) and representative sample will lend more credence to your claims about any patterns observed in the results.

Internet Surveys.   You can reach respondents online in the following ways:

1. E-mail
2. Social media like Facebook
3. Listservs, discussion groups
4. Posting survey link on a blog or Web page

Of these, targeted e-mail and online discussion groups of relevant people are likely to be the most productive. Marketing specialists often buy e-mail lists, an unlikely option for the undergraduate. That's why posting a link to your survey on a relevant online forum or listserv can be so effective, since you can match the subject of your survey to people who discuss that subject online. You must, of course, first subscribe to one or more of these lists, and it always helps to listen in on the conversation before you make an appeal for survey respondents. Make sure this group is the appropriate one to answer your questions. Try searching Google Groups to find potential respondents.

Posting a link to your survey on Facebook or Twitter will get it out to potentially many more people, but you should expect a very low response rate.

Fieldwork: Research on What You See and Hear

My daughter Julia, as a senior in high school, belonged to the school's theater group, performing in plays and taking theater classes. She enjoyed it. But she also claimed that certain qualities distinguished "theater kids" from other kinds. How did she come to these conclusions? By hanging out with the theater crowd. To use a more academic phrasing, Julia was a "participant-observer," though there was certainly no method involved. We all make judgments about social groups, inferences that come from experience. Usually there's nothing systematic about this process, and sometimes these judgments are unfair.

Yet the data that comes from observation, particularly if we take care to collect and document it, can be a rich vein to mine. This kind of data is also relevant to research in the social sciences and humanities and even to research essays in composition courses. Suppose, for instance, that your research question focuses on comparing crowd behavior at college and high school football games. How can you research that essay *without* observing a few games? If your topic has anything do to with subcultures or social groups—say, international students on your campus or the snowboarding community—fieldwork can be invaluable.

Preparing for Fieldwork

The kind of fieldwork you're able to do for your essay simply won't be the more rigorous and methodologically sophisticated work that academic ethnographers, anthropologists, or sociologists do. For one thing, you don't have the time it requires. But you can collect some useful observations for your paper. There are three tools for this you might find useful:

1. *Notebook.* You can't do without this. For convenience, you might choose a pocket notebook rather than a full-size one.
2. *Digital camera.* Use your camera or smartphone to take pictures of the site you're observing and the people participating in an activity for later study. Also photograph objects (ethnographers call these "artifacts") that have symbolic or practical significance to the people you're observing.
3. *Digital recorder.* Use it for interviews and other recording in the field. (Remember to ask permission to record interviewees.) Smartphones these days can fulfill both your recording and your video needs.

Where you go to conduct field observations of course depends on your topic. Typically you choose a physical space in which people in particular social or cultural groups meet to participate in meaningful (to them) activities. If your research is on the high school theater group as a subculture, you might go to rehearsals, auditions, or perhaps a cast party. A researcher interested in adult video gaming addiction might spend a few evenings watching gamers do their thing at someone's home. An essay on Kwanzaa, an African American holiday tradition, might observe some families participating in its rituals.

Notetaking Strategies

What do you look for and how do you document it? Well, that depends on your project. Generally, of course, the task is to watch what people do and listen to what they say. More specifically, though, consider the following:

• *Look for evidence that confirms, contradicts, or qualifies the theories or assertions you've read about in your research.* Is it true that when they're not playing, adult video gamers can appear irritable and depressed? Do dogs that are punitively corrected during a training class demonstrate submissive behavior?

• *Look and listen to what people say during moments with particular significance for participants.* How do fans behave when the referee doesn't call the foul? What does one gamer say to another when she beats him?

- *Describe "artifacts"—things that people in the situation typically use.* A skater's skateboard. The objects in an actor's dressing room. The clothing traditionally worn by women celebrating Kwanzaa.

When you take notes, consider using the double-entry journal system that is discussed in detail in the next chapter. Use the left-facing page of your notebook to scribble your observations and the right-facing page to later freewrite about what strikes you about these observations. Make sure that you clearly indicate when you are quoting someone and when you are describing something.

Using What You See and Hear

Unless your research topic is an ethnography—an investigation that describes and interprets the activities of a cultural group in the field—it's likely that you will use your own fieldwork in your essay in a relatively limited way. Still, it can really be worth the effort. For example, fieldwork can be especially useful to:

- *Give your topic a face.* Nothing makes a problem or idea more meaningful than *showing* how it affects people. Can you use your descriptions of individuals (perhaps along with your interviews) to show rather than simply explain why your topic is significant?

- *Make a scene.* Observations in the field give you the ingredients of a scene: In a particular time and place, people are *doing something.* If what they are doing is significant and relevant to your research question, you can describe the place, the people, the action, and even the dialogue. Few techniques give writing more life.

- *Incorporate images.* Depending on the nature of your project, the digital pictures you take in the field can be powerful illustrations of what you're writing about.

- *Develop a multimodal research essay.* Using the digital recordings you made in the field and free editing software like Audacity, you can create a podcast of your research essay, even incorporating music. You can use free software like Microsoft Photo Story to use images, text, and voice narration to present your findings.

EXERCISE 16.2.3　DataViz: Tell a Story with Facts

By week's end, you should have a learned enough about your project to be surprised. Maybe you thought something is true when you started only to discover it isn't. Maybe you encountered some information or some perspective on the problem that few people know. Maybe there's some fascinating data that highlights the need to solve the problem or answer the question. Information, when effectively selected and arranged, can turn these discoveries into stories that have the potential to not just enlighten but to surprise, and one of the most dramatic mediums for factual storytelling these days is the infographic.

Infographics help people *visualize* information. They can explain a process, highlight a trend or interesting finding, or make an argument; but they do this through *showing,* not just telling. Imagine, for example, that I want to highlight the trend of songbird declines in the

United States. I could simply illustrate this with a bar graph. But I could also illustrate it using a visual metaphor. Maybe I could have a row of bird silhouettes (passenger pigeons?) that get smaller and smaller, correlating with overall population declines over time. Even without the exact data on declines, the visualization dramatizes them for an audience.

To end the week, design a simple infographic from the research you've gathered so far that uses graphics, images, graphs, and texts to dramatize a key finding, trend, process, or argument relevant to your research topic. I'm not a designer, and I'm guessing you aren't either, so these infographics likely won't be appropriate for you to Tweet to the world. But fortunately, there are some free online programs that can help you with design. The best of these is infogr.am, which provides templates, charts, and maps that might prove useful. To see what one student did using the program, see Figure 16.2.11.

As you design your infographic, keep the following things in mind:

1. **Keep it simple.** You're not trying to visualize your entire topic but only the small part of it that you find interesting. Less is more.
2. **Minimize text.** Let the visual representations carry the load.
3. **Use metaphor.** Think about the things that typically symbolize how people see your subject. An infographic on the problem of prison overpopulation might use graphics of jail bars or prison stripes, one on the issue of American spending habits might use a pink piggy bank, and so on.

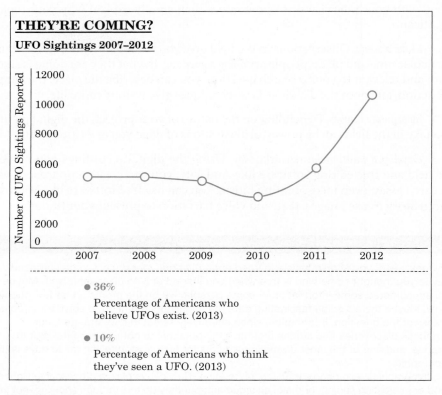

FIGURE 16.2.11 A simple infographic on the trend of increased UFO sightings. This was created with the online program infogram.

4. **Have good data.** It should be reliable, relevant, and *interesting*.

5. **Tell a story.** You're not just illustrating information, you're using it to dramatize a finding, process, trend, or argument. It should have a beginning, middle, and end and, ultimately, an implied or explicit point (e.g., songbirds are disappearing because of habitat destruction, and we have to do something about it!).

Your instructor may ask you to submit your infographic with a bibliography of sources.

16.3 USING YOUR SOURCES

In this section, you will learn to:

- Practice notetaking as a conversation with a source.

- Identify different types of borrowing from a source, which of these risk plagiarism, and what to do about it.

- Understand the triad of notetaking strategies—paraphrase, summary, and quotation—and use them in your own notes.

- Consider several techniques for notetaking that encourage written conversations with sources, and choose one that works for you as a research writer.

- Learn some advanced methods for researching on the Web or in the library, and use them to find additional information on your inquiry topic.

- Draft an annotated bibliography that explains and evaluates key sources on your topic.

Writing in the Middle

Tim's inquiry question explores the impact that an adult's addiction to video games has on family and friends. He spends a week collecting research, mostly printing out articles from library databases and Web sites. Tim skims things, underlining a line or a passage from time to time, but for the most part he's like a bear in a blueberry patch, voraciously collecting as much information as he can. This is all in preparation for the writing, which he'll postpone until right before the paper is due.

Sound familiar? This is certainly similar to the way I always did research.

Here's how I would rewrite this scene for Tim: Tim is still hungrily collecting information about video gaming addiction, *but as he collects it, he's writing about what he's found.* Tim's notebook is open next to his laptop, and he's jotting down quotations and summaries and maybe an interesting fact or two. He's also marking up the electronic copy, highlighting passages of an article he might want to return to, or cutting and pasting relevant passages into an open Word document. Then, when he's done reading the article, Tim writes furiously in his notebook for 10 minutes or so, exploring his reaction to what he found.

I now believe that the writing that takes place in the *middle* of the research process—the notetaking stage—may be as important as, if not more important than, the writing that takes place at the end—composing the draft. Writing in the middle helps you take possession of your sources and establish your presence in the draft. It sharpens your thinking about your topic, and it is the best cure for unintentional plagiarism.

I realize I have a sales job to do on this. Writing in the middle, particularly if you've been weaned on notecards, feels like busywork. "It gets in the way of doing the research," one student told me. "I just want to collect as much stuff as I can, as quickly as I can. Notetaking slows me down." Though it may seem inefficient, writing as you read may actually make your research *more* efficient. Skeptical? Read on.

Conversing

I went to dinner the other night at a friend of a friend's house, and while the hosts were lovely people, one of them talked too much. You know "conversations" like that? You say something like, "As a matter of fact, I'd love to go to Italy in June" or "The Chicago Cubs, what can you say about the Chicago Cubs?"; and before you can continue the thought, the person you're talking to takes your offhanded comment and runs with it for the next 10 minutes, while you smile and nod and wish you were somewhere else. That's how I think of the notes I took while writing research papers in high school. This time around, I'm hoping you'll disinvite yourself from that kind of dinner party.

Writing as you read is a genuine conversation between you and a source. If you imagine the qualities of a good conversation, you probably realize that they don't include just nodding and smiling while someone holds forth. On the contrary, a conversation involves a back-and-forth. You hear something that makes you think of something else, and then someone responds, and then you make a new connection with another idea or experience. It's a dialogue.

We don't often engage in a dialogue when we read to write. If we write at all, we mostly just write stuff down that the source said. This squanders some of the power of the writing process, which, yes, involves our recording things but, more importantly, allows us *to make meaning* and to follow our own words about a subject to see what we have to say about it. This is the power I hope you'll harness when you use writing to engage in conversations with what you read.

But first, let me show you how this can work for you.

EXERCISE 16.3.1 Getting into a Conversation with a Fact

Through writing, facts can ignite thought, if we let them. They can help us discover what we think and refine our point of view. But for this to happen, you have to interact with information. Rather than a monologue—simply jotting down what an author is saying—you engage in a conversation—talking *with* an author: questioning, agreeing, speculating, wondering, connecting, arguing. You can do this in your head, but it's far more productive to have this dialogue through writing.

Let's try it.

I'm going to share with you two facts—one at a time—that together start to tell an interesting story about gender, beauty, and culture. Each fact will be a prompt for about 5 minutes of fastwriting in which you explore your thinking about the fact.

STEP 1: How do women see men's "attractiveness"? *Harper's Magazine* recently reported the following:

> **Portion of men whose attractiveness is judged by U.S. women to be "worse than average": 4/5**

What do you make of this? Does it surprise you? Assuming it's true, how would you explain it? If you doubt it's true, why? Fastwrite your response for 5 minutes.

STEP 2: Now that you've done 5 minutes of "thinking through writing" about how women view men, consider how men view women's "attractiveness."

> **Portion of women whose attractiveness is judged by U.S. men to be "worse than average": 2/5**

What do you make of men's more generous attitude toward women? Does this surprise you? How might you explain both "facts"? Together, what does this information say to you about gender and "attractiveness"? Fastwrite for 5 minutes, exploring these questions.

As you reread your two fastwrites, do you see any consistent line of thought developing? If someone asked you what you thought about these two facts, what would you say?

In a small way, you've just practiced a method of notetaking that can help you make sense of information you encounter when you read for your research project or read any other text you want to think about. Later in this chapter, I'll show you something called the "double-entry journal," which is a system for using this technique. But in this exercise, you have practiced the essence of writing in the middle: seeing information as the beginning of a conversation, not the end of one.

Exploring your reaction to what you read during an open-ended fastwrite is only part of using information to discover what you think. You must also *understand* what you're reading. Most *good* conversations make demands on both speakers. The most important of these is simply to listen carefully to what the other person is saying, even (and perhaps especially) if you don't agree. In couples therapy there's a method to help this along called "say back"—each partner has to listen first and then repeat what he or she heard the other say. Response or reaction comes later. Researchers entering into a conversation with their sources need to engage in the same practice: You need to listen or read carefully, first making an effort to understand a subject or an author's arguments or ideas and then exploring your response to them, as you did earlier in this exercise.

The academic equivalent of "say back" is paraphrasing or summarizing, something we'll look at in more detail later in this chapter. Both are undervalued skills, I think, that require practice.

Informally writing your responses is a way to hold up your end of a conversation with a source, but when you actually *use* sources in your essay, you have an obligation to use them responsibly. Beyond quoting source material accurately, citing the right page numbers, and spelling names correctly, you're obligated to represent the source's ideas fairly. This includes making it clear which ideas and words come from the source and which come from you. Frankly, this takes practice. Give it a try in Exercise 16.3.2.

> EXERCISE 16.3.2   "Say Back" to a Source
>
> Read the following brief essay on "what college is for" by the President of Amherst College, and then write a paragraph summary of what it says, highlighting what you think are the main ideas. This time, leave out any comments you have about the ideas in the piece; just try to "say back" as accurately as you can what you think the writer is saying.
>
> **What Is College For?**
>
> *Carolyn A. (Biddy) Martin*
>
> *President of Amherst College*
>
> College is for the development of intelligence in its multiple forms. College is the opportunity for achievement, measured against high standards. College is preparation for the complexities of a world that needs rigorous analyses of its problems and synthetic approaches to solving them. College is for learning how to think clearly, write beautifully, and put quantitative skills to use in the work of discovery. College is for the cultivation of enjoyment, in forms that go beyond entertainment or distraction, stimulating our capacity to create joy for ourselves and others. College is for leave-taking, of home and of limiting assumptions, for becoming self-directed, while socially responsible.
>
> In his 2005 commencement speech at Kenyon College, the brilliant writer and Amherst graduate David Foster Wallace ('85), defined the value of the liberal arts in the following terms: "The real, no bullshit value of your liberal-arts education is how to keep from going through your comfortable, prosperous, respectable lives dead, unconscious, a slave to your head and to your natural default settings."
>
> For all the tragic irony of Wallace's point, given his own premature death, his admonition holds. A spate of recent books have enjoined us to distinguish between our natural default settings and our ability to reason on the basis of evidence—between what Daniel Kahneman calls, for example, our "fast" and "slow" thinking, or the automatism housed in one part of our brain and the ability to reflect in another.
>
> College is for finding a calling, or many callings, including the calls of friendship and love. It is for the hard work of experimentation, failure, reflection, and growth. It is about the gains we make and the losses that come with them. In an age of sound bites and indignation, college is for those who are brave enough to put at risk what they think they know in recognition of the responsibility we have to one another and to those still to come.

A Taxonomy of Copying

My colleague Casey Keck, a linguist, studied how students paraphrase sources and ways to describe students' brushes with plagiarism. Casey notes that there are four kinds of borrowing:

- **Near copy:** About half of the borrowed material is copied from the source, usually in a string of phrases. The bolded phrases are lifted verbatim from "What Is College For?", the essay in the above exercise.

  *Example: Students shouldn't necessarily go to college just to focus on a particular job but also to prepare for **the complexities of a world that needs rigorous analyses** and to **create joy for ourselves and others.***

- **Minimal revision:** Less than half but more than 20 percent is copied from the original. Notice that the quotation marks appropriately signal at least one borrowed phrase from the original.

  *Example: Martin says David Foster Wallace **defined** what it means to go to college as learning to avoid being "a slave to your head" and being **brave enough** to **risk what they think they know.***

- **Moderate revision:** Less than 20 percent is copied from the original, and mostly individual words are mentioned only once in the source.

  *Example: Martin says that college is the search for a **calling,** but this isn't necessarily a professional one. It includes a willingness to try new things and risk both **failure** and **growth**.*

- **Substantial revision:** Though the paraphrase might include a few general words that are used a few times in the original text, there are no copies of phrases or unique words that appear in the source.

  Example: According to Martin, college is an opportunity to reimagine ourselves—to break with old ways of thinking, and find delight in something other than the usual "distraction" and "entertainment."

Evaluate your own summary of the "What Is College For?" essay to see if any of it involves borrowing from the original source in these four categories. Remember, this is just practice!

Plagiarism Q & A

1. **So I can't take *any* words from the original source?** Yes, of course you can, but try to steer clear of unique words, and especially avoid using the same string of words unless you put them in quotation marks.

2. **If I add an attribution tag (e.g., "According to _____,"..., or _____ argues that...") or include a citation, does that mean I can copy things from a source?** Attribution tags and citations are really useful for your readers and are a good way to credit authors for their ideas, but they aren't licenses to use source material without the usual signals—like quotation marks—that you've copied something.

3. **Is it a problem if I paraphrase a source and follow pretty much the same structure of the original in terms of the order of ideas?** Technically, that is a form of plagiarism, and practically speaking, it's far better to restate a source in the order that reflects what *you* think are the important ideas.

4. **How do I credit the same information that I found in, say, four different books?** You may not have to. Check out the "common knowledge" exception on page 484.

What Is Plagiarism?

Each college or university has a statement in the student handbook that offers a local definition. But that statement probably includes most or all of the following forms of plagiarism:

1. Handing in someone else's work—a downloaded paper from the Internet or one borrowed from a friend—and claiming that it's your own.
2. Handing in the same paper for two different classes.
3. Using information or ideas from any source that are not common knowledge and failing to acknowledge that source.
4. Using the exact language or expressions of a source and not indicating through quotation marks and citation that the language is borrowed.
5. Rewriting a passage from a source, making minor word substitutions, but retaining the syntax and structure of the original.

The Common Knowledge Exception

While you always have to tell readers what information you have borrowed and where it came from, things that are "common knowledge" are excluded from this. But what is "common knowledge"? The answer, in part, is considering what is common knowledge to *whom*. Each field makes different judgments about that. In addition, knowledge is constantly changing, so what may be accepted fact today could be contested tomorrow. What's the undergraduate researcher to do? Scholar Amy England suggests that you consider something common knowledge if you find the exact same information in four or more different sources.

5. **I've got a lot of my own ideas about my topic. Do I risk plagiarizing if someone else has the same ideas but I don't know about it?** No, you can't know what you don't know. But the point of research is that it helps *expand* your ideas about a topic. If you encounter a source that repeats an idea you already hold, look more closely to see what you didn't already know: a fresh context, a slightly different angle, a new bit of supporting evidence. Then think again. Can you revise your own ideas, discovering new insights that do reflect your own thinking?

Why Plagiarism Matters

It may seem that concern over plagiarism is just a lot of fuss that reflects English teachers' obsession with enforcing rules. In reality, the saddest days I've ever had as a writing teacher have always been when I've talked with a student about a paper she downloaded from the Internet or borrowed from her roommate. Most instructors hate dealing with plagiarism.

Deliberate cheating is, of course, an ethical issue, but the motive for carefully distinguishing between what is yours and what you've borrowed isn't just to "be good." It's really about making a gesture of gratitude. Research is always built on the work that came before it. As you read and write about your topic, I hope that you come to appreciate the thoughtful writing and thinking of people before you who may have given you a new way of seeing or thinking.

Knowledge is a living thing (see Figure 16.3.1), growing like a great tree in multiple directions, adding (and losing) branches that keep reaching higher toward new understandings. As researchers we are tree climbers, ascending the branches in an effort to see better. It's only natural that as we make this climb, we feel grateful for the strength of the limbs supporting us. Citing and acknowledging sources is a way of expressing this gratitude.

The Notetaker's Triad: Quotation, Paraphrase, and Summary

Taylor is writing a paper on plastics in the ocean, and from the European Environment Commission Web site, she cuts and pastes the following text into a Word document:

> Marine litter is a global concern, affecting all the oceans of the world. Every year, approximately 10 billion tons of litter end up in the ocean world wide, turning it into the world's biggest landfill and thus posing environmental, economic, health, and aesthetic problems. Sadly, the persistence of marine litter is the result from poor practices of solid waste management, lack of infrastructure, and a lack of awareness of the public at large about the consequences of their actions.*

She likes the passage—it succinctly states the problem of ocean pollution and even includes a powerful statistic: 10 billion tons of garbage end up in the world's oceans each year. Now, what can she do with it?

FIGURE 16.3.1 As researchers, we're tree climbers, standing on branches that other researchers before us have grown. Citation identifies the wood we're standing on that has helped us to see further into our topic.

*From http://ec.europa.eu/environment/water/marine/pollution.htm. © European Union, 1995–2011. Reproduction is authorized.

Consider her choices:

1. Do nothing. Set the passage aside and hope there will be a place in her paper where she can digitally dump the whole thing or part of it.
2. Rewrite all or part of it in her own words. Set the rewrite aside and hope to weave it into her paper later.

Student writers often face this dilemma, and in the digital age, when it's easy to cut and paste text, choice #1 is the odds-on favorite. Just collect and dump. What this usually means in the draft research essay is a quotation. In some cases, this is justified. Perhaps the material *is* so well said that you want the voice of the source to speak for itself. But more often, a cut-and-paste quotation—particularly an extended one—looks like a sign of surrender: Instead of actively guiding the reader through information, the writer opts to take a nap.

What about choice #2? How might Taylor rewrite the passage to establish herself as a reliable guide?

> None of the world's oceans are spared from pollution, notes the European Environment Commission, which also reports that 10 billion tons of garbage are dumped in the world's oceans every year. They now represent "the world's biggest landfill" ("Marine Pollution Awareness").

In the rewrite, Taylor mines the original passage selectively, emphasizing what she thinks is important but without misrepresenting what was said. Here is a writer who is controlling information rather than being controlled by it.

The relationship between a source and a research writer is often complex, for various reasons. Consider how difficult it can be to read someone else's words, make an effort to understand what they mean, and then find your own words to restate the ideas. What's worse is that sometimes the authors are experts who use language you may not easily grasp or use reasoning in ways you can't easily follow. And then there are those authors who write so beautifully, you wonder how you could possibly say it better. Finally, you might fear that somehow you will goof and accidentally plagiarize the source's ideas or words.

One useful, if somewhat crude, way of describing how a writer might take possession of the information she gathers is in terms of three approaches you've no doubt heard of before: paraphrase, summary, and quotation. These are useful to learn about, not only so that you know the rules for how to employ them, but, perhaps more important, so that you can see each as a different way of interacting with what you read. Ultimately, they are tools that keep you in the game.

Paraphrasing

In Exercise 16.3.2, you practiced "say back," a technique that helps many married couples who may be headed for divorce. As I mentioned, *paraphrase* is the academic equivalent of this therapeutic method for getting people to listen to each other. Try

to say in your own words—and with about the same length as the author said it—
what you understand the author to mean. This is hard, at first, because instead of
just mindlessly quoting—a favorite alternative for many students—you have to
think. Paraphrasing demands that you make your own sense of something. The time
is well worth it. Why? Because not only are you lowering the risk of unintentional
plagiarism and being fair to the source's ideas, *you are also essentially writing a fragment
of your draft.*

To put it most simply, at the heart of paraphrasing is this very simple idea: *Good
writers find their own ways of saying things.*

Summarizing

In order to sell a movie to Hollywood, a screenwriter should be able to summarize
what it's about in a sentence. "*Juno* is a film about a smart, single, pregnant teenager
who finds unexpected humor in her situation but finally finds that her wit is not
enough to help her navigate the emotional tsunami her pregnancy triggers in the
lives of those around her." That statement hardly does justice to the film—which is
about so much more than that—but I think it basically captures the story and its
central theme.

Obviously, that's what a *summary* is: a reduction of longer material into a brief
statement that captures a basic idea, argument, or theme from the original. Like paraphrasing, summarizing often requires careful thought. This is especially the case
when you're trying to capture the essence of a whole movie, article, or chapter that's
fairly complex. Many times, however, summarizing involves simply boiling down a
passage—not the entire work—to its basic idea.

While a summary can never be purely objective, it needs to be fair. After all, each
of us will understand a text differently, but at the same time we have to do our best to
represent what a source is actually saying without prejudice. That's particularly a
challenge when you have strong feelings about a topic.

Quoting

I'll never forget the scene from the documentary *Shoah,* an 11-hour film about the
Holocaust, that presents an interview with the Polish engineer of one of the trains
that took thousands of Jews to their deaths. As an old man still operating the same
train, he was asked how he felt about his role in World War II. He said quietly, "If you
could lick my heart, it would poison you."

It would be difficult to restate the Polish engineer's comment in your own words.
But more important, it would be stupid even to try. Some of the pain and regret and
horror of that time in history are embedded in that one man's words. You may not
come across such a distinctive quote as you read your sources this week, but be alert to
how authors (and those quoted by authors) say things. Is the prose unusual, surprising,
or memorable? Does the writer make a point in an interesting way? If so, jot it down in
your journal or cut and paste it into a digital file, making sure to signal the borrowed
material with quotation marks.

There are several other reasons to quote a source as you're taking notes.

- To bring in the voice, not just the ideas, of a notable expert on your topic.
- To quote someone who says something effectively that supports a key point you're trying to make.
- When you're writing an essay that uses primary sources—a literary text, a transcript, and so on—quoted material is essential.

As a general rule, however, the college research paper should contain no more than 10 or 20 percent quoted material. This principle sometimes gets ignored because it's so easy to just copy a passage from a source and paste it into an essay. But keep in mind that a writer who quotes does not really need to think much about and take possession of the information, shaping it and allowing herself to be shaped by it. Still, you can retain a strong presence in your work even when using the words of others if you remember to do the following:

1. *Quote selectively.* You need not use all of the passage. Mine phrases or sentences that are particularly distinctive, and embed them in your own prose.
2. *Provide a context.* The worst way to use a quote is to just drop it into a paragraph without attribution or comment. If you're going to bring someone else's voice into your work, you should, at the very least, say who the source is and perhaps indicate why what this person says is particularly relevant to what you're saying.
3. *Follow up.* In addition to establishing a context for a quotation, seize the chance to analyze, argue with, amplify, explain, or highlight what is in the quotation.

As an example of effective use of quotation, consider the following excerpt from Bill Bryson's book *At Home: A Short History of Private Life*. Bryson is especially talented at telling compelling nonfiction stories using research, and here he explains the fears of people in the nineteenth century about being buried alive. In this case, Bryson incorporates a "block quotation"—that is, the passage he quotes is set off and indented, as is required in MLA style for passages of more than four [*MLA Handbook*, p. 94] lines.

> According to one report, of twelve hundred bodies exhumed in New York City for one reason or another between 1860 and 1880, six showed signs of thrashing or other postinternment distress. In London, when the naturalist Frank Buckland went looking for the coffin of the anatomist John Hunter at St. Martin-in-the-Fields Church, he reported coming upon three coffins that showed clear evidence of internal agitation (or so he was convinced).... A correspondent to the British journal *Notes and Queries* offered this contribution in 1858:
>
> > A rich manufacturer named Oppelt died about fifteen years since at Reichenberg, in Austria, and a vault was built in the cemetery for the reception of the body by his widow and children. The widow died about a month ago and was taken to the same tomb; but, when it was opened for the purpose, the coffin of her husband was found open and empty, and the skeleton discovered in the corner of the vault in a sitting posture.
>
> For at least a generation such stories became routine in even serious periodicals. So many people became morbidly obsessed with the fear of being interred before their time that a word was coined for it: *taphephobia*.

Notice that Bryson provides a context for his quotation—the name of the source—and then follows up the quoted passage by noting that the story it tells is typical of nineteenth-century fears of being buried alive. He also notes that the anecdote is an illustration of what was then called taphephobia. Bryson's book is not an academic work, so you don't see citations, something that you will incorporate into your own essay, but you can see how a powerful quotation can bring the work to life, especially when it's sandwiched within the commentary of a writer who chooses to allow another voice to speak.

Notetaking

There's the skills part of notetaking—knowing how to cite, summarize, paraphrase, and quote correctly—and then there's the more interesting, harder part—making *use* of what you're reading to discover what you think. So far, we've talked about this latter process using the metaphor of conversation. In Exercise 16.3.1, you tried out this idea, responding in writing to facts about gender and notions of "attractiveness." This conversation metaphor doesn't originate with me. Lots of people use it to describe how all knowledge is made. One theorist, Kenneth Burke, famously explained that we might imagine that all scholarship on nearly any subject is much like a parlor conversation between people in the know (see the box "The Unending Conversation" below). These are the experts who, over time, have contributed to the discussions about what might be true and who constantly ask questions to keep the conversation going.

As newcomers to this conversation, we don't really have much to contribute. It's important that we listen in so that we begin to understand what has already been said and who has said it. But at some point, even novices like us are expected to speak up. We're not there to simply record what we hear. We're writers. We're supposed to discover something to say.

The Unending Conversation

Imagine that you enter a parlor. You come late. When you arrive, others have long preceded you, and they are engaged in a heated discussion, a discussion too heated for them to pause and tell you exactly what it is about. In fact, the discussion had already begun long before any of them got there, so that no one present is qualified to retrace for you all the steps that had gone before. You listen for a while, until you decide that you have caught the tenor of the argument; then you put in your oar. Someone answers; you answer him; another comes to your defense; another aligns himself against you, to either the embarrassment or gratification of your opponent, depending upon the quality of your ally's assistance. However, the discussion is interminable. The hour grows late, you must depart. And you do depart, with the discussion still vigorously in progress.

Kenneth Burke

Fortunately, we rarely enter the parlor empty handed. We have experiences and other prior knowledge that are relevant to the conversation we're listening in on. For example, you certainly know something about the subject of Thomas Lord's essay, "What? I Failed? But I Paid for Those Credits! Problems of Students Evaluating Faculty." After all, you've probably filled out an evaluation or two for a course you've taken. But clearly, Lord, as a science educator, has spent considerably more time than you considering whether these evaluations are useful for judging the quality of teaching. Yet college writers, even if they have limited expertise, are expected to speak up on a topic they're writing about, entering the conversation by raising questions, analyzing arguments, speculating, and emphasizing what they think is important.

EXERCISE 16.3.3   Dialogic Notetaking: Listening In, Speaking Up

Drop into the conversation that Thomas Lord has going in his essay, and, drawing on what you've learned so far, use your journal writing to listen in and speak up.

STEP 1:
1. Begin by listening in. Read Thomas Lord's essay once straight through. Underline and mark passages that you think are:
   a. important to your understanding of the article,
   b. puzzling in some way,
   c. surprising, or
   d. connected with your own initial ideas and experiences.
2. Reread the opening paragraph, the last few paragraphs, and all of your marked passages; then, without looking at the article, compose a three- or four-sentence summary of what you understand to be the most important thing the article is saying. Write this down on the left-hand page of your notebook.
3. Find two passages in the article that you think are good examples of what you state in your summary. Copy these on to the left-hand page of your notebook, too. Or if you're doing this on your computer, use the Table function to create two columns, and use the left one.

STEP 2: Now speak up. Use the right-hand side of your notebook to explore your thinking about what Lord is saying. Look on the left-hand pages to remind yourself of some of his ideas and assertions. This is an open-ended fastwrite, but here are some prompts to get you writing and thinking:

- Tell the story of your thinking:
  - *Before I read about this topic, I thought _____, and then I thought _____, and then _____, and then...but now I think _____.*
- Consider ways you've begun to think differently:
  - *I used to think _____, but now I'm starting to think _____.*
- Try both believing and doubting:
  - *The most convincing points Lord makes in his essay are _____. or Though I don't necessarily agree with Lord, I can understand why he would think that _____.*
  - And then: *The thing that Lord ignores or fails to understand is _____. or The least convincing claim he makes is _____ because _____.*

- Consider questions:
  - *The most important question Lord raises is _____.*
  - *The question that he fails to ask is _____.*

Discuss in class how this notetaking exercise worked. What went well? What was difficult? How did your initial thoughts influence your reading of the article? Did your thinking change? Which of these techniques will you continue to use in your notetaking?

What? I Failed? But I Paid for Those Credits! Problems of Students Evaluating Faculty*

Thomas Lord

Thomas Lord (trlord@grove.iup.edu) is a professor in the Department of Biology at the Indiana University of Pennsylvania in Indiana, Pennsylvania.

Late one afternoon several days ago, I was startled by a loud rap on my office door. When I opened it, I immediately recognized a student from the previous semester clutching the grade slip he had just received in the mail. Sensing his anger and frustration, I invited him in to discuss his scores. I was surprised that he had not anticipated the failing grade because his exam scores were abysmal, his class work was marginal, and his attendance was sporadic. When I scooted my chair over to my computer to open the course's spreadsheet to review his grade, he told me he didn't have an argument with the test, class, and attendance records. His reason for coming to see me was to ask how he could get his refund. He had, after all, paid for the credits, right? I was astonished. In all my years in higher education, this was the first time I had been asked for a refund.

A day later over lunch, a colleague remarked that with the nation's troublesome economy, many universities have turned to the business model of running the institution. "The business model," he acknowledged, "focuses on financial efficiency while maintaining a quality product."

"Perhaps so," another colleague responded, "but the principal foundation of the business model is the notion of satisfying the customer. Because the products of a college are its graduates, it requires the college to meet their expectations for both a quality education and a gratifying experience. This is nearly impossible if the college wants to retain its integrity and high standards."

Furthermore, what students expect from their college experience varies greatly. A quality, highly respected education is, of course, always desirable, but

*"What? I Failed? But I Paid for Those Credits! Problems of Students Evaluating Faculty" by Thomas Lord from *Journal of College Science Teaching*, November/December 2008. Used by permission of the National Science Teachers Association.

(Continued)

that's about as common as the expectations get. Some college students relish the liberal challenges universities can provide, some look for a cultural experience, and others simply want to be trained for a career. A large number of undergraduates seek strong intercollegiate athletic or theater programs, and some students are most interested in an exciting social life. This diversity is where the difficulty lies. With such an assortment of demands and expectations, it's simply not possible for any institution to provide it all and maintain a student-as-consumer philosophy. Many universities have tried, and in so doing, have undercut their reputation. Several decades ago, education theorist David Reisman (1981) wrote, "This shift from academic merit to student consumerism is one of the two greatest reversals of direction in all the history of American Higher Education; the other being the replacement of the classical college by the modern university a century ago."

Despite Reisman's statement, the student-as-consumer philosophy has become more widely spread in academic institutions over the last two decades, and with it has come a tendency for students to have a stronger voice in higher education (d'Apollonia and Abrami 1997). It is common nowadays for student representatives to serve on university committees. Students are often consulted on ventures that include curriculum, discipline, regulation, and campus construction. In many schools, segments of the institution's governance are shared with students. My institution, for example, retains two students on the University Executive Board.

But by far the greatest number of student voices impacting the institution is in the evaluation of the instructors. The practice was first implemented at Purdue University in 1927, when surveys were distributed to students in a sociology class to solicit their opinions of the course (Remmers 1927). The surveys were not shared with the administration, but were retained by the professors as feedback for self-improvement. Two years later, Remmers revised the surveys to include "student ratings of their instructor's teaching and what they have learned in the course." The researcher reported his finding at a national professional meeting, and soon other universities began soliciting instructor ratings on their campuses. Course and instructor evaluations remained benign until the 1960s, when students discovered the power their united voices could make in higher education. During this time, students began vocalizing their resistance to the war in Vietnam, the ills of the environment, and the materialism of society. It was a time of student free speech about ethical, cultural, and racial issues. Suddenly, evaluations of instructors and courses became more about student satisfaction than about a professor's instructional effectiveness.

———

When the driving mechanism for faculty evaluations shifts from educating to pleasing, many problems occur. "Student evaluations of their professors are impacted heavily by student perception," states Professor Stanley Fish, dean emeritus at the University of Illinois (2007). "When student experiences

(Continued)

in classes do not match their prior expectations, they react in negative ways. Students may begin to boycott classes they're unhappy with, they may write complaint letters to administrators, or they may challenge the academic integrity of their professors. Some students may become so disrespectful of the professor that they circulate their feelings in the press, on the internet, and over the airways." In 1965, for example, students at the University of California–Berkeley generated a review of teacher performance in a manual entitled *The Slate Supplement,* and sold it at the campus bookstore. "Most of the opinions in the manual were ill-informed and mean-spirited," recalls Fish. "The opinions weren't from professionals in the field but transient students with little or no stake in the enterprise who would be free (because they were anonymous) to indulge any sense of grievance they happened to harbor in the full knowledge that nothing they said would ever be questioned or challenged. The abuse would eventually affect the careers and livelihoods of faculty members especially the young, nontenured professors" (Selvin 1991). In addition, with the negative exposure, university officials became alarmed that the dissatisfaction would lead to students dropping their courses or leaving the university altogether. With the mounting anxieties, many instructors countered by lowering the expectations in their courses. A survey of faculty found 70% of professors believe that their grading leniency and course difficulty bias student ratings, and 83% admitted making their course easier in response to student evaluations (Ryan, Anderson and Birchler 1980).

This was nicely demonstrated when Peter Sacks, a young journalism instructor, was hired on a tenure track at a small northwest college. At the end of the first semester, Sacks, an accomplished writer but not yet an accomplished teacher, found himself in trouble with student evaluations. When he started, Sacks resolved to maintain a high quality in his courses by emphasizing critical thinking about issues. Although he found it extremely difficult, he stuck with his plan for the entire semester, and as a consequence, received terrible student evaluations. Fearing that he would lose his tenure-track appointment after the spring term, he decided to change his tactics and attempt to achieve higher evaluations by deliberately pandering to his students. At the end of his three-year trial, he had dramatically raised his teaching evaluations and gained tenure. Sacks shamelessly admits he became utterly undemanding and uncritical of his students, giving out easy grades, and teaching to the lowest common denominator (1986). Other researchers have confirmed that lenient grading is the most frequently used faculty strategy to counter abusive student assessment (Howard and Maxwell 1982; Greenwald 1997).

Another problem with the business model is that students truly believe they're paying for their credits and not their education. Consumers are used to paying for merchandise that can later be returned for a refund with no questions asked. The student confusion over this probably resides in the way

(Continued)

universities charge pupils for the credits they're taking (at least for students attending part time or over the summer). If, for example, a high school biology teacher decided to upgrade his or her knowledge of wildflowers and enrolled in a three-credit course at a local college on spring flora, the teacher would be charged for the three credits. If the teacher decided to continue the learning the following semester on summer wildflowers, he or she would again pay for the three credits. It's not hard, therefore, to see how the idea of paying for credits rather than earning them came about.

A final reason why student evaluations are an unreliable way to assess faculty is that most students simply don't know what good teaching is. Undergraduates generally have a vision of how college teaching is conducted from depictions in movies or hearing tales from former students. The most common view is that professors stand before a class and recite, write on the chalkboard, or use PowerPoint slides to get across the information students should know in the lesson (McKeachie 1992).

I asked my students what they thought made a great instructor and was told the best professors move unhurriedly through their notes, speaking at a slow-to-moderate pace, explaining the information the students need to learn. One student told me that good professors don't get sidetracked by superficial chunks of information and don't waste time off the subject. Some students also suggested that competent professors are entertaining when they lecture and frequently use demonstrations and videos to back up their presentations. Many class members said the best professors repeat several times the items that are the most salient and hold review sessions before each exam to reaffirm the important content.

Most contemporary theorists, however, tell us that top instructors don't do most of those things. According to education leaders, competent teachers seldom lecture to a gallery of passive students, but provide experiences and directions that actively challenge class members to think and discover information (Handelsmen et al. 2004). Practiced professors believe understanding is the driving force for learning and spend a great amount of preclass time orchestrating team-based learning situations for the upcoming class. Proponents of student-centered instruction acknowledge that active participation in classes and discovery-based laboratories help students develop the habits of mind that drive science (Udovic et al. 2002). Furthermore, while traditional instructors create factual recall questions for their exams where students reiterate what they were told in class, contemporary teachers challenge students to discover the answers through application, synthesis, or evaluation (Huitt 2004). Quality teachers understand what agronomist George Washington Carver meant in 1927 when he wrote, "I know nothing more inspiring than discovering new information for oneself" (Carver 1998).

Students also believe that the best professors don't expect class members to know information that the professor hasn't covered in lecture. Students

(Continued)

don't seem to realize that education is the art of using information, not the art of restating it. College graduates must understand that once they're out of school, they'll depend on their education to get them through life. Often will they have to address unfamiliar questions. As I've stated previously, "Once they're out of college, students can't fall back on the answer, 'I don't know 'cause it wasn't covered by my professor'" (Lord 2007).

Enough has been written on this matter that colleges and universities should justify why they continue to use student evaluations to assess their faculty. "The answer is already known," answers Cahn (1986). "Institutions of higher education provide faculty evaluations to students to assess student satisfaction. Not only are the evaluations easy to grade and inexpensive to administer, but they give the impression of objectivity in comparison with more subjective measures such as letters from observers since student evaluations produce definite numbers."

"The role of the university is leadership, not a servant of consumer demands as the current business model requires," states Wilson (1998). "Universities certainly have a responsibility for the safety, well-being, and satisfaction of the people they serve, but they also have a responsibility to educate the people as well. With their dignity and reputation on the line, the most important responsibility is to certify that their graduates are truly educated. Under the consumer model, the goals of satisfaction and education are sometimes in conflict. It is important, therefore, that the metaphor of students as consumers be replaced by the metaphor of students as apprentices" (Haskell 1997).

References

Cahn, S. 1986. *Saints and scamps: Ethics in academia.* Totowa, NJ: Rowman and Littlefield.

Carver, G.W. 1998. *The all-university celebration.* Iowa City, IA: University Press.

d'Apollonia S., and P. Abrami. 1997. Navigating student ratings of instruction. *American Psychologist* 52 (11): 1198–1208.

Fish, S. 2007. Advocacy and teaching. *Academe* 93 (4): 23–27.

Greenwald, A.G. 1997. Validity concerns and usefulness of student ratings. *American Psychologist* 52 (11): 1182–86.

Handelsman, J., D. Ebert-May, R. Beichner, P. Burns, A. Chang, R. DeHann, J. Gentile, S. Luffefer, J. Stewart, S. Tukgnab, and W. Wood. 2004. Scientific thinking. *Science* 304 (5670): 521–22.

Haskell, R. 1997. Academic freedom, tenure and student evaluation of faculty: Galloping polls in the 21st century. *Education Policy Analysis Archives* 5 (6): 43.

Howard, G., and S. Maxwell. 1982. Linking raters' judgments. *Evaluation Review* 6 (1): 140–46.

(Continued)

...continued What? I Failed? But I Paid for Those Credits! **Thomas Lord**

Huitt, W. 2004. Bloom et al's taxonomy of the cognitive domain. *Educational Psychology Interactive.* http://chiron.valdosta.edu/whuitt/col/cogsys/bloom. html. Valdosta, GA: Valdosta University Press.

Lord, T. 2007. Putting inquiry to the test: Enhancing learning in college botany. *Journal of College Science Teaching* 36 (7): 56–59.

McKeachie, W. 1992. Student ratings: The validity of use. *American Psychologist* 52 (11): 1218–25

Reisman, D. 1981. *On higher education: The academic enterprise in an era of rising student consumerism.* San Francisco: Jossey Bass.

Remmers, D. 1927. Experimental data on the Purdue rating scale. In *Student ratings of instructors: Issues for improving practice,* eds. M. Theall and J. Franklin. 1990. San Francisco: Jossey Bass.

Ryan, J., J. Anderson, and A. Birchler. 1980. Student evaluation: The faculty responds. *Research in Higher Education* 12 (4): 395–401.

Sacks, P. 1986. *Generation X goes to college.* LaSalle, IL: Open Court Press.

Selvin, P. 1991. The raging bull at Berkeley. *Science* 251 (4992): 368–71.

Wilson, R. 1998. New research casts doubt on value of student evaluations of professors. *Chronicle of Higher Education* 44 (19): A2–A14.

Udovic, D., D. Morris, A. Dickman, J. Postlethwait, and P. Wetherwax. 2002. Workshop biology: Demonstrating the effectiveness of active learning in an introductory biology course. *Bioscience* 52 (3): 272–81.

Notetaking Techniques

In the first edition of *The Curious Researcher,* I confessed to a dislike of notecards. Apparently, I'm not the only one who feels that way. Mention notecards, and students often tell horror stories. It's a little like talking about who has the most horrendous scar, a discussion that can prompt participants to expose knees and bare abdomens in public places. One student even mailed me her notecards—50 bibliography cards and 53 notecards, all bound by a metal ring and color coded. She assured me that she didn't want them back—ever. Another student told me she was required to write 20 notecards a day: "If you spelled something wrong or if you put your name on the left side of the notecard rather than the right, your notecards were torn up and you had to do them over."

While it's true that some writers find notecards useful (and most teachers aren't finicky about their being done "correctly"), I'm convinced that notecards are too small for a good conversation. On the contrary, they seem to encourage "data dumps" rather than dialogue (see Figure 16.3.2).

But what's the alternative? You've already practiced one approach in the previous exercise, "Listening In, Speaking Up." There you used opposing sides of a notebook or Word document to summarize your understanding of an essay and collect

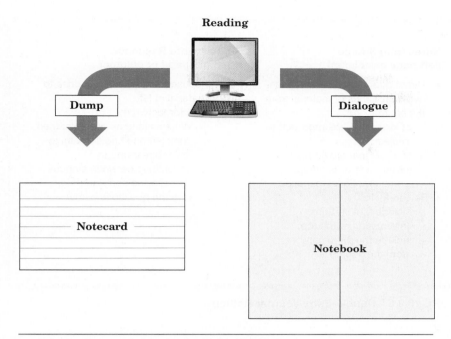

FIGURE 16.3.2　Notecards versus Notebooks

relevant passages, and then you told the story of your thinking about the reading. This is *knowledge making* rather than dump truck driving—you are going beyond simply recording and collecting information to actually *doing* something with it. You'll also practice a technique called the "double-entry" journal.

The Double-Entry Journal

The double-entry approach (see Figure 16.3.3) is basically this: Use opposing pages of your research notebook or opposing columns in a Word document—two columns and one row for each source. At the top of the page for each source, write down the bibliographic information for that source. Then, using the left side or column, compile your notes from a source—paraphrases, summaries, quotes. Put appropriate page numbers in the margin next to borrowed material or ideas. Then on the right side, comment on what you collected from each source. Imagine that the line down the middle of the page—or the spiral binder that divides opposing pages—is a table at which you sit across from an author with something to say about a topic you're interested in. Take care to listen to what the author says through paraphrase, summary, and quotation on the left, and then on the right respond with a fastwrite in which you give your own commentary, questions, interpretations, clarifications, or

**Notes from Source
(left page or column)**

- Direct quotations, paraphrases, and summaries of material from the source:
  - of ideas that are important to project
  - of ideas that are surprising or puzzling or generate some emotional response
- Be careful to:
  - include bibliographic information at the top;
  - include the page number from the source.

**Fastwrite Response
(right page or column)**

- Focused fastwrite in response to material at left
- Tips for fastwrite:
  - Write as long as possible; then look left and find something else to respond to.
  - Try shifting between stances of believing and doubting.
  - Use the questions below.

FIGURE 16.3.3 Double-Entry Journal Method

even feelings about what you heard. Your commentary can be pretty open ended, responding to questions such as the following:

- What strikes you? What is confusing? What is surprising?
- If you assume that this is true, why is it significant?
- If you doubt the truth or accuracy of the claim or fact, what is the author failing to consider?
- How does the information stand up to your own experiences and observations?
- Does it support or contradict your thesis (if you have one at this point)?
- How might you use the information in your paper? What purpose might it serve?
- What do you think of the source?
- What further questions does the information raise that might be worth investigating?
- How does the information connect to other sources you've read?

Refer to this list of questions (and any others that occur to you) as a prompt for the writing on the right side of your journal (or right column of your Word document). There are a variety of ways to approach the double-entry journal. If you're taking notes on the printout of an article or a photocopy from a book, try reading the material first and underlining passages that seem important. Then, when you're done, transfer some of that underlined material—quotes, summaries, or paraphrases—into the left column of your journal. Otherwise, take notes in the left column *as* you read.

While you take notes, or after you've finished, do some exploratory writing in the right column. This territory belongs to you. Here, through language, your mind and heart assert themselves over the source material. Use your notes in the left column as a trigger for writing in the right. Whenever your writing stalls, look to the left. The process is a little like watching tennis—look left, then right, then left, then right. Direct your attention to what the source says and then to what *you* have to say about the source. Keep up a dialogue.

Figures 16.3.4 and 16.3.5 illustrate how the double-entry journal works in practice. Note these features:

- Bibliographic information is recorded at the top of the page. Do that first, and make sure it's complete.
- Page numbers are included in the far-left margin, right next to the information that was taken from that page. Make sure you keep up with this as you write.
- While the material from the source in the left column may be quite formal or technical, the response in the right column should be informal and conversational. Try to write in your own voice. Find your own way to say things. And don't hesitate to use the first person: *I*.
- The writers often use their own writing to try to question a source's claim or understand better what that claim might be (e.g., "What the authors seem to be missing here…" and "I don't get this quote at all…").
- Seize a phrase from your source, and play out its implications; think about how it pushes your own thinking or relates to your thesis.
- In Figures 16.3.4 and 16.3.5, the writers frequently pause to ask themselves questions—not only about what the authors of the original sources might be saying but also what the writers are saying to themselves as they write. Use questions to keep you writing and thinking.

What I like about the double-entry journal system is that it turns me into a really active reader as I'm taking notes for my essay. That blank column on the right, like the whirring of my computer right now, impatiently urges me to figure out what I think through writing. All along, I've said the key to writing a strong research paper is *making the information your own*. Developing your own thinking about the information you collect, as you go along, is one way to do that. Thoughtful notes are so easy to neglect in your mad rush to simply take down a lot of information. The double-entry journal won't let you neglect your own thinking; at least it will remind you when you do.

The Research Log

The research log is an alternative to the double-entry journal that promotes a similar "conversation" between writer and source but with a few differences. One is that, like a Tonight Show host, the researcher starts with a monologue and always gets the last word. The standard format of the research log can serve as a template, that can be retrieved whenever you're ready to take notes on another source. Those notes can

Prior, Molly. "Bright On: Americans' Insatiable Appetite for Whiter-Than-White Teeth Is Giving Retailers Something to Smile About." *Beauty Biz* 1 Sept. 2005: 36–43. Print.

Teeth are no longer just for eating with—their appearance is becoming more important as a factor in a person's image, and they need to be perfectly white. (36)

Cosmetics companies are now entering territory once reserved for dentists as more and more people care mostly about the aesthetics of their teeth and smile. (36)

"Sephora is so enthusiastic about the [tooth-whitening] category, it named 'smile' its fifth retail pillar, joining the four others (makeup, fragrance, skin care and hair care) earlier this year." (37)

"The trend has shed its clinical beginnings and assumed a new identity, smile care. Its new name has been quickly adopted by a growing troupe of retailers, who hope to lure consumers with a simple promise: A brighter smile will make you look younger and feel more confident." (37)

Instead of going to the dentist and taking care of their teeth so they function well, people are investing a cosmetic interest in their teeth. People selling tooth-whitening products hope people associate whiter, more perfect teeth with higher self-esteem and social acceptance. (40)

"What says health, youth and vitality like a great smile?" (40)

I have noticed the increasing amount of importance that people put on the whiteness of their teeth, but this also seems to have increased with the amount of advertising for whitening products on TV and in magazines. I wonder if the whole thing is profit driven: Hygiene companies wanted to make more money, so instead of just selling toothbrushes and toothpaste, they created a whitening product and then worked to produce a demand for it. I almost feel really manipulated, like everyone's teeth were fine the way they naturally existed, and then all of the sudden a big company decided it needed to create a new product and sell it by making us feel bad about our smiles, and thus bad about ourselves.

The whole thing is sad, because once something becomes the societal "norm," we start to become obligated to do it. If everyone's teeth are beige, it's no problem when yours are too. But when everyone has sparkling white teeth, then it looks funny if you let yours stay brown. It either says "I don't have the money to whiten my teeth," or "I don't care about my appearance."

Sometimes it feels people might also judge you as being dirty, because white teeth seem healthier and cleaner than brown teeth, or lazy, for not spending the time to whiten your teeth. All those things are negative, and create a negative cloud around our teeth where we once felt good, or at least ambivalent. I don't like the way I'm being told my smile isn't good enough the way it is. I feel like when I smile it should just be about showing happiness and conveying that to others, not a judgment about me as a person.

FIGURE 16.3.4   Amanda's Double-Entry Journal. Here, Amanda concentrates on thinking through the implications of the summaries and quotations she collected from an article on teeth whitening.

Greenbaum, Jessica B. "Training Dogs and Training Humans: Symbolic Interaction and Dog Training." *Anthrozoos* 23.2: 129–141. Web. 10 Jan. 2010.

"The 'traditional' dominance-based method of training endorses obedience by using a human-centric approach that places dogs in a subordinate position in order to maintain a space in the family. The 'reward-based' behavior modification method promotes a dog-centric approach that highlights companionship over dominance...." (129)

Article seems to capture the essence of the debate: Is a well-behaved dog a product of dominance or companionship? Why can't it be both? One of the things that always strikes me about these binaries—either/or—is that it ignores both/and. Dogs will always have some kind of unequal relationship with their owners. Right? They have to. And won't they try to sort out, in their own way, the question of who is in charge?

"The methods we use to train our dogs reflect our perceptions of relationships between human and non-human animals. The socially constructed status of dogs, as pet or companion, influences the philosophy, methods, and training skills used." (129)

This seems key: "the socially constructed status of dogs" has an enormous influence on how we construe our relationship with them. Greenbaum draws the distinction as between "pet" and "companion." Behind those general terms is a whole set of ways in which we "socially construct" pets. A pet can be a companion, right? It doesn't necessarily imply subservience? I keep returning to the binaries that theorists draw. This is exactly the same thing that I notice with dog trainers themselves. There is a "right" and "wrong" way, and this divide is typically described as it is here: between positive reinforcement and negative reinforcement.

Mead discounted idea that animals can engage in symbolic communication with humans: "the ability to think was the ability to say." But article, using Sanders, argues that in a sense, pet owners "speak for" their animals. Sanders's research on police dogs, however, also highlighted the "ambiguity" of dog ownership—they are both companions and "tools." Subjective beings and objective things. (130)

This idea that we "speak for animals" strikes home, and I imagine that people like me who constantly give dogs and cats a human voice are more likely to favor "human-centric" methods. How can you put a shock collar on a dog that can talk back? But I never thought about this "ambiguity" between dogs as "tools" and "companions." Though wouldn't this be mostly true of people who train dogs for particular purposes? Is this ambiguity typical of most pet owners who don't?

FIGURE 16.3.5 **Double-Entry Journal.** Here's a double-entry journal entry that uses Word's Table feature to respond to an article I was reading on theories of dog training. I could copy and paste quotes from the original article, a PDF file, and drop them into the left column. Also notice, however, that I rely on summaries as well. Page numbers in parentheses follow borrowed material.

then be easily dropped into a draft as needed, using the Cut and Paste feature of your word processing program.

The basic approach is this:

1. Take down the full bibliographic information on the source—article, book chapter, Web page, or whatever (see Figure 16.3.6). Then read the source, marking up your personal copy in the usual fashion by underlining, making marginal notes, and so on.

2. Your first entry will be a fastwrite that is an *open-ended response* to the reading under the heading "First Thoughts." For example, you might begin by playing the "believing game," exploring how the author's ideas, arguments, or findings are sensible, and then shift to the "doubting game," looking for gaps, questions, and doubts you have about what the source says. You could write a response to any or all of the questions suggested for the double-entry journal.

3. Next, mine the source for nuggets. Take notes under the heading "Notes." These are quotations, summaries, paraphrases, or key facts you collect from the reading. They are probably some of the things you marked as you read the source initially. Make sure you include page numbers that indicate in the source where the material in your notes came from.

4. Finally, follow up with one more fastwrite under the heading "Second Thoughts." This is a second, *more focused* look at the source in which you fastwrite about what stands out in the notes you took. Which facts, findings, claims, or arguments that you jotted down shape your thinking now? If the writing stalls, skip a line, take another look at your notes, and seize on something else to write about.

Narrative Notetaking

This is the simplest method of all. As you read, mark up or annotate your source in the ways you usually do. After you read through it carefully, you will fastwrite a rapid summary for at least one full minute, beginning with the following prompt (see Figure 16.3.7):

> What I understand this to be saying is ....

Skip a line, and begin a second episode of fastwriting. Tell the story of your thinking, a narrative of thought that begins with what you initially might have believed about the topic covered in your source, and then how that thinking was influenced by what you read. This time, scribble (or type) for as long as you can without stopping, beginning with this prompt:

> When I first began reading this, I thought _____, and now I think _____.

Whenever your writing stalls, repeat the prompt again, inserting another discovery from your reading.

Project: Belief in Alien Abduction

Source: Kelley-Romano. "Mythmaking in Alien Abduction Narratives." *Communication Quarterly* 54.3 (August 2006): 383-406

Date: 11 November 2013

First Thoughts:
This article argues that alien abduction stories are essentially myths, and by this she doesn't mean necessarily "untrue," but that they are stories that a growing number of people tell themselves for the same reasons we've always told myths: They are instructive. Through interviews with 130 people who claim to have been abducted, Kelley-Romano identifies four of the most common narratives. These include the "salvation" narrative (aliens are coming to save us from ourselves), the "hybridization" narrative (they need us to reproduce with them and save their own kind)....What I find so interesting about this is that instead of dismissing alien abduction stories as tales told by crazy people, the author argues that they are actually mythical stories that can tell us a lot about not only the people who believe them but also the state of our culture....

Notes:
"An examination of this fascinating and significant phenomenon has the potential to inform our understanding of symbolic practices—exploring what it means to believe, and how we come to know. Most importantly, unlike religions and other codified systems of belief, the alien abduction myth—the Myth of Communion—is still developing. Beginning with the supposed crash of a UFO at Roswell in 1947 and fueled by the abduction of Betty and Barney Hill in 1961, believers in the abduction phenomenon have produced a set of narratives that continues to increase in complexity in both form and function." (384)

Unlike religious myth, the "alien abduction myth" is fluid—the narrative "continues to increase in complexity." (384)

The five elements of myth: heroes, "narrative form," "archetypal language," and focus on a particular place and time. (386)

There is a difference between myths and other kinds of stories like folk tales and fairy tales because myths are "accepted as true" by their believers. (387)

. . .

Second Thoughts:
As I think about my research question, this idea of the "myth of communion"—the alien abduction narrative that suggests that aliens are trying to integrate humanity into the "cosmos"—seems the most powerful explanation of why these stories seem to cultivate believers like religions do. As the author points out, believers who embrace this "myth of communion" see something "sacred" about the whole thing. Narrators who embrace the "myth of communion" view other alien abduction stories as relatively unenlightened, even "transcendent." The author really emphasizes how the need for such myths comes during certain times, and in the case of the "communion myth," this seems to be a time when people feel they need to be "rescued"....

FIGURE 16.3.6   Research Log

Focusing Question: How has cosmetic dentistry changed the way we think of the smile, and what are the repercussions?

Source: Walker, Rob. "Consumed; Unstained Masses." *New York Times*, 2 May 2004. Web. 10 Apr. 2009.

Rapid Summary (one minute):
What I understand this article to be saying is that the American public is getting more and more vain, as evidenced by the fact that tooth whitening is growing in popularity. While only celebrities used to modify the appearance of their teeth, now average people are doing it. Because of the value of appearance in our society, once we realize we can modify the way we look to our advantage, we seem to flock to it quickly. That's what's happening with the whole trend of smile care—we're using whiteners to change the way our teeth look so maybe we will be judged more profitably. And when a large percentage of society decides to buy something, there will always be corporations and retailers standing alongside to reap a profit.

Narrative of Thought (six minutes):
Before I started reading this article I thought that it was the capitalistic profit motive that had introduced whitening products and created a consumer demand for them. Now I understand that all of us as consumers have an equal responsibility with the companies that make and market such products, because we're the ones that buy them and change our standards of beauty. That makes me think that this is a complicated issue. While it's frustrating to feel like I can never be attractive enough, because the standard of attractiveness to which I'm held keeps getting harder and harder to meet, I'm the one that is interested in meeting it in the first place. While it would be easy to denigrate that as vanity, however, I can also see that being judged by others as attractive does have actual benefits, be it a higher salary or better treatment from strangers. In that case I'm put in a tough spot—I can work against the culture that tells me I don't look the right way, and feel negatively judged, or I can conform to it, and feel disappointed that I folded to social pressure. This isn't just an issue about people whitening their teeth for fun, it's about how society changes its standards and how quickly we assimilate to them—and why.

FIGURE 16.3.7 Amanda's Narrative Notes

Online Research Notebooks

These days, academic researchers frequently work with digital documents, especially PDF files. While it's always a good idea to print out hard copies of anything you use, it's also convenient to annotate and mark up electronic copies. In addition to highlighting passages, it's also possible with some software to insert comments. These can be much like responses in the double-entry journal.

The problem is that most of the software that can annotate PDF files isn't free. For example, while anyone can download Adobe Reader to read PDF documents, you might need to buy Adobe Acrobat to annotate them. There is, however, some free software that can help you organize your digital research files and attach documents to them. That way, you can attach your notes for each source to the digital original. The downside, of course, is that these notes aren't keyed to particular passages in the source, but the software is still useful for researchers. Here's a list of a few you might try:

1. *Zotero* (http://zotero.org). This is a favorite software for research because it not only organizes digital documents in project folders but also organizes citation information for each source. Zotero is an add-in that only works on the Firefox browser.

2. *Evernote* (http://evernote.com). You can organize your research sources and associated notes and then upload them so they're accessible everywhere you have an Internet connection. The program also runs on all kinds of devices—iPads, iPhones, PCs, Androids, and so on. In addition, Evernote has a function that allows you to search your notes by tags or titles.

3. *Google Docs* (http://google.com). Google Docs is the standard for many users who want to organize (and share) documents, and it's even more useful now that it allows documents like PDFs and Word files to remain in their native formats. As with Evernote, you can access your Google Docs wherever you have an Internet connection.

When You're Coming Up Short: More Advanced Searching Techniques

During week three of a research project, students often hit a wall. This is the week when students announce, "I can't find anything on my topic! I need to find another one." Their frustration is real, and it often has to do with that moment in a creative process when motivation sinks as the difficulties arise. For student researchers, these difficulties include a lot of things, like trying to remember citation details, worrying about plagiarism, wondering if there's enough time to wait for those interlibrary loan books to come in, and confronting problems with the project's focus or research question. But the problem is rarely that there is not enough information on the topic.

I take that back. Sometimes it *is* a problem, but it's usually one of the easiest to solve: You just need to exploit the many techniques that help researchers to dig more deeply. Here's where advanced searching techniques pay off (see Figure 16.3.8). We'll look briefly at each of these.

Advanced Library Searching Techniques

These advanced library searching techniques are listed in the order you might try them.

1. *Vary search terms.* Try using some search terms suggested by your research so far. You might, for instance, try searching using the names of people who have published on your topic.

2. *Search other databases.* Okay, so you've tried a general subject database like Academic OneFile and even a specialized database like PsycINFO. But have

Library	Internet	Alternative Sources
• Vary search terms	• Vary search terms	• Search blogs
• Search other databases	• Use advanced search features	• Search images
• Check bibliographies	• Use multiple search engines	• Listen to archived radio and podcasts
• Use interlibrary loan	• Watch videocasts	• Search iTunes U
• Troll government documents		• Visit local organizations or libraries
• Ask a librarian		

FIGURE 16.3.8   More Advanced Searching Techniques

you tried another general database like Academic Search Premier or another specialized database like InfoTrac Psychology? Broaden your coverage.

3. *Check bibliographies.* Academic books and articles always include a list of references at the end. These can be gold mines. Look at all the sources that you've collected so far and scan the titles in the bibliographies that seem promising. Find these by searching the library databases.

4. *Consider using interlibrary loan services.* Your campus library will get you that article or book it doesn't have by borrowing the materials from another library. This is an incredibly useful service, often available online. These days, delivery of requested materials can take as little as a few days!

5. *Troll government documents.* The U.S. government is the largest publisher in the world. If your research question is related to some issue of public policy, then there's a decent chance you'll find some government documents on the subject. Try the site USA.gov (see Figure 16.3.9), a useful index to the gazillions of government publications and reports.

6. *Ask a reference librarian for help.* If you do, you won't be sorry.

Advanced Internet Searching Techniques

It's more likely that you've tapped out relevant sources on the Internet before you've tapped out those in the library—most of us like to begin with the Internet. But make sure that you've tried some of the following search strategies on the Web.

1. *Vary search terms.* By now, you've gathered enough information on your topic to have some new ideas about terms or phrases that might yield good results. Say you're researching the origins of American blues music, and you discover that among its many traditions is something called the Piedmont style. Try searching using that phrase in quotation marks. Also consider doing Web searches on the names of experts who have contributed significantly to the conversation on your topic.

FIGURE 16.3.9   USA.gov is a useful starting point for a search of government documents on your topic.

2. *Use advanced search features.* Few of us use the advanced search page on Google and other search engines. By habit, we just type in a few terms in the simple search window. But advanced searching will allow you to exploit methods that will give you better results—things like phrase searching in conjunction with Boolean operators like AND and OR.

3. *Use multiple search engines.* Don't call for retreat until you've gone beyond Google. Try Yahoo!, Ask.com, and similar search engines. Also try specialized search engines that are relevant to your subject (see Section 16.2).

Thinking Outside the Box: Alternative Sources

Sometimes you need to be creative. Try searching for sources on your research question in places you hadn't thought to look.

1. *Search blogs.* It's easy to dismiss blogs as merely self-indulgent musings of people with nothing better to do, but some blogs are written by people who really know what they're talking about. Bloggers can be vigilant observers of

new developments, breaking news stories, and cutting-edge opinion. There are a number of specialized search engines to scour the blogosphere. Perhaps the best is http://technorati.com.

2. *Search images.* Another source of material you may not have thought of is images available on the Internet. A photograph of a collapsed school building following the 2008 earthquake in central China will do much to dramatize your essay on the vulnerability of buildings to such a disaster. Or a historical essay on lynching in the South might be more powerful with a picture of a murder from the Library of Congress archives (especially see http://memory .loc.gov/). Your campus library may also have a collection of digital images relevant to your project. Remember that if you use them in your essay, images need to be cited like any other source.

3. *Archived radio or podcasts.* Suppose your research question focuses on Martin Luther King Jr. Why not listen to an interview of Taylor Branch, the man who wrote a three-volume biography of the civil rights leader? You can find it on NPR.org. National Public Radio is a particularly good source for material for academic projects. There are also a variety of search engines that will help you find podcasts on nearly any subject.

4. *Check out YouTube.* It isn't just about laughing babies anymore. YouTube is a rich archive of video that can provide material on many topics. For the project on Martin Luther King Jr., for example, you might watch a video of his last speech. There are, of course, other sites that archive video, too. Truveo (http://www.truveo.com/) will help you search them all.

5. *Search iTunes U.* Across the United States, colleges and universities are going online through Apple's iTunes U, putting up video and audio speeches, lectures, and other academic content. You can find iTunes U on iTunes, of course, and you can do a keyword search on multiple sites using "power search." The term "global warming" produced 90 hits, including lectures, opinions, and reports from some of America's top universities.

6. *Local organizations.* The reference librarians on our campus routinely refer students to the state historical society or state law library when relevant to their projects. Local organizations can be rich sources of not only published information but also interviews and artifacts.

EXERCISE 16.3.4   Building an Annotated Bibliography

Reading to write starts with a very practical motive: *Can I use this source to develop my ideas and argument or to explore my topic?* With this in mind, the most skillful readers intuitively know that there are three kinds of readings they need to do (see Figure 16.3.10): First, they need to understand what the source is saying (yes, even if they disagree with it); second, they need to try to place what they've read in the context of what they already know about the topic; and finally, they need to imagine how some of the reading might be *used* in their own writing. This is the kind of reading that will help you develop a certain kind of *annotated bibliography*—in this case, a preliminary list of relevant sources, each of which has a brief summary and evaluation attached to it.

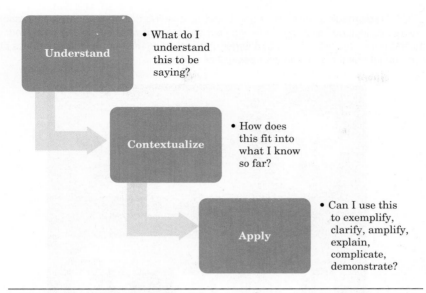

FIGURE 16.3.10   Reading Strategy for Building an Annotated Bibliography

Imagine, for instance, that you were researching these questions: What is the relationship between gender and reactions to facial expressions? Do men and women react differently to expressions of facial emotion? The literature—and conventional wisdom—seem to confirm the view that women are more intuitive than men, and that they have a higher "emotional intelligence." Might a partial explanation for this be that women are better at recognizing facial expressions, including subtle ones that communicate feeling? You find an article[1] in an academic database in which the researchers show 133 students in an undergrad course a series of pictures like this one (see p. 510), which includes a variety of facial expressions related to anger, contempt, disgust, fear, happiness, sadness, and surprise. Are both men and women equally competent in recognizing the emotions behind these facial expressions, including the more subtle emotions? Here are some of the results:

1. **Understand.** It's clear that, up to a point, women are better than men at recognizing the feeling behind a facial expression, particularly more subtle feelings. But the study also qualifies this finding by suggesting that when it comes to "highly expressive" expressions, there is no difference between women and men.
2. **Contextualize.** If you had been doing research on this topic, you'd recognize that this study looks at only a small aspect of what psychologists call "emotional competence." It doesn't fully explain whether women have an advantage over men in this ability. It does seem to confirm, however, your own experience that men can be emotional blockheads until things get really out of hand emotionally.
3. **Apply.** The graph is pretty clear. Why not use it to emphasize the idea that women seem to be better than men at recognizing more subtle emotions?

[1]Hoffman, Holger, Henrik Kessler, Tobias Eppel, Stefanie Rukavina, and Harold C. Traue. "Expression Intensity, Gender, and Facial Emotion Recognition: Women Recognize Only Subtle Facial Emotions Better than Men." *Acta Psychologica* 135 (2010): 278–83.

These three readings give you a good start on building a short paragraph annotation of the article that includes all three elements: your summary of what the source says, your comments about how the article fits into a larger understanding of your topic, and a guess about how you might use the article in your essay. For example:

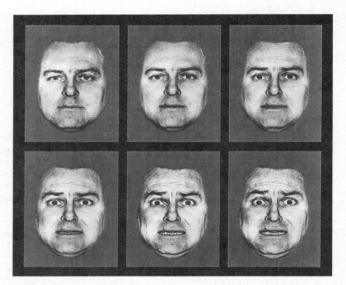

Note. The image on the upper left is the neutral face (0% intensity); the image on the lower right is the full-blown emotional face (100% intensity).

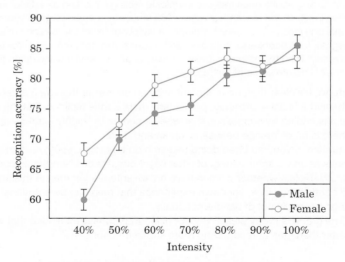

Note. Error bars depict standard errors

Sample Evaluative Annotation

1. Hoffman, Holger, Henrik Kessler, Tobias Eppel, Stefanie Rukavina, and Harold C. Traue. "Expression Intensity, Gender, and Facial Emotion Recognition: Women Recognize Only Subtle Facial Emotions Better than Men." *Acta Psychologica* 135 (2010): 278–83.

   This article investigates whether there is a "female advantage" over men when it comes to the ability to recognize facial expressions that imply emotion. This question is a part of larger investigations about "emotional competence" and whether it's related to gender. Conventional wisdom and the popular press suggest women are better at feelings than at reason. My research poses the question of whether, if true, this emotional "advantage" might be related to women's sensitivity to emotional facial expressions. This article, which reports on two studies of college students, seems to confirm it: Women who were quickly shown images of actors with a range of six different emotions, from subtle to "full-blown," were much better than men at detecting the less intense expressions. At higher intensities there was no difference between men and women. A graph in the article might be particularly dramatic evidence of this in my essay.

End the week by writing annotations like this for a handful of the best sources you've found so far. Cite the sources as best you can, but focus especially on your annotations.

Unit 5

Writing Styles

Visual texts, like word-based ones, can be read in multiple ways. This photograph can be "read" as a classic depiction of the great American sport. But after you read David Sirota's essay in this chapter about baseball and race, come back to this photograph and see if you notice anything new, or if you "read" it in new ways.

17

Informative Writing

EXPLAINING is a frequent purpose for writing. Explaining goes beyond investigating the facts and reporting information; it analyzes the component parts of a subject and then shows how the parts fit in relation to one another. Its goal is to clarify for a particular group of readers *what* something is, *how* it happened or should happen, and/or *why* it happens.

Explaining begins with assessing the rhetorical situation: the writer, the occasion, the intended purpose and audience, the genre, and the cultural context. As you begin thinking about a topic, keep in mind your own interests, the expectations of your audience, the possible genre you might choose (essay, article, pamphlet, multigenre essay, website), and the cultural or social context in which you are writing or in which your writing might be read.

Explaining any idea, concept, process, or effect requires analysis. Analysis starts with dividing a thing or phenomenon into its parts. Then, once you explain the various parts, you put them back together (synthesis) to explain their relationship or how they work together.

> **" Become aware of the two-sided nature of your mental make-up: one thinks in terms of the connectedness of things, the other thinks in terms of parts and sequences. "**
>
> —Gabriele Lusser Rico,
> Author of *Writing the Natural Way*

Taken from *The Prentice Hall Guide for College Writers*, Eleventh Edition by Stephen P. Reid and Dominic DelliCarpini.

> "What [a writer] knows is almost always a matter of the relationships he establishes, between example and generalization, between one part of a narrative and the next, between the idea and the counter idea that the writer sees is also relevant. "
>
> —Roger Sale, Author of *On Writing*

Because its purpose is to teach the reader, *expository writing,* or writing to explain, should be as clear as possible. Explanations, however, are more than organized pieces of information. Expository writing contains information that is focused by your point of view, by your experience, and by your reasoning powers. Thus, your explanation of a thing or phenomenon makes a point or has a thesis: This is the *right* way to define *happiness.* This is how one *should* bake lasagne or do a calculus problem. To make your explanation clear, you use specific support: facts, data, examples, illustrations, statistics, comparisons, analogies, and images. Your thesis is a *general* assertion about the relationships of the *specific* parts. The support helps your reader identify the parts and see the relationships. Expository writing teaches the reader by alternating between generalizations and specific examples.

Techniques for Explaining

> "The main thing I try to do is write as clearly as I can. "
>
> —E. B. White, Journalist and coauthor of *Elements of Style*

Since explaining must always consider how much the audience you are addressing already knows, you must first assess your rhetorical situation. Below are techniques for writing explanations that are sensitive to your audience's needs.

Techniques for Explaining

Technique	Tips on How to Do It
Considering (and reconsidering) your purpose, audience, genre, and social context	As you change your *audience* or your *genre,* you must change how you explain something as well as how much and what kind of evidence you use.
Getting the reader's attention and stating the thesis	Devise an accurate but interesting *title.* Use an attention-getting *lead-in.* State the *thesis* clearly.
Defining key terms and describing *what* something is	Analyze and define by *describing, comparing, classifying* and/or *giving examples.*
Identifying the steps in a process and showing *how* each step relates to the overall process	Describe *how* something should be done or *how* something typically happens.

| Describing causes and effects and showing *why* certain causes lead to specific effects | • Analyze how several causes lead to a *single effect,* or show how a single cause leads to *multiple effects*. |
| Supporting explanations with specific evidence | • Use descriptions, examples, comparisons, analogies, images, facts, data, or statistics to *show* what, how, or why. |

EXPLAINING *WHAT*: DEFINITION

17.1
Understand techniques for defining key terms

Explaining *what* something is or means requires showing the relationship between it and the *class* of beings, objects, or concepts to which it belongs. *Formal definition,* which is often essential in explaining, has three parts: the thing or term to be defined, the class, and the distinguishing characteristics of the thing or term. The thing being defined can be concrete, such as a turkey, or abstract, such as democracy.

Thing or Term	Class	Distinguishing Characteristics
A turkey is a	bird	that is large, has brownish plumage and a bare, wattled head and neck; it is widely domesticated for food.
Democracy is	government	by the people, exercised directly or through elected representatives.

Frequently, writers use *extended definitions* to establish how they are using a key term. This is important, as it helps writers come to terms with a particular audience. The following extended definition of democracy, written for an audience of college students and appearing in a textbook, begins with the etymology of the word and then explains—using analysis, comparison, example, and description—what democracy is and what it is not.

Since democracy is government of the people, by the people, and for the people, a democratic form of government is not fixed or static. Democracy is dynamic; it adapts to the wishes and needs of the people. The term *democracy* derives from the Greek word *demos,* meaning "the common people," and *-kratia,* meaning "strength or power" used to govern or rule. Democracy is based on the notion that a majority of people creates laws and then everyone agrees to abide by those laws in the interest of the common good. In a democracy, people are not ruled by a king, a dictator, or a small group of powerful individuals. Instead, people elect officials who use the power temporarily granted to them to govern the society. For example, the people may agree that their government should raise money for defense, so the officials levy taxes to support an army. If enough people decide, however, that taxes for defense are too high, then they request that their elected officials change the laws or they elect new officials. The essence of democracy lies in its responsiveness:

Formal definition

Description: What democracy is

Etymology: Analysis of the word's roots

Comparison: What democracy is not

Example

Formal definition

Democracy is a form of government in which laws and lawmakers change as the will of the majority changes.

More typically, extended definitions are informal and are followed by examples that illustrate and explain the concept. In the following definition, Caterina Fake, the founder of Flickr and Hunch, defines on her blog the social phenomenon of FOMO.

FOMO and Social Media

Caterina Fake, cofounder of Hunch and Flickr.

I've been watching Twitter and Ditto feeds of people at SxSW [South by Southwest], and, from a distance, I get a distinct sense of the social anxiety and FOMO that's going on there. "FOMO" stands for "Fear of Missing Out" and it's what happens everywhere on a typical Saturday night, when you're trying to decide if you should stay in, or muster the energy to go to the party. At SxSW I see people wondering if they're at the wrong party—the party where they are is lame, feels uncool, has too much brand advertising or doesn't have anyone there they'd want to hook up with—and so they move on to the next party where they have to wait in line too long, can't get a beer, or don't find their friends, and so move on to the next venue where . . . and so on.

FOMO is a great motivator of human behavior, and I think a crucial key to understanding social software, and why it works the way it does. Many people have studied the game mechanics that keep people collecting things (points, trophies, check-ins, mayorships, kudos). Others have studied how the neurochemistry that keeps us checking Facebook every five minutes is similar to the neurochemistry fueling addiction. Social media has made us even more aware of the things we are missing out on. You're home alone, but watching your friends status updates tell of a great party happening somewhere. You are aware of more parties than ever before. And, like gym memberships, adding Bergman movies to your Netflix queue and piling up unread copies of the *New Yorker*, watching these feeds gives you a sense that you're participating, not missing out, even when you are.

EXPLAINING *HOW*: PROCESS ANALYSIS

17.2
Understand techniques for explaining a process

Explaining how something should be done or how something happens is called process analysis. There are two kinds of process analysis: *prescriptive* and *descriptive*.

- *Prescriptive* analyses: Typically, prescriptive processes involve a "how to" explanation—how to cook a turkey, how to tune an engine, how to get a job. The analysis is "prescriptive" because it explains the right way to do something to get the best results.
- *Descriptive* analyses: Usually, descriptive process analyses simply explain how something typically happens without suggesting that this is the right way or best way to do something.

In both prescriptive and descriptive process analyses, you analyze a process—dividing the sequence into steps or parts—and then show how the parts contribute to and explain the whole process.

Cookbooks, automobile-repair manuals, instructions for assembling toys or appliances, and self-improvement books are all examples of *prescriptive* process analysis. Writers of recipes, for example, begin with analyses of the ingredients and the steps in preparing the food. Then they carefully explain how the steps are related, how to avoid problems, and how to serve mouth-watering concoctions. Farley Mowat, naturalist and author of *Never Cry Wolf,* gives his readers the following detailed recipe for creamed mouse. Mowat became interested in this recipe when he decided to test the nutritional content of the wolf's diet. "In the event that any of my readers may be interested in personally exploiting this hitherto overlooked source of excellent animal protein," Mowat writes, "I give the recipe in full."

Souris à la Crème

Ingredients:

One dozen fat mice	Salt and pepper	One cup white flour
Cloves	One piece sowbelly	Ethyl alcohol

Skin and gut the mice, but do not remove the heads; wash, then place in a pot with enough alcohol to cover the carcasses. Allow to marinate for about two hours. Cut sowbelly into small cubes and fry slowly until most of the fat has been rendered. Now remove the carcasses from the alcohol and roll them in a mixture of salt, pepper and flour; then place in frying pan and sauté for about five minutes (being careful not to allow the pan to get too hot, or the delicate meat will dry out and become tough and stringy). Now add a cup of alcohol and six or eight cloves. Cover the pan and allow to simmer slowly for fifteen minutes. The cream sauce can be made according to any standard recipe. When the sauce is ready, drench the carcasses with it, cover and allow to rest in a warm place for ten minutes before serving.

Explaining *how* something happens or is typically done involves a *descriptive* process analysis. It requires showing the chronological relationship between one idea, event, or phenomenon and the next—and it depends on close observation. As she proposed her research project on the Ebola virus, Paige Koch developed this description of how the mutation of viruses makes vaccines less than fully effective.

Viruses tread a very thin line between living and nonliving. They possess a few traits that consider them as living organisms; namely, they have the ability to mutate. Mutating means that the genome of a virus is able to change from generation to generation, rather by random happenstance or by being introduced to a new gene from the outside environment. Ebola happens to be an RNA virus, the type that has the higher rate of mutations (the other type, DNA viruses, are much more stable). For this reason, the Ebola virus has the potential to be just different enough for a vaccine to be ineffective. A good example of this is the influenza virus. Every time flu season returns, a new vaccine is made available. But the vaccine does not guarantee 100% immunity from the flu. Vaccines offered for the flu virus are made with the most prevalent strains of influenza from the previous year, protecting from just those strains. Influenza mutates and changes at a quick enough rate that there is always a new strain by the time a vaccine is created from the last strain. That is why the flu has not been wiped out of existence yet—the virus changes too quickly for scientists to keep up. Thankfully, influenza does not have consequences as serious as Ebola-Zaire does. Ebola, unfortunately, also has potential to mutate as quickly as the influenza virus does. If scientists cannot keep up with the virus, then a vaccine would be exponentially harder to produce.

EXPLAINING *WHY*: CAUSAL ANALYSIS

17.3
Understand techniques for explaining causes

Explaining *why* something occurs can be the most fascinating—and difficult—kind of expository writing. Answering the question "why" usually requires analyzing *cause-and-effect relationships.* The causes, however, may be too complex or intangible to identify precisely. We are on comparatively secure ground when we ask *why* about physical phenomena that can be weighed, measured, and replicated under laboratory conditions. Under those conditions, we can determine cause and effect with precision.

Fire, for example, has three *necessary* and *sufficient* causes: combustible material, oxygen, and ignition temperature. Without each of these causes, fire will not occur (each cause is "necessary"); taken together, these three causes are enough to cause fire (all three together are "sufficient"). In this case, the cause-and-effect relationship can be illustrated by an equation:

Cause 1	+	Cause 2	+	Cause 3	=	Effect
(combustible material)		(oxygen)		(ignition temperature)		(fire)

Analyzing both necessary and sufficient causes is essential to explaining an effect. You may say, for example, that wind shear (an abrupt downdraft in a storm) "caused" an airplane crash. In fact, wind shear may have *contributed* (been necessary) to the crash but was not by itself the total (sufficient) cause of the crash: an airplane with enough power may be able to overcome wind shear forces in certain circumstances. An explanation of the crash is not complete until you analyze the full range of necessary *and* sufficient causes, which may include wind shear, lack of power, mechanical failure, and even pilot error.

Cause-and-effect relationships are particularly tricky to prove. What kind of evidence do we need to prove that A causes B? The following short opinion article shows how racial prejudice in major league baseball affects umpires' judgment in calling balls and strikes. In support of his claim of cause and effect, David Sirota cites extensive statistical evidence from 3.5 million pitches over a period of four years to demonstrate that racial prejudice still exists and that it impairs the judgment of umpires. After reading Sirota's essay. you might look back at the photograph on the first page of this chapter to see if you notice any new details.

How Baseball Explains Modern Racism

David Sirota

David Sirota, a political commentator and syndicated columnist, is the author of *Back to Our Future: How the 1980s Explain the World We Live in Now.* The syndicated article below first appeared in many newspapers nationally in October 2011.

Despite recent odes to "post-racial" sensibilities, persistent racial wage and 1 unemployment gaps show that prejudice is alive and well in America. Nonetheless, that truism is often angrily denied or willfully ignored in our society, in part because prejudice is so much more difficult to recognize on a day-to-day basis. As opposed to the Jim Crow era of white hoods and lynch mobs, 21st century American bigotry is now more often an unseen crime of the subtle and the reflexive—and the crime scene tends to be the shadowy nuances of hiring decisions, performance evaluations, and plausible deniability.

Thankfully, though, we now have baseball to help shine a light on the prob- 2 lem so that everyone can see it for what it really is.

Today, Major League Baseball games using the QuesTec computerized 3 pitch-monitoring system are the most statistically quantifiable workplaces in America. Match up QuesTec's accumulated data with demographic information about who is pitching and who is calling balls and strikes, and you get the indisputable proof of how ethnicity does indeed play a part in discretionary decisions of those in power positions.

This is exactly what Southern Methodist University's researchers did when 4 they examined more than 3.5 million pitches from 2004 to 2008. Their findings say as much about the enduring relationship between sports and bigotry as they do about the synaptic nature of racism in all of American society.

First and foremost, SMU found that home-plate umpires call dispropor- 5 tionately more strikes for pitchers in their same ethnic group. Because most home-plate umpires are white, this has been a big form of racial privilege for white pitchers, who researchers show are, on average, getting disproportionately more of the benefit of the doubt on close calls.

Second, SMU researchers found that "minority pitchers reacted to umpire 6 bias by playing it safe with the pitches they threw in a way that actually harmed their performance and statistics." Basically, these hurlers adjusted to the white umpires' artificially narrower strike zone by throwing pitches down the heart of the plate, where they were easier for batters to hit.

Finally, and perhaps most importantly, the data suggest that racial bias is 7 probably operating at a subconscious level, where the umpire doesn't even recognize it.

To document this, SMU compared the percentage of strikes called in QuesTec- 8 equipped ballparks versus non-QuesTec parks.

(Continued)

...continued How Baseball Explains Modern Racism, **David Sirota**

Researchers found that umpires' racial biases diminished when they knew   9
they were being monitored by the computer. Same thing for high-profile moments. During those important points in games when umpires knew fans were more carefully watching the calls, the racial bias all but vanished. Likewise, the same-race preference was less pronounced at high-attendance games, where umps knew there would be more crowd scrutiny.

Though gleaned from baseball, these findings transcend athletics by pro-   10
viding a larger lesson about conditioned behavior in an institutionally racist society.

Whether the workplace is a baseball diamond, a factory floor or an office,   11
when authority figures realize they are being scrutinized, they are more cognizant of their own biases—and more likely to try to stop them before they unduly influence their behavior. But in lower-profile interludes, when the workplace isn't scrutinized and decisions are happening on psychological autopilot, pre-programmed biases can take over.

Thus, the inherent problem of today's pervasive "post-racial" fallacy. By   12
perpetuating the lie that racism doesn't exist, pretending that bigotry is not a workplace problem anymore, and resisting governmental efforts to halt such prejudice, we create the environment for our ugly subconscious to rule. In doing so, we consequently reduce the potential for much-needed self-correction.

Warming Up: Journal Exercises

The following exercises ask you to write explanations. Read all the exercises and then write on the three that interest you most. If another idea occurs to you, write about it.

1 **Writing Across the Curriculum.** Write a one-paragraph explanation of an idea, term, or concept that you have discussed in a class that you are currently taking. From biology, for example, you might define *photosynthesis* or *gene splicing*. From psychology, you might define *psychosis* or *projection*. From computer studies, you might define *cyberspace* or *morphing*. First, identify someone who might need to know about this subject. Then give a definition and an illustration. Finally, describe how the term was discovered or invented, what its effects or applications are, and/or how it works.

2 **Collaborating with peers.** Since explanations are not written in a vacuum, it is worthwhile to determine what people know, don't know, and perhaps know differently about your topic. Before you begin collecting details, talk with some of your peers, individually or in groups, to gauge what they already know about your topic. That might help you decide how much, and what kind of, details you will need to include in an explanation.

③ Novelist Ernest Hemingway once defined *courage* as "grace under pressure." Using this definition, explain how you or someone you know showed this kind of courage in a difficult situation.

④ Choose a skill that you've acquired (for example, operating a machine, playing a sport, drawing, counseling others, dieting) and explain to a novice how he or she can acquire that skill. Reread what you've written. Then write another version addressed to an expert. What parts of your original version can you leave out? What must you add?

⑤ Explaining is not only about *what;* sometimes it is about *why.* Try writing an explanation about why, as you see it, a recent local or national event took place. Help readers see the event in a new way.

Sometimes writers use standard definitions to make a larger point. Suze Orman, in "How to Take Control of Your Credit Cards," defines the key financial terms "interest rate," "credit history," "monthly minimum payment," and "FICO credit score" to help readers learn how to control their financial health. As you read this piece, consider how you might define key terms in your writing to explain why a course of action is advisable.

How to Take Control of Your Credit Cards

Suze Orman

The author of several best-selling books, including *The Money Book for the Young, Fabulous & Broke* (2005) and *Women and Money: Owning the Power to Control Your Destiny* (2007), Suze Orman was born in 1951 in Chicago, earned a degree in social work from the University of Illinois, and started her career not as a financial expert but as a waitress. Six of her books have been *New York Times* best sellers. "How to Take Control of Your Credit Cards" appeared originally as one of her regular columns for *Money Matters* on Yahoo! Finance.

I'm all for taking credit where credit is due, but when it comes to credit   1
cards, way too many of you are overdoing it. For Americans who don't pay their entire credit card bill each month, the average balance is close to $4,000. And when we zoom in on higher-income folks—those with annual incomes between $75,000 and $100,000—the average balance clocks in at nearly $8,000. If you're paying, say, 18 percent interest on an $8,000 balance, and you make only the 2 percent minimum payment due each month, you are going to end up paying more than $22,000 in interest over the course of the 54 years it will take to get the balance down to zero.

That's absolute insanity.   2

And absolutely unnecessary.   3

(Continued)

If you have the desire to take control of your credit card mess, you can. It's   *4*
just a matter of choice. I am not saying it will be easy, but there are plenty of
strategies that can put you on a path out of credit card hell. And as I explain
later, even those of you who can't seem to turn the corner and become credit
responsible on your own, can get plenty of help from qualified credit counseling services.

How to Be a Credit Card Shark

If you overspend just because you like to buy buy buy on credit, then you   *5*
are what I call Broke by Choice. You are willfully making your own mess. I am
not going to lecture you about how damaging this is; I'm hoping the fact that
you're reading this article means you are ready to make a change.

But I also realize that some of you are Broke by Circumstance. I actually tell   *6*
young adults in the dues-paying stage of their careers to lean on their credit
cards if they don't yet make enough to always keep up with their bills. But the
key is that if you rely on your credit cards to make ends meet, you must limit the
plastic spending to true necessities, not indulgences. Buying groceries is a necessity. Buying dinner for you and your pals at a swank restaurant is an indul-
gence you can't afford if it will become part of your unpaid credit card balance.

But whether you are broke by choice or by circumstance, the strategy for   *7*
getting out of credit card debt is the same: to outmaneuver the card companies
with a strategy that assures you pay the lowest possible interest rate, for the
shortest possible time, while avoiding all of the many snares and traps the card
companies lay out for you.

Here's how to be a Credit Card Shark.   *8*

Take an Interest in Your Rate

The average interest rate charged on credit cards is 15 percent, with plenty   *9*
of folks paying 18 percent, 20 percent, or even more. If you carry a balance on
any credit cards, your primary focus should be to get that rate down as low as
possible.

Now then. If you have a FICO score of at least 720, and you make at least the   *10*
minimum payment due each month, on time, you should be able to negotiate
with your current credit card issuer to lower your rate. Call'em up and let them
know you plan to transfer your entire balance to another card with a lower
rate—more on this in a sec—if they don't get your rate down.

If your card issuer doesn't step up to the plate and give you a better deal,   *11*
then do indeed start shopping around for a new card with a sweet intro offer.
For those of you with strong FICO scores, a zero-rate deal ought to be possible.
You can search for top card deals at the Yahoo! Finance Credit Card Center.

Don't forget, though, that the key with balance transfer offers is to find out   *12*
what your rate will be when the intro period expires in six months to a year. If

your zero rate will skyrocket to 20 percent, that's a crappy deal, unless you are absolutely 100 percent sure you will get the balance paid off before the rate changes. (And if you got yourself into card hell in the first place, I wouldn't be betting on you having the ability to wipe out your problem in just six months. . . .)

Once you are approved for the new low- or zero-rate card, move as much of **13** your high-rate balances onto this new card. But don't—I repeat, do NOT—use the new card for new purchases. Hidden in the fine print on these deals are provisions stating, first, that any new purchases you make on the card will come with a high interest rate, and second, that you'll be paying that high interest on the entirety of your new purchase charges until you pay off every last cent of the balance transfer amount. This, to put it mildly, could really screw up your zero-rate deal. So please, use the new card only to park your old high-rate debt, and not to shop with.

Another careless mistake you can make is to cancel your old cards. Don't **14** do that either. Those cards hold some valuable "history" that's used to compute your FICO credit score. If you cancel the cards, you cancel your history, and your FICO score can take a hit. If you are worried about the temptation of using the cards, just get out your scissors and give them a good trim. That way you can't use 'em, but your history stays on your record.

Coddle Your New Card

When you do a balance transfer, you need to protect your low rate as if it **15** were an endangered species—because if the credit card issuer has anything to say about it, it will be. Look, you don't really think the card company is excited about charging you no interest, do you? How the heck do they make money off of that? They only offer up the great deal to lure you over to their card. Then they start working overtime trying to get you to screw up so they have an excuse to change your zero interest rate, often to as much as 20 percent or more.

And the big screw-up they are hoping you don't know about is buried down in **16** the fine print of your card agreement: make one late payment and you can kiss your zero deal good-bye. Even worse is that card companies are now scouring all your credit cards—remember, they can check your credit reports—to see if you have been late on any card, not just their card. So even if you always pay the zero-rate card on time, if you are late on any other card, your zero deal can be in jeopardy.

That's why I want you to make sure every credit card bill is paid ahead of **17** schedule. Don't mail it in on the day it is due; that's late. Mail it in at least five days early. Better yet, convert your card to online bill pay so you can zap your payments over in time every month. And remember, it's only the minimum monthly payment that needs to be paid. That's not asking a lot.

Dealing with High-Rate Debt

Okay, I realize not everyone is going to qualify for these low-rate balance **18** transfer deals, so let's run through how to take control of your cards if you are stuck with higher rates.

(Continued)

...continued How to Take Control of Your Credit Cards, **Suze Orman**

I want you to line up all your cards in descending order of their interest 19
rates. Notice I said the card with the highest interest rate comes first. Not the
one with the biggest balance.

Your strategy is to make the minimum monthly payment on every card, on 20
time, every month. But your card with the highest interest rate gets some special
treatment. I want you to pay more than the minimum amount due on this card.
The more you can pay, the better; but everyone should put in, at the minimum,
an extra $20 each month. Push yourself hard to make that extra payment as
large as possible. It can save you thousands of dollars in interest charges over
time.

Keep this up every month until your card with the highest rate is paid off. 21
Then turn your attention to the card with the next highest rate. In addition to
the usual monthly minimum payment due on that second card, I want you to
add in the entire amount you were previously paying on the first card (the one
that's now paid off). So let's say you were paying a total of $200 a month on your
original highest-rate card, and making a $75 monthly minimum on the second
card. Well, now you are going to fork over $275 a month to the second card.
And, of course, you'll continue to make the minimum monthly payment due on
any other cards. Once your second card is paid off, move on to the third. If your
monthly payment on that second card was $275, then that's what you should
add to the minimum payment due on your third card. Get the idea? Rinse and
repeat as often as needed, until you have all your debt paid off. For some of you
this may take a year, for others it may take many years. That's okay. Just get
yourself moving in the right direction and you'll be amazed how gratifying it is
to find yourself taking control of your money rather than letting it control you.

And be sure to keep an eye on your FICO credit score. As you pay down 22
your card balances—and build a record of paying on time—your score is indeed
going to rise. Eventually your score may be high enough to finally qualify for a
low-rate balance transfer offer.

Questions for Writing and Discussion

1 Writers of effective explaining essays focus their thesis for a specific audience.
Describe the audience Suze Orman addresses in her essay. Which sentences help
you identify this audience? Which sentences in Orman's essay most clearly
express her thesis?

2 Explaining essays typically use definition of terms, explanation of processes, and
analyses of causes and effects. Identify at least one example of each of these
strategies in Orman's essay. In each case, decide whether the information
Orman gives is clear to you. Where do you need additional information or
clarification?

3 Two strategies that Orman uses to connect with her readers are addressing them in the second person, "you," and using informal language such as "you and your pals," "call 'em up," "more on this in a sec," and "sweet intro offer." Find other examples of informal language in her essay. Does this language work for her audience? Does it make the essay more lively and readable for you? Is this language appropriate in an essay about finances? Explain.

4 Find an offer for credit cards that you, a friend, or a family member has recently received. Study the fine print. Then, in your own words, explain what the fine print means in language that another member of your class can understand. Is Orman right about the "many snares and traps" that the card companies set for their customers?

Sometimes writers use standard definitions to make a larger point. Suze Orman, in "How to Take Control of Your Credit Cards," defined key financial terms like "interest rate," "credit history," "monthly minimum payment," and "FICO credit score" to help readers learn how to control one's financial health. As you read, try to assess how well she is able to instruct you about these financial concepts. Do you feel better informed after reading her essay?

In the piece that follows, Deborah Tannen explains how teaching strategies might affect men and women differently. In "How Male and Female Students Use Language Differently," Tannen attempts to explain classroom phenomena through gender studies. As you read her essay, you might think about your own classes. Do men talk more than women? Does the teacher's style in some classes seem to be more gender-inclusive than others? How clearly—and convincingly—does Tannen seem to explain underlying gender issues that could help to explain your own experiences?

As you read this piece, consider how you might define key terms or explain background concepts to better explain why a course of action is advisable.

How Male and Female Students Use Language Differently

Deborah Tannen

Everyone knows that men and women communicate differently, but Deborah Tannen, a linguist at Georgetown University, has spent her career studying how and why their conversational styles are different. Tannen's books include her best-selling *You Just Don't Understand: Women and Men in Conversation* (1990) and *I Only Say This Because I Love You* (2001). In the following article from the *Chronicle of Higher Education,* Tannen applies her knowledge of conversational styles to the classroom.

When I researched and wrote my latest book, *You Just Don't Understand:* 1 *Women and Men in Conversation,* the furthest thing from my mind was reevaluating my teaching strategies. But that has been one of the direct benefits of having written the book.

(Continued)

The primary focus of my linguistic research always has been the language of everyday conversation. One facet of this is conversational style: how different regional, ethnic, and class backgrounds, as well as age and gender, result in different ways of using language to communicate. *You Just Don't Understand* is about the conversational styles of women and men. As I gained more insight into typically male and female ways of using language, I began to suspect some of the causes of the troubling facts that women who go to single-sex schools do better in later life, and that when young women sit next to young men in classrooms, the males talk more. This is not to say that all men talk in class, nor that no women do. It is simply that a greater percentage of discussion time is taken by men's voices.

The research of sociologists and anthropologists such as Janet Lever, Marjorie Harness Goodwin, and Donna Eder has shown that girls and boys learn to use language differently in their sex-separate peer groups. Typically, a girl has a best friend with whom she sits and talks, frequently telling secrets. It's the telling of secrets, the fact and the way that they talk to each other, that makes them best friends. For boys, activities are central: their best friends are the ones they do things with. Boys also tend to play in larger groups that are hierarchical. High-status boys give orders and push low-status boys around. So boys are expected to use language to seize center stage: by exhibiting their skill, displaying their knowledge, and challenging and resisting challenges.

These patterns have stunning implications for classroom interaction. Most faculty members assume that participating in class discussion is a necessary part of successful performance. Yet speaking in a classroom is more congenial to boys' language experience than to girls', since it entails putting oneself forward in front of a large group of people, many of whom are strangers and at least one of whom is sure to judge speakers' knowledge and intelligence by their verbal display.

Another aspect of many classrooms that makes them more hospitable to most men than to most women is the use of debate-like formats as a learning tool. Our educational system, as Walter Ong argues persuasively in his book *Fighting for Life* (Cornell University Press, 1981), is fundamentally male in that the pursuit of knowledge is believed to be achieved by ritual opposition: public display followed by argument and challenge. Father Ong demonstrates that ritual opposition—what he calls "adversativeness" or "agonism"—is fundamental to the way most males approach almost any activity. (Consider, for example, the little boy who shows he likes a little girl by pulling her braids and shoving her.) But ritual opposition is antithetical to the way most females learn and like to interact. It is not that females don't fight, but that they don't fight for fun. They don't *ritualize* opposition.

Anthropologists working in widely disparate parts of the world have found contrasting verbal rituals for women and men. Women in completely unrelated cultures (for example, Greece and Bali) engage in ritual laments: spontaneously produced rhyming couplets that express their pain, for example, over the loss of

(Continued)

loved ones. Men do not take part in laments. They have their own, very different verbal ritual: a contest, a war of words in which they vie with each other to devise clever insults.

When discussing these phenomena with a colleague, I commented that I see 7
these two styles in American conversation: many women bond by talking about troubles, and many men bond by exchanging playful insults and put-downs, and other sorts of verbal sparring. He exclaimed: "I never thought of this, but that's the way I teach: I have students read an article, and then I invite them to tear it apart. After we've torn it to shreds, we talk about how to build a better model."

This contrasts sharply with the way I teach: I open the discussion of read- 8
ings by asking, "What did you find useful in this? What can we use in our own theory building and our own methods?" I note what I see as weaknesses in the author's approach, but I also point out that the writer's discipline and purposes might be different from ours. Finally, I offer personal anecdotes illustrating the phenomena under discussion and praise students' anecdotes as well as their critical acumen.

These different teaching styles must make our classrooms wildly different 9
places and hospitable to different students. Male students are more likely to be comfortable attacking the readings and might find the inclusion of personal anecdotes irrelevant and "soft." Women are more likely to resist discussion they perceive as hostile, and, indeed, it is women in my classes who are most likely to offer personal anecdotes.

A colleague who read my book commented that he had always taken for 10
granted that the best way to deal with students' comments is to challenge them; this, he felt it was self-evident, sharpens their minds and helps them develop debating skills. But he had noticed that women were relatively silent in his classes, so he decided to try beginning discussion with relatively open-ended questions and letting comments go unchallenged. He found, to his amazement and satisfaction, that more women began to speak up.

Though some of the women in his class clearly liked this better, perhaps 11
some of the men liked it less. One young man in my class wrote in a questionnaire about a history professor who gave students questions to think about and called on people to answer them: "He would then play devil's advocate ... *i.e.,* he debated us. ... That class *really* sharpened me intellectually. ... We as students do need to know how to defend ourselves." This young man valued the experience of being attacked and challenged publicly. Many, if not most, women would shrink from such "challenge," experiencing it as public humiliation.

A professor at Hamilton College told me of a young man who was upset 12
because he felt his class presentation had been a failure. The professor was puzzled because he had observed that class members had listened attentively and agreed with the student's observations. It turned out that it was this very agreement that the student interpreted as failure: since no one had engaged his ideas by arguing with him, he felt they had found them unworthy of attention.

(Continued)

So one reason men speak in class more than women is that many of them 13
find the "public" classroom setting more conducive to speaking, whereas most
women are more comfortable speaking in private to a small group of people
they know well. A second reason is that men are more likely to be comfortable
with the debate-like form that discussion may take. Yet another reason is the
different attitudes toward speaking in class that typify women and men.

Students who speak frequently in class, many of whom are men, assume that 14
it is their job to think of contributions and try to get the floor to express them. But
many women monitor their participation not only to get the floor but to avoid
getting it. Women students in my class tell me that if they have spoken up once or
twice, they hold back for the rest of the class because they don't want to dominate.
If they have spoken a lot one week, they will remain silent the next. These different ethics of participation are, of course, unstated, so those who speak freely assume that those who remain silent have nothing to say, and those who are reining
themselves in assume that the big talkers are selfish and hoggish.

When I looked around my classes, I could see these differing ethics and hab- 15
its at work. For example, my graduate class in analyzing conversation had twenty
students, eleven women and nine men. Of the men, four were foreign students:
two Japanese, one Chinese, and one Syrian. With the exception of the three
Asian men, all the men spoke in class at least occasionally. The biggest talker in
the class was a woman, but there were also five women who never spoke at all,
only one of whom was Japanese. I decided to try something different.

I broke the class into small groups to discuss the issues raised in the readings 16
and to analyze their own conversational transcripts. I devised three ways of dividing the students into groups: one by the degree program they were in, one by gender, and one by conversational style, as closely as I could guess it. This meant that
when the class was grouped according to conversational style, I put Asian students
together, fast talkers together, and quiet students together. The class split into
groups six times during the semester, so they met in each grouping twice. I told
students to regard the groups as examples of interactional data and to note the different ways they participated in the different groups. Toward the end of the term, I
gave them a questionnaire asking about their class and group participation.

I could see plainly from my observation of the groups at work that women 17
who never opened their mouths in class were talking away in the small groups.
In fact, the Japanese woman commented that she found it particularly hard to
contribute to the all-woman group she was in because "I was overwhelmed by
how talkative the female students were in the female-only group." This is particularly revealing because it highlights that the same person who can be "oppressed" into silence in one context can become the talkative "oppressor" in
another. No one's conversational style is absolute; everyone's style changes in
response to the context and others' styles.

Some of the students (seven) said they preferred the same-gender groups; 18
others preferred the same-style groups. In answer to the question "Would you

(Continued)

have liked to speak in class more than you did?" six of the seven who said yes were women; the one man was Japanese. Most startlingly, this response did not come only from quiet women; it came from women who had indicated they had spoken in class never, rarely, sometimes, and often. Of the eleven students who said the amount they had spoken was fine, seven were men. Of the four women who checked "fine," two added qualifications indicating it wasn't completely fine: One wrote in "maybe more," and one wrote, "I have an urge to participate but often feel I should have something more interesting/relevant/wonderful/intelligent to say!!"

I counted my experiment a success. Everyone in the class found the small groups interesting, and no one indicated he or she would have preferred that the class not break into groups. Perhaps most instructive, however, was the fact that the experience of breaking into groups, and of talking about participation in class, raised everyone's awareness about classroom participation. After we had talked about it, some of the quietest women in the class made a few voluntary contributions, though sometimes I had to ensure their participation by interrupting the students who were exuberantly speaking out.   19

Americans are often proud that they discount the significance of cultural differences: "We are all individuals," many people boast. Ignoring such issues as gender and ethnicity becomes a source of pride: "I treat everyone the same." But treating people the same is not equal treatment if they are not the same. . . .   20

In a class where some students speak out without raising hands, those who feel they must raise their hands and wait to be recognized do not have equal opportunity to speak. Telling them to feel free to jump in will not make them feel free; one's sense of timing, of one's rights and obligations in a classroom, are automatic, learned over years of interaction. They may be changed over time, with motivation and effort, but they cannot be changed on the spot. And everyone assumes his or her own way is best. When I asked my students how the class could be changed to make it easier for them to speak more, the most talkative woman said she would prefer it if no one had to raise hands, and a foreign student said he wished people would raise their hands and wait to be recognized.   21

My experience in this class has convinced me that small-group interaction should be part of any class that is not a small seminar. I also am convinced that having the students become observers of their own interaction is a crucial part of their education. Talking about ways of talking in class makes students aware that their ways of talking affect other students, that the motivations they impute to others may not truly reflect others' motives, and that the behaviors they assume to be self-evidently right are not universal norms.   22

The goal of complete equal opportunity in class may not be attainable, but realizing that one monolithic classroom-participation structure is not equal opportunity is itself a powerful motivation to find more-diverse methods to serve diverse students—and every classroom is diverse.   23

Questions for Writing and Discussion

1 In her essay, Deborah Tannen states and then continues to restate her thesis. Reread her essay, underlining all the sentences that seem to state or rephrase her main idea. Do her restatements of the main idea make her essay clearer? Explain.

2 Explaining essays may explain *what* (describe and define), explain *how* (process analysis), and/or explain *why* (causal analysis). Find one example of each of these strategies in Tannen's essay. Which of these three is the dominant shaping strategy? Support your answer with references to specific sentences or paragraphs.

3 Effective explaining essays must have supporting evidence—specific examples, facts, quotations, testimony from experts, statistics, and so on. Choose four consecutive paragraphs from Tannen's essay and list the kinds of supporting evidence she uses. Based on your inventory, rate her supporting evidence as weak, average, or strong. Explain your choice.

4 Does the style of Tannen's essay support her thesis that men and women have different ways of communicating? Does Tannen, in fact, use a "woman's style" of writing that is similar to women's conversational style? Examine Tannen's tone (her attitude toward her subject and audience), her voice (the projection of her personality in her language), and her supporting evidence (her use of facts and statistics or anecdotal, contextual evidence). Cite specific passages to support your analysis.

Tips for Transferring Skills

The writing techniques discussed in this chapter can be used in many other situations you will face as a college writer and beyond. To reinforce these techniques, and to really put them to use, you should find ways to apply and practice them on other occasions and in other classes. Here are tips for using these techniques in a variety of writing situations.

1. In this chapter you learned about the uses of explanatory or "expository" writing. One crucial use of these skills will be in your science classes, where you often attempt to explain a chain of cause and effect. As you complete writing tasks such as lab reports, you can use the "causal chain" technique discussed on page 535.

2. One key premise of the social sciences is that "correlation does not prove causation." That is, even if two phenomena occur together, it does not mean that one has necessarily caused the other. As you write in social science classes such as sociology or psychology, use your lead-in sentences to explain the relationships between phenomena in ways that do not make unsupportable claims of causation.

3. One of the most basic—and most crucial—forms of explanation is the definition. When you write in other classes, be sure that you carefully define the ways that you use terms. For example, in a literature paper, you might define a key literary technique before showing how it is used in a story or poem. In a history class, you could explain how you define a term like "war" before arguing whether attempts to fight terrorism are "war." In each case, the explanatory definitions you use are key to the argument you will build.

4. Understanding how explanatory writing works can also make you a better reader. As you complete a reading assignment for another class, annotate the text or make notes in your journal that point out the use of explanatory techniques such as process analysis, definition, causal analysis, and so forth. That can help you see the subtle differences in how these techniques are used in various fields of study.

Explaining: Writing Processes

Using Explaining in Your Writing Processes

The techniques in this chapter can help you to *explain* what something means or is, *how* it should be done or *how* it occurs, and *why* something occurs. These writing techniques can help you to explain something as clearly as possible for your audience by analyzing, showing relationships, and demonstrating with examples, facts, illustrations, data, or other information. These skills will all be important facets of solving problems and building arguments through your writing as well.

As you develop a topic, use the grid below to think about the audience and genre that best fit that topic. Once you've chosen an audience, think about how much they know about the subject. Are they experts, novices, or somewhere in between? What specifically do they already know? What are they least likely to know?

Audience	Possible Genres for Explaining
Personal Audience	Class notes, annotations in a textbook, journal entry, blog, scrapbook, social networking page, explanatory video or podcast
Academic Audience	Expository essay, academic analysis and synthesis, journal entry, forum entry on class site, multimedia document
Public Audience	Column, letter, or article in a magazine, newspaper, online site, newsletter, explanatory video, or multimedia document

CHOOSING A SUBJECT

17.4
Use strategies for choosing a topic that requires explanatory writing

❝You can write about anything, and if you write well enough, even the reader with no intrinsic interest in the subject will become involved. **❞**

—Tracy Kidder,
Novelist

If one of your journal entries suggests a likely subject, go on to the collecting and shaping strategies. If you still need an interesting subject, consider the following suggestions.

- Think of the writing assignment you are currently working on and revisit your prewriting. Does your prewriting contain ideas that you might define or explain, processes suitable for how-to explanations, or causes or effects that you could analyze and explain for a certain audience?

- **Writing Across the Curriculum.** Reread your notes from another class in which you have an upcoming examination. Select some topic, idea, principle, process, famous person, or event from the text or your notes. Investigate other texts, popular magazines, or journals for information on that topic. If appropriate, interview someone or conduct a survey. Explain this principle or process to a member of your writing class.

- **Community Service Learning.** If you are doing a community service learning project, consider a writing project explaining the agency's mission to the public or to a potential donor. You might also write an article for a local or campus newspaper explaining a recent contribution the agency has made to the community.

- Write an artistic, cultural, historical, or social explanation of a visual image or a set of visual images. One excellent website for famous photographs is the Pulitzer site at http://www.gallerym.com. Decide on a particular audience, genre, and context appropriate for the photograph.

- Choose a current controversy and, instead of arguing for one side or the other, explain the different points of view. Who are the leading figures or groups representing each position? Choose a particular audience, genre, and context, and explain what each person or group has to gain or lose and how their personal investments in the topic determine their position.

COLLECTING

17.5
Use collecting strategies to gather reliable information

Questions

Once you have a tentative subject and audience, consider which of the following will be your primary focus (all three may be relevant).

- *What* something means or is
- *How* something occurs or is done (or should be done)
- *Why* something occurs or what its effects are

Focus on Definition To explain *what* something is, jot down answers to each of the following questions. The more you can write on each question, the more details you'll have for your topic.

- What are its class and distinguishing characteristics?
- What is its etymology?
- How can you describe it?
- What examples can you give?
- What are its parts or its functions?
- What is it similar to? What is it *not*?
- What figurative comparisons apply?
- How can it be classified?
- Which of the above is most useful to your audience?

Focus on Process Analysis To explain *how* something occurs or is done, answer the following questions.

- What are the component parts or steps in the whole process?
- What is the exact sequence of steps or events?
- Are several of the steps or events related?
- If steps or events were omitted, would the outcome change?
- Which steps or events are most crucial?
- Which steps or events does your audience most need to know?

Focus on Causal Analysis To explain *why* something occurs or what its effects are, consider the following questions.

- Which are the necessary or sufficient causes?
- Which causes are remote in time, and which are immediate?
- What is the order or sequence of the causes? Do the causes occur simultaneously?
- What are the effects? Do they occur in a sequence or simultaneously?
- Do the causes and effects occur in a "chain reaction"?
- Is there an action or situation that would have prevented the effect?
- Are there comparable things or events that have similar causes or effects?
- Which causes or effects will need special clarification for your audience?

Branching

Often, *branching* can help you analyze your subject visually. Start with your topic and then subdivide each idea into its component parts. The resulting analysis will not only help generate ideas but may also suggest ways to shape an essay.

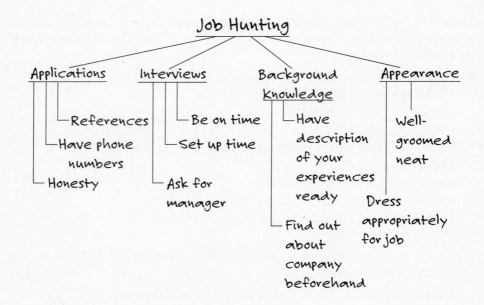

Observing

If you can observe your subject, try drawing it, describing it, or taking careful notes. Which senses can you use to describe it—sight, sound, touch, smell, taste? If it is a scientific experiment that you can reproduce or a social situation you can reconstruct, go through it again and observe carefully. As you observe it, put yourself in your readers' shoes: What do you need to explain to them?

Remembering

Your own experience and memory are essential for explaining. *Freewriting, looping,* and *clustering* may all generate detailed information, good examples, and interesting perspectives that will make your explanation clearer and more vivid. (See Chapter 15 for an explanation of looping and clustering.)

Reading

When you find written texts about your subject, be sure to use your active reading strategies. You may need only a few sources if you reread them carefully. Write out a short summary for each source. Respond to each source by analyzing its effectiveness, agreeing or disagreeing with its ideas, or interpreting the text. The quality of your understanding is more important than the sheer number of sources you cite.

Investigating

Use sources available in the library, textbooks containing relevant information, or interviews with teachers, participants, or experts. Interview your classmates about their own subjects for this assignment: Someone else's subject may trigger an idea

66 Readers may be strangers who have no immediate reason to care about your writing. They want order, clarity, and stimulation. 99

—Elizabeth Cowan **Neeld,** Teacher and author

that you can write about or may suggest a fresh approach to the subject you have chosen.

SHAPING AND DRAFTING

17.6
Use shaping and drafting strategies to choose an effective organization

As you think about ways to organize and develop your essay, be sure to reread your assignment and reconsider your purpose and audience. Limit your subject to create a *narrowed* and *focused* topic. You will not be able to cover everything you've read, thought, or experienced about your topic, so choose the most interesting ideas—for you and for your audience—and then try the following strategies.

Shaping Strategies

Do you want to . . .	Consider using these rhetorical modes or strategies:
define key terms or concepts?	definition, classification, example (p. 543)
describe how a process works?	chronological order (p. 545)
explain relationships between causes and effects?	causal analysis, example (p. 546)
structure your essay so your reader understands your thesis and can follow your explanation?	an introduction, thesis, essay map, and paragraph transitions; also consider multimedia options such as websites, audio, or video to explain or illustrate your point. (pp. 548–550)

Audience, Genre, and Medium

An essay directed at a general audience composed of peers like your classmates is just one possibility. A letter to the editor, a pamphlet for a community agency, a job analysis for your employer, an article for a local or school newspaper, a posting or response to a listserve, or an essay for students in your major are other possibilities. Once you have a tentative audience and genre, you'll have a better idea about how to organize your explanation. Reread your assignment for specific suggestions and guidelines about audience and genre.

Definition and Classification

An essay explaining *what* something means or is can be shaped by using a variety of definition strategies or by classifying the subject.

Definition itself is not a single organizing strategy; it supports a variety of strategies that may be useful in shaping your essay: description, analysis of parts or function, comparison/contrast, development by examples, or figures of speech such as simile, metaphor, and analogy.

Research Tips

Review your audience, purpose, and possible focus. Which of the following four research strategies would help you gather information on your topic?

1. Direct *observation* (see Chapter 15)
2. Use of *memories* and personal experience (see Chapter 15)
3. *Field research* including interviews and surveys
4. *Library/Internet* research

As you do your research, keep the following in mind:

- Save all your *links* or *Word files* or make *photocopies* or *printouts* of all the sources that you plan to cite in your essay.
- Be sure to *write all relevant bibliographic information,* such as author, date publisher, place of publication, journal title, and volume and issue numbers in your Word files or on the photocopies or printouts. Note the website sponsor and your access date for Web sources.
- When you cite sources in your text, be sure to *introduce* the sources.
- Make sure your direct quotations are *accurate* word-for-word transcriptions.

Classification, on the other hand, is a single strategy that can organize a paragraph or even a whole essay quickly. Observers of human behavior, for example, love to use classification. Grocery shoppers might be classified by types: racers (the ones who seem to have just won forty-five seconds of free shopping and run down the aisles filling their carts as fast as possible), talkers (the ones who stand in the aisles gossiping forever), penny-pinchers (who always have their calculators out and read the unit price labels for everything), and dawdlers (who leave their carts crosswise in the aisles while they read twenty-nine different soup can labels). You can write a sentence or two about each type or devote a whole paragraph to explaining a single type.

Example

Development by example can illustrate effectively what something is or means, and it can also help explain how or why something happens. Usually, an example describes a specific incident that *shows* or *demonstrates* the main idea. In the following paragraph from *Mediaspeak,* Donna Woolfolk Cross explains what effects soap operas can have on addicted viewers. This paragraph is developed by several examples—some described in detail, others referred to briefly.

> Dedicated watchers of soap operas often confuse fact with fiction . . . Stars of soap operas tell hair-raising stories of their encounters with fans suffering from this

affliction. Susan Lucci, who plays the promiscuous Erica Kane on "All My Children," tells of a time she was riding in a parade: "We were in a crowd of about 250,000 traveling in an antique open car moving ver-r-ry slowly. At that time in the series I was involved with a character named Nick. Some man broke through, came right up to the car and said to me, 'Why don't you give me a little bit of what you've been giving Nick?'" The man hung onto the car, menacingly, until she was rescued by the police. Another time, when she was in church, the reverent silence was broken by a woman's astonished remark, "Oh, my god, Erica prays!"

Voice and Tone

Writers use voice and tone to shape and control whole passages, often in combination with other shaping strategies. In the following paragraph, Toni Bambara, author of *The Salt Eaters* and numerous short stories, explains *what* being a writer is all about. This paragraph is shaped both by a single extended example and by Bambara's voice speaking directly to the reader.

> When I replay the tapes on file in my head, tapes of speeches I've given at writing conferences over the years, I invariably hear myself saying—"A writer, like any other cultural worker, like any other member of the community, ought to try to put her/his skills in the service of the community." Some years ago when I returned south, my picture in the paper prompted several neighbors to come visit. "You a writer? What all you write?" Before I could begin the catalogue, one old gent interrupted with—"Ya know Miz Mary down the block? She need a writer to help her send off a letter to her grandson overseas." So I began a career as the neighborhood scribe—letters to relatives, snarling letters to the traffic chief about the promised stop sign, nasty letters to the utilities, angry letters to the principal about that confederate flag hanging in front of the school, contracts to transfer a truck from seller to buyer, etc. While my efforts have been graciously appreciated in the form of sweet potato dumplings, herb teas, hair braiding, and the like, there is still much room for improvement—"For a writer, honey, you've got a mighty bad hand. Didn't they teach penmanship at that college?" Another example, I guess, of words setting things in motion. What goes around, comes around, as the elders say.

Chronological Order and Process Analysis

Writers use chronological order to help explain how something is typically done. In her essay "How to Take Control of Your Credit Cards," Suze Orman uses transitional words to signal the successive stages in the process she suggests. In the following sentences, the italicized words mark the chronological stages of this process.

> *Keep this up every month* until your card with the highest rate is paid off. *Then* turn your attention to the card with the next highest rate. *In addition* to the usual monthly minimum payment due on that second card, I want you to add in the entire amount you were previously paying on the first card (the one that's now paid off). So let's say you were paying a total of $200 a month on your original highest-rate card, and making a $75 monthly minimum on the second card. Well, *now* you are going to fork over $275 a month to the second card. And, of course, you'll *continue* to make the minimum monthly payment due on any other cards. *Once* your second card is

paid off, move on to the third. If your monthly payment on that second card was $275, then that's what you should add to the minimum payment due on your third card. Get the idea? Rinse and *repeat* as often as needed, until you have all your debt paid off. For some of you this may take a year, for others it may take many years. That's okay. Just get yourself moving in the right direction and you'll be amazed how gratifying it is to find yourself taking control of your money rather than letting it control you.

Causal Analysis

In order to explain *why* something happens or what the effects of something are, writers often use one of three patterns of cause and effect to shape their material.

Shaping Your Points: Several Causes, One Effect

In the case of fire, for example, we know that three causes lead to a single effect. These causes do not occur in any special sequence; they must all be present at the same time. For historical events, however, we usually list causes in chronological order.

Sometimes one cause has several effects. In that case, we reverse the pattern:

Shaping Your Points: One Cause, Several Effects

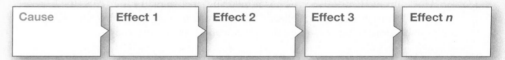

Tips for Integrating Images

For your explaining essay, you may wish to integrate images (photographs, graphics, or charts), and you may wish to modify your document design. To integrate images with your text, first consider your rhetorical situation.

- **What is your purpose?** Does the visual contribute to your thesis or main idea, or would it be just a distraction?
- **Who is your audience?** Is the image appropriate for your target audience? Would it make your document more appealing or attractive?

Would it offend? Would it amuse? Would it make your point in a way that words could not?

- **What is your intended genre?** Look at other examples of your genre (essay, pamphlet, web page, article, advertisement, brochure, laboratory report, letter, flyer). How do they use images or graphics?
- **What is the social/cultural context of your text?** Consider whether the subject, topic, or issue you are discussing could or should be illustrated with an image or a certain document design.

Use search engines and library sources to find images relevant to your topic. Start with an image search on Google or Yahoo!, but don't forget that your library has a wealth of online image databases. If you're looking for paintings or fine art, check websites for museums around the world. Having several potential images enables you to choose the one most effective for your rhetorical situation.

Finally, don't forget about your document design. Start with your purpose, audience, and genre. Consider how the genre you have selected uses the following document features.

- **Columns** Would a text with two columns work for your purpose?
- **Margins and white space** Avoid overcrowding words, images, and graphics on a page. Use margins and white space to emphasize key parts of your text.
- **Fonts** Use a font appropriate to your purpose, genre, and audience. Times New Roman and Palatino Linotype are widely accepted, but do you need **Franklin Gothic Demi** for particular parts of your text? For special situations, perhaps consider a script face such as Felt Tip or a bolder face such as TRADE GOTHIC.
- **Sidebars** If appropriate for your text, use a sidebar for emphasis or to add related information.

> Is the image appropriate for your target audience? Does the image contribute to your thesis?

For example, an explanation of the collapse of the economy following the stock market crash of 1929 might follow this pattern. The crash (itself a symptom of other causes) led to a depreciated economy, widespread unemployment, bankruptcy for thousands of businesses, and foreclosures on farms. An essay on the effects of the crash might devote one or two paragraphs to each effect.

In the third pattern, causes and effects form a pattern of chain reactions. One cause leads to an effect that then becomes the cause of another effect, and so on:

Shaping Your Points: Causal Chain

We could analyze the circumstances that led to the rise of the extremist group ISIS (the Islamic State in Iraq and Syria). We could trace the series of actions and reactions that allowed for the quick growth and strength of what at first seemed just a small splinter group. Such an analysis would show how each political action and governmental decision in the Middle East and elsewhere contributed to a causal chain that led to the major crisis that this group has come to represent.

Introduction and Lead-in

The first sentences of the introductory paragraph of an essay are often the hardest to write. You want to get your reader's attention and focus on the main idea of your essay, but you don't want to begin, boringly, with your thesis statement. Several kinds of opening sentences are designed to grab your reader's interest. Consider your topic to see if one of these strategies will work for you.

A Personal Example

I knew my dieting had gotten out of hand, but when I could actually see the movement of my heart beating beneath my clothes, I knew I was in trouble.

—Nancie Brosseau, "Anorexia Nervosa"

A Description of a Person or Place

It's still there, the Chinese school on Yale Street where my brother and I used to go. Despite the new coat of paint and the high wire fence, the school I knew ten years ago remains remarkably, stoically the same.

— Elizabeth Wong, "The Struggle to Be an All-American Girl"

A Striking Question or Questions

Do nonhuman animals have rights? Should we humans feel morally bound to exercise consideration for the lives and well-being of individual members of other animal species? If so, how much consideration, and by what logic?

— David Quammen, "Animal Rights and Beyond"

A Common Error or Mistaken Judgment

There was a time when, in my search for essences, I concluded that the canyonland country has no heart. I was wrong. The canyonlands did have a heart, a living heart, and that heart was Glen Canyon and the golden, flowing Colorado River.

—Edward Abbey, "The Damnation of a Canyon"

Lead-in, Thesis, and Essay Map

The introduction to an explaining essay usually contains these features:

- **Lead-in:** An example, description, startling statement, statistic, short narrative, allusion, or quotation to get the reader's interest *and* focus on the topic the writer will explain.
- **Thesis:** Statement of the main idea; a "promise" to the reader that the essay will fulfill.
- **Essay map:** A sentence, or part of a sentence, that *lists* (in the order in which the essay will discuss them) the subtopics for the essay.

In her essay on anorexia nervosa, Nancie Brosseau's introductory paragraph has all three features.

I knew my dieting had gotten out of hand, but when I could actually see the movement of my heart beating beneath my clothes, I knew I was in trouble. At first, the family doctor reassured my parents that my rapid weight loss was a "temporary phase among teenage girls." However, when I, at fourteen years old and five feet tall, weighed in at sixty-three pounds, my doctor changed his diagnosis from "temporary phase" to "anorexia nervosa." Anorexia nervosa is the process of self-starvation that affects over 100,000 young girls each year. Almost 6,000 of these girls die every year. Anorexia nervosa is a self-mutilating disease that affects its victim both physically and emotionally.

> Lead-in: Startling statement
>
> Description
>
>
>
> Statistics
> Thesis and essay map

The essay map is contained in the phrase "both physically and emotionally": The first half of the essay discusses the physical effects of anorexia nervosa; the second half explains the emotional effects. Like a road map, the essay map helps the reader anticipate what topics the writer will explain.

Paragraph Transitions and Hooks

Transition words and paragraph hooks are audience cues that help the reader shift from one paragraph to the next. These connections between paragraphs enable the reader to see the relationships of the various parts. Transition words—*first, second, next, another, last, finally,* and so forth—signal your reader that a new idea or a new part of the idea is coming up. In addition to transition words, writers often tie paragraphs together by using a key word or idea from one paragraph in the first sentence of the next paragraph to "hook" the paragraphs together.

The following paragraphs from Deborah Tannen's essay illustrate how transition words and paragraph hooks work together to create smooth connections between paragraphs.

> The research of sociologists and anthropologists . . . has shown <u>that girls and boys learn to use language differently</u> in their sex-separate peer groups. Typically, <u>a girl</u> has a best friend with whom she sits and talks, frequently telling secrets. It's the telling of secrets, the fact and the way that they talk to each other, that makes them best friends. <u>For boys</u>, activities are central: their best friends are the ones they do things with. Boys also tend to play in larger groups that are hierarchical. High-status boys give orders and push low-status boys around. So boys are expected to use language to seize center stage: by exhibiting their skill, displaying their knowledge, and challenging and resisting challenges.
>
> These patterns have stunning implications for classroom interaction. Most faculty members assume that participating in class discussion is a necessary part of successful performance. Yet speaking in a classroom is more congenial to boys' language experience than to girls', since it entails putting oneself forward in front of a large group of people, many of whom are strangers and at least one of whom is sure to judge speakers' knowledge and intelligence by their verbal display.
>
> Another aspect of many classrooms that makes them more hospitable to most men than to most women is the use of debate-like formats as a learning tool. . . .

Body Paragraphs

Body paragraphs in expository writing are the main paragraphs in an essay, excluding any introductory, concluding, or transition paragraphs. They often contain these features:

- **Topic sentence.** To promote clarity and precision, writers often use topic sentences to announce the main ideas of paragraphs. The main idea should be clearly related to the writer's thesis. A topic sentence usually occurs early in the paragraph (first or second sentence) or at the end of the paragraph.
- **Unity.** To avoid confusing readers, writers focus on a single idea for each paragraph. Writing unified paragraphs helps writers—and their readers—concentrate on one point at a time.
- **Coherence.** To make their writing flow smoothly from one sentence to the next, writers supplement their shaping strategies with coherence devices: repeated key words, pronouns referring to key nouns, and transition words.

One body paragraph from Deborah Tannen's essay illustrates these features. The first sentence is the *topic sentence*, which focuses our attention on the key idea to be discussed in the paragraph: "girls and boys learn to use language differently." The paragraph has *unity* because it follows this topic sentence by first describing how girls use language and then discussing how boys use language. Paragraph *coherence* is achieved by focusing on the one idea of different language use, and by discussing first the girls' use of language and then the boys' use of language—as forecast, or promised, in the topic sentence.

The research of sociologists and anthropologists . . . has shown that girls and boys learn to use language differently in their sex-separate peer groups. Typically, a girl has a best friend with whom she sits and talks, frequently telling secrets. It's the telling of secrets, the fact and the way that they talk to each other, that makes them best friends. For boys, activities are central: their best friends are the ones they do things with. Boys also tend to play in larger groups that are hierarchical. High-status boys give orders and push low-status boys around. So boys are expected to use language to seize center stage: by exhibiting their skill, displaying their knowledge, and challenging and resisting challenges.

Before you begin drafting, reconsider your purpose and audience. What you will explain depends on what your audience needs to know or what would demonstrate your point most effectively. The thesis statement you write in an explanatory essay usually states your topic, and at the same time it helps the audience understand how and why it is useful for them to have this information.

As you work from an outline or from an organizing strategy, remember that all three questions—*what, how,* and *why*—are interrelated. When you are writing about causes, for example, an explanation of *what* the topic is and *how* the causes function may be necessary to explain your subject clearly. As you write, balance your sense of plan and organization with a willingness to pursue ideas that you discover as you write. Be ready to change course if you discover a more interesting idea or angle.

REVISING

As you revise your explaining essay, concentrate on making yourself clear, on illustrating with examples where your reader might be confused, and on signaling the relationship of the parts of your essay to your reader.

17.7
Use revision strategies to assure clear explanations

Guidelines for Revision

- **Review your purpose, audience, and genre.** Will your purpose be clear to your target audience? Should you modify your chosen genre to appeal to your audience?

- **Review possibilities for visuals or graphics.** What additions or changes to images might be appropriate for your purpose, genre, or audience?

- **Compare your thesis sentence with what you say in your conclusion.** You may have formed a clearer statement of your thesis near the end of your paper. Revise your original thesis sentence to make it clearer, more focused, or more in line with what your essay actually says.

- **Explaining means *showing* and *demonstrating* relationships.** Be sure to follow general statements with *specific examples, details, facts, statistics, memories, dialogues,* or other *illustrations*.

> **❝I wish he would explain his explanation.❞**
>
> —Lord Byron,
> Poet

- **In a formal definition, be sure to state the class of objects or concepts to which the term belongs.** Avoid ungrammatical writing, such as "Photosynthesis is *when* plants absorb oxygen" or "The lymphatic system is *where* the body removes bacteria and transports fatty cells."

- **Avoid introducing definitions with "Webster says. . . . "** Instead, read definitions from several dictionaries and give the best or most appropriate definition.

- **Collaborating with peers.** One of the best ways to assure that explanations are clear is to have others read them to see if your point comes across. Ask a peer to read your piece, then ask her or him to explain to you key elements from the essay. Were your main points understood?

- **Don't mix categories when you are classifying objects or ideas.** If you are classifying houses *by floor design* (ranch, bilevel, split-level, two-story), don't bring in other categories, such as passive-solar, which could be incorporated into any of those designs.

- **In explaining *how* something occurs or should be done, be sure to indicate to your audience which steps are *most important*.**

- **In cause-and-effect explanations, avoid post hoc fallacies.** This term comes from the Latin phrase *post hoc, ergo propter hoc:* "After this, therefore because of this." For example, just because Event B occurred after Event A, it does not follow, necessarily, that A caused B. If, for example, statistics show that traffic fatalities in your state declined after the speed limit on interstate highways was increased, you should not conclude that higher speeds caused the reduction in fatalities. Other causes—increased radar patrols, stiffer drunk-driving penalties, or more rigorous vehicle-maintenance laws—may have been responsible.

- **As you revise to sharpen your meaning or make your organization clearer, use appropriate transitional words and phrases to signal the *relationships among the parts of your subject*.**

  —*To signal relation in time:* before, meanwhile, later, soon, at last, earlier, thereafter, afterward, by that time, from then on, first, next, now, presently, shortly, immediately, finally

  —*To signal similarity:* likewise, similarly, once again, once more

  —*To signal difference:* but, yet, however, although, whereas, though, even so, nonetheless, still, on the other hand, on the contrary

  —*To signal consequences:* as a result, consequently, therefore, hence, for this reason

USING EXPLAINING TO REDEFINE A PHENOMENON

As you have learned in this chapter, explaining is not always an attempt to teach an audience about an unfamiliar concept or phenomenon. In many cases, it is really about explaining why the audience's views on that topic are incomplete or misinformed.

That is, we explain not only to inform, but to help an audience understand things differently. For example, student Chris Blakely decided to write his essay on white-collar crime to help readers better understand how serious these crimes can be—that they are not just "white lies." To do so, he explains the collapse of financial institutions, such as AIG, and the revelation of pyramid schemes, such as the one perpetrated by Bernie Madoff, which cost investors $65 billion. After gathering information about the nature of white-collar crime and its effects, Blakely then focuses two examples: the Enron collapse and the Adelphia Communications scandal. His purpose was to explain what white-collar crime is and how its effects can be more devastating than those of street crime. As his essay overview explains, he also wrote a graphic novel to help make his point more visually and memorably for his audience. Sample pages from his graphic novel appear on the next page.

Student Writing

White Lies: White-Collar Crime in America

Chris Blakely

Chris Blakely decided to write his essay on white-collar crime after the collapse of financial institutions such as AIG and the revelation of pyramid schemes such as the one perpetrated by Bernie Madoff that cost investors $65 billion. After gathering information about the nature of white-collar crime and its effects, Blakely decided to focus on two examples: the Enron collapse and the Adelphia Communications scandal. His purpose was to explain what white-collar crime is and how its effects can be more devastating than those of street crime. As his essay overview explains, he also wrote a graphic novel to help make his point more visually and memorably for his audience. Sample pages from his graphic novel appear on the next page.

ESSAY OVERVIEW

In this paper, I planned to analyze the state of white collar crime and how it is perceived by the general public and the justice system. I found in my early research that white-collar criminals are perceived as less of a threat than street criminals (Holtfreter et al.). This helped me to realize that public perception needs to change—and helping to change that perception was the main goal of my paper. I first needed to define white-collar crime, which I limited to cases where an employee of a public company engaged in illegal activity that seems to benefit that person and the company, but in the end harms the company, its employees, and its stockholders. I found examples of crime on a large scale, such as the Enron, Tyco, and WorldCom scandals, to show how damaging white-collar crime can be at its highest levels.

(Continued)

...*continued* White Lies: White-Collar Crime in America, **Chris Blakely**

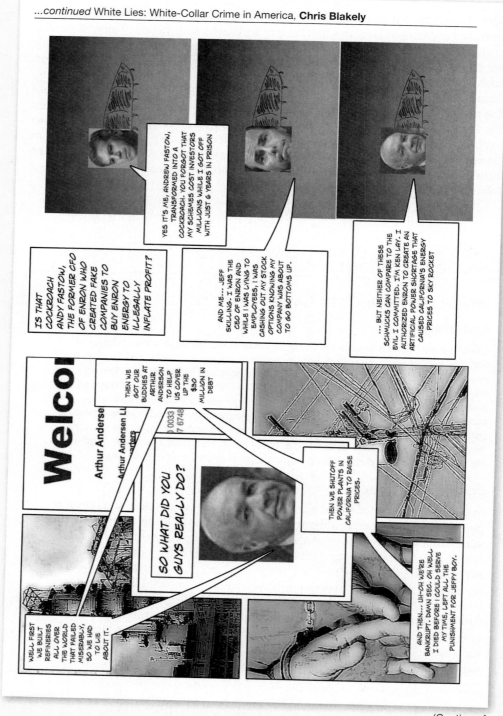

(Continued)

Understanding this type of crime first became important to me when I found that, "according to the Federal Bureau of Investigation, white-collar crime is estimated to cost the United States more than $300 billion annually" (Legal Information Institute). Despite a recent rise in white-collar crime awareness, I was outraged that the justice system had not shifted its efforts to reduce white-collar crime. How are white-collar criminals getting away with $300 billion every year? What happens to the employees when companies go bankrupt as a result of this crime? It is necessary to understand all types of crime so that society can treat all criminals in a fair and just manner.

I also wanted to understand why people didn't take white-collar crime seriously, so the second part of my paper used studies, mainly one by Florida State University, which look at public perception of white-collar crime. I wanted to show how white-collar crime can be just as damaging to the general public as street crime. This part helped to validate my thesis and show that this paper is exigent.

One major audience for this paper is business students. It will be their decisions that shape the business world, and the ethical decisions they make could reduce white-collar crime. It will be their bosses, coworkers, and corporations committing white-collar crime—and maybe asking them to participate. If they have a better understanding of the term, as well as a sense of how damaging it can be, businesses may act more ethically.

Considering the audience of students, I then created a short graphic novel about a CEO who is tempted to commit white-collar crime, but is dissuaded after meeting characters like Jeff Skilling, Dennis Kozlowski, and Karl Marx. My graphic novel, "Hope for America," looks at the illegal activity orchestrated by the CEOs of Enron. I wanted readers to be intrigued but not overwhelmed by the magnitude of the crimes. I felt that the graphic novel, which I created by learning and using the program "Comic Life," would be a great medium for presenting the information because it can be informal and is driven by visuals. It is also a much faster way for the audience to understand my point than reading a research paper—and maybe can interest them in later reading more details.

FINAL DRAFT

1   In the prosperous days before the current economic crisis, stories about misdoings among corporate executives got little more than a nod and a wink; businesspeople, it seemed, were expected to cut corners and bend the rules in seeking the profits expected of their shareholders. After all, were these "real" crimes?

Question introduces readers to the key definition that informs this explanatory essay

2   But times have changed. In the face of growing unemployment, numerous bankruptcies, and shrinking retirement funds, suddenly the public (and the justice system) have turned their attention—and sometimes their rage—toward the white-collar criminal. Joe Nacchio, CEO of Qwest Communication, has been sentenced to six years in federal prison; Bernie Madoff, who pled guilty to defrauding clients out of some $65 billion, has faced not only criminal penalties but also death threats; and bonuses paid to executives at the American International Group (AIG) have caused public outrage by citizens and legislators. But while

Shows the exigency of the topic

(Continued)

these and countless other abuses have finally caught the public and governmental eye, white-collar crime is no new phenomenon. A look back at the all-but-forgotten Aldephia Communications scandal and the Enron debacle before that demonstrates how, despite the spectacular headlines, we largely ignored this building storm until it was too late.

Thesis statement previewed

On March 27, 2002, John Rigas and his executive board at Adelphia prepared for a routine financial check by the Securities and Exchange Commission. The investigation disclosed that the Rigas family had illegally co-borrowed $2.3 billion from the company. To cover the loans, it was estimated that Adelphia would have to borrow $1 billion. In response, investors pushed Adelphia's stock down 30% the very next day. Adelphia's shares were temporarily taken off the market and by summer the company filed for bankruptcy. On July 24, 2002, Rigas and his sons were arrested in New York City. Rigas's son Tim was sentenced to twenty years, while his father was given fifteen years for securities fraud (Cauley). After his trial, John Rigas maintained that, "It was a case of being in the wrong place at the wrong time. If this happened a year before, there would have been no headlines" (Cauley). In other words, Rigas felt that few would have noticed his actions if he had been caught before Enron and other corporate scandals of 2001 were exposed. And perhaps he was right.

Explains the way this crisis unfolded

The Adelphia story would be a tragedy in its own right, but when it is looked at in conjunction with companies like Enron, WorldCom, Tyco, Global Crossing, Qwest, Xerox, and several other Fortune 500 companies that went bankrupt after white-collar crime was exposed, a pattern of corruption that has existed for many years emerges. In the film *Enron: The Smartest Guys in the Room*, Bethany Mclean, a co-author of the book of the same title, shows a significant problem with how white-collar crime is perceived: "The Enron story is so fascinating because people perceive it as a story that's about numbers, that it's somehow about all these complicated transactions. In reality it's a story about people, and it's really a human tragedy" (Gibney).

Explains a possible misconception that the author wishes to build upon

By explaining the human costs behind these white collar crimes, I hope to show why the public must pay attention to this public scourge. First, I want to show how the sentencing of these criminals, as compared to the sentencing of street criminals, sends the wrong message about the serious nature of white-collar crime. Second, I hope to demonstrate that public perception of white-collar crime is flawed and out of sync with the personal tragedies that crime causes.

States purpose and thesis, and previews the organization of the essay

The term *white-collar crime* was originally coined by Edward Sutherland in 1939. Sutherland defined white-collar crime as "crime committed by a person of respectability and high social status in the course of their occupation" (Strader 1). Recently, sociologists and criminologists have debated what crimes are considered white-collar. Often, the term refers to a crime committed in the course of a person's occupation—no matter the social class. But, as Sutherland suggests, true white-collar crime is that which has a great impact upon society.

Uses definition to explain the key concept

White-collar crime is often very difficult to detect. The crimes take place in private offices where there are rarely eye-witnesses. The government has to base

3

4

5

6

7

(Continued)

their prosecution on complex paper trails instead of concrete evidence (Strader 1-4). Also, white-collar criminals of high social status are able to hire better-trained, more experienced lawyers. This makes convicting white-collar criminals much more difficult than convicting street criminals.

Because white-collar crimes are often not given due attention, it is difficult for the majority of Americans to understand their financial complexity. Understanding the methods used to commit the crimes, however, is not nearly as important as recognizing the damage that is done to countless employees who lose everything that they worked years to accomplish. Americans need to realize that their ignorance of the effects of white collar crime has allowed the American justice system to be unfairly lax in the way it treats white-collar criminals.

8 — Provides reason why this essay's explanations are necessary

If we compare white-collar crime to a typical armed robbery, we can see the inequality of the current justice system. For example, compare the sentencing of John Rigas to that of three Kentuckians who robbed a small grocery store. In November 2007, Morgan Wallace, 30, entered the grocery store with a handgun and demanded money. Geneva S. Goodin and Megan Johnston assisted in the escape before the three were apprehended on a highway near the scene of the crime. All three were held in a detention center after the robbery. On April 11, 2008, Wallace and Goodin were sentenced to ten years in prison while Johnston was sentenced to five years ("Three Plead"). Unlike Rigas, Wallace, Goodin, and Johnston were not able to obtain bail money so that they could go to their homes before their trial. The three robbers were arrested, tried, and convicted within five to six months. That period is a stark contrast to the five years of freedom that Rigas was allowed before a judge requested he begin his jail time (Cauley). There is also a clear disparity in the punishment that was handed out in relation to the damage of the crimes to society. The amount that the Kentuckians made off with was not disclosed, but it is certainly a miniscule amount compared with the $2.3 billion that Rigas gained, followed by the millions of dollars that were lost to shareholders. However, Wallace's term is only five years shorter than that of John Rigas, and there was no stipulation that the sentence could be as short as two years (as with Rigas's case), if Wallace's health declined.

9 — Uses comparison/contrast

The Rigas case is important in its own right, but it is impossible to explain the devastation caused by white-collar crime without also examining the Enron scandal. In January 2001, Enron was the seventh largest corporation in America. Enron had built oil-extracting stations all over the world, but most of them were performing terribly. However, instead of accurately releasing the correct financial statistics, Enron's executives included prospective profits in its bottom line. Enron and its accounting firm, Arthur Anderson, were able to hide the fact that Enron was $30 million in debt. Enron's CFO, Andy Fastow, created fake partnerships that would buy energy from Enron, in order to increase Enron's value. However, Fastow was merely working under Kenneth Lay, the founder of the company, and Jeffrey Skilling, the CEO. When investors started to question Enron's finances, Enron was not able to provide legitimate documentation for their profits. The final straw was when Enron began shutting down power plants in California in order to create artificial power shortages to increase the price of energy. Then the SEC began to inquire into Enron. In response, Enron began to

10 — Explains the importance of this case toward understanding white collar crime's effects

(Continued)

...continued White Lies: White-Collar Crime in America, **Chris Blakely**

Demonstrates causal chain

release massive restatements, and Arthur Anderson began to shred documents concerning Enron. Six weeks after the investigations began, Enron filed for bankruptcy (Gibney). Ken Lay passed away before he could be sentenced. Jeff Skilling was sentenced to twenty-four years and $60 million in fines; however, he was allowed to keep his $5 million mansion and $50 million in stocks and bonds. Andy Fastow was sentenced to just six years in prison.

The difference between Enron and other corporate scandals is that no other company has ever been so high and fallen with such damaging consequences. While Adelphia was partially bought up by Time Warner (Cauley), Enron completely collapsed. The stock value went from $90.75 at its peak to just $.08 after the company filed for bankruptcy. Five thousand employees lost their jobs, along with $800 million in pension funds. It is also important to remember that not all of the damage was financial. Enron employees and investors were personally affected. After losing their jobs, former employees were forced to deal with the stress that surrounds finding a new job and making ends meet while providing for a family. The employees went from having a secure future in a successful company to being unemployed with most of their stock and their retirement funds erased. Enron was white-collar crime at its worst.   11

Reinforces exigency by explaining the effects upon real people

These personal tragedies are often lost in the extravagant numbers and complex business practices. As a result of the fraud committed by a small group of men, thousands of people lost their livelihood. This problem cannot be considered an isolated incident. Doing that would ignore the damage that white-collar crime has already done and foster ignorance of future corporate fraud. As Ben Lerach, the chief attorney for Enron employees stated, "It's the same old adage; if it looks too good to be true, then it is. Enron was making millions of dollars out of nowhere, and no one inside the company was there to stand up and question where this money was coming from" (Gibney). But is the public aware?   12

Question used to transition into the next topic

Following these high-profile white-collar crimes, researchers took specific interest in how white-collar crime is perceived by the general public. Researchers at the College of Criminology at Florida State University published a study in February 2008 that addressed this topic. In preliminary research it was found that white-collar crime costs the United States about $250 billion per year, whereas personal, or "street crimes," and household crimes account for only $17.6 billion lost. Despite this large disparity, the focus of criminal justice authorities and criminologists has been on explaining and preventing personal crime.   13

Uses published survey research to demonstrate public opinion on the topic

A study by researchers at Cal State and the University of Florida published in February 2007 provides more data on the topic. Researchers used data from a national phone poll of 1,106 participants and found that three-quarters of the sample believed that street criminals were more likely to be caught and more likely to receive a harsher punishment. The sample was split on who *should* receive a harsher punishment. This study suggests that while the public may believe all criminals should receive the same punishment, it is clear that Americans believe white-collar criminals will receive less of a punishment (Schoepfer).   14

(Continued)

Interesting conclusions can be drawn from both of these studies. From the   *15*
Florida State study, participants believed that in a case where a white-collar criminal and a street criminal commit crimes of equal financial damage, the street
criminal should receive a harsher punishment. This may be because street crime
is usually a crime where the victim is personally involved in a confrontation,
whereas white-collar crime is a more indirect form of victimization. However, it
is obvious, due to the large gap in total damages, that white-collar criminals are
acting more frequently and doing more financial damage than street criminals.
The second study shows that the public acknowledges a disparity in the sentencing of white-collar and street criminals, yet no major reforms have attempted to
change this pattern. These studies show that public perception is inaccurate as
based on the threat that each type of crime poses financially.

Explains the importance of the research cited

The American business model is an institution that has shown sustainability   *16*
and reliability for the past two hundred years. However, it is through this institution that Americans are stealing nearly fifteen times more money than through
conventional street crimes. The devastating effects of white-collar crime need to
be discussed by all Americans and addressed in a systematic way. The current
outrage is not sufficient for a long-term fix. People lock their doors when they
leave their houses, but they see no problem in putting ninety percent of their
401k stock options into one company. White-collar crime has produced real
damage, and without change in public opinion, there are no signs that it will decline. Understanding white-collar crime now can prevent or reduce the damage
that white-collar crime inflicts on America.

Builds toward conclusion about the insidious nature of this phenomenon

Reinforces the importance of both the topic and his explanations of it.

Works Cited

Cauley, Leslie. "John Rigas Tells His Side of the Adelphia Story." *USA Today*. Gannett, 10 Apr. 2008. Web. 12 Apr. 2009.

Legal Information Institute. "White-Collar Crime." *Cornell University Law School*. N.D. Web. 13 November 2014. https://www.law.cornell.edu/wex/white-collar_crime

"Former Enron CEO Skilling Gets 24 Years." *Associated Press*. Associated Press, 23 Oct. 2006. Web. 11 Apr. 2009.

Gibney, Alex, dir. *Enron: The Smartest Guys in the Room*. Perf. Peter Coyote. Jigsaw, 2005. Film.

Holtfreter, Kristy, et al. "Public Perception of White-Collar Crime." *Journal of Criminal Justice* 36:1 (2008): 50–60. Print.

Meier, Barry. "Founder of Adelphia Is Found Guilty of Conspiracy." *New York Times*. New York Times, 8 July 2004. Web. 13 Apr. 2009.

Schoepfer, Andrea, et al. "Do Perceptions of Punishment Vary between White Collar and Street Crimes?" *Journal of Criminal Justice* 35:2 (2007): 151–63. Print.

Strader, Kelly. "Understanding White Collar Crime." *Understanding White Collar Crime*. New York: Mathew Bender, 2002. 1–13. Print.

"Three Plead Guilty in Store Robbery." *McCreary County Voice*. McCreary County Voice, 11 Apr. 2008. Web. 13 Apr. 2009.

Questions for Writing and Discussion

1 In his essay overview, Chris Blakely says his purpose is to change public perception about the effects of white-collar crime. Cite at least two specific sentences from his essay where Blakely states this purpose.

2 Explaining essays typically use definition, process analysis, and cause-and-effect reasoning to demonstrate the main points. Reread Blakely's essay. Then cite examples of all of these strategies from his paper. Which of the strategies is most closely related to his purpose or thesis? Explain.

3 In an explaining essay, transitions from paragraph to paragraph help to clarify the subject for the audience. Review the section on "Paragraph Transitions and Hooks" in this chapter (pages 543–544). Then find two places where Blakely makes clear and smooth transitions from one paragraph to the next. Identify the transition words and hooks he uses to connect these paragraphs.

4 Review the selections from Blakely's graphic novel. How do the scenes he depicts relate to the subject and purpose of his essay? Do the cartoon-like pictures and captions make white-collar crime seem humorous? How do Blakely's images and captions convey the seriousness of these crimes? Explain, citing specific images and dialogue.

Applying What You Have Learned

1 Write an extended definition of an object or phenomenon that goes beyond its conventional definition to show its social impact, and which helps a specific audience understand that impact more fully. For example, you might write a definition of social media to shows that it is not just a technology, but a change in how humans relate to one another. Or you could write a definition of an automobile that shows that it really represents American freedom rather than being just a mode of transportation. Highlight the key elements and characteristics of the thing or phenomenon you are defining in order to move readers toward the purposeful definition you have in mind. Start by identifying your audience and purpose, then consider how you might collect key details that will help you create this extended redefinition. As you shape, draft, and revise your essay, keep that audience and purpose in mind.

Using multimedia. The definition of a thing or phenomenon can be greatly enhanced by vivid examples that show the reader its key features. Multimedia can strengthen your definition when you include visual or auditory examples. Images can help the reader see how an object affects those who interact with it, and video or audio clips can provide the chance to see and hear the deeper effects of a phenomenon that you want to redefine more broadly. Imagine, for example, how audio clips of people talking about their cars could help you make the case about how automobiles represent freedom, or how text boxes with social media excerpts could visually demonstrate the relationships found in social media.

② Describe a process for completing a task that you have mastered, but which others seem to struggle with. For example, you might find changing the oil in your car a very simple job, but you know that many others find it daunting and spend money unnecessarily on professional oil changes. Or you might find that older Americans who could connect with their families through Facebook avoid it because they don't know how to get started. Write a process essay that helps a specific audience learn the simple steps to becoming proficient at doing something that will benefit them. First assess the audience's needs and what causes them to avoid doing something. Then, collect details about how this process can be made simple, and shape them into a clear set of steps, drafting an essay that uses techniques in this chapter such as chronology and transitions to help readers move smoothly through the process. As you revise, ask members of your intended audience to try out the process you describe to see whether parts of it may be unclear.

Using multimedia. Showing how to do something is often greatly enhanced by illustrations, audio descriptions, and video. If you seek information on the Web for how to do something, for example, you will often find sites that provide a video or a set of images with audio voiceover. To enhance the process you have written about in your process essay—or to present your explanation without written text altogether—use visual, auditory, or video media to illustrate the process. In doing this, you will still need to outline a clear set of steps and organize them chronologically, using the same techniques you use as a writer.

③ Demonstrate how one phenomenon was (or continues to be) the cause of another. For example, you might want to show that the passing of a law has caused unintended consequences (raising the legal drinking age has in fact caused teens to drink more) or how a recent trend has affected specific facets of society in ways that have not adequately been considered. Remember that, as this chapter makes clear, showing a cause-and-effect relationship can be difficult (because one event preceded another doesn't mean that one caused the other). As you collect information, look for specific details that will show that one event had a real influence on another. As you shape and draft, use connections to organize your piece in a way that reinforces that cause-and-effect relationship.

Using multimedia. Because causation is often a difficult case to make, using visual depictions that demonstrate the relationship between events or phenomena can be useful. Charts, graphs, and other visual representations of both quantitative and qualitative data help your reader envision relationships. Using as a model the "causal chains" diagrams on pages 540–542, prepare a chart that illustrates the connections between cause and effect on the topic you are explaining. Or draw a graph that shows how the growth or decline of one phenomenon mirrors the growth or decline of another.

Parliament comes from the same root as *parlor*, which means "to speak" (from the French, *parler*). A parliament, like a parlor, is a place where people come together to speak to one another—to argue or debate the issues of the day. That is why the seats in legislatures like this one (and in our living rooms) are usually arranged to face one another. In this chapter, you'll learn several forms of argument that are meant to lead to productive outcomes as participants in a debate face one another.

Persuasive Writing

W HEN people argue with each other, they often become highly emotional or confrontational. Recall the last heated argument you had with a friend or family member: at the end of the argument, perhaps one of you stomped out of the room, slammed the door, and didn't speak to the other for days. In the aftermath of such a scene, you felt angry with the other person and with yourself. Neither of you came close to achieving what you wanted when you began the argument. Rather than understanding each other's point of view and working out your differences, you effectively closed the lines of communication.

When writers construct written arguments, however, they try to avoid the emotional outbursts that often turn arguments into displays of temper. Strong feelings may energize an argument—few of us make the effort to argue without an emotional investment in the subject—but written argument stresses the fair presentation of opposing or alternative arguments. Because written arguments are public, they take on a civilized manner. They implicitly say, Let's be reasonable. Let's look at the evidence on all sides. Before we argue for our position, let's put all the reasons and evidence on the table so everyone can see what's at stake.

> **Give me liberty to know, to utter, and to argue freely according to conscience, above all liberties.**
>
> —John Milton,
> Poet

> **All writing . . . is propaganda for something.**
>
> —Elizabeth Drew,
> Writer and critic

Taken from *The Prentice Hall Guide for College Writers*, Eleventh Edition by Stephen P. Reid and Dominic DelliCarpini.

As writers construct written arguments, they carefully consider the rhetorical situation:

- What is the social or cultural context for this issue?
- Where might this written argument appear or be published?
- Who is the audience, and what do they already know or believe?
- Do readers hold an opposing or alternative viewpoint, or are they more neutral and likely to listen to both sides before deciding what to believe?

An effective written argument creates an atmosphere of reason, which encourages readers to examine their own views clearly and dispassionately. When successful, such argument convinces rather than alienates an audience. It changes people's minds or persuades them to adopt a recommended course of action.

Techniques for Writing Arguments

A written argument is similar to a public debate between attorneys in a court of law or between members of Congress who represent different political parties. It begins with a debatable issue: Is this a good bill? Should we vote for it? In such debates, one person argues for a position or proposal, while the other argues against it. The onlookers (the judge, the jury, members of Congress, the public) then decide what to believe or what to do. This is why, as in the opening image of this chapter, we see legislatures designed in ways that encourage participants to argue an issue face to face.

Written argument, however, is not identical to a debate. *In a written argument, the writer must play all the roles.* The writer is above all the person arguing for the claim. But the writer must also represent what the opposition might say. In addition, the writer must make sure the argument follows appropriate rules. Depending on the audience, certain arguments or types of evidence are more or less effective. The writer needs to anticipate the responses of the audience and respond to them as well.

Written argument, then, represents several points of view, responds to them reasonably and fairly, and gives reasons and evidence that support the writer's claim. An effective written argument uses the techniques described in the box on the facing page.

In an article titled "Active and Passive Euthanasia," James Rachels claims that active euthanasia may be defensible for patients with incurable and painful diseases. The following paragraphs from that article illustrate the key features of argument.

Opposing position

       The distinction between active and passive euthanasia is thought to be crucial for medical ethics. The idea is that it is permissible, at least in some cases, to withhold treatment and allow a patient to die, but it is never permissible to take any direct action designed to kill the patient. This doctrine seems to be accepted by most doctors. . . .

Claim

       However, a strong case can be made against this doctrine. In what follows I will set out some of the relevant arguments, and urge doctors to reconsider their

Audience

views on this matter.

Techniques for Arguing

Technique	Tips on How to Do It
Analyzing the *rhetorical situation*	• Review your purpose, audience, genre, occasion, and context to understand how to write your essay. Pay particular attention to your *audience.* Knowing what your audience already knows and believes will help you persuade them.
Focusing on a *debatable* claim	• Make this claim the *thesis* of your paper.
Representing and evaluating the *opposing points of view* on the issue fairly and accurately	• The key to a successful arguing paper is *anticipating and responding* to the most important alternative or opposing positions.
Arguing reasonably *against opposing arguments* and *for your claim*	• Respond to or refute alternative or opposing arguments. Present the best arguments supporting your claim. Argue reasonably and fairly.
Supporting your claims with sufficient *evidence*	• Use firsthand observations; examples from personal experience; results of surveys and interviews; graphs, charts, and visuals; and statistics, facts, and quotations from your reading.

To begin with a familiar type of situation, a patient who is dying of incurable cancer of the throat is in terrible pain, which can no longer be satisfactorily alleviated. He is certain to die within a few days, even if present treatment is continued, but he does not want to go on living for those days, since the pain is unbearable. So he asks the doctor for an end to it, and his family joins in the request.   *Argument for claim*

Example

Suppose the doctor agrees to withhold treatment, as the conventional doctrine says he may. The justification for his doing so is that the patient is in terrible agony, and since he is going to die anyway, it would be wrong to prolong his suffering needlessly. But now notice this. If one simply withholds treatment, it may take the patient longer to die, and so he may suffer more than he would if more direct action were taken and a lethal injection given. This fact provides strong reason for thinking that, once the initial decision not to prolong his agony has been made, active euthanasia is actually preferable to passive euthanasia, rather than the reverse. To say otherwise is to endorse the option that leads to more suffering rather than less, and is contrary to the humanitarian impulse that prompts the decision not to prolong his life in the first place.   *Example*

Argument against opposition

CLAIMS FOR WRITTEN ARGUMENT

18.1

Understand what kinds of claims are debatable

The thesis of your argument is a *debatable claim*. Opinions on both sides of the issue must have some merit. Claims for a written argument usually fall into one of four categories: claims of fact, claims about cause and effect, claims about value, and claims about solutions and policies. A claim may occasionally fall into several categories or may even overlap categories.

Claims of Fact or Definition

These claims are about facts that are not easily determined or about definitions that are debatable. If I claim that a Lhasa apso was an ancient Chinese ruler, you can check a dictionary and find out that I am wrong. A Lhasa apso is, in fact, a small Tibetan dog. There is no argument here. But people do disagree about some supposed "facts": Are polygraph tests accurate? Do grades measure achievement? People also disagree about definitions: Gender discrimination exists in the marketplace, but is it "serious"? What is discrimination, anyway? And what constitutes "serious" discrimination?

In "'American Gothic,' Pitchfork Perfect," a review of Grant Wood's famous painting, Paul Richard opens with a claim of fact and definition (the complete essay appears in Chapter 13). His claim is that *American Gothic* is an American emblem or icon. Although reviews typically contain claims of value, Richard begins his essay with a claim of fact or definition, arguing that the painting is a visual manifestation of the American dream.

> Is "American Gothic" America's best-known painting? Certainly it's one of them. Grant Wood's dual portrait—with its churchy evocations, its stiffness and its pitchfork—pierced us long ago, and got stuck into our minds. Now, finally, it's here.
>
> "American Gothic," which hasn't been in Washington in 40 years, goes on view today at the Renwick Gallery of the Smithsonian American Art Museum. By all means, take it in—although, of course, you have already.
>
> It should have gone all fuzzy—it's been parodied so often, and parsed so many ways—but the 1930 canvas at the Renwick is as sharp as ever. Its details are finer than its travesties suggest, its image more absorbing. . . .
>
> The picture with a pitchfork is an American unforgettable. Few paintings, very few, have its recognizability. Maybe Whistler's mother. Maybe Warhol's soup can. Maybe Rockwell's Thanksgiving turkey. They're national emblems, all of them, visual manifestations of the American dream.

Claims About Cause and Effect

- Testing in the schools improves the quality of education.
- Capital punishment does not deter violent crime.

Unlike the claim that grades affect admission to college—which few people would deny—the above claims about cause and effect are debatable. Do tests ultimately improve students' education, or do they just make students better test-takers? The deterrent effect of capital punishment is still an arguable proposition, with reasonable arguments on both sides.

In a selection from her book *The Plug-In Drug: Television, Children, and the Family*, Marie Winn argues that television has a negative effect on family life. In her opening paragraphs she sets forth both sides of the controversy and then argues that the overall effect is negative.

Television's contribution to family life has been an equivocal one. For while it has, indeed, kept the members of the family from dispersing, it has not served to bring them *together*. By its domination of the time families spend together, it destroys the special quality that depends to a great extent on what a family does, what special rituals, games, recurrent jokes, familiar songs, and shared activities it accumulates.

"Like the sorcerer of old," writes Urie Bronfenbrenner, "the television set casts its magic spell, freezing speech and action, turning the living into silent statues so long as the enchantment lasts. The primary danger of the television screen lies not so much in the behavior it produces—although there is danger there—as in the behavior it prevents: the talks, the games, the family festivities and arguments through which much of the child's learning takes place and through which his character is formed. Turning on the television set can turn off the process that transforms children into people."

Claims About Value

- Boxing is a dehumanizing sport.
- Internet pornography degrades children's sense of human dignity.

Claims about value typically lead to evaluative essays. All the evaluating strategies discussed in Chapter 13 apply here, with the additional requirement that you must anticipate and respond to alternative or opposing arguments. The essay that claims that boxing is dehumanizing must respond to the argument that boxing is merely another form of competition that promotes athletic excellence. The claim that pornography degrades children's sense of dignity must respond to the claim that restricting free speech on the Internet would cause greater harm.

In "College Is a Waste of Time and Money," the teacher and journalist Caroline Bird argues that many students go to college simply because it is the "thing to do." For those students, Bird claims, college is not a good idea.

Nowadays, says one sociologist, you don't have to have a reason for going to college; it's an institution. His definition of an institution is an arrangement everyone accepts without question; the burden of proof is not on why you go, but why anyone thinks there might be a reason for not going. The implication is that an 18-year-old . . . should listen to those who know best and go to college.

I don't agree. I believe that college has to be judged not on what other people think is good for students, but on how good it feels to the students themselves.

I believe that people have an inside view of what's good for them. If a child doesn't want to go to school some morning, better let him stay at home, at least until you find out why. Maybe he knows something you don't. It's the same with college. If high-school graduates don't want to go, or if they don't want to go right away, they may perceive more clearly than their elders that college is not for them.

Claims About Solutions or Policies

- Pornography on the Internet should be censored.
- Both texting and cell phone use while driving should be against the law.

Claims about solutions or policies sometimes occur *along with* claims of fact or definition, cause and effect, or value. Because grades do not measure achievement (argue that this is a fact), they should be abolished (argue for this policy). Boxing is a dehumanizing sport (argue this claim of value); therefore, boxing should be banned (argue for this solution). Claims about solutions or policies involve all the strategies used for problem solving, but with special emphasis on countering opposing arguments: "Although advocates of freedom of speech suggest that we cannot suppress pornography on the Internet, in fact, we already have self-monitoring devices in other media that could help reduce pornography on the Internet."

In *When Society Becomes an Addict,* psychotherapist Anne Wilson Schaef argues that our society has become an "Addictive System" that shares many characteristics with alcoholism and other addictions. Advertising becomes addictive, causing us to behave dishonestly; the social pressure to be "nice" can become addictive, causing us to lie to ourselves. Schaef argues that the solution for our social addictions begins when we face the reality of our dependency.

> We cannot recover from an addiction unless we first admit that we have it. Naming our reality is essential to recovery. Unless we admit that we are indeed functioning in an addictive process in an Addictive System, we shall never have the option of recovery. Once we name something, we own it. . . . Remember, to name the system as addict is not to condemn it: It is to offer it the possibility of recovery.
>
> Paradoxically, the only way to reclaim our personal power is by admitting our powerlessness. The first part of Step One of the AA [Alcoholics Anonymous] Twelve-Step Program reads, "We admitted we were powerless over alcohol." It is important to recognize that admitting to powerlessness over an addiction is not the same as admitting powerlessness as a person. In fact, it can be very powerful to recognize the futility of the illusion of control.

APPEALS FOR WRITTEN ARGUMENT

18.2
Understand how rhetorical appeals support arguments

To support their claims and respond to opposing arguments, writers use *appeals* to the audience. Argument uses three important types of appeals: to *reason* (logic and evidence support the claim), to *character* (the writer's good character itself supports the claim), and to *emotion* (the writer's expression of feelings about the issue may support the claim). Effective arguments will emphasize the appeal to reason but may also appeal to character or emotion.

Appeal to Reason

An appeal to reason depends most frequently on *inductive logic,* which is sometimes called the *scientific method.* Inductive logic draws a general conclusion from personal observation or experience, specific facts, reports, statistics, testimony of authorities, and other data.

> **❝Mere knowledge of the truth will not give you the art of persuasion. ❞**
>
> —Plato,
> *Phaedrus*

Inductive Logic In inductive logic, a reasonable conclusion is based on a *sufficient* quantity of accurate and reliable evidence that is selected in a *random* manner to reduce human bias or to take into account variation in the sample. The definition of *sufficient* varies, but generally the number must be large enough to convince your audience that your sample fairly represents the whole subject.

Let's take an example to illustrate inductive reasoning. Suppose you ask a student, one of fifty in a Psychology I class, a question of value: "Is Professor X a good teacher?" If this student says, "Professor X is the worst teacher I've ever had!" what conclusion can you draw? If you avoid taking the class based on a sample of one, you may miss an excellent class. So you decide to gather a *sufficient sample* by polling twenty of the fifty students in the class. But which twenty do you interview? If you ask the first student for a list of students, you may receive the names of twenty other students who also hate the professor. To reduce human or accidental bias, then, you choose a random method for collecting your evidence: As the students leave the class, you give a questionnaire to two out of every five students. If they all fill out the questionnaires, you probably have a *sufficient* and *random* sample.

Finally, if the responses to your questionnaire show that fifteen out of twenty students rate Professor X as an excellent teacher, what *valid conclusion* should you draw? You should not say, categorically, "X is an excellent teacher." Your conclusion must be restricted by your evidence and the method of gathering it: "Seventy-five percent of the students polled in Psychology I believe that Professor X is an excellent teacher."

Claim	Professor X is an excellent psychology teacher
Reason #1:	Professor X is an excellent teacher because she gives stimulating lectures that students rarely miss. ***Evidence:*** Sixty percent of the students polled said that they rarely missed a lecture.
Reason #2:	Professor X is an excellent teacher because she gives tests that encourage learning rather than sheer memorization. ***Evidence:*** Seventy percent of the students polled said that Professor X's essay tests required thinking and learning rather than memorization.

Most arguments use a shorthand version of the inductive method of reasoning. A writer makes a claim and then supports it with *reasons* and representative *examples* or *data*.

Appeal to Character

An appeal based on your good character as a writer can also be important in argument. (The appeal to character is frequently called the *ethical appeal* because readers make a value judgment about the writer's character.) In a written argument, you show your audience—through your reasonable persona, voice, and tone—that you are a person who abides by moral standards that your audience shares: You have a good reputation, you are honest and trustworthy, and you argue "fairly."

A person's reputation often affects how we react to a claim, but *the argument itself* should also establish the writer's trustworthiness. You don't have to be a Mahatma Gandhi or a Mother Teresa to generate a strong ethical appeal for your claim. Even if your readers have never heard your name before, they will feel confident about your character if you are knowledgeable about your subject, present opposing arguments fairly, and support your own claim with sufficient, reliable evidence.

At the most basic level, your interest in the topic and willingness to work hard can improve your ethical appeal. Readers can sense when a writer cares about his or her subject, when a writer knows something about the topic, about the rhetorical or cultural context, and about the various viewpoints on a topic. Show your readers that you care about the subject, and they will find your arguments more convincing. Show you care by

- using sufficient details and specific, vivid examples.
- including any relevant personal experience you have on the topic.
- including other people's ideas and points of view and by responding to their views with fairness and tact.
- organizing your essay so your main points are easy to find and transitions between ideas are clear and logical.
- revising and proofreading your essay.

Readers know when writers care about their subjects, and they are more willing to listen to new ideas when the writer has worked hard and is personally invested in the topic.

Appeal to Emotion

Appeals to emotion can be tricky because, as we have seen, when emotions come in through the door, reasonableness may fly out the window. Argument emphasizes reason, not emotion. Emotional appeals designed to *deceive* or *frighten* people or to *misrepresent* the virtues of a person, place, or object have no place in rational argument. But emotional appeals that illustrate a truth or movingly depict a reality are legitimate and effective means of convincing readers.

Combined Appeals

Appeals may be used in combination. Writers may appeal to reason and, at the same time, establish trustworthy characters and use legitimate emotional appeals. The following excerpt from *The Seneca Falls Resolution* uses all three appeals to support its argument for the rights of women. (See Chapter 12 for an extended analysis of its use of rhetorical appeals.) Its author, Elizabeth Cady Stanton, draws on the ethos of a respected document, The Declaration of Independence, to make its own argument for women's rights. It uses logos appeal to show how justice is derived from the rights from "the consent of the governed." And it uses pathos appeal to show the "long train of abuses" and "injuries" has adversely affected women. All of these are used in support of its thesis: women have the right to claim an equal status in property and in law.

When, in the course of human events, it becomes necessary for one portion of the family of man to assume among the people of the earth a position different from that which they have hitherto occupied, but one to which the laws of nature and of nature's God entitle them, a decent respect to the opinions of mankind requires that they should declare the causes that impel them to such a course.

We hold these truths to be self-evident: that all men and women are created equal; that they are endowed by their Creator with certain inalienable rights; that among these are life, liberty, and the pursuit of happiness; that to secure these rights governments are instituted, deriving their just powers from the consent of the governed. Whenever any form of government becomes destructive of these ends, it is the right of those who suffer from it to refuse allegiance to it, and to insist upon the institution of a new government, laying its foundation on such principles, and organizing its powers in such form, as to them shall seem most likely to effect their safety and happiness. Prudence, indeed, will dictate that governments long established should not be changed for light and transient causes; and accordingly all experience hath shown that mankind are more disposed to suffer, while evils are sufferable, than to right themselves by abolishing the forms to which they were accustomed. But when a long train of abuses and usurpations, pursuing invariably the same object evinces a design to reduce them under absolute despotism, it is their duty to throw off such government, and to provide new guards for their future security. Such has been the patient sufferance of the women under this government, and such is now the necessity which constrains them to demand the equal station to which they are entitled.

The history of mankind is a history of repeated injuries and usurpations on the part of man toward woman, having in direct object the establishment of an absolute tyranny over her. To prove this, let facts be submitted to a candid world.

He has never permitted her to exercise her inalienable right to the elective franchise.

He has compelled her to submit to laws, in the formation of which she had no voice.

He has withheld from her rights which are given to the most ignorant and degraded men — both natives and foreigners.

Having deprived her of this first right of a citizen, the elective franchise, thereby leaving her without representation in the halls of legislation, he has oppressed her on all sides.

He has made her, if married, in the eye of the law, civility dead.

He has taken from her all right in property, even to the wages she earns.

Ethos appeal, using language and authority of the Declaration of Independence

Logos appeal, establishing the purposes of the Declaration as based in "the opinions of mankind"

Borrows ethos from the Declaration of Independence

Logos and ethos established based on the roots of the U.S. government

Establishes pathos for the plight of women

The author states her thesis: that women have the right to assert an equal status.

Pathos appeal

Combines pathos and logos, as this action is made to seem both cruel and imprudent

APPROACHES TO ARGUMENT

While productive argument is meant to bring people together to discuss and resolve a debatable issue, the approach we take should keep in mind the special circumstances of the situation. In this section, we will examine two effective forms of argument that can be applied, as appropriate, to written arguments. Both forms of argument attempt to overcome the problems faced when participants in an argument cannot find ways to listen to one another in a civil, productive way. "The Argument Culture" by Deborah Tannen and the questions that follow it can help you to think more about the contexts that will influence how you approach argumentative writing.

The Argument Culture

Deborah Tannen

A professor of linguistics at Georgetown University, Deborah Tannen is also a best-selling author of many books on discourse and gender, including *You Just Don't Understand: Women and Men in Conversation* (1990), *The Argument Culture: Moving from Debate to Dialogue* (1998), and *You Were Always Mom's Favorite!* (2010). In the following essay from *The Argument Culture*, Tannen tries to convince her readers that adversarial debates—which typically represent only two sides of an issue and thus promote antagonism—create problems in communication.

Balance. Debate. Listening to both sides. Who could question these noble 1
American traditions? Yet today, these principles have been distorted. Without thinking, we have plunged headfirst into what I call the "argument culture."

The argument culture urges us to approach the world, and the people in it, 2
in an adversarial frame of mind. It rests on the assumption that opposition is the best way to get anything done: The best way to discuss an idea is to set up a debate; the best way to cover news is to find spokespeople who express the most extreme, polarized views and present them as "both sides"; the best way to settle disputes is litigation that pits one party against the other; the best way to begin an essay is to attack someone; and the best way to show you're really thinking is to criticize.

More and more, our public interactions have become like arguing with a 3
spouse. Conflict can't be avoided in our public lives any more than we can avoid conflict with people we love. One of the great strengths of our society is that we can express these conflicts openly. But just as spouses have to learn ways of settling their differences without inflicting real damage, so we, as a society, have to find constructive ways of resolving disputes and differences.

The war on drugs, the war on cancer, the battle of the sexes, politicians' turf 4
battles—in the argument culture, war metaphors pervade our talk and shape

(Continued)

our thinking. The cover headlines of both *Time* and *Newsweek* one recent week are a case in point: "The Secret Sex Wars," proclaims *Newsweek*. "Starr at War," declares *Time*. Nearly everything is framed as a battle or game in which winning or losing is the main concern.

The argument culture pervades every aspect of our lives today. Issues from   5
global warming to abortion are depicted as two-sided arguments, when in fact most Americans' views lie somewhere in the middle. Partisanship makes gridlock in Washington the norm. Even in our personal relationships, a "let it all hang out" philosophy emphasizes people expressing their anger without giving them constructive ways of settling differences.

Sometimes You Have to Fight

There are times when it is necessary and right to fight—to defend your country or yourself, to argue for your rights or against offensive or dangerous ideas or actions. What's wrong with the argument culture is the ubiquity, the knee-jerk nature of approaching any issue, problem or public person in an adversarial way.   6

Our determination to pursue truth by setting up a fight between two sides   7
leads us to assume that every issue has two sides—no more, no less. But if you always assume there must be an "other side," you may end up scouring the margins of science or the fringes of lunacy to find it.

This accounts, in part, for the bizarre phenomenon of Holocaust denial.   8
Deniers, as Emory University professor Deborah Lipstadt shows, have been successful in gaining TV air time and campus newspaper coverage by masquerading as "the other side" in a "debate." Continual reference to "the other side" results in a conviction that everything has another side—and people begin to doubt the existence of any facts at all.

The power of words to shape perception has been proved by researchers in   9
controlled experiments. Psychologists Elizabeth Loftus and John Palmer, for example, found that the terms in which people are asked to recall something affect what they recall. The researchers showed subjects a film of two cars colliding, then asked how fast the cars were going; one week later they asked whether there had been any broken glass. Some subjects were asked, "How fast were the cars going when they bumped into each other?" Others were asked, "How fast were the cars going when they smashed into each other?"

Those who read the question with "smashed" tended to "remember" that   10
the cars were going faster. They were also more likely to "remember" having seen broken glass. (There wasn't any.) This is how language works. It invisibly molds our way of thinking about people, actions and the world around us.

In the argument culture, "critical" thinking is synonymous with criticizing.   11
In many classrooms, students are encouraged to read someone's life work, then rip it to shreds.

When debates and fighting predominate, those who enjoy verbal sparring   12
are likely to take part—by calling in to talk shows or writing letters to the editor. Those who aren't comfortable with oppositional discourse are likely to opt out.

(Continued)

...continued The Argument Culture, **Deborah Tannen**

How High-Tech Communication Pulls Us Apart

One of the most effective ways to defuse antagonism between two groups   13
is to provide a forum for individuals from those groups to get to know each other personally. What is happening in our lives, however, is just the opposite. More and more of our communication is not face to face, and not with people we know. The proliferation and increasing portability of technology isolates people in a bubble.

Along with the voices of family members and friends, phone lines bring   14
into our homes the annoying voices of solicitors who want to sell something—generally at dinnertime. (My father-in-law startles phone solicitors by saying, "We're eating dinner, but I'll call you back. What's your home phone number?" To the nonplused caller, he explains, "Well, you're calling me at home; I thought I'd call you at home, too.")

It is common for families to have more than one TV, so the adults can watch   15
what they like in one room and the kids can watch their choice in another—or maybe each child has a private TV.

E-mail, and now the Internet, are creating networks of human connection   16
unthinkable even a few years ago. Though e-mail has enhanced communication with family and friends, it also ratchets up the anonymity of both sender and receiver, resulting in stranger-to-stranger "flaming."

"Road rage" shows how dangerous the argument culture—and especially   17
today's technologically enhanced aggression—can be. Two men who engage in a shouting match may not come to blows, but if they express their anger while driving down a public highway, the risk to themselves and others soars.

The Argument Culture Shapes Who We Are

The argument culture has a defining impact on our lives and on our   18
culture.

- **It makes us distort facts,** as in the Nancy Kerrigan-Tonya Harding story. After the original attack on Kerrigan's knee, news stories focused on the rivalry between the two skaters instead of portraying Kerrigan as the victim of an attack. Just last month, *Time* magazine called the event a "contretemps" between Kerrigan and Harding. And a recent joint TV interview of the two skaters reinforced that skewed image by putting the two on equal footing, rather than as victim and accused.

- **It makes us waste valuable time,** as in the case of scientist Robert Gallo, who co-discovered the AIDS virus. Gallo was the object of a groundless four-year investigation into allegations he had stolen the virus from another scientist. He was ultimately exonerated, but the toll was enormous. Never mind that, in his words, "These were the most painful and horrible years of my life." Gallo spent four years fighting accusations instead of fighting AIDS.

(Continued)

- **It limits our thinking.** Headlines are intentionally devised to attract attention, but the language of extremes actually shapes, and misshapes, the way we think about things. Military metaphors train us to think about, and see, everything in terms of fighting, conflict and war. Adversarial rhetoric is a kind of verbal inflation—a rhetorical boy-who-cried-wolf.
- **It encourages us to lie.** If you fight to win, the temptation is great to deny facts that support your opponent's views and say only what supports your side. It encourages people to misrepresent and, in the extreme, to lie.

End the Argument Culture by Looking at All Sides

How can we overcome our classically American habit of seeing issues in absolutes? We must expand our notion of "debate" to include more dialogue. To do this, we can make special efforts not to think in twos. Mary Catherine Bateson, an anthropologist at Virginia's George Mason University, makes a point of having her class compare three cultures, not two. Then, students are more likely to think about each on its own terms, rather than as opposites. 19

In the public arena, television and radio producers can try to avoid, whenever possible, structuring public discussions as debates. This means avoiding the format of having two guests discuss an issue. Invite three guests—or one. Perhaps it is time to re-examine the assumption that audiences always prefer a fight. 20

Instead of asking, "What's the other side?" we might ask, "What are the other sides?" Instead of insisting on hearing "both sides," let's insist on hearing "all sides." 21

We need to find metaphors other than sports and war. Smashing heads does not open minds. We need to use our imaginations and ingenuity to find different ways to seek truth and gain knowledge through intellectual interchange, and add them to our arsenal—or, should I say, to the ingredients for our stew. It will take creativity for each of us to find ways to change the argument culture to a dialogue culture. It's an effort we have to make, because our public and private lives are at stake. 22

Questions for Writing and Discussion

❶ List three controversial topics currently in the news. Then choose one of those topics and explain the two "sides" of the argument. Now, imagine a third point of view: How is it different from the first two positions? Does coming up with a third position help you think creatively about how to resolve the dispute? Explain.

❷ In her essay, Tannen outlines the nature of the problem with the "argument culture." What kinds of impediments does she suggest exist to formulating a reasonable argument in the current environment? Have you noticed these kinds of problems in media discussions of current issues, such as those on cable news or talk radio shows? What might you do as a writer to avoid them?

③ In what ways does Tannen critique "pro/con" debates—debates that set up only two possible "sides" in a debate? Why does she feel that looking at an issue in this way limits the ways we can approach argument? How does that approach shape "who we are" as we participate in an argument?

④ According to Tannen, the language we choose and the metaphors we use affect our perceptions of the world. Where does Tannen discuss how words or metaphors shape our perceptions? What examples does she give? Considering Tannen's analysis of language styles, what kinds of things might you avoid in your own writing style?

⑤ Tannen also addresses how arguments are affected by what she calls "High-Tech Communication." In your own experience, how does argument via social media differ from face-to-face argument? What might you learn about productive methods of argument from this difference?

Rogerian Argument

Traditional argument assumes that people are most readily convinced or persuaded by a confrontational "debate" on the issue. As Tannen's essay suggests, the argument becomes a kind of struggle or "war" as the writer attempts to "defeat" the arguments of the opposition. The purpose of a traditional argument is thus to convince an undecided audience that the writer has "won a fight" and emerged "victorious" over the opposition.

In fact, there are many situations in which a less confrontational and adversarial approach is more effective. Particularly when the issues are highly charged or when the audience is the opposition, writers may more effectively use negotiation rather than confrontation. *Rogerian argument*—named after psychologist Carl Rogers—is a kind of negotiated argument where understanding and compromise replace the traditional, adversarial approach. Rogerian, or *nonthreatening*, argument opens the lines of communication by reducing conflict. When people's beliefs are attacked, they instinctively become defensive and strike back. As a result, the argument becomes polarized: The writer argues for a claim, the reader digs in to defend his or her position, and no one budges.

To avoid this polarization, Rogerian arguments work toward a compromise. As Rogers says, "This procedure gradually achieves a mutual communication. Mutual communication tends to be pointed toward solving a problem rather than toward attacking a person or group." Rogerian argument, then, imitates not a courtroom debate but the mutual communication that may take place between two people. Whereas traditional argument intends to change the actions or the beliefs of the opposition, Rogerian argument works toward changes *in both sides* as a means of establishing common ground and reaching a solution.

Rogerian argument is appropriate in a variety of sensitive or highly controversial situations. You may want to choose Rogerian argument if you are an employer requesting union members to accept a pay cut to help the company avoid bankruptcy. Similarly, if you argue to husbands that they should assume responsibility for half the housework, or if you argue to Anglo-Americans that Spanish language and culture should play a larger role in public education, you may want to use a Rogerian strategy. By showing that you empathize with the opposition's position and are willing to compromise, you create a climate for mutual communication.

Rogerian argument makes a claim, considers the opposition, and presents evidence to support the claim, but in addition, it avoids threatening or adversarial language and promotes mutual communication and learning. A Rogerian argument uses the following strategies.

- **Avoiding *a confrontational stance.*** Confrontation threatens your audience and increases their defensiveness. Threat hinders communication.
- **Presenting your *character* as someone who understands and can empathize with the opposition.** Show that you understand by restating the opposing position accurately.
- **Establishing *common ground* with the opposition.** Indicate the beliefs and values that you share.
- **Being willing *to change your views.*** Show where your position is not reasonable and could be modified.
- **Directing your argument toward *a compromise or workable solution.***

Note: An argument does not have to be either entirely adversarial or entirely Rogerian. You may use Rogerian techniques for the most sensitive points in an argument that is otherwise traditional or confrontational.

In his essay "Animal Rights Versus Human Health," biology professor Albert Rosenfeld illustrates several features of Rogerian argument. Rosenfeld argues that animals should be used for medical experiments, but he is aware that the issues are emotional and that his audience is likely to be antagonistic. Rosenfeld avoids threatening language, represents the opposition fairly, grants that he is guilty of *speciesism*, and says that he sympathizes with the demand to look for alternatives. He indicates that his position is flexible and grants that there is some room for compromise, but he is firm in his position that some animal experimentation is necessary for advancements in medicine.

It is fair to say that millions of animals—probably more rats and mice than any other species—are subjected to experiments that cause them pain, discomfort, and distress, sometimes lots of it over long periods of time.... All new forms of medication or surgery are tried out on animals first. Every new substance that is released into the environment, or put on the market, is tested on animals....

States opposing position fairly and sympathetically

In 1975, Australian philosopher Peter Singer wrote his influential book called *Animal Liberation*, in which he accuses us all of "speciesism"—as reprehensible, to him, as racism or sexism. He freely describes the "pain and suffering" inflicted in the "tyranny of human over nonhuman animals" and sharply challenges our biblical license to exercise "dominion over the fish of the sea, and over the fowl of the air, and over every living thing that moveth upon the Earth."

States opposing position fairly

Well, certainly we are guilty of speciesism. We do act as if we had dominion over other living creatures. But domination also entails some custodial responsibility. And the questions continue to be raised: Do we have the right to abuse animals? To eat them? ... To keep them imprisoned in zoos—or, for that matter, in our households? Especially to do experiments on these creatures who can't fight back?

Acknowledges common ground

Sympathetic to opposing position

Suggests
compromise position

Hardly any advance in either human or veterinary medicine—cure, vaccine, operation, drug, therapy—has come about without experiments on animals. . . . I certainly sympathize with the demand that we look for ways to get the information we want without using animals. Most investigators are delighted when they can get their data by means of tissue cultures or computer simulations. But as we look for alternative ways to get information, do we meanwhile just do without?

The Toulmin Method of Argument

In *The Uses of Argument* (1958), British philosopher Stephen Toulmin identified six concepts that can be helpful as we analyze the logic of an argument.

- **Data:** The evidence gathered to support a particular claim.
- **Claim:** The overall thesis the writer hopes to prove. This thesis may be a claim of fact or definition, of cause and effect, of value, or of policy.
- **Warrant:** The statement that explains why or how the data support the writer's claim.
- **Backing:** The additional logic or reasoning that, when necessary, supports the warrant.
- **Qualifier:** The short phrases that limit the scope of the claim, such as "typically," "usually," or "on the whole."
- **Exceptions:** Those particular situations in which the writer does not or would not insist on the claim.

Example of a Toulmin Analysis We can illustrate each of these six concepts using Cathleen A. Cleaver's argument against Internet pornography in her essay, "The Internet: A Clear and Present Danger?" that appears later in this chapter. The relationship of the data, warrant, and claim are shown here.

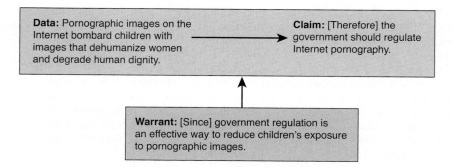

Data: Pornographic images on the Internet bombard children with images that dehumanize women and degrade human dignity.

Claim: [Therefore] the government should regulate Internet pornography.

Warrant: [Since] government regulation is an effective way to reduce children's exposure to pornographic images.

- **Backing:** Government regulation already exists in print, radio, and television media, so it should be extended to the Internet.
- **Qualifier:** *In most cases,* the government should regulate pornography on the Internet. (Cleaver does not use a qualifier for her claim; this is a qualifier she might use.)

- **Exceptions:** Government regulations must protect children, but *where children are not involved, regulation may not be as urgent.* (Cleaver implies this exception, since she focuses her argument only on pornography's effect on children.)

Using the Toulmin Model Applying the Toulmin model of argument to written texts can help us as readers and writers if we follow a few guidelines. First, the Toulmin model is especially helpful as we critically read texts for their logical strengths and weaknesses. As we become better critical readers, we are likely to make our own arguments more logical and thus more persuasive. Second, as we critically read texts, not all of us find the same warrant statements because there can be several ways of explaining a logical connection between the data and the stated claim. Third, applying the Toulmin model and using warrants, backing, qualifiers, and exceptions becomes more important when our readers are likely to disagree with the claim.

Just as Rogerian argument tries to reduce conflict in adversarial situations through mutual communication and a strong appeal to character, the Toulmin model helps communicate in adversarial contexts by being especially reasonable and logical. If our readers already agree that pornography on the Internet is a bad thing, we need to give only a few examples and go straight to our claim. But if readers have a strong belief in free speech on the Internet, we need to qualify our claim and make our warrants—the connections between the data and the claim—as explicit and logical as possible. We may also need to state backing for the warrant and note the exceptions where we don't want to press our case. The more antagonistic our readers are, the more we need to be as logical as possible. The Toulmin model is just one approach that can help bolster the logic of our argument.

> **❝** A society which is clamoring for choice [is] filled with many articulate groups, each arguing its own brand of salvation. **❞**
>
> —Margaret Mead,
> Anthropologist

Warming Up: Journal Exercises

The following exercises ask you to practice arguing. Read all of the exercises and then write on three that interest you. If another idea occurs to you, write about it.

1. **Collaborating with peers.** From the list of "should" statements, choose one that relates to your experience and freewrite for ten minutes. When you finish your freewriting, compare your responses with those of peers. How do their thoughts impact your own?

- Handguns should not be permitted on college campuses.
- Using a cell phone or texting while driving should be outlawed.
- Bicyclists should be subject to regular traffic laws, including DWI.
- High-quality child care should be available to all working parents at employer's expense.
- Punishments for plagiarism in college courses need to be more strict.
- Organic foods need to meet a single, national standard.
- Every adult citizen in the United States should be required to purchase health insurance.

② Controversial subjects depend as much on the audience as they do on the issue itself. Make a short list of your everyday activities: eating, reading, socializing, discussing ideas. For one of these activities, imagine people who might find what you do immoral, illogical, unjust, or unhealthy. What claim might they make about your activity? What reasons or evidence might they use to argue that your activity should be abolished, outlawed, or changed? Write for five minutes arguing *their* point of view.

③ **Writing Across the Curriculum.** Grades are important, but in some courses they get in the way of learning. Choose a course that you have taken and write an open letter to the school administration, arguing for credit/no-credit grading in that course. Assume that you intend to submit your letter to the campus newspaper.

④ Arguments for academic or public audiences should focus on a *debatable* claim—that is, a claim about which knowledgeable people might disagree. Sometimes, however, even the notion of what constitutes a "debatable claim" is debated. Read and analyze the Doonesbury cartoon. What controversies does the cartoon suggest are not really controversies? How does Garry Trudeau use irony to make his point?

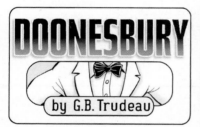

MULTIGENRE CASEBOOK ON NEW MEDIA

18.4
Read and synthesize
a variety of texts

The texts in this casebook represent a snapshot of the ongoing conversation and debate about the uses and abuses of social media and the Internet. These texts raise many questions about how social media and the Internet affect our lives.

Cathleen A. Cleaver, in "The Internet: A Clear and Present Danger?" (which was originally delivered as a speech at Boston University), asks us to consider whether the Internet presents serious risks to our finances, our children, and our values. A pie chart, "Social Networking Gets Most Online Time," adds to the seriousness of those questions, graphically illustrating just how much time we spend in online environments. Then a series of pieces ask us to consider specific potential risks of new media. Jennifer Holladay, in her magazine article "Cyberbullying," and Danah Boyd and Alice Marwick, in their op-ed piece "Bullying as True Drama," help us to consider the effects of social media gone awry and possible ways of responding to this threat. Of course, with such threats come calls for censorship as a method of alleviating the danger. Miguel Helft's newspaper article, "Facebook Wrestles with Free Speech and Civility," examines the efforts of Facebook's "hate and harassment team" to find the line between First Amendment rights and the risks of hate speech that can be accelerated by social media.

The casebook then turns to another key argument concerning new media: the credibility (or lack thereof) of the information available through crowdsourced sites such as Wikipedia. An academic journal article by Neil L. Waters ("Why You Can't Cite Wikipedia in My Class") and an online article by Mark Wilson ("Professors Should Embrace Wikipedia") open a conversation about whether such sites should be prohibited in serious, academic research, or whether academia should embrace the potential for using opensourced sites to teach key research and writing skills. Finally, Nicholas Carr's newspaper article "Does the Internet Make You Dumber" (with an accompanying illustration), examines the research of neuroscientists who suggest that surfing the Internet might be affecting our mental discipline in favor of our species' "instinctive distractedness."

These texts are meant to open the conversation about contemporary Internet and social media sites, to start you thinking critically about your own online habits and the effects of Internet use on people throughout the world.

In addition to thinking critically about the arguments in each of the texts, analyze the texts rhetorically. Are the authors making claims of fact or definition, cause and effect, value, or policy? Does each document make an argument and consider alternative points of view? (Are any of the texts simply informative without making an argument?) What appeals—to reason, to character, to emotion—do the authors make? Consider also how the writers construct or address their audience: Who do they think their reader is? What do they believe their readers already know or believe? What strategies do they think will convince or persuade their readers?

Finally, after you have read these texts, consider how the genre of the document—essay or article in a journal or magazine, oral presentation, blog on a website, visual, or graphic—affects the argument of the document. Do the visuals or graphics make appeals as strong—or stronger—than the written texts? As you consider how to incorporate multimedia into your own writing, consider how each genre will contribute to your goal of convincing or persuading your audience.

The Internet: A Clear and Present Danger?

Cathleen A. Cleaver

Cathleen Cleaver has written extensively on issues relating to children and the Internet, in newspapers and magazines such as *USA Today, Newsday,* and the *Congressional Quarterly Researcher*. The following essay was originally a speech given at Boston University as part of a College of Communication Great Debate. In this speech, she argues that some industry and government regulation of the Internet is necessary.

- Someone breaks through your firewall and steals proprietary informa- 1 tion from your computer systems. You find out and contact a lawyer who says, "Man, you shouldn't have had your stuff online." The thief becomes a millionaire using your ideas, and you go broke, if laws against copyright violation don't protect material on the Internet.

- You visit the Antiques Anonymous website and decide to pay their hefty 2 subscription fee for a year's worth of exclusive estate sale previews in their private online monthly magazine. They never deliver and, in fact, never intended to—they don't even have a magazine. You have no re-course, if laws against fraud don't apply to online transactions.

- Bob Guccione decides to branch out into the lucrative child porn market 3 and creates a Teen Hustler website featuring nude adolescents and pre-teens. You find out and complain, but nothing can be done, if child por-nography distribution laws don't apply to computer transmissions.

- A major computer software vendor who dominates the market develops his 4 popular office software so that it works only with his browser. You're a small browser manufacturer who is completely squeezed out of the market, but you have to find a new line of work, if antitrust laws don't apply online.

- Finally, a pedophile e-mails your son, misrepresenting himself as a 5 twelve-year-old named Jenny. They develop an online relationship and one day arrange to meet after school, where he intends to rape your son. Thankfully, you learn in advance about the meeting and go there your-self, where you find a forty-year-old man instead of Jenny. You flee to the police, who'll tell you there's nothing they can do, if child-stalking laws don't apply to the Internet.

The awesome advances in interactive telecommunication that we've wit- 6 nessed in just the last few years have changed the way in which many Americans communicate and interact. No one can doubt that the Internet is a technological revolution of enormous proportion, with outstanding possibilities for human advancement.

As lead speaker for the affirmative, I'm asked to argue that the Internet 7 poses a "clear and present danger," but the Internet, as a whole, isn't dangerous. In fact, it continues to be a positive and highly beneficial tool, which will un-doubtedly improve education, information exchange, and commerce in years

(Continued)

to come. In other words, the Internet will enrich many aspects of our daily life. Thus, instead of defending this rather apocalyptic view of the Internet, I'll attempt to explain why some industry and government regulation of certain aspects of the Internet is necessary—or, stated another way, why people who use the Internet should not be exempt from many of the laws and regulations that govern their conduct elsewhere. My opening illustrations were meant to give examples of some illegal conduct which should not become legal simply because someone uses the Internet. In looking at whether Internet regulation is a good idea, I believe we should consider whether regulation is in the public interest. In order to do that, we have to ask the question: Who is the public? More specifically, does the "public" whose interests we care about tonight include children?

Children and the Internet

Dave Barry describes the Internet as a "worldwide network of university, government, business, and private computer systems, run by a thirteen-year-old named Jason." This description draws a smile precisely because we acknowledge the highly advanced computer literacy of our children. Most children demonstrate computer proficiency that far surpasses that of their parents, and many parents know only what their children have taught them about the Internet, which gives new relevance to Wordsworth's insight: "The child is father of the man." In fact, one could go so far as to say that the Internet is as accessible to many children as it is inaccessible to many adults. This technological evolution is new in many ways, not the least of which is its accessibility to children, wholly independent of their parents. 8

When considering what's in the public interest, we must consider the whole public, including children, as individual participants in this new medium. 9

Pornography and the Internet

This new medium is unique in another way. It provides, through a single avenue, the full spectrum of pornographic depictions, from the more familiar convenience store fare to pornography of such violence and depravity that it surpasses the worst excesses of the normal human imagination. Sites displaying this material are easily accessible, making pornography far more freely available via the Internet than from any other communications medium in the United States. Pornography is the third largest sector of sales on the Internet, generating $1 billion annually. . . . 10

There is little restriction of pornography-related activity in cyberspace. While there are some porn-related laws, the specter of those laws does not loom large in cyberspace. There's an implicit license there that exists nowhere else with regard to pornography—an environment where people are free to exploit others for profit and be virtually untroubled by legal deterrent. Indeed, if we consider cyberspace to be a little world of its own, it's the type of world for which groups like the ACLU have long fought but, so far, fought in vain. 11

(Continued)

...*continued* The Internet: A Clear and Present Danger, **Cathleen A. Cleaver**

I believe it will not remain this way, but until it changes, we should take the opportunity to see what this world looks like, if for no other reason than to re-assure ourselves that our decades-old decisions to control pornography were good ones. — 12

With a few clicks of the mouse, anyone, any child, can get graphic and often violent sexual images—the kind of stuff it used to be difficult to find without ex-ceptional effort and some significant personal risk. Anyone with a computer and a modem can set up public sites featuring the perversion of their choice, whether it's mutilation of female genitals, eroticized urination and defecation, bestiality, or sites featuring depictions of incest. These pictures can be sold for profit, they can be sent to harass others, or posted to shock people. Anyone can describe the fan-tasy rape and murder of a specific person and display it for all to read. Anyone can meet children in chat rooms or via e-mail and send them pornography and find out where they live. An adult who signs onto an AOL chat room as a thirteen-year-old girl is hit on thirty times within the first half hour. — 13

All this can be done from the seclusion of the home, with the feeling of near anonymity and with the comfort of knowing that there's little risk of legal sanction.... — 14

Beyond the troubling social aspects of unrestricted porn, we face the reality that children are accessing it and that predators are accessing children. We have got to start considering what kind of society we'll have when the next genera-tion learns about human sexuality from what the Internet teaches. What does unrestricted Internet pornography teach children about relationships, about the equality of women? What does it teach little girls about themselves and their worth? — 15

Opponents of restrictions are fond of saying that it's up to the parents to deal with the issue of children's exposure. Well, of course it is, but placing the burden solely on parents is illogical and ineffective. It's far easier for a distribu-tor of pornography to control his material than it is for parents, who must, with the help of software, search for and find the pornographic sites, which change daily, and then attempt to block them. Any pornographer who wants to can easily subvert these efforts, and a recent Internet posting from a teenager wanting to know how to disable the filtering software on his computer received several effective answers. Moreover, it goes without saying that the most sophis-ticated software can only be effective where it's installed, and children will have access to many computers that don't have filtering software, such as those in libraries, schools, and at neighbors' houses. — 16

Internet Transactions Should Not Be Exempt

Opponents of legal restrictions often argue simply that the laws just cannot apply in this new medium, but the argument that old laws can't apply to changing technology just doesn't hold. We saw this argument last in the early '80s with the advent of the videotape. Then, certain groups tried to argue that, since you — 17

(Continued)

can't view videotapes without a VCR, you can't make the sale of child porn videos illegal, because, after all, they're just plastic boxes with magnetic tape inside. Technological change mandates legal change only insofar as it affects the justification for a law. It just doesn't make sense that the government may take steps to restrict illegal material in *every* medium—video, television, radio, the private telephone, *and* print—but that it may do nothing where people distribute the material by the Internet. While old laws might need redefinition, the old principles generally stand firm.

18 The question of enforcement usually is raised here, and it often comes in the form of: "How are you going to stop people from doing it?" Well, no law stops people from doing things—a red light at an intersection doesn't force you to stop but tells you that you should stop and that there could be legal consequences if you don't. Not everyone who runs a red light is caught, but that doesn't mean the law is futile. The same concept holds true for Internet laws. Government efforts to temper harmful conduct online will never be perfect, but that doesn't mean they shouldn't undertake the effort at all.

19 There's clearly a role for industry to play here. Search engines don't have to run ads for porn sites or prioritize search results to highlight porn. One new search engine even has sex as the default search term. Internet service providers can do something about unsolicited e-mail with hotlinks to porn, and they can and should carefully monitor any chat rooms designed for kids.

20 Some charge that industry standards or regulations that restrict explicit pornography will hinder the development of Internet technology. But that is to say that its advancement depends upon unrestricted exhibition of this material, and this cannot be true. The Internet does not belong to pornographers, and it's clearly in the public interest to see that they don't usurp this great new technology. We don't live in a perfect society, and the Internet is merely a reflection of the larger social community. Without some mitigating influences, the strong will exploit the weak, whether a Bill Gates or a child predator.

Conclusion: Technology Must Serve Man

21 To argue that the strength of the Internet is chaos or that our liberty depends upon chaos is to misunderstand not only the Internet but also the fundamental nature of our liberty. It's an illusion to claim social or moral neutrality in the application of technology, even if its development may be neutral. It can be a valuable resource only when placed at the service of humanity and when it promotes our integral development for the benefit of all.

22 Guiding principles simply cannot be inferred from mere technical efficiency or from the usefulness accruing to some at the expense of others. Technology by its very nature requires unconditional respect for the fundamental interests of society.

23 Internet technology must be at the service of humanity and of our inalienable rights. It must respect the prerogatives of a civil society, among which is the protection of children.

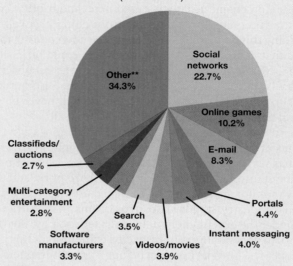

Social Networking Gets Most Online Time

Americans spend nearly a quarter of their time online on social networking sites and blogs—up form 15.8 percent a year ago. That is far more than any other sector and also more time than is spent on e-mail and online games combined.

Top 10 Sectors by Share of U.S. Internet Time
(June 2010)

Other** 34.3%

Social networks 22.7%

Online games 10.2%

E-mail 8.3%

Classifieds/ auctions 2.7%

Multi-category entertainment 2.8%

Software manufacturers 3.3%

Search 3.5%

Videos/movies 3.9%

Instant messaging 4.0%

Portals 4.4%

*Figures do not total 100 due to rounding
**74 remaining online categories visited from PCs/laptops
Source: "What Americans Do Online: Social Media and Games Dominate Activity," Nielsen, August 2010.

Cyberbullying

Jennifer Holladay

First published in 2010, this essay appeared in *Teaching Tolerance,* a magazine published by the Southern Poverty Law Center (SPLC). Jennifer Holladay acts as the senior adviser for strategic affairs at SPLC. Founded in 1971, the SPLC's published mission includes three pillars: fighting hate, teaching tolerance, and seeking justice. Its mission is to "ensure that the promise of the civil rights movement became a reality for all."

(Continued)

Phoebe Prince is loved by her peers. At least, now she is. Hundreds of people 1
have supported her on Facebook. Taylor Gosselin wrote, "Your story touched
my heart." Dori Fitzgerald Acevedo added, "I am so glad we are not letting this
get swept under the carpet."

"This" is what some might call bullicide—suicide by bullying. 2

Before Phoebe Prince hanged herself, she was a new student at South Hadley 3
(MA) High School. She reportedly dared to date boys whom others thought
should be off limits to her.

Girls at Phoebe's school reportedly called her a "whore" and a "bitch," vi- 4
ciously harassing her in person and on Facebook. At least one student gloated
after Phoebe took her own life, "I don't care that she's dead."

Phoebe's tormentors have since been dubbed the "Mean Girls," after the 5
clique in the 2004 Tina Fey–scripted movie. And for the Mean Girls of South
Hadley, the consequences of their purported actions have been severe. They are
now maligned across the Internet, from postings on Facebook to the comment
areas of news websites worldwide.

The Mean Girls, along with two male students, also face criminal charges 6
for allegedly bullying Phoebe. Since then, it's become clear that Phoebe's reasons for taking her own life were complicated. She struggled with depression
and had even attempted suicide once before. But the bullying she endured definitely had an impact.

New Term, Old Concept

The word cyberbullying didn't even exist a decade ago, yet the problem is per- 7
vasive today. Simply put, cyberbullying is the repeated use of technology to
harass, humiliate, or threaten. When people take to the keyboard or cell phone
and craft messages of hate or malice about a specific person, cyberbullying is
emerging. And unlike traditional bullying, it comes with a wide audience.

"You can pass around a note to classmates making fun of a peer, and it stays 8
in the room," said Sheri Bauman, director of the school counseling master's degree program at the University of Arizona. "But when you post that same note
online, thousands can see it. The whole world becomes witness and is invited to
participate."

Anywhere from one-third to one-half of youths have been targeted by cy- 9
berbullies. And those experiences produce damaging consequences—from a
decline in academic performance to suicide.

"Our study of upwards of 2,000 middle school students revealed that cyber- 10
bullying victims were nearly twice as likely to attempt suicide compared with
students not targeted with online abuse," said Sameer Hinduja, study co-author
and founder of the Cyberbullying Research Center. "Cyberbullying clearly
heightens instability and hopelessness in adolescents' minds."

Findings like these lend a sense of urgency to anti-cyberbullying efforts. 11
Legally speaking, those efforts can be tricky for school administrators. The judi-
ciary has long struggled to balance freedom of speech against the darker side of
digital communication.

(Continued)

...*continued* Cyberbullying, **Jennifer Holladay**

Is Cyberbullying Largely a Problem for Girls?

Conventional wisdom suggests that boys are more likely to bully in person and girls to bully online. But Sheri Bauman notes that "cyberbullying is a new area of inquiry, and it's just hard to draw definitive conclusions from the research that's currently available," she said.

What is clear is that cyberbullying, like traditional bullying, is about power. "Students attempt to gain social status through cyberbullying," said Bauman. Sameer Hinduja says that gaining social status often means tearing someone else down, and boys and girls often do that differently.

"Girls tend to target each other with labels that carry particular meanings for them," said Hinduja. Labels like "slut," "whore," and "bitch" are common within girl-to-girl cyberbullying. The main tactic of boy cyberbullies who attack other boys is to accuse them of being gay. "The amount of abuse boys encounter because of real or perceived sexual orientation is pronounced," Bauman said.

12 More and more though, courts and law enforcement send the message that cyberbullying will not be tolerated. For instance, in March 2010, California's Second Appellate District concluded that online threats against a student were not protected speech and allowed a civil lawsuit against the alleged perpetrators, their parents, and school officials to proceed.

13 The notion that schools must respond to behavior that takes place off campus and online may seem a tall order. But schools are coming to understand that bullies don't just attack in the cafeteria or on the playground. "Wherever kids go with their computers or phones, which is nearly everywhere, the bullies come with them," said Bauman.

14 A 2010 study by the Henry J. Kaiser Family Foundation found that technology access among children has skyrocketed since 1999. Today, 93% of children ages 8 to 18 have computers at home, 66% have cell phones, and 76% own another multimedia device, such as an iPod.

15 These tools give them access to a dizzying array of social media. Some, such as Twitter and Facebook, are well known among parents and teachers. Others, such as Formspring, fly well below the radar of most adults. Yet sites like Formspring can create the biggest headaches. Formspring offers its users total anonymity. That makes it at once a huge draw for curious teenagers and a nearly perfect medium for cyberbullies.

Relieving the Drama

16 The ostensible boundary between off-campus behavior and school life evaporated for Highline Academy, a K-8 charter in Denver, last spring when a conflict fueled by Facebook posts ultimately led to a physical altercation. In the wake of the incident, Highline officials spoke with students in meetings and issued a packet of information to parents and guardians about cyberbullying and Internet safety. Still, a new Facebook page soon appeared, with a growing stream of posts about a student involved in the altercation.

17 "As a community, we needed to step back from the incident and relieve some of the drama," principal Greg Gonzales said. He asked every parent to support a 48-hour moratorium on Facebook activity at home and to discuss the use of the social networking site with their children.

(Continued)

Gonzales and colleagues also placed personal phone calls to parents of students who had engaged in the online conversations. "It may be outside our jurisdiction to dictate what students do on their own time, but it was important to let parents know we'd discovered their child had engaged in cyberbullying or inappropriate conversations about the incident," Gonzales said. "Numerous parents came back to us and said, 'I had no idea'—no idea what their child was doing online, or even that they had a Facebook page." 18

A 2009 study from Common Sense Media found that parents nationally underestimate children's use of social networking sites and often are unaware of how they are used. Thirty-seven percent of students, for example, admitted they'd made fun of a peer online, but only 18% of parents thought their child would do so. 19

Getting in Front of the Problems

The Seattle Public School District took a proactive stance last year when it launched a pilot curriculum to prevent cyberbullying in junior high and middle schools. 20

Mike Donlin, senior program consultant who led the curriculum's development, says the district created its own resources rather than use off-the-shelf products, ensuring that the resources would be easy to use and integrate into existing curricula. "There also was the issue of cost," he said. "We believed we could create something great with far less expense." 21

Unlike many programs that address cyberbullying piecemeal—focusing only on Internet safety skills, for example—the Seattle curriculum attacked the entire problem by using the four most promising prevention practices: 22

- Debunking misperceptions about digital behavior,
- Building empathy and understanding,
- Teaching online safety skills, and
- Equipping young people with strategies to reject digital abuse in their lives.

The Seattle curriculum also recognizes the importance of parental engagement by offering take-home letters and activities. 23

Academically, the curriculum focuses on writing, which boosts student skills in a tested area, while allowing the program to discard common, ineffective practices. Instead of asking students to sign a pre-crafted pledge, for example, the curriculum prompts them to write personal contracts for themselves about their online behavior. 24

The curriculum also educates teachers about cyberbullying and introduces language they can share with students. "We couch lessons in a way that resonates for teachers, too," said Donlin. "So, we use the Golden Rule. We use the old-fashioned mantra 'don't kiss and tell' to address sexting." 25

Still, some information requires repeated explanation. Some might wonder, for example, why the curriculum prompts students to try to see things from the bully's perspective. "A student can be a victim, a bystander, and a bully in different moments," Donlin explained. "Maybe a child was bullied at school this 26

(Continued)

morning, but gets online later and bullies back. Roles shift. Technology gives them tremendous freedom and power to reach out and touch in nearly every moment, for good or evil."

Learning to resist the urge to "bully back" is important, as is unlearning some 27 common myths about being online. Kids often think they can be anonymous, or that what they do on the Internet is fleeting. Both ideas are mistaken. The Library of Congress, for example, is archiving all Twitter messages sent from March 2006 forward. Even the "mean tweets" will be immortalized for future generations. "Everything students do online reflects on them, permanently," says Donlin.

For teachers, a common stumbling block revolves around First Amend- 28 ment protections and discomfort about corralling students' speech. Donlin believes that should not be a problem. "We have Second Amendment rights to possess weapons, but that doesn't mean we allow children to bring guns to school," he observed. "When it comes to cyberbullying, we're still talking about school safety."

Bullying as True Drama

Danah Boyd and Alice Marwick

Published in *The New York Times* in 2011, this essay examines the phenomenon that led to the death of a 14 year-old boy who was "cyberbullied." It was authored by Danah Boyd, a senior researcher at Microsoft Research and a research assistant professor at New York University, and Alice Marwick, who at the time was a postdoctoral researcher at Microsoft Research and a research affiliate at Harvard University.

The suicide of Jamey Rodemeyer, the 14-year-old boy from western New York 1 who killed himself last Sunday after being tormented by his classmates for being gay, is appalling. His story is a classic case of bullying: he was aggressively and repeatedly victimized. Horrific episodes like this have sparked conversations about cyberbullying and created immense pressure on regulators and educators to do something, anything, to make it stop. Yet in the rush to find a solution, adults are failing to recognize how their conversations about bullying are often misaligned with youth narratives. Adults need to start paying attention to the language of youth if they want antibullying interventions to succeed.

Jamey recognized that he was being bullied and asked explicitly for help, 2 but this is not always the case. Many teenagers who are bullied can't emotionally afford to identify as victims, and young people who bully others rarely see themselves as perpetrators. For a teenager to recognize herself or himself in the adult language of bullying carries social and psychological costs. It requires acknowledging oneself as either powerless or abusive.

(Continued)

In our research over a number of years, we have interviewed and observed 3 teenagers across the United States. Given the public interest in cyberbullying, we asked young people about it, only to be continually rebuffed. Teenagers repeatedly told us that bullying was something that happened only in elementary or middle school. "There's no bullying at this school" was a regular refrain.

This didn't mesh with our observations, so we struggled to understand the 4 disconnect. While teenagers denounced bullying, they—especially girls— would describe a host of interpersonal conflicts playing out in their lives as "drama."

At first, we thought drama was simply an umbrella term, referring to vary- 5 ing forms of bullying, joking around, minor skirmishes between friends, break-ups and makeups, and gossip. We thought teenagers viewed bullying as a form of drama. But we realized the two are quite distinct. Drama was not a show for us, but rather a protective mechanism for them.

Teenagers say drama when they want to diminish the importance of some- 6 thing. Repeatedly, teenagers would refer to something as "just stupid drama," "something girls do," or "so high school." We learned that drama can be fun and entertaining; it can be serious or totally ridiculous; it can be a way to get attention or feel validated. But mostly we learned that young people use the term drama because it is empowering.

Dismissing a conflict that's really hurting their feelings as drama lets teen- 7 agers demonstrate that they don't care about such petty concerns. They can save face while feeling superior to those tormenting them by dismissing them as desperate for attention. Or, if they're the instigators, the word drama lets teenagers feel that they're participating in something innocuous or even funny, rather than having to admit that they've hurt someone's feelings. Drama allows them to distance themselves from painful situations.

Adults want to help teenagers recognize the hurt that is taking place, which 8 often means owning up to victimhood. But this can have serious consequences. To recognize oneself as a victim—or perpetrator—requires serious emotional, psychological and social support, an infrastructure unavailable to many teenagers. And when teenagers like Jamey do ask for help, they're often let down. Not only are many adults ill-equipped to help teenagers do the psychological work necessary, but teenagers' social position often requires them to continue facing the same social scene day after day.

Like Jamey, there are young people who identify as victims of bullying. But 9 many youths engaged in practices that adults label bullying do not name them as such. Teenagers want to see themselves as in control of their own lives; their reputations are important. Admitting that they're being bullied, or worse, that they are bullies, slots them into a narrative that's disempowering and makes them feel weak and childish.

Antibullying efforts cannot be successful if they make teenagers feel vic- 10 timized without providing them the support to go from a position of victimization to one of empowerment. When teenagers acknowledge that they're being

(Continued)

...*continued* Bullying as True Drama, **Danah Boyd and Alice Marwick**

bullied, adults need to provide programs similar to those that help victims of abuse. And they must recognize that emotional recovery is a long and difficult process.

But if the goal is to intervene at the moment of victimization, the focus should be to work within teenagers' cultural frame, encourage empathy and help young people understand when and where drama has serious consequences. Interventions must focus on positive concepts like healthy relationships and digital citizenship rather than starting with the negative framing of bullying. The key is to help young people feel independently strong, confident and capable without first requiring them to see themselves as either an oppressed person or an oppressor.   11

> **❝The way today's students will do science, politics, journalism, and business next year and a decade from now will be shaped by the skills they acquire in using social media and by the knowledge they gain of the important issues of privacy, identity, community, and the role of citizen media in democracy.❞**
>
> —Howard Rheingold, Author of *Smart Mobs*

Facebook Wrestles with Free Speech and Civility

Miguel Helft

Miguel Helft first published this essay in *The New York Times* in December 2010. Helft writes largely about Internet companies in his role as a business desk reporter for that publication. He has also written on topics related to business and technology for a number of other publications, and has experience as a software engineer. In addition to a Masters degree in Computer Science, he holds a B.A. in Philosophy.

Palo Alto, Calif.—Mark Zuckerberg, the co-founder and chief executive of Facebook, likes to say that his website brings people together, helping to make the world a better place. But Facebook isn't a utopia, and when it comes up short, Dave Willner tries to clean up.   1

Dressed in Facebook's quasi-official uniform of jeans, a T-shirt and flip-flops, the 26-year-old Mr. Willner hardly looks like a cop on the beat. Yet he and his colleagues on Facebook's "hate and harassment team" are part of a virtual police squad charged with taking down content that is illegal or violates Facebook's terms of service. That puts them on the front line of the debate over free speech on the Internet.   2

"Facebook has more power in determining who can speak and who can be heard around the globe than any Supreme Court justice, any king or any president," said Jeffrey Rosen, a law professor at George Washington University who has written about free speech on the Internet. "It is important that Facebook is exercising its power carefully and protecting more speech rather than less."   3

But Facebook rarely pleases everyone. Any piece of content—a photograph, video, page or even a message between two individuals—could offend somebody. Decisions by the company not to remove material related to Holocaust denial or pages critical of Islam and other religions, for example, have annoyed   4

(Continued)

advocacy groups and prompted some foreign governments to temporarily block the site.

Some critics say Facebook does not do enough to prevent certain abuses, 5 like bullying, and may put users at risk with lax privacy policies. They also say the company is often too slow to respond to problems.

For example, a page lampooning and, in some instances, threatening vio- 6 lence against an 11-year-old girl from Orlando, Fla., who had appeared in a music video, was still up last week, months after users reported the page to Facebook. The girl's mother, Christa Etheridge, said she had been in touch with law enforcement authorities and was hoping the offenders would be prosecuted.

"I'm highly upset that Facebook has allowed this to go on repeatedly and to 7 let it get this far," she said.

A Facebook spokesman said the company had left the page up because it 8 did not violate its terms of service, which allow criticism of a public figure. The spokesman said that by appearing in a band's video, the girl had become a public figure, and that the threatening comments had not been posted until a few days ago. Those comments, and the account of the user who had posted them, were removed after the *New York Times* inquired about them.

Facebook says it is constantly working to improve its tools to report abuse 9 and trying to educate users about bullying. And it says it responds as fast as it can to the roughly two million reports of potentially abusive content that its users flag every week.

"Our intent is to triage to make sure we get to the high-priority, high-risk 10 and high-visibility items most quickly," said Joe Sullivan, Facebook's chief security officer.

(*Continued*)

In early October, Mr. Willner and his colleagues spent more than a week 11 dealing with one high-risk, highly visible case; rogue citizens of Facebook's world had posted antigay messages and threats of violence on a page inviting people to remember Tyler Clementi and other gay teenagers who have committed suicide, on so-called Spirit Day, Oct. 20.

Working with colleagues here and in Dublin, they tracked down the ac- 12 counts of the offenders and shut them down. Then, using an automated technology to tap Facebook's graph of connections between members, they tracked down more profiles for people, who, as it turned out, had also been posting violent messages.

"Most of the hateful content was coming from fake profiles," said James 13 Mitchell, who is Mr. Willner's supervisor and leads the team. He said that because most of these profiles, created by people he called "trolls," were connected to those of other trolls, Facebook could track down and block an entire network relatively quickly.

Using the system, Mr. Willner and his colleagues silenced dozens of troll 14 accounts, and the page became usable again. But trolls are repeat offenders, and it took Mr. Willner and his colleagues nearly 10 days of monitoring the page around the clock to take down over 7,000 profiles that kept surfacing to attack the Spirit Day event page.

Most abuse incidents are not nearly as prominent or public as the defacing 15 of the Spirit Day page, which had nearly 1.5 million members. As with schoolyard taunts, they often happen among a small group of people, hidden from casual view.

On a morning in November, Nick Sullivan, a member of the hate and ha- 16 rassment team, watched as reports of bullying incidents scrolled across his screen, full of mind-numbing meanness. "Emily looks like a brother." (Deleted) "Grady is with Dave." (Deleted) "Ronald is the biggest loser." (Deleted) Although the insults are relatively mild, as attacks on specific people who are not public figures, these all violated the terms of service.

"There's definitely some crazy stuff out there," Mr. Sullivan said. "But you 17 can do thousands of these in a day."

Facebook faces even thornier challenges when policing activity that is con- 18 sidered political by some, and illegal by others, like the controversy over WikiLeaks and the secret diplomatic cables it published.

Last spring, for example, the company declined to take down pages related 19 to "Everybody Draw Muhammad Day," an Internetwide protest to defend free speech that surfaced in repudiation of death threats received by two cartoonists who had drawn pictures of Muhammad. A lot of the discussion on Facebook involved people in Islamic countries debating with people in the West about why the images offended.

Facebook's team worked to separate the political discussion from the at- 20 tacks on specific people or Muslims. "There were people on the page that

(Continued)

were crossing the line, but the page itself was not crossing the line," Mr. Mitchell said.

Facebook's refusal to shut down the debate caused its entire site to be 21 blocked in Pakistan and Bangladesh for several days.

Facebook has also sought to walk a delicate line on Holocaust denial. The 22 company has generally refused to block Holocaust denial material, but has worked with human rights groups to take down some content linked to organizations or groups, like the government of Iran, for which Holocaust denial is part of a larger campaign against Jews.

"Obviously we disagree with them on Holocaust denial," said Rabbi 23 Abraham Cooper, associate dean of the Simon Wiesenthal Center. But Rabbi Cooper said Facebook had done a better job than many other major websites in developing a thoughtful policy on hate and harassment.

The soft-spoken Mr. Willner, who on his own Facebook page describes his 24 political views as "turning swords into plowshares and spears into pruning hooks," makes for an unlikely enforcer. An archaeology and anthropology major in college, he said that while he loved his job, he did not love watching so much of the underbelly of Facebook.

"I handle it by focusing on the fact that what we do matters," he said. 25

Why You Can't Cite Wikipedia in My Class

Neil L. Waters

This essay first appeared in *Communications of the ACM*, a magazine for computer professionals, in September 2007. Its author, Neil Waters, is the Kawashima Professor of Japanese Studies and a professor of history at Middlebury College, a liberal arts institution in Vermont.

The case for an online opensource encyclopedia is enormously appealing. 1 What's not to like? It gives the originators of entries a means to publish, albeit anonymously, in fields they care deeply about and provides editors the opportunity to improve, add to, and polish them, a capacity not afforded to in-print articles. Above all, open sourcing marshals legions of unpaid, eager, frequently knowledgeable volunteers, whose enormous aggregate labor and energy makes possible the creation of an entity—Wikipedia, which today boasts more than 1.6 million entries in its English edition alone—that would otherwise be far too costly and labor-intensive to see the light of day. In a sense it would have been technologically impossible just a few years ago; open sourcing is democracy in action, and Wikipedia is its most ubiquitous and accessible creation.

Yet I am a historian, schooled in the concept that scholarship requires ac- 2 countability and trained in a discipline in which collaborative research is rare. The idea that the vector-sum products of tens or hundreds of anonymous

(Continued)

collaborators could have much value is, to say the least, counterintuitive for most of us in my profession. We don't allow our students to cite printed general encyclopedias, much less open-source ones. Further, while Wikipedia compares favorably with other tertiary sources for articles in the sciences, approximately half of all entries are in some sense historical. Here the qualitative record is much spottier, with reliability decreasing in approximate proportion to distance from "hot topics" in American history [1]. For a Japan historian like me to perceive the positive side of Wikipedia requires an effort of will.

I made that effort after an innocuous series of events briefly and improbably propelled me and the history department at Middlebury College into the national, even international, spotlight. While grading a set of final examinations from my "History of Early Japan" class, I noticed that a half-dozen students had provided incorrect information about two topics—the Shimabara Rebellion of 1637–1638 and the Confucian thinker Ogyu Sorai—on which they were to write brief essays. Moreover, they used virtually identical language in doing so. A quick check on Google propelled me via popularity-driven algorithms to the Wikipedia entries on them, and there, quite plainly, was the erroneous information. To head off similar events in the future, I proposed a policy to the history department it promptly adopted: "(1) Students are responsible for the accuracy of information they provide, and they cannot point to Wikipedia or any similar source that may appear in the future to escape the consequences of errors. (2) Wikipedia is not an acceptable citation, even though it may lead one to a citable source."

The rest, as they say, is history. The Middlebury student newspaper ran a story on the new policy. That story was picked up online by *The Burlington Free Press*, a Vermont newspaper, which ran its own story. I was interviewed, first by Vermont radio and TV stations and newspapers, then by the *New York Times*, the *Asahi Shimbun* in Tokyo, and by radio and TV stations in Australia and throughout the U.S., culminating in a story on NBC Nightly News. Hundreds of other newspapers ran stories without interviews, based primarily on the *Times* article. I received dozens of phone calls, ranging from laudatory to actionably defamatory. . . .

In the wake of my allotted 15 minutes of Andy Warhol-promised fame I have tried to figure out what all the fuss was about. There is a great deal of uneasiness about Wikipedia in the U.S., as well as in the rest of the computerized world, and a great deal of passion and energy have been spent in its defense. It is clear to me that the good stuff is related to the bad stuff. Wikipedia owes its incredible growth to open-source editing, which is also the root of its greatest weakness. Dedicated and knowledgeable editors can and do effectively reverse the process of entropy by making entries better over time. Other editors, through ignorance, sloppy research, or, on occasion, malice or zeal, can and do introduce or perpetuate errors in fact or interpretation. The reader never knows whether the last editor was one of this latter group; most editors leave no trace save a whimsical cyber-handle.

(Continued)

Popular entries are less subject to enduring errors, innocent or otherwise, 6
than the seldom-visited ones, because, as I understand it, the frequency of visits
by a Wikipedia "policeman" is largely determined, once again, by algorithms
that trace the number of hits and move the most popular sites to a higher priority. The same principle, I have come to realize, props up the whole of the Wiki-
world. Once a critical mass of hits is reached, Google begins to guide those who
consulted it to Wikipedia before all else. A new button on my version of Firefox
goes directly to Wikipedia. Preferential access leads to yet more hits, generating
a still higher priority in an endless loop of mutual reinforcement.

It seems to me that there is a major downside to the self-reinforcing cycle of 7
popularity. Popularity begets ease of use, and ease of use begets the "democratization" of access to information. But all too often, democratization of access to
information is equated with the democratization of the information itself, in the
sense that it is subject to a vote. That last mental conflation may have origins
that predate Wikipedia and indeed the whole of the Internet.

The quiz show "Family Feud" has been a fixture of daytime television for 8
decades and is worth a quick look. Contestants are not rewarded for guessing
the correct answer but rather for guessing the answer that the largest number of
people have chosen as the correct answer. The show must tap into some sort of
popular desire to democratize information. Validation is not conformity to
verifiable facts or weighing of interpretations and evidence but conformity to
popular opinion. Expertise plays practically no role at all.

Here is where all but the most hopelessly postmodernist scholars bridle. 9
"Family Feud" is harmless enough, but most of us believe in a real, external
world in which facts exist independently of popular opinion, and some interpretations of events, thoroughly grounded in disciplinary rigor and the weight
of evidence, are at least more likely to be right than others that are not. I tell my
students that Wikipedia is a fine place to search for a paper topic or begin the
research process, but it absolutely cannot serve subsequent stages of research.
Wikipedia is not the direct heir to "Family Feud," but both seem to share an element of faith—that if enough people agree on something, it is most likely so.

What can be done? The answer depends on the goal. If it is to make Wikipe- 10
dia a truly authoritative source, suitable for citation, it cannot be done for any
general tertiary source, including the *Encyclopaedia Britannica*. For an anonymous
open-source encyclopedia, that goal is theoretically, as well as practically, impossible. If the goal is more modest—to make Wikipedia more reliable than it
is—then it seems to me that any changes must come at the expense of its open-
source nature. Some sort of accountability for editors, as well as for the originators of entries, would be a first step, and that, I think, means that editors must
leave a record of their real names. A more rigorous fact-checking system might
help, but are there enough volunteers to cover 1.6 million entries, or would
checking be in effect reserved for popular entries?

Can one move beyond the world of cut-and-dried facts to check for logical 11
consistency and reasonableness of interpretations in light of what is known

...continued Why You Can't Cite Wikipedia in My Class, **Neil L. Waters**

about a particular society in a particular historical period? Can it be done without experts? If you rely on experts, do you pay them or depend on their voluntarism?

I suppose I should now go fix the Wikipedia entry for Ogyu Sorai 12 (en.wikipedia.org/wiki/Ogyu_Sorai). I have been waiting since January to see how long it might take for the system to correct it, which has indeed been altered slightly and is rather good overall. But the statement that Ogyu opposed the Tokugawa order is still there and still highly misleading [2]. Somehow the statement that equates the samurai with the lower class in Tokugawa Japan has escaped the editors' attention, though anyone with the slightest contact with Japanese history knows it is wrong. One down, 1.6 million to go.

References

1. Rosenzweig, R. Can history be open source? *Journal of American History 93,* 1 (June 2006), 117–146.
2. Tucker, J. (editor and translator). *Ogyu Sorai's Philosophical Masterworks.* Association for Asian Studies and University of Hawaii Press, Honolulu, 2006, 12–13, 48–51; while Ogyu sought to redefine the sources of Tokugawa legitimacy, his purpose was clearly to strengthen the authority of the Tokugawa shogunate.

Professors Should Embrace Wikipedia

Mark Wilson

Offering a counterpoint to Neil Waters' essay, this piece was first published in *Inside Higher Ed* in April 2008. Its author, Mark A. Wilson, is the Lewis M. and Marian Senter Nixon Professor of Natural Sciences and Geology at The College of Wooster. How does his vision of what Wikipedia can be differ from what you have been told about the site? Is it feasible? Does his argument adequately answer Waters' negative take on Wikipedia?

When the online, anyone-can-edit Wikipedia appeared in 2001, teachers, espe- 1 cially college professors, were appalled. The Internet was already an apparently limitless source of nonsense for their students to eagerly consume—now there was a website with the appearance of legitimacy and a dead-easy interface that would complete the seduction until all sense of fact, fiction, myth and propaganda blended into a popular culture of pseudointelligence masking the basest ignorance. . . .

Now the English version of Wikipedia has over 2 million articles, and it has 2 been translated into over 250 languages. It has become so massive that you can

(Continued)

type virtually any noun into a search engine and the first link will be to a Wikipedia page. After seven years and this exponential growth, Wikipedia can still be edited by anyone at any time. A generation of students was warned away from this information siren, but we know as professors that it is the first place they go to start a research project, look up an unfamiliar term from lecture, or find something disturbing to ask about during the next lecture. In fact, we learned too that Wikipedia is indeed the most convenient repository of information ever invented, and we go there often—if a bit covertly—to get a few questions answered. Its accuracy, at least for science articles, is actually as high as the revered *Encyclopaedia Britannica*, as shown by a test published in the journal *Nature*.

It is time for the academic world to recognize Wikipedia for what it has become: a global library open to anyone with an Internet connection and a pressing curiosity. The vision of its founders, Jimmy Wales and Larry Sanger, has become reality, and the librarians were right: the world has not been the same since. If the Web is the greatest information delivery device ever, and Wikipedia is the largest coherent store of information and ideas, then we as teachers and scholars should have been on this train years ago for the benefit of our students, our professions, and that mystical pool of human knowledge.   3

What Wikipedia too often lacks is academic authority, or at least the perception of it. Most of its thousands of editors are anonymous, sometimes known only by an IP address or a cryptic username. Every article has a "talk" page for discussions of content, bias, and organization. "Revert" wars can rage out of control as one faction battles another over a few words in an article. Sometimes administrators have to step in and lock a page down until tempers cool and the main protagonists lose interest. The very anonymity of the editors is often the source of the problem: how do we know who has an authoritative grasp of the topic?   4

That is what academics do best. We can quickly sort out scholarly authority into complex hierarchies with a quick glance at a vita and a sniff at a publication list. We make many mistakes doing this, of course, but at least our debates are supported with citations and a modicum of civility because we are identifiable and we have our reputations to maintain and friends to keep. Maybe this academic culture can be added to the Wild West of Wikipedia to make it more useful for everyone?   5

I propose that all academics with research specialties, no matter how arcane (and nothing is too obscure for Wikipedia), enroll as identifiable editors of Wikipedia. We then watch over a few wikipages of our choosing, adding to them when appropriate, stepping in to resolve disputes when we know something useful. We can add new articles on topics which should be covered, and argue that others should be removed or combined. This is not to displace anonymous editors, many of whom possess vast amounts of valuable information and innovative ideas, but to add our authority and hard-won knowledge to this growing universal library.   6

The advantages should be obvious. First, it is another outlet for our scholarship, one that may be more likely to be read than many of our journals. Second, we   7

(Continued)

...*continued* Professors Should Embrace Wikipedia, **Mark Wilson**

are directly serving our students by improving the source they go to first for information. Third, by identifying ourselves, we can connect with other scholars and interested parties who stumble across our edits and new articles. Everyone wins.

I have been an open Wikipedia editor now for several months. I have enjoyed   8
it immensely. In my teaching I use a "living syllabus" for each course, which is a kind of academic blog. (For example, see my History of Life course online syllabus.) I connect students through links to outside sources of information. Quite often I refer students to Wikipedia articles that are well sourced and well written. Wikipages that are not so good are easily fixed with a judicious edit or two, and many pages become more useful with the addition of an image from my collection (all donated to the public domain). Since I am open in my editorial identity, I often get questions from around the world about the topics I find most fascinating. I've even made important new connections through my edits to new collaborators and reporters who want more background for a story.

For example, this year I met online a biology professor from Centre College   9
who is interested in the ecology of fish on Great Inagua Island in the Bahamas. He saw my additions and images on that Wikipedia page and had several questions about the island. He invited me to speak at Centre next year about evolution–creation controversies, which is unrelated to the original contact but flowed from our academic conversations. I in turn have been learning much about the island's living ecology I did not know. I've also learned much about the kind of prose that is most effective for a general audience, and I've in turn taught some people how to properly reference ideas and information. In short, I've expanded my teaching.

Wikipedia as we know it will undoubtedly change in the coming years as all   10
technologies do. By involving ourselves directly and in large numbers now, we can help direct that change into ever more useful ways for our students and the public. This is, after all, our sacred charge as teacher-scholars: to educate when and where we can to the greatest effect.

Does the Internet Make You Dumber?

Nicholas Carr

This essay was first published in 2010 in *The Wall Street Journal*, one of the preeminent publications for the business world. Its author, Nicholas Carr, is a well-known authority on technology and culture and has written for *The Atlantic*, *The Wall Street Journal*, *The New York Times*, *Wired*, *Nature*, *MIT Technology Review*, and many other periodicals. He is also the author of *The Shallows: What the Internet Is Doing to Our Brains*, a 2011 Pulitzer Prize finalist and a *New York Times* bestseller. More recently, he has published the *The Glass Cage: Automation and Us*. Carr has consistently pushed readers to

(Continued)

consider the larger implications of our reliance upon computers, and how computer technology is changing the way we think.

The Roman philosopher Seneca may have put it best 2,000 years ago: "To be everywhere is to be nowhere." Today, the Internet grants us easy access to unprecedented amounts of information. But a growing body of scientific evidence suggests that the Net, with its constant distractions and interruptions, is also turning us into scattered and superficial thinkers.   1

The picture emerging from the research is deeply troubling, at least to anyone who values the depth, rather than just the velocity, of human thought. People who read text studded with links, the studies show, comprehend less than those who read traditional linear text. People who watch busy multimedia presentations remember less than those who take in information in a more sedate and focused manner. People who are continually distracted by emails, alerts and other messages understand less than those who are able to concentrate. And people who juggle many tasks are less creative and less productive than those who do one thing at a time.   2

The common thread in these disabilities is the division of attention. The richness of our thoughts, our memories and even our personalities hinges on our ability to focus the mind and sustain concentration. Only when we pay deep attention to a new piece of information are we able to associate it "meaningfully and systematically with knowledge already well established in memory," writes the Nobel Prize–winning neuroscientist Eric Kandel. Such associations are essential to mastering complex concepts.   3

When we're constantly distracted and interrupted, as we tend to be online, our brains are unable to forge the strong and expansive neural connections that give depth and distinctiveness to our thinking. We become mere signal-processing units, quickly shepherding disjointed bits of information into and then out of short-term memory.   4

In an article published in *Science* last year, Patricia Greenfield, a leading developmental psychologist, reviewed dozens of studies on how different media technologies influence our cognitive abilities. Some of the studies indicated that certain computer tasks, like playing video games, can enhance "visual literacy skills," increasing the speed at which people can shift their focus among icons and other images on screens. Other studies, however, found that such rapid shifts in focus, even if performed adeptly, result in less rigorous and "more automatic" thinking.   5

In one experiment conducted at Cornell University, for example, half a class of students was allowed to use Internet-connected laptops during a lecture, while the other had to keep their computers shut. Those who browsed the Web performed much worse on a subsequent test of how well they retained the lecture's content. While it's hardly surprising that Web surfing would distract students, it should be a note of caution to schools that are wiring their classrooms in hopes of improving learning.   6

> **❝The popularity of Web 2.0 is evidence of a tide of credulity and misinformation that can only be countered by a culture of respect for authenticity and expertise in all scholarly, research, and educational endeavors.❞**
>
> —Michael Gorman, "Web 2.0: The Sleep of Reason"

(Continued)

Ms. Greenfield concluded that "every medium develops some cognitive skills at the expense of others." Our growing use of screen-based media, she said, has strengthened visual-spatial intelligence, which can improve the ability to do jobs that involve keeping track of lots of simultaneous signals, like air traffic control. But that has been accompanied by "new weaknesses in higher-order cognitive processes," including "abstract vocabulary, mindfulness, reflection, inductive problem solving, critical thinking, and imagination." We're becoming, in a word, shallower. 7

In another experiment, recently conducted at Stanford University's Communication Between Humans and Interactive Media Lab, a team of researchers gave various cognitive tests to 49 people who do a lot of media multitasking and 52 people who multitask much less frequently. The heavy multitaskers performed poorly on all the tests. They were more easily distracted, had less control over their attention, and were much less able to distinguish important information from trivia. 8

The researchers were surprised by the results. They had expected that the intensive multitaskers would have gained some unique mental advantages from all their on-screen juggling. But that wasn't the case. In fact, the heavy multitaskers weren't even good at multitasking. They were considerably less adept at switching between tasks than the more infrequent multitaskers. "Everything distracts them," observed Clifford Nass, the professor who heads the Stanford lab. 9

It would be one thing if the ill effects went away as soon as we turned off our computers and cellphones. But they don't. The cellular structure of the human brain, scientists have discovered, adapts readily to the tools we use, including those for finding, storing and sharing information. By changing our habits of mind, each new technology strengthens certain neural pathways and weakens others. The cellular alterations continue to shape the way we think even when we're not using the technology. 10

The pioneering neuroscientist Michael Merzenich believes our brains are being "massively remodeled" by our ever-intensifying use of the Web and related media. In the 1970s and 1980s, Mr. Merzenich, now a professor emeritus at the University of California in San Francisco, conducted a famous series of experiments on primate brains that revealed how extensively and quickly neural circuits change in response to experience. When, for example, Mr. Merzenich rearranged the nerves in a monkey's hand, the nerve cells in the animal's sensory cortex quickly reorganized themselves to create a new "mental map" of the hand. In a conversation late last year, he said that he was profoundly worried about the cognitive consequences of the constant distractions and interruptions the Internet bombards us with. The long-term effect on the quality of our intellectual lives, he said, could be "deadly." 11

What we seem to be sacrificing in all our surfing and searching is our capacity to engage in the quieter, attentive modes of thought that underpin 12

(Continued)

contemplation, reflection and introspection. The Web never encourages us to slow down. It keeps us in a state of perpetual mental locomotion.

It is revealing, and distressing, to compare the cognitive effects of the 13 Internet with those of an earlier information technology, the printed book. Whereas the Internet scatters our attention, the book focuses it. Unlike the screen, the page promotes contemplativeness.

Reading a long sequence of pages helps us develop a rare kind of mental 14 discipline. The innate bias of the human brain, after all, is to be distracted. Our predisposition is to be aware of as much of what's going on around us as possible. Our fast-paced, reflexive shifts in focus were once crucial to our survival. They reduced the odds that a predator would take us by surprise or that we'd overlook a nearby source of food.

To read a book is to practice an unnatural process of thought. It requires us 15 to place ourselves at what T. S. Eliot, in his poem "Four Quartets," called "the still point of the turning world." We have to forge or strengthen the neural links needed to counter our instinctive distractedness, thereby gaining greater control over our attention and our mind.

It is this control, this mental discipline, that we are at risk of losing as we 16 spend ever more time scanning and skimming online. If the slow progression of words across printed pages damped our craving to be inundated by mental stimulation, the Internet indulges it. It returns us to our native state of distractedness, while presenting us with far more distractions than our ancestors ever had to contend with.

Questions for Writing and Discussion

❶ The rhetorical occasion for Cleaver's argument was a debate sponsored by the College of Communication at Boston University. In her essay, can you find evidence (word choice, vocabulary, sentence length, tone, use of evidence, use of appeals) that suggests that her original *genre* was a speech and that her *audience* was college students, college faculty, and members of the community? Cite evidence from the essay showing where Cleaver uses debate elements appropriate for this genre and makes appeals to this audience.

❷ Both Jennifer Holladay in "Cyberbullying" and Danah Boyd and Alice Marwick in "Bullying as True Drama" make recommendations for responding to cyberbullying. Explain how their recommendations are similar and how they differ. Based on your own experience with social networking and cyberbullying, explain which of their recommendations would be most effective and why.

❸ Although the First Amendment to the Constitution says that "Congress shall make no law . . . abridging freedom of speech," certain kinds of speech are not permitted, including speech that incites actions that cause harm to others (shouting "fire" in a crowded arena). Based on Miguel Helft's "Facebook Wrestles with Free Speech and Civility," explain how Facebook's policies do or do not meet First Amendment guidelines. (Check a U.S. government site such as http://www.uscourts.gov for specific cases related to free speech in social media.) Just because Facebook users agree to a contract, can Facebook still censor language that it believes constitutes "hate or harassment"?

4 Neil Waters in "Why You Can't Cite Wikipedia in My Class" and Mark Wilson in "Professors Should Embrace Wikipedia" represent nearly opposing points of view. According to each author, what are the proper uses and limitations of Wikipedia? Citing examples from both articles, explain what uses of Wikipedia they agree on and then exactly how their recommendations differ.

5 Review Chapter 12 on strategies for doing a rhetorical analysis. Then analyze Nicholas Carr's "Does the Internet Make You Dumber?" for its key rhetorical strategies. How effectively does Carr state his purpose for his selected audience? What appeals to logos, ethos, or pathos does Carr make? Which of his appeals are most or least effective? Are his conclusions logically supported by his review of the research?

6 Analyze the cartoon below, "The Evolution of Communication," by Mike Keefe. What argument about the Internet or social media does this cartoon make? How do the cartoon's elements (composition, focal points, and narrative) help make this argument? Explain how this argument is similar to or different from Nicholas Carr's argument.

Tips for Transferring Skills

The writing techniques discussed in this chapter can be used in many other situations you will face as a college writer and beyond. To reinforce these techniques, and to really put them to use, you should find ways to apply and practice them on other occasions and in other classes. Here are tips for using these techniques in a variety of writing situations.

1. While we often think about "arguing" as something different from academic writing, just about all the writing you do in college involves argument. In science classes, you argue that your results are valid; in history class, that your interpretation of historical events is accurate; in literature class, that your reading of a text is reasonable. As you write in each of your classes, pay attention to how various assignments ask you to use skills of argument, and how the conventions of argument are similar or different across disciplines.

2. As you read articles assigned in other classes, read each one a second time, in order to consider the Toulmin model of argument. Note its use of data, claims, warrants, backing, qualifiers, and exceptions. Are there specific kinds of data that seem to be most valued in that field? Is there a clear claim or thesis from the start? Also note the ways that claims are "qualified," and what "exceptions" are pointed out. In the end, try to understand why writers in the field build arguments in this way.

3. Though we sometimes hear politics described as "a bunch of rhetoric," and while politics can be filled with personal attacks, in reality, political argument is often the means for getting things done. As you become aware of, and engaged in, topics of debate on your campus or in your community, consider using the Rogerian style of argument to convince others of your point of view without attacking their beliefs.

4. The Casebook in this chapter examines social media and its effects. There is no doubt that the types of arguments that exist out there in cyberspace can be quite different from traditional paper-based arguments. As you surf the social media sites that you frequent, try to come up with your own theory of Web-based argument for particular kinds of sites. How are arguments made on Facebook? On Instagram? On Twitter? This exercise can help you to become a more thoughtful user of social media, and to build arguments appropriate to a variety of media.

Arguing: Writing Processes

Using Arguing in Your Writing Processes

As you encounter debatable topics that catch your interest or relate to your personal experience, the techniques of argument examined in this chapter can help you to engage in key conversations, both orally and in writing. To become more skilled in argument, examine possible claims of fact or definition, value, cause and effect, or policy. If the claim is debatable, you may have a focus for your argument. Remember also to think about your possible audience. Who needs to be convinced about your argument? Who has the power to change the status quo? Are there multiple perspectives or stakeholders involved in this issue? Is there a compromise position you should argue for? How might your understanding of your audience change your claim? It is usually best to narrow your audience to a local group that might be influential. And remember to choose a genre and medium that best fit your purpose and audience. Use the following grid to help brainstorm combinations of audience and genre effective for your purpose and topic.

Audience	Possible Genres for Arguing
Personal Audience	Class notes, journal entry, blog, scrapbook, social networking page
Academic Audience	Academic essay, researched argument, examination essay, debate script, forum entry on class site, journal entry, website, or multimedia document
Public Audience	Letter to the editor, column, blog, article, or critique in a newspaper, online site, magazine, newsletter, graphic novel, website, or multimedia document

CHOOSING A SUBJECT

18.5

Use strategies for choosing a debatable topic

If a journal entry suggests a possible subject, do the collecting and shaping strategies. Otherwise, consider the following ideas.

- Review your journal entries and the papers you have already written for this class. Test their subjects for an arguable claim that you could make, opposing arguments you could consider, and an appropriate audience for an argumentative piece.
- **Writing Across the Curriculum.** Brainstorm ideas for argumentative subjects from the other courses you are currently taking or have taken. What

controversial issues have you discussed in your classes? Ask current or past instructors for controversial topics relating to their courses.

- Newspapers and magazines are full of controversial subjects in sports, medicine, law, business, and family. Browse current issues or online magazines, looking for possible subjects. Check news items, editorials, and cartoons. Look for subjects related to your own interests, your job, or your experiences.

- Interview friends, family, or classmates. What controversial issues affect their lives most directly? What would they most like to change about their lives? What has irritated or angered them most in the recent past?

- **Community Service Learning.** If you are doing a community service learning project, consider one of these topics: (1) Which of the agency's activities best meet the goals of the agency? Write an essay to the agency coordinator recommending a reallocation of resources to the most effective activities. (2) How might agency volunteers more usefully serve the agency in future projects? Write to your project coordinator recommending improvements that would better meet the dual goals of academic learning and agency service.

> **❝** You can write about anything, and if you write well enough, even the reader with no intrinsic interest in the subject will become involved. **❞**
>
> —Tracy Kidder, Novelist

COLLECTING

Narrowing and Focusing Your Claim

Narrow your subject to a specific topic, and sharpen your focus by applying the "Wh" questions. If your subject is "grades," your responses might be as follows.

18.6
Use collecting strategies to narrow and focus your claim

Subject: Grades

- **Who:** College students
- **What:** Letter grades
- **When:** In freshman and sophomore years
- **Where:** Especially in nonmajor courses
- **Why:** What purpose do grades serve in nonmajor courses?

Determine what claim or claims you want to make. Make sure that your claim is *arguable*. (Remember that claims can overlap; an argument may combine several related claims.)

Claim of Fact or Definition

- Letter grades exist. (not arguable)
- Employers consider grades when hiring. (slightly arguable, but not very controversial)
- Grades do not measure learning. (very arguable)

Claim About Cause or Effect

- Grades create anxiety for students. (not very arguable)
- Grades prevent discovery and learning. (arguable)

Claim About Value

- Grades are not fair. (not very arguable: "fairness" can usually be determined)
- Grades are bad because they discourage individual initiative. (arguable)
- Grades are good because they give students an incentive to learn. (arguable)

Claim About a Solution or Policy

- Grades should be eliminated altogether. (arguable—but difficult)
- Grades should be eliminated in humanities courses. (arguable)
- Grades should change to pass/fail in nonmajor courses. (arguable—and more practical)

Focusing and narrowing your *claim* helps determine what evidence you need to collect. Use your observing, remembering, reading, and investigative skills to gather the evidence. ***Note:*** An argumentative essay should not use only abstract and impersonal evidence. *Your experience* can be crucial to a successful argumentative essay. Start by doing the *remembering* exercises. Your audience wants to know not only why you are writing on this particular *topic,* but also why it is of interest to *you.*

Remembering

Use *freewriting, looping, branching,* or *clustering* to recall experiences, ideas, events, and people who are relevant to your claim. If you are writing about grades, brainstorm about how *your* teachers used grades, how you reacted to specific grades in one specific class, how your friends or parents reacted, and what you felt or thought. These prewriting exercises will help you understand your claim and give you specific examples that you can use for evidence.

Analyzing Statistics

Whether you are evaluating statistical sources in an essay that you are reading or choosing statistical data to use as evidence for a claim in your own essay, use the following questions to help you determine the relevance, validity, and bias of the statistics.

- Who is the author or the group responsible for gathering or presenting the information? Do they have a bias or point of view?
- What is the date of the study or survey? Are the data still relevant?

- For a survey or poll, what is the sample size (number of respondents) and sample selection (demographic group selected)? Is the sample large enough to give reliable results? Was the group randomly selected? Are certain key groups not included?
- Analyze the wording of the questions asked in the poll or survey. Are the questions relatively neutral? Do the questions lead respondents to a certain conclusion?
- Are the conclusions drawn justified by the data? Are the conclusions exaggerated or overgeneralized?

Observing

If possible for your topic, collect data and evidence by observing, firsthand, the facts, values, effects, or possible solutions related to your claim. *Repeated* observation will give you good inductive evidence to support your argument.

Investigating

For most argumentative essays, some research or investigation is essential. Because it is difficult to imagine all the valid counterarguments, interview friends, classmates, family, coworkers, and authorities on your topic. From the library, gather books and articles that contain arguments in support of your claim. ***Note:*** As you do research in the library, save, electronically or on paper, key passages from relevant sources to hand in with your essay. If you cite sources, list them on a Works Cited page following your essay.

SHAPING AND DRAFTING

As you plan your organization, reconsider your rhetorical situation. Will the *genre* you have selected (researched essay, letter to the editor, blog, website, brochure, PowerPoint presentation) help carry out your *purpose* for your intended audience? Is there a relevant *occasion* (meeting, anniversary, or response to news item) that your writing might focus on? What is the *cultural, social,* or *political context* for your writing? Finally, reconsider your *audience.* Try imagining one real person who might be among your readers. Is this person open-minded and likely to be convinced by your evidence? Does this person represent the opposing position? If you have several alternative positions, are there individual people who represent each of those positions? After reconsidering your rhetorical situation, try the shaping strategies that follow.

18.7
Use shaping and drafting strategies to organize a logical argument

Shaping Strategies

Do you want to . . .	Consider using these rhetorical modes or strategies:
write an argument with just one opposing position?	list "pro" and "con" arguments in two columns (p. 604)
write an argument with several alternative positions or solutions?	draw a circle of alternative positions (p. 605)
outline your argument using classical structure?	organizing arguments (pp. 605–608)
develop your argument with several supporting reasons?	developing arguments (p. 608)

List "Pro" and "Con" Arguments

Write out your *claim,* then list the arguments for your position (pro) and the arguments for the opposing positions (con). After you have made the list, match up arguments by drawing lines, as indicated in this lists below.

When pro and con arguments match, you will be able to argue against the con and for your claim at the same time. When arguments do not match, you will need to consider them separately. Also keep in mind the limitations of pro/con arguments suggested by Deborah Tannen's essay.

Claim: *Grades should be changed to pass/fail in nonmajor courses.*

PRO	CON
Grades inhibit learning by putting too much emphasis on competition.	Grades actually promote learning by setting students to study as hard as possible.
Grade competition with majors in the field can be discouraging.	Students should be encouraged to compete with majors. They may want to change their own major and need to know whether they can compete.
Pass/fail grading encourages students to explore nonmajor fields.	Students who don't have traditional grading won't take nonmajor courses seriously.
Some students do better without the pressure of grades; they need to find out whether they can motivate themselves without grades, but they shouldn't have to risk grades in their major field to discover that.	

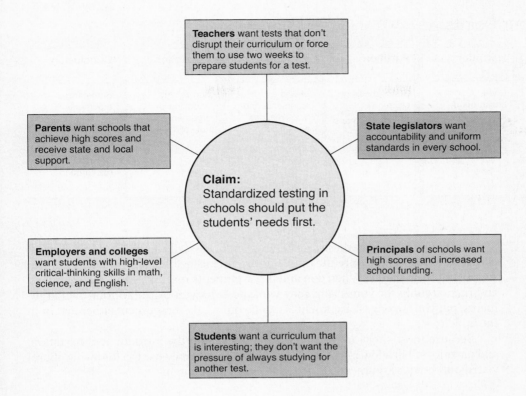

Draw a Circle of Alternative Positions

If you are considering multiple alternative positions, put your claim in the middle of a circle and indicate the various positions or stakeholders outside the circle. This diagram will help you identify the most important positions in the debate and thereby help you organize your writing.

Once you have a diagram that includes all the major alternative positions or stakeholders, decide the focus of your argument. For your purpose, audience, and context, you may want to focus on the different goals of teachers, students, and parents. Or you may want to suggest how teachers, students, and parents should organize and force legislators to change standardized testing or change how schools are funded based on test results.

Organizing Arguments

For more than two thousand years, writers and speakers have been trying to determine the most effective means to persuade audiences. One of the oldest outlines for a successful argument comes from classical rhetoric. The six-part outline is intended as a guideline rather than a rigid list; test this outline to see if it will work for *your* argument.

Shaping Your Points: Classical Argument

Introduction	Narration	Partition	Argument	Refutation	Conclusion
Announces subject Gets reader's interest Establishes trust in the writer	Gives background, context, statement of problem, or definition	States thesis or claim Outlines or maps argument	Makes arguments and gives reasons and evidence for the claim	Shows why opposing arguments are not valid	Summarizes argument Suggests solution Ties into the introduction or background

Most arguments have these features, but not necessarily in this order. Some writers prefer to respond to or refute opposing arguments before giving the reasoning in support of their claims. When con and pro arguments match, refuting an argument and then arguing for your claim may work best. As you organize your own arguments, put your strongest argument last and your weakest argument either first or in the middle.

Because most short argumentative essays contain the introduction, narration, and partition all in a few introductory paragraphs, you may use the following abbreviated outlines for argument.

Shaping Your Points: Abbreviated Argument Pattern 1

Introductory paragraph(s)	Your arguments	Refutation of opposing arguments	Concluding paragraph(s)
Attention getter Background Claim or thesis	Gives arguments and reasons and evidence to support them	Shows why opposing arguments are not valid	Summarizes argument Ties into the introduction or background

Shaping Your Points: Abbreviated Argument Pattern 2

Introductory paragraph(s)	Refutation of opposing arguments	Your arguments	Concluding paragraph(s)
Attention getter Background Claim or thesis	Shows why opposing arguments are not valid	Gives arguments and reasons and evidence to support them	Summarizes argument Ties into the introduction or background

Shaping Your Points: Abbreviated Argument Pattern 3

Introduction	Refutation of first opposing argument	Refutation of second opposing argument, etc.	Additional arguments	Concluding paragraph(s)
Attention getter Background Claim or thesis	Refutes first opposing argument that matches your first argument	Refutes second opposing argument that matches your second argument, etc.	Makes arguments and gives reasons and evidence for the claim	Summarizes argument Ties into the introduction or background

For Rogerian arguments, you can follow one of the above outlines, but the emphasis, tone, and attitude will be different.

Shaping Your Points: Rogerian Argument

Introduction	Opposing arguments	Your arguments	Concluding paragraph(s)
Attention getter and background Claim or thesis (often downplayed to reduce threat) Appeal to character (crucial)	States opposing arguments fairly Shows where, how, or when those arguments may be valid Establishes common ground	States your position fairly Shows where, how, or when your arguments are valid	Presents compromise position States your solution to the problem Shows its advantages to both sides

Developing Arguments

Think of your argument as a series of *because* statements, each supported by evidence, statistics, testimony, expert opinion, data, specific examples from your experience, or a combination of these elements.

THESIS OR CLAIM: *Grades should be abolished in nonmajor courses.*

Reason 1	Because they may keep a student from attempting a difficult non-major course *Statistics, testimony, data, and examples*
Reason 2	Because competition with majors in the field can be discouraging *Statistics, testimony, data, and examples*
Reason 3	Because grades inhibit students' learning in nonmajor fields *Statistics, testimony, data, and examples*

You can develop each reason using a variety of strategies. The following strategies may help you generate additional reasons and examples.

Definition	Define the crucial terms or ideas. (What do you mean by *learning?*)
Comparison	Compare the background, situation, and context with similar contexts. (What other schools have tried pass/fail grading for nonmajor courses? How has it worked?)
Process	How does or should a change occur? (How do nonmajors become discouraged? How should a school implement pass/fail in grading?)

These strategies may help you develop an argument coherently and effectively. If several strategies are possible, consider which would be most effective for your audience.

You will never really know "enough" about your subject or have "enough" evidence. At some point, however, you must stop collecting and start your draft. (The most frequent problem in drafting an argumentative essay is delaying the actual writing too long, until the deadline is close). This is when you should have at least a "working" thesis—the main point that you want to argue. While your thesis might change or develop as you draft, having a working thesis will help keep you focused.

For argumentative essays, start with a working order or sequence and sketch an outline on paper or in your head. Additional examples and appeals to reason, character, or emotion may occur to you as you develop your argument or refute opposing arguments. In addition, if you have done some research, have your notes, photocopies of key data, statistics, quotations, and citations of authorities close at hand. As you write, you will discover that some information or arguments don't fit into the flow of your essay. Don't force arguments into your draft when they no longer belong.

> "No one can write decently who is distrustful of the reader's intelligence, or whose attitude is patronizing."
>
> —E. B. White, Essayist

Research Tips

When you draft an arguing essay, don't let citations or direct quotations over-power your own argument. Two tactics will keep you in control of your argument:

First, always avoid "unidentified flying quotations" by *sandwiching* your quotations. *Introduce* quotations by referring to the author, the source, and/or the author's study. *Follow* quotations with a sentence explaining how the author's evidence supports your argument.

Second, keep your direct quotations *short*. If possible, reduce a long passage to one sentence and incorporate the quoted material in the flow of your own language. For example, in the essay that appears earlier in this chapter, Nicholas Carr writes:

> Only when we pay deep attention to a new piece of information are we able to associate it "meaningfully and systematically with knowledge already well established in memory," writes the Nobel Prize-winning neuroscientist Eric Kandel.

REVISING

Argumentation is the most public of the purposes for writing. The rhetorical situation (purpose, audience, genre, occasion, and cultural context) plays a crucial role. As you revise, look at this larger context, not just at phrasing, words, or sentences. Test your argument by having friends or classmates read it. Explain your claim, your focus, and your intended audience, genre, and context. Ask them to look for counter-arguments that you have omitted or for weaknesses, omissions, or fallacies in logic. But don't automatically change your draft in response; follow only the advice that makes your overall purpose more effective for your audience.

18.8
Use revision strategies to evaluate the quality of your argument

Guidelines for Revision

- **When you finish your draft, reconsider the elements of the rhetorical situation** (writer, purpose, audience, genre, occasion, cultural context). Look at the big picture. What needs changing? What needs to be added? What parts are repetitious or ineffective?
- **Collaborating with peers.** Ask a class member or friend to read your draft to determine the intended audience for your argument. See which arguments your reader thinks would not be effective for your audience.

- **Use the Toulmin model to evaluate your essay.** Is your claim clearly stated? Does your claim have a qualifier? Do you note exceptions to your claim? Do you have warrant statements explaining how your data support your reasons and claim?
- **Which of your *because* arguments are most effective?** Least effective? Should you change the outline or structure that you initially chose?
- **Revise your draft to avoid fallacies or errors in reasoning.** Errors in logic create two problems: They can destroy your rational appeal and open your argument to a logical rebuttal, and they can weaken your credibility—and thus reduce your appeal to your character. (Review the list of fallacies below.)
- **Support your reasons with evidence: *data, facts, statistics, quotations, observations, testimony, statistics, or specific examples from your experience.*** Check your collecting notes once again for further evidence to back up your weakest argument. Is there a weak or unsupported argument that you should omit?
- **Signal the major arguments and counterarguments in your partition or map.** Between paragraphs, use clear transitions and paragraph hooks.
- **Could your essay be improved by visuals or special formatting?** Reconsider your genre and audience. If visuals might make your essay more effective, do a search on the computer. If you need help formatting your essay, check with a peer, a computer lab assistant, or your instructor.
- **If you cite sources in your essay, check the *accuracy* of your statistics, quotations, and source references.**
- **Revise sentences to improve conciseness and clarity.**
- **Edit sentences for grammar, punctuation, and spelling.**

Revising Fallacies in Logic

Be careful to avoid using any of the common fallacies in logic described here. Reread your draft or your peer's draft and revise as appropriate to eliminate these illogical forms of argument.

- **Hasty generalization:** Conclusion not justified by sufficient or unbiased evidence. If Mary tells you that Professor Paramecium is a hard grader because he gave her 36 percent on the first biology test, she is making a hasty generalization. It may be *true*—Prof P. may be a difficult grader—but Mary's logic is not valid because she cannot logically draw that conclusion from a sample of one.
- **Post hoc ergo propter hoc:** Literally, "after this, therefore because of this." Just because B *occurred after* A does not mean that A *necessarily caused* B. You washed your car in the morning, and it rained in the afternoon. Though we

joke about how it always rains after we wash the car, there is certainly no causal relationship between the two events.

- **Genetic fallacy:** Arguing that the origins of a person, object, or institution determine its character, nature, or worth. Like the post hoc fallacy, the genetic fallacy is an error in causal relationships.

This automobile was made in Detroit. It'll probably fall apart after 10,000 miles. He speaks with a funny German accent. He's really stupid, you know. He started Celestial Seasonings Herb Teas just to make a quick buck; it's only another phony yuppie product.

The second half of each statement *may* or *may not* be true; the logical error is in assuming that the origin of something will determine its worth or quality. Stereotyping is frequently caused by a genetic fallacy.

- **Begging the question:** Loading the conclusion in the claim. Arguing that "pornography should be banned because it corrupts our youth" is a logical claim. However, saying that "filthy and corrupting pornography should be banned" is begging the question: The conclusion that the writer should *prove* (that pornography corrupts) is assumed in the claim. Other examples: "Those useless psychology classes should be dropped from the curriculum"; "Everyone knows that our ineffective drug control program is a miserable failure." The writers must *prove* that the psychology classes are useless and that the drug program is a failure.

- **Circular argument:** A sentence or argument that restates rather than proves. Thus, it goes in a circle: "President Reagan was a great communicator because he had that knack of talking effectively to the people." The terms in the beginning of the sentence (*great communicator*) and the end of the sentence (*talking effectively*) are interchangeable. The sentence ends where it started.

- **Either/or:** An oversimplification that reduces the alternatives to only two choices, thereby creating a false dilemma. Statements such as "Love it or leave it" attempt to reduce the alternatives to two. If you don't love your school, your town, or your country, you don't have to leave: A third choice is to change it and make it better. Proposed solutions frequently have an either/or fallacy: "Either we ban boxing or hundreds of young men will be senselessly killed." A third alternative might be to change boxing's rules or equipment.

- **Faulty comparison or analogy:** Basing an argument on a comparison of two things, ideas, events, or situations that are similar but not identical. Although comparisons or analogies are often effective in argument, they can hide logical problems. "We can solve the meth problem the same way we reduced the DWI problem: Attack it with increased enforcement and mandatory jail sentences." Although the situations are similar, they are not identical. The DWI solution will not necessarily work for drugs. An analogy is an extended comparison that uses something simple or familiar to explain something complex or less familiar. "Solving a mathematics problem is like baking a cake: You have to take it one step at a time. First, you assemble your ingredients or your known data. . . ." Like baking, solving a problem does involve a process; unlike baking, however, mathematics is more exact. Changing the amount of flour in a recipe by 1 percent will not make the cake fall; changing a numeric value by 1 percent, however, will ruin the whole problem. The point, however, is not to avoid comparisons or analogies. Simply make sure that your conclusions are qualified; acknowledge the *differences* between the two things compared as well as the similarities.

- **Ad hominem (literally, "to the man"):** An attack on the character of the individual or the opponent rather than his or her opinions, arguments, or qualifications: "Susan Davidson, the prosecuting attorney, drinks heavily. There's no way she can present an effective case." This is an attack on Ms. Davidson's character rather than an analysis of her legal talents. Her record in court may be excellent.

- **Ad populum (literally, "to the people"):** An emotional appeal to positive concepts (God, mother, country, liberty, democracy, apple pie) or negative concepts (fascism, atheism) rather than a direct discussion of the real issue: "If you are a true American, you should be in favor of tariffs to protect the garment industry."

- **Red herring:** A diversionary tactic designed to avoid confronting the key issue. *Red herring* refers to the practice of dragging a smelly fish across the trail to divert tracking dogs away from the real quarry. A red herring occurs when writers avoid countering an opposing argument directly: "Of course equal pay for women is an important issue, but I wonder whether women really want to take the responsibility that comes with higher paying jobs. Do they really want the additional stress?"

Using Argument to Seek Common Ground

This chapter focuses upon the ways that argument can be used to think through conflicting ideas, evaluate the strength of those ideas, and reach some common ground—even when fundamental disagreements remain. Strong argumentative writing thus seeks to help the audience see a full spectrum of possible perspectives before using critical thinking, evaluation, and skills of argument to help readers reach a shared conclusion with the writer.

In the essay that follows, Leah Miller takes on a topic that has long been debated: the use of animals for scientific experiments. While some believe, quite stridently, that doing so is unethical and cruel, others believe that the benefit to human beings outweighs our responsibility to animals. As a topic that has a great amount of emotion surrounding it, as well as a great amount of credible scientific evidence, animal testing lends itself to argumentative writing that needs to negotiate conflict and find grounds to help those with a range of opinions come to a consensus. Miller's essay raises some of the key issues surrounding this subject by reviewing the literature, and then asserts a conclusion based on the expert opinions she provides and most values. Note how she uses elements of both the Toulmin and Rogerian forms of argument.

One way to build a strong argument ourselves is to examine and evaluate the arguments made by other writers. To prepare for the argument that she would build about the necessity of animal testing in medical science, Leah Miller first did a review of the literature, pulling from the articles she had read the key arguments, and then seeing how they spoke to each other. This allowed her to develop the central points of debate.

Article	Main arguments	Notes
"Animal Testing: Is It Worth It?" by Geoff Watts	• Examines how much scientific progress made by performing tests on animals. • States that new methods, such as testing on human cells, have proven more accurate and valuable toward medical advancement.	This piece explains alternatives to live animal testing and considers their accuracy. This alternative might be even more viable in the future— but are we there yet?
"Suffering for Science: Animal Testing," anonymous, the *Economist*	• A new rule in Europe in 2008 helps protect animals used in scientific tests. • Politicians chose to limit the conditions in which great apes can be tested on to help preserve the population. They banned the use of animals captured in the wild and allowed only animals who were raised in a laboratory setting to be used. • They required that any experiment that causes mild or severe pain to an animal must first be approved.	This article looks at the legislation on animal testing in the European union that was passed in 2008. It provides insight into new protections for animals that ensure ethical use. This might be important to help skeptics see that media portrayals are not always accurate.
"Animal Testing: TV or Not TV," by Tipu Aziz, John Stein, and Ranga Yogeshwar	• The authors take two sides on the idea of publicly announcing scientific breakthroughs that have used animals in experiments. Aziz and Stein take on the idea that someone has to inform the public about medical research, even if they receive threats, as many scientists have. • Yogeshwar takes on the idea that scientists should not announce research on TV because the programming of animal abuse will likely impact the viewers more than scientists discussing a disease that has been cured with the help of animal testing.	This article discusses an important part of the debate, looking at how animal testing is portrayed in the media. That can help us better understand the reasons why some misinformation about testing might be out there. The article includes opposing views of the debate, so allows me to see how the ideas interact.

(Continued)

"About Animal Testing: Humane Society International," published by the Humane Society	• The authors discuss animal testing as a whole: what it is, the alternatives, and what they believe is wrong with it. • They also discuss the reliability of animal testing, deciding that there are better alternatives to it.	This source has a clear agenda because of the Humane Society's mission. It captures a set of ideas held by many who believe that animal testing should be banned.
"Why We Should Accept Animal Testing," by Elizabeth Fisher	• Fisher talks about how animals are beneficial in scientific testing. • She says while the use of in vitro and non-animal methods can prove useful, most medical breakthroughs have been made through the use of animal testing. • She says that without animal testing, we would not have as much medical knowledge as we do today	This article represents the view of most of the scientific community, in that it demonstrates that animal testing is still the most viable method of medical research—at the present.

Student Writing

Animal Testing Is Still Necessary

Leah Miller

Lays out the contested ground of the argument

Acknowledges counterarguments but states thesis clearly

Lays out the organization of the argument

Provides fair explanation of alternatives

Uses definition to explain

Provides range of arguments on the topic

The idea of using animals for scientific and cosmetic testing has been debated for many years. Many scientists still believe that it is a necessary aspect of most scientific testing, while animal rights groups and many members of the public believe that there are other methods that could prove more accurate while also preserving the animal population. While there are many valid ethical and practical concerns about animal testing, I believe that when regulated correctly, it remains beneficial for advancing medical science. I will examine a number of arguments against medical science as well as responses to those arguments.   *1*

The first argument against animal testing is that other reliable methods exist. In-vitro medical testing, for example, tests biological reactions and processes in a controlled environment within a laboratory instead of in a living organism. While in-vitro testing is the most common alternative to animal testing, the method known as in-silico exists as well. In-silico medical testing uses computer-generated programs and models to demonstrate how a living organism will react to different products or medications. One of those who believe animal testing remains necessary is Elizabeth Fisher, who argues that animal testing is necessary to science because very few medical breakthroughs have been made with in-vitro methods. The Humane Society disagrees with Fisher, believing that human genes,   *2* proteins, and tissues are much easier to work with and are more humane. The Humane Society also suggests that just because animal testing was beneficial in the past does not mean that it is necessary today, when science is always looking for new advances. They suggest that in-vitro methods may be exactly what science needs to further progress. However, as Watts argues, most medical researchers use animal methods because that is still considered the most reliable form of testing.

The reliability of animal testing is indeed a major concern among the scientific community. Some believe that animal testing is not nearly as reliable as in-vitro methods, while others believe that animal testing remains necessary to science. The Humane Society, for example, explains how very little medical advancement has been made, despite the use of animal testing. While thousands of tests have been performed to test the effectiveness of stroke medication, they suggest, only one of those tests has proved reliable enough to be used on humans. The Humane Society further argues that research has shown that more than half of successful experiments in animals have failed when used on human subjects. Fisher, however, believes that medical progress still depends on animal testing, demonstrating that new medications for the treatment of Progeria and diabetes have been developed thanks to animal tests. The Humane Society also argues that the biological processes of animals and humans are far too different to depend solely on animal testing. Watts, however, demonstrates that many animals used in scientific research have been genetically modified, or had genes removed, in order to make their bodies react similarly to those of humans. This modification makes such animals more reliable for testing purposes than other animals. In the end, while the reliability of animal testing is still in question, until it is shown to be less reliable than other methods, it will most likely continue to be used throughout the world.

Another issue faced by the scientific community is how the public will react to the use of medications developed through animal testing. Although many people will use a medication despite its developmental history, there are some who may choose not to use a medication that was tested on animals because of the ways animal testing is portrayed by animal rights activists. Fisher's article notes that less than 0.2% of medical tests are performed on cats, dogs, and monkeys; however, these animals are often pictured when the public thinks of animal tests. As Fisher notes, those who provide graphic arguments against animal testing rarely depict actual test subjects such as rats, birds, fish, and mice. Ranga Yogeshwar agrees, pointing out in an article that the public does not get the whole story of animal testing from television, but only the negative view the media paints. He says the public is fed emotional ads that advocate an end to animal testing, ads that influence viewers more than a scientific story of a new medication's being developed through animal testing. Tipu Aziz and John Stein believe that scientists should share their work with the public in order to change the way that animal testing is viewed; despite threats, they suggest, scientists should respect

3

4

Draws conclusion based on the evidence presented

Creates transition to new topic

Shows key debate points

Writer identifies herself with "the scientific community"

Provides response to ethical concerns

(Continued)

...continued Animal Testing is Still Necessary, **Leah Miller**

their research enough to put it out for the public to see. This is a key argument, for it is important that the public be informed about exactly what animal testing entails. It is too easy to get caught up in disturbing images on TV of animals cramped in small cages being mistreated, without realizing that in most cases, animals are treated much more ethically.

Indeed, there are laws and rules which aim to protect the welfare of animals   5
used in scientific tests. The Humane Society discusses how the European Union's encouragement of the 3Rs—the principles of replacement, reduction, and refinement—has helped to reduce the number of animals who endure extreme mistreatment in scientific tests. An essay in the *Economist* also discusses the idea of the 3Rs and new laws adopted in Europe in 2008 to expand on the type of animal testing allowed. For example, a rule was developed that great apes may be used in testing only when the test is being conducted to preserve the primate community or when tests are necessary to evaluate medications that may help cure humans diseases. The rules also dictate that experiments that would cause mild to severe pain in animals must have approval from their national authority before being conducted. Fisher also discusses Europe's regulations regarding the use of animals in scientific tests, asserting that these laws are adequate enough to prevent the use of animals in unnecessary tests. The fact that Europe is taking necessary measures to make sure that animals are not mistreated and are used only when necessary supports the argument that animal testing can be carried out ethically.

There seems to be a consensus, then, that the use of animals in unnecessary   6
testing or in unethical ways should be stopped. However, while some believe that animals should be eliminated from scientific testing completely—because other methods exist that could be more accurate while also preserving the animal population—medical science has not yet reached that point. Using animals in scientific tests should continue, as long as medical progress is being made, especially now that laws in Europe and the European Union have made animal testing there more humane and regulated. While we still see many negative ads against animal testing, the real methods used in scientific testing are not as widely known—and they seem to have become much more humane. For these reasons, until the success of other methods can be seen to be reliable, we must continue animal testing, while also continuing to insure that the practice is regulated to minimize the suffering of test subjects.

Works Cited

"About Animal Testing: Humane Society International." *RSS*. N.p., n.d. Web. 9 Nov. 2014.

Aziz, Tipu, John Stein, and Ranga Yogeshwar. "Animal Testing: TV or Not TV?" *Nature* 24 Feb. 2011: 457–459. Web. 5 Nov. 2014.

Counters pathos-based arguments with logos appeal

Transitions to discussion of ethics protections

Builds toward conclusion

Acknowledges part of counterargument to build consensus

Reiterates thesis and reasoning

Fisher, Elizabeth. "Why We Should Accept Animal Testing." *Huffington Post*. N.p., 17 July 2013. Web. 9 Nov. 2014.

"Suffering for Science: Animal Testing." *Economist* 9 May 2009: 76(EU). *Biography in Context*. Web. 5 Nov. 2014.

Watts, Geoff. "Animal Testing: Is It Worth It?" *JSTOR*. BMJ: British Medical Journal, 27 Jan. 2007. Web. 3 Nov. 2014.

Questions for Writing and Discussion

1 What audience(s) does Miller seem to be addressing? How much does she assume they already know about the topic? What indications are there that Miller is addressing what they might already believe? How does she avoid alienating her audience?

2 Miller attempts to bring together various perspectives on animal testing—not just "pro" and "con," but views that consider science, media, and politics. How does she bring those various pieces together? How does she build transitions between one perspective and another?

3 What opposing arguments does Miller consider? Find three examples where she seems to respond to arguments that differ from her own. How do her responses seem to use a Rogerian approach, attempting to form consensus rather than discord? Does she draw on a Toulmin approach, using claims, warrants, and evidence at any spot in this essay?

Applying What You Have Learned

1 While argument is often seen as "a matter of opinion," effective argument really involves being informed on a topic and the consensus of facts surrounding a topic. Write an essay or some other form of document that helps an uninformed or under-informed audience change their perspective on a topic by learning more about recent research on the topic For example, you might demonstrate to an audience who believe that single-sex parenting is injurious to children that studies prove the contrary. Or you might demonstrate, using reliable evidence, that those who argue that climate change is undeniably caused by human actions that there is contrary evidence that should affect their views. Choose a topic that is current and debatable. Then collect reliable evidence that should influence your audience's perspective on the topic—even if it it has not up to this point. Finally, shape and draft your essay in ways that acknowledge their views and yet help them consider why those views might be somewhat (or drastically) different if they were to consider recent evidence.

Using multimedia. While facts and the arguments we build from them are often in words, arguments are also made implicitly by graphs, charts, and other visual aids. After you have collected evidence that you believe should change your audience's perspectives, build accompanying visual arguments—graphs, charts, images, or multimedia visuals—that, along with a caption, make parts of your case at a glance. You could use textboxes to reinforce your main points, as in Holladay's essay on cyberbullying, or to highlight key quotations. Consider carefully where to place these enhancements on the page.

2 Two essays in this chapter's Casebook discuss the dangers of cyberbullying. But as Miguel Helft demonstrates in his article, issues related to free speech are also part of the picture. Write an argument that takes a position on the level of censorship that should be instituted on social media or the Internet more generally. Narrow and focus your topic on a specific phenomenon or feature of cybercommunication. Then collect research on the topic as well as examples from social media sites that can help build your argument. As you shape and draft your essay, consider your audience's likely reaction if you were to use elements of Rogers's or Toulmin's approach to argument. Will your audience be moved by clear data, claims, and warrants, or is consensus-building and meeting your audience halfway more advisable? You can also ask those questions as you revise your stylistic choices.

Using multimedia. The articles in this chapter and your own arguments in this assignment use words to present a case about "true drama" played out on the Internet. But to help your audience fully understand what goes on in cyberspace, it might be more effective to present the experiences of those who have been bullied more directly. You could do audio and/or video interviews, collecting individuals' uncomfortable experiences in cyberspace, and present them in ways that capture the pathos inherent in those experiences. Or you could use excerpts from social media—or links to those discussions—to illustrate the need for censorship, free speech, or some middle ground.

3 This chapter's essays on Wikipedia question whether this source of information is useful, reliable, or counterproductive. Write an argument that demonstrates your own informed opinions and experiences with using open-sourced sites like Wikipedia and other user-developed sites such as Yahoo Answers. Narrow your topic and develop a thesis that takes a position on whether these sources enhance or detract from an informed society, collecting examples that illustrate why they are, or are not effective ways to advance knowledge on a given topic. Shape and draft your essay in ways that address your audience's predispositions toward the topic. As you revise your piece, collaborate with peers to test out the arguments that you are building.

Using multimedia. In order to better understand how "crowd-sourced" sites like Wikipedia work, try this: First, search a topic that you have been studying. When you get to an article, click on the "View History" tab at the top. This will allow you to compare various versions of the article as it has been edited by users. Once you learn about this process, you might try editing the article to make it more accurate; then see if others do further edits as well. Does this process make you feel that Wikipedia is more or less reliable than you first thought? Use these experiments in the media to help enhance your own argument about a site's usefulness through firsthand experience with it.

Unit 6

Writing for Your Career

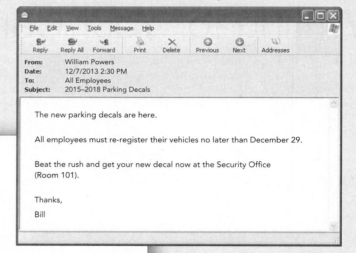

From: William Powers
Date: 12/7/2013 2:30 PM
To: All Employees
Subject: 2015–2018 Parking Decals

The new parking decals are here.

All employees must re-register their vehicles no later than December 29.

Beat the rush and get your new decal now at the Security Office (Room 101).

Thanks,

Bill

GREENE'S

New Acres Mall   Tallahassee, FL   32301

June 16, 2013

Mr. William Britton
55-A Jackson Road
Tallahassee, FL 32301

Dear Mr. Britton:

We appreciate your continued patronage of Greene's. We note, however, that your charge account is now $565.31 overdue and that we have not received your monthly payment since April.

If you have recently sent in your payment, please ignore this friendly reminder. If not, we would appreciate a minimum remittance of $50.00 at your earliest convenience.

19

Workplace Correspondence: Memos, E-mail, and Business Letters

Learning Objective

When you complete this chapter, you'll be able to use basic format and organization patterns to write effective memos, e-mail messages, and business letters.

UNTIL fairly recently, the memo was perhaps the most common form of workplace correspondence. Along with the business letter, the memo was fundamental to office procedure. Any large company, agency, or other organization would generate thousands of such documents daily. Now, however, the memo—and, to a lesser extent, the business letter as well—has been largely replaced by e-mail. To provide historical context, this chapter explores the connections among the memo, e-mail, and the business letter, and explains how to handle each.

Taken from *Workplace Communications: The Basics,* Sixth Edition by George J. Searles.

MEMOS

Traditionally, the memo was a vehicle for internal or "intramural" communication—a message from someone at Company X to someone else at Company X. The memo may have been written to one person or to a group, but it was almost always a form of in-house correspondence.

Although the usual purpose of a memo was to inform, often its function was to create a written record of a request or other message previously communicated in person, over the phone, or through the grapevine.

Accordingly, a memo was usually quite direct in approach. It would come to the point quickly and not ramble on. A good memo would focus sharply, zooming in on what the reader needed to know. Depending on the subject, a memo would make its point in three or four short paragraphs: a concise introduction, a middle paragraph or two conveying the details, and perhaps a brief conclusion. But some memos were as short as one paragraph or even one sentence. Like so many other features of workplace communications, memo length was determined by purpose and audience.

Although minor variations did exist, practically all memos shared certain standard format features:

- The word *Memo, Memorandum,* or some equivalent term at or near the top of the page.
- The TO line, enabling the memo to be "addressed," and the FROM line, enabling it to be "signed."
- The DATE line.
- The SUBJECT line, identifying the topic. Like a newspaper headline but even more concisely, the SUBJECT line would orient and prepare the reader for what was to follow. A good subject line answers this question: "In no more than three words, what is this memo really about?"
- Of course, the message or content of the memo. As explained earlier, three or four paragraphs were usually sufficient.

The memo in Figure 19.1 embodies all these features and provides an opportunity to explore the principle of *tone*, which will be discussed in Chapter 20.

The personnel manager picked her words carefully to avoid sounding bossy. She says "You *may want* to send him a . . . card," not "You *should* send him a . . . card," even though that's what she really means. As will be discussed in Chapter 20, a tactful writer can soften a recommendation, a request, or even a command simply by phrasing it in a diplomatic way. In this situation, an employee's decision whether to send a card would be a matter of personal choice, so the memo's gentle tone is particularly appropriate. But the same strategy can also be used when conveying important directives you definitely expect the reader to follow.

For the sake of convenience in situations where a paper memo may still be preferable to e-mail, most word-processing programs include at least one preformatted memo form, called a *template*. The template automatically generates formatted headings and inserts the date. The writer simply fills in the blanks.

M E M O R A N D U M

DATE: May 11, 2013

TO: All Employees

FROM: Susan Lemley, Manager, Personnel Department *SL*

SUBJECT: James Mahan

As many of you already know, James Mahan of the maintenance department was admitted to Memorial Hospital over the weekend and is scheduled to undergo surgery on Tuesday.

Although Jim will not be receiving visitors or phone calls for a while, you may want to send him a "Get Well" card to boost his spirits. He's in Room 325.

We'll keep you posted about Jim's progress.

From line was often initialed

Paragraph-breaks segment content

FIGURE 19.1 • Basic Memo Format

E-MAIL

Because an e-mail is essentially just an electronic memo, practically everything that's already been said here about traditional memos also applies to e-mail.

By now, almost everyone is famliar with how to use e-mail. Typically, a worker logs on to the system by typing his or her username and a secure password that prevents unauthorized access. New e-mail is stored in the inbox and, once read, can be deleted, saved for future reference, printed, answered, or forwarded—or a combination of these options. To respond to a message, the writer simply inserts the new message above the existing one. To create an entirely new e-mail, the writer brings up a blank template on the screen, ready to be completed. When the writer finishes the message, it's sent to as many other users as the writer wishes—one or everyone—depending on how the To line has been addressed. The new e-mail is also stored in the writer's electronic Sent file and can be kept there indefinitely for future reference. Figure 19.2 is a typical e-mail memo, similar to those you will see in Chapter 20.

There are good reasons e-mail has been so widely adopted since becoming generally available in the 1990s. On the most obvious level, it's incomparably faster than traditional correspondence. In the past, communicating by memo or letter involved five distinct steps:

1. Drafting
2. Typing (usually by a secretary)
3. Proofreading and initialing by the writer
4. Photocopying for the writer's file
5. Routing to the intended reader

Depending on office workload and clerical staffing levels, this process could be very time-consuming. With e-mail, however, all five steps are compressed into one, permitting speedy communication. Additionally, e-mail allows for rapid-fire exchanges, and the most recent transmittal can reproduce a complete record of all that has gone before. When you're engaged in a lengthy back-and-forth e-mail "conversation," however, the focus of the discussion will most likely evolve. So it's smart to continuously revise the subject line to reflect that fact.

Despite its many obvious advantages, e-mail can also create some problems. One major drawback is that the very ease with which e-mail can be generated encourages overuse. Sometimes a simple phone call is more efficient, even if voice mail is involved. In the past, a writer would not bother to send a memo without good reason; too much time and effort were involved to do otherwise. Now, though, much needless correspondence is produced. Many of yesterday's writers would wait until complete information on a given topic had been received, organized, and considered before acting on it or passing it along. But today, it's not uncommon for many e-mails to be written on the same subject, doling out the information piecemeal, sometimes within a very short time span. The resulting fragmentation wastes the energies of writer and reader alike and increases the possibility of confusion, often because of premature response. One way to minimize this danger is to scan your entire menu of incoming messages, taking special note of multiple mailings from the same source, before responding to any.

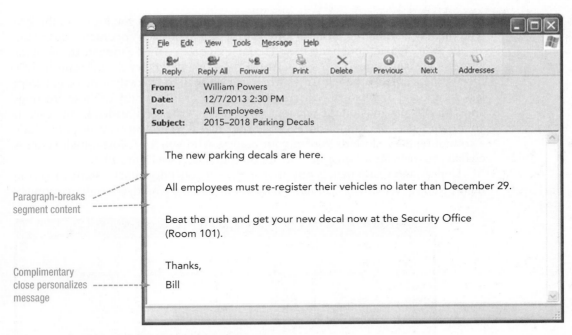

Paragraph-breaks segment content

Complimentary close personalizes message

FIGURE 19.2 • E-mail

Similarly, e-mails about sensitive issues are often dashed off "in the heat of battle," without sufficient reflection. In the past, most writers had some time to reconsider a situation before reacting. There was usually the option of revising or simply discarding a memo if, upon proofreading, it came to seem a bit too harsh or otherwise inappropriate. The inherent rapidity of e-mail, however, all but eliminates any such opportunity for second thoughts. In addition, hasty composition causes a great many keyboarding miscues, omissions, and other fundamental blunders. These must then be corrected in subsequent messages, creating an inefficient proliferation of "e-mail about e-mail." Indeed, hurried writing combined with the absence of a secretarial "filter" has given rise to a great deal of embarrassingly bad prose in the workplace. You risk ridicule and loss of credibility unless you closely proofread every e-mail before sending it. Make sure that the information is necessary and correct and that all pertinent details have been included. Be particularly careful to avoid typos, misspellings, faulty capitalization, sloppy punctuation, and basic grammatical errors. Virtually all e-mail systems include spell-checkers; although not foolproof, they help minimize typos and misspellings. Similarly, grammar checkers can detect basic sentence problems.

When you're creating an e-mail, the To and From lines are handled somewhat differently from those on a memo. Depending on the characteristics of the system you're using, the To line mTay include only the receiver's name (or e-mail address), omitting the receiver's title and/or department. This is because an e-mail message is electronically transmitted (rather than being physically delivered) to the intended reader, appearing on that person's screen shortly after you send it. Likewise, your name (or e-mail address) is automatically activated as soon as you log on to the system, thereby eliminating the need for you to type it in on each document you create.

Be aware that although the To and From lines on an e-mail eliminate the need for a letter-style salutation ("Dear Ms. Bernstein") or complimentary close ("Yours truly"), most writers employ these features when using e-mail to make their messages seem less abrupt and impersonal. The relative formality or informality of these greetings and sign-offs depends on the relationship between writer and reader. In any case, if your own e-mail name and address don't fully reveal your identity, you *must* include a complimentary close to inform your readers who you are. Most e-mail systems enable you to create a "signature file" for this purpose. (See Figure 19.3.)

Understand that e-mail is not private. Recent court decisions—some involving high-profile government scandals—have confirmed the employer's right to monitor

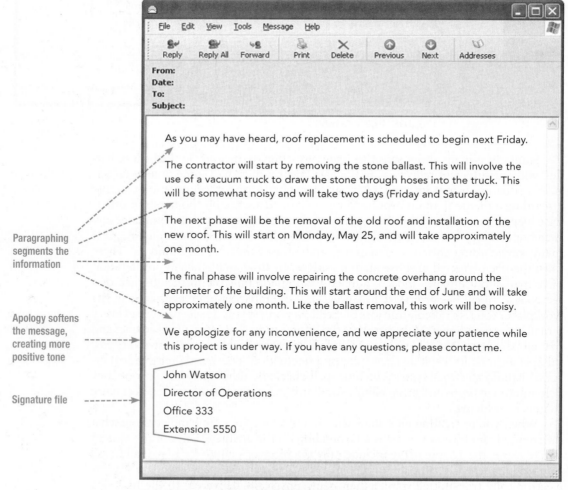

FIGURE 19.3 • E-mail with Signature File

Tech Tips

Despite its seemingly informal, spontaneous nature, e-mail is no less "official" and permanent than a memo printed on paper. Therefore, it's important to use this medium thoughtfully, efficiently, and responsibly. These guidelines will help:

- Resist the temptation to forward chain letters, silly jokes, political rants, pornographic images, and the like. This not only wastes people's time but, in certain circumstances, can also be hazardous to your professional health.

- Never forward legitimate e-mail to other readers without the original writer's knowledge and permission. The message may have been intended for you alone.

- When responding to a mass mailing, do not click Reply All unless there's a valid reason to do so; reply only to the sender.

- Some readers routinely ignore attachments, so don't create one if you can build the information into the body of the e-mail, where it's more likely to be read. If that's not practical, provide a one- or two-sentence summary in the body of the e-mail to prompt the reader to open the attachment. Because very large attachments can clog readers' accounts, it's better to send a hard copy of such material.

- Remember that e-mail is only partially able to convey "tone of voice." For this reason, voice mail or actual conversation is often preferable, allowing your reasoning and feelings to be understood more accurately. This is especially true in complicated or delicate situations, particularly those involving negative messages—the denial of a request, for example.

- Never attempt to communicate when angry. Observe the standard rules of e-mail etiquette. Avoid "flaming" (openly hostile or abusive comments, whether directed at the reader or at a third party). The fact that you're communicating electronically doesn't exempt you from accepted norms of workplace courtesy.

or inspect workers' e-mail (and Internet activity). Indeed, it's not uncommon for workers to be fired for impropriety in this regard. A good rule of thumb is, "Don't say it in an e-mail unless you'd have no problem with it appearing on the front page of your company newsletter." In some situations, a given message may be entirely appropriate but may contain highly sensitive information. In such cases, the best choice may be a paper memo personally delivered in a sealed envelope.

As will be discussed in Chapter 20, the company e-mail network is no place for personal messages or an excessively conversational style. Many employers provide a separate e-mail "bulletin board" on which workers can post and access announcements about garage or vehicle sales, carpooling, unwanted theater and sports tickets, and the like. Such matters are appropriate only as bulletin board content.

Now that nearly all organizations are online, e-mail is no longer just an intramural communications medium; indeed, it's beginning to rival the business letter as the major form of correspondence across company boundaries. When you're sending e-mail to readers at other locations, tone takes on even greater importance than usual. Because the writer and the reader probably do not know each other personally, a higher level of courteous formality is in order. Additionally, the subject matter is often more involved than that of in-house correspondence, so e-mail sent outside the

Checklist _____

Evaluating a Memo or E-mail

A Good memo or e-mail

____ Follows a standard format;

____ Includes certain features:

☐ Date line (appears automatically in e-mail)

☐ To line, which includes the name and often the title and/or department of the receiver

☐ From line, which includes the name (appears automatically in e-mail) and often the title and/or department of the sender; on a paper memo, the From line must be initialed by the writer before the memo is sent

☐ Subject line, which is a clear, accurate, but brief statement of what the message is about

____ Is organized into paragraphs (one is often enough) covering the subject fully in an orderly way;

____ Includes no inappropriate content;

____ Uses clear, simple language;

____ Maintains an appropriate tone—neither too formal nor too conversational;

____ Contains no typos or mechanical errors in spelling, capitalization, punctuation, or grammar.

workplace is commonly longer and more fully developed than messages intended for coworkers. And outside e-mail nearly always includes a letter-style salutation and complimentary close unless the writer and the reader have established an ongoing professional relationship.

To sum up, e-mail is no different from any other form of workplace communication in requiring close attention to audience, purpose, and tone—not to mention ethical considerations. Just as you would after composing a conventional memo on paper, assess your e-mail by consulting the checklist above.

BUSINESS LETTERS

Business letters are typically used for *external* communication: a message from someone at Company X to someone elsewhere—a customer or client, perhaps, or a counterpart at Company Y. As mentioned earlier, however, e-mail is now often used in situations that in the past would have required letters, and this trend is increasing. Nevertheless, countless letters are still written every day for an enormous variety of reasons. Some of the more typical purposes of a letter are to do the following:

- Ask for information (inquiry)
- Sell a product or service (sales)

- Purchase a product or service (order)
- Request payment (collection)
- Voice a complaint (claim)
- Respond to a complaint (adjustment)
- Thank someone (acknowledgment)

Figures 19.5 through 19.8 provide some examples.

Regardless of its purpose, however, every letter includes certain essential components that appear on the page in the following sequence:

1. Writer's address (often preprinted on letterhead) at the top of the page. (Figure 19.4 lists standard abbreviations used in letter writing.)
2. Date (like e-mail, letters sent by fax are also automatically imprinted with the exact *time* of transmission)
3. Inside address (the full name, title, and address of the receiver)
4. Salutation, followed by a colon (avoid gender-biased salutations such as "Dear Sir" or "Gentlemen")
5. Body of the letter, using the three-part approach outlined later in this chapter
6. Complimentary close ("Sincerely" is best), followed by a comma
7. Writer's signature
8. Writer's name and title beneath the signature
9. Enclosure line, if necessary, to indicate item(s) accompanying the letter

Along with these standard components, all business letters also embrace the same three-part organization:

1. A brief introductory paragraph establishing context (by referring to previous correspondence, perhaps, or by orienting the reader in some other way) and stating the letter's purpose concisely
2. A middle section (as many paragraphs as needed) conveying the content of the message by providing all necessary details presented in the most logical sequence
3. A brief concluding paragraph politely requesting action, thanking the reader, or providing any additional information pertinent to the situation

Table 19.1 provides guidance in applying this three-part approach in each of the basic letter-writing situations.

Format

Over the years, letters have been formatted in various ways. Today, however, "full block" style is the norm. As shown in Figures 19.5 through 19.8, full block style requires that every line (including the date, the receiver's address, the salutation, the complimentary close, and the sender's name) begin at the left margin. If, as in Figure 19.7, the sender's address isn't preprinted on letterhead, it should also begin at the left margin.

Note also that in full block style, even the first line of each paragraph begins at the left margin rather than being indented.

Alabama	AL	Kentucky	KY	Ohio	OH
Alaska	AK	Louisiana	LA	Oklahoma	OK
Arizona	AZ	Maine	ME	Oregon	OR
Arkansas	AR	Maryland	MD	Pennsylvania	PA
California	CA	Massachusetts	MA	Puerto Rico	PR
Colorado	CO	Michigan	MI	Rhode Island	RI
Connecticut	CT	Minnesota	MN	South Carolina	SC
Delaware	DE	Mississippi	MS	South Dakota	SD
District of Columbia	DC	Missouri	MO	Tennessee	TN
		Montana	MT	Texas	TX
Florida	FL	Nebraska	NE	Utah	UT
Georgia	GA	Nevada	NV	Vermont	VT
Hawaii	HI	New Hampshire	NH	Virginia	VA
Idaho	ID	New Jersey	NJ	Washington	WA
Illinois	IL	New Mexico	NM	West Virginia	WV
Indiana	IN	New York	NY	Wisconsin	WI
Iowa	IA	North Carolina	NC	Wyoming	WY
Kansas	KS	North Dakota	ND		

Avenue	AVE	Expressway	EXPY	Parkway	PKWY
Boulevard	BLVD	Freeway	FWY	Road	RD
Circle	CIR	Highway	HWY	Square	SQ
Court	CT	Lane	LN	Street	ST
Turnpike	TPKE				

North	N	West	W	Southwest	SW
East	E	Northeast	NE	Northwest	NW
South	S	Southeast	SE		

Room	RM	Suite	STE	Apartment	APT

FIGURE 19.4 **Standard Abbreviations**

Source: U.S. Postal Service.

TABLE 19.1 Letter Content Guidelines

Letter Type	Introduction	Middle Paragraphs	Conclusion
Inquiry	Briefly explain the reason for your inquiry, and clearly identify what you're inquiring about.	Provide all relevant details about your inquiry. Concretely specify what you want to know, why the reader should provide this information, and what you'll use it for. If you have more than one question, create a bulleted or numbered list.	Thank the reader in advance for complying with your request. If you must have a reply by a certain date, specify it. Make sure you've provided all the information the reader will need to reply (address, phone number, e-mail address). It's a good idea to provide a stamped, self-addressed envelope.
Sales	Get the reader's attention, perhaps by asking a question, describing a situation, presenting an interesting fact, or using a quotation, and state what you're selling.	Provide all relevant details about the product or service you're selling and create an incentive by explaining to the reader the advantages of purchasing.	Thank the reader in advance for becoming a customer and make sure you've provided all the information the reader will need to place an order (price list or catalog, order form, address, Web site, phone number, e-mail address).
Order	Establish that this is indeed an order letter, and state what you want to purchase.	Provide all relevant details about your order (product numbers, prices, quantities, method of payment, etc.). A table is often the best format for presenting this information.	Thank the reader in advance for filling the order. If you must have the product or service by a certain date, specify it. Make sure you've provided all the information the reader will need to ship the order (address, billing address, method of delivery).

(Continued)

TABLE 19.1 Letter Content Guidelines (continued)

Letter Type	Introduction	Middle Paragraphs	Conclusion
Collection	Open with a polite but firm reminder that the reader's payment is overdue. (In a second or third collection letter, the tone of the introduction can be more urgent.)	If you have not already done so in the introduction, provide all the relevant details about how much is owed, when it was due, and when it must be paid to avoid penalty, but acknowledge the possibility of error at your end.	Repeat the payment request and encourage the reader to contact you with any concerns or to discuss payment options. Make sure you've provided all the information the reader will need to respond (address, phone number, e-mail address). It's a good idea to include a stamped, self-addressed envelope.
Claim	Provide some background information, but come quickly to the point, identifying the problem.	Politely provide all relevant details about what has gone wrong and what you want the reader to do about it. If appropriate, provide copies of bills, receipts, contracts, etc.	Thank the reader in advance for correcting the problem and make sure you've provided all the information the reader will need to contact you (address, phone number, e-mail address).
Adjustment	Thank the reader for bringing the problem to your attention, and if the complaint is justified, apologize.	If the complaint is justified, explain what you'll do to fix the problem. If not, tactfully explain why you must deny the claim.	Thank the reader again for writing to you and provide reassurances that everything will be satisfactory in the future.
Acknowledgment	Briefly explain why you are writing the acknowledgment and identify the person, group, or situation you're commending.	Provide all relevant details about why the person, group, or situation deserves commendation.	Conclusions vary greatly depending on the nature of the situation. Commonly, you'll thank the reader for considering the remarks and invite a reply. In such cases, make sure you've provided all the information the reader will need to contact you (address, phone number, e-mail address).

THE
WEEKLY NEWS
P.O. Box 123
Littleton, NY 13300
Telephone (315) 555-1234 • Fax (315) 555-4321

February 24, 2013

Chief Joseph Kealy
Littleton Police Department
911 Main St.
Littleton, NY 13300

Dear Chief Kealy:

It is our understanding that a Littleton resident, Mr. Alex Booth,
is the subject of an investigation by your department, with the
assistance of the county district attorney. In keeping with the
provisions of the New York Freedom of Information Law, I'm
requesting information about Mr. Booth's arrest.

This information is needed to provide our readership with
accurate news coverage of the events leading to Mr. Booth's
current situation. *The Weekly News* prides itself on fair, accurate,
and objective reporting, and we're counting on your assistance
as we seek to uphold that tradition.

Because the police blotter is by law a matter of public record,
we appreciate your full cooperation.

Sincerely,

Nancy Muller

Nancy Muller, Reporter

Single-spacing
within each
block of print

Double-spacing
between blocks

Additional spacing
to accommodate
signature

FIGURE 19.5 • Inquiry Letter in Full Block Style

New Acres Mall   Tallahassee, FL   32301

June 16, 2013

Mr. William Britton
55-A Jackson Road
Tallahassee, FL 32301

Dear Mr. Britton:

Opening paragraph creates context, states purpose. → We appreciate your continued patronage of Greene's. We note, however, that your charge account is now $565.31 overdue and that we have not received your monthly payment since April.

Middle paragraph provides details. → If you have recently sent in your payment, please ignore this friendly reminder. If not, we would appreciate a minimum remittance of $50.00 at your earliest convenience.

Last paragraph concludes politely, includes contact information. → If you have any questions about your account, please call me at 555-0123, ext. 123.

Sincerely,

Heather Sutcliffe

Heather Sutcliffe
Credit Services Department

FIGURE 19.6 • Collection Letter in Full Block Style

41 Allan Court
Tucson, AZ 86700
June 30, 2013

Consumer Relations Department
Superior Foods, Inc.
135 Grove St.
Atlanta, GA 30300

Dear Superior Foods:

Opening paragraph provides background, identifies problem.

Superior microwave dinners are excellent products that I've purchased regularly for many years. Recently, however, I had an unsettling experience with one of these meals.

Middle paragraph provides details.

While enjoying a serving of Pasta Alfredo, I discovered in the food what appeared to be a thick splinter of wood. I'm sure this is an isolated incident, but I thought your quality control department would want to know about it.

Last paragraph concludes politely.

I've enclosed the splinter, taped to the product wrapper, along with the sales receipt for the dinner. May I please be reimbursed $4.98 for the cost?

Sincerely,

George Eaglefeather

George Eaglefeather

Enclosures

FIGURE 19.7 • Consumer Claim Letter in Full Block Style

135 Grove St., Atlanta, GA 30300 • (324) 555-1234

July 7, 2013

Mr. George Eaglefeather
41 Allan Court
Tucson, AZ 86700

Dear Mr. Eaglefeather:

Opening paragraph
thanks reader,
apologizes for
problem.

Thank you for purchasing our product and for taking the time to contact us about it. We apologize for the unsatisfactory condition of your Pasta Alfredo dinner.

Middle paragraph
provides solution
to problem.

Quality is of paramount importance to all of us at Superior Foods, and great care is taken in the preparation and packaging of all our products. Our quality assurance staff has been notified of the problem you reported. Although Superior Foods doesn't issue cash refunds, we have enclosed three coupons redeemable at your grocery for complimentary Superior dinners of your choice.

Last paragraph
concludes politely.

We appreciate this opportunity to be of service, and we hope you'll continue to enjoy our products.

Sincerely,

John Roth

John Roth
Customer Services Department

Enclosure line.

Enclosures (3)

FIGURE 19.8 • Adjustment Letter in Full Block Style

Tech Tips

Letters and other documents are often sent by a facsimile (fax) machine—basically, a scanner with a modem that converts documents into digital data that's then transmitted over telephone lines to the receiver's fax machine, which prints out a hard copy. Like e-mail, this technology has the obvious advantage of speed; a letter that might take two or three days to arrive by conventional mail can be received instantaneously by fax.

But whenever you fax anything, you must fax a cover memo along with it. In this memo, you should include any additional information that might be necessary to orient the reader and indicate how many pages (including the cover memo itself) you have included in the transmission so the reader will know whether there's anything that was sent but not received. You should also include your fax number, telephone number, and e-mail address so the reader has the option of replying. here's an example:

DONROC, INC.
36 Clinton St., Collegeville, NY 13323
FAX

DATE: November 9, 2013 (3:15 p.m.)

TO: John Lapinski, Main Office Comptroller (fax #212-123-4567)

FROM: Mark Smith, Branch Office Manager (fax #212-891-0111)
            Telephone 212-555-2595, e-mail msmth@sarge.com

SUBJECT: Cosgrove Letter

PAGES: 2

Here's Michael Cosgrove's letter of November 3. Let's discuss this at Thursday's meeting.

As shown, a full block letter is single-spaced throughout, with double spacing between the blocks of print. A common practice is to triple- or even quadruple-space between the complimentary close and the sender's name to provide ample room for the sender's signature.

A fairly recent development in letter writing is the open punctuation system, in which the colon after the salutation and the comma after the complimentary close are omitted. A more radical change is the trend toward a fully abbreviated, "no punctuation, all capitals" approach to the inside address. This derives from the U.S. Postal Service recommendation that envelopes be so addressed to facilitate computerized scanning and sorting. Because the inside address has traditionally matched the address on the envelope, such a feature may well become standard, at least for letters sent by conventional mail rather than by electronic means. Indeed, many companies using "window" envelopes have already adopted this style.

As mentioned earlier, more and more companies are communicating with each other by e-mail and other forms of electronic messaging rather than by business letter. The letter is still preferred, however, for more formal exchanges, especially those in which speed of delivery isn't a major factor. In situations involving individual customers and clients (some of whom may still rely on conventional mail), the business letter is also the best choice. At least for the immediate future, therefore, the letter will continue to be a major form of workplace correspondence, although its role will almost certainly undergo further redefinition as various forms of electronic communication become increasingly widespread.

Like all successful communication, a good letter must employ an appropriate tone. Obviously, a letter is a more formal kind of communication than in-house correspondence because it's more public. Accordingly, a letter should uphold the image of the sender's company or organization by reflecting a high degree of professionalism. However, although a letter's style should be polished, the language should be natural and easy to understand. The key to achieving a readable style— in a letter or in anything else you write—is to understand that writing shouldn't sound pompous or "official." Rather, it should sound much like ordinary speech— shined up just a bit. Whatever you do, avoid stilted, old-fashioned business clichés. Strive instead for direct, conversational phrasing. One way to achieve this is to use active rather than passive verbs. Instead of saying, for example, "Your report has been received," it's better to say "We have received your report." Here's a list of overly bureaucratic constructions, paired with "plain English" alternatives:

Cliché	Alternative
As per your request	As you requested
Attached please find	Here is
In lieu of	Instead of
Please be advised that X	X
Pursuant to our agreement	As we agreed
Until such time as	Until
We are in receipt of	We have received
We regret to advise you that X	Regrettably, X

If you have a clear understanding of your letter's purpose and have analyzed your audience, you should experience little difficulty achieving the appropriate tone for the situation. In addition, if you have written your letter following full-block format and if you have used clear, accessible, and mechanically correct language, your correspondence will likely accomplish its objectives. As noted earlier, you must scrupulously avoid typos and mechanical errors in memos and e-mails. This is equally important when you compose letters intended for outside readers, who will take their business elsewhere if they perceive you as careless or incompetent. Always proofread carefully, making every effort to ensure that your work is error-free, and consult the following checklist.

Checklist ──

Evaluating a Business Letter

A good letter

___ Follows full block format;

___ Includes certain features:

    ☐ Sender's complete address

    ☐ Date

    ☐ Receiver's full name and complete address

    ☐ Salutation, followed by a colon

    ☐ Complimentary close ("Sincerely" is best), followed by a comma

    ☐ Sender's signature and full name

    ☐ Enclosure notation, if necessary

___ Is organized into paragraphs, covering the subject fully in an orderly way:

    ☐ First paragraph establishes context and states the purpose

    ☐ Middle paragraphs provide all necessary details

    ☐ Last paragraph politely achieves closure

___ Includes no inappropriate content;

___ Uses clear, simple language;

___ Maintains an appropriate tone, neither too formal nor too conversational;

___ Contains no typos or mechanical errors in spelling, capitalization, punctuation, or grammar.

Exercises

EXERCISE 19.1

You're the assistant to the personnel manager of a metals fabrication plant. Monday is Labor Day, and most of the 300 employees will be given a paid holiday. The company is under pressure, however, to meet a deadline. Therefore, a skeleton force of 40—all in the production department—will be needed to work on the holiday. Those who volunteer will have the option of being paid overtime at the standard time-and-a-half rate or receiving two vacation days. If fewer than 40 employees volunteer, others will be assigned to work on the basis of seniority, with the most recently hired employees chosen first. The personnel manager has asked you to alert affected employees. Write an e-mail.

EXERCISE 19.2

You're a secretary at a regional office of a state agency. Normal working hours for civil service employees in your state are 8:30 a.m. to 4:30 p.m., with a lunch break from 12:00 to 12:30 p.m. During the summer, however, the hours are 8:30 a.m. to 4:00 p.m., with lunch unchanged. Summer hours are in effect from July 1 to September 2. It's now mid-June, and the busy office supervisor has asked you to remind employees of the summer schedule. Write a memo to be posted on the main bulletin board and sent via e-mail.

EXERCISE 19.3

You work in the lumberyard of a building supplies company. Every year during the July 4 weekend, the town sponsors the Liberty Run, a 10K (6.2-mile) road race. This year, for the first time, local businesses have been invited to enter five-member teams to compete for the Corporate Cup. The team with the best combined time takes the trophy. There will be no prize money involved but much good publicity for the winners. Because you recently ran the Boston Marathon, the company president wants you to recruit and organize a team. It's now April 21. Better get started. Write an e-mail.

EXERCISE 19.4

You're an office worker at a large paper products company that has just installed an upgraded computer system. Many employees are having difficulty with the new software. The manufacturer's representatives will be onsite all next week to provide training. Because you're studying computer technology, you've been asked to serve as liaison. You must inform your coworkers about the training, which will be delivered in Conference Room 3 from Monday through Thursday in eight half-day sessions (9:00 a.m. to 12:00 p.m. and 1:00 to 4:00 p.m.), organized alphabetically by workers' last names as follows: A–B, C–E, F–I, J–M, N–P, Q–SL, SM–T, and U–Z. Workers unable to attend must sign up for one of two makeup sessions that will be held on Friday. You must ensure that everyone understands all these requirements. Write a memo to be posted on all bulletin boards and sent via e-mail.

EXERCISE 19.5

You're the manager of the employee cafeteria at a printing company. For many years, the cafeteria has provided excellent service, offering breakfast from 7:00 a.m. to 8:30 a.m. and lunch from 11:00 a.m. to 2:00 p.m. It also serves as a breakroom, selling coffee, soft drinks, and snacks all day. But the cafeteria is badly in need of modernization. Work is scheduled to begin next Wednesday. Naturally, the cafeteria will have to be closed while renovations are in progress. Employees will still be able to have lunch and breaks, however, because temporary facilities are being set up in Room 101 of Building B, a now-vacant area formerly used for storage. The temporary cafeteria will provide all the usual services except for breakfast. Obviously, employees need to know about the situation. Write an e-mail.

Proofread and rewrite the following memo, correcting all errors.

MEMORANDUM

DATE: September 8, 2013

TO: All Employes

FROM: Roger Sammon, Clerk
             Medical Recrods Department

SUBJECT: Patricia Klosek

As many of you allready know. Patricia Klosik from the Medical records Depratment is retiring next month. After more then thirty years of faithfull service to Memorial hospital.

A party is being planed in her honor. It will be at seven oclock on friday October 23 at big Joes Resturant tickets are $50 per person whitch includes a buffay diner and a donation toward a gift.

If you plan to atend please let me no by the end of next week try to get you're check to me by Oct 9

EXERCISE 19.7

A consumer product that you especially like is suddenly no longer available in retail stores in your area. Write the manufacturer a letter ordering the product.

EXERCISE 19.8

Pretend you've received the product ordered in Exercise 19.7, but it's somehow unsatisfactory. Write the manufacturer a claim letter expressing dissatisfaction and requesting an exchange or a refund.

EXERCISE 19.9

Team up with a classmate, exchange the claim letters you each wrote in response to Exercise 19.8, and then write adjustment letters to each other.

EXERCISE 19.10

The writer of the following letter has adopted a highly artificial and self-important style. Rewrite the letter to convey the message in "plain English."

County Building, Northton, MN 55100

November 9, 2013

Ms. Sally Cramdon
359 Roberts Road
Northton, MN 55100

Dear Ms. Cramdon:

We are in receipt of your pay stubs and your letter of 4 November 2013 and have ascertained a determination re: your application for food stamp eligibility.

Enclosed please find a photocopy of food stamp budget sheet prepared by this office on above date, counterindicating eligibility at this point in time. Per county eligibility stipulations, it is our judgment that your level of fiscal solvency exceeds permissible criteria for a household the size of your own (four persons).

In the subsequent event that your remuneration should decrease and remain at the decreased level for a period of thirty (30) calendar days or more, please do not hesitate to petition this office for a reassessment of your eligibility status at that juncture.

Very truly yours,

William Hanlon

William Hanlon
Casework Aide

20

The Keys to Successful Communication: Purpose, Audience, and Tone

Purpose

Audience

Tone

Exercises

Learning Objective

When you complete this chapter, you'll be able to employ the three-step writing process (prewriting, writing, rewriting) to identify your communication purpose and your audience and achieve the appropriate tone in every workplace writing situation.

EVERY instance of workplace writing occurs for a specific reason and is intended for a particular individual or group. Much the same is true of spoken messages, whether delivered in person or by phone. Therefore, both the purpose and the audience must be carefully considered to ensure that the tone of the exchange will be appropriate to the situation. Although this may seem obvious, awareness of purpose, audience, and tone is crucial to ensuring that your communication will succeed. Equally important is the need to understand that writing

Taken from *Workplace Communications: The Basics*, Sixth Edition by George J. Searles.

is actually a three-step process involving not only the writing itself but also prewriting and rewriting. This chapter concentrates on these fundamental concerns, presents a brief overview of the basic principles involved, and provides exercises in their application.

PURPOSE

Nearly all workplace writing is done for at least one of three purposes: to create a record, to request or provide information, or to persuade. For example, a caseworker in a social services agency might interview an applicant for public assistance to gather information that will then be reviewed in determining the applicant's eligibility. Clearly, such writing is intended both to provide information and to create a record. On the other hand, the purchasing director of a manufacturing company might write a letter or e-mail inquiring whether a particular supplier can provide materials more cheaply than the current vendor. The supplier will likely reply promptly. Obviously, the primary purpose here is to exchange information. In yet another setting, a probation officer composes a pre-sentencing report intended to influence the court to grant probation to the offender or impose a jail sentence. The officer may recommend either, and the report will become part of the offender's record, but the primary purpose of this example of workplace writing is to persuade.

At the prewriting stage of the writing process—before you attempt to actually compose—you must first do some *thinking* in order to identify which of the three categories of purpose applies. Ask yourself, "Am I writing primarily to create a record, to request or provide information, or to persuade?" Once you make this determination, the question becomes, "Summarized in one sentence, what am I trying to say?" To answer, you must zoom in on your subject matter, focusing on the most important elements. A helpful strategy is to employ the "Five W's" that journalists use to structure the opening sentences of newspaper stories: Who, What, Where, When, Why. Just as they do for reporters, the Five W's will enable you to get off to a running start.

AUDIENCE

Next, ask yourself, "Who will read what I have written?" This is a crucial part of the prewriting stage of the communication process.

An e-mail, letter, report, or oral presentation must be tailored to its intended audience; otherwise, it probably won't achieve the desired results. Therefore, ask yourself the following questions before attempting to prepare any sort of formal communication:

- Am I writing to one person or more than one?
- What are their job titles and/or areas of responsibility?
- What do they already know about the specific situation?

- Why do they need this information?
- What do I want them to do as a result of receiving it?
- What factors might influence their response?

Because these questions are closely related, the answers will sometimes overlap. A good starting point for sorting them out is to classify your audience by level: layperson, expert, or executive. The layperson doesn't possess significant prior knowledge of the field, whereas an expert obviously does. An executive reader has decision-making power and, one hopes, considerable expertise. By profiling your readers or listeners this way, you'll come to see the subject of your planned communication from your audience's viewpoint as well as your own. You'll be better able to state the purpose of your communication, provide necessary details, cite meaningful examples, achieve the correct level of formality, and avoid possible misunderstandings, thereby achieving your desired outcome.

In identifying your audience, remember that workplace communications fall into four broad categories:

- **Upward communication:** Intended for those above you in the hierarchy. (Example: An e-mail reply to a question from your supervisor.)
- **Lateral communication:** Intended for those at your own level in the hierarchy. (Example: A voice mail to a coworker with whom you're collaborating.)
- **Downward communication:** Intended for those below you in the hierarchy. (Example: An oral reminder to an intern you've been assigned to train.)
- **Outward communication:** Intended for those outside your workplace. (Example: A letter to someone at a company with which you do business.)

These differences will influence your communications in many ways, particularly in determining format. For in-house communications (the first three categories), the memo was traditionally the preferred written medium. The memo has now been almost totally replaced by e-mail. For outward communications, such as correspondence with clients, customers, or the general public, the standard business letter has been the norm. Business letters are either mailed or transmitted by fax machine. Even for outward communications, though, e-mail is often the best choice because of its speed and efficiency. If a more formal document is required, a confirmation letter can always be sent later.

TONE

As Table 20.1 reflects, the drafting stage of the three-part writing process is the least complicated. If you've devoted enough time and attention to prewriting, you'll know what you intend to say, you'll have *enough* to say, and you'll know what goes where, so you'll be able to compose fairly quickly. Indeed, at the drafting stage, you should simply push ahead rather than stopping to fine-tune because it's best not to disrupt the flow of your ideas. Of course, if you notice an obvious miscue (a typo, for example), it's OK to correct it, but keep the emphasis on completing the draft before you run

TABLE 20.1 Writing: A Three-Step Process

Prewriting	Drafting	Rewriting
• Identify your purpose and your intended audience. • Decide what needs to be said. • Choose the most appropriate format (e-mail, letter, report).	• Create a first draft, concentrating on content rather than fine points of mechanics, style, and tone.	• Consider the organization of the content. • Check for accuracy, completeness, and ethical validity. • Revise for style, striving for concision and simplicity. • Adjust the tone to suit the audience. • Edit for mechanical errors (typos, spelling, grammar, punctuation).

out of time and energy. Any additional polishing that may be needed can be done at the final, most challenging stage of the process, rewriting.

Nobody produces good writing on the first try. You *must* rewrite. But rewriting involves far more than simply correcting mechanical errors. For example, what may have seemed sufficient and logical at the drafting stage might now strike you as much less so. Therefore, you might want to add something here and there or take something out. How about organization?

- Are the individual words in each sentence precisely the right ones, and is each exactly where it belongs?
- Are the sentences in each paragraph presented in the best possible order?
- Are the paragraphs in the best sequence, or should they be rearranged?

In addition, you should look for ways to tighten your style by avoiding wordiness and expressing yourself as simply and directly as possible. Very importantly, is your tone appropriate to your purpose and your intended reader?

Your hierarchical relationship to your reader will play a major role in determining your tone, especially when you're attempting to convey "bad news" (the denial of a request from an employee you supervise, for example) or to suggest that staff members adopt some new or different procedure. Although such messages can be phrased in a firm, straightforward manner, a harsh voice or belligerent attitude is seldom productive.

Any workforce is essentially a team of individuals cooperating to achieve a common goal: the mission of the business, organization, or agency. A high level of collective commitment is needed for this to happen. Ideally, each person exerts a genuine effort to foster a climate of shared enthusiasm. But if coworkers become defensive or resentful, morale problems inevitably develop, undermining productivity. In such a situation, everyone loses.

Therefore, don't try to sound tough or demanding when writing about potentially sensitive issues. Instead, appeal to the reader's sense of fairness and cooperation. Phrase your sentences in a nonthreatening way, emphasizing the reader's viewpoint by using a reader-centered (rather than a writer-centered) perspective. For obvious reasons, this approach should also govern your correspondence intended for readers outside the workplace.

Here are some examples of how to creatively change a writer-centered perspective into a reader-centered perspective:

Writer-Centered Perspective	**Reader-Centered Perspective**
If I can answer any questions, I'll be happy to do so.	If you have any questions, please ask.
We shipped the order this morning.	Your order was shipped this morning.
I'm happy to report that . . .	You'll be glad to know that . . .

Notice that changing *I* and *we* to *you* and *your* personalizes the communication. Focusing on the reader is also known as the "you" approach. Another important element of the you approach is the use of *please, thank you,* and other polite terms.

Now consider Figures 20.1 and 20.2. Both e-mails have the same purpose—to change a specific behavior—and both address the same audience. But the first version adopts a writer-centered approach and is harshly combative. The reader-centered revision, on the other hand, is diplomatic and therefore much more persuasive. The first is almost certain to create resentment and hard feelings, whereas the second is far more likely to gain the desired results.

In most settings, you can adopt a somewhat more casual manner with your equals and with those below you than with those above you in the chain of command or with persons outside the organization. But in any case, avoid an excessively conversational style. Even when the situation isn't particularly troublesome and even when your reader is well-known to you, remember that "business is business." Although you need not sound stuffy, it's important to maintain a certain level of formality. Accordingly, you should never allow personal matters to appear in workplace correspondence. Consider, for example, Figure 20.3, an e-mail in which the writer has obviously violated this rule. Although the tone is appropriately respectful, the content should be far less detailed, as in the revised version shown in Figure 20.4.

A sensitive situation awaits you when you must convey unpleasant information or request assistance or cooperation from superiors. Although you may sometimes yearn for a more democratic arrangement, every workplace has a pecking order that you must consider as you choose your words. Hierarchy exists because some individuals—by virtue of more experience, education, or access to information— are in fact better positioned to lead. Although this system sometimes functions imperfectly, the supervisor, department head, or other person in charge will respond better to subordinates whose communications reflect an understanding of this basic reality. Essentially, the rules for writing to a person higher on the ladder are the same as for writing to someone on a lower rung. Be focused and self-assured, but use the "you" approach, encouraging the reader to see the advantage in accepting your recommendation or granting your request.

An especially polite tone is advisable when addressing those who outrank you. Acknowledge that the final decision is theirs and that you are fully willing to abide by

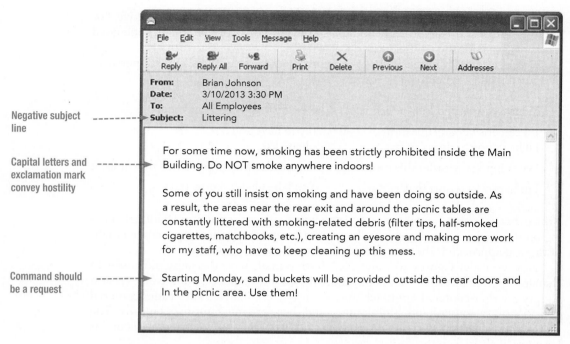

Negative subject line

Capital letters and exclamation mark convey hostility

Command should be a request

FIGURE 20.1 • Original E-mail

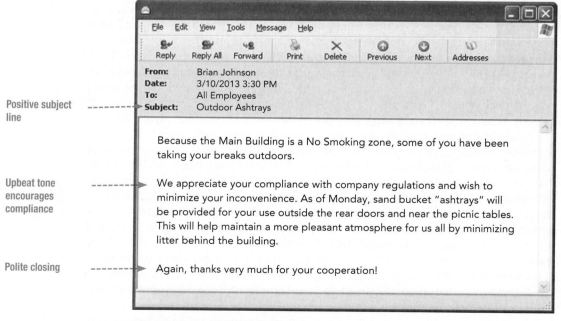

Positive subject line

Upbeat tone encourages compliance

Polite closing

FIGURE 20.2 • Revised E-mail

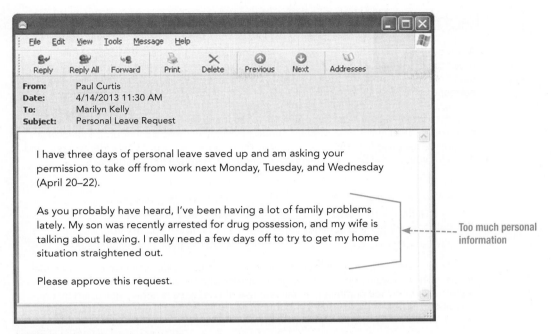

FIGURE 20.3 • Original E-mail

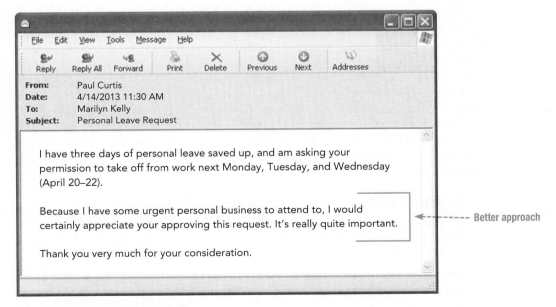

FIGURE 20.4 • Revised E-mail

Tech Tips

A slangy, vernacular style is out of place in workplace writing, as are expletives and any other coarse or vulgar language. Something that may seem clever or humorous to you may not amuse your reader and will probably appear foolish to anyone reviewing the correspondence later. Keep this in mind when sending e-mail, a medium that seems to encourage looser, more playful phrasing.

Avoid abbreviations and acronyms hatched in Internet chat rooms and other informal contexts such as instant messaging. Although inventive, most are inappropriate for the workplace because they may not be readily understood—especially by older workers and those for whom English is not their native language. Here are ten examples.

BTW: by the way	IRL: in real life
FWIW: for what it's worth	OTOH: on the other hand
HAND: have a nice day	TMOT: trust me on this
IMHO: in my humble opinion	TTYTT: to tell you the truth
IOW: in other words	WADR: with all due respect

At the same time, *technical* acronyms specific to particular businesses and occupations facilitate dialogue among employees familiar with those terms. As with so many aspects of workplace communications, the use of acronyms is largely governed by considerations of audience, purpose, and tone.

that determination. This can be achieved either through "softening" words and phrases (*perhaps, with your permission, if you wish*) or simply by stating outright that you'll accept whatever outcome may develop. For example, consider the e-mails in Figures 20.5 and 20.6. Although both say essentially the same thing, the first is completely inappropriate in tone, so much so that it would likely result in negative consequences for the writer. The second would be much better received because it properly reflects the nature of the professional relationship.

Communicating with customers or clients also requires a great deal of sensitivity and tact. When justifying a price increase, denying a claim, or apologizing for a delay, you'll probably create an unpleasant climate unless you present the facts in a gentle manner. Always strive for the most upbeat, reader-centered wording you can devise. Here are some examples of how to rephrase negative content in more positive, reader-centered terms:

Negative Wording	**Positive Wording**
We cannot process your claim because the necessary forms have not been completed.	Your claim can be processed as soon as you complete the necessary forms.
We do not take phone call after 3:00 p.m. on Fridays.	You may reach us by telephone on Fridays until 3:00 p.m.
We closed your case because we never received the information requested in our letter of April 2.	Your case will be reactivated as soon as you provide the information requested in our April 2 letter.

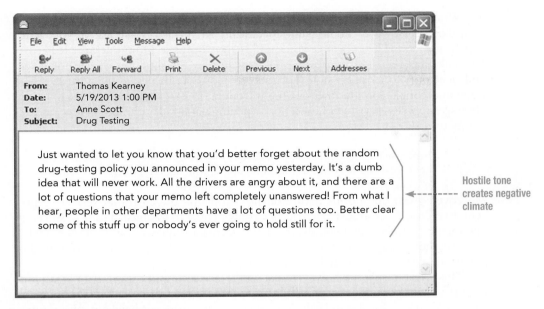

FIGURE 20.5 • Original E-mail

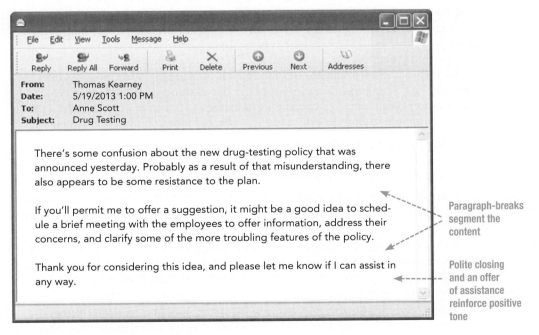

FIGURE 20.6 • Revised E-mail

When the problem has been caused by an error or oversight on your part, be sure to apologize. However, do not state specifically what the mistake was or your letter may be used as evidence against you should a lawsuit ensue. Simply acknowledge that a mistake has occurred, express regret, explain how the situation will be corrected, and close on a conciliatory note. For example, consider the letter in Figure 20.7. The body and conclusion are fine, but the introduction practically invites legal action. Here's a suggested revision of the letter's opening paragraph, phrased in less incriminating terms:

> Thank you for purchasing our product and for taking the time to contact us about it. We apologize for the unsatisfactory condition of your Superior microwave dinner.

Moreover, given the serious nature of the complaint, the customer services representative should certainly have made a stronger effort to establish a tone of sincerely apologetic concern. As it stands, this letter seems abrupt and rather impersonal—certainly not what the context requires. (For a much better handling of this kind of situation, see the adjustment letter in Figure 19.8.)

This is not to suggest, however, that workplace communications should attempt to falsify reality or dodge responsibility. On the contrary, there's a moral imperative to uphold strict ethical standards. Recent corporate misdeeds have put ethical questions under the spotlight and greatly increased the public's appetite for investigative reporting by the media. The online *Encyclopedia Brittanica* defines *ethics* as "the discipline concerned with what is morally good and bad, right and wrong." Essentially, ethics involves choosing honesty over dishonesty, requiring us to act with integrity even when there would be short-term gains for behaving otherwise. Ethical communication must therefore be honest and fair to everyone involved.

By their nature, workplace communications can greatly affect people's lives. Accordingly, customers and clients, investors, taxpayers, and workers themselves should be able to treat such materials as accurate, reliable, and trustworthy—in short, ethical. But those documents fail the ethics test if corrupted by any of the following tactics:

- **Suppression of information:** The outright burying of data to hide inconvenient truths. (Example: A company fails to reveal product-testing results that indicate potential danger to consumers.)

- **Falsification or fabrication:** Changing or simply inventing data to support a desired outcome. (Example: A company boasts of a fictitious enterprise to lure investors into supporting a new venture.)

- **Overstatement or understatement:** Exaggerating the positive aspects of a situation or downplaying negative aspects to create the desired impression. (Example: A public-opinion survey describes 55 percent of the respondents as a "substantial majority" or 45 percent as "a small percentage.")

- **Selective misquoting:** Deleting words from quoted material to distort the meaning. (Example: A supervisor changes a report's conclusion that "this proposal will seem feasible only to workers unfamiliar with the situation" to "this proposal will seem feasible . . . to workers.")

135 Grove St., Atlanta, GA 30300 (324) 555-1234

October 13, 2013

Mr. Philip Updike
246 Alton St.
Atlanta, GA 30300

Dear Mr. Updike:

We are sorry that you found a piece of glass in your Superior microwave dinner. ◄------ Wording is
Please accept our assurances that this is a very unusual incident.   too explicit

Here are three coupons redeemable at your local grocery store for complimentary Superior dinners of your choice.

                                                                                            Positive tone
We hope you will continue to enjoy our fine products. ◄---------- despite negative
                                                                                            situation

Sincerely,

John Roth

John Roth
Customer Services Dept.

Enclosures (3)

FIGURE 20.7 • Letter to Customer

- **Subjective wording:** Using terms deliberately chosen for their ambiguity. (Example: A company advertises "customary service charges," knowing that "customary" is open to broad interpretation.)
- **Conflict of interest:** Exploiting behind-the-scenes connections to influence decision making. (Example: A board member of a community agency encourages the agency to hire her company for paid services rather than soliciting bids.)
- **Withholding information:** Refusing to share relevant data with coworkers. (Example: A computer-savvy employee provides misleading answers about new software to make a recently hired coworker appear incompetent.)
- **Plagiarism:** Taking credit for someone else's ideas, findings, or written material. (Example: An employee assigned to prepare a report submits a similar report written by someone at another company and downloaded from the Internet.)

Workers must weigh the consequences of their actions, considering their moral obligations. If this is done in good faith, practices such as those outlined in the preceding list can surely be avoided. Decisions can become complicated, however, when obligations to self and others come into conflict. Workers often feel pressure to compromise personal ethical beliefs to achieve company goals. All things being equal, a worker's primary obligation is to self—to remain employed. But if the employer permits or requires actions that the employee considers immoral, an ethical dilemma is created, forcing the worker to choose among two or more unsatisfactory alternatives.

For example, what if an employee discovers that the company habitually ignores Occupational Safety and Health Administration (OSHA) or Environmental Protection Agency (EPA) standards? As everyone knows, whistle-blowing can incur heavy penalties: ostracism, undesirable work assignments, poor performance reviews—or even termination. Although the Sarbanes-Oxley Act of 2002 prohibits such retribution, it's quite difficult to actually prove retaliation unless the worker is prepared for potentially lengthy and expensive legal combat with no guarantee of success and the added threat of countersuit. And even if the attempt does succeed, the worker must then return to an even more hostile climate. Should the person seek employment elsewhere, blacklisting may have already sabotaged the job search.

There are no easy resolutions to ethical dilemmas, but we all must be guided by conscience. Obviously, this can involve some difficult decisions. By determining your purpose, analyzing your audience, and considering the moral dimensions of the situation, you'll achieve the correct tone for any communication. As we have seen, this is crucial for dealing with potentially resistive readers (especially those above you in the workplace hierarchy) and when rectifying errors for which you're accountable. In all instances, however, a courteous, positive, reader-centered, and ethical approach leads to the best results.

Exercises

Revise each of the following three communications to achieve a tone more appropriate to the purpose and audience.

SOUTHEAST INSURANCE COMPANY

Southeast Industrial Park   Tallahassee, FL 32301
Telephone: (850) 555-0123   FAX: (850) 555-3210

November 9, 2013

Mr. Francis Tedeschi
214 Summit Avenue
Tallahassee, FL 32301

Dear Mr. Tedeschi:

This is to acknowledge receipt of your 11/2/13 claim.

Insured persons entitled to benefits under the Tallahassee Manufacturing Co. plan effective December 1, 2005, are required to execute statements of claims for medical-surgical expense benefits only in the manner specifically mandated in your certificate holder's handbook.

Your claim has been quite improperly executed, as you have neglected to procure the Physician's Statement of Services Rendered. The information contained therein is prerequisite to any consideration of your claim.

Enclosed is the necessary form. See that it's filled out and returned to us without delay or your claim cannot be processed.

Yours truly,

Ann Jurkiewicz

Ann Jurkiewicz
Claims Adjustor

Enclosure

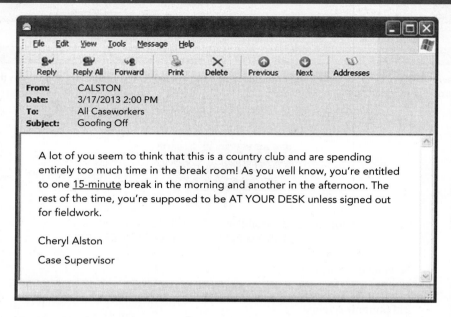

From: CALSTON
Date: 3/17/2013 2:00 PM
To: All Caseworkers
Subject: Goofing Off

A lot of you seem to think that this is a country club and are spending entirely too much time in the break room! As you well know, you're entitled to one <u>15-minute</u> break in the morning and another in the afternoon. The rest of the time, you're supposed to be AT YOUR DESK unless signed out for fieldwork.

Cheryl Alston

Case Supervisor

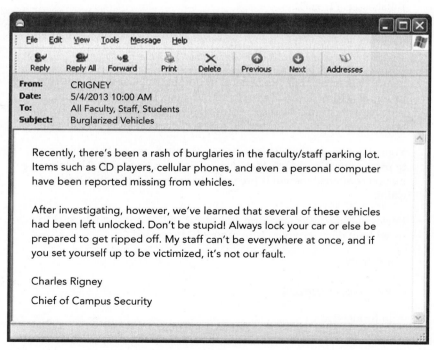

From: CRIGNEY
Date: 5/4/2013 10:00 AM
To: All Faculty, Staff, Students
Subject: Burglarized Vehicles

Recently, there's been a rash of burglaries in the faculty/staff parking lot. Items such as CD players, cellular phones, and even a personal computer have been reported missing from vehicles.

After investigating, however, we've learned that several of these vehicles had been left unlocked. Don't be stupid! Always lock your car or else be prepared to get ripped off. My staff can't be everywhere at once, and if you set yourself up to be victimized, it's not our fault.

Charles Rigney

Chief of Campus Security

Revise each of the following three communications to eliminate inappropriate tone and/or content.

The Turnpike Mall • Turnpike East • Augusta, ME 04330

February 18, 2013

Ms. Barbara Wilson
365 Grove St.
Augusta, ME 04330

Dear Ms. Wilson:

Your Bancroft's charge account is $650.55 overdue. We must receive a payment immediately.

If we don't receive a minimum payment of $50 within three days, we'll refer your account to a collection agency, and your credit rating will be permanently compromised.

Send a payment at once!

Sincerely,

Michael Modoski

Michael Modoski
Credit Department

EXERCISE 20.2 (continued)

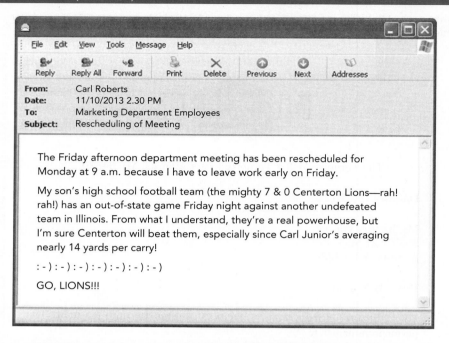

From: Carl Roberts
Date: 11/10/2013 2.30 PM
To: Marketing Department Employees
Subject: Rescheduling of Meeting

The Friday afternoon department meeting has been rescheduled for Monday at 9 a.m. because I have to leave work early on Friday.

My son's high school football team (the mighty 7 & 0 Centerton Lions—rah! rah!) has an out-of-state game Friday night against another undefeated team in Illinois. From what I understand, they're a real powerhouse, but I'm sure Centerton will beat them, especially since Carl Junior's averaging nearly 14 yards per carry!

:-):-):-):-):-):-):-)

GO, LIONS!!!

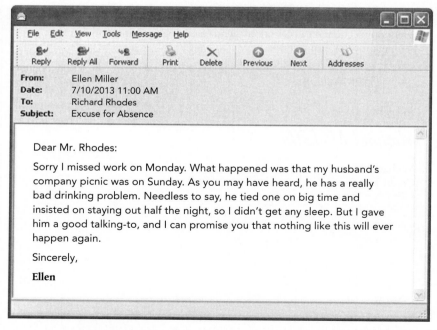

From: Ellen Miller
Date: 7/10/2013 11:00 AM
To: Richard Rhodes
Subject: Excuse for Absence

Dear Mr. Rhodes:

Sorry I missed work on Monday. What happened was that my husband's company picnic was on Sunday. As you may have heard, he has a really bad drinking problem. Needless to say, he tied one on big time and insisted on staying out half the night, so I didn't get any sleep. But I gave him a good talking-to, and I can promise you that nothing like this will ever happen again.

Sincerely,

Ellen

EXERCISE 20.3

Revise each of the following two letters to eliminate wording that might create legal liability.

133 Court St.   Olympia, WA 98501

January 16, 2013

Mr. Robert Ryan
352 Stegman St.
Olympia, WA 98501

Dear Mr. Ryan:

We have received your letter of January 6, and we regret that the heating unit we sold you malfunctioned, killing your tropical fish worth $1,500.

Because the unit was purchased more than three years ago, however, our storewide warranty is no longer in effect, and we are therefore unable to accept any responsibility for your loss. Nevertheless, we are enclosing a Fin & Feather discount coupon good for $20 toward the purchase of a replacement unit or another product of your choice.

We look forward to serving you in the future!

Sincerely,

Sandra Kouvel

Sandra Kouvel
Store Manager

Enclosure

High Rollers Bikes & Boards

516 Bridge St. • Phoenix, AZ 85001

August 17, 2013

Mr. Patrick Casey
252 Sheridan St.
Phoenix, AZ 85001

Dear Mr. Casey:

We're sorry that the bicycle tire we sold you burst during normal use, causing personal injury that resulted in lingering lower back pain.

Certainly, we will install a replacement tire free of charge if you simply bring your bicycle into our shop any weekday during the hours of 9 a.m. to 5 p.m.

Thank you for purchasing your bicycle supplies at High Rollers!

Sincerely,

Monica Lamb

Monica L.amb
Store Manager

Index